BELIEF
IN THE
SEA

To my wife Monica –
without whose loving support and
encouragement this book would
never have been written

BELIEF IN THE SEA

STATE ENCOURAGEMENT OF BRITISH MERCHANT SHIPPING AND SHIPBUILDING

By

MICHAEL DAVIES
T.D., LL.B., Ph.D.
Solicitor, former partner Norton Rose

LLP

LONDON NEW YORK HAMBURG HONG KONG
LLOYD'S OF LONDON PRESS LTD.
1992

Lloyd's of London Press Ltd.
Legal Publishing and Conferences Division
One Singer Street, London, EC2A 4LQ

USA AND CANADA
Lloyd's of London Press Inc.
Suite 308, 611 Broadway
New York, NY 10012 USA

GERMANY
Lloyd's of London Press GmbH
59 Ehrenbergstrasse
2000 Hamburg 50, Germany

SOUTH EAST ASIA
Lloyd's of London Press (Far East) Ltd.
Room 1101, Hollywood Centre
233 Hollywood Road
Hong Kong

First published in Great Britain 1992

British Library Cataloguing in Publication Data

A catalogue record
for this book is available
from the British Library

ISBN 1-85044-204-5 × (used for another title)
1 850444226 (on back cover)

Text set in 10 on 12 Linotron Sabon by
Rowland Phototypesetting Ltd,
Bury St Edmunds, Suffolk
Printed in Great Britain by
WBC Print Ltd.
Bridgend, Mid Glamorgan

FOREWORD

Dr Michael Davies has chosen an opportune time to produce this original and instructive book. First British shipbuilding and now British shipowning have declined almost into insignificance. Dr Davies has written a scholarly and detailed account of the history of the relationship between these two industries and Government. Dr Davies is singularly well qualified to do this. For over a quarter of a century he practised as a lawyer in the specialised field of ship finance: for more than the last 10 of those 25 years, he was generally acknowledged to be the leading expert in the City of London on all legal aspects of his subject.

For 15 years I had the good fortune to work with Michael Davies, first at Botterell & Roche and following that firm's amalgamation with Norton Rose in 1960, at Norton, Rose, Botterell & Roche. Outstanding intellectual capacity, allied with clarity of expression and thoroughness of research, were ever-evident features of his work. All of these are amply testified to by his book, which I unreservedly commend to all who have any interest in the history, or hopes for the recovery, of the British shipping industry.

London, December 1991

DOUGLAS HAMILTON.
Senior Partner, Norton Rose

CONTENTS

TABLE OF CASES

TABLE OF STATUTES

INTRODUCTION

THE FIRST ARTICLE OF AN ENGLISHMAN'S POLITICAL CREED

Until the period from 1979 to the present day, during which, in spite of the serious decline in the British merchant marine, the Government has resolutely adopted a laissez-faire posture, British maritime policy has, for some five centuries, been characterised by a notable consistency of purpose. After a rudimentary beginning at the end of the fourteenth century and then, with a growing national recognition of England's dependence on the sea, from the Tudor period onwards, successive Governments have actively pursued policies designed to encourage the growth of merchant shipping, the supply of trained seamen and the expansion of shipbuilding in the firm belief that maritime power was necessary to ensure both the safety of the realm and its commercial prosperity. The nature of the measures taken has varied widely from time to time according to the prevalent political, economic and social circumstances but there has been no deviation from the objectives which the policies sought to attain.

In the closing years of the seventeenth century George Savile, Marquess of Halifax, introduced his Rough Draft of a New Model at Sea by declaring to his fellow Englishmen that they were confined to an Island, by God Almighty, not as a penalty but a Grace and that accordingly the "First Article of an Englishman's political creed must be that he believeth in the Sea". Savile was preaching to the converted; some three decades earlier the purpose underlying England's long established protectionist maritime policy, designed to achieve both profit and power by discrimination in favour of the English flag, had been epitomised in the resounding preamble to the Navigation Act 1660 which declared its objective to be "For the increase of shipping and the encouragement of the navigation of this nation wherein under the good providence and protection of God the wealth, safety and strength of this kingdom is so much concerned". The protectionist philosophy enshrined in the Carta Maritima of 1660 was far from being innovatory. In 1381, long before England had become a truly seafaring nation, the first of the Navigation Acts, intended "to increase the Navy of England which is now greatly diminished", provided that Englishmen were only to ship their merchandise in English ships. At the end of the fifteenth century Henry VII, as evidenced by the Navigation Acts passed in the early part of his reign, had care, as Bacon put it, "to make his realm potent as well by sea as by land" and this policy, directed towards the achievement of maritime supremacy, was enthusiastically and vigorously developed during the reigns of Henry VIII and Elizabeth I.

By the end of the sixteenth century, as a result of the Navigation Acts and other measures of flag discrimination passed under the Tudors, English ships were required to be wholly owned and largely crewed by the King's subjects in England, Wales or Ireland, the domestic coasting trade was reserved exclusively to English ships, certain goods could only be imported in English ships and other goods were subjected to higher import duties if imported in foreign ships. In addition there had been support for the English fishing industry, then, as now, a valued nursery for seamen, bounties were given for the building of larger ships and steps were taken to increase home supplies of shipbuilding materials and naval stores.

The Navigation Act 1660, with later supplementary measures, enlarged, clarified and made more effective the existing protectionist principles and continued for nearly 200 years as one of the main pillars of the mercantile system. The whole of Britain's colonial and coasting trades and the greater part of her foreign imports were exclusively reserved to ships which were British owned, British built and largely British crewed; Britain was also made the main entrepôt for the export to foreign countries of all the more valuable colonial products and for the import into the colonies of foreign produce. The Navigation Laws succeeded in their objectives of encouraging the growth of British shipping, the supply of British seamen and the development of British shipbuilding; in the latter part of the seventeenth century the weight of contemporary opinion regarded the Act of 1660 as "one of the choicest and most prudent Acts that ever was made in England" and in 1820 a Commons Select Committee had no doubts about the great national advantages derived from the Navigation Laws "in their effects on the maritime greatness and power of the Kingdom".

In the early 1820s, as a result of the growing influence of free trade ideas, there were some minor relaxations of the Navigation Laws but the main protectionist principles established in 1660 and subsequently were largely retained in the Navigation Act 1825 which consolidated and codified the "Law of Navigation of the British Empire". Over the next 20 years, in spite of increasing pressure from the free traders, the British shipping interest, with its deeply held belief in the absolute necessity of protectionism, was strong enough to resist any serious erosion of the navigation system but although, in 1845, the Navigation Laws were again re-enacted without opposition or even debate, it was soon apparent that protectionism had had its day. In 1846 the Corn Laws were repealed and the Navigation Laws were then left conspicuously isolated as the last bastion of a discredited mercantile system. In 1847 the free traders launched the Parliamentary campaign which, after more than two years of bitter struggle, was to culminate in the repeal of those Navigation Laws which even a leading free trader conceded "had been defended by some of our greatest statesmen and eulogised by some of our wisest philosophers and historians".

So in 1850 a free trade Parliament wrought a complete and radical change in the character of British maritime policy; the centuries old protectionism was wholly discarded and foreign shipowners and shipbuilders were free to compete on equal commercial terms. The free traders were convinced that the British maritime industries, having already achieved world supremacy and having ceased to be under threat of foreign retaliatory measures, were no longer in need of protection and were well placed to take full advantage of the confidently anticipated increase in both British and foreign trade. British shipowners and shipbuilders on the other hand viewed the future with much foreboding; although British tonnage was substantially in excess of the aggregate of the tonnage of all the other principal maritime countries, there were doubts as to whether British ships and crews were of sufficient quality to meet the unrestricted foreign competition, particularly that from America, and in addition British owners, unlike their foreign competitors, were burdened with an ever-growing number of new and stringent statutory obligations regarding ship design and construction, the quality of seamanship and the safety, health and welfare of crews and passengers.

After an uncertain and disappointing start, when at first it seemed that the misgivings of the British owners might have been well founded, the abandonment of protectionism proved to be fully justified. From 1860 onwards both shipping and shipbuilding increasingly prospered and at the turn of the century none could dispute the world predominance of the British maritime industries; in 1890 the tonnage of the British Empire represented well over half of the total world fleet and for the years 1892–94 the annual average output of British shipyards represented over 81 per cent of world output. However, this success was only partly attributable to the policy of free trade; other factors of even greater significance were the ability of British yards to build better and cheaper steamships, the competitive advantages gained from the rapid expansion of coal exports, the British development of the Shipping Conference system and, not least, the enterprise of the leading Victorian shipowners and shipbuilders.

Even during the great free trade era between 1850 and 1914, the prevailing doctrine of laissez-faire did not inhibit the Government from giving substantial support to particular sectors of the shipping and shipbuilding industries. There was no question of reverting to a policy of flag discrimination but nevertheless the payments made, from 1837 onwards, to a number of leading liner companies under the Government postal contracts, did undoubtedly contain an element of bounty which both encouraged the establishment of rapid steamship services on regular routes and also stimulated the building in British yards of larger and more advanced steamships. Towards the end of the century there were also some Admiralty subventions to procure the building of fast ships which would be available as fleet auxiliaries and in 1903 there was a more significant change of policy when the Government made substantial loans to Cunard for the building of *Mauretania* and *Lusitania* and in order to avoid the possibility of Cunard falling under American control.

The Great War was also the great watershed: 1914 marked the end of an era and the ascendancy of the British maritime industries was never to be the same as in the pre-war golden days of Empire. The war-time losses of British merchant ships, more than 9 million gross tons, were far in excess of those of the rest of the world and the surviving fleet had suffered from the hardness of war employment and the postponement of renewals and overhauls. In 1918 both the Government and shipowners were united in believing that the wastage of war should be replaced with the utmost dispatch and, notwithstanding the high cost of building new ships, this objective was achieved without any State aid; by 1921 the merchant fleet had been restored to its pre-war level but, owing to the growth of foreign tonnage, the British share of world tonnage was far below what it had been in 1914.

The short uneasy years between the two World Wars marked the beginning of another radical change in British maritime policy. Although the Government, and most British owners, still resolutely adhered to the principle of "freedom of the seas—in the sense of equal treatment of all flags in all ports", severe trade depressions combined with state-aided foreign competition drove the Government into providing, for the first time, general direct financial assistance to the hard pressed British shipowners and shipbuilders. Incentives for the building of new ships in British yards were given through the medium of Treasury guarantees of commercial loans at low interest and Government loans were given to Cunard to finance the building of *Queen Mary* and *Queen Elizabeth* but, Cunard apart, prior to 1934 British owners still did not seek either financial aid or protective measures. Eventually the depressed state of the industry, especially the tramp sector, forced the shipowners to request the Government to grant temporary aid and in 1935 general operating subsidies were, for the first time ever, paid to tramp shipowners; in addition, to alleviate the shipbuilding depression, there was a "scrap and build" scheme under which Government loans were made available to finance the building of new ships for British owners in British yards.

In 1939, under threat of war again, there was concern as to whether the merchant fleet and shipbuilding capacity would be sufficient to meet wartime needs. The Government rejected demands for a revival of the Navigation Laws but, on grounds of national security, accepted the necessity for financial aid; this comprised further tramp subsidies, shipbuilding loans and grants, a liner defence scheme and provision for the establishment of a Government-owned merchant ship reserve. Thus in this pre-Second World War period it was again demonstrated that, when the need arose, the State, without reviving the protectionist principles of the old Navigation Laws, was still prepared to give general financial aid to ensure that the maritime industries were maintained in sufficient strength.

British merchant ship losses in the Second World War, nearly 12 million gross tons, were even greater than in the Great War but by 1949, again without any State assistance, the fleet had been restored to above its pre-war level and stood at 18 million gross tons. Until 1957 British shipowners, assisted by favourable trading conditions, enjoyed a rare period of prosperity but, in spite of the 1954 introduction of tax investment allowances for new ships, the growth of U.K. tonnage between 1949 and 1957 was disappointingly low—less than 7 per cent compared with a growth in world tonnage of over 28 per cent during the same period.

Owing largely to a fall in the level of world trade and an excessive over-ordering of new tonnage by foreign owners, there was a severe shipping depression between 1958 and 1963 and although, in the following years, the freight market showed some modest improvement, the level of U.K. tonnage remained stagnant and between 1958 and 1968 achieved a growth of only 8 per cent compared with a growth in world tonnage of 79 per cent over the same period. During the 1960s British shipping also had to contend with increasing external problems. The main evil was foreign flag discrimination, particularly cargo preference, but there were other causes for concern such as the continuing reservation of certain foreign coastal trades, the growth of subsidised Third World fleets, attacks against the British conference lines, non-commercial intervention from Eastern Bloc shipping and competition from the tax-free flags of convenience. The difficulty was how best to counter these various threats; neither the Government nor most British owners favoured a return to protectionism but diplomatic action at national and international level produced little amelioration.

In the post-war period up to 1958 British shipbuilders received an abundance of new orders from home and abroad but the industry failed to increase output to meet the demand and from 1958 onwards the serious deterioration in the financial position of the industry was causing increasing concern. At a time when world shipbuilding output was continually rising, British output remained stagnant at a low annual figure of around 1 million tons gross; in addition the British yards were losing some of their traditional home and foreign customers and were failing to attract the flags of convenience owners because foreign yards were quoting lower fixed prices, shorter and firmer delivery dates and more favourable credit terms. Eventually, in 1963, the Government, for the first time since 1939, decided that financial support had to be given; export credit facilities for new ships were improved and Government loans totalling £75 million were given for the building of new ships for U.K. owners in U.K. yards. These measures resulted in a substantial number of new orders for the ailing shipbuilders—without them it is likely that many yards would not have survived—but it was soon apparent that the underlying malaise had not been cured and in 1965 the Government appointed the Geddes Shipbuilding Inquiry Committee to make an exhaustive investigation into the fundamental problems of the industry.

The 1966 Report of the Geddes Committee recommended a major structural reconstruction of the shipbuilding industry to make it more efficient and competitive. The Report was accepted by the Government and the Shipbuilding Industry Act 1967 provided for the making of substantial grants and loans to facilitate a reorganisation of the industry into larger groups and authorised the giving of Government guarantees up to £200 million in respect of bank loans to U.K. shipowners to finance new U.K. built ships. This 1967 Credit Scheme was so successful that, to meet the demand, the limit for the guaranteed loans was progressively increased and by 1975 had reached £1400 million; in addition there was a special Government loan of £24 million to Cunard to finance the building of *Queen Elizabeth* 2.

By 1970 the structural reorganisation of the shipbuilding industry into a smaller number of larger compact groups had been more or less completed and shortage of orders was no longer a problem; improvement in world trade, the new credit facilities and the availability of cash investment grants all combined to produce a surge of new orders which in the three years 1968 to 1970, amounted in total to 6.5 million gross tons. Unfortunately the industry still seemed incapable of raising output to meet demand; the Geddes Committee had hoped that annual output would rise to over 2 million tons gross but in the event output between 1967 and 1971 remained static at an average of 1.1 million tons gross per annum. To make matters worse a combination of inadequate investment, poor productivity, lossmaking contracts and bad labour relations resulted in a continuing and increasing deterioration in the financial position of almost all U.K. yards; to prevent closures both Labour and Conservative Governments felt compelled to provide additional financial support which in the period 1967 to 1972 amounted to well over £100 million.

Whilst the shipbuilding industry was thus still struggling to survive, the position of British shipping showed a marked improvement. In July 1967, some 12 months after the end of a long and damaging seamen's strike, the Labour Government appointed a Committee of Inquiry under Lord Rochdale to review the organisation, structure, operation and efficiency of the U.K. shipping industry; over the previous eight years profitability had been low, foreign fleets had been growing rapidly whilst the U.K. fleet stood still and there was a suspicion that British ship management was lacking in enterprise. Some three years later, when the Rochdale Committee completed their comprehensive Report, the situation had greatly changed for the better; encouraged by improving world trade, the 1965 introduction of free depreciation, the readily available credit facilities under the 1967 scheme and, not least, by the payment from 1966 onwards of cash investment grants in place of taxation investment allowances, British owners, showing what the Rochdale Committee characterised as "a new spirit of enterprise", placed large orders for new tonnage in both British and foreign yards. As a result, by 1973, the U.K. merchant fleet had increased by more than 50 per cent over the 1968 figure —a rise comparable to the percentage increase of world tonnage over the same period.

From 1972 onwards to 1977 the decline in the fortunes of the shipbuilding industry continued and again both Conservative and Labour Governments were compelled to give further financial support. The Industry Act 1972 authorised the making of construction grants to shipbuilders which eventually totalled almost £50 million and, under the same Act, selective financial assistance was given by the Conservative Government in the period 1972 to 1974 to prevent insolvencies in certain yards. Early in 1974 a Labour Government, committed to the nationalisation of shipbuilding, came to power but more than three years was to elapse before the industry was taken into public ownership. In the interim the Government had to provide further financial aid and early in 1977 an invervention fund was established so that grants could be made to bridge the widening gap between U.K. prices and those of foreign yards outside the European Community.

Eventually, in March 1977, after a prolonged struggle in both Commons and Lords, the Labour Government procured the passing of the Aircraft and Shipbuilding Industries Act 1977 under which (*inter alia*) all the major British shipbuilding companies, other than the already State-owned Harland and Wolff, became wholly owned subsidiaries of a new public corporation named "British Shipbuilders". Public ownership did not solve the industry's problems which, in many respects, remained the same as before nationalisation; there were still the falling order books, poor productivity, declining output, increasing foreign competition and the world surplus of both shipping tonnage and shipbuilding capacity. For each of its four financial periods up to 1980/81 British Shipbuilders sustained losses of amounts (after crediting receipts from the intervention fund) varying between £50 million and £110 million and the Conservative Government decided that the shipbuilding industry must be returned to the private sector. By early 1986 all the warship yards had been privatised and by the end of 1989 the merchant yards still remaining after enforced closures were also back in private hands. In little more than 10 years British Shipbuilders has cost the taxpayer around £2 billion and it remains to be seen whether the newly privatised shipbuilding industry can survive and prosper without Government financial support and, if the need should arise, whether such support will be forthcoming.

The British shipping industry is also faced with a difficult and uncertain future. By the end of 1975 the United Kingdom registered fleet (500 grt and over) had attained an all time high level of almost 52 million deadweight tons

(9.7 per cent of world tonnage) but since then, although world tonnage for many years continued to rise, U.K. tonnage declined every year and by December 1986 had fallen to 11.2 million deadweight tons (1.8 per cent of world tonnage); the reduction in trade due to the world recession, the excessive over-supply of world tonnage—particularly tankers and bulk carriers, unfair foreign competition, a fall in competitiveness mainly owing to high U.K. manning costs and an unfavourable tax regime all combined to impose severe financial pressures on U.K. owners who, in order to survive, severely restricted their ordering of new ships and were forced into selling existing tonnage abroad (mainly to foreign competitors rather than to scrap yards) or, in some cases, to flag out to British overseas territories or foreign registries.

Between 1986 and 1989 the decline continued; by mid-1989 the U.K. owned trading fleet (500 grt and above) totalled 15.7 million dwt of which only 8 million dwt was registered in the U.K. and Crown Dependencies. There was a corresponding serious fall in the number of trained British seamen—from 73,400 in 1975 to around 22,000 in 1989. Many believe that there is now a need, more urgent than perhaps any time since the repeal of the Navigation Laws, for active Government encouragement to enable the ageing British fleet to be revived and modernised; but so far the appeals of the shipowners, and, even more significant, the views of many others both within and outside Parliament who have only the national interest at heart, appear to have fallen on deaf ears.

Since 1979 the Government have adhered to the view that there is no economic argument which would justify special assistance to the shipping industry and at the present time continue to maintain that the U.K. owned fleet, even at its much reduced level, would still be able to meet national defence requirements. Outside Government circles there is a near unanimous opinion that, both on strategic and economic grounds, the U.K. owned fleet is deficient, in both ships and trained British seafarers, to meet the country's needs in an emergency and that the decline will inevitably continue unless the Government gives the shipping industry support commensurate with that given to foreign shipowners, both in the Community and elsewhere, by their governments. It remains at present a matter for conjecture as to whether the Government can be persuaded to recognise the historical significance of the support which Parliament has from time immemorial consistently given to the merchant navy and to demonstrate its belief in the sea by taking the positive measures now needed "to increase the Navy of England which is now greatly diminished".

CHAPTER 1

THE WEALTH, SAFETY AND STRENGTH OF THE KINGDOM

"There must be a beginning of any great matter"[1]—so to begin at the beginning, 1381, in which year Parliament passed the first Navigation Law (5 Ric. II, stat I, c.3) and gave statutory recognition to the idea of a protectionist maritime policy. It was only a small beginning, and probably not a very successful one, but nevertheless it was the first real manifestation in England of the spirit of protectionism—the idea that the increase of English shipping and the attainment of maritime supremacy could best be achieved by measures of discrimination in favour of the English flag. The idea was developed and refined by numerous Tudor statutes and reached maturity in the great Navigation Acts of 1651 and 1660; thereafter, for some two centuries, the British maritime industries flourished under an exclusive navigation system which debarred foreign competition entirely from Britain's colonial and coasting trades and to a large extent from the carriage of her imports.

The preamble to the Navigation Act 1381 complained, as do the preambles of many later Navigation Acts, of the great decay of English shipping which the Commons attributed to the requisitioning of merchant shipping by Edward III for service in his wars against the French,[2] the non-payment of requisition hire and the King's policy of favouring foreign merchants. The Act's purpose was "to increase the navy[3] of England which is now greatly diminished" and provided that none of the King's subjects should ship any merchandise going out or coming within the realm of England except in English ships.[4] Owing to the scarcity of suitable English ships and seamen the Act caused serious problems for English merchants and its calamitous effect on foreign trade must have been recognised since, in the

1. "but the continuing unto the end until it be thoroughly finished yields the true glory". (Francis Drake 1587).

2. By virtue of a naval success against the French, Edward claimed the title of Lord of the English Sea but he did little to encourage English shipowners and merchants.

3. In the fourteenth century, and for some 200 years thereafter, the expression "navy" was used as meaning all English ships and not, as in more recent times, the Royal Navy of fighting ships.

4. Foreign merchants, even though resident in England, were free to ship their goods in foreign ships.

following year 1382, a further Act[5] was passed which modified the 1381 Act by allowing English merchants to use foreign vessels if "able and sufficient" English ships could not be found in the port where the merchant carried on his business.

It appears that English shipowners must have taken advantage of their monopoly by charging their fellow countrymen prohibitively high freights and, in an attempt to counteract this abuse, a third statute was passed in 1390[6] which again provided that English merchants must ship their goods in English vessels within the realm but only if the shipowners took not more than "reasonable gains for the freights". No attempt was made to define what was to be considered as "reasonable" and this must have been not only a fruitful source of dispute between shipowners and shippers but also a loophole to enable shippers to evade the restriction. In any case since, at this time, the use of foreign shipping was absolutely necessary for England's foreign trade, it was impossible for the Ricardian statutes to be wholly effective but they may have achieved a limited success since otherwise the need for amending legislation would hardly have arisen.

For the next hundred years little was done to encourage English shipping[7] but in 1485, the first year of the reign of Henry VII, a Navigation Act[8] was passed which, as replaced and elaborated upon by a further Act of 1488[9], established a new principle that was to remain a feature of English maritime policy until the middle of the nineteenth century. The main object of these two Acts was to prohibit the import of Gascon wines and Toulouse wood otherwise than in ships belonging to the King's subjects in England, Ireland and Wales[10] but the Acts also stipulated that the crews of such ships must "for the more part" be English, Irish or Welsh—this latter requirement being made to ensure a larger supply of trained native seamen and to prevent foreign ships masquerading as English. The Acts also revived the old Ricardian legislation by providing that English subjects were prohibited from having any of their merchandise carried in foreign vessels if sufficient English shipping was available.

The King took care to ensure that in both Acts all his prerogatives, including his important dispensing powers, were expressly reserved. Henry VII, sparingly

5. 6 Ric. II, stat. I, c.8.
6. 14 Ric. II, c.6.
7. An Act of 1452 (31 Hen. VI) provided that English merchants who shipped their goods in Mediterranean owned vessels should pay the same alien duties as those imposed on foreigners. In 1463 Edward IV's Parliament passed an Act (3 Edw. IV, c.1) which substantially re-enacted the Ricardian legislation but the Act was only valid for five years and was not renewed.
8. I Hen. VII, c.8.
9. 4 Hen. VII, c.10.
10. Thus, foreign, as well as English, merchants were required to import wine and wood into England only in English ships.

and for political objectives, and subsequently Henry VIII, on a much larger scale and mainly to increase the royal revenues, granted dispensations from the restrictions imposed by these Acts and permitted limited use of foreign ships[11]. The legislation did not thereby become a dead letter; on the contrary, as Professor Harper points out,[12] "the dispensations show that the laws were being enforced rather than that they were inoperative. If merchants could have traded freely without special permission, they would not have gone to the trouble and expense of procuring it". Subsequently an Act of Henry VIII[13], passed in 1515 "for the maintenance of the King's navy", sought to strengthen the observance of the Navigation Acts of Henry VII and declared void all future royal licences granting exemptions from importing wine and wood in English ships.[14]

In 1531 came Henry VIII's second Navigation Act[15] which recited that "the multitude of ships which until this time has been not only a great defence and surety to this Realm of England in time of war but also a high commodity to all the subjects of the same for transporting and conveyance of merchandise in and from the Realm is now marvellously decayed so that within few years there shall be few Englishmen who shall be expert in the seas". The Act then declared that the Navigation Laws of Richard II and Henry VII should stand in their full strength force and effect and also prohibited the importing of Gascon wines between October and February with the intention of preventing losses of English ships during the stormy season. Not surprisingly England's protectionist policy awakened some foreign hostility and in 1534 an Act was passed[16] giving the King power, during his life, to set aside the Act of 1531 by Proclamation when he thought fit and to revive it at will. Early in 1539, at a time when there were fears of an invasion from the Netherlands, the King by Proclamation[17] declared that for a period of seven years foreigners might trade with England without paying the higher rate alien duties but in the following year a further Navigation Act[18] made it clear that foreigners were only entitled to the privilege of paying the same duties as Englishmen did if their goods were shipped in English bottoms.

The preamble to the Navigation Act 1540 gave a comprehensive explanation

11. For details of these and later Tudor dispensations see "Dispensing Powers and Defence of the Realm" by E.F. Churchill in *Law Quarterly Review*, Vol. 148, p. 412.

12. L. A. Harper, *The English Navigation Laws* (p. 22) (Columbia University Press, 1939).

13. 7 Hen. VIII, c.2.

14. Nevertheless dispensations continued to be granted by Henry VIII, Edward VI and Elizabeth I.

15. 23 Hen. VIII, c.7.

16. 26 Hen. VIII, c.10.

17. Proclamation No. 189 in *Tudor Royal Proclamations* (Vol. I) Ed. P. L. Hughes and J. F. Larkin. (Yale University Press, 1964).

18. 32 Hen. VIII, c.14.

of the importance of English shipping[19] and then declared that the navy was "marvellously decayed" because, in spite of the Act of 1531, the laws against importing in foreign ships were not being obeyed. The Act accordingly confirmed the Navigation Acts of 1381, 1382 and 1488 and declared them to be in full force and effect and, in order to overcome the "reasonable freights" problem arising from the imprecise wording of the Ricardian statute of 1390, introduced a novel provision fixing specific maximum freight rates for various commodities in various trades subject to the shipowner's right to higher freights in time of war and to a reduction in the maximum freights if so agreed between the shipowner and shipper. The Act also provided that the privileges for long accorded to the German merchants of the Hanseatic League should only apply if their goods were shipped in English vessels or in vessels of their own territories.[20]

In the reign of Edward VI and at the beginning of the reign of Elizabeth I there occurred what appeared to be statutory relaxations of the protectionist policy. An Act of 1552[21] repealed that part of the Navigation Act 1488 prohibiting imports of wine and wood in foreign ships and declared that any vessel of a friendly country could import these commodities between 1st February and 1st October[22]; but the repeal did not affect that part of the 1488 Act which provided that no Englishman should use a foreign ship if English tonnage was available. Then a far more drastic Act of 1558[23] totally repealed the Acts of Richard II and the 1488 Act of Henry VII but the preamble suggests that it was a short term conciliatory move to appease foreigners who were taking retaliatory action against English shipping. The Act only lasted for five years and did assist English shipping by providing that all goods (except corn) shipped in vessels that were not English owned and manned should be subject to the extra aliens duty.

Four years later, in 1562, came an Act,[24] "touching political constitutions for the maintenance of the Navy", which not only expressly restored the statutes of Henry VII but seems to have been regarded as bringing back into

19. "And whereas the Navy or multitudes of ships of this Realm in times past hath been and yet is very profitable, requisite, necessary and commodious as well for the intercourse and concourse of merchants transporting their wares and merchandise and a great defence and surety of this Realm in time of war as well to offend as defend, and also the maintenance of many masters, mariners and seamen, making them expert and cunning in the art and sciences of shipmen and sailing and they their wives and children have had their living of and by the same and also hath been the chief maintenance and support of the Cities, Towns, villages, havens and creeks near adjoining unto the sea coasts."

20. An early example of the principle of "direct trade", i.e. that in the trade between two countries goods should only be carried in the ships of those countries.

21. 5 & 6 Edw. VI, c.18.

22. This relaxation may have been made because there were not sufficient English ships to provide an adequate service. There may also have been diplomatic reasons.

23. 1 Eliz. I, c.13.

24. 5 Eliz. I, c.5—"For the better maintenance and increase of the navy of the realm of England."

force the older Ricardian Navigation Acts. The 1562 Act also introduced an important new provision—the exclusive reservation of the English coasting trade to English owned ships having English masters—and this monopoly of the English coasting trade was to continue as one of the basic principles of English shipping policy until 1854 when an Act was passed[25] opening the trade to foreign vessels.

In addition to the measures for inhibiting foreign competition, the Tudors also recognised the need for increasing the supply of trained seamen and to this end steps were taken to encourage the English fishing industry. A statute of 1541[26] forbade Englishmen to buy fish abroad or at sea for resale in England and an Act passed in 1544,[27] the first of the so-called "Political Lent" statutes, ordained meatless days[28] "for the good of men's souls" and so that English fishermen might have more employment. Elizabeth I also pursued this policy of giving maximum encouragement to the fishing industry and the measures taken to develop the English fisheries as the main source of supply of both ships and trained seamen and the attempts to restrict foreign fish imports formed the keystone of Cecil's shipping policy. A large part of the Act of 1562 was devoted to the fishing industry and it was provided that Englishmen should be free to export English caught fish in English ships for four years without paying customs duty. This privilege was extended by an Act of 1571[29] and further statutes to foster the expansions of the fishing industry were passed in 1581 and 1598.[30]

Action was also taken to encourage the building in England of larger ships and to improve the supply of naval stores. Henry VII revived the practice, commenced around 1450 in the reign of Henry VI, of paying bounties of five shillings a ton to builders of vessels of 100 tons or more[31] and this practice was continued by Henry VIII who also encouraged the growing of hemp and flax. Cecil's shipping policy also included support for shipbuilding; the bounty system was continued on a more regular basis, there were several statutes designed to conserve timber[32], the apprentice laws were changed by the Act of 1562 to encourage the training of shipwrights, the Act of 1558 sought to encourage the building of larger ships by prohibiting small coasters from engaging in foreign trade and, to ensure that when ships were built they remained in English ownership, a Royal Proclamation of 1559[33] prohibited the sale of ships to foreigners.

25. 17 & 18 Vict., c.5.
26. 33 Hen. VIII, c.2.
27. 2 & 3 Edw. VI, c.19.
28. Fish was to be eaten on Fridays, Saturdays, Ember Days and in Lent.
29. 13 Eliz. I, c.11.
30. 23 Eliz. I, c.7 and 39 Eliz. I, c.10
31. The recipients of bounty were prohibited from selling their ships to foreigners except with the King's permission.
32. 1 Eliz. I, c.15, 23 Eliz. I, c.5, 27 Eliz. I, c.19 and 35 Eliz. I, c.11.
33. Proclamation No. 463 in *Tudor Royal Proclamations* (Vol. II), *op. cit.*.

Elizabethan measures to assist shipping also included the construction of harbours, the suppression of piracy and the encouragement of agriculture so as to provide more corn for export but only in English ships.[34] In addition when, during the latter part of the sixteenth century, the earlier English Trading Companies were incorporated,[35] the opportunity was taken of protecting English shipping interests by inserting in the Charters a requirement for the use of English ships and crews or by giving customs privileges if goods were imported in English vessels; furthermore the long distance trading of the Chartered Companies encouraged the building of larger ships and created employment for more seamen.

There can be no doubt that the various policies devised by Cecil for encouraging the increase in English shipping proved successful. During the Elizabethan period the English merchant fleet showed substantial growth in numbers, the size of ships and total tonnage; in 1572 there were 1,383 vessels having an aggregate tonnage of 50,816 but only 10 years later, in 1582, there had been an increase to 1,642 vessels having an aggregate tonnage of 66,827.[36] This rate of growth was not, however, maintained in the first half of the seventeenth century which was a period of relative stagnation[37]; it was not so much that the early Stuarts failed to take further measures to foster the merchant marine but rather that the steps taken were not adequate to counteract the ever increasing Dutch competition.

As early as the first two years of the reign of James I there were no less than three statutes and a Royal Proclamation for the benefit of shipping. The first Act[38] permitted exports of malt and barley in English ships only, the second Act[39] was another "fish eating" measure and another statute[40] limited the manufacture of sail cloth to skilled workers; there was also a Royal Proclamation of 1604[41] yet again forbidding the sale of vessels to foreigners without royal permission. In 1605 there were two further Acts; the first was an anti-monopolistic measure[42] designed to curb the Chartered Companies and the second[43] was to encourage the export of beer. In the following year

34. The Act of 1562 which permitted the export of grain was expressed to be "for the maintenance of the Navy".

35. Charters were granted to the Muscovy Company (1553), the Eastland Company (1579), the Levant Company (1592) and the East India Company (1600).

36. 1572 and 1582 are the only years for which reasonable reliable statistics are available—see "The Growth of English Shipping 1572–1922 by A. P. Usher in the *Quarterly Journal of Economics* Vol. 42 (1929).

37. *Ibid.*

38. 1 Jac. I, c.25

39. 1 Jac. I, c.29

40. 1 Jac. I, c. 24—in which the Navy is referred to as "the chiefest strength of this Realm (next to God and his Highness)".

41. Proclamation No. 44 in *Stuart Royal Proclamations* (Vol. I), Ed. J. F. Larkin and P. L. Hughes (Oxford University Press, 1973).

42. 3 Jac. I, c.6.

43. 3 Jac. I, c.11.

James' First Charter to the Virginia Company originated what was later to be one of the most fundamental of English shipping policies by establishing the right of England to control the destination of the trade of her Colonies and to prevent their goods from being shipped direct to foreign countries.[44]

Between 1606 and the commencement of the Civil War there were no further shipping statutes but the ever growing supremacy of Dutch shipping prompted a number of Royal Proclamations—mostly aimed against the Dutch. In 1615 a Proclamation[45] gave what was, presumably, a necessary reminder that the old Navigation Laws remained in force and were to be obeyed and also ordered that no goods were to be imported from the Mediterranean except in English ships of the Levant Company. Proclamations made in 1619 and 1624[46] prohibited the import of tobacco except in English ships from Virginia and other Colonies and also prohibited the growing of tobacco in England or Ireland. Meanwhile in 1620 the importance of the increasing coal export trade to the development of English shipping was recognised by English vessels being given a preferential advantage in the export duties on coal and in 1622 a Proclamation[47] ordered the Eastland Company (which had been ignoring the 1615 Proclamation) to ship all their imports in English vessels. There was another 1622 Proclamation[48] prohibiting mariners and shipwrights from serving foreigners and further Proclamations to enforce this prohibition were made by James I in 1623 and 1625[49] and by Charles I, also in 1625,[50] in the first week of his reign.

By 1625 Holland had become unquestionably the leading seafaring nation of the world; England was her only competitor for maritime supremacy but the Dutch shipping tonnage was far greater than that of England and Dutch ships dominated the Baltic and North Sea trades, were powerful in the Mediterranean and Far East and were even beginning to penetrate into England's trade with her own American and West Indian Colonies. Thus there was every reason for Charles I to encourage the growth of English shipping and his efforts to this end, for the most part without the assistance of Parliament,[51] added to the basic principles which were later to be the foundations of the Navigation Acts of 1651 and 1660.

In 1625 Charles I issued a Proclamation[52] for the "well manning and arming" of ships and this was probably designed to prevent the capture of English

44. Subsequently the Privy Council ruled that no commodities from Virginia should be carried to any foreign port until they had first been landed in England and customs duty paid.

45. Proclamation No. 148, *Stuart Royal Proclamations* Vol. I., *op. cit.*

46. Proclamations Nos. 203 and 257, *ibid.*

47. Proclamation No. 228, *ibid.*

48. Proclamation No. 230, *ibid.*

49. Proclamation Nos. 240 and 267, *ibid.*

50. Proclamation No. 4 in *Stuart Royal Proclamations* (Vol. II), Ed. J. F. Larkin (Oxford University Press, 1983).

51. There were no sittings of Parliament between 1629 and 1640.

52. Proclamation No. 32 *Stuart Royal Proclamations* (Vol. II), *op. cit.*.

merchant ships and to supply the Royal Navy with seamen trained in the use of weapons. In 1626 there was a Privy Council order that fish caught by English subjects in the waters of England, Newfoundland and New England were to be carried only in English ships and in the same year a Royal Proclamation[53] revived the practice of paying bounties for the building of larger ships of 200 tons or more. A Proclamation of 1629[54] ordered that all imports of French wine should be made only in English or French vessels,[55] another 1629 Proclamation[56] again prohibited the sale of ships to foreigners and a further Proclamation in 1630[57] ordered English subjects to use only English ships for Baltic imports and exports and declared that the provisions of the old Navigation Laws relating to trade in foreign ships were to be strictly enforced.

Attempts were also made to prevent the Dutch from trading with the English Colonies and to ensure that England received exclusively the benefits of colonial produce. The Privy Council ordered Virginia to send all her produce to England and not to allow any foreigners, the Dutch in particular, to trade in the Colony with shipping. Maryland's Charter required that all her produce should be sent to England and the Admiralty were ordered to ensure that English vessels coming from the Colonies should unload their cargoes in London before going to any foreign country. Thus the Proclamations and Orders by Charles I and his Council show a clear recognition that England's maritime policy should be directed to ensuring that England had a monopoly of her colonial trade and that the Dutch should be excluded not only from trade with the English Colonies but also from the carriage of foreign imports into England.

Notwithstanding the injunctions issued by Charles I, in 1643 Virginia passed an Act allowing the Dutch to trade with the Colony in Dutch ships and it was becoming apparent that, in spite of the attempts to prevent it, the Dutch were securing an increasing share of the English colonial carrying trade. In a conciliatory move, the Commonwealth Parliament in 1646 gave the Colonists the right to import goods from England free of duty for three years provided the Colonists did not allow their produce to be exported otherwise than in English ships. This concession failed to produce the desired effect and was accordingly followed in 1650 by an Act[58] which not only forbade the inhabitants of Virginia, Barbados, Bermuda and Antigua to trade with "any people

53. Proclamation No. 41, *ibid.*
54. Proclamation No. 118, *ibid.*
55. Another early example of the principle of "direct trade".
56. Proclamation No. 119 *Stuart Royal Proclamations* (Vol. II), *op cit.*.
57. Proclamation No. 124, *ibid.*
58. Act of 3rd October 1650 (Vol. II) in *Acts and Ordinances of the Interregnum 1642–1660* Ed. C. H. Firth and R. S. Rait (3 vols. London, 1911), pp. 425–429. The concept at that time of the relationship between the mother country and her Colonies is clearly shown by the preamble to this Act which recited that there were, in divers places in America, Colonies "which were planted at the cost, and settled by the people, and by authority of this Nation, which are and ought to be subordinate to, and dependent upon, England; and hath ever since the planting there have been and ought to be, subject to such laws, orders and regulations as are or shall be made by the Parliament of England".

whatsoever" but also, in a clause aimed directly at the Dutch, forbade any foreign ship to trade with any English Colony in America except by licence from Parliament or the Council of State.

By the middle of the seventeenth century it had become increasingly apparent that the confused and complex system of Navigation Laws and other protective measures stretching back to the time of Richard II, which few understood and many disobeyed, were failing to achieve their primary objective of excluding foreign ships from the carriage of English and colonial imports and exports; in particular it was all too clear that the existing measures, full of loopholes and ambiguities, had done nothing to prevent the continuing growth of Dutch shipping and the increasing Dutch penetration into English and colonial trade. For political and economic reasons, the joint considerations of power and plenty, something had to be done and, by drawing upon established principles and profiting from past mistakes, the Commonwealth Councils of State and Trade succeeded in evolving a relatively simple formula, concentrating on the control of imports, which was intended to achieve both political power and economic wealth by securing for English ships a monopoly of the colonial trade and a larger share of the remainder of the world's carrying trade.

The Commonwealth Navigation Act of 1651[59] accordingly first provided that no goods of the growth, production or manufacture of Asia, Africa or America should be imported into England or into any English possession except in English owned vessels of which the master was English and also most of the crew. The Act then stipulated that goods of the growth, production or manufacture of Europe should be imported into England or any of its possessions only in English owned vessels[60] or in vessels owned by people of the country where the goods were grown, produced or manufactured or by people of the country in which was located the port where the goods were usually first shipped.[61] By these provisions, which applied to aliens and Englishmen alike and were aimed directly against Dutch trade and shipping, the Dutch were excluded from the English colonial trade, were prohibited from carrying to England any goods from foreign countries in Asia, Africa or America and were greatly restricted in the European goods which they were permitted to ship to England or her possessions.

The 1651 Act also repeated the earlier Elizabethan restriction prohibiting aliens from engaging in the English coasting trade and, to encourage English

59. Act of 9th October 1651 in *Acts and Ordinances of the Interregnum* (Vol. II), pp. 559–562. The Act was passed "for the Increase of the Shipping and the Encouragement of the Navigation of this Nation which, under the good Providence and Protection of God, is so great a means of the Welfare and Safety of this Commonwealth", and applied to England, Ireland, all English Islands and the Colonies.

60. In the case of imports from Europe the 1651 Act did not require English owned vessels to have an English master or English crew.

61. The Act also provided that merchandise imported into England must be brought directly from the country of its production or from the port where it was usually first shipped.

fisheries and the supply of trained seamen, it was provided that fish of the kind "usually fished for and caught" by the English, and all fish oil, whale fins and whale bone, should not be imported into England or her possessions unless caught by English owned and English manned ships and that no fish was to be exported from England or her possessions otherwise than in English owned and English manned ships. The Act did not formally repeal the former Navigation Laws but after 1651 the older measures were, for all practical purposes, ignored.

When Charles II was restored to the throne in May 1660 the Navigation Act 1651, along with the remainder of the Commonwealth legislation, ceased to have validity but, even if this had not happened, there was no doubting the need for further and better planned legislation. A major deficiency in the 1651 Act was that no provision had been made for registering the ownership and nationality of ships and the task of identifying a ship was made all the more difficult by the fact that the Act did not require that an English owned ship should also be English built[62] and that in the European import trade there was no stipulation that the master and most of the crew of an English ship had themselves to be English. Thus if a master swore that his ship was English owned who could prove otherwise—and in consequence it was found to be impossible to enforce the provisions of the Act relating to imports from Europe and nearly as difficult to enforce those provisions relating to the Colonies where, in New England particularly, there were widespread evasions. In short the 1651 Act had conspicuously failed to diminish, still less extinguish, Dutch superiority at sea and in commerce.

The importance which the Convention Parliament attached to the need for a rapid and more effective replacement of the 1651 Act is evidenced by the fact that the great Navigation Act 1660[63] was passed within a few months of the King's return from exile. Many of the clauses of the new Act comprised no more than a better drafted expression of the principles established in 1651 and earlier but the 1660 Act, as supplemented by further statutes passed by the Cavalier Parliament in the early years of the Restoration, was in every respect a marked improvement on its predecessor. The main thrust of the 1660 Act was still, as in 1651, the compulsory direction of imports into English ships but, in place of the 1651 general prohibitions against foreign tonnage, there were particular discriminations in respect of specified commodities and this formula proved to be more capable of enforcement and consequently a more effective weapon against the Dutch.

Before considering in detail the principal shipping provisions of the Navigation Act and subsequent legislation, it is convenient, by way of introduction, to mention that for the purposes of the Act the expression "English ships" was

62. In the mid-seventeenth century a large number of English owned vessels were Dutch built.
63. 12 Car. II, c.18–sometimes hereafter referred to as the "Navigation Act".

to be regarded as meaning ships wholly owned by the people of England, Ireland, Wales or Berwick[64] and that the Act defined an "English built ship" as a ship built in England, Ireland, Wales, Guernsey, Jersey, Berwick or in the English possessions in Asia, Africa or America[65]. However a ship only qualified as an English ship or an English built ship if the master and at least three quarters of the crew were English, Welsh or Irish.[66]

In order to secure for English shipping a monopoly of the colonial trade, Section 1 of the Navigation Act provided that all imports and exports of English possessions in Asia, Africa or America were to be carried either in English ships or in ships built and belonging to the Colonies[67] and Section 2 prohibited any foreigners from trading as a merchant or factor in any of these English possessions. Then, for the purpose of ensuring that England became the staple for the raw materials and commodities most needed by the mother country, Section 18 of the Act provided that certain "enumerated commodities" produced in the English possessions outside Europe should only be exported to England or Ireland[68] or another English possession.[69] The enumerated commodities were those most required for home industries and consumption: they originally comprised sugar, tobacco, cotton wool, indigo, ginger, fustick or other dyeing wool but over the following 100 years this list was changed by both additions[70] and relaxations.[71]

The Navigation Act had only made England the staple for the more valuable

64. After the 1707 Act of Union (6 Anne, c.11) ships owned by Scottish subjects were also treated as "English" ships.

65. After 1707 ships built in Scotland were also deemed to be "English built" ships and by Acts passed in 1747 (20 Geo II c.45) and 1766 (7 Geo. III, c.45) duly condemned prize ships and ships built in the Isle of Man were also to be regarded as "English built".

66. After 1707 the master and crew could be Scots. In 1662 the Statute of Frauds (14 Car. II, c.11) provided that the crew could include colonial subjects and made it clear that the three quarters proportion had to be maintained throughout the voyage—a provision difficult in practice to enforce.

67. In this section of the 1660 Act there was no requirement that English owned ships had to be English built but on the other hand colonial owned ships did have to be colonial built.

68. By an Act of 1671 (22 & 23 Car. II, c.26) the shipping of enumerated commodities to Ireland was prohibited. In 1696 an Act (7 & 8 Will. III, c.22) even prohibited the export of non-enumerated commodities from the Colonies to Ireland but this particular bar was removed by an Act of 1731 (4 Geo. II, c.15). Eventually an Act of 1780 (20 Geo. III, c.10) put Ireland in a position of equality with England as regards trade with the Colonies in the West Indies, America and Africa and finally by the Act of Union of 1800 (40 Geo. III, c.67) Ireland was put on the same footing as England for all trade purposes.

69. To prevent evasions of this section in the American Colonies, an Act of 1672 (25 Car. II, c.7) placed a duty on the enumerated commodities if they were shipped from one Colony to another Colony unless security was given that they would be shipped to England from the second Colony and not sent direct to Europe as had apparently been happening frequently.

70. By Acts of 1704 (3 & 4 Anne cc. 5 & 10) rice, molasses and naval stores were added and further additions were made by Acts of 1721 (8 Geo. I, cc. 15 & 18) and 1763 (4 Geo. III, c.15).

71. Acts passed between 1730 and 1770 permitted exports of rice to Southern Europe and other parts of America. An Act of 1739 (12 Geo. II, c.30) allowed the Sugar Colonies to send their staple products to foreign countries but only in British ships and subject to stringent conditions.

colonial exports but in 1663 the Staple Act[72] extended the principle of the staple by providing that, with certain minor exceptions,[73] no commodity grown, produced or manufactured in Europe should be imported into the English Colonies unless it had first been brought to and landed in England by lawful shipping lawfully manned and thereafter carried to the Colonies in an English owned and English built vessel manned as required by the Navigation Act.

Having dealt comprehensively with the colonial trade, steps were then taken to encourage English shipping, hopefully at the expense of the Dutch, in the important and growing long distance non-colonial trades. Section 3 of the Navigation Act provided that no goods or commodities of the growth, production or manufacture of any part of Asia, Africa or America were to be imported into England, Wales or Ireland except in English ships or in ships belonging to the peoples in the English Colonies. In addition, in order to prevent these foreign goods being brought in Dutch or other foreign ships to Europe and then transhipped for import into England, Section 4 of the Act provided that the goods could only be imported into England directly from the country of growth, production or manufacture or from the port of usual first shipment.[74]

As regards imports from Europe, the authors of the 1660 Act devised a different approach; in general European goods and products could be imported into England in any ships from any place but there was an important exception in Section 8 which provided that certain "enumerated articles" had to be carried either in an English ship or in a ship of the country in which the specified goods were grown, produced or manufactured or in a ship of the country in which the port of usual first shipment was located.[75] The "enumerated articles", which comprised, in value, about half of English imports from Europe, included all Russian goods, masts, timber, pitch, tar, rosin, hemp, flax, raisins, figs, prunes, olive oil, corn or grain, sugar, potash, wine, vinegar

72. 15 Car. II, c.7—Sections 5 and 6. The objects of the Act not only deal with the importance of the Colonies from the point of view of shipping but also clearly illustrate what at that time was the mother country's economic policy in relation to her dependencies.

73. The original exceptions were salt for the Newfoundland fisheries, wine from Madeira and the Azores and horses and provisions from Scotland and Ireland. Further small exceptions were added by statutes passed between 1705 and 1776.

74. There were some exceptions to the general rule requiring direct shipment. Sections 12 and 13 of the Act permitted imports from East Indian and Mediterranean countries even though not of the produce of those countries but only in English owned and English built ships. Bullion could be freely imported from any place in any ship and prize goods could also be freely imported but only in English ships. Further exceptions were made during the eighteenth century—see Harper, *op. cit.* pp. 391 *et seq.*

75. Foreign ships carrying the enumerated articles had not only to be owned by people of the exporting country but also to have been built there and to have as masters and three quarters of the crew people of the country in question. This prevented Dutch seamen crewing ships of other countries.

and brandy and also currants and Turkish goods.[76] To give English shipping further protection against competition from Dutch and Hanseatic entrepôts and also to protect certain colonial products, Section 23 of the Statute of Frauds 1662[77] absolutely prohibited the import into England in any ship from a port of the Netherlands or Germany of certain specified commodities—for the most part not grown or produced in those countries.[78]

The Navigation Act continued the 100-years-old prohibition against foreign participation in the English coastal trade; Section 6 provided that the trade should be restricted exclusively to English owned ships with master and at least three quarters of the crew English.[79]

In addition to the benefits received from this detailed code of flag discrimination and the establishment of England as the staple for colonial exports and imports, substantial advantages accrued to the English maritime industries from the preferential system of customs duties and bounties which was created from the time of the Restoration and onwards. The Subsidy Act 1660[80] contained a Book of Rates which laid down preferential duties for various goods imported or exported in vessels which were both English owned and English built.[81] The Navigation Act[82] also provided that imported fish, fish oil and whale products were to pay double aliens duties if not brought in English ships, that qualified foreign ships importing into England any of the European enumerated articles were to be subject to aliens duties and that French ships entering an English port should pay a tonnage duty of five shillings per ton until France discontinued levying tonnage duties on English ships.

As far as exports were concerned, there was a particularly heavy duty imposed by the Book of Rates on coal exported in foreign ships or in English owned but foreign built ships and from an English point of view this was so beneficial that it gave English owned and English built ships a near monopoly of the substantial coal export trade. In addition, by an Act of 1672,[83] a substantial bounty was paid on corn exported in English owned and English crewed

76. English ships importing currants and Turkish goods were also required to have been built in England but otherwise English ships importing the enumerated articles did not have to be English built.

77. 14 Car. II, c.11

78. By the Treaty of Breda in 1667 this prohibition was relaxed so as to permit the Dutch to import into England in Dutch ships goods grown, produced or manufactured in Lower or Upper Germany. Some further exceptions were made during the eighteenth century—see Harper, *op. cit.*, p. 407.

79. By an Act of 1794 (34 Geo. III, c.68) it was provided that all, instead of three-quarters, of the crew of a coasting trade vessel must be British.

80. 12 Car. II, c.4.

81. Section 7 of the Navigation Act provided that these vessels only qualified for the preferential rates if, for the whole of the voyage, the master and at least three-quarters of the crew were English.

82. Sections 5, 9 and 17.

83. 25 Car. II, c.1—subsequently extended by an Act of 1688 (1 Will. & Mar c.12).

ships and this also made it nearly impossible for foreign ships to compete in this export trade. As Professor Ralph Davis comments[84]: "These two financial regulations, affecting the great short distance export trades, have attracted only a fraction of the attention which has been given to the Navigation Acts: but by effectively excluding the competition of Dutch ships which were so well suited to the carriage of corn and coal from England they had an influence on the development of the shipping industry comparable to that of the Navigation Acts themselves".

For the purposes of both the Subsidy Act and the Navigation Act it was necessary that the ownership and build of a vessel should be ascertainable and, with a view to preventing evasion, Section 10 of the Navigation Act provided that all foreign-built ships owned by English subjects had to be registered in order to qualify for the privileges granted to English ships. This modest beginning of a registration system was extended by an Act of 1696[85] which provided that all colonial imports and exports had to be carried in ships that were both English owned and English built and that all English and colonial ships intended for the colonial trade had to be registered. This was the first official Register of English owned and English built ships but it applied only to ships engaged in the colonial trade and it was not until 1786 that a Registration Act[86] made it compulsory for every British built ship over 15 tons owned by British subjects to be registered.[87] The 1786 Act also stated that neither foreigners nor British subjects resident outside His Majesty's Dominions were eligible to be owners of British ships and further provided that all ships not qualified as British ships were to be deemed alien ships even though owned by British subjects.[88]

Apart from the earlier shipbuilding bounties and the provisions in the Subsidy Act 1660 restricting the preferential customs duties to English built ships, prior to the Navigation Act 1660 there had been no direct statutory encouragement for the building of ships in England and indeed the Navigation Act itself was passed specifically for the increase of shipping and the supply of seamen and provided little by way of support for English shipbuilding. However, once the Navigation Act had been passed, Parliament soon turned its attention to shipbuilding; later in 1660 an Act for setting up the Post Office[89] provided that English mail should only be carried by sea from England in English built

84. *The Rise of the English Shipping Industry in the 17th and 18th Centuries* (London, 1962), p. 311.

85. 7 & 8 Will III c.22—the Imperial Act of Frauds.

86. 26 Geo. III, c.60.

87. Registration was made mandatory with a view to preventing the evasions of the Navigation Laws which were still taking place—particularly in the Colonies.

88. British subjects were not prohibited from owning foreign built ships but such ships, being deemed to be alien ships, were not entitled to the privileges of British built ships and could not be registered.

89. 12 Car. II, c.35.

ships navigated by English seamen[90] and the shipping legislation passed during the remainder of the seventeenth century, and in the eighteenth century as well, clearly indicates that, to an ever increasing extent, Parliament came to realise that the shipyards of a nation were the cradle of its sea power.[91]

The Statute of Frauds 1662[92] provided that only ships built in His Majesty's Dominions, except for foreign built ships bought by English subjects before October 1662 and registered under the Navigation Act or ships condemned as lawful prizes, should enjoy the privileges of English ships and that all other ships, even though English owned and English manned, should be deemed alien and subject to alien duties[93]; the Act also granted preferential customs duties for certain types of ships[94] built within His Majesty's Dominions for the next seven years. In the following year further preferences were accorded to English built ships by the Staple Act 1663[95] which not only stipulated that all colonial imports from Europe had to be carried from England to the Colonies in English built ships but also permitted the export of coal from England or Wales to the Colonies and provided that only a small fraction of the normal export duties on coals should be payable provided that the coal was shipped in English built vessels which were English manned as required by the Navigation Act.

During the remainder of the seventeenth century there were a number of further statutory measures to encourage the building of ships in England. By Acts of 1670 and 1694[96] further bounties, in addition to those provided for in the Statute of Frauds, were given for the building of larger and stronger ships and by an Act of 1685[97] foreign-built ships were virtually excluded from the English coastal trade by the imposition of an extra duty of five shillings per ton for every coasting voyage by a foreign built ship thereafter bought by English owners.[98] There was also an Act of 1663[99] to improve supplies of hemp and flax, an Act of 1668[100] to increase and preserve timber for shipbuilding and

90. This 1660 Act was partially repealed in 1710 by 9 Anne, c.16 but the 1710 Act contained a similar provision regarding the carriage of English mail overseas and remained in force until 1871.

91. H. C. Hunter, *How England got its Merchant Marine 1066–1776* (New York, 1935).

92. 14 Car. II, c.11—Section 6.

93. A restrictive interpretation was placed upon this section. Ships which were English owned, English manned but foreign built after 1662 and registered as such were treated as still qualifying for the privileges of English ships under the Navigation Act but were liable to the higher rates of duties imposed on alien ships.

94. Ships were required to have three decks, 30 pieces of ordnance and ammunition in proportion.

95. 15 Car. II, c.7.

96. 22 & 23 Car. II, c.1 and 5 & 6 Will. & Mar., c.24.

97. 1 Jac. II, c.18.

98. An extra duty of 12 pence per ton was also imposed on foreign-built ships already employed in the coasting trade.

99. 15 Car. II, c.15.

100. 19 & 20 Car. II, c.8.

in 1696 there was a valuable boost given by the Imperial Act of Frauds[101] which provided that English built shipping was to have a monopoly in all colonial import and export trades.[102]

During the eighteenth century the needs of war prompted a number of statutes designed to ensure an adequate supply of shipbuilding materials. By an Act of 1704[103] bounties were to be paid to anyone importing specified naval stores from the Colonies in English ships, Acts of 1713 and 1746[104] imposed heavy import duties on foreign sail-cloth and measures passed in 1731 and 1736[105] encouraged the manufacture of British sail-cloth and provided that every British built ship was to be initially equipped with British made sail-cloth. Steps were also taken to safeguard supplies of timber; an Act of 1721[106] allowed lumber to be imported free of duty and in 1763[107] bounties were given on imports of American lumber into Britain for shipbuilding.

Finally the Registration Act 1786[108] gave United Kingdom and colonial shipbuilders the privilege of what amounted to a captive British market; the Act provided that, after 1st April 1786 and subject to minor exceptions,[109] a British owned and British crewed ship was only entitled to be registered and to enjoy the privileges granted to British ships by the Navigation Act 1660 and subsequent legislation if such ship had been wholly built and fitted out in His Majesty's Dominions. There can be little doubt that all the measures, culminating in the 1786 Act, which had been taken since 1660 to encourage the U.K. and colonial shipbuilding industries ultimately had the intended effect but success was only gradually achieved. In the 15 years following the Restoration some foreign ships had been purchased, a large number of foreign-built ships had fallen into English hands as a result of the Dutch wars and, by virtue of royal dispensations, many foreign-built ships had been "Englished" and granted all the privileges of English built ships.[110] Thus in 1675, following the ending of the Dutch wars, perhaps as much as half of English owned merchant tonnage was foreign-built but the years of peace brought a significant change

101. 7 & 8 Will III c.22.

102. The only permitted exceptions were duly condemned prize ships and, for three years only, foreign-built ships employed in bringing naval stores.

103. 3 & 4 Anne, c.10. This Act was continued in 1713 (12 Anne, c.9) and, after lapsing, was revived in 1729 (2 Geo. II, c.35).

104. 12 Anne, c.16 and 19 Geo. II, c.27.

105. 4 Geo. II, c.27 and 9 Geo. II, c.27.

106. 8 Geo. I, c.12.

107. 4 Geo. III, c.11.

108. 26 Geo. III, c.60.

109. Ships built in a foreign country before May 1786 and belonging at that date to British subjects were allowed to continue to enjoy the privileges to which they were entitled under the existing laws.

110. *Law Quarterly Review*, Vol. 148, p. 423. Although the Navigation Act 1660 did not reserve to the Crown a right to dispensations, Charles II continued to grant dispensations under the Royal Prerogative.

and it has been estimated that in 1688 the proportion of foreign built tonnage was not more than one-fifth and almost certainly much less.[111]

Towards the end of the seventeenth century English shipwrights, instead of concentrating on their traditional and expensive defensible ships, began to produce ships, along the lines of the highly successful and competitive Dutch flyboats, which were both cheaper to build and cheaper to operate. This important technical change, coupled with the exclusive reservation of the colonial trade to English or colonial-built ships, ensured that throughout the eighteenth century the proportion of foreign built tonnage continued to diminish although English shipbuilders faced keen competition from the Colonies where building costs were less. In 1774 it was estimated that nearly a third of British owned ships were American built[112] but purchases by English owners from America ended in 1776 when the shipbuilding Colonies became "foreign" for the purposes of the Navigation Laws and by 1792 96.2 per cent of all English ships were English built.[113]

In the eighteenth century measures, often prompted by the exigencies of war, were taken to ensure an adequate supply of seamen. An Act of 1703[114] bound shipowners to take apprentices in accordance with a scale based on the tonnage of the ships and, to assist the important coastal coal trade, a valuable nursery for seamen, exempted from impressment the master, mate and a limited number of seamen on ships in that trade. A later Act of 1703[115] provided that, for the duration of the war,[116] only half, instead of three quarters, of the crew of English ships needed to be English and in 1776 and 1777, during the War of Independence, there were two statutes[117] which temporarily relaxed the Navigation Act and allowed three-quarters of the crew of a British ship to be foreigners. On the other hand an Act of 1794[118] provided that no British ship registered under the Registration Act 1786 could import or export any goods unless navigated by a British master and three quarters British crew.

After the Restoration, although the Political Lent was no longer enforced, the policy of encouraging the fishing industry, still recognised as an important source for ships and trained seamen, was continued by such methods as prohibiting imports of certain kinds of foreign caught fish, imposing heavy duties on fish allowed to be imported in foreign ships, freeing from duties salt required for curing fish, supporting the whaling industry and giving bounties for the export of some kinds of fish in English ships. Colonial fisheries were also

111. Ralph Davis, *op. cit.*, p. 52.
112. *Ibid.*, p. 68.
113. Harper, *op. cit.*, pp. 359 and 361.
114. 2 & 3 Anne, c.6.
115. 2 & 3 Anne, c.19.
116. The War of the Spanish Succession.
117. 16 Geo. III, c.20 and 17 Geo. III, c.34.
118. 34 Geo. III, c.68.

actively helped by Acts of 1730 and 1732[119] to encourage the fisheries of New York and Newfoundland. Although some of the measures were economic failures and the attempt to challenge the Dutch fishing supremacy in the North Sea met with little success, nevertheless there was a substantial increase in the numbers of trained seamen.[120]

The Declaration of American Independence in 1776, which broke British shipping's colonial monopoly in relation to the thirteen Colonies that formed the United States, marks a convenient point at which to consider to what extent, over a period of more than 100 years, the Navigation Act 1660 had succeeded in the attainment of its principal objective—"the increase of shipping and the encouragement of navigation". Unfortunately it is not possible to arrive at firm figures for England's total shipping tonnage in the 40-year period between 1660 and 1700 during which the Navigation Act might be expected to have had a significant effect but it seems likely that the figures in 1660 were somewhere between 160,000 and 200,000 tons and that by 1702, when a survey was made, the tonnage figure had substantially increased to somewhere between 267,000 and 323,000 tons.[121] During the eighteenth century a steady further increase in tonnage was maintained and by 1788, when the figures following compulsory registration under the 1786 Act first became available, total United Kingdom registered tonnage, nearly all built in England or the Colonies, was 1,278 million tons.[122] There are no records that can help in ascertaining to what extent the numbers of seamen increased after 1660 but, bearing in mind the normal statutory requirement that at least three-quarters of the crew had to be British, the substantial increase in British tonnage must have involved at least an equally substantial increase in British seamen.

Thus, by the last quarter of the eighteenth century, there was no doubting the supremacy of British shipping[123] but nevertheless the immediate consequence of the American revolution was to provoke a strong feeling that British shipping and shipbuilding needed more than ever to retain its centuries old navigation system; in particular the influential British shipping interests were convinced that they still required not only their imperial monopoly but also the protection in other trades to which they had for so long been accustomed if they were to maintain their supremacy against American and other foreign

119. 3 Geo. II, c.12 and 5 Geo. II, c.28.

120. For the numbers employed in the fishing industry generally see Harper, *op. cit.*, pp. 329 *et seq.*

121. The lower of the two figures for 1660 and 1702 are those calculated by Harper (*op. cit.*, pp. 326 *et seq.*) and the higher figures in each case are those calculated by Davis (*op. cit.*, p. 15 and Appendix A). Between 1660 and 1700 the ratio of English to foreign vessels in England's foreign trade also substantially improved—see Usher, *op. cit.*, Table II.

122. B. R. Mitchell and Phyllis Deane, *Abstract of British Historical Statistics* (Cambridge, 1962), p. 217.

123. Notwithstanding the fact that, following the Declaration of Independence, the British merchant marine had been reduced by about one-third which represented the ships belonging to the thirteen new States.

competition. So, although the changes brought about by the War of Independence and the industrial revolution, coupled with the growing influence of the new free trade philosophy, were to bring about the gradual decline and eventual abolition of the entire mercantile system of which the Navigation Acts constituted such an essential element, before 1820 there was no serious erosion of the original Carolean principles underlying the navigation system but there were some modifications and most, though not all, of these were relaxations.

The American colonial revolt resulted in the passing, between 1774 and 1776, of Acts[124] whose purpose was first to restrict and then to prohibit completely all trade between the mother country and her rebellious Colonies. In 1783, after the Treaty of Versailles, the trading prohibition was removed[125] but Pitt's introduction of a Bill to allow more liberal trading for United States' vessels with Great Britain and her Colonies[126] provoked fierce opposition, Pitt's ministry went out of office before the Bill could be passed and in the next administration Fox and his supporters accepted that the sacred principles of the Navigation Laws should not be breached. Pitt's Bill was dropped and in its place an Act of 1783[127] empowered the King to regulate trade with the newly recognised United States by Order in Council. Under this Act Orders were made allowing the import and export between the British West Indian Colonies and the United States of a limited number of enumerated goods but in British ships only; in 1788 a further Act[128] put this trade on a more permanent basis but American ships were still prohibited and the permitted list of goods was not extended.

Between 1783 and 1797 the trade between Great Britain and the United States was also regulated by Orders in Council but, following the conclusion of a Treaty of Amity, Commerce and Navigation in 1794, an Act of 1797[129] provided that American produce might be imported into Great Britain[130] either in British vessels or in ships built in the United States, wholly owned by U.S. citizens and manned by a U.S. master with at least three-quarters of the crew also U.S. citizens.[131] However the 1797 Act imposed a tonnage duty on American vessels and a discriminating customs duty on the goods they carried; it was not until the conclusion of further Conventions of Commerce and

124. 14 Geo. III, c.19, 15 Geo. III, cc. 10 & 18 and 16 Geo. III, c.5.

125. By 23 Geo. III, c.26.

126. Pitt's Bill would have allowed United States' ships to trade with Great Britain on the same footing as other foreign ships but only paying the same duties as British ships. In addition the Bill would have permitted American ships to import American goods into the British Colonies and to export any colonial produce to the United States.

127. 23 Geo. III, c.39.

128. 28 Geo. III, c.6.

129. 37 Geo. III, c.97.

130. By an Act of 1801 (41 Geo. III, c.95) into Ireland as well.

131. The 1797 Act also permitted the United States to trade with the British Colonies in the East Indies and an Act of 1807 (47 Geo. III, Sess. 2, c.95) regulated the trade between the United States and the British possessions on the North American continent.

Navigation in 1815 and 1818[132] that reciprocal treatment between British and American ships was established by abolishing the differential duties previously levied not only by Britain but by the United States as well in respect of direct voyages between the two countries.[133]

Between 1776 and 1820 the principle that all the colonial enumerated commodities should only be exported in British ships to the United Kingdom was generally maintained but there were a few small relaxations[134] and in addition some small exceptions were made to the general rule that European goods could only be imported into the Colonies from the United Kingdom.[135] On the other hand all East Indian products had still to be imported into the American and African Colonies from the United Kingdom[136] and, apart from the limited trade between the West Indian Colonies and the United States sanctioned by the Act of 1788, there were only a few products which the British Colonies in the West Indies and South America were allowed to import from British North America or from the European Colonies in America. There was however one small breach in the golden rule that colonial trade should be restricted to British ships; by a "free port" Act of 1765,[137] as supplemented by further similar Acts and culminating in a consolidating statute of 1805,[138] certain nominated British colonial ports in the West Indies and North America were opened to foreign vessels of a particular type which were permitted to bring into these free ports specified produce from the foreign owned American Colonies.

A few more minor exceptions were made to the Navigation Act rule requiring direct shipment of United Kingdom imports from foreign countries in Asia, Africa and America but almost all the goods covered by these exceptions had to be brought in English built ships. On the other hand a new restriction was imposed; the Navigation Act had allowed direct import from Europe of goods of Asian, African or American growth which had been manufactured in Europe

132. The Act providing for their enforcement was passed in 1819–59 Geo. III, c.54 which also permitted U.S. vessels to carry goods from the United Kingdom to British possessions in the East Indies.

133. The rights of importing their produce into the United Kingdom given to the United States by the Acts of 1797 and 1801 led to the granting in 1808 and 1811 of similar trading rights to the Portuguese possessions in Southern America—48 Geo. III, cc. 11 & 109 and 51 Geo. III, c.47.

134. For example an Act of 1816 (56 Geo. III, c.91) allowed Dutch residents of certain West Indian islands, formerly Dutch Colonies, to ship their products direct to Holland and further Acts of 1815 and 1817 (55 Geo. III, c.29 and 57 Geo. III, c.4) permitted all North American colonial produce and many of the products of the Sugar Colonies to be shipped direct to Malta and Gibraltar.

135. The North American Colonies were allowed to import certain specified produce from Malta and Gibraltar, European ports south of Cape Finisterre and the Azores and Madeira. The Sugar Colonies were also permitted to import goods from Malta and Gibraltar and corn from Europe south of Cape Finisterre.

136. This stipulation had been made in 1720 by 7 Geo. I, st. 1 c.21.

137. 6 Geo. III, c.49.

138. 45 Geo. III, c.57.

but by an Act of 1779[139] it was provided that, subject to certain limited exceptions, the produce of Asia, Africa or America manufactured in any foreign country was not to be imported into the United Kingdom unless manufactured in the country of its growth or in the country where the goods were first shipped for transportation.

Prior to 1820 there was no substantial departure from the rules governing the carriage of the enumerated articles from Europe to the United Kingdom or the prohibition of certain imports from the Netherlands and Germany but there were a few small relaxations. An Act of 1782[140] permitted the import from the Netherlands or Germany of Hungarian and German drugs and also Hungarian, Austrian and German wines and silk; the same Act also permitted the import of the enumerated articles in ships which were the property of subjects under the same sovereign as the sovereign of the country of growth, production or manufacture.[141]

The British coasting trade continued to be reserved exclusively to British owned and British built vessels with the master and, after 1794,[142] the whole of the crew British and, apart from temporary relaxations prompted by the exigencies of war,[143] the requirements of the Navigation Laws regarding the manning of other British ships by British seamen were fully maintained and the employment of seamen was encouraged by the payment of bounties and prize money. The fishing industry was still looked upon as a valuable nursery for seamen and continued to receive statutory encouragement. By an Act of 1809[144] it was provided that all fish caught by British subjects in British owned and British built fishing vessels might be imported into the United Kingdom duty free. Bounties continued to be given for the encouragement of herring fishing and curing and by Acts of 1802 and 1806[145] bounties were also given to the Greenland whale fisheries and the Newfoundland fisheries.

When, following the French Revolutionary and Napoleonic Wars, peace came at last in 1815, the United Kingdom had attained an immensely strong commercial position and her shipping, still benefiting from the protection and preference conferred by the little changed Navigation Laws, had increased substantially both in absolute and relative terms. As a result of the damage done to Dutch and French shipping during the Wars and the handicaps and loss of trade sustained by United States' shipping after 1776 through the operation of the Navigation Acts, from which the shipping of the former

139. 19 Geo. III, c.48.
140. 22 Geo. III, c.78
141. This 1782 Act did not include the usual requirement that the foreign ships must also have been built in the foreign country in question and be crewed by the people of that country. This matter was rectified in 1787 by 27 Geo. III, c.19.
142. 34 Geo. III, c.68.
143. 33 Geo. III, c.26 and 43 Geo. III, c.64.
144. 49 Geo. III, c.98.
145. 42 Geo. III, c.26 and 46 Geo. III, c.103.

American Colonies had previously derived substantial benefits, Britain had obtained a near monopoly which practically secured much of the shipping trade of the world.

Over the 30 years following the Registration Act 1786, the tonnage of the British merchant fleet had almost doubled and by 30th September 1816 stood at 2.504 million tons[146]; in addition the clearances of British shipping from ports in Great Britain during the five years 1816–20 were, on average, 83.7 per cent of the total clearances in that period.[147] So "a century and a half of conflict, which began with the first Dutch War and the promulgation of the Navigation Acts, had ended by placing Great Britain in a position of supremacy as regards ships, colonies and commerce such as even seventeenth century Holland had never enjoyed".[148]

146. Mitchell and Deane, *op. cit.*, p 217.

147. C. E. Fayle, *History of the World's Shipping Industry* (London, 1934), p. 197. The total clearances of British shipping during the five years 1816–1820 were nearly 42 per cent greater than in the five years 1788–1792.

148. *Ibid.*

CHAPTER 2

PROTECTIONISM ABANDONED

In view of the world predominance which, by 1815, British shipping had attained, it was not surprising that the protagonists of free trade should campaign for the entire abolition of the navigation system on the grounds that the British shipping industry could stand on its own feet and was no longer in need of the artificial protection that it had enjoyed for more than a century and a half. However those in political power during the period between 1820 and 1845, particularly Peel, Canning and Huskisson, still felt that the Navigation Laws made an important contribution to the defensive strength of the country and the maintenance of the close links between Britain and the Colonies; they therefore concluded that the time was not yet ripe for abolition but that some changes were required. As a result substantial inroads were made into the Navigation Laws and the system of protective tariffs and imperial preference but nevertheless when, in 1845, an Act[1] consolidated and codified the Navigation Laws for the third time since 1825[2] many of the more fundamental protectionist principles established in 1660 were still retained.

The first real momentum for a radical change in British foreign commercial policy came in 1820 when Alexander Baring, the merchant banker, presented to the Commons a petition from the merchants of London calling for relaxation of the protective tariffs and greater freedom for foreign commerce.[3] The petition led to the appointment by Lords and Commons of Select Committees on Foreign Trade and in their Report of 18th July 1820[4] the Commons Committee, after paying tribute to the beneficial effect of the Navigation Laws on the growth of shipping which had rendered the Laws "objects of attachment and veneration to every British subject", proposed some limited relaxations to relieve commerce from a few of the more onerous restrictions.[5]

1. 8 & 9 Vict., c.88
2. The first consolidation was in 1825 (6 Geo. IV, c.109) and the second in 1833 (3 & 4 Will. IV, c.54)—see further *infra*.
3. For the text of the petition see P. Debs. NS, Vol. 1, cc.179–182.
4. Parl. Papers 1820 (300) Vol. 2.
5. The Committee emphasised that their proposals were not to be regarded as advising any "remission of that protective vigilance under which the shipping and navigation of the kingdom have so eminently grown and flourished".

The Commons Committee was reappointed in 1821 and in their Report of 9th March 1821[6] they dealt exclusively with the rates of import duty on timber which, since 1809, had given a strong preference to Canadian timber as against timber from Northern Europe; the Committee, whilst recognising the importance of the Canadian timber trade to British shipping, recommended that the differential should be reduced by £1 and, in spite of strong opposition from both British shipowners and Canadian timber interests, legislative effect was quickly given to this modest reduction in imperial preference.[7]

In 1822 there was a series of five Acts[8] to implement (*inter alia*) the modifications of the Navigation and Colonial Laws recommended in the 1820 Report of the Commons Committee. The first of these measures was an Act[9] repealing a large number of pre-1660 statutes, including all the remaining Navigation Laws prior to 1660, and in the second Act[10] "desecrating hands were placed upon the venerable Act of 1660".[11] The Act repealed the provisions in the Navigation Act 1660[12] requiring U.K. imports of goods from foreign countries in Asia, Africa and America to be directly imported in British ships only and those regulating the import of the European enumerated articles, the provisions in the Statute of Frauds 1662[13] prohibiting certain imports from the Netherlands or Germany and treating British owned but foreign built ships as alien and also repealed that part of 19 Geo. III, c. 48 which required that imported manufactured goods from Asia, Africa or America must have been manufactured in the country of growth or first shipment.

The third Act in the series[14] made some modifications to the principles established in 1660 but otherwise much of the statute comprised re-enactments to fill the repealed provisions of the Navigation Act 1660. With a view to encouraging the United Kingdom's entrêpot trade, it was provided that foreign goods of Asia, Africa and America could be imported in British ships from Europe for warehousing and re-export but if the goods were for use in the United Kingdom import from Europe was still prohibited. The former import prohibitions of certain European goods were not restored and all European countries were thus put on a footing of equality as regards their trades with the United Kingdom. Two additions, tallow and tobacco, were made to the

6. Parl. Papers 1821 (186), Vol. 6.
7. By 1 & 2 Geo. IV, c.37.
8. 3 Geo. IV, cc. 41, 42, 43, 44 and 45—sponsored by Wallace, Vice-President of the Board of Trade and often referred to as "Wallace's Acts".
9. 3 Geo. IV, c.41.
10. 3 Geo. IV, c.42.
11. Alexander Brady, *William Huskisson and Liberal Reform* (Oxford University Press, 1928), p. 89.
12. Sections 3, 4 and 8.
13. Section 23 and part of Section 6.
14. 3 Geo. IV, c.43—sometimes referred to as the Navigation Act 1822.

original list of European enumerated articles[15] but an important relaxation was made by a provision that the enumerated articles could be imported into the United Kingdom in a foreign ship owned and built in the country from which the goods were imported and navigated by crews of that country.[16] In recognition of the independence recently gained by former Spanish Colonies in South America and the West Indies, trading privileges relating to imports into the United Kingdom, similar to those already granted to the United States and Portugal, were extended to these new countries.

The next Act[17] regulated and extended trade between British possessions in America and the West Indies and foreign countries or foreign possessions in America and the West Indies. After repealing many earlier statutes, the Act provided that certain listed articles (but no others) might be imported into the named British colonial free ports[18] direct from any foreign country in North or South America or any foreign islands in the West Indies of which the articles were the growth produce or manufacture either in British ships or ships of the foreign exporting country.[19] It was further provided that the produce of the British Dominions and other goods legally imported into the free ports could be exported from the free ports to any foreign place in America or the West Indies in British ships or foreign ships of the importing country[19] but goods exported in foreign ships had to be taken direct to the country to which the ship belonged. Legally imported listed articles could also be exported to other British Colonies in America or the West Indies or to the United Kingdom but in British ships only. Power was reserved for the King in Council to prohibit intercourse with any foreign country if privileges similar to those granted by the Act were not allowed to British vessels trading with that country.

The last of the five Acts[20] relaxed the rules governing the trade between the British Colonies in America and the West Indies and other parts of the world. Some earlier Acts were repealed and the Act then provided firstly that any articles grown, produced or manufactured in the British American or West Indian Colonies might be exported in British ships direct to any foreign port in Europe or Africa or to Gibraltar, Malta or the Channel Islands and secondly that certain listed articles might be exported from any European or African foreign port or from Gibraltar, Malta or the Channel Islands to British American or West Indian Colonies in British ships. A further statute later in 1822[21]

15. After 1822 there were some further additions to the list but some items were struck off.

16. This modified Section 8 of the Navigation Act 1660 which had provided that European goods carried in a foreign ship from its own country had to be the produce of that country.

17. 3 Geo. IV, c.44.

18. Power was reserved to the King in Council to add to the list of free ports.

19. To qualify, the foreign ships had to be built in the country in question and owned and navigated by the inhabitants of that country.

20. 3 Geo. IV, c.45.

21. 3 Geo. IV, c.119.

regulated the trade between Canada and the United States; certain United States' goods were allowed to be imported into Canada by land or inland navigation and permission was also given for the produce of the British Dominions to be exported from Canada to the United States in British or American vessels if the export was by sea.

At the end of 1822 Huskisson was appointed President of the Board of Trade and shortly afterwards there was an amending and consolidating Act dealing with the registration of British ships.[22] Since the Registration Act 1786 there had been several statutory modifications[23] but administrative problems still arose and it was decided that there should be a consolidating statute. The 1823 Act did not however involve any departure from the basic principles laid down in 1786; it was still the policy to confine the privileges of British ships to ships wholly built in the British Dominions, duly registered, wholly owned by resident British subjects and navigated by a British master with at least three-quarters of the crew also British.

In 1823 there were also two statutes relating to crews on British ships. The first of the Acts[24] was intended to increase the number of trained seamen and provided that after 1st January 1824 every British ship of more than 80 tons should have on board one or more apprentices proportionate to the tonnage of the ship.[25] The second Act[26] declared that lascar seamen should not be regarded as British mariners for the purpose of 34 Geo. III, c. 68[27] but the King was empowered to vary this stipulation in time of war and it was also provided that, if a ship with lascars as part of the crew had a British master and not less than four British seamen for every 100 tons registered (and pro rata), then such ship was to be deemed duly navigated according to law even though the number of British seamen should be less than three-quarters of the total crew.[28] In addition there was a Warehousing Act 1823[29] which, as a further step towards Wallace's goal of "making this country the general depot, the great emporium of the commerce of the world",[30] allowed foreigners to deposit goods in British warehouses and then to export them free of duty.

However, from the point of view of British shipping, the most significant change in 1823 resulted from the legislation which Huskisson initiated with a view to granting to the ships of those foreign countries willing to reciprocate the same treatment as was accorded to British ships in respect of customs

22. 4 Geo. IV, c.41—the Registration Act 1823.
23. 27 Geo. III, c.19, 34 Geo. III, cc. 42 & 68, 35 Geo. III, c.58 and 37 Geo. III, c.63.
24. 4 Geo. IV, c. 25—Ships' Apprentices Act 1823.
25. The maximum was five apprentices for a ship of 700 tons or more.
26. 4 Geo. IV, c.80
27. This 1794 Act had provided that British ships could not import or export any article unless navigated by British subjects.
28. This Act also consolidated and amended the laws regulating trading to and from places within the limit of the East India Company's Charter.
29. 4 Geo. IV, c.24.
30. P. Debs. NS, Vol. 5, c.1292.

duties and port charges in British ports. For many years an important feature of the mercantile system, although it was not strictly part of the Navigation Laws, had been that foreign vessels bringing to the U.K. or re-exporting legally permissible goods were required to pay higher import duties and port charges and to receive lower drawbacks, bounties and allowances than would have been the case had the goods been carried in British vessels. Thus there was a preference for British shipping even in trades in which foreign ships could participate without offending the Navigation Laws, but Huskisson considered that commerce would benefit if the equal treatment already accorded to the United States and Portugal were to be extended to other countries[31]; furthermore, by the early 1820s, European maritime powers were becoming strong enough to threaten retaliation against British shipping and indeed Holland and Prussia had already taken retaliatory action.

The Reciprocity Act 1823[32] empowered the King in Council to enter into reciprocity treaties with foreign countries whereby, providing British ships were given equality of treatment in those countries, foreign ships carrying goods of a kind which they were legally entitled to import or export into or from the United Kingdom or British Dominions should pay the same duties as British vessels and would likewise receive the same drawbacks, bounties and allowances.[33] A supplementary Reciprocity Act of 1824[34] gave power to authorise the payment by foreign ships of the same tonnage duties as were paid by British vessels provided the foreign country gave equal treatment to British vessels.[35] From 1824 onwards reciprocity treaties were concluded with most of the maritime countries in Europe[36] and with many of the new South American Republics but these treaties did not alleviate in any way the restrictions imposed on foreign ships by the Navigation Laws since they merely gave the same treatment in respect of customs and tonnage duties to goods legally shipped in foreign ships as was accorded to goods shipped in British ships.[37]

Between 1824 and 1849 there was constant argument between the free traders and the protectionists, the majority of British shipowners being in the latter category, as to the effect of the reciprocity treaties on the growth of

31. See Huskisson's speech on 6th June 1823—P. Debs. NS, Vol. 9, c.795.

32. 4 Geo. IV, c.77.

33. Power was also given to levy additional duties on goods in foreign vessels if the foreign country in question imposed higher duties on goods imported in British vessels. Acting under this power Huskisson, in 1824, took retaliatory action against American shipping—see P. Debs. NS, Vol. 10, c.154.

34. 5 Geo. IV, c.1.

35. Under this 1824 Act also there was power to impose higher tonnage duties on foreign ships belonging to countries which imposed higher tonnage duties on British ships.

36. The text of the first treaty, that with Prussia on 2nd April 1824, is given in *Hertslet's Collection of Treaties and Conventions relating to Commerce and Navigation* Vol. III (London, 1840), pp. 353–355.

37. Not all the treaties gave complete equality of treatment because in some cases the foreign country was not willing to grant full equality to British ships.

British and foreign shipping and their respective participations in the so called "protected" and "unprotected" trades. The statistics show[38] that from 1824 to 1838 there was no significant absolute growth in British tonnage and although, between 1838 and 1849, British tonnage increased substantially[39] so that Britain was still well ahead of her main competitors, in terms of relative growth the position was far from comforting; between 1830 and 1850 United States' foreign trade tonnage increased by some 167 per cent but over the same period the increase in the tonnage of the British Empire was only 67 per cent.[40] Furthermore the figures for British and foreign tonnage entering the United Kingdom before and during reciprocity show that in comparative terms British shipping was losing ground; the yearly average of British tonnage entering the United Kingdom during reciprocity (1824–49) increased 76.6 per cent as compared with the average for the eight preceding years but the corresponding increase in entries of foreign tonnage was 131 per cent.[41]

The year 1825 marked the culmination of the legislative measures for the reform of the navigation and trade systems which had commenced with Wallace's Acts of 1822 and which had been continued by Huskisson in 1823 and 1824. The main legislative event of 1825 was the passing of the Customs Consolidation Acts[42] -a series of 12 statutes sponsored by Huskisson which have been described as "by far the greatest feat in the consolidation of the statute law that had ever been made".[43] The first Act in the series[44] repealed well over 400 statutes relating to the Customs covering a period from 1393 to 1824 including substantially all the Navigation Laws then remaining in force.[45] The following three Acts provided a new set of rules for the management and general regulation of the Customs[46] and codified the law relating to smuggling.[47] There was then enacted the most comprehensive single statute in the history of the Navigation Laws since 1660—the Navigation Act 1825[48] "For the Encouragement of British Shipping and Navigation" in which it was declared that the Act should come into operation on 1st January 1826 and that it should "constitute and be the Law of Navigation of the British Empire".

38. Mitchell and Deane *op. cit.*, pp. 217–218.

39. The figures for British tonnage were: 1824: 2,349,000 tons; 1838: 2,421,000 tons and 1849: 3,486,000 tons.

40. See "Tables of the Progress of Merchant Shipping 1820–1880", Parl. Papers 1881 (125), Vol. 82.

41. Harper, *op. cit.*, p. 351.

42. 6 Geo. IV, cc. 105 to 116. For the Commons debates on these Acts see P. Debs. NS, Vol. 12, cc. 1097 and 1196 and Vol. 13 cc. 1215, 1277 and 1347.

43. W. S. Holdsworth, *A History of English Law*, Vol. 13 (London, 1938), p. 262.

44. 6 Geo. IV, c.105.

45. Amongst the repeals were those sections of the Navigation Act 1660 and the Statute of Frauds 1662 which still remained on the statute book, the Navigation Act 1822, the Colonial Trade Acts of 1822, the Registration Act 1823 and the Ships' Apprentices Act 1823.

46. 6 Geo. IV, cc. 106 and 107.

47. 6 Geo. IV, c.108.

48. 6 Geo. IV, c.109.

The Navigation Act 1825 was mainly a codifying and consolidation measure which, in much improved form, re-enacted the Navigation Laws as amended by Wallace's Acts of 1822 and, although a few further relaxations were introduced, it needs to be emphasised that many of the fundamental protectionist principles established in 1660 were still retained. The entire imperial trade, including the coastal trade of the United Kingdom and the Colonies, was still exclusively reserved for British ships, there was still, in practical terms, a near monopoly for British ships in the carriage of long distance imports from foreign countries of Asia and Africa and some degree of preference in imports from foreign America, the general prohibition against importing non-European produce from Europe (even in British ships) was retained and British shipping was still favoured to some extent by the modified regulations governing the import of the European enumerated goods. Moreover there were no relaxations of the rules governing the ownership of British ships and their manning by British masters and seamen nor of the requirement that a British ship had to be British built.

As regards imports into the United Kingdom from Europe, the 1825 Act provided a further relaxation whereby the enumerated goods could be brought in any ship if such goods were only to be warehoused in Great Britain for re-exportation and there was also some widening of the exceptions to the maintained general rule prohibiting the import from Europe of Asian, African or American goods for use in the United Kingdom.[49] The Act retained the general rule that goods that were the produce of foreign countries in Asia, Africa and America were not to be imported in foreign ships but it was now provided that such produce could be imported for use in the United Kingdom either in British ships or in ships of the country of which the goods were the produce and from which they were imported.[50] An earlier statute of 1825[51] had already eased the rules governing imports into the British possessions abroad from foreign countries and the Navigation Act carried the liberalising process a stage further by permitting foreign goods to be imported into any British possession in Asia, Africa or America in foreign ships[52] provided they were "ships of the country of which the goods are the produce and from which the goods are imported".[53]

The next statute in the series, an Act for the registering of British vessels,[54]

49. If these goods were being imported for warehousing and re-exportation they could be brought in British or any foreign ships.

50. This extended to all countries in the three continents the privileges already granted to the United States, Portugal, Spanish America and the Spanish West Indies. Goods for warehousing and re-exportation could be brought in British or any foreign ships.

51. 6 Geo. IV, c.73.

52. This privilege given to foreign ships was limited by 6 Geo. IV, c.114—see *infra*.

53. There was no freedom for foreign ships generally to bring in goods to the British Colonies for warehousing and re-exportation.

54. 5 Geo. IV, c.110—Registration Act 1825.

was almost identical to the repealed Registration Act 1823 and there was then an Act[55] imposing new customs duties; the duties were lowered, simplified and consolidated but the duties on foreign imports still gave substantial protection to British manufacturers and a significant amount of imperial preference for all the more important colonial products.[56] Then came an Act[57] which dealt with the bonded warehouses and this was followed by an Act[58] granting certain bounties and allowances which drastically reduced the list of goods still entitled to receive export bounties.[59]

The purpose of the following statute, the British Possessions Act 1825,[60] was to regulate the trade of the British possessions abroad; certain of its provisions supplemented the Navigation Act 1825[61] and, in effect, formed part of the imperial Navigation Code. The 1822 legislation had still left some restrictions on colonial exports[62] but by this 1825 Act these were removed and the foreign export trade of the Colonies was no longer subject to any limitations except that first the trade was only to be through the free ports and secondly the countries of the foreign vessels trading to the Colonies were required to give similar privileges to British ships.[63] The Possessions Act also provided for the levying of duties on the import of certain goods into the Colonies and the table of duties showed a significant preference to the produce and manufacture of the United Kingdom and her Colonies; thus the heavier taxation of foreign imports meant that in practice the mother country retained much of the old monopoly which had been abandoned in 1822 and this in turn benefited British ships in which all exports from the United Kingdom to the Colonies had still to be carried.[64]

Whilst there can be little doubt that the modification made to the Navigation Laws by Wallace's Act of 1822 and the Customs Consolidation Acts 1825, together with the reciprocity treaties and the treaties admitting foreign ships to colonial trade, all combined to favour foreign shipping, particularly in the short sea trades between the United Kingdom and the Continent, at the

55. 6 Geo. IV, c.111—Customs Duties Act 1825.

56. This imperial preference not only assisted the Colonies but also benefited British shipping through its imperial monopoly.

57. 6 Geo. IV, c.112.

58. 6 Geo. IV, c.113.

59. Bounties were only to be given for the export of cordage, linen and sail-cloth and for the re-export of sugar.

60. 6 Geo. IV, c.114.

61. For example the Possessions Act provided that the foreign imports into the Colonies permitted by the Navigation Act should only be through the designated free ports.

62. Colonial exports to foreign countries in Europe and Africa had to be carried in British ships.

63. This requirement for equality of treatment applied to both colonial exports and imports. Treaties opening colonial foreign trade to foreign ships were made with a number of European and South American countries but no treaty was ever made with Holland because the Dutch would not grant reciprocal privileges to British ships.

64. Navigation Act 1825, s.7.

expense of the British, nevertheless British shipping still retained exclusively the profitable imperial trade, the coastal trades of the United Kingdom and Colonies and the greater part of the long distance trades with Asia, Africa and America.

However the powerful and well organised British shipping interest which, with the landed interest, provided the backbone of protectionism[65] vehemently believed that without protection they could not compete with foreign shipowners and that the Reciprocity Acts and the 1825 legislation would inevitably lead to the decay and ruin of British shipping; the shipowners regarded Huskisson as their chief enemy and he was condemned as insensitive to the special position which the industry deserved[66] in spite of the fact that Huskisson's speeches in the Commons[67] showed clearly that his objectives did not include the destruction of the navigation system. Huskisson accepted "the necessity of preserving our ascendancy of the ocean and thereby sustaining the high station in the rank of nations which that ascendancy more than any other circumstance has given to this country" and he viewed the navigation laws as having a two-fold object—"First to create and maintain in this country a great commercial Marine and secondly—(an object not less important in the eyes of statesmen)—to prevent any one other nation from engrossing too large a portion of the navigation of the rest of the world". Huskisson also strongly defended the imperial shipping monopoly—"All intercourse between the mother country and the colonies, whether direct or circuitous, and all intercourse of the colonies with each other will be considered as a coasting trade to be reserved entirely and absolutely to ourselves".

The shipping interest in the Commons, though small numerically, was very strongly organised and comprised "a recognised parliamentary group, voting together and always alert to resist anything which might hurt their interests".[68] At the beginning of 1826, a time of general trade and shipping depression, the shipowners presented numerous petitions to Parliament "all asserting the impossibility of competition, the inequalities of the reciprocity treaties, the vast increase of foreign and the rapid decline of British shipping and demanding the reimposition of protecting duties on British bottoms".[69] On 12th May 1826 the Commons debated "the Navigation Laws—State of the Shipping

65. Lucy Brown, *The Board of Trade and the Free Trade Movement 1830–42* (Oxford, 1958), p. 176.

66. Barry Gordon, *Economic Doctrine and Tory Liberalism 1824–1839* (London, 1979), p. 103.

67. On 21st March 1825 (P. Debs. NS, Vol. 12, c.1097) when introducing the 1825 legislation, on 12th May 1826 (P. Debs. NS, Vol. 15, c.1144) in a debate on "Navigation Laws—State of the Shipping Interest" and on 7th May 1827 (P. Debs., Vol. 17, c.619) in a debate on "the State of the British Commercial Shipping Interest".

68. Lucy Brown, *op. cit.*, p. 175.

69. W. Smart, *Economic Annals of the Nineteenth Century 1821–1830* (London, 1917), p. 374.

Interest"[70] and Huskisson convinced the majority of the House that British shipping was far from being "in a state of decay", that the policy of reciprocity was fully justified and that the shipowners' problems were only temporary and partly due to their overbuilding of new ships.

A year later there was another Commons debate[71] on a motion for the appointment of a Select Committee to inquire into the depressed state of the British Shipping Interest but, after the shipping spokesmen had criticised the reciprocity treaties and renewed their demand for protection, Huskisson "taking point after point in detail, tore the statements made by the shipowners to pieces"[72] and the motion was thereupon withdrawn. In June 1828, shortly after Huskisson's unexpected resignation from office, there was a further Commons debate on the motion that "this House cannot view the diminution of registered tonnage and the numbers of seamen employed without concern"[73] but the motion was negatived without a discussion. Lastly, in 1830, another petition by London shipowners was debated in both Lords and Commons[74]; on this occasion Wellington successfully defended Huskisson's reforms and maintained that the relaxation of the Navigation Laws had not harmed the shipping industry.

The shipowners' failure, between 1826 and 1830, to convince Parliament of their need for protection did not deter them from continuing their efforts. In 1831,[75] and again in 1835, they succeeded in defeating proposals for reducing the protection given to Canadian timber,[76] in 1833 their complaints of unfair competition formed a considerable part of the evidence taken by the Select Committee on Manufactures, Commerce and Shipping[77] and in 1837 they played a leading part in defeating a private member's Bill to implement the recommendations contained in the 1836 Report of the Select Committee on the Causes of Shipwrecks.[78] Later, in 1844, the shipowners procured the appointment of a Select Committee to inquire into the state and condition of the Merchant Marine[79] and from 1847 they conducted a long and bitter campaign against the proposed repeal of the Navigation Laws.

In spite of the persistence with which the shipowners pursued their campaign both in Parliament and the country, they failed to persuade successive Tory

70. P. Debs. NS, Vol. 15, c.1144.
71. On 7th May 1827—P. Debs. NS, Vol. 17, c.592.
72. Smart, *op. cit.*, p. 426.
73. Debate on 17th June 1828. P. Debs., Vol. 19, c.1416.
74. P. Debs. NS, Vol. 24, cc. 453 and 660.
75. P. Debs. 3 Ser., Vol.2, c.414.
76. The 1835 proposals were contained in the Report of the Select Committee on Timber Duties, Parl. Papers 1835 (519) Vol. 19.
77. Parl. Papers 1833 (690) Vol. 6.
78. Parl. Papers 1836 (567) Vol. 17. The shipowners also successfully opposed similar recommendations in 1843 by another Select Committee on Shipwrecks—see First Report of the 1843 Committee, Parl. Papers 1843 (549) Vol. 9 and p. 56 *infra*.
79. P. Debs. 3 Ser., Vol. 75, c.274 and Parl. Papers 1844 (545) Vol. 8.

and Whig governments to reverse the measures which Huskisson had carried through but it may well be that the political and commercial strength of the shipping interest contributed to the fact that after 1825 no significant further relaxations of the Navigation Laws took place prior to their repeal in 1849 although there was new legislation relating to seamen and the carriage of passengers. Early in 1826 there was an Act to give effect to Treaties of Commerce with South American countries,[80] later in the same year there was an Act which relaxed slightly the rules governing the import from Europe of goods produced in Asia or Africa[81] and in 1827 a further Act made a number of changes in the list of European enumerated goods.[82] Apart from a Passengers Act in 1828, there was no further legislation relating to the Navigation and Trade Laws until 1833 when, somewhat surprisingly, there was a further series of 11 Customs Consolidation Acts.[83] The first of these statutes was a repealing Act and the remaining 10 statutes were, subject to small modifications, repetitions of the corresponding 1825 legislation. The Navigation Act 1833 only differed from its predecessors by incorporating the changes effected in 1826 and 1827 and there were only a few minor changes in the Registration Act 1833. The British Possessions Act 1833 was also much the same as the corresponding 1825 Act and thus in general the main principles of the Navigation Laws remained unchanged.

Between 1833 and 1845[84] there were only a few relatively modest relaxations of the Navigation Laws[85] but during this period there was some much needed legislation relating to British seamen and the carriage of passengers on British ships. In 1835 there were two statutes to improve the supply of British seamen; the first Act[86] established a register of all merchant seamen, regulated their terms of service and provided for the compulsory carrying of apprentices[87] whilst the second Act[88] encouraged the voluntary enlistment of seamen in the Royal Navy by the giving of bounties and by limiting the period of service. In

80. 7 Geo. IV, c.5. These Treaties involved a small amendment to section 15 of the Navigation Act 1825.

81. 7 Geo. IV, c.48. This Act also restored the Ships' Apprentices Act 1823 which had been inadvertently repealed by 6 Geo. IV, c.105.

82. 7 & 8 Geo. IV, c.56. The changes resulted in substantial net additions to the list.

83. 3 & 4 Will. IV, cc.50–60. It seems that in the nineteenth century the legislature was inclined to revise the entire code at rather short intervals; there was to be a further re-enactment only 12 years later (8 & 9 Vict., cc. 84–94). On the understanding that the Bills of 1833 were a simple and pure consolidation without any change they were passed without any debate (P. Debs. 3 Ser. 1833, Vol. 9, c.5).

84. The year in which the next series of Customs Consolidation Acts were enacted.

85. See 1 & 2 Vict., c.113; 3 & 4 Vict., c.95 and 6 & 7 Vict., c.84.

86. 5 & 6 Will. IV, c.19—repealed but largely re-enacted in 1844 by a further Act (7 & 8 Vict., c.112) amending and consolidating the laws relating to merchant seamen.

87. The Ships' Apprentices Act 1823 was repealed but Section 31 of this 1835 Act provided that every ship over 80 tons had to carry apprentices in proportion to its tonnage with a maximum of five apprentices for ships over 700 tons.

88. 5 & 6 Will. IV, c.24.

the same year there was a further Passengers Act[89] which repealed the Passengers Act 1828 and greatly extended the previous statutory requirements regarding the numbers of passengers that could be carried and the supply of food, water and medicines. However experience showed there were still serious deficiencies and abuses and these led to the passing in 1842 of a more severe Passengers Act[90]; even the advocates of free trade felt bound to concede that the state of the passenger trade necessitated an exceptional degree of Government control over merchant shipping in this special area.

Before the last consolidation of the Navigation Laws in 1845 an important new kind of Government encouragement for one sector of British shipping manifested itself in the period from 1837 onwards. This took the form of payments to certain British owners for the carriage of mail overseas and although these postal subventions, or postal subsidies as they were sometimes misleadingly called, were payments under contracts in return for services, in the early days at any rate the amounts paid were more than were commercially justified for the work performed and did undoubtedly contain some element of bounty.[91]

Prior to 1837 all overseas mail services from the United Kingdom had been controlled by the Admiralty but the service was carried out entirely by sailing vessels and was notoriously slow and irregular. Steamships were still then regarded by many as unreliable new-fangled inventions which, owing to their excessive coal consumption and higher capital cost, could not compete commercially with sailing ships in the carriage of bulk cargoes over long distances.[92] However early in 1837 two steam enthusiasts, Willcox and Anderson,[93] commenced a regular steamship service from London to Portugal, Gibraltar and Spain and in August of that year they concluded a contract with the Government to carry each week the whole of the Peninsular mail for the sum of £29,600 per annum.[94]

In the following year the Admiralty invited tenders for an Atlantic mail

89. 5 & 6 Will. IV, c.53. The first statutory attempt to improve the conditions under which passengers were carried by sea had been an Act of 1803 (43 Geo. III, c.56). There were four amending Acts between 1817 and 1823 and a consolidation Act in 1825 (6 Geo. IV, c.116). A detailed account of the many Passenger Acts between 1803 and 1872 is given by Oliver Macdonagh in *A Pattern of Government Growth* (London, 1961).

90. 5 & 6 Vict., c.107—amended in 1847 by 10 & 11 Vict., c.103 and again in 1848 by 11 & 12 Vict., c.6.

91. Many years later, in the Second Report of a Select Committee on Steamship Subsidies (Parl. Papers 1902 (385) Vol. 9) an attempt was made to define and distinguish the expressions "subvention", "subsidy" and "bounty".

92. See H. J. Dyos and D. H. Aldcroft, *British Transport* (Leicester, 1969), pp. 238–239.

93. Later to be the founders of the Peninsular and Oriental Steam Navigation Company ("P & O") incorporated by Royal Charter in 1840.

94. This mail service, thanks partly to the subsidy, was such an unqualified success that in 1840 Willcox and Anderson won a contract for the regular carriage of the Indian mail as far as Alexandria; this involved a further subvention of £34,200 per annum and led to the incorporation of P & O.

service and in 1839 the contract was won by Samuel Cunard who thereupon formed the British & North American Royal Mail Steam Packet Company—subsequently renamed the Cunard Steam Ship Company. For this mail service to Canada (Halifax) and the United States (Boston) Cunard was paid an annual subvention of £55,000, which by 1841 had been increased to £80,000, and thus began the close and most favoured relationship between Cunard and the Government which, in various ways, has continued up to the present day.[95] Then in 1840 the Pacific Steam Navigation Company was paid a relatively modest postal subvention for the carriage of mails between Central and South American ports and in 1842 the Royal Mail Steam Packet Company was awarded a contract for the delivery of mail to the West Indies, Gulf of Mexico and southern United States. Royal Mail received an initial subvention of £240,000 per annum, increased in 1852 to £270,000 per annum; the payment undoubtedly contained a large element of subsidy without which Royal Mail, regarded at that time as highly inefficient, would probably not have survived.

The reason underlying the Melbourne Government's new policy was not so much to assist struggling steamship owners in achieving commercial viability but rather to provide a more economical and efficient mail service and to encourage the development of more rapid communication with the Colonies and foreign commercial centres. Nevertheless the Government recognised and accepted that, in order to achieve a fast and regular overseas mail service by steamship, it was necessary for the payments under the early mail contracts to contain some element of bounty since without this support the liner owners would not have been able to earn sufficient revenue to meet the high costs of steamship operation. So, as Thornton puts it,[96] "the commercial importance of the decision to contract for the mail cannot be too strongly emphasized . . . the new mail policy of the British Government remained unique for ten years and in those years it gave British ocean steam shipping a start it never lost".

Since "rapid postal communication has mainly, and in fact necessarily, followed the lines of great commercial traffic"[97] there is little doubt that the new mail system did greatly encourage the growth of the British steamship liner trades and was largely responsible for the British dominance in these trades up to 1914. Moreover at a time when British sailing vessels were suffering severely from American competition in the Atlantic and other unprotected trades, there can also be little doubt that the British success in eventually recapturing the all important Atlantic liner trades from the Americans was, to a significant extent, due to the Government's postal subvention policy. In

95. Other British shipping lines strongly opposed the Government preference shown to Cunard (see F. E. Hyde, *Cunard and the North Atlantic 1840–1973* (London, 1975), p. 34. The grievances of the Great Western Shipping Company led in 1846 to the appointment of a Select Committee to consider Cunard's Atlantic Contract—see p. 72 *infra*.

96. R. H. Thornton, *British Shipping*, 1st edn. (Cambridge, 1939), p. 25.

97. Second Report of the 1902 Select Committee on Steamship Subsidies, *op. cit.*

addition this policy was also of benefit to the British shipbuilding industry since the subventions were only paid for services by British built steamships and this encouraged a more rapid expansion and development of steam vessels.

In 1845, after an interval of only 12 years since the last consolidation, Parliament passed yet another series of Customs Consolidation Acts[98]; as had been the case in 1833, the 11 Bills passed through both Houses without any debate. The first of the 1845 Acts repealed all the Customs Consolidation Acts of 1833 and also repealed, in whole or in part, more than 20 Customs and Shipping Acts which had been passed between 1833 and 1845. The following 10 statutes followed exactly the same general pattern as the corresponding 1833 legislation but incorporated the relatively minor amendments which had been made to that legislation since 1833. Thus, apart from some small relaxations, the Navigation Act 1845,[99] the Registration Act 1845[100] and the British Possessions Act 1845[101] were largely re-enactments of their 1833 predecessors and so the main principles of the British Navigation Laws remaining in force in 1845 were not only little changed from what they had been in 1825 but still in substance retained many of the more important protectionist rules which had originated in the seventeenth century.[102]

Looking, with the benefit of hindsight, at the political history of the Navigation Laws during the next four years, it is perhaps surprising that in a Parliament comprising many members strongly committed to the principle of free trade there was no opposition of any kind to the 1845 re-enactments. However, as Sir John Clapham observes, "there seems as yet to have been a tacit assumption that a navigation law was an inevitable part of British policy"[103] and he suggests that the lack of opposition may have been "partly because some of its sections were obsolete; partly because trade had for generations been adjusted to it; partly because it was so intricate and technical that only a few official persons and a few inquirers in political economy understood it, the code had escaped the critical notice of eager and informed free traders".[104] On the other hand the anti-protectionists may have thought that tactically it was best to concentrate first on securing the repeal of the Corn Laws and further reductions in imperial preference in the belief that it would then be easier to attack the Navigations Laws as the last remaining bastion of the mercantile system. If this was their political judgement, in the event it proved correct;

98. 8 & 9 Vict., cc. 84–94.

99. 8 & 9 Vict., c.88.

100. 8 & 9 Vict., c.89.

101. 8 & 9 Vict., c.93.

102. A useful summary, prepared by the Board of Trade, giving a comparative view of the state of the Navigation Laws in 1660 and 1847 is to be found in the Appendix to the 5th Report of the Commons Select Committee on the Navigation Laws dated 17th July 1847, Parl. Papers 1847 (678), Vol. 10.

103. J. H. Clapham, "The Last Year of the Navigation Acts", *English Historical Review*, Vol. 25 (1910).

104. J. H. Clapham, *Economic History of Modern Britain*, Vol. 1 (Cambridge, 1967), p. 501.

1845 was the calm before the storm and the reprieve of the Navigation Laws was only short-lived.

During the three years prior to 1845 Peel's Government, which had come to power in 1841, carried through a drastic revision of the commercial tariff which had been recommended in the 1840 Report of a Select Committee on Import Duties[105]; protective import duties were substantially reduced—in some cases eliminated—and, in differing degrees, the imperial preferences on timber, coffee and sugar were also reduced. Then, in June 1846, just before Peel's resignation, the Corn Laws were virtually abandoned by the so-called Repeal Act[106] and before the end of the 1846 session Lord John Russell's new Whig administration introduced Bills for the gradual equalisation of the import duties on colonial and foreign sugar[107] and empowering the colonial legislatures of America and Mauritius to reduce or repeal the preferential import duties in favour of British goods.[108]

These free trade measures of 1842 to 1846 undermined the whole basis of the mercantile system and, to the eyes of those opposed to protection, conspicuously exposed the Navigation Laws as an inconsistent anachronism. In January 1847, as a consequence of the potato famine and harvest failure, there was a Commons debate[109] on the temporary suspension of the Navigation Laws and an Act was passed permitting, for a limited period, import into the United Kingdom for home use of corn, other cereals and potatoes from any country in any ship however navigated "anything in the Law of Navigation to the contrary in any wise notwithstanding".[110] Although, in the course of this debate, no Government spokesmen suggested that anything more than a temporary suspension was in mind, some two weeks later the Government were supporting a Commons motion,[111] sponsored by J. L. Ricardo,[112] that "a Select Committee be appointed to inquire into the operation and policy of the Navigation Laws".

Although opposed by Disraeli and other protectionists voicing the views of shipowners and the Royal Navy, Ricardo's motion was eventually carried by a comfortable majority. The Select Committee, chaired by Milner Gibson, Vice-President of the Board of Trade, worked with commendable zeal and expedition; before the end of the 1847 session they had submitted to the House

105. Parl. Papers 1840 (601), Vol.5.

106. 9 & 10 Vict c.22. The import duty was not entirely abolished although, as from 1st February 1849, it was brought down to a nominal amount of one shilling a quarter.

107. 9 & 10 Vict c.63—Sugar Duties Act 1846. In the course of the Commons debate Lord John Russell stated that he did not propose, in any respect, to alter the Navigation Laws (P. Debs. 3 Ser., Vol.87, c.1326).

108. 9 & 10 Vict c.94.

109. P. Debs. 3 Ser. Vol. 89 cc. 210 & 275.

110. The Act (10 Vict., c.2) permitted imports in foreign ships up to September 1847 but this was later extended to 1st March 1848 by a further Act (10 & 11 Vict., c.86).

111. P. Debs. 3 Ser., Vol. 89, c.1007.

112. Author of the *Anatomy of the Navigation Laws* (London, 1847).

no less than five Reports containing the huge volume of evidence which had been taken[113] but the Committee failed to reach any conclusions. At the beginning of 1848 the protectionists, believing the majority in the Commons to be against them, moved their campaign to the House of Lords and in February 1848[114] the Lords appointed their own Select Committee to inquire into the policy and operation of the Navigation Laws. The Lords Committee also took a vast amount of evidence which was submitted to the House in three Reports between May and August 1848[115] but, like their Commons counterpart, the Lords Committee reached no conclusion.[116]

On 15th May 1848, undeterred by the fact that the Lords Committee was still taking evidence, the Commons debated a Government motion for going into Committee of the whole House on the Navigation Laws.[117] Labouchere, President of the Board of Trade, summarised the Government proposals which involved the repeal of most of the Navigation Act 1845, except that British ships would still have to be wholly British owned, the United Kingdom coasting and fishing trades and the colonial coasting trade would still be confined to British ships and the British crew requirement would be retained, the repeal of the stipulation in the Registration Act 1845 that a British ship must be wholly of the build of some part of the British Dominions and the abandonment of the compulsory apprenticeship system; he did however emphasise that the retaliatory powers of the Queen in Council[118] would be retained.

The main arguments advanced by the Government's supporters, who included Peel and Gladstone, in favour of the abolition of the navigation system were the commercial advantages of free trade and the benefits which would accrue to British shipping from the confidently predicted expansion of commerce; the strength of colonial opinion[119]; the increasing success of British shipping in the unprotected trades; the complaints of foreign powers[120]; the offers of reciprocity by the United States and what Peel described as the mutilated and shattered state of the Navigation Laws. The Conservative Opposition's arguments against repeal centred on the danger to the security of the realm and Harries, a former Chancellor of the Exchequer and the leading spokesman for the shipping interest, proposed the following resolution—"That it is essential to the national interests of the country to maintain the

113. Parl. Papers 1847 (232), (246), (329), (556) and (678), Vol. 10.

114. P. Debs. 3 Ser., Vol. 96, c.1313.

115. Parl. Papers 1847–48. HL (340), (431) and (754). Vol. 20. Part 2.

116. They asked to be reappointed in the next session so that they might give an Opinion but the Committee were not reappointed.

117. P. Debs. 3 Ser., Vol. 98, cc. 988–1005. Predictably the debate proved to be lengthy and was continued on 29th March and on 1st, 2nd, 8th and 9th June (P. Debs. 3 Ser., Vol. 99, cc. 9–70, 179–234, 251–326, 510–559 and 573–673).

118. As then set forth in 4 Geo. IV, c.77, 5 Geo. IV, c.1 and 8 & 9 Vict., c.90 (section 8).

119. See the petitions from Canada, Jamaica and Trinidad appended to the Third Report of the Lords' Select Committee, Parl. Papers 1847–48 (754) Vol. 20., Part 2.

120. There were threats of retaliation by Prussia and other German States.

fundamental principles of the existing Navigation Laws subject to such modifications as may be best calculated to obviate any proved inconvenience to the commerce of the United Kingdom and its dependencies without danger to our national strength".

The protectionists feared that American and other foreign competition in the trades that would become unprotected would lead to a serious decline both in the absolute and relative growth of British shipping and in the numbers of British seamen. The mercantile marine was still regarded by the Admiralty and many others as the nursery of the Royal Navy in times of peace and an essential source of reserve manpower in times of war.[121] The Opposition also had serious misgivings as to the effect which repeal would have on the British shipbuilding industry; it was well established that wooden sailing ships of first quality could be built much more cheaply in America and certain other foreign countries and it was feared that, if British owners were no longer required to have their ships British built, a serious decline in British shipbuilding would ensue and it would be difficult for the shipyards to meet the needs of the Royal Navy particularly in wartime. Disraeli and other protectionists also doubted whether the United States, Prussia and other foreign competitors would voluntarily reciprocate by abolishing such of their own restrictions as corresponded to those imposed by British Navigation Laws; it was argued that the correct policy should be to make only piecemeal relaxations in favour of any country that would give Britain equivalent treatment.[122]

In the end after protracted and heated debate, Harries' resolution was negatived and there was a substantial Whig/Peelite majority of 117 for going into Committee on the Navigation Laws; the Repeal Bill was then introduced but no further proceedings on it were taken until February 1849. In the meantime the Government, having noted that even some of their supporters were concerned that foreign powers might not reciprocate, arranged for a circular note to be sent by the Foreign Secretary to a large number of foreign governments outlining the restrictions which it was proposed to remove and enquiring as to what reciprocal action would be taken. The replies were, for the most part, far from reassuring[123]; in particular the United States repeated the warning made in November 1847 by the American Ambassador[124] that, even if American ships were admitted to the British imperial trade, though not to the United Kingdom's coastal trade, British ships would still not be admitted to the United States' reserved coastal trade which the Americans treated as covering not only

121. The Report of an Admiralty Committee (Appendix 9 of the Third Report of the Lords' Select Committee) showed that over the previous few years two-fifths of the Royal Navy's petty officers and seamen came from the merchant service.

122. Gladstone, a supporter of repeal, also favoured a policy of conditional relaxation.

123. For the text of Palmerston's note and the replies received from various foreign government see Command (1029), (1030), (1036), (1038), (1041) and (1048), Parl. Papers 1849, Vol. 51.

124. See "Exchange of Correspondence—Lord Palmerston and the American Ambassador", Parl. Papers 1847–48 (901) Vol. 59.

the voyages between their extensive Atlantic and Pacific coasts but also direct traffic with America's overseas possessions such as the Philippines.

On 14th February 1849 the Repeal Bill was brought in to the Commons[125] and the Second Reading took place on 9th and 12th March 1849.[126] The arguments of both free traders and protectionists were much the same as they had been in 1848 but there was on this occasion a more significant contribution from Gladstone[127] who reiterated his view that the giving of privileges to foreign ships should be conditional upon similar privileges being simultaneously given to British ships and also severely criticised the Bill's reserve powers of retaliation which he claimed were dishonest to foreign powers and unfair to British shipowners since the Government had admitted that the retaliatory clause would be called into operation only exceptionally in cases of extreme necessity and was really intended to be a dead letter.[128] Gladstone's criticisms were supported by the Opposition but the Government were averse to the idea of separate reciprocal negotiations with each foreign power and the Bill passed its Commons Second Reading with a majority of 56. The Bill came up for its Third Reading in the Commons on 23rd April 1849[129] and, after Lord John Russell in his winding up speech had expressed confidence that there would be fair and equal reciprocations both by the United States[130] and most of the European countries, the Bill passed its Third Reading with a slightly larger majority of 61.

The Bill then went to the House of Lords where the Second Reading took place on 7th May 1849.[131] There was no commercial shipping interest in the Lords and the opposition arguments concentrated on the adverse effect which repeal would have on national defence. Lord Brougham, normally an advocate of free trade, argued[132] that the Government were giving away the "quid" without the "quo" and inquired of his peers "Are you prepared to abandon a system to which you owe so precious a possession, not only the foundation of your glory but the bulwark of your strength and the protection of your very existence as a nation". Lord Stanley, also arguing for conditional relaxation, asked whether it was advisable "to throw down and destroy utterly and altogether that system of laws which for two hundred years at least has been looked upon by the people of the country as the basis of our national greatness

125. P. Debs. 3 Ser., Vol. 102, cc. 680–741.

126. P. Debs. 3 Ser., Vol. 103, cc. 464–534 and 540–629.

127. *Ibid.*, cc. 551–552.

128. In 1851 the Government turned down Lord Stanley's plea that retaliatory action should be taken (P. Debs. 3 Ser., Vol. 117, c.847) and in fact the powers of retaliation were never exercised.

129. P. Debs. 3 Ser., Vol. 104, cc. 622–706.

130. In the event British ships were not admitted to the United States' "coastal" trade which, to this day, remains reserved to American ships.

131. P. Debs. 3 Ser., Vol. 104, c.1316.

132. *Ibid.*, c.1339.

and the foundation of our naval strength".[133] As in the case of the Battle of Waterloo, the outcome of the Lords' Second Reading debate was "the nearest run thing you ever saw in your life"[134]; the repealers won by a margin of only 10 votes[135] and of those in favour of repeal 11 were bishops.[136] The Third Reading in the Lords was on 12th June 1849[137] when, after a short debate, the Repeal Bill was passed without a division.

The Royal Assent to the Repeal Bill was given on 26th June 1849 and amongst the statutory measures repealed by the Repeal Act 1849[138] were the whole of the Navigation Act 1845[139]; the provisions in the Registration Act 1845[140] that no ship should be registered as a British ship unless wholly built in the British Dominions and disqualifying ships repaired abroad; the provisions in the British Possessions Act 1845[141] relating to trading into and out of the colonial free ports and limiting the privileges of foreign ships trading to the Colonies; the requirement for carrying apprentices[142]; and the various statutory provisions empowering the Queen in Council to take retaliatory measures against foreign countries which were discriminating against British ships or goods.[143]

The Repeal Act swept away almost all the centuries old exclusive trading privileges which British shipping had enjoyed and ended the British shipbuilders' monopoly. The only trades which the Act still reserved for British registered ships were the United Kingdom's domestic coastal and fishing trades[144] and the coasting trades of every British possession in America, Africa and Asia.[145] The monopoly of the home trades only lasted until 1854 when an Act was passed[146] admitting foreign ships to these trades and the reservation of the colonial coasting trades was ended by the Merchant Shipping (Colonial) Act 1869[147] although subsequently the legislatures of some of the Commonwealth countries restricted their coasting trades to ships flying the British flag.

133. P. Debs. 3 Ser., Vol. 105, cc. 83–84.
134. The Duke was present and voted in favour of repeal.
135.

Contents:	Present: 105	Proxies: 68	Total: 173
Non-Contents:	Present: 119	Proxies: 44	Total: 163

136. Lord Winchelsea, a naval officer, maintained that the Bill only passed through the interference of these prelates in a secular matter of which they were profoundly ignorant.
137. P. Debs. 3 Ser., Vol. 106, c.11.
138. 12 & 13 Vict., c.29.
139. 8 & 9 Vict., c.88.
140. 8 & 9 Vict., c.89.
141. 8 & 9 Vict., c.93.
142. 7 & 8 Vict., c. 112, s.37.
143. 4 Geo. IV, c.77, 5 Geo c. 1; 8 & 9 Vict., c. 90, s.8 and 5 & 6 Vict., c. 14, s.8.
144. 12 & 13 Vict., c.29, ss. 2 and 3.
145. *Ibid.*, s.4.
146. 17 & 18 Vict., c.5.
147. 32 & 33 Vict., c.11 which left the Colonies free to deal with their own coasting trades.

The Act did still provide that no ship was to be regarded as a British ship unless duly registered under the Registration Act 1845 and navigated as such and retained the requirement that all British ships in the domestic coasting and fishing trades must have a British master and wholly British crews and that all other British ships must have a British master and three quarters of the crew British.[148] However the continuation of this long established British crew requirement also proved short lived since it was ended in 1853 by the Merchant Shipping Law Amendment Act.[149] The Act also maintained the long established exclusion of foreigners from the owning of British ships by providing[150] that the only individual persons who were eligible to be the owners of a British ship[151] were either natural born British subjects or persons naturalised or made denizens and there was no repeal of the rules, first laid down in 1786, that if any such person was not resident in the British dominions he was not entitled to own a British ship unless he was "a Member of some British Factory or Agent for or Partner in any House or Co-Partnership actually carrying on trade in Great Britain or Ireland."[152]

Although the powers of retaliation against foreign ships given by earlier Acts were repealed, the 1849 Act, under the heading of Reciprocity, did provide[153] first that if a foreign country restricted the voyages of British ships or the goods they might import or export the Queen in Council might restrict the privileges of the ships of that country by imposing similar disabilities and secondly that the Queen in Council might impose additional duties (of tonnage or on goods) on foreign ships so as to countervail any disadvantage to which British trade or navigation might be subjected by the imposition of foreign charges or duties greater than those imposed on the vessel of the foreign country in question or the goods carried in such vessel. These retaliatory powers were repealed by the Customs Consolidation Act 1853[154] but they were re-enacted in the same Act[155] without any significant changes and then,

148. 12 & 13 Vict., c.29, s.7. Provision was also still made (*ibid.*, s.9) for the proportion of seamen to be altered by Proclamation but the definition of British crew now included both lascars and also any foreigners who had served on British warships in war time for three years (*ibid.*, s.8). There was the same proviso that if there was one British seaman for every 20 tons of a ship's tonnage the ship was to be deemed duly navigated even if the number of foreign seamen exceeded one quarter of the whole crew.

149. 16 & 17 Vict., c.131, s.31.

150. 12 & 13 Vict., c.29, s.17.

151. There was no reference in this section to ownership of a British ship by a British company and in all the Registration Acts between 1786 and 1845 the eligibility for ownership of a British ship was limited to "His Majesty's subjects" and there were only oblique references to corporate ownership. However, in 1846, the Court of Queen's Bench held that a British corporation was a British subject within the meaning of Section 5 of the Registration Act 1845 (see *R.* v. *Arnaud*, 9 QB 806) and subsequently the Merchant Shipping Act 1854 for the first time dealt affirmatively with corporate ownership.

152. Registration Act 1845, s.12.

153. By Sections 10 and 11.

154. 16 & 17 Vict., c.107.

155. Sections 324 and 325.

although never invoked, remained on the statute book until 1974 when provision for their repeal was made by the Merchant Shipping Act 1974.[156]

Since the abandonment of protectionism marked such a radical change in the British Government's traditional maritime policy and was a major turning point in the history of the British maritime industries, 1850 is perhaps the opportune moment at which to take a retrospective look at Britain's centuries-old navigation system and to consider the contentious question as to the success or otherwise of those laws which in 1776 had caused Adam Smith to modify his free trade doctrine to the extent of conceding that "As defence is of much more importance than opulence, the Act of Navigation is perhaps the wisest of all the commercial regulations of England".[157] Certainly the question as to whether or not the Navigation Laws were beneficial has been the subject of much controversy and widely conflicting opinions have been expressed by contemporary observers, nineteenth century politicians and modern historians; so, in attempting to reach a correct conclusion, one must endeavour first to determine and isolate the primary objectives of the Navigation Acts and then to ascertain whether, through the operation of the Acts, such objectives were in fact attained.

At least up to the end of the seventeenth century the primary purpose of the Navigation Laws was political rather than economic. The legislation prior to 1660 was manifestly directed to the strengthening of national defence and, for an island nation, it was natural that shipping should be regarded as "the chiefest strength of this Realm".[158] Thus the Navigation Acts of 1651 and 1660 were only continuing a well established policy and putting it into a better organised and more readily enforceable form; nothing could be plainer or more succinct than the identical words used in both Acts to denote their objectives—"the increase of shipping and the encouragement of the navigation of this nation" -and it is manifest that, although it was also hoped to achieve commercial prosperity, the main purpose of the 1660 Act and the subsequent shipping legislation of the seventeenth century was to ensure the safety and strength of the realm by encouraging a greater supply of ships and seamen and the expansion of English shipbuilding. So, did the Navigation Act of 1660 achieve its objectives? In respect of the period from 1660 to 1776 in which the Act might have been expected to exert its most beneficial influence, it can certainly be established that shipping tonnage increased substantially in both absolute and relative terms, that there was an increase in the supply of trained seamen and a significant development of shipbuilding[159] but the question

156. The 1974 Act gave the Government extensive retaliatory powers considerably more far-reaching than those in the 1853 Act. No order was ever made under Section 24(2) of the 1974 Act for the repeal of Sections 324 and 325 of the 1853 Act and it was not until 1986 that the whole of this 1853 Act was repealed by the Statute Law Repeals Act 1986.

157. Adam Smith, *An Inquiry into the Nature and Causes of the Wealth of Nations* (1776), Ed. J. S. Nicholson (London, 1884), Book 4, Chapter 2.

158. 1 Jac. I, c.24—though only next to God and the King!

159 See pp. 25 and 26 *supra*.

remains as to whether the Navigation Laws were the main cause of this achievement.

During the period of some 100 years from the passing of the 1660 Act there were indeed some contemporary critics of the Navigation Laws[160] but their main complaints centred on the harmful economic effects on trade which it was not the primary purpose of the Laws to benefit. On the other hand, during the same period, there were many contemporary writers[161] who were firm in their opinion that the Navigation Laws were not only successful in achieving their main objective, the increase of shipping and seamen, but were also beneficial in promoting the increase of trade; Sir Joseph Child, one of the strongest supporters of the Navigation Laws, in 1669 expressed the opinion that "in relation to Trade, Shipping, Profit and Power" the Act of 1660 was "one of the choicest and most prudent Acts that ever was made in England"[162] —a view echoed by Adam Smith a century later. Even in the changed circumstances after 1776, following the secession of the American Colonies, liberal opinion in Parliament during the 1820s favoured no more than a modest relaxation of the Navigation Laws to meet the new conditions; the Prime Minister, Lord Liverpool, emphasised that Wallace's Acts of 1822 involved as little change as possible in the original principles of the Navigation Laws and Huskisson's subsequent modifications still left British ships with protection in the most important trades.

The conclusions reached by modern historians differ as sharply as those of the contemporary writers. Cunningham, who in the fourth and fifth editions of his work[163] modifies the views he had expressed in earlier editions, criticises the malign effects of the 1660 Act on trade but reluctantly concedes that it probably did contribute to the rapid expansion of the mercantile marine. Lipson[164] views the economic consequences of the Act with disfavour and argues that credit for the expansion of tonnage should not be given to the Act but Fayle,[165] while also criticising the Act's adverse effects on trade, does concede that credit for the great part of the increase in English shipping may fairly be given to the secure employment provided by the Plantation trade. On the other hand Sir William Holdsworth is categorical in his opinion that the

160. See particularly Roger Coke, *Discourse of Trade* (London, 1670); Philanglus (anon), *Britannia Languens* (London, 1680); Mathew Decker, *Causes of the Decline of Foreign Trade* (London, 1750).

161. Including Samuel Fortrey, *England's Interest and Improvement* (Cambridge, 1663); William Petty, *Essays in Political Arithmetic* (London, 1699); Francis Brewster, *Essays on Trade and Navigation* (London, 1695); Charles D'Avenant, *Political and Commercial Works* (London, 1695) and Adam Anderson, *The Origins of Commerce* (London, 1765).

162. *A New Discourse of Trade*, 4th edn. (London, 1740), pp. 121 and 123.

163. William Cunningham, *The Growth of English Industry and Commerce in Modern Times*, 5th edn. (Cambridge, 1910).

164. E. Lipson, *Economic History of England*, 12th edn. (London, 1959).

165. *History of the World's Shipping Industry*, *op. cit.*, pp. 189–191.

Act of 1660 was successful[166] and his view is shared by several other modern historians[167] who, after analysing the trade and shipping statistics, have unhesitatingly reached the conclusion that the pre-eminent position that British shipping had attained by the latter part of the eighteenth century was largely due to the encouragement given by the Navigation Laws not only to shipping but to the supply of seamen and the development of shipbuilding as well.

Hunter refers to the 1660 Act as being "the centre of controversy for a long time" but adds that "its principles were to prevail for nearly two hundred years . . . and the fact remains that under it there began a steady growth of the British merchant marine that was to continue until the long coveted sea supremacy was Britain's in actuality". Dickerson asserts that, after a century of experience with the Navigation Act, "even the most ardent advocate of free trade must admit that the system had worked" and that the shipping regulations "had given England by 1769 the greatest merchant marine in the world and a reservoir of sailors nearly equal to the combined numbers of seamen in all the other nations of western Europe". Professor Davis emphasises that the great expansion of English shipping between 1660 and 1700 was in vessels for foreign trade and that this expansion was brought about by the reservation of the long trans-Atlantic trade for English ships and by eliminating Dutch competition for the carriage of timber cargoes from Norway and the Baltic.

Professor Harper devotes the whole of his penultimate chapter to what he describes as weighing the evidence and his final summing up is in agreement with the preponderance of contemporary opinion and the conclusion reached by the majority of modern historians and in recent American Government Reports[168]: "the Navigation Acts should be judged as we would judge any physical mechanism—with relation to the end it is designed to accomplish. Judged by this standard, the Acts were successful. When entrusted with the task of developing England's maritime power, they were called upon to foster English shipping, to aid in training English seamen, to develop English shipbuilding and to preserve English trade. The evidence demonstrates that they benefited England's shipping, seamen and shipbuilding. Her trade prospered and even gained in comparison with that of her rivals. Different measures might have proved to be of greater benefit in advancing any one, but the secret of the Navigation Acts' success was the degree to which they protected all elements of maritime greatness."

However, while accepting the conclusion that up to the end of the eighteenth century the Navigation Laws had succeeded in meeting their prime objectives,

166. *A History of English Law*, Vol. 6, *op. cit.*, p. 318.

167. H. C. Hunter, *How England got its Merchant Marine*, *op. cit.*; L. A. Harper, *The English Navigation Laws*, *op. cit.*; O. M. Dickerson, *The Navigation Acts and the American Revolution* (Philadelphia, 1951); Ralph Davis, *The Rise of the English Shipping Industry*, *op. cit.*

168. G. M. Jones, *Government Aid to Merchant Shipping* (U.S. Department of Commerce, 1925); J. E. Saugstad, *Shipping and Shipbuilding Subsidies* (U.S. Department of Commerce, 1932).

the question remains as to whether, in the very different political and economic climate of the mid-nineteenth century, the Navigation Laws had not only ceased to be necessary for encouraging the growth of a merchant marine whose tonnage exceeded that of all the rest of the world but had instead become such a discouragement to the expansion of British commerce and industry that Parliament was justified in deciding that the needs of the time demanded not the continuance of the Navigation Laws in a substantially modified form, which even some of the most convinced protectionists were prepared to concede was necessary, but rather an entire abrogation of the navigation system.

Unlike in this respect the controversy on the merits of the Navigation Laws in earlier times, and even without the benefit of hindsight as regards the dramatic growth of the British maritime industries in the second half of the nineteenth century, it is now generally accepted that in 1849 Parliament reached the right conclusion in deciding that the Navigation Laws had become obsolete and were doing more harm than good. A powerful dissenter from this view is Holdsworth[169] who considered that those who supported the repeal of the Act ignored or denied the danger to national security and concentrated on its commercial disadvantages but the argument of the Whig Administration and its Peelite supporters was that the increase of trade that they confidently expected would flow from the removal of the artificial restrictions would in turn increase a British marine whose existing superiority placed it in a privileged position to take advantage of new and enlarged trading opportunities; they saw freedom of trade, and the benefits that would accrue from it by way of an increase in the national wealth and a more favourable balance of trade, as a positive contribution to national security.

Although, even as late as the debates in 1848, a leading advocate of repeal could still describe the Navigation Laws as having "long been regarded among us with a reverence only inferior to that which we are accustomed to pay to those immortal statutes which are the bulwarks and safeguards of our constitutional liberties",[170] the navigation system had to go because it was no longer needed or appropriate; as Trevelyan puts it[171] "The time had come when this artificial support, which had been praised in its day by Adam Smith, could be dispensed with by the full grown strength of the British mercantile marine". Indeed it was the very success of the Navigation Laws in the period up to the end of the eighteenth century which led to their demise in the very different commercial world of the mid-nineteenth century.

169. See *History of English Law*, Vol. 15, *op. cit.*, pp. 6–10 and his Rhodes Lecture at University College, London, on 25th February 1918 entitled "The Relation between Commercial Legislation and National Defence Historically Considered".

170. P. Debs. 3 Ser., Vol. 98, c.992.

171. *History of England*, 3rd edn. (London, 1945), p. 626.

CHAPTER 3

FREE TRADE—BUT HARDLY LAISSEZ-FAIRE

On 1st January 1850 the Repeal Act came into effect and the Law of Navigation of the British Empire, under which British ships had for so long been protected, was almost completely abrogated. It was indeed the *dies irae* for the British shipping interest—diehard protectionists almost to a man—and, burdened with the complacency engendered by centuries of protection, it was hardly surprising that initially many British owners viewed with despondency, if not despair, the prospect of meeting the challenge of unrestricted foreign competition. British shipbuilders also had now to accept that ships built abroad were eligible for registration as British ships and that the quality and lower cost of American and other foreign built sailing ships might prove a strong inducement for British owners to forsake their traditional domestic ties.

In 1850 the net tonnage of the merchant navy of the British Empire was 4.233 million, that of the United Kingdom was 3.565 million and that of all the other principal maritime countries (United States foreign trade ships only) was 3 million[1]; small wonder that the advocates of repeal were confident that, with the expansion of world commerce which they rightly predicted, British shipping would not only retain their traditional hold on the routes which had for so long been protected but would also secure a dominant position in the rapidly developing new trades. However, whilst there was no gainsaying the supremacy of the British merchant fleet in terms of tonnage, both sail and steam,[2] the reforming zeal of the free traders may have resulted in insufficient consideration being given to other factors affecting the condition and the competitiveness of the British mercantile marine which to others had rightly become a cause for serious concern. In the years leading up to the repeal of the Navigation Laws American foreign trade tonnage had been growing at a far more rapid rate than British tonnage and British sailing ships had been suffering severely from American competition in the Atlantic and other unprotected trades; the inroads that the Americans were making into trades that had

1. Cd. 7033, Table 11, Parl. Papers 1913, Vol. 60.

2. In 1850 world sea-going steam tonnage (U.S. foreign trade ships only) totalled 253,650 tons, of which 168,474 tons were U.K. owned (Cd. 7033, Table 11).

formerly been a near monopoly for British ships were attributable not only to American superiority in the design and quality of their sailing ships and their lower building costs but also, no less in importance, to the higher level of efficiency of American masters, officers and crews.

As the 1970 Report of Lord Rochdale's Committee observed,[3] in the early nineteenth century the lot of most British seafarers was unenviable—"At sea they had a life of danger, privation and squalor on ships that were often unseaworthy: ashore they were frequently at the mercy of crimps and other exploiters". The Act of 1835[4] had made some improvements in the seamen's condition of service but there was still "little to be proud of in the British mercantile marine. The ships were vastly inferior, as ships, to the American . . . There was little direct recruitment of officers. Masters were illiterate, navigation crude and unscholarly and, except in the aristocratic and uneconomic conditions of the East Indiamen, the employment of hands was beggarly and harsh."[5] In 1836 the Report of a Commons Select Committee inquiring into the Causes of Shipwrecks[6] stated that the most frequent and generally accepted causes of shipwrecks were the drunkenness and incompetence of British masters and officers; the Committee recommended the formation of a Mercantile Marine Board to superintend all the affairs of the merchant navy and compulsory examinations for masters and mates but the Government, strongly supported by the shipping interest, opposed a private member's Bill to implement the Report and so no action was taken. The high level of shipwrecks continued and in 1843 the Report of another Commons Select Committee on Shipwrecks[7] emphasised the incompetence and negligence of masters and mates but, as in 1836, no effect was given to the Committee's recommendation for compulsory examinations which the still powerful shipping interest considered would be an unwarranted intrusion into their affairs.[8]

In July 1843 James Murray, a Foreign Office official, wrote a circular letter to the British Consuls at a large number of foreign ports requesting reports on the character and conduct of British masters and seamen and how they compared with foreign officers and seamen. The replies received from the Consuls in 23 foreign countries were almost unanimously adverse; there were repeated references to the drunkenness and incompetence of British masters and mates, their ignorance of navigation and their total deficiency in education. Murray thereupon wrote to Lord Canning, the Foreign Secretary, emphasising that the character of British shipping had declined and suggested that, instead of

3. Report of the Committee of Inquiry into Shipping (Chairman, Lord Rochdale), Cmnd. 4337, (para 788) Parl. Papers 1969–70, Vol. 27.

4. 5 & 6 Will. IV, c.19.—see p. 41 *supra*.

5. R. H. Thornton, *British Shipping*, 2nd edn. (Cambridge, 1959), pp. 21–22.

6. Parl. Papers 1836 (567) Vol. 17.

7. Parl. Papers 1843 (549) Vol. 9.

8. In 1845 the Board of Trade did issue regulations for the voluntary examination of masters and mates but the response was poor.

responsibility for the merchant service being spread over many Government departments, there should be established a Department of Commercial Marine, with sole responsibility, in order to remedy the defects "and keep up the character which Great Britain has for years maintained of supremacy in commercial navigation and enterprise".[9] Early in 1844 Murray's proposals were passed to the Board of Trade whose Minute Book recorded "consideration postponed"[10]; another Merchant Shipping Act of that year[11] did little to remedy the defects and, as Sir Hubert Smith puts it[12]: "Responsibilities [for the mercantile marine] were scattered among nine different Departments which administered with very imperfect powers a mass of uncodified laws, many of them obsolescent and some of them conflicting. Hence conditions in the British Mercantile Marine went from bad to worse, until the enquiries of 1843 revealed a startling state of inferiority to foreign shipping which could not be allowed to continue."

In the event six more years were to elapse before Parliament took some action. Meantime there was further disquieting evidence submitted in 1844 to a Commons Select Committee inquiring into the state and condition of the mercantile marine[13] and in 1847 the British Consuls abroad, in response to a request from the then Foreign Secretary Lord Palmerston, again made a number of highly adverse reports. Based on the Consuls' replies James Murray submitted a further Memorandum[14] in which, after pointing out how poorly British masters and crews compared with their foreign counterparts, he repeated the suggestion, already made three years earlier, for forming a Department "to take entire cognizance of all matters relating to Merchant Seamen and Shipping". Once again there was no immediate response; between 1847 and 1849 Parliament was too preoccupied with the highly contentious question of the repeal of the Navigation Laws.

However, even to a Government committed to free trade, it was manifest that action had to be taken and that "the two essential preliminaries for dealing effectively with the situation were to centralise in one Department the responsibility for dealing with merchant shipping and to consolidate in one statute the piecemeal legislation relating thereto".[15] The repeal of the Navigation Laws and the consequent exposure of British shipping to unrestricted

9. Murray's letter to the Consuls, their replies and Murray's letter to Canning are all included in the "Papers relating to the Commercial Marine of Great Britain" presented to both Houses of Parliament in 1847 (Parl. Papers 1847–48 (913) Vol. 59).

10. Sir H. L. Smith, *The Board of Trade* (London, 1928), p. 104.

11. 7 & 8 Vict., c.112. Although this Act was passed only five years before the repeal of the Navigation Laws, the preamble still recited in the familiar and hallowed words that "the Prosperity, Strength and Safety of Her Majesty's Dominions do greatly depend on a large, constant and ready supply of seamen".

12. Sir H. L. Smith, *op.cit.*, p. 102.

13. See the Committee's First Report, Parl. Papers 1844 (545) Vol. 8.

14. Palmerston's letter, the replies from the Consuls and Murray's Memorandum are also reproduced in Parl. Papers 1847–48 (913) Vol. 59.

15. Sir H. L. Smith, *op. cit.* p. 103.

foreign competition made it essential to correct a situation in which it was clear that "British shipping was being left behind by many of its rivals as regards the design and fitting of the ships, the training, discipline and treatment of the crews and the professional education of the officers".[16] At last, in 1850, the Mercantile Marine Act[17] was passed "for improving the conditions of Masters, Mates and Seamen and maintaining discipline in the Merchant Service" and, for the first time, the Board of Trade was given sole responsibility for all matters, other than carriage of passengers, relating to the merchant navy.[18]

It was not only in relation to the well-being and efficiency of seamen that the free traders found themselves compelled by humanitarian considerations and practical necessity to provide for more effective State intervention. Between 1803 and 1848 there had been a number of statutes designed to improve the health and safety conditions for passengers, especially emigrants, on British merchant ships[19] but the vast increase in the numbers of emigrants between 1847 and 1849 revealed many imperfections in the protective legislation. A Passengers Act of 1849[20] did bring about some improvements but it was still a comparative failure—largely owing to the intolerable burden placed on the few and poorly paid executive officers of the Emigration Commissioners who were responsible for its administration. Early in 1851 the Commons appointed a Select Committee to inquire into the operation of the Passenger Acts and the Committee's Report[21] concluded that the existing legislation did not give adequate guarantees of safety, decency or health; the Committee made a wide range of recommendations and most of these were subsequently embodied in the Passengers Act 1852[22] which conferred exceptionally wide discretionary powers upon the Emigration Commissioners[23] and placed heavy responsibilities upon the shipowners and their masters.

After the passing of the Mercantile Marine Act 1850 there remained the complex task of codifying the multifarious laws applicable to merchant ships and their crews. Preparatory work on a major consolidating and amending measure began in 1850 but it was clear, particularly having regard to the need for constant consultation with shipowners and other interested parties, that it

16. *History of the World's Shipping Industry*, *op. cit.*, p. 232.

17. 13 & 14 Vict., c.93.

18. The 1850 Act provided (*inter alia*) for the compulsory examination of masters and mates. Prior to the Act Britain was the only maritime power which had no code of laws to regulate the conduct and test the competency of those who navigated her merchant ships.

19. See p. 42 *supra*.

20. 12 & 13 Vict., c.33.

21. Parl. Papers 1851 (632), Vol. 19.

22. 15 & 16 Vict., c.44.

23. The Emigration Commissioners remained responsible for the implementation of the passenger legislation until 1872 when administration of the Passenger Acts then in force was transferred to the Board of Trade by the Merchant Shipping Act 1872 (35 & 36 Vict., c.73).

would be some years before the drafting of the Bill could be completed; in the meantime a free trade Parliament continued its active intervention into the affairs of the merchant marine. The Steam Navigation Act 1851[24] provided (*inter alia*) for passenger carrying steam vessels to be inspected twice yearly by the Board of Trade and for iron steamers to be built with water-tight compartments and the Customs Consolidation Act 1853[25] re-enacted the reciprocity provisions and powers of retaliation against foreign shipping which had been contained in the Repeal Act 1849. Statutes passed in 1853 and 1854 brought to an end two of the most ancient features of the Navigation System which had survived repeal in 1849; the Merchant Shipping Law Amendment Act 1853[26] repealed the centuries old requirement for the manning of British ships by British masters and British crews[27] and the Coastal Trade Act 1854[28] opened to foreign ships the coasting trade of the United Kingdom and Channel Islands which had been exclusively reserved to domestic shipping since 1562.[29]

At last, in May 1854, the long awaited Merchant Shipping Bill came before the Commons for its Second Reading[30] but it is certainly no grounds for criticism that the task which the newly created Mercantile Marine Department of the Board of Trade, and in particular its Secretary T. H. Farrer,[31] commenced in 1850 was not completed until 1854; on the contrary, the time taken in perfecting the Bill's 548 Clauses and many Schedules had been well spent. The Bill quickly passed through all its stages in both Houses with very little debate and received the Royal Assent on 16th August 1854 without a single amendment having been made; by any reckoning this was a remarkable achievement for a complex piece of legislation which may well have been, at the time, the longest Act on the Statute Book.

The Merchant Shipping Act 1854[32] stood the test of time remarkably well and can still fairly be regarded as the most important of the many Merchant Shipping Acts which followed it; although subjected to many amendments over the following 40 years, it remained the principal Act and continued to provide the general framework within which merchant shipping was controlled and administered until it was superseded by the next major consolidating measure—the Merchant Shipping Act 1894[33] which remains to this day the principal Merchant Shipping Act. It would be inappropriate—indeed

24. 14 & 15 Vict., c.79.
25. 16 & 17 Vict., c.107, ss.324–326, 330 and 331—see p. 50 *supra*.
26. 16 & 17 Vict., c.131., s.31.
27. First introduced in 1488 by 4 Hen. VII, c.10—see p. 10 *supra*.
28. 17 & 18 Vict., c.5.
29. By 5 Eliz., c.5.—See p. 13 *supra*.
30. P. Debs. 3 Ser., Vol. 133, c.571.
31. Mr Farrer (later Lord Farrer) was subsequently appointed in 1866 Permanent Secretary of the Board of Trade and continued to serve with distinction in that capacity until 1893.
32. 17 & 18 Vict., c.104.
33. 57 & 58 Vict., c.60.

impossible—here to attempt even an outline study of the 1854 Act but the breadth of its scope and the extent of the duties imposed on the Board of Trade can be gauged by the following list of the 11 parts into which the Act was divided, namely: the general functions of the Board of Trade; the conditions to be complied with by British ships including their ownership; measurement and registration; the relationship between masters and seamen; safety and the prevention of accidents; pilotage; lighthouses; the Mercantile Marine Fund; casualties and salvage; liability of shipowners; legal procedure and miscellaneous.

In view of the prevailing political philosophy the 1854 Act naturally did not revive any of the old monopolistic measures for protecting British shipping and shipbuilding against foreign competition but, even with free trade at its zenith, Parliament retained the ancient principle, first established nearly 500 years earlier[34] and continued until 1988, that only ships wholly owned by British subjects should be entitled to be treated as British ships and to enjoy the privileges attaching to the British flag. Section 18 of the Act provided that ships belonging wholly to natural born British subjects qualified as British ships regardless as to where their owners were resident[35] and that a ship also qualified as a British ship if she belonged wholly to a body corporate established under, subject to the laws of, and having its principal place of business in the United Kingdom or some British possession. Thus, in order to be eligible for owning a British ship, a company had not only to be incorporated in the United Kingdom or some British possession but had also to have its principal place of business there; this meant, and still means, that the residence of the British owning company—i.e. the place where the central control and management of its business was genuinely located—had to be either in the United Kingdom or in some British possession. However, if that condition was satisfied, then the fact that some, or even all, of the shares in the company were owned by foreigners did not itself disqualify the company from being registered as the owners of a British ship.[36] This fundamental principle of excluding foreigners from the privilege of owning British ships was retained by Parliament 40 years later in Section 1 of the Merchant Shipping Act 1894 which remained in force until 1988.

By 1854 the legislative activity of Parliament in the field of merchant shipping, no less than 15 statutes since 1849, presented British owners with some major problems. The centuries-old system designed to encourage and protect British shipping had been swept away and, although the Crown still retained its statutory power of retaliation against foreign shipping, this power could

34. By the Navigation Act 1381 (5 Ric. II, stat. I, c.3.)—see p. 9 *supra*.

35. Under the ship registration laws in force between 1786 and 1854 a British subject was not normally eligible to own a British ship unless he was also resident within the British Dominions. —see p. 50 *supra*.

36. So held by the Court of Queen's Bench in 1846—see *R.* v *Arnaud*, 9 QB 806 (English Reports, Vol. 115).

only be exercised if there was unfair foreign discrimination against British ships; in the debates between 1847 and 1849 the Government had indicated that it was unlikely that retaliatory action would be taken—and in the event it never was. In addition to being shorn of protection, the merchant marine was simultaneously burdened with a quite unprecedented volume of parental, or in the eyes of the owners grandmotherly, legislation which subjected the owners to stringent and often minutely detailed regulations governing such matters as standards of construction, equipment and navigation, safety of life and goods at sea, passenger and crew conditions, seaworthiness and so on; indeed there were few aspects relating to the building and operating of British ships which escaped the attention of the legislators and in respect of which a high standard was imposed on the unhappy British owners some of whom, not always the least efficient, felt that Parliament was hardly assisting them in their efforts to meet the ever growing and unrestricted competition from foreign shipping which did not have to comply with such onerous statutory requirements.

Another constraint which handicapped British owners in the years following repeal resulted from the fact that, contrary to the Government's confident expectations, the United States and other foreign maritime powers failed to reciprocate by abolishing such of their own restrictions as corresponded to those hitherto imposed by the British Navigation Laws. During the debates on the Repeal Bill the protectionists, and even a free trader such as Gladstone, had argued in favour of a policy of conditional relaxation of the Navigation Laws so that there should only be piecemeal concessions in favour of foreign countries which reciprocated by giving Britain equivalent treatment. The Government, however, was sure that, once the British Navigation Laws had been repealed, foreign maritime powers would voluntarily reciprocate but in the event the fears of Gladstone and the protectionists were proved to be justified; the United States, France and Russia continued to exclude British ships from their coastal trades, which were so extensive as to be analogous to the unrestricted British imperial trade, and France, Spain and the United States continued to charge high differential duties on goods imported in British ships. In 1851 London shipowners presented a petition to the Commons stating that the United States and most European countries had failed to reciprocate[37] and in the same year a petition to the Lords from Liverpool shipowners requested the Government to exercise their power of retaliation[38] but the Government refused to accede and contended that retaliation would do more harm than good.

How then, in the decade following the repeal of the Navigation Laws, did British shipowners react to the challenge presented by the complete removal

37. P. Debs. 3 Ser., Vol. 116, c.304.
38. *Ibid.*, Vol. 117, c.847.

of their trading privileges and the subjection of their far from efficient industry to onerous and every increasing statutory regulations? Although there were some, notably the more progressive owners in London and Liverpool, to whom "the possibility of being driven off the sea, or perhaps it may be the stimulus given by the loss of protection, brought out the best fighting qualities",[39] there were many more who failed to shed their complacency and mistakenly concentrated their efforts on what proved to be the impossible task of trying to put the clock back.

In the first half of the 1850s British owners were to some extent cushioned against the full impact of unrestricted foreign competition by the exceptional demand for shipping created firstly by the discovery of gold in Australia and the greatly increased flow of emigration which this brought about and secondly by the military needs resulting from the Crimean War and the troubles in India. This proved to be only a transitory period of prosperity and in the second half of the decade there was a surplus of shipping in consequence of overbuilding and a trade depression on both sides of the Atlantic; both these factors inevitably had a prejudicial effect on the demand for tonnage but nevertheless at the Annual General Meeting of the General Shipowners Society in June 1858 those present "still held the strange delusion that the repeal of the Navigation Laws and the absence of foreign reciprocity were the main causes of suffering rather than the general commercial depression".[40]

In December 1858 there was a special meeting in London of British shipowners from all the major ports at which, since there seemed little hope of persuading Parliament to reverse its free trade policy, it was decided to address a petition to the Queen.[41] Predictably the Address began by reciting the ruinous state of depression into which the British shipping interest was plunged and emphasised that, at the time of the repeal of the Navigation Laws, the shipowners had expressed their belief that this misguided policy was "fraught with danger to the supremacy of British navigation and to the natural defence of the British Empire". The Address then stated that since 1854 the British owners had been exposed to all the severity of unequal competition with the shipping of every foreign State and requested the Queen to exercise her powers of retaliation under the Customs Consolidation Act 1853 because British navigation was in many cases impeded by foreign States imposing prohibitions and restrictions which were totally at variance with the reciprocity contemplated when the Navigation Laws were repealed.

The petition was referred to the Board of Trade who, in March 1859,

39. A. W. Kirkaldy, *British Shipping—its History, Organisation and importance* (London, 1914).

40. W. S. Lindsay, *History of Merchant Shipping and Ancient Commerce*, Vol. 3 (London, 1874–76, 4 Vols.) p. 262. Lindsay was himself a leading shipowner and a Member of Parliament.

41. C.2494. Parl. Papers, 1859 Vol. 25. Address to the Queen and subsequent correspondence in reference thereto.

rejected the shipowners' request for the taking of retaliatory action. The Board accepted that France, Spain and Portugal restricted British shipping in their foreign trades but considered that, since the ships of these countries engaged to such a negligible extent in the United Kingdom's foreign trade, no purpose would be served by retaliation. The Board also accepted that many foreign countries reserved their coasting trades and that there would be justification for excluding their ships from the United Kingdom's coasting trade but it was felt that such retaliatory action would be valueless since that trade, in theory open to the world since 1854, was in practice still virtually monopolised by British shipping. The Board's view was that the shipping depression was not attributable to the withdrawal of protection from British ships but was due to the general commercial crisis and the cessation of the abnormal demand for shipping created by the Russian war and the disturbances in British India. It was therefore suggested that British shipping and shipbuilding would be assisted by the repeal of the differential duty on timber as the raw material of shipbuilding and that in addition British shipping should be relieved by the abolition of passing tolls and other local dues.

Not surprisingly the owners were far from content with the Board of Trade's reply and indeed the progress of British shipping in the decade following the repeal, when compared with American (foreign trade) shipping and the shipping of Norway, Britain's most dangerous rival in Europe, certainly gave no cause for satisfaction. Although, in this period, the British dominance in steamships was beginning to make an impact in certain limited trades such as the carriage of passengers and mails, in terms of world tonnage and trade the steamer was still relatively insignificant[42] and the main concern of most British owners was the competition from foreign sailing ships, particularly American and Norwegian. Between 1850 and 1860 U.K. tonnage (sail and steam) had increased by 30.67 per cent but the corresponding United States foreign trade tonnage had increased by 60.57 per cent and the increase in Norwegian tonnage amounted to 87.36 per cent.[43] In the same period there was likewise a significant increase in the extent to which foreign tonnage was participating in the United Kingdom's foreign trade; the total tonnage (sail and steam) entered and cleared with cargoes had grown from some 12 million in 1850

42. In 1860 steamships (454,000 tons in total) still represented less than one-tenth of total U.K. tonnage and the proportion of world steam tonnage in relation to total world tonnage was very much less (see Cd. 7033, Table 11).

43. The comparative tonnage figures (sail and steam) in 1850 and 1860 (see Cd. 7033, Table 11) were as follows:

	1850	*1860*
United Kingdom	3,565,133	4,658,687
United States (foreign trade)	1,585,711	2,546,237
Norway	298,315	558,927

to around 20.84 million in 1860—an increase of 73.35 per cent—but the breakdown between British and foreign tonnage showed that the participation of foreign tonnage had increased by 118 per cent as compared with an increase in the British participation of only 50.75 per cent.[44]

In the summer of 1859 another meeting of British shipowners took place in London and the owners present, still believing that British shipping needed protection to counter the foreign challenge, decided to campaign not only for retaliatory action but also for a restoration of their pre-1850 monopoly of the imperial carrying trade. On 31st January 1860 the Commons approved a motion, proposed by W. S. Lindsay, for the appointment of a Select Committee to inquire into the state of merchant shipping, the operation of the burdens and restrictions affecting it and of certain statutes including particularly the Merchant Shipping Act 1854.[45] The Committee, of which Lindsay and others from shipping constituencies were members, took a massive amount of evidence and made their Report to the House later in the same year.[46] The Committee were unanimously of the opinion that it would be impossible to reverse the established policy of free trade and that any proposal for re-establishing an exclusive monopoly of the carrying trade to and from our colonial possessions must, both on political and commercial grounds, be rejected. It was also felt that it would be difficult to enforce reciprocity by retaliatory action but the Government was urged to take more aggressive diplomatic action to secure general reciprocity and the abolition of foreign restrictions against British shipping. The Committee did not consider that the shipping depression was due to the repeal of the Navigation Laws but attributed it to the various commercial factors beyond the control of the Government.

The Report concluded with proposals for easing some of the shipowners' domestic burdens; it was recommended that shipping should be exempt from light dues, which should be borne by the nation, that passing tolls should be abolished, local taxes and stamp duties modified and that there should be a voluntary pilotage system. Legislative action was quickly taken to give effect to the Committee's recommendations on passing tolls and local dues[47] and in

44. C.144 and C.145, Parl. Papers 1870, Vol. 68. See also John Glover's "Address to the Statistical Society" in 1863, *Journal of the Statistical Society*, Vol. 26 (March 1863). The exact figures were as follows:

Nationality	*Tonnage* *1850*	*1860*	*Increase per cent*
British	8,039,308	12,119,454	50.75
Foreign	3,981,366	8,718,464	118.00
Total	12,020,674	20,837,918	73.35
Proportion of foreign	33.2	41.9	
Proportion of British	66.8	58.1	
	100.00	100.00	

45. P. Debs. 3 Ser., Vol. 156, c.332.

46. Parl. Papers 1860 (530), Vol. 13.

47. 24 & 25 Vict., c.47—Harbour and Passing Tolls Act 1861.

1862 provision was made for a voluntary pilotage system[48] but no change was made in the system of light dues. No retaliatory measures were taken against any foreign State under the Customs Consolidation Act 1853 and, although negotiations with the French eventually brought some easing of their discrimination against British shipping,[49] diplomatic efforts achieved no relaxation of the United States' monopoly of their extensive so-called coasting trade. No other Government action was taken, but in spite of this the anguished voices of the shipowners now at last fell silent; no longer was there a demand for a return to the pre-1850 golden age of protection—and for good reason. The end of 1860 marked a turning point for British shipping and the beginning of the decline of American competition; the erstwhile diehard protectionists were soon to become the most ardent of free traders.

Meanwhile how were the shipbuilders facing up to the unwelcome situation resulting from the fact that as from 1st January 1850 there was no longer any statutory requirement that a ship had to have been built in the British Dominions in order to be eligible for registration as a British ship? One of the main fears of those who opposed the repeal of the Navigation Laws was that the British shipbuilding industry, so essential to the strength of the navy, would suffer a serious decline as a result of the loss of their hitherto captive domestic market. In the middle of the century the output of the United States' shipyards was about equal to that of the British and, with American builders having ready access to cheaper supplies of timber and the ability to produce sailing ships which were unquestionably far superior in design and performance, it seemed that British builders would be hard put to challenge the unrestricted foreign competition; indeed, in the early 1850s, some of the more progressive British owners were not slow to take advantage of their unaccustomed freedom and hastened both to place orders for new sailing ships with American builders and to acquire second-hand American built vessels.

However, even in the first decade following repeal, before the advent of the iron steamships had made any marked impact on world shipbuilding, there was a beginning, slow at first but soon increasing rapidly, of a resurgence of British shipbuilding. Some of the better British builders were prepared to learn from the American example and there was a gradual improvement in design but the more significant change in the situation was brought about by the growing demand by British owners for new steamships; between 1850 and 1860 there was not only a substantial increase, some 58.5 per cent, in the total tonnage of new ships produced by British yards but, far more important, their

48. 25 & 26 Vict., c.63—Merchant Shipping Act Amendment Act 1862.

49. See correspondence respecting the operation of French Navigation Laws on British shipping (Parl. Papers 1867 (3773) Vol. 74), P. Debs. 3 Ser., Vol. 185, c.108 and the Shipping Dues Exemption Act 1867 (30 Vict., c.15).

output of new steamships was trebled.[50] Whilst the end of protection may have given a stimulus, it was the near simultaneous beginning of the triumph of the iron (and later steel) steamship over the wooden sailing ship which was soon to make the British yards pre-eminent; as an American Government Report, published many years later, emphasised,[51] by the middle of the nineteenth century "the iron industry of England had been extensively developed for a number of years" . . . and "the application of steam to industry was further advanced in England than in the United States. England had therefore in the manufacture of iron steamships an advantage similar to that which the United States had in the manufacture of wooden sailing vessels." Moreover the success of the British yards was not only attributable to the favourable economic factors; it was due also to the skill and enterprise of the Victorian shipbuilders and marine engineers, to the willingness of the leading British liner owners to operate ocean-going steamships and the early financial support supplied by the Government mail contracts.[52]

From 1860 onwards the growing superiority of the British yards in the production of steamships was paralleled by a remarkable surge in the tonnage of steamships on the British register; the statistics showed[53] that in 1875 the total tonnage on the U.K. register stood at approximately 6.1 million of which steamship tonnage amounted to just under 2 million—more than quadruple its level in 1860. In contrast the tonnage (sail and steam) of the United States foreign trade fleet in 1875 had fallen to some 1.5 million tons, a million tons below the 1860 level, and the tonnage of American foreign trade steamships was relatively insignificant—192,000 in 1875 compared with 97,000 in 1860. Moreover between 1860 and 1870 British tonnage (sail and steam) entered and cleared with cargoes in the U.K.'s foreign trade had increased by over 83 per cent whereas the increase of foreign tonnage in that trade over the same period was only seven per cent, so that the British proportion of the trade had risen to 70.3 per cent in 1870 compared with 58.1 per cent in 1860.[54]

The growth in the British steam fleet between 1860 and 1875 was only a beginning; over the next 15 years, with the steamship becoming of ever increasing importance, the progress continued and by 1890 the steam tonnage on the U.K. register stood at over 5 million tons whereas the steam tonnage of all the other principal maritime countries (U.S. foreign trade ships only) was just

50. C.144 and C.145. The tonnage figures were as follows:

Year	*Sail*	*Steam*	*Total*
1850	119,111	14.584	133,695
1860	158,172	53,796	211,968

51. *Government Aid to Merchant Shipping*, *op. cit.*

52. See A. K. Cairncross and J. R. Parkinson, "The Shipbuilding Industry". Chapter 12 of the *Structure of British Industry*, Ed. Duncan Burn (Cambridge, 1958).

53. Parl. Papers 1881 (125), Vol. 82., Tables 7 and 8.

54. For the detailed figures see Glover's "Address to the Statistical Society" in 1872, *Journal of the Statistical Society*, Vol. 353 (June 1872).

below 3 million tons.[55] The output of steam tonnage from the British yards also showed remarkable growth; in 1883 the output was just over 744,000 tons—an increase of 1,283 per cent since 1860. What then were the combination of circumstances which, after 1860, were so swiftly to bring about such a sensational improvement in the absolute and relative growth of the British maritime industries, to what extent can credit be given to the free traders who brought protectionism to an end and what part was played by Government intervention into the affairs of shipping and shipbuilding during the second half of the nineteenth century?

Certainly those who had advocated the repeal of the Navigation Laws could claim that the progress of British shipping and shipbuilding from 1860 onwards had more than justified the case that they had made in the debates of 1847–49 and had likewise confounded most of the arguments of their protectionist opponents. As the free traders had confidently predicted, there had been a vast expansion in British and world trade and, once the shipowners had overcome the initial shock and rid themselves of their complacency, the British merchant fleet with its rapidly growing steamship component was well placed to acquire an ever greater proportion of world commerce. Protectionist misgivings as to the adverse effect which repeal would have on the shipbuilding industry were soon falsified by events. Likewise their fears that the supply of British seamen for the Royal Navy would be dangerously diminished was proved to have been misplaced; although, during the second half of the century, there was a steady increase in the proportion of foreign seamen serving in British ships,[56] the foreign proportion never reached the one quarter figure permitted under the Navigation Laws and there was still an ample number of British merchant seamen available for recruitment to the Royal Navy Volunteer Force which was established in 1859 following the recommendation of a Royal Commission.[57]

So, after 1860, when the shipowners had bestirred themselves, improved their efficiency and were resolved to meet the foreign competition head on, both contemporary observers and modern historians are unanimous as to the beneficial effects that had flowed from freedom of trade. In 1874 Lindsay had no doubt that "the freedom of our laws has given an impetus to maritime commerce far beyond the most sanguine hopes of those who, a quarter of a century ago, most strenuously advocated the policy of free trade"[58] and Thornton emphasises the "profound and salutary effect" of the combined legislation of 1849–50 which, more than any other single factor, promoted the growth

55. United States foreign trade steam tonnage only—see Cd. 7033, Table 11.

56. For the detailed figures see Parl. Papers 1881 (125), Table 25 and Cd. 7033, Table 25.

57. C.2469 Parl. Papers 1859 (1st Sess), Vol. 6. The new force was established by the Royal Naval Reserve (Volunteer) Act 1859 (22 & 23 Vict., c.40) and by the Officers of the Royal Naval Reserve Act 1863 (26 & 27 Vict., c.69).

58. *History of Merchant Shipping*, Vol. 3, *op. cit.*, pp. 420–421.

of the English maritime industry during the latter part of the nineteenth century and "resulted in the gradual elimination of the more casual elements in the industry".[59] In the main only the best of the Victorian shipowners survived the repeal and their enterprise, conservative financial policies and the close personal attention that they gave to every facet of their ship operations were qualities that contributed in no small measure to the success achieved by the British mercantile marine.

However, whilst not detracting from the vital contribution made by the repeal of the Navigation Laws and the general policy of free trade, the predominant position which the British maritime industries were soon to attain was also attributable to other developments and circumstances which were unlikely to have been uppermost in the minds of those who in 1847–49 had so ardently campaigned for freedom of the seas. Undoubtedly the most important factor in the rapid growth of British shipping and shipbuilding after 1860 was the ever increasing change in the methods of ship construction. The change from sail and wood to steam and iron—and after 1875 from iron to steel—was of inestimable benefit to British shipping and conversely was a major reason for the sudden decline of American competition. The Report of the 1860 Select Committee had emphasised that steamers could be built in the United Kingdom at much less expense and were greatly superior to any produced abroad and so, as the Report of a Board of Trade Departmental Committee stated more than half a century later,[60] "The modern position of the United Kingdom as the great shipowning and shipbuilding country of the world dates from the substitution of steam for sailing power and of iron and steel for wood. Once the discoveries of the industrial revolution were applied to the instruments of sea transport, the resources of the United Kingdom in coal and iron and their proximity to good shipbuilding sites furnished the means for a great expansion."

Another factor of great significance to the growth of British shipping, and one closely connected with the steamship itself, was the export of coal. Britain was fortunate in having indigenous coal supplies of a quality ideal for bunkers and, by establishing coal depots all over the world which had to be constantly restocked, British ships employed in bringing ever increasing supplies of raw materials to the United Kingdom had the great advantage of being able to earn freight on their outward voyages instead of having to travel in ballast. Thus coal exports[61] gave British owners a keen competitive edge and played an essential part in the evolution and development of the tramp steamers which in the years leading up to the Great War comprised more than half of the British merchant fleet.

59. *British Shipping*, 2nd edn., *op. cit.*, pp. 38 and 40.

60. Cd. 9092 (Final Report, Part 2), Parl. Papers 1918, Vol. 13.

61. In 1860 coal exports amounted to 7.3 million tons; by 1890 they had grown to 30.1 million tons and by 1913 they had risen to 76.68 million tons.

So, as Glover told the Statistical Society in 1872, "Iron and coal have enabled us to recover our place as the greatest among the maritime carriers -and our engineers and shipbuilders have made such splendid use of these two minerals in the production of carrying machines as to deserve the pre-eminence which our flag has won". To put it shortly, Britain could build steamers better and cheaper than anybody else and since, from 1870 onwards, the superiority of the steamship over the sailing ship in most trades was becoming increasingly apparent, there was bound to be a tremendous upsurge in British shipping and shipbuilding. The decline of American competition, resulting from the reluctance of American owners to turn to steam and accelerated by the consequences of the Civil War and the development of the American West, and the fact that the European maritime countries were far behind in the construction and operation of steamships, put the British owners, with their experience and enterprise, in a uniquely favourable position to retain their hold on the imperial routes which they had for so long monopolised when the Navigation Laws were in force and to acquire not only the trade lost by the Americans but also a major share in the new and expanding trades which were becoming of increasing importance.

Apart from the beneficial effects flowing from the repeal of the Navigation Laws which enabled the better British owners to take the fullest advantage of their technical lead at a time of enormous expansion in world trade, to what extent, in the second half of the nineteenth century, did the Government seek to intervene, directly or indirectly, in the affairs of the British maritime industries? Certainly successive Governments did not allow the generally accepted political belief in the principle of laissez-faire to inhibit them from building vigorously upon the legislation of the early 1850s which had culminated in the Merchant Shipping Act 1854. Over the following 40 years, ending in the second major consolidation of 1894, there was almost unceasing Parliamentary activity affecting the operations of the mercantile marine but the legislation was of a character far removed from the statutes of the navigation system; no longer did the preambles declare that the measures were taken for the encouragement of British shipping and indeed many owners felt that this was an era of Parliamentary discouragement.

Having once, somewhat belatedly, accepted responsibility for the welfare of passengers and crews, Parliament pursued its task with unremitting zeal and between 1854 and 1894 there were no fewer than 43 statutes which in various ways extended and modified the provisions of the 1854 Act with the object of improving the welfare of passengers and crew, ensuring the competence of officers and seamen and reducing losses at sea resulting from unseaworthiness or overloading. Notwithstanding this spate of legislation, in 1875 there were complaints in Parliament and elsewhere that merchant sailors had been neglected and that with free trade had come in a system of laissez-faire with respect to British shipping and seamen. Farrer was requested to investigate the position and, in his Report to the President of the Board of Trade on legislation concerning Merchant Ships and Seamen covering the period 1835–75,[62] he detailed, with comments, the statutes passed, nearly 50 in number, and the Reports of Select Committees and Royal Commissions during the period under review. As Farrer observed, if things had not turned out well it had not been for want of legislative and administrative interference and he concluded by stating "It will thus be seen that in almost every year during the period I have taken, a period commencing long before the repeal of the Navigation Laws and lasting for more than a quarter of a century since that repeal, there have been laws introduced and passed and Committees or Commissions appointed to consider matters affecting the welfare and safety of our shipping and seamen".

Perhaps the real anxiety was not so much the extent of Government intervention as its effectiveness; the legislation requiring compulsory examination of masters, mates and engineers was not retrospective and their effects were accordingly not immediate. In 1869 Reports from British Consulates abroad regarding the general condition of British seamen[63] showed that there was still plenty of room for improvement and in 1874 evidence given by the Board of Trade to a Royal Commission on Unseaworthy Ships[64] showed that no less than 65 per cent of the wrecks and casualties (excluding collisions) over the period 1856–72 resulted from the faults of the master, crew or pilot. Nevertheless from 1870 onwards there was a steady improvement in the professional ability and standards of education of merchant navy masters and officers which was the result not only of the statutory requirements for the holding of certificates of competence but also by reason of the higher standards imposed by the leading shipowners—especially the liner companies. There was also some improvement, though not so marked, in the quality of British seamen, particularly those enjoying the benefit of continuous employment with the liner companies, but even after the turn of the century the seamen's conditions of service on many tramp ships still left much to be desired as regards such matters as accommodation, sanitary arrangements and rates of pay.

Over the period from 1855 to 1870 there were increasing allegations that many ships were being sent to sea in an unsafe condition, overloaded and sometimes overinsured; the Merchant Shipping Acts 1871 and 1873[65] made it a misdemeanour for a shipowner to send an unseaworthy ship to sea, provided for compulsory marking and recording of a vessel's draught and empowered the Board of Trade to carry out a survey if the Board itself or any third party had reason to believe that, by reason of a ship's defective condition or as a

62. C.1398. Parl. Papers 1876, Vol.66.

63. C.630 Parl Papers 1872, Vol. 53.

64. See Final Report of the Royal Commission, Appendix 68, C.1027, Parl. Papers 1874, Vol. 34.

65. 34 & 35 Vict., c.110 and 36 & 37 Vict., c.85.

result of overloading or improper loading, the ship was unfit to proceed to sea without serious danger to human life. The 1874 Royal Commission considered that the Board of Trade's powers of survey and detention were adequate and, after referring to the fact that officers of the Board of Trade had admitted that many Acts designed to secure safety of life at sea had been mischievous and should be modified or repealed, the Commission concluded that "the amount of legislation and the multiplicity of details connected with shipping that are now regulated by law have not been altogether successful and it seems that the results aimed at are hardly attainable by Acts of Parliament". The Commission also endeavoured to grapple with the problem of overloading but reluctantly concluded that, with the then present state of knowledge, they could not recommend any enactment for establishing a fixed load line and could not prescribe any universal rule for the safe loading of all vessels.

Following the recommendations of the Commission, the Merchant Shipping Act 1876[66] endeavoured to promote safety of life at sea in part by increasing the responsibility of the owners and in part by increasing the powers and obligations of the Board of Trade but the load line requirements of the Act, particularly as regards the less responsible owners, were a valueless safeguard since it was left to the owners themselves to select the position of the mark which they were obliged to place on the ship's side. Eventually, in 1885, the Report of a Load Line Committee[67] stated that it had become practicable to frame general rules concerning freeboard which would prevent dangerous overloading without interfering with trade and recommended that a compulsory load line should be enforced. The Committee's recommendation was endorsed in 1887 in a Report by a Royal Commission inquiring into the extent and cause of the loss of ships and lives at sea since 1874[68] and subsequently the Merchant Shipping Act 1890[69] provided for the compulsory marking of load lines on British ships as approved by the Board of Trade. The 1887 Royal Commission's Report revealed that from 1874 to 1883 there had been a marked increase in the losses of British ships and the lives of those employed in them[70] and the Commission concluded that "the hopes and intentions of Parliament to reduce loss of life at sea by the various Acts and through the powers entrusted to the Board of Trade have not been successful and that all the measures adopted have hitherto had little or no effect".

Although, during the second half of the nineteenth century, Parliament was so much preoccupied in imposing statutory regulations on the none too grateful shipowners who, not surprisingly, regarded the new controls as a poor substitute for the protection they had lost and felt that Parliament was hardly

66. 39 & 40 Vict., c.80.
67. C.4566 Parl. Papers 1887, Vol. 43.
68. C.5227 *ibid.*
69. 53 Vict., c.9.
70. The detailed figures are in Appendix 2 of the Report.

assisting them in resisting competition from foreign owners who were not burdened with such stringent statutory requirements, nevertheless there remained a limited, but important, sector of the shipping industry which, even after the repeal of the Navigation Laws, continued to receive Government support against foreign competition. There was, of course, no question of any erosion of the policy of unrestricted free trade, indeed it was some of Britain's principal foreign competitors who now still clung to protectionism, but the Government was not prevented by its political philosophy from continuing the new form of encouragement to British shipping which had been initiated in 1837 when, for the first time, the Government had placed a contract for the carriage of mail overseas by privately owned steamships instead of leaving all overseas mail services to be carried out by Admiralty sailing ships.[71]

However, even before the repeal of the Navigation Laws, the early mail contracts became increasingly subject to Parliamentary scrutiny. In July 1846 a Select Committee was appointed to inquire into the circumstances connected with the granting of Cunard's first trans-Atlantic contract[72] and in their Report[73] the Committee concluded that the arrangement had been made on terms advantageous to the public service but added that they did not wish to express any opinion as to whether a more advantageous one might not have been made had the tender been thrown open to public competition. In 1849 a Select Committee was appointed to inquire into the Contract Packet Service,[74] in 1851 another Select Committee was appointed to consider steam communication with India, China, Australia and New Zealand[75] and in the same year the Admiralty appointed Commissioners to examine harbours in Ireland suitable for an Irish packet station.[76] Then, in 1853, following complaints by the Post Office that the payments made by the Admiralty under their contracts with Cunard were far in excess of the postage paid on the mails carried, the Treasury appointed a Committee, under the chairmanship of the Postmaster-General, Lord Canning, to enquire into the whole process of the contract packet system.

The Canning Committee examined in detail all the existing mail contracts and agreed with the Post Office contention that the payments to Cunard and most of the other shipowners were substantially in excess of the sea postage.[77] However in their Report[78] the Committee accepted that there

71. For details of the early mail contracts see pp. 42–44 *supra*.
72. See P. Debs. 3 Ser. Vol. 87, c.1412.
73. Parl. Papers 1846 (563), Vol. 15.
74. For the Committee's Report see Parl. Papers 1849 (571), Vol. 12.
75. For the Committee's Reports see Parl. Papers 1851 (372 and 605), Vol. 21.
76. For the Commissioner's Report see C.1391, Parl. Papers 1851, Vol. 25.
77. In the case of Cunard the sea postage was £121,000 per annum compared with the contract payment of £188,000.
78. Parl. Papers 1853 (195), Vol. 95.

were other reasons of national importance which had hitherto justified payment of subventions greater than the cost of carrying the mails; in wording redolent of the sentiments underlying the recently repealed Navigation Laws, it was stated that the objects of the mail contracts were "to afford a rapid, frequent and punctual communication with those distant parts which feed the main arteries of British commerce and with the most important of our foreign possessions; to foster maritime enterprise; and to encourage the production of a superior class of vessel which would promote the convenience and wealth of the country in time of peace and assist in defending the shores against hostile aggression". The Committee concluded that the expectations of the Government's policy had not been disappointed, that the cost of meeting these objectives had not been excessive and that the service had been performed more cheaply by contract than by government agency; however, while accepting that subsidies were necessary in the early days, it was considered that they could now be dispensed with. Lastly the Committee laid down the principles which should govern the formation and renewal of contracts and in particular stressed that there was no need for long-term contracts and that in most cases there should be open competition.

The views of the Canning Committee appear to have made very little impression on the Admiralty and the Treasury. In 1857 Cunard, at that time under severe competitive pressure from the American Collins Line, requested a renewal of their trans-Atlantic contract although their current contract was not due to expire until 1862. The Post Office strongly opposed the renewal but, fortunately for Cunard, "the Admiralty and the Treasury were on its side"[79] and the contract was renewed for a further 10 years at the same rate. In response to the objection of the Post Office, the Secretary of the Admiralty wrote that "the best course for ensuring a satisfactory performance will be to prolong the contract—keeping the superiority of the British line appears to my Lords to be of national importance"; at the time the Admiralty still regarded the mail ships as an important naval reserve and the contract provided that the ships had to be structurally strong enough to carry the largest guns and to be capable of acceptable speeds.

In 1859 a further Select Committee was appointed to inquire into the mail contracts and in their Report[80] the Committee severely criticised the lack of liaison between Government departments, the failure to pursue the policies recommended by the Canning Committee and the lack of any effective Parliamentary control. The renewal of the Cunard contract was subjected to particularly adverse comment and it was stated that the practice of renewing contracts to existing holders had been carried to an extent

79. *Cunard and the North Atlantic*, *op. cit.*, p. 36.
80. Parl. Papers 1860 (328), Vol. 14.

which should no longer be sanctioned; it was also considered that on the U.K.—North America route no subsidies were required to secure a regular, speedy and efficient postal service. The Committee was so unimpressed by the Admiralty's conduct that, following its recommendation, an Act was passed in 1860[81] to vest control of existing and future contracts in the Post Office and a Treasury Minute approved the principles that the Packet Service should be self supporting and that long-term contracts should as far as possible be avoided.

Another debate on mail contracts took place in March 1868[82] during which the practice of giving fixed subsidies to special lines of steamers was generally condemned but, although the Chancellor of the Exchequer stated that he was desirous to see the postal service across the Atlantic self supporting, nine months later the Postmaster General entered into new trans-Atlantic contracts with Cunard and Inman at rates still far in excess of the sea postage. This provoked a further Commons debate in March 1869[83] during the course of which it was pointed out that the Government had made a contract with North German Lloyd which only involved payment of the sea postage and which was determinable on six months' notice. The debate concluded with the appointment of yet another Select Committee to inquire into the Cunard/Inman contracts; in their Report[84] the Committee stated that there was no longer any need for a fixed subsidy over a term of years for the U.K.—United States sea post and recommended that the contracts be disapproved[85]; the Government disregarded the recommendation and the contracts were ratified.

Shortly afterwards, in July 1869, the Commons resolved that in future all mail contracts should be made subject to the condition that they should not be binding until approved by a resolution of the House.[86] From then onwards the payments under the various mail contracts gradually came to represent a more realistic assessment of the actual value of the services to be performed[87] and in general the carriage of mails brought no more than a reasonable margin of profit to the liner owners. Thus, although there is no doubting the importance of the early mail contracts in furthering the setting up and development of the British steamship lines, from about 1870 onwards the element of bounty in the postal subventions was progressively reduced; in 1870 the annual subvention was around £1.2 million but by 1880 it had fallen substantially to about £664,000.[88] Moreover it must be borne

81. 23 & 24 Vict., c.6.
82. P. Debs. 3 Ser., Vol. 190, c.2010.
83. *Ibid.*, Vol. 194, c.1281.
84. Parl. Papers 1868–69 (106), Vol. 6.
85. The contracts contained an express power of disallowance by the House of Commons.
86. P. Debs. 3 Ser., Vol. 197, c.1818.
87. For details of the sea mail contracts 1860–85 see Howard Robinson, *Carrying British Mail Overseas* (London, 1964), Chapter 20 and Sir Evelyn Murray, *The Post Office* (London, 1927) pp. 57–59.
88. Parl. Papers 1890–91 (33), Vol. 48.

in mind that it was only the liner companies, and but a few of them, who received the postal subventions; the ships involved in the mail contracts only represented a small fraction, probably no more than five per cent, of the steam tonnage under the British flag and up to 1914 the tramp ships which made up the greater part of the British merchant fleet received no Government financial aid of any kind.

It was not for overseas mail services alone that Government payments were made to some of the liner owners. Between 1883 and 1885 the Admiralty hired a number of liners for use as auxiliary cruisers and troop transports but these were commercial transactions with the rate of hire reflecting the prevailing emergency conditions and containing no element of bounty. In 1887 the Admiralty decided that, instead of hiring ships *ad hoc* to meet emergencies, it was preferable to make arrangements in advance; contracts were entered into with Cunard and White Star Line under which the Admiralty paid subventions in order to obtain prior rights for the use or purchase, at agreed figures, of certain high-speed vessels suitable for use as armed merchant cruisers and the Admiralty considered this to be "an economical arrangement so far as the public expenditure is concerned".[89] Subsequently similar arrangements were made with other liner companies but since all the vessels held at Admiralty disposal had to be ready for service at short notice, were required to have uneconomically fast speeds and had to be specially constructed and equipped to fit them for naval use, it does not seem that the owners received any significant non-commercial benefits.

From 1870 onwards British shipbuilders also benefited from the ever growing number of Admiralty orders for new naval vessels which were required both as replacements for the ships which, with the advent of steam and the rapid development in armaments, had become obsolete and also to meet the increasing menace of German naval strength.[90] It has been suggested that this naval building programme was a form of concealed Government support for the shipbuilding industry[91] but, whilst the naval contracts were no doubt profitable and increased the prosperity that the shipbuilders were enjoying from the flood of orders for British and foreign merchant ships—and foreign orders for war ships as well—there were sound strategic reasons for the Admiralty programme and there seems to be no evidence that the Government intended to confer any bounty on the shipbuilders who in any case were far

89. "Subventions of Merchant Steamers for State Purposes", C.5006, Parl. Papers 1887, Vol. 52.

90. The vast scale of the naval building programme is shown by various Admiralty Returns—see for example Parl. Papers 1895 (260) and (460) Sess. 2, Vol. 65.

91. S. Pollard, *The Economic History of British Shipbuilding 1870–1914* (University of London Thesis, 1951). See also his article "Laissez-faire and Shipbuilding", *Economic History Review*, 2nd Series, Vol. 5, (1952–53).

from needing any artificial support. In 1884 the Report of a Committee inquiring into contract conditions for the building of naval ships[92] stated that the building of warships in private yards should be encouraged and its scope widened but there was no suggestion that the contracts included any subsidy for the builders; three years later the Report of an Admiralty Committee on Naval Contracts[93] was critical of Admiralty methods in the placing of contracts in private yards but again there was no indication that there was any hidden bounty in the prices agreed.

It can thus fairly be concluded that, amongst the many factors which contributed to the remarkable resurgence of the British maritime industries from 1860 onwards, Government financial support, which was limited to the decreasing bounty element in the mail contracts, was of relatively little significance and only benefited the few favoured liner companies which continued to receive the postal subventions. In general the British mercantile marine and shipbuilding industry prospered without any State protection or subsidy; as Fayle sums it up[94]—for 70 years prior to the outbreak of the Great War "British shipping had been left to compete, strictly on its own merits, in the freight markets of the world . . . The suggestion, sometimes made at home and abroad, that the great expansion of British shipping since the repeal of the Navigation Laws was due to the payment of subsidies by the Government will not bear the most cursory examination. It is based largely upon a confusion between subventions paid to shipping companies in return for the performance of specific services and subsidies or bounties granted for the encouragement of shipping as a matter of commercial policy."

By 1890 there could be no doubting the predominant position that British shipping and shipbuilding had achieved. In that year the tonnage on the U.K. register (sail and steam) stood at just under 8 million tons which represented 44.3 per cent of the total world fleet[95] and, in terms of steam tonnage alone, which amounted to over 5 million tons, the U.K. share was no less than 60.6 per cent.[96] For the years 1892–1894 the annual average output of British shipyards (sail and steam) represented over 81 per cent of world output.[97] In addition, over the previous 30 years, British shipping (sail and steam) had greatly increased its share of the total tonnage entered and cleared with cargoes in the U.K.'s foreign trade; in 1860 the British proportion of the trade had been 58.1 per cent but by 1890 it had risen to 73.85 per cent.[98]

92. C.4219. Parl. Papers 1884–85, Vol. 14.
93. C.4987. Parl. Papers 1887, Vol. 16.
94. C. E. Fayle, *The War and the Shipping Industry* (London, 1927), p. 21.
95. Cd. 7033, Table 11. United States overseas trade ships only. The proportion for the British Empire was 53.3 per cent.
96. *Ibid.* The British Empire's share was approximately 65 per cent.
97. Cd. 9092, 2nd Report.
98. For the detailed figures see Glover's "Address to the Royal Statistical Society" in 1892, *Journal of the Royal Statistical Society*, Vol. 55 (June 1892).

However, notwithstanding their wide margin of supremacy, from 1880 onwards the British maritime industries began to feel the effect of keen international competition from their principal foreign maritime rivals. In the liner trades the threat to British supremacy came mainly from Germany and Japan and, to a lesser extent, from France, Italy and Holland whilst in the tramp trades there were the beginnings of a serious challenge from Norway and Greece. In shipbuilding the foreign threat was not yet significant but there were signs of growing competition from the yards of France, Germany, Italy, the United States and Japan.

Although the British maritime industries neither sought nor received any general operating or construction subsidies, the same could not be said of some of their main foreign competitors. In 1880, in reply to a Commons question from David MacIver, a director of Cunard, the Government confirmed that the French were about to pass a law providing for a bounty of 1½ francs per ton on every ton of new shipping built in France for each 1,000 miles traversed in voyages to and from France.[99] Four years later the President of the Board of Trade stated that there had been some increase in French shipbuilding and that there had been movements of British shipyard workers to France[100]; subsequently, in 1886, the Government confirmed that the Italian government had passed a law for the payment of bounties on Italian ships.[101]

By 1888 increasing British anxiety regarding the impact of foreign subsidised competition was reflected in a House of Commons Address asking for "A return of the various European Countries giving bounties or subsidies for the construction or running of ships". Reports were duly published in 1889[102] but the information concerning the direct and indirect aid that was being given to their shipping by a number of foreign governments[103] did not provoke the British Government into any departure from their policies of free trade and non-intervention. As the President of the Board of Trade had stated some three years previously,[104] Her Majesty's Government "while disapproving of any interference with trade, whether by bounties or protective duties, are not aware that they have any means of inducing or compelling foreign governments to abandon them. They have no intention of entering upon a war of tariffs against bounties."

So for the time being at any rate, British shipowners and shipbuilders had

99. P. Debs. 3 Ser., Vol. 253., c.539. The French had already imposed a protective tax (*surtaxe d'entrepôt*) on foreign imports which had been first landed in another country before arriving in France; this tax affected British shipping more unfavourably than that of any other country—see P. Debs. 3 Ser., Vol. 254, c.177.

100. P. Debs. 3 Ser., Vol. 293, c.353.

101. *Ibid.*, Vol. 302, c.310.

102. C.5667, Parl. Papers 1889, Vol. 76.

103. Reports were made in respect of Austria-Hungary, Belgium, Bulgaria, Denmark, France, Germany, Greece, Italy, Montenegro, Netherlands, Portugal, Rumania, Russia, Servia, Spain, Sweden and Turkey.

104. P. Debs. 3 Ser., Vol. 303, c.300.

to accept that the Government had no intention of exercising their statutory powers of retaliation under the Customs Consolidation Act 1853 or even of pursuing any diplomatic campaign; presumably the Government felt that the British margin of supremacy was so great that the foreign challenge, even when stimulated by subsidies and protective measures, could be safely disregarded. Nevertheless, from 1890 onwards, those in Parliament concerned with safeguarding British maritime interests were constantly watchful of the growing encroachment of foreign shipping and shipbuilding as a result of their national policies and endeavoured to ensure that no corrective action was lacking that might prevent the British mercantile marine or national security from being seriously threatened by the increasing scale of financial and other forms of encouragement that certain foreign governments were giving to their own shipping and shipbuilding industries.

CHAPTER 4

BRITANNIA RULES THE WAVES

In the last decade of the nineteenth century and up to the beginning of the Great War there was no gainsaying the supremacy of British merchant shipping in terms of both quantity and quality. Although during this period there was growing competition from some of the foreign maritime countries, at the outbreak of war in 1914 the British mercantile marine was still indisputably "the largest, the most up to date and the most efficient of all the merchant navies of the world".[1]

The steam tonnage registered under the British flag in 1895 was far greater than the seagoing steam tonnage of the rest of the world[2] and although by June 1914 the relative superiority of the British Empire had diminished, Britain and her overseas possessions still owned nearly 48 per cent of the world's seagoing steam tonnage.[3] The superior quality of British tonnage was no less marked; British owners continually pursued a policy of selling their older ships to foreign flags and replacing them with the larger and more efficient ships that the British yards could readily supply.[4]

As regards the crews of British merchant ships, at the turn of the century there was some concern at the increasing proportion of foreigners employed on British ships[5] and in 1901 the Board of Trade appointed a Committee to inquire into the situation. In its Report[6] the Committee attributed the relative decrease of British merchant seamen to the superior attractiveness of shore employment and considered that an improvement in conditions on board ship would result in the recruitment of more British seamen but no statutory effect

1. Cd. 9092, Final Report.
2. The 1895 figures (see Cd. 7033) were: British Empire 6,544,455 net tons; World Total* 10,599,460 net tons.

* Excluding U.S. steam tonnage not registered for foreign trade and the steam tonnage of Portugal and Greece for which figures were not available.

3. Cd. 9092, Final Report, para. 13.
4. At the end of 1913 nearly 68 per cent of British steam tonnage had been built since 1900 —see Cd. 7616, Parl Papers 1914, Vol. 82.
5. See Cd. 7033. In 1895 the proportion was 17.96 foreign for every 100 British but by 1901 the proportion had increased to 21.76.
6. Cd. 1607. Parl. Papers 1903, Vol. 62.

was given to any of the Committee's recommendations until 1906[7] and in the meantime the statistics for 1903 showed that the proportion of foreigners had increased to 22.88 per cent. However in the event 1903 proved to be the turning point; from then onwards the numbers of British seamen increased both absolutely and relatively so that by 1912 the total had increased by some 32,000 since 1903 and the proportion of foreign seamen had fallen to 14.84 per cent. Thus, shortly before the outbreak of war, there was a sufficient supply of British seamen to provide for the wartime needs of both the merchant service and the Royal Navy.[8] Moreover the quality of British crews was now unsurpassed; as Thornton puts it[9]: "British Officers, engineers and seamen had established at last a reputation which was unrivalled for sound navigation, technical skill and loyal service . . . on every point of seafaring practice and technique the accepted standard was seldom anything but a copy of the British".

The dominant position which British shipping had attained also owed much to the high quality of British shipowners. Many of them had long and proud traditional ties with the sea and, although they were often fiercely independent men and in some cases not over-caring as to their seamen's conditions on board ship, their expertise, industry and enterprise were recognised and admired throughout the maritime world. There were, of course, some exceptions but, as Thornton emphasises, "the vast majority of British ships were well found and well managed"; British owners "in a very real sense formed an aristocracy of commerce and lived up to the best meaning of that word by their public-spirited management and the extreme prudence and conservation of their finance".

The supremacy of British shipping in the period leading up to the Great War was also reflected in the trading position. The official statistics showed that in 1895 British shipping (sail and steam) represented a proportion of nearly 73 per cent of the net tonnage entered and cleared, with cargoes and in ballast, at United Kingdom ports from and to foreign countries and British possessions.[10] In relation to the total trade of the world, as represented by the entrances of vessels with cargoes and in ballast at the ports of all countries in the year 1911-12, it was calculated that 41 per cent of the actual entrances were British flag including 85 per cent in the inter-imperial trade, 52 per cent in the Empire's foreign trade and 24 per cent in the trade between foreign

7. Merchant Shipping Act 1906 (6 Ed. VII, c.48).

8. Following the Report of a Naval Reserve Committee (Cd. 1491. Parl. Papers 1903, Vol. 40) the Naval Forces Act 1903 (3 Ed. VII, c.6) had empowered the Admiralty to raise a Royal Naval Volunteer Reserve comprising men not normally employed full time in sea-going pursuits and had removed the statutory limit of 30,000 for the Royal Naval Reserve of Merchant Seamen.

9. *British Shipping*, 2nd Edn., p. 80.

10. Cd. 7033. By 1913 the share of the British flag had fallen but it was still a formidable 57 per cent.

countries.[11] As regards the world's seaborne trade, as represented by the value of imports into all countries in 1912, it was estimated that British shipping carried about 52 per cent of this total trade including 92 per cent of the inter-imperial trade, 63 per cent of the trade between the Empire and foreign countries and 30 per cent of the trade between foreign countries.[12]

The supremacy of the British shipbuilding industry was likewise indisputable. For the years 1892–94 the annual average output of the merchant ships from British Empire yards was 1.008 million tons which represented 81.6 per cent of the annual average world output and although, from 1894 onwards, the output of foreign shipbuilders increased relatively at a greater rate than that of British shipbuilders, for the years 1910–14 the annual average output of merchant ships from British yards was 1.695 million tons which was still as much as 61.9 per cent of average world output for the same period.[13] Although, at the turn of the century, it was a rare event for British owners to order new tonnage abroad,[14] substantial orders for new tonnage were placed by foreign owners with British yards and the dominant position of British built steam tonnage is clearly illustrated by the extent to which the world's merchant navies depended on British shipbuilders; it was estimated that in 1901–02 about 70 per cent in number of the world's steamships had been built in U.K. shipyards[15] and in respect of the years 1909–13 an average of 22.4 per cent of U.K. output was for registration abroad.[16]

The production of the United Kingdom shipyards in this pre Great War period was far from being confined to merchant ships; warship building had become a profitable source of business for a limited number of specialist shipbuilders. In the twenty years or so leading up to the Great War the race for naval superiority was on and the Admiralty warship building programme was of a dimension never remotely equalled before or since. Between 1892 and 1914 no less than 2,576 warships were built in the United Kingdom[17] and, although many were constructed in the Royal Dockyards, a substantial proportion were built for the Royal Navy under contract in private shipyards.[18] During the period 1901 to 1913 the warships launched for the Admiralty amounted in total to around 1.782 million displacement tons, of which over 61 per cent had been built in private yards, and the expenditure on naval new

11. Cd. 9092, Final Report.
12. *Ibid.*
13. For detailed figures see Cd. 9092, Second Report.
14. In 1901–02 no less than 99 per cent of steamships on the U.K. register had been built in the U.K.
15. See *Economic History of British Shipbuilding*, *op. cit.*, p. 401.
16. L. Jones, *Shipbuilding in Britain* (Cardiff, 1957), Table 29.
17. *Economic History of British Shipbuilding*, *op. cit.*
18. Between 1900 and 1914 the share of the private yards in the warship tonnage built annually was hardly ever less than 50 per cent and in some years it was substantially more—see *Shipbuilding in Britain*, *op. cit.*, Table 33.

construction in this period was approximately £142 million.[19] In addition to the Admiralty programme British shipyards also built a substantial number of warships for foreign countries which did not have the domestic capability to build their own; between 1896 and 1913 the warships launched for foreign account amounted in total to over 447,000 displacement tons.[20]

Thus, during the period of some 20 years prior to the Great War, the predominance of the British mercantile marine and the United Kingdom's shipbuilding industry cannot be disputed; but to what extent was the growth in the tonnage registered under the British flag and in the output of the United Kingdom shipyards attributable to any artificial stimulus or protectionist policies on the part of the British Government? Certainly there was no departure from the principle of free trade; foreign shipping remained free to compete in all trades, including coastal and inter-imperial, on at least equal terms with British ships and foreign shipbuilders were equally free to compete for British orders. Likewise no general bounty or subsidy was granted to aid the construction or operation of British merchant ships and so it remains to consider in what other ways the British Government supported the domestic maritime industries and the extent to which such support was of real significance in contributing to British maritime supremacy.

In the case of shipbuilding, British yards, like most of their foreign competitors, were allowed to import free of duty any materials required for the construction and equipment of new vessels or for the repair of existing ships but this was only one element in the general British free trade policy under which, if they so wished, British shipowners were free to import foreign built vessels without payment of duty. Otherwise the principal non-commercial factor which in this period materially contributed to the growth and prosperity of the British shipbuilding industry, or rather that section to whom the building of warships and their armaments was entrusted, was the Admiralty building programme but there appears to be nothing in the contemporary official records to suggest that the Government regarded the Admiralty contracts as a form of indirect support for the industry.

The cost of the naval building programme was provided for in the normal Admiralty estimate, and there is no suggestion that any of the contract payments were of the nature of a subvention. The Report of the Committee which was appointed in 1902 to inquire into the Arrears of Naval Shipbuilding[21] included an examination of the expenditure incurred but there was no allegation that the contract prices were unduly liberal. From time to time there was considerable political opposition to what some regarded as an unnecessary

19. "Statistical Abstracts of the U.K. 1911–13 and 1914–17 and Admiralty Returns Parl. Papers 1912–13 (300), Vol. 53 and 1914 (410), Vol. 54.

20. See Appendix 2 of Chapter 4 of *Survey of Metal Industries* (HMSO, 1927) prepared by the Balfour Committee on Industry and Trade.

21. Cd. 1055, Parl. Papers 1902, Vol. 61.

and extravagant naval building programme but it was not suggested that either the scale of the programme or the extent to which the work was entrusted to private yards was prompted by any intention on the part of the Government to confer bounty on the relatively few shipbuilders concerned.

There were however some other Government activities which were undoubtedly of benefit to the technical progress of the shipbuilding and marine engineering industries. As Jones emphasises,[22] "Most of the credit for the technical improvements in design, for the introduction of new techniques in construction and for the advance of the science of naval architecture generally must go to the Royal Dockyards", but on the other hand it has to be recognised that the Admiralty efforts were naturally directed to improvements in naval construction and design and that their effects on merchant shipbuilding in general, though doubtless beneficial, were only incidental. Shipbuilding design was also substantially affected by the considerable volume of merchant shipping legislation but the main purpose of the far-reaching safety, passenger and tonnage regulations was the improvement of standards of safety and welfare rather than any direct intention of changing the traditional practices of old-fashioned shipbuilders.

It therefore seems reasonable to conclude that the Admiralty shipbuilding programme was motivated solely by the Government's policy of renewing and expanding the British fleet and that, since the capacity of the Royal Dockyards was quite insufficient to meet the demand, the major share of the new naval construction had to be entrusted to the private yards. Thus, apart from the freedom from import duty on shipbuilding materials, there seems to be no evidence of any direct or indirect Government support for British shipbuilding. Nor indeed is there anything to suggest that aid was sought or needed; although by 1914 the shipbuilding industries of Germany, Japan and the United States had developed sufficiently to meet their own national merchant shipping and warship requirements, the technical lead of the United Kingdom in iron, steel, naval architecture and marine engineering combined with the high capacity of British shipyards were such that, without any artificial support, Britain could still fairly claim to be the steamship builder of the world.

Turning now to the British shipping industry, it must be conceded that in this 20-year period from 1894 to 1914 there was some degree of financial support from the Government but an examination of the amount of such aid and the extent to which it was attributable to services rendered suggests that Government assistance only made a relatively modest contribution to the growth of British tonnage. In particular it needs to be emphasised that "the direct financial aid extended by the British Government has at no time reached more than 5 per cent of the tonnage under the British flag and has not benefited

22. *Shipbuilding in Britain*, *op. cit.*, pp. 14 *et seq.* See also "Laissez-faire and Shipbuilding", *op. cit.*

the hundreds of cargo ships that have been the main source of strength of the British merchant marine and the chief reliance of British industry and trade".[23]

The most conspicuous form of Government support was, as it had been for the previous 50 years, the postal subventions but, in view of the worldwide range of the mail services performed and the other obligations imposed by the contract conditions with regard to composition of crews, frequency, regularity and speed of service, the amount of the postal subventions paid to a limited number of liner companies does not appear unduly large. In 1895 the total gross payment was £775,000[24] and in 1902 the Report of a Commons Select Committee[25] stated that in 1901 the mailship subsidies were running at the rate of £756,000 per annum which the Committee considered to be almost certainly in excess of the full postal value although no attempt was made to estimate the amount of the bounty involved. In respect of the year 1906–07 a Parliamentary Return[26] showed that the total sum for foreign and colonial mail services had fallen to a gross amount of £558,000 and for 1912–13 a further Parliamentary Return[27] revealed that 10 British liner companies and two British railway companies had received between them a total payment of £610,000.[28]

By the turn of the century, if not earlier, it is probable that the payments to the liner companies under the postal contracts had become no more than what was fairly due for the services rendered. Official pronouncements certainly betray no desire to confer bounty on the shipowners; in a Commons debate in 1901 Gerald Balfour, President of the Board of Trade, stated that British shipping companies only received what he termed "legitimate subsidies", i.e. subsidies "given for services rendered and representing the value of such services"[29] and eight years later, in 1909, the Report of the Royal Commission on Shipping Rings[30] regarded "as the settled policy of this country that the sums paid under the postal contracts should merely cover the services rendered in carrying the mails". Writing in 1927[31] the position was summed up by Sir Evelyn Murray who, as Secretary to the Post Office since 1914, was both well qualified to express an opinion and also unlikely to put an unduly favourable gloss on the value of the liner companies services; after referring to the views of the 1853 and 1860 Committees that it was no longer necessary to subsidise

23. *Government Aid to Merchant Shipping*, *op. cit.*, p. 51.

24. See 41st Report of the Postmaster General, C.7852, Parl. Papers 1895. Vol. 26.

25. Select Committee on Foreign Shipping Subsidies, Second Report, Parl. Papers 1902 (385), Vol. 9.

26. Parl. Papers 1907 (359), Vol. 47.

27. Parl. Papers 1914 (156), Vol. 70.

28. The principal payments were £305,000 to P & O, £68,000 to Cunard, £62,900 to Royal Mail and £44,600 to Canadian Pacific.

29. P. Debs. 4 Ser., Vol. 92, c.1173.

30. Cd. 4668, Parl. Papers 1909, Vol. 47.

31. *The Post Office*, *op. cit.*, p. 58.

contractors,[32] he stated: "Post Office policy gradually moved in this direction. The element of subsidy disappeared from the British mail contracts and for many years past the contract payments have represented no more than a fair equivalent for services rendered . . . acceptance of the contract conditions as to regularity and speed entitles the shipping company to reasonable remuneration in addition to a payment of freightage for the actual conveyance of the mails."

In addition to the mail contracts, the Admiralty continued the practice of contracting with certain liner owners for the hire or purchase of specified ships for use as armed cruisers in time of war. In 1902 a Parliamentary Report[33] showed that 48 ships were then under contract of which only 18 were in receipt of annual subventions totalling £103,750 and due to expire in 1905–06. The amounts paid were in line with the recommendations in the Report of an Admiralty Committee on Mercantile Cruisers[34] and, since the vessels had to be constructed and manned to comply with Admiralty requirements, it seems improbable that the subventions contained any significant element of bounty bearing in mind that these naval requirements "lessened the freedom of the shipowner in dealing with his property, demanded extra expense in construction and, by adding to the weight of the fabric, lessened the earning power of the ship".[35]

With one notable exception the Admiralty subventions had ceased altogether by April 1906; the exception was, of course, Cunard and the event which prompted the then unprecedented financial arrangements made in 1903 between the Government and Cunard was the imminent possibility of Cunard falling under American control—a circumstance considered so potentially disastrous that it was "to occupy Parliament, off and on but sometimes very intensively, for some eighteen months, to come at least four times before the Cabinet; and to engross the heads of five departments of state in long and intricate negotiations".[36]

In 1901 an American trust named International Mercantile Marine Company ("IMM") had acquired from Ellermans a controlling interest in the British Leyland Line and early in 1902 IMM had entered into an Agreement with (*inter alios*) the Oceanic Steam Navigation Company to acquire the British White Star Line; at about the same time IMM purchased other British and American shipping lines, acquired a controlling interest in the Holland America Line and entered into working agreements with the German Hamburg-Amerika Line and Norddeutscher Lloyd. The formation of this formidable American

32. See pp. 72–74 *supra*.
33. Parl. Papers 1902 (218), Vol. 92.
34. Cd. 1379 Parl. Papers 1902. Vol. 92.
35. B. W. Guisberg, "Shipping Subsidies", *Journal of the Statistical Society*, Vol. 64 (1901).
36. V. Vale, "The Government and the Cunard Contract of 1903", *Journal of Transport History* (New Series) Vol. 5, No. 1 (February 1979). See also Part IV of Chapter 5 of *Cunard and the North Atlantic*, *op. cit.*

controlled shipping combine not only posed a serious threat to Cunard's North Atlantic trade but also gave rise to fears that IMM would make a bid for control of Cunard.[37] In the latter part of April 1903 Parliamentary concern first centred on the question as to how the IMM/White Star arrangements would affect the White Star ships held at the disposal of the Admiralty as armed merchant cruisers[38] but then on 1st May 1903 there was an adjournment debate[39] to discuss a matter of urgent public importance—namely "the formation of an American Shipping Combination for the purpose of controlling the Shipping Trade in the North Atlantic and its effects on the Maritime and Mercantile interests of the United Kingdom" in the course of which it was suggested that the Government should reintroduce the Navigation Laws.[40]

Between April and July 1902 the Government was much occupied in conducting parallel negotiations with IMM, White Star and Cunard with a view to concluding agreements which would protect Britain's merchant shipping and naval interests and ensure that Cunard at least remained under British control. After protracted negotiations agreement in principle was reached in August 1902 but it was not until a year later that the Cunard and White Star Agreements were signed[41] and approved by both Commons and Lords.[42]

The Government's Agreement with IMM did not remove the potential threat of stronger competition in the North Atlantic[43] but it did go some way towards allaying British fears; the Agreement, which was to last for at least 20 years,[44] provided that White Star and other IMM controlled British shipping companies should continue to be qualified to own British ships, that a majority of their directors should be British, that all officers and a proportion of the crews should be British, that none of the ships should be transferred to a foreign flag and that any of their ships should be hired or sold to the Admiralty if required. On the other hand the Government agreed to treat American controlled British shipping companies on the same footing of general equality with other British shipping companies in respect of any services, naval, military or postal, which

37. In mid-April 1902 IMM did make a formal bid for a controlling interest in Cunard but their offer was rejected by Cunard's Chairman Lord Inverclyde.

38. See P. Debs. 4 Ser., Vol. 106, cc. 1181–83 and 1322–24 and Vol. 107, cc. 30–31 and 426–431.

39. P. Debs. 4 Ser., Vol. 107, c.458.

40. *Ibid.*, c.470. Two weeks later (P. Debs. 4 Ser., Vol. 108, c.384) the Prime Minister, A. J. Balfour, admitted that the possibility of re-enacting the Navigation Laws had been considered by the Government.

41. The Cunard Agreement (Cd. 1703, Parl. Papers 1903, Vol. 36) was signed on 30th July 1903 and the IMM/White Star Agreement (Cd. 1704 Parl. Papers 1903, Vol. 63) was signed on 12th August 1903.

42. P. Debs. 4 Ser., Vol. 127, cc. 1080 and 1137.

43. In the event, mainly owing to poor management, the IMM commercial threat did not prove so serious as had been feared.

44. And thereafter subject to five years notice by either side—but the Government had a right of termination if the IMM Group "pursued a policy injurious to the British Mercantile Marine or British Trade".

the Government might desire to have rendered by the British mercantile marine.

The Cunard Agreement contained elaborate provisions to ensure that Cunard's head office should remain in Great Britain, that the Cunard ships should be maintained under British flag and management with only British officers and at least three quarters British crews and that no foreigner should be allowed to be either a director or shareholder of Cunard. In order to meet the existing German challenge and the serious competition expected from IMM, Cunard was to build in British yards two new passenger ships[45] which were to have an exceptionally fast speed of 24/25 knots and a high technical specification.[46] The construction of these expensive ships was to be financed by a Government loan of £2.6 million[47] repayable over 20 years, carrying an uncommercially low interest rate of 2¾ per cent and secured by a charge over all Cunard's vessels and other assets. Both the new ships and other Cunard vessels were to be at Admiralty disposal for hire or purchase on specified terms and there were restrictions on chartering and the sale of ships abroad. The Agreement was for a period of 20 years from the delivery of the second new ship and the Admiralty were to pay Cunard a subvention of £150,000 per annum, which was in addition to an increased postal subvention of £68,000 per annum for the carriage of mails.

In shipping circles the Agreement was generally regarded as being exceptionally beneficial for the shipowners and there is little doubt that this major Government financial support was of great importance to Cunard; Professor Hyde[48] suggests that "without such aid it is arguable whether the Company would have survived the difficult years 1903–08" and adds that Cunard may only have been saved from coming to the verge of bankruptcy "due to the fact that Cunard was able to capitalise goodwill into a national asset". Political opinion as to whether the Government's arrangements with Cunard were in the national interest was sharply divided.[49] The Liberal opposition argued that the Government had been thrown into an unnecessary panic, that the granting of loans and subventions represented an unwarranted departure from British traditional laissez-faire policy, that it was wrong to confer bounty on Cunard without giving other British liner owners the opportunity to compete and that in relation to Cunard the Government had made a thoroughly bad bargain.

45. Subsequently named *Mauretania* and *Lusitania*.

46. Not only to meet Admiralty requirements for armed merchant cruisers but also to regain the Blue Riband of the Atlantic from the Germans; this the *Mauretania* not only successfully accomplished but continued to hold the Blue Riband for some 20 years.

47. The making of this loan was subsequently authorised by the Cunard Agreement (Money) Act 1904 (4 Ed. VII, c.22).

48. *Cunard and the North Atlantic*, *op. cit.* pp. 157–158.

49. See the debates on 12th August 1903 (P. Debs. 4 Ser., Vol. 127, c.1080), 2nd and 3rd August 1904 (P. Debs. 4 Ser., Vol. 139, cc. 674 and 829) and on 8th August 1904 (P. Debs. 4 Ser., Vol. 139, c.1470).

The Government however contended that prompt action had prevented Cunard being forced into the American combine,[50] that Cunard was the only liner owner with the resources and expertise to operate the new ships, that the subventions were no more than fair compensation to Cunard for building and operating at high speed commercially uneconomic vessels and that the Agreement was profitable and for the benefit of the nation.

However regardless as to which of the parties made the best deal—and perhaps a fair assessment is that both the Government and Cunard achieved their respective objectives—it is clear that the Government's financial assistance to Cunard did represent a radical change in the traditional non-interventionist shipping policies which successive British Governments had followed since the repeal of the Navigation Laws. When sufficiently threatened by external pressure, the Government had showed that, in the national interest, it was prepared to sanction a different form of protectionism—monetary support rather than trading monopolies—to safeguard the predominance of the merchant marine and the defence of the realm. A new principle had been established which thereafter, although it was to lie dormant for some 30 years, was then reactivated[51] and subsequently, both in the years leading up to the Second World War and from 1964 onwards, became an accepted means of support for both British shipping and shipbuilding.

In this pre-Great War period the sole remaining Government payment to a British shipowner was the subsidy of £10,000 per annum granted to Elder Dempster in 1900 under a 10-year Agreement for a steamship service between Jamaica and the United Kingdom[52]; this was, however, a colonial, rather than shipping subvention to encourage the Jamaica fruit trade[53] and, in view of the considerable obligations imposed on the shipowners, it seems unlikely that any bounty for Elder Dempster was given or intended. Thus in the year 1912/13 the only Government payments to British shipowners were represented by postal subventions of £610,000 to some dozen liner owners and the sole Admiralty subvention of £150,000, to Cunard[54]; nothing went to the tramp ships which were estimated to comprise some 60 per cent of British tonnage and even the total of £760,000 paid to the liner owners was in return for postal and Admiralty services of varying kinds and contained little, if any, element of bounty.

In the 1890s, at a time when the great majority of British shipowners

50. From Professor Hyde's account of the whole transaction it seems likely that, if the Government had not intervened, IMM might well have succeeded in taking over Cunard. See also *British Shipping*, 2nd Edn., *op. cit.*, p. 79.

51. For the benefit of Cunard (naturally!)—in connection with the Cunard–White Star merger and the financing of the *Queen Mary* and *Queen Elizabeth*. See Chapter 6 *infra*.

52. Cd. 175, Parl. Papers 1900, Vol. 55.

53. In the 1907 Return on Subsidies (Parl. Papers 1907 (359), Vol. 47) the payments to Elder Dempster were described as charged to the Vote for Colonial Service.

54. Parl. Papers 1914 (156), Vol. 70.

received no Government aid of any kind, there was continuing concern in Parliamentary and shipping circles as to the extent to which the increasing threat to British maritime supremacy from Britain's main foreign competitors was being directly or indirectly aided by state support. Although a Report on foreign shipping subsidies had been made in 1889,[55] in the period of six years, from 1895 to 1901, the Foreign Secretary on no less than three occasions called upon the British Ambassadors in the principal foreign maritime countries to make reports on the support which the governments of those countries were giving to their national maritime industries. These Reports, published in 1895, 1898 and 1901,[56] revealed that, directly or indirectly, the governments of most of these countries did give some measure of artificial assistance to encourage the expansion of their merchant marines and shipbuilding industries.[57]

Direct foreign government aid consisted of construction bounties for the building of new ships—the amount being related to the type, tonnage, engine capacity and cost of the new ship and the location of the yard—and navigation bounties which were paid to the shipowners and which were calculated by reference to such factors as the number of sea miles sailed, the operating routes, the amount of cargo or number of passengers carried and the type, tonnage and speed of the ship. Up to 1914 no general navigation bounties had ever been paid to British shipowners and, apart from the early shipbuilding bounties which had ceased around the end of the seventeenth century,[58] the British Government had likewise given no general construction bounties. By contrast, during the 30 years or so prior to the Great War, the granting of general navigation and construction bounties formed a significant feature of the national shipping policies of a number of other maritime countries.[59]

Apart from this direct aid, there were a number of other means by which foreign governments indirectly supported their maritime industries. By 1900 most maritime countries had adopted the practice, begun in Britain as early as 1838, of paying contract prices for the carriage of their overseas mail to certain of their national shipping lines but, owing to the varying nature of the services to be performed, it is impracticable to assess with any accuracy the element of bounty in any particular postal subvention or even to say with certainty that

55. C.5667, Parl. Papers 1889, Vol. 76—see p. 77 *supra*.

56. C.7898, Parl. Papers 1895 Vol. 103; C.8720, Parl. Papers 1898 Vol. 92 and Cd. 596, Parl. Papers 1901, Vol. 80. A further Report was published in 1913—Cd. 6899, Parl. Papers 1913, Vol. 40.

57. For further details of foreign shipping and shipbuilding subsidies see also the Reports of the Select Committee on Foreign Shipping Subsidies (Parl. Papers 1901 (300), Vol. 8 and 1902 (385), Vol. 9) and the Final Report of the Departmental Committee on Shipping and Shipbuilding (Cd. 9092, Parl. Papers 1918, Vol. 13).

58. The last statute giving a construction bounty was in 1694 (5 & 6 Will. & Mar., c.24)—see. p. 23 *supra*.

59. France had paid both navigational and construction bounties since 1881 and the French example was subsequently followed by Italy, Russia, Austria-Hungary, Japan, Spain and others.

there was some element of bounty. A number of maritime countries also still reserved their coasting trades (in some cases far extended) for their own national ships[60]—a source of grievance to British owners in view of the fact that the British imperial trade had been open to ships of all nations since 1850 and that the reservation of the United Kingdom's coasting trade had ceased in 1854. Other forms of foreign indirect aid included exemption of shipbuilding materials from import duties, preferential railway rates for goods exported in national ships, loans to shipowners at low interest rates or even free of interest, reimbursement of canal and port dues, reservation of registry for home built ships only and tax exemptions for domestic shipping.[61] In the case of Germany alone, their liner companies obtained a significant preference in the North Atlantic emigrant trade as a result of the German government entrusting them with the management of the emigrant control stations.

The 1895, 1898 and 1901 Reports were largely factual and did not reveal what impact foreign aid was having on the British shipping industry. However in 1901 the increase in German trade to East Africa, which was mainly attributable to the subsidies given to the German East Africa shipping line, gave rise to a debate in the House of Commons[62] as a result of which a Select Committee was appointed to inquire into the subsidies to steamship companies and sailing vessels under foreign governments and the effect thereby produced on British trade. The Committee's First Report[63] contained a considerable volume of evidence on both British and foreign aid to shipping[64] and in its Second Report[65] the Committee's main conclusion was that the granting of shipping subsidies by foreign governments had favoured the development of competition against British shipowners and trade upon the principal routes and had assisted in the transfer from British to Continental ports of some branches of foreign and colonial trade but that, notwithstanding foreign subsidies, British steam shipping and trade had in the main held their own and under fair conditions British shipowners were able to maintain the maritime commerce of the United Kingdom.

The Committee also considered that competition by British shipowners upon fair conditions without Government interfering by way of subsidies was more healthy and likely to be more beneficial to the nation and Empire than a State-subsidised and State-controlled system under which the shipowner would

60. These included the United States, France, Italy, Russia, Belgium, Spain and several South American countries.

61. Britain also exempted shipbuilding materials from import duty but otherwise, apart from the 1903 loan to Cunard, at this time gave no other indirect aid to its maritime industries.

62. On 23rd April 1901—P. Debs. 4 Ser., Vol. 92, c.1141.

63. Parl. Papers 1901 (300), Vol. 8.

64. Appendix 36 sets out a comparison, as at 1st August 1901, of the subsidies paid by Great Britain, France, Russia, Germany and the United States. In the case of France, construction and navigation bounties amounted to £72,000.

65. Parl. Papers 1902 (385), Vol. 9.

have to depend less on his own energy and skill and more upon the favour and support of the Government. It was believed that a general system of subsidies other than for services rendered would be costly and inexpedient but there were rare cases justifying subsidies[66] and the Committee thought that there should be a British line to East Africa where there was no direct British service and where British trade was handicapped by the subsidised German East Africa line. With a view to ensuring that British shipowners were able to compete on fair terms with their foreign rivals, the Committee recommended that Board of Trade regulations should be enforced against foreign vessels in British ports, that light dues should be abolished,[67] that action through diplomatic means should be taken to get access for British vessels to restricted foreign coasting trades and that, if need be, regulation for the admission of foreign vessels to the British and Colonial trade of the Empire should be used with the object of securing reciprocal advantage for British shipowners abroad.

British shipowners had for long complained that they were placed in an unfair competitive position because the safety and welfare regulations imposed on them under the Merchant Shipping Acts were more stringent than the corresponding foreign regulations and because the British regulations did not apply for foreign ships using United Kingdom ports. Accordingly, as a result of the recommendation made in the Committee's Second Report, in 1905 a further Select Committee was appointed to consider to what extent the statutory regulations applying to British ships trading to and from ports in the United Kingdom should be made applicable to foreign vessels trading to and from such ports. In their Report[68] the Committee recommended that there should be power to apply in U.K. ports the British load line rules to merchant ships of any country which did not have loading rules substantially equivalent to the British rules; that the provisions of the Merchant Shipping Act 1894 regarding unseaworthy ships should be applied to foreign ships in U.K. ports; that foreign ships with grain cargoes should be subject to the same regulations as British ships and that British rules relating to life-saving appliances should

66. In any case in which the Government granted subsidies the Committee recommended that there should be a small permanent committee to keep the matter under constant review; that subsidised vessels should have adequate speed; that the hire or sale of subsidised vessels should be subject to Government permission; that a majority of the directors of the shipping company should be British and that the captain, officers and a proportion of the crew should also be British.

67. The Report of the 1860 Committee to inquire into the State of Merchant Shipping (Parl. Papers 1860 (530), Vol. 13—see pp. 64–65 *supra*) had also recommended that merchant shipping should be exempted from light dues and that these should be borne by the nation. Up to 1902 the Government had taken no action and the recommendation of the 1902 Committee was likewise ignored. In 1918 the Final Report of the Departmental Committee (Cd. 9092) stated that £500,000 per annum was still being levied for general light dues and recommended that the cost of lighting the coast should be borne by the State rather than by merchant shipping; this recommendation has never been implemented.

68. Parl. Papers 1905 (269), Vol. 7.

apply to foreign ships trading with the U.K. Effect was promptly given to all these recommendations by the Merchant Shipping Act 1906.[69]

The reservation by a number of foreign governments of their coastal trades was certainly no new problem; it had been foreseen more than 50 years earlier when, in the course of the debates on the repeal of the Navigation Laws,[70] the Conservative Opposition and even some supporters of repeal such as Gladstone had endeavoured, without success, to persuade the Government that the participation of foreign shipping in the British imperial trade should be conditional upon British shipping being granted reciprocal treatment in relation to the so-called coastal trades of the United States and other countries, such as France and Russia, who reserved for their own ships not only their domestic coasting trade but also the trade with their overseas possessions. In the event the United States and the other foreign countries in question did not reciprocate in the way that the Government had confidently expected and, although in 1860 a Select Committee had urged the Government to use diplomatic measures to secure the abolition of these restrictions,[71] it was apparent from the Second Report of the 1902 Committee on Foreign Subsidies[72] that such diplomatic initiatives as may have been taken between 1860 and 1900 had produced no amelioration in the situation.

In these circumstances the Committee thought that the occasion had come when the qualified reservation of the British imperial coasting trade should be considered by the Government "with a view to reserving the British and colonial coasting trades and the imperial 'coasting' trade within the British Empire to British and Colonial ships and to vessels of those nations who throw open their coasting trade to British and Colonial Ships".[73] Although the Government presumably considered the Committee's suggestion, no action was taken to implement it[74]—possibly because the Government took the view that a diplomatic initiative supported by threats of reserving the coastal trade of the United Kingdom and the inter-imperial trade was unlikely to meet with any success in view of the fact that foreign participation in both these trades was insignificant.[75] Thus at the outbreak of the Great War British vessels were still excluded from the coasting trades of many of the principal maritime countries including the United States and the American possessions, France and her possessions, Holland and her possessions, Russia, Spain, Japan, Brazil and Argentina.[76]

69. 6 Ed. VII, c.48.
70. See pp. 47–48 *supra*.
71. See p. 64 *supra*.
72. Appendix 3 to the Second Report (Parl. Papers 1902 (385), Vol. 9).
73. Second Report, p. 22.
74. There was power to do so under Sections 324 and 325 of the Customs Consolidation Act 1853.
75. In 1913 British shipping monopolised the U.K. coasting trade to the extent of 99.1 per cent, and 92 per cent of the inter-imperial trade was carried in British ships.
76. Cd. 9092, Final Report.

Nevertheless it seems unlikely that, in the 20 years prior to the Great War, these foreign cabotage policies and the various other measures of direct and indirect aid which some of the principal foreign maritime countries gave to their shipping affected significantly the growth of British shipping and its prosperity and competitive position in world trade. In June 1914 the British Empire's merchant navy comprised nearly one half of the world's steam tonnage (12.4 million tons net out of about 26 million) and was four times as large as its nearest and most formidable competitor—the German mercantile marine. The growth of British steam tonnage in the first 14 years of the century was more than 5 million tons net and there is little evidence to suggest that such growth was significantly retarded by the discriminatory shipping policies of foreign governments. Admittedly in this period the share of the world's trade carried in British ships did diminish but this was due more to the natural expansion of both trade and foreign merchant fleets than to foreign artificial aid; and in 1914 British ships still carried more than half of the world's seaborne trade.

There can be no doubt that, in the years immediately prior to the Great War, British shipping, in both the liner and tramp trades, was increasingly feeling the impact of foreign competition but the most severe competitors were not the ships of those countries who gave the largest artificial aid. In the Atlantic liner trades the main threat came from the German lines which received no direct subsidy and whose success was largely attributable to their efficiency and enterprise. In the field of tramp shipping the main challenge to British supremacy came from Scandinavia, Holland and Greece whose shipowners received very little in the way of State assistance. The view expressed by the Rochdale Committee of Inquiry into Shipping fairly sums up the position; their Report stated[77]: "The declining relative importance of the U.K. merchant fleet in the years immediately prior to 1914 can reasonably be regarded as resulting from the economic development of other nations. It would not be fair to attribute it to a failure of enterprise on the part of the U.K. shipowners or to unfair competition from their rivals in this period. While some governments were assisting domestic shipping industries to establish viable enterprises in the face of our well entrenched position, the fleets of few of our main rivals were in receipt of major assistance and most trades of the world were open freely to all commerce. Discrimination in favour of national fleets was comparatively uncommon, except for the reservation of coastal trades (cabotage) by a number of countries."

It thus seems reasonable to conclude that the growth and prosperity of British shipping in this period was not seriously affected by artificial aid to its foreign competitors and equally owed little to British Government support; there was no discrimination against foreign flags, the bulk of the merchant

77. Cmnd. 4337, Parl. Papers 1969–70, Vol. 27.

marine received no State assistance of any kind and, apart from the exceptional Cunard transaction, there remained little, if any, element of bounty in the postal and Admiralty subventions paid to a small number of liner owners. Likewise the British shipbuilding industry's predominant position had been achieved without Government aid; the privilege of importing shipbuilding materials free of duty only put the British shipbuilder into a situation of parity with his main foreign competitors and the warship orders, although important to the development and prosperity of some yards, cannot rightly be classified as a form of State support. As regards foreign shipbuilding competition, the 1918 Departmental Committee[78] had no doubt that "the output of shipyards in the United Kingdom would have been absolutely and relatively greater had foreign governments not artificially encouraged their shipbuilding industries" but nevertheless, largely because British built ships were both cheaper and better, the annual average output of British yards between 1910 and 1914 still represented nearly 62 per cent of the world's total and Britain could still fairly claim to be the steamship shipbuilder of the world.

So in 1914, as the Rochdale Committee pointed out,[79] "there were 18.9 million gross tons of steamship on the U.K. register . . . we were pre-eminent in the liner trades . . . we had a smaller, but still large, share in the tramp trade . . . and a very considerable coastal trade employing hundreds of small vessels". It was as well that this was so; the hundred years of the *Pax Britannica* was about to come to an end and when it did "the whole war effort of Great Britain, a great part of the fighting strength of her allies, depended, directly or indirectly, on the activities of the ships . . . It is no exaggeration to say that the possession by Great Britain of a mercantile fleet much larger than was required for her own minimum essential needs was, above all else, the decisive factor in the war."[80]

Thus, in the forthcoming conflict, perhaps more so than ever previously, Britain's strength depended, as it had in Tudor times, upon having "a multitude of ships as a great defence and surety of the realm in time of war as well to offend as defend"[81] and, as the Departmental Committee emphasised in 1918,[82] "Had the British Empire been dependent during the present war for its shipping facilities upon foreign countries, there would have been no prospect of success. Had British shipyards and marine engineering works not been capable of a great output, it would have been impossible largely to increase our naval strength or to make good any of the damage inflicted on our mercantile marine."

78. Cd. 9092, Second Report.
79. Cmnd. 4337, paras. 27 and 28.
80. *War and the Shipping Industry*, *op. cit.*, pp. 1 and 321.
81. From the preamble to the Navigation Act 1540.
82. Cd. 9092, Second Report, para. 3.

CHAPTER 5

THE GREAT WAR AND ITS AFTERMATH

It is impossible here to attempt even a summary of the outstanding war record of the British mercantile marine; as Thornton rightly says[1]—"On that subject one must write a volume or nothing at all".[2] In recognition of the merchant navy's gallantry it must regretfully suffice to record yet again the tribute in the 1918 Report of the Departmental Committee[3] to the skill, efficiency and seamanship of the officers and men whose courage and devotion during the war ensured the maintenance of the seaborne trade upon which Britain and her Allies so much depended. Nevertheless, in regard to the period of the Great War and its aftermath, it is necessary to examine the many wartime controls to which British shipping and shipbuilding were subjected and to consider the effects which this unprecedented interference with normal commercial operations, the losses of merchant shipping from enemy action or otherwise and the exigencies of war in general had on the British maritime industries during the war, in the immediate post-war period and in the longer term.

Even before the official declaration of war it was apparent that, on the commencement of hostilities, a large number of merchant ships would be immediately required for transports, supplies and naval auxiliary purposes. The rapid obtaining of tonnage required no emergency legislation; from as far back as the thirteenth century Parliament had recognised the power of the Crown to requisition ships and men for national defence and although, in 1914, the Royal Prerogative of requisitioning ships had not been exercised for more than two centuries, it was not doubted that the Crown had a right to resume the exercise of this prerogative.[4] Accordingly on 3rd August 1914 a

1. *British Shipping*, *op. cit.*

2. A concise account of the war record of British shipping is given in Chapter 20 of *War and the Shipping Industry*, *op. cit.* The wartime operations of the merchant navy are dealt with in detail in "The Merchant Navy" by Archibald Hurd (*History of the Great War*. (London, 1921)) and shipping's part in the maintenance of supplies during the war period is described in "Seaborne Trade" by C. E. Fayle (*History of the Great War* (London and New York, 1920–24)). See also *National Service of British Seamen 1914–1919* by Father C. P. Hopkins (London, 1920) and *Allied Shipping Control* by Arthur Salter (Oxford, 1921).

3. Cd. 9092.

4. See "The Power of the Crown to Requisition British Ships in a National Emergency" by W. S. Holdsworth in *Law Quarterly Review*, Vol. XXV (1919) and the decision of the Court of Appeal in *The Broadmayne* (1916) 1 P. 64.

Royal Proclamation[5] authorised the Admiralty to requisition any British ships, as defined in the Merchant Shipping Act 1894, within the British Isles or adjacent waters[6] and provided that the owners should receive payment for the use of their ships on terms to be mutually agreed or, failing agreement, by award of an Arbitration Board. By the end of August 1914 an Admiralty Transport Arbitration Board had been constituted[7] and, after the Board's recommendations regarding rates of hire had been circulated in a Blue Book, what thereafter came to be known as the "Blue Book Rates" were accepted by both the shipowners and the Government.[8]

By January 1915 between 20 and 25 per cent of British ocean-going tonnage[9] was under requisition and, although there was a gradual increase over the next 15 months, by May 1916 only 37 per cent was fully requisitioned whilst 19 per cent was subject to various kinds of direction and the remaining 44 per cent was still free.[10] Thus until 1917 when, following the setting up of a Ministry of Shipping, the new Shipping Controller introduced a policy of more or less universal requisitioning, nearly half the ocean-going tonnage remained free from full requisition and, prior to 1917, this seems to have been deliberate Government policy[11] so as to leave every shipowner with some ships free to take advantage of the favourable freight market on which rates increasingly became far in excess of the Blue Book levels for requisitioned ships. Unfortunately this policy produced highly inequitable results as between different shipowners owing to the fact that in the earlier part of the war the incidence of requisitioning was extremely uneven.[12] However many vessels not under full requisition were far from being at the free disposal of their owners. Early in 1915 the Government requisitioned all the refrigerated space in British liners trading to Australia, New Zealand and South America and later in 1915 the North Atlantic liners were required to reserve up to 50 per cent of their cargo capacity for the carriage of wheat and flour at Blue Book rates. In addition there was a substantial amount of tramp tonnage which, under threat of

5. 1914 No. 1247. On the same date there was another Proclamation (1914 No. 1176) calling out for service the members of the Royal Naval Reserve, the Royal Fleet Reserve and the Royal Naval Volunteer Reserve.

6. Dr Holdsworth considers that the prerogative power extends to the requisition of British ships wherever they may be but in practice most ships were requisitioned in British territorial waters.

7. The Board comprised Government nominees and representatives of shipowners, marine insurers, banking and cargo interests and officers and crews.

8. For details of original and revised Blue Book Rates see Appendix 40 of *War and the Shipping Industry*, *op. cit.*

9. I.e. steamships of 1,600 tons gross or more on the U.K. register.

10. For detailed figures at May 1916 and other selected dates between January 1916 and December 1919 see *War and the Shipping Industry*, *op. cit.*, Appendix 15.

11. See Russell Smith, *Influence of the Great War Upon Shipping* (New York, 1919), p. 155.

12. To some extent this was unavoidable since at the beginning of the war ships had to be requisitioned quickly depending on their availability and without regard to ownership. Subsequently the Admiralty did endeavour to ensure that requisitions were more equitably distributed.

requisition, was "directed" into certain trades or "required" to carry specified Government cargoes.[13]

Shortly after Lloyd George succeeded Asquith in December 1916 there was a fundamental change in the Government's requisitioning policy. Under Section 5 of the New Ministries and Secretaries Act 1916[14] a Ministry of Shipping was created and power was given for the appointment of a Minister of Shipping under the title of Shipping Controller[15] "For the purpose of organising and maintaining the supply of shipping in the national interest". In February 1917 the Government instructed the Controller to "extend the requisitioning of tonnage at Blue Book rates so as to make it general and as nearly as possible universal"; at that time a majority of tramp ships were already under full requisition and most of those nominally free were engaged in "directed" trades but only one third of the liners had been fully requisitioned and it was thus largely the liner owners who felt the main impact of the new policy.[16] The Controller realised that it would be of little avail to requisition the liners alone without the backing of their highly specialised organisations at home and abroad and the solution eventually reached was that the Government would, in effect, requisition both the ships and the services of their owners[17]; so for the last 18 months of the war by far the greater part of the U.K. ocean-going tonnage, both liner and tramp, was under full requisition at Blue Book rates and most of the relatively few so-called free vessels were engaged in "directed" trades.[18]

By virtue of Regulations made under the Defence of the Realm Acts 1914 ("DORA"),[19] from the earliest days of the war the navigation of all British merchant vessels was subject to Admiralty control and, after the first year of war, the shortage of tonnage, caused by such factors as losses from enemy action, decline in output of new merchant ships, port congestion and wasteful use of requisitioned ships, resulted in restrictions being placed on the trading of free ships. In November 1915 all British ships over 500 tons gross were prohibited from carrying cargoes outside the British Empire except by licence

13. Usually at Blue Book rates or at least at rates below the current market level.

14. 6 & 7 Geo. V, c.68.

15. Sir Joseph Maclay, a well known Glasgow shipowner, was appointed Shipping Controller and continued in that office until March 1921 when the Ministry of Shipping was dissolved.

16. For details of the requisitioning position at 28th February 1917 see *War and the Shipping Industry*, *op. cit.*, p. 224.

17. Under this so-called Liner Requisition Scheme the Government had control of the routes and cargoes and were entitled to any operating profit. The owners continued the day to day running of their fleets and retained their valuable organisations. The arrangements rested on the co-operation of the liner owners since in the case of *China Mutual Steam Navigation Company* v *Maclay* ([1918] 1 KB 33) it was held that the Controller had no power to requisition the owners' services.

18. But at no time during the war was there any general requisitioning of vessels engaged in the coasting trade.

19. 4 & 5 Geo. V, c.63 & 5 Geo. V, c.8.

of the Ship Licensing Committee[20] and in February 1916 the licensing system was extended to all voyages. In January 1917, following the creation of the Ministry of Shipping, the licensing system was transferred to the new Ministry[21] and by Regulations made in June 1917[22] the Controller was given not only the right to requisition but was also empowered to make orders as to the nature of trades and traffic, the terms and conditions on which traffic was carried, loading and discharging ports, rates to be charged for freight, hire and carriage of passengers and other matters affecting shipping.

In 1914 the agreed Blue Book rates were higher than those then obtainable in the open market and, although they were less than in the boom years of 1912 and 1913, they gave a better rate of return than the average of the years 1901 to 1911 which had been a period of depression for British and world shipping. So initially the owners of requisitioned ships made a reasonable, though not excessive, trading profit but inevitably war conditions brought about a rapid change of circumstances. By January 1915 the shortage of free tonnage had resulted in the level of open market freights being far in excess of the Blue Book rates whilst on the other hand there had been a sharp increase in operating expenses[23]; consequently the net return from the requisitioned vessels increasingly became more unremunerative whilst at the same time the owners fortunate enough to have free ships were making ever greater profits. The tramp owners asked for an upward revision of the Blue Book rates and, since neither party had envisaged such a rapid and substantial increase in operating costs, the rates for tramp ships were increased by an average of about 16 per cent and the Admiralty also agreed to bear the cost of wages in excess of the August 1914 level.[24]

Even with the upward adjustment in Blue Book rates, the owners of requisitioned vessels did not, in 1915, receive more than a modest net return and in the next two years operating expenses continued to rise to such an extent that in some cases there was no profit after providing for depreciation. Thus it could not be fairly alleged that British shipowners were profiteering from their requisitioned ships but, bearing in mind that until the end of 1916 nearly half the United Kingdom's ocean going tonnage remained free from full requisition, it cannot be denied that in 1915 and 1916, as a result of the enormous rise in

20. A Committee chaired by a shipping lawyer and comprising representatives of shipowners which was appointed by and responsible to the Board of Trade.

21. DORA Regulation 39 DD provided that no ship could proceed to sea without the licence of the Shipping Controller.

22. DORA Regulation 39 BBB.

23. Most requisitioned ships were taken on a time-charter basis so the owners remained responsible for all operating expenses except bunkers and also bore the cost of repairs and marine and war risks insurance.

24. These concessions were made on the understanding that no further claims for increase should be made for the duration of the war but in fact rates increased further as from 1st March 1918.

freights, profits on a prodigious scale were made from the free ships.[25] The general public's indignation at the shipowners' alleged profiteering was exacerbated by the fact that some owners distributed exorbitant dividends instead of retaining profits to meet the ever increasing cost of replacement; in addition, since the excessive level of freights was inevitably reflected in grossly inflated ship values, some shipowners made vast tax free fortunes from the sale or loss of their ships.

The root cause of the freight explosion was the shortage of tonnage but prior to 1917, in spite of pressure from the shipowners, the Government refused either to limit demand by prohibiting non-essential imports or to increase supply by enabling owners to replace their wartime losses with new tonnage.[26] Government action was, however, taken to tax the excess profits of all businesses by the imposition in September 1915 of 50 per cent excess profits duty ("EPD") to be charged for any business account year ending after 4th August 1914 but by chance the shipping community, having had two prosperous years in 1912 and 1913 which formed the datum from which their excess was to be calculated,[27] suffered less from the new EPD than most other sections of the business community. The Government did not respond to pressure for special discriminatory taxation against shipowners' operating and capital profits so that, although the rate of EPD was raised to 60 per cent in April 1916 and again to 80 per cent as from the beginning of 1917, the fact still remained that "Up to this point, the profits made by shipping had been the most notorious and striking of any section of industry and the capital gains of those who sold ships outright were the subject of widespread wonder and disapproval".[28]

However, from 1917 onwards the embarrassment of high shipping profits became increasingly of less importance. The greater part of the ocean-going tonnage was under full requisition on Blue Book rates and the remaining ships were subject to the Shipping Controller's power to direct not only the voyages they were to perform but also the freights that they were to be paid. The shortage of tonnage was alleviated by concentrating ships on the shortest sea routes, severe import restrictions and the building of more new merchant ships. All this resulted in a marked decline in shipping profits in 1917 and 1918.[29]

A further Government control imposed on shipowners as from March 1915 was in relation to the sale of ships to foreigners. Before the war two of the factors which had helped to maintain the high quality of the British merchant

25. For figures showing the remarkable rise in "free" freights see "Merchant Shipping and State Control" by J. Hilton in *Edinburgh Review*, Vol. 1 (1918). For estimates of shipping profits August, 1914 to December, 1916 see *War and the Shipping Industry*, *op. cit.*, Chapter XI.

26. Until the latter part of 1916 the Admiralty, who controlled all shipyards from the outbreak of war, gave absolute priority to warship building and repairs—see further *infra*.

27. See Finance (No. 2) Act 1915, Section 40.

28. Sir J. Stamp, *Taxation during the War* (London, 1932).

29. For details see *War and the Shipping Industry*, *op. cit.*, Appendix 46.

fleet was the sale of obsolete and uneconomic tonnage to foreign flags and the speedy replacement of this old tonnage with new British built ships. In the first six months of the war British owners remained free to sell ships not under requisition to foreign buyers but then the British Ships (Transfer Restriction) Act 1915[30] provided that any transfer of a British ship[31] to anyone not qualified to own a British ship[32] should not have effect unless the transfer was approved by the Board of Trade. Two lacunae in this 1915 statute were filled in the following year by the British Shipping (Transfer Restriction) Act 1916[33] which provided that the Board of Trade's control was also to apply to mortgages of ships to foreigners and to transfers or mortgages of ships to foreign controlled British companies.[34] These two statutory restrictions resulted in a large decrease, as compared with pre-war, in the number of second hand British ships sold to foreign flags[35] but, although this policy did result in a number of old ships remaining on the United Kingdom register[36] and available for use in the war effort, it also meant that at the end of the war the merchant navy had far too many obsolete vessels. As from February 1917 the purchase of ships by British owners was also controlled; a new DORA Regulation[37] prohibited the purchase of any ship or a controlling interest therein without the permission of the Shipping Controller.

There were many other statutory controls, too numerous here to detail, which directly or indirectly affected shipping but brief mention must be made of the Government backed War Risks Insurance Scheme since the State's prompt intervention to solve this problem on the outbreak of war was so important that without it there is every probability that in the early months of the war the greater part of the merchant navy would have been lying idle in port. The difficulty had been foreseen, and referred to a Treasury Committee, as early as 1908 but the Committee had failed to find a solution[38] and it was not until 1913 that a Sub-Committee of the Committee of Imperial Defence was appointed to consider whether a practicable scheme could be devised for the insurance of British ships and cargoes in time of war. In their

30. 5 Geo. V, c.21.

31. But only a British ship registered in the United Kingdom or in any of the British possessions other than India, Canada, Australia, New Zealand, South Africa and Newfoundland.

32. In accordance with Section 1 of the Merchant Shipping Act 1894. Those qualified were British subjects and bodies corporate established under and subject to the laws of some part of the British Dominions and having their principal place of business in those Dominions.

33. 6 & 7 Geo. V, c.42.

34. A British incorporated company having the majority of its shares owned by foreigners could still be qualified to own a British ship if it could establish that its principal place of business was within the British Dominions.

35. The net tonnage sold to foreign buyers over the four years 1915 to 1918 was 174,000 tons. In the years 1911–13 an annual average of nearly 400,000 tons net were sold to foreign buyers.

36. In 1917 DORA Regulation 39 G restricted the transfer of registry of a British ship outside the United Kingdom.

37. Regulation 39 CC.

38. See their Report—Cd. 4161, Parl. Papers 1908, Vol. 58.

Report dated 30th April 1914[39] the Sub-Committee recommended the setting up of a State War Risks Insurance Scheme under which the existing Mutual War Risks Associations would issue their shipowner members with new war risks policies which the State would reinsure to the extent of 80 per cent.[40] On 4th August 1914, coincident with the declaration of war, Agreements, implementing the Sub-Committee's proposals, were signed between the Government and the War Risks Associations[41] and, subject to modifications necessitated by wartime experience, the Scheme continued substantially unchanged until the end of the war except that as from August 1917 the Government assumed responsibility for all war risks losses and likewise received all premiums.[42]

At the outbreak of war all British shipyards were commandeered by the Admiralty and throughout the war period shipbuilding remained under direct Government control. As a result of what is now recognised as a serious error in policy, for at least the first two years of the war the Admiralty insisted upon absolute priority being given to naval building and repairs; far from allowing the commencement of new merchant tonnage, many cargo ships in course of construction at the outbreak of war were left for long periods on the stocks in a half-built state. As a result of this failure to recognise the importance of replacing losses of merchant ships, coupled with the shortage of skilled labour and materials, merchant tonnage launched in 1915 and 1916 amounted in total to only 1.259 million tons gross compared with an output of a little under 2 million tons in 1913.

In December 1916 the advent of the Lloyd George Government heralded a radical change of policy; one of the prime tasks given to the newly appointed Shipping Controller was to quicken the supply of new merchant ships and the Government also decided that all future new buildings should be of approved standard types[43] and that such new vessels should be owned by the Government and operated on the Government's behalf by selected shipowners acting as managers.[44] As a result of these moves the 1917 launchings of merchant

39. Cd. 7560, Parl. Papers 1914, Vol. 70.

40. The premium was to be fixed by the Government and would be payable 80 per cent to the Government and 20 per cent to the War Risks Association.

41. The texts of these Agreements and of certain supplemental Agreements are set out in Cd. 7838, Parl. Papers 1914–16, Vol. 55.

42. There were some who contended that this State Scheme conferred substantial bounty on the shipowners but the premiums were actuarially calculated on normal insurance principles and at the end of the war the State had a profit of more than £16 million on the hulls insured under the Scheme—see Cmd. 98, Parl. Papers 1919, Vol. 32 and *War and the Shipping Industry*, *op. cit.*, Appendix 41.

43. A decision much criticised by shipping and shipbuilding interests but it did result in an increase in production and the standard ships did perform adequately in their service under wartime conditions.

44. The shipowners regarded with some misgiving the building up of a State-owned merchant fleet at a time when they themselves were prohibited from making good their own wartime losses.

ships amounted to 1.163 million gross tons and, although this was an improvement on the two preceding years, the output came nowhere near replacing the merchant tonnage lost by enemy action and marine risks which in 1917 reached a total of over 4 million gross tons.

The Shipping Controller's responsibility for merchant shipbuilding lasted for less than six months since in May 1917 the Government decided that the control of merchant shipbuilding should be transferred back to the Admiralty and that a newly appointed Navy Controller[45] should be in charge of both naval and mercantile shipping. The Naval Controller continued the policy of building standard ships for Government account only in all the traditional shipbuilding centres but in addition he decided, with Government approval, that new State shipyards should be established on the River Severn for the erection of prefabricated standard ships of simplified types.[46] The creation of these new State-owned shipyards provoked strong opposition from British shipbuilders who earlier in 1917 had, at the request of the Shipping Controller, expanded the capacity of their own yards but the Government agreed that there should be no diversion of men or materials from the traditional yards and in the event the 1918 output from these yards improved to 1.6 million gross tons.

It would however be wrong to conclude, on the basis of the low output of new merchant tonnage during the war years, that there was a failure on the part of British shipbuilders to match up to the nation's wartime needs; a fair assessment must take account of the output of naval tonnage and the work done on repairs to naval and merchant ships. No accurate assessment of the extent of the repair work can be attempted but that it was substantial cannot be doubted; moreover the work was so considerable and the urgency so great that repairs often had to be done by yards which normally only built new ships and whose output of new tonnage was thereby diminished. As regards new naval craft, in terms of displacement tons the annual average of launchings by private yards for the four years 1915 to 1918 was 486,000 tons[47] and when this is added to the annual average output of merchant ships for the same years, a little over 1 million tons gross, it is apparent that the total output of new naval and merchant ships between 1915 and 1918 bore fair comparison with the average for the years 1911 to 1913–1.825 million tons gross for merchant ships and 167,646 displacement tons for warships built for British and foreign account.

With the coming of the Armistice on 11th November 1918 it was possible for a final reckoning to be made of the dreadful losses in men and materials

45. The first appointee was Sir Eric Geddes but he was succeeded in July 1917 by Sir Alan Anderson.

46. There were so many problems in establishing these new national yards that by the Armistice not a single ship had even been launched on the River Severn.

47. See "Statistical Abstract for the United Kingdom 1929", Cmd. 3253, Parl. Papers, Vol. 21.

which the British mercantile marine had sustained. Nearly 15,000 officers and men of the merchant service had been lost through enemy action and more than 9 million gross tons of British merchant shipping had been lost through enemy action and marine risks; all foreign shipping losses amounted to approximately 6 million gross tons.[48] The United Kingdom's output of new merchant ships during the war period was only 4.342 million gross tons whilst the output of the British dominions, Allied and neutral countries over the same period amounted to 6,507,231 gross tons so that, owing largely to their concentration on naval work, U.K. output during the war was only 38.6 per cent of world output compared with more than 60 per cent for the period of 1899 to 1914. The net result was that the United Kingdom ended the war with a merchant shipping tonnage about 3.5 million tons less than that registered in June 1914 whilst the tonnage of the rest of the world showed a net gain of over 1.6 million gross tons; so, whereas in June 1914 U.K. merchant shipping stood at 18.892 million gross tons representing 41.6 per cent of the world's sea-going tonnage, by June 1919 U.K. tonnage was reduced to 16.350 million gross tons and its share of world tonnage had fallen to 34.1 per cent.

Quite apart from this severe loss of men and ships, British shipping had a great deal of leeway to make up. Owing to the wartime restrictions on new building and transfers abroad, the fleet at the end of 1918 was, on average, much older than it had been in 1914 and, on account of the deferment of repairs and wartime conditions, of much poorer quality as well. There were many fewer specialised ships of the liner type and much of the war-built tonnage was unsuited to peacetime conditions. In marked contrast the position of Britain's main foreign competitors was far more favourable; during the war they had been able to capture many of the tramp and liner trades which Government controls had forced British shipowners to abandon and, out of the larger profits which they had been able to amass, they were able quickly to replace their relatively modest wartime losses by new buildings from the expanded foreign yards not monopolised by naval work. In addition foreign owners were free to take full advantage of the unprecedented boom in freights between 1919 and 1920 whereas during this period much of British shipping was still subject to Government direction of employment and limitation of freights.

In November 1918 British shipowners and shipbuilders were united in their determination that their industries should be rapidly freed from Government control so that they should be able to make good the ravages of war and restore British shipping and shipbuilding to the dominant position which both industries had attained in 1914. In their Final Report[49] the Departmental

48. "Merchant Tonnage and the Submarine", Cd. 9009 and Cd. 9221, 1918, Vol. 22.
49. Cd. 9092.

Committee emphasised that "the maritime ascendancy of the Empire must be maintained at all costs" and warned that if the restoration of the mercantile marine was not accomplished without delay Britain would have to suffer the consequences that would attend her "decline to the level of a second rate maritime power"[50]—but neither the shipping community nor the Government fully appreciated that the favourable circumstances in which British shipping and shipbuilding had prospered before the war were never to return. There had been so many changes in the general pattern of world trade and so much progress by Britain's traditional and new maritime competitors that the natural desire to recapture our former ascendancy was to prove a dream incapable of fulfilment; Britain did not become a second-rate maritime power but British shipping and shipbuilding were destined never again to attain the imperial splendour of their pre-war position in the maritime world.

Even before the end of the war, a threat to the restoration of the shipowners' pre-war freedom arose from the fact that it was known that nationalisation of shipping had been considered by the Government in 1917 and it was believed that there were some, both within and without Government circles, who favoured post-war nationalisation[51] or alternatively the operation of the existing State owned merchant fleet in competition with private enterprise. The Departmental Committee considered that any scheme of State ownership in either shipping or shipbuilding would be "a blunder of the worst kind"[52] and the Joint Committee also characterised the possibility of peacetime State control as "a disaster".[53] However the Labour Party were believed to be lukewarm in their support for nationalisation and in October 1918 the shipowners' fears were dispelled by an announcement by the Ministry of Shipping that they were prepared to consider tenders for the purchase of some State-owned ships and by a statement in the Commons that the Government did not contemplate the nationalisation of merchant shipping.[54]

In an announcement made on the day after the Armistice[55] the Shipping Controller stated that ships under requisition would be released as soon as possible but that essential military and domestic requirements prevented anything approaching a general release. By February 1919 only 184 seagoing ships had been freed from requisition[56] but from 1st March 1919,

50. The 1917 Report of the Joint Committee of the Chamber of Shipping of the U.K. and the Liverpool Steamship Owners' Association also stated that it was "imperative that the U.K. should replace the wastage of war with the utmost possible dispatch".

51. A leading protagonist was Sir Leo Money, the Parliamentary Secretary to the Ministry of Shipping. See his article "The Nationalisation of Shipping" in *English Review*, Vol. 28 (1919).

52. Cd. 9092, Final Report, paras. 70 and 117.

53. Joint Committee's Report, para. 97.

54. P. Debs. 5 Ser., Vol. 110, c.1116.

55. *The Times*, 12th November 1918.

56. At the Armistice there had been about 2,660 privately owned sea-going ships and 1,400 smaller ships on full requisition.

following a further announcement by the Shipping Controller,[57] the tempo of de-requisitioning increased and by the end of 1919 only 59 privately owned sea-going ships remained under requisition. However the released ships were far from being at the free disposal of their owners for employment on the open market; the Controller had made it clear that there was to be no early relaxation of the controls affecting the employment and earnings of ships no longer under requisition and, for a period of some 18 months following the Armistice, all British ships proceeding to sea, both in the foreign and coasting trades, still required the licence of the Controller.

Throughout 1919 the Controller exercised on a substantial scale his powers to direct the so-called free tramp ships into various essential trades and to limit the amount of their freights. The owners of the released liners were required to agree that up to 50 per cent of their cargo space should be available for Government imports at Blue Book rates and arrangements were also made for insulated space on refrigerated ships to continue to be available for Government meat imports. By these means the Government ensured that tonnage was available, at a level of freight well below the free market rate, for the import of food and other essential commodities but this policy prevented British shipowners from taking advantage of the short-lived boom which began in March 1919 and also delayed the re-entry by British shipping into the trades abandoned during the war.

From March 1920 onwards the market level of freights fell rapidly and in July 1920 the Shipping Controller announced that licences would only be refused in exceptional circumstances and that there would be no further limitation of freights. The arrangements with the liner companies, other than those relating to refrigerated space, ended in August 1920 and in September 1920, the Controller issued a general licence permitting all ships to be fixed freely in any trade.[58] However the Board of Trade's control, under the British Ships (Transfer Restrictions) Acts 1915 and 1916, over the sale of British ships to foreigners continued until August 1921 although in January 1919 it was announced that consideration would be given for permitting the sale abroad of vessels over 15 years old provided that the proceeds of sale were promptly applied towards the acquisition of new tonnage.

On 14th November 1918 the Shipping Controller informed owners that, as and when berths became vacant, shipbuilding for private account could be resumed. In spite of the trading uncertainties at that time and the enormous increase in building costs, British owners, with full Government encouragement, not only hastened to place new orders, but also purchased from the Government 156 completed standard ships and 115 standard ships still in

57. *The Times*, 15th January 1919.

58. The Controller's powers did however continue until his office ceased on 1st April 1921 and in October 1920 he did requisition a number of vessels to meet an emergency resulting from a coastal strike.

course of construction. In addition British owners purchased most of the German ships surrendered under the Treaty of Versailles and further second-hand tonnage was acquired from Scandinavia, Greece, Spain and America. As a result of this programme of building and purchases, the steam and motor tonnage registered in the United Kingdom had by June 1920 risen to 18.1 million tons gross—only 800,000 tons below the 1914 figure.

This rapid acquisition of tonnage at a time when prices were exceptionally high[59] put a severe strain on the financial resources of many British owners. The Government compensation for loss of requisitioned ships and the total loss insurance recoveries that had been received in respect of tonnage sunk during the war often proved quite inadequate to meet the replacement costs. Owning companies had to draw heavily on their reserves built up from post taxation wartime profits but, owing to the unevenness of the burden of requisition and total losses, some owners had earned far more profits than others and there were also those who had failed to husband their profits and total loss recoveries.[60] So, although it was true that foreign competitors had been able to make far higher profits during the war, had received more compensation for lost tonnage and had been able to replace lost ships without delay and at lower cost, in some cases there may well have been substance in the contention that, if carefully preserved, the post taxation wartime profits of British owners should have been sufficient to make good the difference between total loss recoveries and post war replacement costs.[61]

The strong feeling of nationalism engendered by the war did result in a move for the revival of some of the principles underlying the Navigation Acts[62] but in 1918 the majority of British shipowners were as strong in their belief in the freedom of trade as their mid-nineteenth century predecessors had been in their resistance to the repeal of the Navigation Laws. After full consideration the Joint Committee stated that "any return to the general principles of the old Navigation Laws would be against the best interests of our foreign commerce and our Mercantile Marine"[63] and the Departmental Committee expressed the view that the nature of our carrying trade made a policy of flag discrimination undesirable and that "freedom of the seas, in the sense of equal treatment of all flags in all ports, should therefore be a cardinal principle in our post-war policy".[64] There were some owners who felt that the cabotage

59. On average building costs in the 1919/1920 period were reckoned to be at least five times their pre-war level and the price of second-hand tonnage was equally excessive.

60. See Rochdale Committee Report, Cmnd. 4337, para 31.

61. S. G. Sturmey, *British Shipping and World Competition* (London, 1962), pp. 48–52.

62. See W. S. Holdsworth's Rhodes Lecture, *op. cit.* For the arguments against revival see C. E. Fayle's article "The Proposed Revival of the Navigation Acts" in *Edinburgh Review*, Vol. 2 (1918).

63. Joint Committee's Report, para. 56.

64. Cd. 9092, Final Report, para. 397.

policies still pursued by some principal foreign competitors[65] would justify the reservation of British imperial trade and the U.K. coasting trade for the British flag alone but the Departmental Committee disagreed since "without artificial aid of any kind" British shipping had almost a monopoly of the inter-imperial trade and the coasting trades of the Empire and the United Kingdom.[66] So in 1918 Britain adhered to her policy of "freedom of the seas" and it was only in relation to Germany that the Treaty of Versailles[67] made provision to prevent the pre-war abuse of the Emigrant Control Stations by German ship-owning companies.[68]

Apart from Government control and supervision in the areas of safety and health, where it was felt that British standards should be rigorously enforced on foreign ships in British ports, it was the clear desire of British shipowners that there should be the minimum of Government intervention in the affairs of the shipping industry. In particular the majority of owners were opposed to subsidies[69] and, prior to the Trade Facilities Act 1921,[70] there was no general State financial aid for the construction or operation of British ships. However the pre-war mail contracts were revived and although, contrary to the view of the Dominions' Royal Commission that there should be a subsidised imperial mail service,[71] the Departmental Committee had advised that, where possible, exclusive mail contracts with particular lines should be avoided,[72] most of the original mail contracts with the same handful of liner companies and cross-channel ferries were continued but by 1924 the annual total of the postal subventions, around £558,000, was not large in relation to the services rendered[73] and probably contained little, if any, element of bounty. In addition there was some modest and short term aid to coastal shipping whose trade had declined to less than one third of what it had been in 1913 partly owing to the exigencies of war but far more due to unfair subsidised competition from the railways; the Government endeavoured to encourage the diversion of traffic from rail to water by payment of a subsidy to shippers but the scheme

65. British ships were still excluded from the coasting trades of the United States, Russia, France and the French possessions, Holland and the Dutch possessions, Portugal and the Portuguese possessions, Greece, Japan, Brazil and Argentina.

66. Immediately prior to the war some 92 per cent of the imperial trade had been carried in British ships and over 99 per cent of the U.K. coasting trade were British.

67. Cmd. 153 (Article 322), Parl. Papers 1919, Vol. 53.

68. See First Report of the Departmental Committee, Cd. 9092.

69. There were various reasons for this opposition—see *International Sea Transport* by Sir H. O. Mance (London, 1945), p. 120.

70. 11 & 12 Geo. V, c.65—see further *infra*.

71. Final Report, paras. 564–577. Cd 8462, Parl. Papers 1917–18, Vol. 10.

72. Cd. 9092, Final Report, paras. 335–337. The advice of the Departmental Committee was approved by the Imperial Shipping Committee.

73. For details of the subventions paid in 1924 see Parl. Papers 1924 (147), Vol. 13. The total of £558,000 excludes the *Mauretania* payment of £90,000 "for naval purposes" and a subsidy of £30,000 per annum to Hebridean Steamer Services.

only met with limited success and the subsidy was discontinued in June 1920.[74]

Since at the beginning of 1919 world tonnage was well above what it had been in 1914 whereas world trade was well below its pre-war level, it had been thought that a period of surplus tonnage and low freights was likely but in the event, owing to a variety of causes,[75] by March 1919 there was an acute world shortage of shipping and this inevitably resulted in a steep rise in the level of freights. This unexpected and unprecedented boom lasted for some 12 months and in this period many tramp owners made large operating profits but it was only the free ships which benefited and, unfortunately for British owners, for most of the boom period the majority of British ships were still subject to Government control and direction; it was therefore Britain's foreign competitors who were the main beneficiaries.

As a result of the desire to replace tonnage lost in the war and the mistaken belief that the highly favourable market conditions were likely to continue for a considerable period, during 1919 and 1920 there was also a world boom in shipbuilding. British shipbuilders were naturally anxious to re-establish the pre-war supremacy of their industry and, in spite of the high level of building costs, there was a rush of orders from both British and foreign owners and the gross merchant tonnage launched in 1919 and 1920 was 1.620 million tons and 2.056 million tons respectively[76]—the latter figure just exceeding the highest pre-war launching figure of 1.9 million tons in 1913. There was also a high output from the foreign shipyards, particularly in America and Japan, which had greatly expanded their capacity during the war; the gross tonnage launched outside the United Kingdom in 1919 and 1920 amounted to 5.524 million tons and 3.807 million tons[77] respectively and, as a result of this worldwide shipbuilding activity, the world tonnage afloat in June 1920 was 7 million tons greater than in 1914.

The increase in world tonnage, the failure of the revival of world trade to its pre-war level and the gradual disappearance of the factors that had created the artificial shortages in carrying capacity all combined to bring about the disastrous consequences that some of the more cautious British owners had feared. Early in 1920 it became apparent that the total available tonnage was far in excess of the world's carrying requirements; in March 1920 the Chamber of Shipping tramp freight index stood at 141 but by December 1920 it had fallen to 58 and by March 1921 it was as low as 37. This collapse exacted a severe toll on those British owners who had not only paid grossly inflated prices for their recently acquired new and second-hand tonnage but who had

74. For details of the problems of coastal shipping see *Studies of British Transport History 1870–1970* by D. H. Aldcroft, (London, 1974), Chapter 6.

75. See *Studies of British Transport History*, *op. cit.*, Chapter 7.

76. In 1919 94 per cent of the tonnage launched was for U.K. owners but in 1920 only 58.8 per cent was for U.K. account.

77. As a proportion of world launchings, U.K. launchings in 1919 and 1920 were respectively 22.7 per cent and 35.1 per cent compared with an average of 58.7 per cent for 1909–13.

also to carry greatly increased operating costs. Although the effect was delayed, British shipbuilders were no less hardly hit; a large number of contracts were cancelled, there was a dearth of new orders and a consequent steady decline in the tonnage under construction.[78]

By 1921 the gloomy and uncertain future facing world shipping in general, and British shipping in particular, was clearly revealed. Although the gross tonnage of ships registered in the United Kingdom had risen to 19.320 million tons—400,000 tons above the figure for June 1914—world shipping had increased to 58.846 million tons which was more than 13 million tons above the pre-war level; thus whilst the United Kingdom still had, by a wide margin, the largest active merchant fleet, its relative share of world shipping had declined to 32.8 per cent in June 1921 compared with 41.6 per cent in June 1914. It was, however, not only in terms of a decline in its relative tonnage position that the British mercantile marine found itself at a serious disadvantage in meeting the challenge of its foreign competitors. In the period 1919–20, when British owners were hastening to replace their lost tonnage, prices of both new and second-hand ships were grossly inflated[79] and since, unlike some of their foreign competitors, British owners had to meet the replacement costs entirely from their own resources and without any Government assistance, the depletion, if not exhaustion, of their reserves left them ill prepared to endure the depression which started before they were in a position to take advantage of the short lived boom. Another adverse factor was the nature of much of the replacement tonnage; the design of many of the new ships proved to be unsuited to the changing pattern of post-war trade and the second-hand tonnage, particularly the ageing enemy ships and the Government standard ships, was found to be economically uncompetitive in post-war conditions.

The experience of British shipping's main foreign competitors was comparatively far more favourable. They had made far higher profits during the war and had been taxed less heavily, their ship losses had been much smaller and they had received higher compensation, and they had been able to replace tonnage during the war at prices far below those prevailing in 1919/20; in addition at the end of the war they had ample free tonnage available to take full advantage of the 1919/20 boom and to establish themselves in trades which had been an almost exclusive preserve of British ships. Consequently, when the post-war boom and freight rates collapsed in 1921/22, many foreign shipowners could face the future in a relatively strong position whereas the

78. In the last quarter of 1920 ships under construction amounted to 3.731 million gross tons but two years later the figure had declined to 1.617 million gross tons.

79. At the end of 1919 the price of a new ready cargo steamer of 7,500 tons was £232,500 compared with £42,500 in June 1914. In March 1920 the price had risen to a peak of £258,750 but nine months later it had fallen to £105,000 (Balfour Committee, *Survey of Metal Industries*, Appendix V, 1927).

U.K. shipping industry was left with too many companies which were financially ill prepared to weather storms and which were still taking delivery of new ships at prices which could never be recouped.[80]

Largely on account of the dislocation caused by the war, it was estimated that in 1921 world seaborne trade was approximately 89 million tons below its 1913 level[81] whereas world shipping tonnage was more than 13 million tons above its pre-war level; in addition much of the newer tonnage was larger, faster and more efficient than in the pre-war era and it was therefore inevitable that there would be far too many ships chasing far too few cargoes. All shipping was, of course, affected by this decline in world trade but British shipping was particularly hit by the serious contraction of the United Kingdom's trade upon which, even more than pre-war, it greatly depended. The U.K. trade figures, import and export, were 73.6 million tons in 1921 compared with 149.6 million tons in 1913 and tramp shipping had lost much of its important pre-war competitive edge by reason of the drastic reduction in coal exports; in 1913 the total had been 73.4 million tons but in both 1920 and 1921 it was less than 25 million tons. For tramp owners there seemed little hope that their newer ships, built at enormously inflated cost, would be able to operate profitably or even to find employment at all[82]; liner companies also suffered a serious decline in their valuable emigrant traffic as a result of drastic restrictions on immigration imposed by the United States and Canadian governments and by the action of the Italian government in restricting the carriage of Italian emigrants to Italian ships.[83]

The relative decline and parlous financial condition of Britain's maritime industries in the early 1920s did not evoke any request for Government aid but the Government was seriously concerned at the high level of unemployment and initiated legislative action in 1921 which did bring some much needed orders to British shipyards, whose expanded capacity was much under utilised, and incidently assisted shipowners, both British and foreign, to finance the construction of new British built ships. The Trade Facilities Act 1921[84] authorised the Treasury to guarantee the principal and interest of any loan raised within or without the United Kingdom if the Treasury were satisfied that the loan was to be applied towards the payment for capital works and that the application of the loan was calculated to promote employment in the United Kingdom. The 1921 Act also provided that the capital amount of the loans so guaranteed was not to exceed £25 million and that no guarantee should be given after the expiry of 12 months from the commencement of the Act but

80. Rochdale Report, Cmnd 5447, para. 32.

81. See P. Jaffe, "World Trade and British Shipping", Table IV in *Britain and her Export Trade*, Ed. M. Abrams, (London, 1946).

82. In July 1921 over 1,000 ships having a net tonnage of 1.85 million were laid up in U.K. ports.

83. *Cunard and the North Atlantic*, *op. cit.* p. 171.

84. 11 & 12 Geo. V, c.65. The Act commenced on 10th November 1921.

as a result of subsequent legislation,[85] the maximum principal amount of the loan so guaranteed was eventually extended to £75 million and the period during which guarantees could be given was extended to 31st March 1927.

The Treasury guarantees up to the time when the scheme ended amounted to over £71 million[86] and, although shipbuilding was only one of several industries which the Acts were intended to benefit, in the event more than one third of the total of the guarantees given was in respect of shipbuilding.[87] In addition further aid to the Belfast shipyards was given by the Northern Ireland Loan Guarantee Acts 1922–38[88] under which the Ministry of Finance of Northern Ireland was empowered to give guarantees up to an eventual permitted maximum of £14.5 million over periods successively extended to 31st March 1940; here again the powers were almost fully utilised and thus the combined effect of the legislation resulted in the provision of guarantees totalling more than £39 million[89] for the construction of at least 110 ships[90] in British yards. It was however mainly the liner section of the British shipping industry which took this opportunity of raising Government guaranteed loans to replace lost ships and to modernise their fleets[91]; tramp owners, who had already, by 1921, replaced much of their lost tonnage at high cost, felt it was a mistake to encourage additions to the world tonnage surplus and were still traditionally averse to building new ships with borrowed money.

It should perhaps be emphasised that the ships built with the assistance of the Acts were not subsidised by the State. No doubt the availability of a Government guarantee would have facilitated the raising of loans at below the usual interest rate but apart from this interest saving, which in itself cost the State nothing, there was no element of subsidy in the scheme and such was never the Government's intention. Indeed the whole operation of the scheme in respect of both shipbuilding and other industries cost the Government comparatively little; when the scheme was finally wound up in 1962 a Parliamentary Return stated that the contingent liability of the Exchequer had been extinguished and that the total amount paid in fulfilment of guarantees had been some £14 million of which over £13.25 million had been repaid.[92] Thus, at small cost, the scheme brought a welcome increase in activity to British

85. The Trade Facilities and Loan Guarantee Act 1922, the Trade Facilities Act 1924, the Trade Facilities Act 1925 and the Trade Facilities Act 1926.

86. See Parl. Papers 1927 (61), Vol. 13.

87. See *Shipping and Shipbuilding Subsidies*, *op. cit.*, Table 29 and Supplement No. 1.

88. The first in this long line of Northern Ireland statutes was the Loans Guarantee Act (N.I) 1922 (12 & 13 Geo. V, c.22). No less than 16 amending Acts were passed between 1923 and 1938.

89. Loans raised by foreign shipowners represented about 10 per cent of this total amount.

90. *Shipbuilding in Britain*, *op. cit.*, p. 144. The figure may be an under-estimate—see *Shipping and Shipbuilding Subsidies*, *op. cit.*, Tables 49 and 50.

91. See *British Shipping and World Competition*, *op. cit.*, p. 106.

92. Parl. Papers 1961–62 (183), Vol. 25. It was also stated that a further £500,000 was in course of being repaid.

shipyards as a result of increased orders from home and abroad and also encouraged liner owners to increase and modernise their fleets.

In 1922 a Government statement in the Commons[93] made it clear that the mail contract system was to continue virtually unchanged and in 1928 the Postmaster-General entered into new contracts with both Cunard and White Star[94] which provided for increased remuneration "in recognition of the large increase in the volume and cost of conveyance of the mails"; the contracts were approved by the Commons[95] and later in 1928 Commons' approval was also given[96] to the contract with Macbraynes for the maintenance of passenger, cargo and mail services to the Western Highlands and Islands of Scotland.[97] By 1930 the gross annual payments to British shipping companies in respect of postal subventions for overseas mails amounted to £811,572[98] but, as the Balfour Committee had previously pointed out,[99] "with one or two exceptions, Government payments to shipping companies are not subsidies but are for postal services rendered by the companies".[100] By 1937 the annual payments for overseas mails had fallen to £711,343[101] and, as had been the case since the mail contract system had been instituted in 1837, the ships in receipt of these payments only represented a very small part of the British merchant marine.

Prior to the radical change in the Government's shipping policy which was embodied in the British Shipping (Assistance) Act 1935,[102] the Government's only direct financial intervention into the affairs of the shipping industry during the post war period was in relation to only one company. In October 1929 the Board of Cunard decided that at least one ship "of revolutionary design and of great size, power and speed" should be built to replace one or more of their ageing liners and to meet the increasing competition from Germany and France.[103] The first problem was insurance since it was anticipated that the British market would be unable to absorb the whole cost of the new Cunarders and, at Cunard's request, the Government agreed to cover such part of the construction or marine risks as Cunard were unable to place elsewhere. In

93. P. Debs. 5 Ser., Vol. 154, c.810.

94. Parl. Papers 1928 (95) and (96), Vol. 13. Following the subsequent merger of Cunard and White Star in 1933–34 a new contract was made between the Postmaster-General and Cunard White Star—see Parl. Papers 1935–36 (92), Vol. 15.

95. P. Debs. 5 Ser., Vol. 220, c.779.

96. P. Debs. 5 Ser., Vol. 222, c.1662.

97. Parl. Papers 1928–29 (4), Vol. 16.

98. Parl. Papers 1931–32 (7), Vol. 18 (Revenue Dept's Appropriation Accounts, p. 18)

99. In their *Survey of Factors in Industrial and Commercial Efficiency* (HMSO, 1927), p. 385.

100. The exceptions were the annual payment of £90,000 to Cunard in respect of the *Mauretania* under the 1903 Agreement and the small subsidy paid since 1920 to steamers serving the Hebrides.

101. Parl. Papers 1938–39 (19), Vol. 20. (Revenue Dept's Appropriation Accounts, p. 17).

102. See Chapter 6 *infra*.

103. *Cunard and the North Atlantic*, *op. cit.*, p. 203. In the event two new ships were built (both by John Brown) and were named *Queen Mary* and *Queen Elizabeth*.

December 1930 authority for the Government's insurance participation was given by the Cunard (Insurances) Agreement Act 1930[104]—the Government's action being inspired not only by the desire that British shipping should maintain a leading presence in the trans-Atlantic passenger trade but also because the building of the ships would provide much needed employment both at John Brown's yard and for the numerous sub-contractors. However far from this arrangement having any element of subsidy, the Government's foray into marine insurance turned out to be good business for the taxpayer; when the Cunard Insurance Fund was closed on 31st March 1954 there was a final credit in favour of the Government of £880,539 less one small unspecified contingent liability.[105]

The Government's insurance participation eventually turned out to be only a relatively small part of the Government's involvement in the building of new giant liners. By the end of 1931 Cunard's profits had been so adversely affected by the world depression that its financial standing was no longer strong enough to enable it to continue its traditional method of shipbuilding finance[106] and there was no alternative but to suspend work on the first ship. The Cunard Board then proposed that the Government should give financial assistance in the same way as it had in 1903 for the building of the *Mauretania* and *Lusitania* and although, in March 1932, the Government refused to give any help,[107] by the end of that year, following the receipt by the Government of a Report made at its request by Lord Weir,[108] there were signs that the Government was preparing to alter course. The Government's change of mind was prompted, at least in part, by the urgent need to prevent the total financial collapse of the Royal Mail Group which, since 1926, included the White Star Line purchased for £7 million from International Mercantile Marine[109]; by 1931 both White Star Line and Royal Mail itself had defaulted on the payments due in respect of loans guaranteed by the Government under the Trade Facilities Acts and the Royal Mail Group's major creditors, among whom the largest were the British and Northern Ireland Governments and the Bank of England, had become increasingly anxious to find some solution to the Royal Mail Group's desperate position.

Eventually, in the spring of 1933, the Government proposed to Cunard that, if Cunard was willing to rescue the ailing White Star Line, the Government would provide finance for the building of both the new Cunarders. By the

104. 21 Geo. V, c.2. The draft of the Agreement to be made with Cunard was scheduled to the Act and details of the Government's insurance participation were set out in Cmd. 3706, Parl. Papers 1930–31, Vol. 25.

105. Parl Papers 1953–54 (220), Vol. 20.

106. By the use of undistributed profits retained to cover annual depreciation of the fleet and the discounting of bills at modest rates of interest.

107. See P. Debs. 5 Ser., Vol. 262, c.1612.

108. See *Cunard and the North Atlantic*, *op. cit.*, pp. 209, 219 and 367.

109. The American IMM had acquired the White Star Line in 1902—see p. 85 *supra*.

latter part of 1933 negotiations for the merger of the Cunard and White Star fleets had been concluded[110] and the matter was then formalised by an Agreement made on 30th December 1933 between Cunard, Oceanic Navigation Co. Ltd. (who owned the White Star Line) and the Government[111] which provided that a new company, Cunard White Star Ltd., would take over the North Atlantic business, goodwill and ships of Cunard and Oceanic on the terms of the already agreed Memorandum,[112] that the equity capital of Cunard White Star would be allotted 62 per cent to Cunard and 38 per cent to Oceanic and that the Treasury would make loans of up to a maximum of £9.5 million to finance the construction of the two new ships and to provide Cunard White Star with working capital.[113] Further details of the financing arrangements were submitted to Parliament in February 1934[114] and then, after lengthy debates on the enabling Bill,[115] the North Atlantic Shipping Act 1934[116] received the Royal Assent on 28th March 1934.

In May 1934 John Brown were instructed to recommence work, the vessel was launched in September and named *Queen Mary* and in May 1936 she was delivered to Cunard White Star and commenced her North Atlantic service. A contract for the building of the second ship was signed with John Brown in October 1936 and in February 1937 there was a supplemental Agreement between the Treasury and Cunard White Star setting out the terms of the further loans[117]; the second ship was launched in September 1938 and christened *Queen Elizabeth* but she was not delivered, and then only in an incomplete state, until February 1940, some six months after the outbreak of the Second World War. So, as in 1902, Cunard were proved right in relying on their "special relationship" with the Government to provide the finance which was not obtainable elsewhere but the Government could fairly claim that, in the event, this exceptional treatment meted out to Cunard was fully justified; not only did the two "Queens" uphold British supremacy in the North Atlantic in times of peace but, even more important, they rendered a vital war service as British and American troop carriers and thus made a unique contribution

110. See P. Debs. 5 Ser., Vol. 284, c.372. A Memorandum setting out the basic terms for the merger was signed by the Chairmen of Oceanic and Cunard.

111. Cmd. 4502, Parl. Papers 1933–34, Vol. 16.

112. A copy of the Memorandum was set out in the First Schedule to the Agreement. It was stipulated in the Agreement that Cunard White Star should be so constituted as to remain under British control and that all its directors should be British.

113. £3 million was for the completion of the first ship, £5 million for the building of the second ship and £1.5 million for working capital. All the advances were to be repayable on or before 31st December 1975.

114. Cmd. 4516, Parl. Papers 1933–34, Vol. 18.

115. P. Debs. 5 Ser., Vol. 286, cc.608 and 1825 and Vol. 287, cc.486 and 723.

116. 24 Geo. V, c.10. The Act not only authorised the loans but also gave authority for the transfer to Cunard White Star of the benefits and obligations of the Cunard (Insurance) Agreement Act 1930.

117. Cmd. 5397, Parl. Papers 1936–37, Vol. 21. See also Cmd. 5725, Parl. Papers 1937–38, Vol. 21.

to the Allied war effort. Moreover the Treasury loans were paid off many years before their final maturity date[118] and the only real subsidy element was the favourable interest rate which was probably about two per cent below the prevailing commercial rate.

Following the ending, in 1921, of the post-war shipping and shipbuilding boom, the period from 1922 to 1926 was one of almost continued depression for the British maritime industries. World seaborne trade in 1922 and 1923 was still below its pre-war level and the growth thereafter was slow, world tonnage was far above the 1914 level, the freight market was weak,[119] and there was a severe decline in the output of U.K. shipyards[120] and growing foreign competition. Nevertheless, as in the immediate post-war period, there was throughout the 1920s a continuing belief that any financial intervention by the British Government would do more harm than good and that freedom of the seas and non-discrimination was still the policy best calculated to encourage the expansion and prosperity of British shipping and shipbuilding.

In the early 1920s some progress was made in securing international co-operation for measures supporting the principle of non-discrimination. International Conventions signed in 1921 provided for freedom of transit on inland waterways[121] and free exercise of navigation on navigable waterways[122] and a further Convention signed in 1923 granted equality of treatment for all vessels in the maritime ports of the contracting parties.[123] A strong endorsement of the policy of non-discrimination was also made by the 1923 Imperial Economic Conference[124]; the Empire representatives declared that it was their established practice to make no discrimination between the flags of shipping using their ports and that there would be no departure from this practice as regards countries which treated ocean-going shipping under the British flag on a footing of equality with their own national shipping.[125] In 1929 the Balfour Committee in its Final Report[126] emphasised the benefits to British trade resulting from the policy, pursued since the repeal of the Navigation Laws, of treating the merchant shipping of all countries using British ports on exactly the same

118. Nearly £8 million was paid off in 1941 and the balance was paid off in 1944 and 1946.

119. The Chamber of Shipping Freight Index (1920=100) never rose above 40 between the middle of 1921 and the autumn of 1926.

120. Average annual output between 1922 and 1926 was only 968,000 gross tons as compared with an annual average of 1.797 million tons for 1920 and 1921.

121. Cmd. 1992, Parl. Papers 1922, Vol. 24.

122. Cmd. 1993, Parl. Papers 1923, Vol. 24. This Convention did however provide that a riparian State could reserve for its own flag the transport of passengers and goods loaded at one port under its sovereignty and unloaded at another port under its sovereignty.

123. Cmd. 2141, Parl. Papers 1923, Vol. 27.

124. Cmd. 2009, Parl. Papers 1923, Vol. 10.

125. It was however added that if Empire shipping was threatened by foreign discrimination against the British flag, the Empire governments would consult together as the best means of meeting the situation.

126. Cmd. 3282, Parl. Papers 1928–29, Vol. 7.

footing as British ships and regretted that some foreign countries still clung to the practice of various forms of flag discrimination.

Britain's long held aversion to State intervention was shared by some of the traditional maritime powers such as the Scandinavian countries, the Netherlands and Greece but some of Britain's principal foreign maritime competitors were firmly committed to varying forms of State subsidies and other artificial support for their national shipping and shipbuilding and the policy of flag discrimination posed a serious threat to the prosperity of the British maritime industries.[127] The United States Merchant Marine Act 1920 (the "Jones Act") declared it to be the policy of the United States to do whatever was necessary to develop and encourage the maintenance of a merchant marine sufficient to carry the greater portion of its commerce and it was estimated that for the 10 years up to 1930 the cost of the American State-owned fleet was £1,000 million;[127] in addition there were shipbuilding loans at non-commercial rates of interest, postal subsidies far in excess of the cost of the mail services[128] and the continued reservation of the extended American coasting trade. In 1921 the German government set up a Reconstruction Fund under which grants totalling 30 million marks were made available for the rebuilding of the German merchant marine and, as a result of this and other aid, German tonnage, in the period 1921 to 1931, increased more than that of any other country[129] and also had the advantage of being exceptionally up to date. France and Italy paid navigation and construction bounties, Japan aided and protected her shipbuilding industry and all these countries reserved their coastal trades for national ships.

Notwithstanding the adverse impact on British shipping of these nationalistic maritime policies, even after the commencement of the 1929 world depression British shipowners still adhered to the doctrine of what they described as "the four F's"—Freedom of the Seas, Freedom of Ports, Freedom of Trade and Freedom of Contract—but the length of the depression, which lasted for at least five years, and the increasing severity of its impact on British shipping and shipbuilding eventually forced a change in this long-held philosophy. In 1929, whilst tonnage on the U.K. register was only some 1 million tons more than it had been in 1914, the carrying capacity of world shipping was approximately 50 per cent above its pre-war level and, since world trade had only increased by 10 per cent on pre-war figures, tonnage was already vastly in excess of demand. Between 1923 and 1933 the quantum of world trade fell by 90 million tons, world shipping grew by 1 million tons whilst

127. For full details of foreign shipping and shipbuilding subsidies in the inter-war period see the Memorandum appended to the 1939 Report of the Joint Shipping Policy Committee of the Chamber of Shipping and the Liverpool Steamship Owners' Association.

128. In 1930 U.S. mail contract payments totalled U.S. $13,066,441 compared with an estimated cost of U.S. $2,273,000.

129. In 1920 German tonnage had been reduced to 419,438 gross tons but by 1931 it stood at 4.3 million tons—almost up to its pre-war level.

U.K. tonnage slightly declined and U.K. trade fell by over 34 million tons including a fall of over 20 million tons in the all-important coal exports.[130] As a result British shipping laid up in U.K. ports, which in 1929 had been 0.63 million tons (3.3 per cent), had by 1933 increased to 3.21 million tons (18.1 per cent) and for the years 1930–1935 the profits from British tramp operations were so low that the industry was only able to provide some £8 million towards a total depreciation requirement of £18.7 million. There was also inevitably a serious fall in the demand for new ships; in 1929 the tonnage of new ships launched from U.K. shipyards was 1.5 million gross tons but in 1932 and 1933 the corresponding figures were only 187,800 and 133,100 gross tons and in the latter year only five per cent of all the berths in the United Kingdom were occupied.[131]

Despite the continuing and accelerating deterioration in the position of the British maritime industries, even as late as 1932 British shipowners were still clinging to their traditional policies; they still declared their belief in the Freedom of the Seas and they were still generally opposed to subsidies. However in 1932, after being the apostles of free trade for nearly a century, Britain and her Dominions were leaning more and more towards protection and imperial preference and by the end of 1933 the critical condition of British shipping, particularly the tramp section, and of shipbuilding as well forced both the shipping interest and the Government to a change in policy so radical that, when it was foreshadowed in a Commons statement by the President of the Board of Trade in July 1934, a member commented that it was "the most important pronouncement by a Minister of the Crown on shipping since the repeal of the Navigation Laws eighty years ago".[132]

130. In 1933 coal exports had fallen to 42.1 million tons compared with nearly 77 million tons in 1913. Sir Donald Anderson, a leading British shipowner, considered that "the death of the vast U.K. export trade in coal was the greatest single blow that tramp shipping ever suffered" ("British Shipping in 1964", National Provincial Bank Review No. 65 (February, 1964)).
131. *Shipbuilding in Britain*, *op. cit.*, Table XX.
132. P. Debs. 5 Ser., Vol. 291, c.1720.

CHAPTER 6

ECONOMIC NATIONALISM AND RETURN TO PROTECTIONISM

The election of the National Government in the autumn of 1931 resulted in a radical change in Britain's traditional trade policy. As a consequence of the alarming rise in unemployment, the increasingly adverse trade balance and the world banking and financial crisis, Britain, for so long the chief protagonist, abandoned free trade and turned again to protectionism. The Import Duties Act 1932[1] imposed a general *ad valorem* duty of 10 per cent on all imports other than those specifically exempted[2] and those charged under other enactments; there were also specific exemptions for goods from the Dominions and Colonies[3] and, to assist the shipbuilding industry, the Act exempted from duty all imports consigned to a registered shipbuilding yard. In August 1932 protectionism was taken a stage further; at the conclusion of the Imperial Economic Conference held in Ottawa, the United Kingdom entered into Agreements with the Dominions[4] under which further preference was given to U.K. imports of Empire goods and the Ottawa Agreements Act 1932[5] increased the import duties on certain foreign foodstuffs, imposed new duties on certain foreign commodities—notably wheat—and restricted some foreign imports.

The outcome of the Ottawa Conference was a disappointment to British shipowners. The Shipping Policy Committee of the Chamber of Shipping had urged that effective steps should be taken to secure and maintain the objects set forth in the "British shipping" resolution adopted at the Imperial Economic Conference 1923[6] but the Conference ignored this recommendation and indeed paid little or no attention to British shipping policy. Having failed to achieve anything at Ottawa, the Shipping Policy Committee turned its attention to the

1. 22 & 23 Geo. V, c.8 which received the Royal Assent on 29th February 1932.
2. The free list was set out in the First Schedule to the Act. The rate of duty could be raised above 10 per cent by Treasury Order.
3. These were mainly foodstuffs and raw materials. In April 1932 (see P. Debs. 5 Ser., Vol. 264, c.303) the Government rejected a suggestion that imperial preference should only apply if the goods were imported in British ships.
4. Copies of these Agreements are set out in Appendices I to VII of Cmd. 4174 (Parl. Papers 1931–32, Vol. 10) which also contains a summary of the proceedings at the Ottawa Conference.
5. 22 & 23 Geo. V, c.53.
6. See p. 115 and fn 125.

World Monetary and Economic Conference due to be held in London in January 1933 and recommended that the primary concern of the British shipping industry at the Conference should be the removal of trade barriers of every description.[7] When the Economic Conference took place, a sub-committee was appointed to consider (*inter alia*) shipping subsidies and the U.K. delegation proposed a resolution to the effect that subsidising countries should move as rapidly as possible towards the diminution and ultimate abolition of State assistance to shipbuilding and ship operation on competitive routes. However, as the President of the Board of Trade subsequently stated in the House,[8] only the Scandinavian countries, Holland and—"rather grudgingly and full of conditions"—France supported the British anti subsidy policy; all other maritime countries were determined to continue with some form of State assistance to their national maritime industries.

In view of Britain's reversion to a protectionist trade policy, the increasingly depressed state of British shipping and the failure, from the shipping point of view, of the Ottawa Conference, it was not surprising that in the latter part of 1932 there were suggestions, both from within and outside the shipping industry, that there was a need for some measure of protection for British shipping. In a Report made in November 1932 the Shipping Policy Committee suggested, for the first time, that there was a strong case for a temporary counter-subsidy to equate foreign subsidies or lower working costs and, after the disappointing outcome of the World Economic Conference, there was a further hardening of attitude in the recommendations made by the Shipping Policy Committee in a Report made in July 1933.[9] There was no response from the Government and, with the situation continuing to deteriorate, in October 1933 the Council of the Chamber of Shipping appointed a Special Committee to consider the position of British Tramp Shipping.

In their Report made on 23rd November 1933 the Tramp Shipping Committee accepted that the only stable and permanent cure for the preservation of British tramp shipping was the restoration of world trade but, since this was only likely to come slowly and there was no immediate prospect of restricting foreign State aid to shipping, it was recommended that the Government should grant tramp shipping a temporary subsidy with the object of equalising the advantages of foreign competition due to subsidies, depreciated currencies and lower wage costs. In addition the Government were asked to

7. The Committee considered that subsidies and discrimination in favour of ships under the national flag were amongst the most mischievous of trade barriers.

8. P. Debs. 5 Ser., Vol. 284, c.437.

9. These recommendations included (*a*) voyages between Australia and New Zealand to be regarded as coastal and open only to British ships and ships of countries who opened their coastal trade to British ships (*b*) inter-Dominion trade to be reserved for ships of countries which allowed British ships to engage in their inter-Colonial trade and (*c*) the granting of concessions in trade treaties to be dependent upon the elimination or strict limitation of shipping subsidies.

consider the negotiation of new trade agreements providing for the employment of a minimum percentage of British ships, that preference on Empire goods should be confined to goods imported in British ships, discriminating duties on cargo imported in foreign ships, protection for the United Kingdom coastal trade and, as a last resort, the reintroduction of the wartime Government licensing system to promote the employment of British tramp shipping.

On 13th December 1933 there was a Commons debate[10] on a motion by one of the members for Newcastle-upon-Tyne urging the Government to take immediate steps to assist and defend the British shipping and shipbuilding industries. The motion was seconded by Colonel Ropner, a leading British tramp owner, who stated that the fundamental problems facing British shipping were the low level of world trade, excess of world tonnage and the diminution of Britain's share of world trade; he suggested that the artificial support given to foreign shipping could only be met in the short term by a temporary subsidy of £3 million for British tramp shipping.[11] The Government reply, given by Walter Runciman, then President of the Board of Trade and himself previously also a leading British tramp owner, accepted that it was necessary to preserve and foster tramp shipping but emphasised that it was up to the shipping community to find means which would ensure that any financial aid which might be granted was not dissipated. The President added that care must be taken that any form of support did not do more harm than good but made it clear that he would, albeit reluctantly, support a change in Britain's long established shipping policy if it was necessary to prevent the continued existence of an adequate mercantile marine from being imperilled.

Following six months of intensive discussion between the Government and the shipowners, on 3rd July 1934 the President of the Board of Trade made a further statement in the Commons[12] which heralded a radical change in British navigation policy. The Government was prepared to give for one year a tramp shipping subsidy of £2 million "to be used for defensive purposes and aimed at securing the abolition of foreign subsidies and the greater employment of British shipping and seafarers" provided that the shipowners formulated a scheme, satisfactory to the Government, which would prevent the subsidy being dissipated by domestic competition of British ships carrying tramp cargoes and would ensure that the subsidy was effectively directed to securing the greater employment of British tramp shipping at the expense of foreign subsidised shipping; the subsidy was also to be subject to the further condition that British owners should press on foreign owners "the framing of proposals

10. P. Debs. 5 Ser., Vol. 284, c.385.

11. Col. Ropner also suggested that the subsidy should be supplemented by tariff protection, preference for British ships in trade agreements and imperial preferences being restricted to goods imported in British ships.

12. P. Debs. 5 Ser., Vol. 291, c.1720.

tending to adjust the supply of tonnage in the world to demand and thus to raise freight rates once more to a remunerative level".[13]

The President also announced that, in order to benefit not only shipping but shipbuilding as well, the Government intended to introduce a Scrapping and Rebuilding Scheme[14] under which Treasury loans would be given for the building of new ships or the modernising of existing ships[15] on condition that three times as much old tonnage was scrapped; Mr Runciman added that other protective measures[16] might have to be considered "if the proposals outlined do not succeed in lessening the menace to the British Mercantile Marine" and, in a debate on the Government's measures which took place a few days later,[17] the speeches from the shipping experts on the Government back benches tended to favour a stronger "out and out policy of protection".[18]

During the next four months the shipowners produced a detailed scheme to meet the Government conditions applicable to the subsidy and when the next session of Parliament was opened in November 1934 the Government was able to publish details of both the subsidy and the scrapping and rebuilding scheme.[19] On 4th December 1934, after a lengthy debate,[20] the British Shipping (Assistance) Money Resolution was passed and the British Shipping (Assistance) Bill was given a formal First Reading. The debate of the Second Reading of the Bill took place on 14th December 1934[21] and, after a Labour Opposition amendment regretting the lack of measures to ensure fair wages, good working conditions and employment of British seamen in place of foreigners[22] had been negatived, the Bill was given an unopposed Second Reading. Following the Committee stage of the Bill,[23] when a number of Opposition amendments were defeated, the Bill passed its Third Reading by a majority of 147 to 37 on 1st February 1935[24] and

13. The Government simultaneously informed the major foreign maritime powers that it was willing to enter into negotiations with foreign governments subsidising their shipping with a view to reaching an agreement which would enable the proposed British subsidy to be withdrawn; but nothing came of this initiative.

14. Brief details of the Scheme were given in Cmd. 4647, Parl Papers 1933–34, Vol. 18. The Scheme was to apply to all tramp ships and certain types of general cargo liners.

15. All work was to be carried out at yards in Great Britain.

16. Such as reservation of inter-imperial trades or preferential treatment in Empire ports for British ships and their cargoes.

17. P. Debs. 5 Ser., Vol. 292, c.179.

18. One speaker suggested the reimposition of the Navigation Laws but the Government considered this would be mistaken policy under present day conditions.

19. "Memorandum on Financial Resolution re Assistance to British Shipping", Cmd. 4754, Parl. Papers 1934–35, Vol. 14.

20. P. Debs. 5 Ser., Vol. 295, c.1417.

21. *Ibid.*, Vol. 296, c.711.

22. However the Government statistics showed that the proportion of foreigners employed on British ships had gone down every year since 1903 when the proportion was nearly 23 per cent compared with only 2 per cent in 1933–35.

23. P. Debs. 5 Ser., Vol. 296, c.1408.

24. *Ibid.*, Vol. 297, c.681.

the British Shipping (Assistance) Act 1935[25] received the Royal Assent on 26th February 1935.

Part I of the Act dealt with the subsidy and Section 1(1) provided that "For the purpose of helping the owners of vessels registered at ports in the United Kingdom to compete with foreign shipping in receipt of subsidies from foreign Governments" the Board of Trade, subject to Treasury direction and upon recommendations made by the Tramp Shipping Subsidy Committee ("TSSC"),[26] was authorised to pay "to the owners eligible for subsidy under this part of the Act"[27] subsidies in respect of tramp voyages[28] or parts of tramp voyages carried out in 1935. The subsidies were not to exceed, in the aggregate, £2 million but the maximum figure was subject to reduction if the average freight for 1935 proved to be a figure higher than 92 per cent of the average freight for 1929.[29] No subsidy was to be paid for any voyage wholly between ports within the United Kingdom, Irish Free State, Isle of Man and the Channel Islands.[30]

Part II of the Act[31] contained the Scrap and Build Scheme and provided that if the Board of Trade, after consultation with the Ships Replacement Committee ("SRC"),[32] were satisfied that the carrying out of proposals for demolition and for building or modernising vessels submitted by a person qualified to own a British ship[33] would promote the general interest of British shipping, the Board might approve the proposals[34] and, with the consent of the Treasury and on the recommendation of the SRC, make an advance to that person to enable him to build or modernise the vessels. Vessels had to be demolished in the United Kingdom[35] and such demolition had to be in the proportion of two gross tons for every gross ton built or of one gross ton for every gross ton modernised. Vessels had to be built or modernised in Great Britain and

25. 25 Geo. V, c.7.

26. A statutory committee whose functions were to consider applications for subsidy and make recommendations to the Board of Trade. The TSSC comprised six tramp owners, two liner owners and one independent Government nominee.

27. To be eligible for subsidy a vessel had to comply with the conditions set out in Sections 1(2) and 6(1) of the Act.

28. I.e. "voyage in the course of which all the cargo carried is carried under charter party but does not include any voyage during the course of which more than 12 passengers are carried".

29. Taking the average tramp freight rate index for 1929 as 100, Cmd. 4754 provided that if the index for 1935 turned out to be less than 100 the total subsidy would be £250,000. for every unit below 100 subject to a maximum of £2 million.

30. Further details for calculating and paying the subsidy were set out in Cmd. 4754.

31. Which came into operation on 18th March 1935.

32. This was an advisory committee appointed for the purposes of Part II of the Act by the Board of Trade with the concurrence of the Treasury.

33. In accordance with Section 1 of the Merchant Shipping Act 1894. In the event all applicants were shipowning companies incorporated and having their principal place of business in the United Kingdom.

34. The statutory requirements regarding the proposals were set out in Section 3(1) of the Act. All tramp ships qualified for Part II and some cargo liners as well, provided they were not engaged in short sea trades nor constructed for the carriage of more than 12 passengers.

35. Unless the Board of Trade otherwise agreed.

registered at a port in the United Kingdom. Advances were not to exceed in the aggregate £10 million, no advance was to be made after 26th February 1937 and advances were to be secured by first mortgages on the new or modernised vessels, bear interest at a rate not in excess of 3 per cent per annum and be repayable within a period not exceeding 12 years.

The way in which the subsidy arrangements worked out in practice and their impact on the prosperity of British shipping can best be traced through the six-monthly reports which the Tramp Shipping Advisory Committee ("TSAC")[36] were required to make to the President of the Board of Trade. The first Report of the TSAC,[37] made on 25th July 1935 in respect of the six months ending 30th June 1935, emphasised that the Committee had been faced with trading conditions so adverse that, to avoid disaster, prompt action was imperative; this took the form, first, of a minimum freight scheme for the River Plate trade[38] and, when this proved successful, the establishment of equally successful minimum freight schemes for the St. Lawrence and Australian trades. An essential feature of the schemes was the regulation of the volume of tonnage in the various trades and a strict control on the number of ballast voyages by unfixed tonnage outward from the United Kingdom; the Report also pointed out that the minimum freights had stopped rate cutting by subsidised foreign ships and that, with the aid of the subsidy, British ships were able to compete. The Committee described its actions as "without precedent in the history of modern shipowning in times of peace" and concluded that in its first six months the Act had saved the British tramp shipping industry from collapse, prevented large transfers of British ships to foreign flags and made possible a movement for international co-operation which could prove of lasting value.

The second Report of the TSAC,[39] made on 25th January 1936 in respect of the six months ending 31st December 1935, showed that although, compared with 1934, there had been a slight improvement in the volume of world trade and, compared with 1929, a slight decrease in the amount of world tonnage, there was still in 1935 a surplus of supply over demand of 24 per cent; nevertheless, although the subsidy had not had time to take full effect, the minimum freight schemes had continued to operate with conspicuous success[40] and had resulted in the employment of many more British ships and crews. Even before the end of 1935 the Government had announced[41] that

36. The constitution and functions of the TSAC were set out in detail in Cmd. 4754.

37. Cmd. 5004, Parl. Papers 1934–35, Vol. 11.

38. This was the main tramp trade and by February 1935 the rate had fallen to 12 shillings per ton which meant that the freight was 25 per cent less than the cost of the voyage. The new scheme, backed by cargo interests and foreign shipowners, established a minimum freight of 16 shillings and sixpence and between 14th February and 25th July 1935 nearly 600 charters were signed with no violation except for one foreign ship.

39. Cmd. 5084, Parl. Papers 1935–36, Vol. 13.

40. Since mid-February 1935, 1,482 vessels had been chartered under the schemes and not a single British vessel had been chartered below the minimum rate.

41. P. Debs. 5 Ser., Vol. 307, c.713.

Parliament would be asked to make available for 1936 a further subsidy of £2 million on the same general terms and conditions as for 1935 and early in February 1936 there was published the British Shipping (Continuance of Subsidy) Memorandum on the Financial Resolution providing for the continuance of the Tramp Shipping Subsidy.[42] The debate on the Financial Resolution took place on 11th February 1936[43] and was followed within a period of one month by the carrying through of all stages of the British Shipping (Continuance of Subsidy) Bill 1936.[44] British shipping's continued need of the subsidy to counteract the "baneful effect of foreign shipping subsidies" was not seriously disputed but the Labour Opposition criticised the lack of effective public control of the subsidy and suggested that shipowner members on the Government side were feathering their own nest; however the published Statement of the Distribution of the Tramp Shipping Subsidy in 1935[45] showed that, although the larger tramp groups such as Ropners and Runcimans had received substantial payments, the subsidy had been widely distributed throughout the industry and the smaller owners had in fact received the most.

The progress of the British shipping industry in 1936, supported by the subsidies paid under the British Shipping (Continuance of Subsidy) Act 1936[46] is fully documented in the Third and Fourth Reports of the TSAC[47] During 1936 there were many increases in the minimum rates[48] and there had been more fixtures above the minimum with the result that the Index of Tramp Shipping Freight Rates (1929=100) had risen to an average of 90.79 for 1936,[49] British shipping laid up in U.K. ports in June 1936 was only 60,000 gross tons compared with 3.5 million gross tons in June 1932, unemployment among masters and officers had been reduced and there was practically no unemployment among British white seamen.[50] The Committee emphasised that full and complete effect had been given to all conditions of the subsidy and that freight co-operation between British and foreign owners had saved the markets from collapse, restored confidence and stabilised freights on a moderately rising curve.

The Fourth Report did however point out that there was still much leeway to be made up since six lean years had resulted in the industry being faced

42. Cmd. 5082, Parl. Papers 1935–36, Vol. 13.

43. P. Debs. 5 Ser., Vol. 308, c.773.

44. See P. Debs. 5 Ser., Vol. 308, c.2011; Vol. 309, c.1355 and Vol. 310, c.745.

45. Cmd. 5129, Parl. Papers 1935–36, Vol. 13. The total of the subsidies distributed for 1935 was £1,989,999.

46. 26 Geo. V, and 1 Edw. VIII, c.12 which received the Royal Assent on 9th April 1936.

47. Cmd. 5291, Parl. Papers 1935–36, Vol. 13 and Cmd. 5363, Parl. Papers 1936–37, Vol. 13.

48. The rates had originally been fixed to cover operating costs and had been gradually increased to cover depreciation and interest.

49. For the three previous years the index figures were 72.9 for 1933, 75.83 for 1934 and 76.28 for 1935.

50. It was also pointed out that there had been strict compliance with National Maritime Board wages and agreements.

with gigantic arrears of depreciation[51] which had to be met if the mercantile marine was to be maintained even at its present strength.[52] Dealing with future prospects the Committee stated that tonnage and trade were nearing equilibrium but that, although trade agreements had done much to increase British exports, new or revised agreements should specifically safeguard the interests of shipping as the principal export industry.[53] Nevertheless two years' experience of the Subsidy Acts and the system of freight co-operation had shown Government policy in granting the subsidy to be fully justified in the results which had saved British tramp shipping from collapse, stopped abnormal sales abroad, increased employment and benefited shipbuilding and ancillary trades; so, in the view of the Committee, "the Acts have thus exactly fulfilled the purpose for which they were temporarily sought viz: to bridge the gap between the period of exceptional depression and returning prosperity".

Notwithstanding the substantial rise in the freight market that had been taking place in the last quarter of 1936, on 11th November 1936 the President of the Board of Trade announced in the House that the Government proposed similar shipping subsidy arrangements for 1937[54] but, although the announcement was welcomed by Government supporters, two weeks later, in an adjournment debate,[55] a motion was proposed from the Government back benches to the effect that further measures were necessary to protect British shipping against foreign competition.[56] A "Memorandum on the Financial Resolution for the Continuance of the Tramp Shipping Subsidy" was published in January 1937[57] and in the subsequent debate on the Financial Resolution[58] there was no indication that, apart from the subsidy, the Government intended to give any further protection to British shipping; on the contrary the Government expressed the hope that in 1937 the level of freights would be so high that in fact no subsidy would be payable[59] and made it clear that in any case it was not intended to continue the subsidy after 1937. All stages of the British

51. The TSAC had carried out a financial investigation which revealed the seriousness of the depreciation position—see Table VI of the Committee's Fourth Report.

52. World gross tonnage in June 1936 was 65 million compared with 45.5 million in 1914. U.K. tonnage had decreased from around 19 million in 1914 to around 17 million in 1936.

53. A bilateral trade agreement made in June 1939 between the U.K. and the U.S.A. (Cmd. 6048, Parl. Papers 1938–39, Vol. 28) provided that the goods in question were to be transported in the vessels of the two States on a 50:50 basis but many trade agreements with foreign countries did not specifically protect British shipping interests.

54. P. Debs. 5 Ser., Vol. 317, c.878.

55. *Ibid.*, Vol. 318, c.495.

56. It was suggested that to some extent there should be a reversion to the Navigation Acts and in particular it was proposed that there should be a reservation of the U.K. coasting trade. There was no Government reply to the debate.

57. Cmd. 5357, Parl. Papers 1936–37, Vol. 21. The amount of the subsidy and the conditions attaching to it were to be the same as for 1936 except that in 1937 there were to be no interim quarterly payments.

58. P. Debs. 5 Ser., Vol. 319, c.1331.

59. No subsidy was payable if the Freight Index was above 100—see Cmd. 4754.

Shipping (Continuance of Subsidy) Bill 1937 were carried through between 2nd February and 1st March 1937[60] and the British Shipping (Continuance of Subsidy) Act 1937,[61] which was in substance the same as the 1936 Act, received the Royal Assent on 25th March 1937. In the same month a Statement was published giving details of the subsidy payments made in 1936.[62]

In the event no subsidy was paid for 1937; the Fifth Report of the TSAC[63] in respect of the first six months of 1937 showed that for this period the Freight Index Figure had been 135.7, far above the 1929 level, and the figure for the whole year turned out even higher at 140.4. The subsidy provisions of the British Shipping (Assistance) Acts 1935 to 1937 ceased at the end of 1937 and in May 1938 the TSAC issued its Sixth and Final Report[64] in which it summarised the main results of the three years during which the Acts had been in operation. The matters emphasised in the Committee's review were the value of the co-operation between British tramp and liner owners and the effective foreign support, the advance of freight rates to a level which covered operating costs, depreciation and a small return on capital, supply of tonnage being adjusted to demand, the elimination of unemployment of officers and crews and increased employment in shipbuilding and ancillary trades and the restoration of confidence to British tramp shipping enabling it to stand on its own feet again. The Report concluded with an account of the measures which had been voluntarily taken by all British owners in the tramp trade to secure future co-operation; there was a binding agreement[65] to comply with minimum freight schemes, restrictions on unfixed tonnage sailing in ballast, agreed forms of charter and N.M.B. scales of pay and the Committee observed that it was the first time in the history of British shipping that it had proved possible to unite the whole industry in support of the principle of co-operation.

Meanwhile the working out of the Scrap and Build Scheme over its authorised period of two years from 26th January 1935 had fallen far short of expectations; the published Accounts[66] showed that total advances of £3,548,154 (out of a permitted maximum of £10 million) had been made for the building of 50 new vessels[67] aggregating 186,000 gross tons subject to

60. P. Debs. 5 Ser., Vol. 319, c.1854 and Vol. 321, c.96.

61. 1 Edw. VIII and 1 Geo. VI, c.21.

62. Cmd 5420, Parl. Papers 1936–37, Vol. 16. The total for 1936 was £1,991,015.

63. Cmd. 5555, Parl. Papers 1936–37, Vol. 13.

64. Cmd. 5750, Parl. Papers 1937–38, Vol. 13.

65. Subscribed to by the owners of 93 per cent of tramp tonnage over 2,500 tons and by the owners of 120 tramp ships under 2,500 tons. The Scheme was approved by all the liner owners concerned and was also adopted by most of the principal European shipowners.

66. Accounts for the period ended 31st March 1936. Parl. Papers 1936–37 (8), Vol. 16. Accounts for periods ended 31st March 1937 and 31st March 1938. Parl Papers 1937–38(1) and (145), Vol. 16.

67. No advances were made for modernisation. Out of the 50 new vessels, 36 of a tonnage of 176,186 gross tons were deep sea tramps, five were smaller ships built for the Baltic trade and seven were small coasting tramps.

demolition of 97 vessels aggregating 386,625 gross tons.[68] The Report of the Ships Replacement Committee published in May 1937[69] stated that the main reason why not more use was made of the Scheme was the scarcity of scrap tonnage since few applicants had tonnage of their own for scrapping and out of the 97 vessels scrapped 91 were bought in the open market, many from foreign owners, at an increasingly heavy premium over scrap value. Another difficulty was that the SRC refused to accept for demolition tonnage which was already out of commission and too old to be really competitive and, with the strong improvement in the freight market in the autumn of 1936, the scrap position became almost impossible and many proposals had to be abandoned.[70]

There were other factors which militated against the success of the scheme. Parts I and II of the 1935 Act were to some extent incompatible since the very success of the TSAC in bringing about an improvement in freights resulted in owners being reluctant to scrap ships which had become capable of profitable operation; it seems likely that without the scrapping requirement many more new ships would have been built. Moreover there were some tramp owners, traditionally disinclined to build with borrowed money, who considered that the interest rates on the loans were too high. Nevertheless, although the outcome of the scheme was disappointing, the SRC could fairly claim that 50 modern, fast and economical ships had been built, a substantial amount of obsolete tonnage had been scrapped and the shipbuilding industry had received a much needed boost.[71]

During the first six months of 1938 it became clear that the high market rates of 1937 had been only a flash in the pan; the peak had been reached in September 1937 and for the next nine months there was a general downward trend with the result that for the first half of 1938 tramp freights were back to a level at which the full subsidy would have been payable had the British Shipping (Assistance) Acts 1935–37 remained in force. The decline was due to a fall in world trade[72] and an increase in world tonnage[73] so that once again it was the old story of too many ships chasing too little cargo. Thus there was renewed concern regarding the economic position of British shipping but, in

68. Since foreign shipbreakers were paying much more than their British counterparts, the Board of Trade eventually allowed an unrestricted market for the disposal of scrap tonnage.

69. Cmd. 5459, Parl. Papers 1936–37, Vol. 13.

70. The SRC considered applications for 95 new vessels but nearly half of these were rejected by SRC or abandoned by the owners.

71. The tonnage of merchant vessels launched from British yards increased appreciably in 1936 and 1937 as compared with the previous two years. The figures were 459,877 in 1934, 499,011 in 1935, 856,257 in 1936 and 920,822 in 1937. There was also a marked decrease in shipyard unemployment.

72. The League of Nations quantum of world trade (1929=100) fell from 97 in 1937 to 89 in 1938.

73. Between July 1935 and July 1938 world tonnage increased by over 3 million gross tons. In the same period U.K. tonnage as a whole increased by 400,000 gross tons but U.K. tramp tonnage declined by 100,000 gross tons.

the aftermath of the Munich crisis of March 1938, there was even greater anxiety as to whether the decline of the British maritime industries might endanger national security if, as seemed increasingly probable, the United Kingdom should once again be plunged into a major war.

Comparing the position of British shipping in 1938–39 with what it had been in 1913–14, there was clearly both an absolute and relative decline in tonnage and a marked diminution in British shipping's share of world trade. Steam and motor tonnage registered in the United Kingdom was approximately 1 million gross tons less in June 1939 than it had been in 1914[74] whereas the steam and motor tonnage of the remainder of the world (excluding the British Dominions) had in the same period risen by nearly 22.5 million gross tons so that the United Kingdom's share of the world fleet had fallen from 43.8 per cent in 1914 to 27.3 per cent in 1939. Britain's share of the world seaborne trade had fallen from a pre-Great War figure of 50 per cent to around 40 per cent in 1936, the United Kingdom's export trade in almost all the inter-war years was well below its pre Great War level[75] and British shipping's share of the United Kingdom's import trade was substantially lower than in 1913.[76]

The decline of British shipping in the inter-war years was certainly in part due to adverse circumstances wholly or largely outside the control of British owners who were far from having recovered from the unparalleled losses sustained in the Great War, the grossly inflated cost of their post-war replacements and the severity of the slumps of the early 1920s and 30s. In the contemporary opinion of British owners themselves, the main cause of the depressed state of British shipping was a combination of the lack of growth in world trade, the vast increase, unjustified in economic terms, of foreign shipping,[77] higher British capital and operating costs and the unfair competition resulting largely from the policies of foreign governments in providing shipping and shipbuilding subsidies and encouraging flag discrimination of various kinds.[78]

There can be little doubt that in many trades British owners were placed at a disadvantage by reason of the artificial aid given to many of their principal foreign competitors. By 1933 foreign subsidies were running at the rate of £33 million a year and British shipping suffered especially from the subsidies given

74. But since, between 1914 and 1939, U.K. tanker tonnage had increased by nearly 2 million gross tons, U.K. dry cargo tonnage in1939 was some 3 million tons less than in 1914.

75. Tramp shipping suffered severely from the decline in coal exports—38.2 million tons in 1938 compared with 76.7 million tons in 1913. The liner trades suffered from the fall in non-coal exports (9.8 million tons in 1933 compared with 16.9 million tons in 1913) and from the severe decline in emigrant traffic.

76. Partly due to foreign governments giving subsidies and encouraging c.i.f. shipments in national ships.

77. Not only was the volume grossly in excess of the world's seaborne trade requirements; the improvements resulting from technical progress meant an increase in the effective carrying capacity of post-war built ships.

78. The Parliamentary shipping debates show that, with few exceptions, there was general agreement with the shipowners' analysis of their own problems.

to the ships of France, Germany, Italy, Japan and the United States; the ships of these countries substantially increased their share of the U.K. import trade, American ships gained a much higher proportion of the United States' trade and the severe competition experienced by British shipping in the Far East was considered to be mainly due "to the advent of new German and Italian vessels built with heavy subsidies".[79] In addition foreign shipping had the advantage of indirect aids, preferences and action tending to divert cargo into ships of the national flag so that, whilst British ships enjoyed no trade protection, "in varying degrees the foreign seafaring nations of the world were reverting to the practices which had prevailed at the time of the Navigation Acts".[80] The United States, France, Japan and many other lesser maritime powers still reserved their coastal trades,[81] it was the recently declared policy of the United States[82] that American ships should carry a substantial portion of the United States' foreign trade and Russia had announced its intention to build up its mercantile marine with the object of carrying the whole of her imports and exports to the exclusion of non-Russian vessels.[83]

However in certain areas within their control it must be conceded that some British owners failed to meet the challenge created by the new trading conditions of the inter-war years and appeared content to conduct their affairs in the belief that British shipping was inherently superior and that all would be well once "normal" (i.e. pre-war) conditions returned.[84] Apart from their ventures into the comparatively new field of cruising, British liner owners, cushioned by the conference system, seemed to await complacently, with vessels slower than those of their principal competitors, the better times which were never to return. Tramp owners clung to both their traditional ships and their traditional trades; unlike the Scandinavians and the Dutch, there was a reluctance to switch from coal to oil fuel and from steam to the diesel engine[85] and likewise, in spite of the loss of their coal exports, British owners were slow to get into the ever growing oil trade.[86] This British failure cannot be laid at the door of subsidised competition; in the inter-war period Norway and other non-subsidising countries were quick to enter new trades with fast and

79. "British Shipping in the Orient". 38th Report of the Imperial Shipping Committee (HMSO, 1939).

80. G. B. A. Behrens, *Merchant Shipping and the Demands of War* (HMSO, 1955), p. 2.

81. In the case of the United States and France the coastal trade was still artificially extended to include voyages between the mother country and overseas territories.

82. See the preamble to the U.S. Merchant Marine Act 1936.

83. See 1938 "Memorandum of the Chamber of Shipping on British Shipping and Trade with Russia". By 1938 the whole of the British liner trade between the U.K. and Russia had been eliminated and cargoes carried in British tramp ships drastically reduced.

84. See generally *British Shipping and World Competition*, *op. cit.*, Chapter IV.

85. With the result that most British tramps were slower and less economical than their principal competitors.

86. See Rochdale Report, (Cmnd. 4337, para. 37). In 1914 the United Kingdom owned more than half of the world's tankers but by 1938 the proportion had fallen to one quarter.

specialised ships[87] whilst the policies of British owners appeared conservative, over-cautious and lacking in the spirit of adventurous enterprise which had characterised British shipping in the pre-war years.

The decline of British shipbuilding during the inter-war years was no less marked. Prior to the war British yards had built around 60 per cent of the world merchant tonnage but the average proportion in the five years 1933–37 was only 37.5 per cent; in 1913 output had been over 2 million tons but from 1931 to 1938 output had only in one year, 1938, been as much as 1 million tons and in most other years had fallen far below this level. In theory, at least, British yards still had the capacity for a far greater output,[88] notwithstanding the yard closures effected during the 1930s by National Shipbuilders' Security Limited,[89] but, with so many skilled workers having left the industry and the rate of unemployment still abnormally high, there was concern as to whether it would be physically possible to achieve rapidly the large increase of output that would be needed in the event of an outbreak of war.

The shipbuilding decline was partially attributable to factors outside the builders' control; depressed world trade led to a marked falling off in orders for new tonnage and British owners, still suffering from the high cost of their post-war replacements, were reluctant to place new orders in the shipping depression of the early 1930s. Moreover, since British building costs were much higher than on the Continent or in Japan, more British owners were building abroad and fewer foreign owners were placing orders in British yards. Nevertheless British shipbuilders cannot be absolved from all blame; although they were handicapped by the increase in foreign shipbuilding capacity and foreign subsidies, British builders failed to modernise the equipment in their yards and still pursued out-of-date production methods. British labour costs were high owing mainly to bad organisation of work and delays caused by inter-union disputes. British marine engineers were slow to adopt technical improvements particularly in relation to the diesel engine and in consequence diesel machinery in Britain was far more expensive than on the Continent. All these, and other, factors, many of them within the control of the builders, placed the British shipping industry in a weak competitive position.[90]

Although, in the shipping crisis of the early 1930s, shipowners had suggested

87. See Cmnd. 4337, para. 40 and *International Sea Transport*, *op. cit.*, p. 81.

88. In 1928 the Balfour Committee's *Survey of Metal Industries* estimated the U.K.'s annual shipbuilding capacity at about 3 million tons. In 1938 the Shipbuilding Conference estimated that the maximum productive merchant work capacity of U.K. yards was about 2 million tons per annum but at that date 55 per cent of the available berths were unoccupied.

89. A company formed in 1930 by the leading British shipbuilders for the purchase and dismantling of redundant and obsolete shipyards in order to achieve a more efficient and slimmed-down industry. For details of the activities of the company during the 1930s see *Shipbuilding in Britain*, *op. cit.*, pp. 133–140.

90. For a detailed examination of the reasons for the decline of British shipbuilding during the inter-war years see *Shipbuilding in Britain*, *op. cit.*, Chapter III.

that the Government should consider whether Britain still possessed a well-balanced mercantile marine for supplying the nation in case of an emergency,[91] it was not until the time of Munich that the Committee of Imperial Defence first considered the relationship in any future war between demand for ships and the effective available supply. The question was then referred to the Mercantile Marine Department of the Board of Trade who, on the assumption that only British tonnage would be available, reached the conclusion that British ships would be able to import 48 million tons of dry cargo in the first year of war. Since the anticipated import need was 47 million tons it appeared there would be enough shipping and the Board of Trade's judgement was accepted by the Committee of Imperial Defence.[92]

Notwithstanding these sanguine conclusions, Parliamentary concern regarding the decline in the maritime industries and their ability to meet the country's needs in wartime continued to be expressed from both sides of the House. In a debate on 7th March 1938[93] on the 1938 Defence White Paper[94] the Minister for Co-ordination of Defence was challenged on his recent statement[95] that cargo carrying capacity was as effective as in 1914 and in a further debate on 15th June 1938[96] repeated doubts were expressed as to the sufficiency of Britain's shipping and shipbuilding resources in an emergency and calls were made for a return to the Navigation Laws and customs preference for goods carried in British ships. With the fear of war growing stronger, the state of the merchant navy was raised yet again in a debate on 8th July 1938[97] and, although the Government did not accept the suggestions that there should be discriminatory measures along the lines of the Navigation Acts, Oliver Stanley, who had succeeded Runciman as President of the Board of Trade, suggested that the shipping industry should itself consider in what ways it could best be helped and added that, when the industry had completed its task, the Government would not be unsympathetic "to the claims of an industry upon which the greatness of Britain was built in the past and upon which it must rest in the future".

Shipowners responded with alacrity to the Government's invitation and in January 1939 there was submitted to the Government a Report of the Joint Shipping Policy Committee of the Chamber of Shipping and Liverpool Steamship Owners' Association embodying the proposals for the support of British shipping which had resulted from an exhaustive investigation covering all

91. 1933 Memorandum of the Chamber of Shipping Policy Committee.
92. *Merchant Shipping and the Demands of War*, *op. cit.*, pp. 35–38.
93. P. Debs. 5 Ser., Vol. 332, c.1657.
94. Cmd. 5682, Parl. Papers 1937–38, Vol. 17. The White Paper made no reference to the merchant navy.
95. P. Debs. 5 Ser., Vol. 331, c.1123.
96. *Ibid.*, Vol. 337, c.232.
97. *Ibid.*, Vol. 338, c.799.

sections of the industry.[98] The Joint Committee described their proposals "as best able to secure the welfare of the British Mercantile Marine in the face of severe and increasing competition, largely itself State-aided or artificially fostered" but the Report made it clear that most British owners still believed in freedom of trade and did not therefore recommend a return to Navigation Acts policy[99]; in the main the proposals called for financial support only[100] but on a much more extensive basis than in 1935.

After the Government had considered the recommendations of the Joint Shipping Policy Committee,[101] the President of the Board of Trade made a statement to the House on 28th March 1939 of Government policy regarding shipping and shipbuilding[102] and at the beginning of July 1939 the Government published a White Paper containing its proposals for the assistance of British shipping and shipbuilding.[103] The Second Reading of the British Shipping (Assistance) Bill 1939[104] took place on 19th July 1939[105] and the debate was opened by Oliver Stanley who, after referring to the 1934 debate leading up to the British Shipping (Assistance) Act 1935, emphasised the one great difference between that period and 1939: in 1934 the debates had ranged entirely on economic lines but "to-day over the whole of our debate lies the shadow of a possible great national emergency. To-day we cannot think of the shipping industry of the country only as a desirable asset in time of peace; we have to think of it as a vital service in time of war, of war which may be upon us within measurable time." The President then outlined the main provisions of the Bill as amplified and supplemented by Cmd. 6060.[106]

98. The main Report was accompanied by a series of reports prepared by Fact Finding Committees which comprised:
Report of the Deep Sea Tramp Fact Finding Committee
Summary of Replies to Deep Sea Liner Questionnaire
Report of the Near Continental Trades and Russia Fact Finding Committee
Report of the Coasting Fact Finding Committee
Report of the Tanker Fact Finding Committee
Report on Shipping and Shipbuilding
Memorandum on Shipping and Shipbuilding Subsidies.

99. British coasting tramp owners did however advocate the reservation of the U.K. coasting trade.

100. But in the case of the Near Continental Trades it was urged that the Government should insist on a proportion of Russian timber imports being carried in British ships and should negotiate for British shipping to be used to a greater extent for timber imports from other countries and for coal exports to Near Continental countries.

101. Together with the Imperial Shipping Committee's Report on "British Shipping in the Orient".

102. P. Debs. 5 Ser., Vol. 345., c.1853.

103. Cmd. 6060, Parl. Papers 1938–39, Vol. 18.

104. Parl. Papers 1938–39, Vol. 1.

105. P. Debs. 5 Ser., Vol. 350, c.465.

106. The Government's proposals did not include everything that the shipowners had asked for but on the other hand the Bill did include some new provisions to meet the possibility of a national emergency.

Once again there were to be operating subsidies for the tramp voyages[107] by eligible vessels[108] but on this occasion the period was to be for five years from 1st January 1940, the subsidy was not to exceed £2.75 million per annum and was to be payable only to persons qualified under the Merchant Shipping Act 1894 to own a British ship and whose principal place of business was in the United Kingdom. The White Paper set out the conditions which tramp shipowners were required to fulfil[109] and laid down in detail the manner in which the duration of voyages was to be ascertained, the methods of calculating and paying the subsidy and the procedure for settlement of disputes.[110]

Again, as under the 1935 Assistance Act, there were to be Board of Trade loans, up to a maximum, in the aggregate, of £10 million in respect of the building in Great Britain of general trading vessels contracted after 22nd March 1939 but under the 1939 Bill there was no scrapping requirement and, to encourage the quick placing of new orders, the Board of Trade was also authorised to make grants, not exceeding in the aggregate £2.5 million, towards the cost of building in the United Kingdom general trading vessels ordered after 28th March 1939 but the Board had to be satisfied that the construction of the ship would promote the general interests of British shipping and shipbuilding and the new vessel had to be completed by 31st December 1941.[111] The detailed conditions applicable to the shipbuilding loans and grants were set out in the White Paper which, in an attempt to bring some measure of stability to the shipbuilding industry, also provided for the setting up of a Joint Committee of shipowners and shipbuilders whose task was to devise some means for securing the more regular ordering of new tonnage by British owners in British yards.

Another novel feature of the 1939 Bill was the provision of support for liner shipping; the Board of Trade was empowered, within a period of two years, to give financial assistance, up to a total of £10 million, to help liner owners to compete with foreign shipping in receipt of official subsidies or assistance[112] but subject to the proviso that a liner service should only be assisted if it had been discontinued or substantially curtailed and that the Board considered it to be in the national interest that assistance should be given.[113]

107. Defined in the same way as in the 1935 Act.

108. I.e. any ship employed in the carriage of commercial cargoes other than liquid in bulk but excluding ships with substantial insulated space, fishing vessels, tugs or similar craft.

109. These included co-operation between British owners and the promotion of international measures to adjust supply of tonnage to demand.

110. In general terms the subsidy conditions were similar to those in the 1935 Act but there were significant differences in detail.

111. These grants undoubtedly achieved their objective—namely the quick placing of new orders. Within one month the Board of Trade had been notified of firm or probable orders for 190 ships.

112. I.e. shipping directly or indirectly assisted by a foreign government or by a local or public authority in a foreign country.

113. The detailed procedures applicable to this Liner Defence Scheme were set out in the White Paper.

In addition, for the first time, the Bill provided for the establishment of a Government owned reserve of merchant ships[114]; the Board of Trade was empowered to expend up to £2 million in the purchase of vessels registered in the United Kingdom for the purpose of creating a reserve to be kept in use for an emergency and, both to enable this Merchant Ship Reserve to be built up and to curtail depletion of British tonnage generally, the sale or mortgage to any unqualified person[115] of vessels of specified classes registered in the United Kingdom was prohibited.[116] The Board was authorised to make regulations whereby the specified classes of vessels were not to cease to be registered in the United Kingdom except with the Board's consent and, if such consent was refused, the Board was required to offer to purchase the vessel on terms to be agreed or, in default of agreement, to be settled by arbitration.

After the Bill had been given its Second Reading it was committed to a Committee of the whole House but no further progress on the Bill was made prior to the outbreak of war on 3rd September 1939 and on 3rd October 1939 Stanley stated in the House[117] that it was not intended to proceed with the Bill but that nevertheless the Government would consider applications for building loans in respect of contracts made between 29th March and 3rd October which were in the national interest; he added that the Government were reviewing the shipbuilding grants position but that the other schemes covered by the Bill were unnecessary or inapplicable in wartime. Subsequently, in October 1940, the Ministry of Shipping[118] published a "Memorandum on the War-Time Financial Arrangements between the Government and British Shipowners"[119] which (*inter alia*) dealt with shipbuilding loans and grants; the Memorandum stated that approval had been given for loans to 39 owners for sums aggregating £4,817,005 in respect of the building of 55 vessels having a gross tonnage of 239,822 and an estimated building cost of £6,311,295 and that authority had also been given for the payment of initial building grants, estimated at £320,000, involving about 100 vessels.

Thus, although the 1939 Bill never reached the statute book, it did achieve part of its purpose; the shipbuilding industry received a substantial number of much needed orders and there was a valuable accretion to the merchant navy's

114. This radical change was viewed by some shipowners with misgivings.

115. Any person not qualified under the Merchant Shipping Act 1894 to be the owner of a British ship.

116. Any vessel sold or mortgaged in defiance of this prohibition was subject to forfeiture to the Crown under Section 76 of the Merchant Shipping Act 1894.

117. P. Debs. 5 Ser., Vol. 351, c.1793.

118. Pursuant to the Ministers of the Crown (Emergency Appointments) Act 1939 and S.R. & O. 1939 No. 1425, in October 1939 the Ministry of Shipping was established as a separate Government department. In May 1941 all the functions of the Ministry of Shipping (and also those of the Ministry of Transport) were transferred to the newly created Ministry of War Transport (S.R. & O. 1941 No. 654).

119. Cmd. 6218, Parl. Papers 1939–40, Vol. 7.

tonnage. Without this assistance, and the other financial support and encouragement which the Government had given to the British maritime industries during the inter-war years,[120] there can be no doubt that the state of British shipping and shipbuilding in 1939 would have been that much worse. Nevertheless at the outbreak of the Second World War there were many who, in spite of Government reassurances, given in June 1938, that the position in regard to the available supply of merchant shipping was not unsatisfactory,[121] had serious misgivings as to whether the available dry cargo and tanker tonnage would be adequate to meet the military and civil demands of war and whether the shipyards would be able to supply the needs of the Navy, increase the merchant fleet and effect the necessary repairs and replacements resulting from enemy action.

120. Under the Trade Facilities Acts 1921 to 1926, the Northern Ireland Loan Guarantee Acts 1922 to 1938, the Cunard (Insurance) Agreement Act 1930, the North Atlantic Shipping Act 1934 and the British Shipping (Assistance) Acts 1935 to 1937.

121. See the speech of the Parliamentary Secretary to the Board of Trade in the debate on 15th June 1938—P. Debs. 5 Ser., Vol. 337, c.232.

CHAPTER 7

THE FOURTH SERVICE AT WAR AGAIN

In September 1939 the conflict was renewed and once again, after an all too short breathing space of 20 years, the men and ships of the merchant navy were called upon to fulfil their vital role as the Fourth Arm of Britain's defences. As Churchill succinctly put it, "Without ships we cannot live: without ships we cannot conquer"; for, even more so than in the Great War, the role of merchant ships during the Second World War in carrying the offensive to the enemy was an essential factor in the ultimate victory. The civil and military demands resulted in our resources, both in men and ships, being strained to the uttermost and the tragic consequence was that in the Second World War around 32,000 British seamen lost their lives as a direct or indirect result of enemy action—a casualty rate more than double that sustained between 1914 and 1918. However, as in the case of the Great War, it is necessary to resist the temptation of adding to the already comprehensive coverage of the general history of the merchant navy in the Second World War[1]; here the investigation must be limited to the impact made upon the British maritime industries by Government controls and policies during the emergency, wartime losses and wartime economic influences.

How then, in 1939, did the state of the British maritime industries measure up to the awesome task which lay ahead; for, as Roskill emphasises,[2] the merchant navy "must be adequate to feed our home population, to bring in the raw materials needed by our industries, to carry our exports overseas and to transport our armies and their multifarious supplies to the theatres where they are required to fight. Nor is the Merchant Navy by itself enough. It must be supported by an adequate shipbuilding and ship repairing industry

1. In the *Official History of the Second World War* (U.K. Civil Series, Ed. Sir Keith Hancock) *Merchant Shipping and the Demands of War*, *op. cit.* deals mainly with dry cargo shipping, *Oil* by D. J. Payton Smith (HMSO, 1971) covers tankers, *Inland Transport* by C. I. Savage (HMSO, 1957) covers coastal shipping; merchant shipbuilding is dealt with in *British War Production* by H. M. Postan (HMSO, 1952) and *British War Economy* by W. K. Hancock and M. M. Gowing (HMSO, 1949) deals with certain aspects of both shipping and shipbuilding. For an account of naval operations see *The War at Sea* by Stephen Roskill (HMSO, 1954). See also *British Merchantmen at War* by J. L. Hodson (HMSO, 1945) and *Statistical Digest of the War* (HMSO, 1951).

2. *The War at Sea*, *op. cit.*, Vol. 1, p. 7.

to enable losses to be replaced and damaged ships to be returned rapidly to the service."

At the outbreak of the Second World War U.K. gross tonnage was 17,891,134 compared with 19,256,766 in June 1914 but in 1939 tanker tonnage was nearly 3 million, as compared with only 833,000 in 1914, so that in 1939 U.K. dry cargo tonnage was some 3.5 million tons less than it had been in 1914; even allowing for the improvements in speed and efficiency, some experienced shipping men doubted the Board of Trade opinion[3] that British dry cargo tonnage alone would be able to meet the wartime civil and military requirements. Likewise, although U.K. tanker tonnage was nearly four times greater than it had been in 1914, the probable wartime requirement was generally reckoned to be beyond the capacity of British tankers alone[4]; there was also some concern regarding the adequacy of coastal tonnage since there was a shortage of small handy vessels of between 1,000 and 4,000 gross tons.[5] In addition there were misgivings as to whether British shipyards would be able both to supply the additional and replacement tonnage which the Royal and Merchant Navies would require and also to effect with expedition the increasing volume of ship repairs which would inevitably result from enemy action and the strains of wartime operations; the output of merchant ships in 1938—at just over 1 million tons the best of the decade—was about half the 1913 level and although, in theory, there was ample surplus capacity, the shortage of skilled labour was a serious restrictive factor.[6]

Although, in their pre-war consideration of the shipping problem, the Government had mistakenly concluded that there would be no shortage of tonnage, it was nevertheless realised that a prompt and extensive degree of Government control would be essential in order to ensure the total commitment of British shipping and shipbuilding to the war effort. To this end, well before war became imminent, plans had been made to set up a Ministry of Shipping,[7] drafts of the necessary emergency legislation had been prepared,[8] restrictions on the transfer of British ships abroad had been embodied in the British Shipping (Assistance) Bill 1939[9] and, to avoid the stagnation of shipping on the outbreak of war, arrangements had been made in advance for the

3. See p. 132 *supra*.
4. *Oil*, *op. cit.*, p. 57.
5. See the 1938 Report of the Coasting Fact Finding Committee. In a Memorandum submitted by the Board of Trade to the Royal Commission on Transport in 1930 the importance of an efficient and adequate coasting shipping service in times of war was emphasised—see Cmd. 3751, para. 483, Parl. Papers 1930–31, Vol. 17.
6. The state of the shipbuilding industry in the 1930s is summarised in *British Industries and their Organisation* by G. C. Allen, 5th edn. (London, 1970) pp. 126 *et seq*. See also *Factories and Plant* by W. Hornby, (U.K. Civil Histories of the Second World War, HMSO, 1958) pp. 36 *et seq*.
7. *Merchant Shipping and the Demands of War*, *op. cit.*, p. 38.
8. *British War Economy*, *op. cit.*, pp. 83–84.
9. See p. 135 *supra*.

insurance of ships. As regards the latter it was clearly essential that, as in the Great War, the major share of war risks insurance should be borne by the Government and, following discussion between all the interests concerned, the Government published in April 1939 a Provisional Scheme for Re-Insurance by the Board of Trade in respect of King's Enemy Risks on Cargoes destined for discharge in or shipped from the United Kingdom[10] and in July 1939 a draft Agreement between the Board of Trade and the War Risks Associations for the Re-Insurance of British Ships against King's Enemy Risks by the Board of Trade.[11] Following its Second Reading on 17th July 1939,[12] the War Risks Insurance Bill quickly passed through all its stages and the War Risks Insurance Act 1939[13] received the Royal Assent on 4th August 1939. In the following month the Board of Trade concluded Agreements with all the War Risks Associations[14] under which (*inter alia*) the Board of Trade agreed to reinsure 80 per cent of each Association's war risks liability.[15]

In August 1939 it was also decided that, even prior to the outbreak of war, it was necessary for the Government to be invested with exceptional statutory powers to meet the emergency and accordingly on one day, 24th August 1939, the Emergency Powers (Defence) Bill passed through all its stages[16] and in the evening received the Royal Assent. The Emergency Powers (Defence) Act 1939[17] empowered the King, by Order in Council,[18] to make such Defence Regulations as were necessary and expedient "for securing the public safety, the defence of the realm, the maintenance of public order and the efficient prosecution of any war in which His Majesty may be engaged and for maintaining supplies and services essential to the life of the community"; and, without prejudice to this generality, express powers were conferred whereby the Defence Regulations could provide for the taking possession or control of any property and the acquisition of any property other than land. These express powers were clearly wide enough to cover the control, requisition and acquisition of ships and, although the powers conferred by the Act were declared to be "in addition to and not in derogation of the powers exercisable by virtue of the prerogative of the Crown", it is apparent that in 1939 it was decided that shipping should be controlled under statutory powers instead of,

10. Cmd. 6002, Parl. Papers 1938–39, Vol. 21.
11. Cmd. 6058, *ibid.*
12. P. Debs. 5 Ser., Vol. 350, c.51.
13. 2 & 3 Geo. VI, c.57.
14. Parl. Papers 1938–39 (182) to (194), Vol. 21.
15. Fundamental changes were made to these Agreements in May 1940—see fn. 70 *infra.*
16. P. Debs. 5 Ser., Vol. 351, c.63.
17. 2 & 3 Geo. VI, c.62. The 1939 Act was amended on 22nd May 1940 by the Emergency Powers (Defence) Act 1940 (3 & 4 Geo. VI, c.20) and was further amended on 1st August 1940 by the Emergency Powers (Defence) (No. 2) Act 1940 (3 & 4 Geo. VI, c.45).
18. Every Order in Council making Defence Regulations had to be laid before Parliament and was subject to annulment by either House within 28 days.

as in 1914 and up to the end of 1916, by the exercise of the Royal Prerogative.[19]

On 25th August 1939 the Government published the Defence (General) Regulations[20] and, in relation to shipping, the most important were Regulations 43 to 52,[21] which were grouped in Part III were under the head of "Ships and Aircraft" and Regulations 53 and 54 in Part IV which dealt (*inter alia*) with the requisition and acquisition of shipping. However neither the Defence Act nor the Defence Regulations contained any provision for assessing compensation in respect of the exercise of powers of requisition or acquisition and this lacuna was filled by the Compensation (Defence) Act 1939[22] which, as regards shipping, laid down the formulae to be used for calculating the compensation to be paid for the requisitioning of ships or the taking of space or accommodation in ships and provided that, in default of agreement,[23] claims for compensation were to be determined by a Shipping Claims Tribunal.

Three other measures relevant to shipping were also rushed through Parliament on 1st September 1939 and the first of these was the Import, Export and Customs Powers (Defence) Act 1939[24] which conferred a general power on the Board of Trade to control imports and exports of any goods, including the carriage coastwise or shipment of ships' stores. The next statute, the Ships and Aircraft (Transfer Restrictions) Act 1939,[25] applied to all British ships except those registered in a Dominion or India or Burma; Section 1 provided that, except with the consent of the Board of Trade, it should be unlawful to transfer or mortgage any ship or any share therein and Section 2 imposed restrictions on the transfer of a ship's port of registry—the object being to prevent the weakening of the national effort by transferences of ships from the British Registry.[26] Lastly there was the Ministers of the Crown (Emergency Appointments) Act 1939[27] which was designed to facilitate the creation

19. It is not clear why in 1939 the Government decided that requisitioning of ships should not be effected, as it had been in 1914, by Order in Council under the Royal Prerogative. Possibly there were doubts as to the Crown's right to requisition outside territorial waters and it was therefore thought safer to rely on statutory powers. Section 3 of the Act expressly authorised the requisitioning of British ships (other than Dominion, Indian or Southern Rhodesian ships) wherever they might be.

20. S.R. & O. 1939 No. 927.

21. During the course of the war a large number of additional Regulations concerning shipping were inserted in various places between the original Regulations 43 and 52.

22. 2 & 3 Geo. VI, c.75 which, with seventeen other statutes, passed through Parliament and received the Royal Assent on 1st September 1939.

23. Rates of hire in respect of requisitioned vessels were eventually agreed between the Government and shipowners' representatives—see Cmd. 6218, pp. 145 *et seq. infra.*

24. 2 & 3 Geo. VI, c.69.

25. 2 & 3 Geo. VI, c.70. Although the Act provided that it was to continue until the date "declared to be the end of the emergency for the purposes of the Act" no such declaration was ever made and in the event the Act continued in force until the end of 1974.

26. P. Debs. 5 Ser, Vol.351, c.176. The President of the Board of Trade acknowledged that under the Act permission was required for the transfer from one British owner to another but gave an assurance that there was no intention to use this power to prevent ordinary legitimate transactions between *bona fide* owners.

27. 2 & 3 Geo. VI, c.77.

of new wartime Ministers; at the outset of war Govenment responsibility for merchant shipping was still vested in the Mercantile Marine Department of the Board of Trade but on 13th October 1939 a Ministry of Shipping was set up by Order in Council[28] and on 19th October 1939 a further Order in Council[29] transferred to the Minister of Shipping all the functions of the Board of Trade with reference to shipping.

Government shipping policy at the commencement of the Second World War was markedly different from what it had been in 1914. In the case of the Great War the policy of general requisitioning of British ships was not introduced until the war had been running for two and a half years and it took one and a half years of war before there was even a general licensing control.[30] In 1939 the Government was resolved that, as far as possible, it should learn and profit from the mistakes of the past and, although there were some initial errors of judgement, in general the control of shipping in the Second World War was significantly more successful and equitable than it had been in the Great War; one reason for this was that in its pre-war planning the Government had ensured that, when war came, it would have far wider statutory powers of control over shipping operations and trading than it had possessed in 1914.

With a view to securing that British ships were only used in such manner as the competent authority[31] considered expedient in the interests of the defence of the realm, Defence Regulation 46 (Control of Trade by Sea) empowered the competent authority to order that a British ship should not proceed to sea[32] except under the authority of a licence which might be granted subject to limitations and conditions with respect to the trades in which a ship might be engaged and the voyages which might be undertaken, the class of cargoes or passengers which might be carried, the hiring of the ship and the terms on which cargoes or passengers might be carried. In addition orders might be given directing the U.K. port (or the place in that port) to which a ship was to go or for determining the class of goods or passengers to be put on board or taken off at such port.

Under Defence Regulation 53 (Requisition of Ships) the competent authority was empowered to requisition a vessel or anything on board a vessel in the United Kingdom or to requisition a British ship[33] or anything on board a

28. The Ministers of the Crown (Minister of Shipping) Order 1939 (S.R. & O. 1939 No. 1425).

29. The Ministry of Shipping (Transfer of Functions) Order 1939 (S.R. & O. 1939 No. 1480).

30. See pp. 96–97 *supra*.

31. At the outbreak of war the "competent authority" for shipping under the Defence Regulations was the Board of Trade. After the creation of the Ministry of Shipping in October 1939, the Minister of Shipping became the competent authority (by virtue of S.R. & O. 1939 No. 1500) and when the Ministry of Shipping was merged in the Ministry of War Transport in May 1941, the Minister of War Transport became the competent authority (S.R. & O. 1942 No. 381).

32. The control also extended to the coastal trade.

33. Other than a British ship registered in any Dominion or in India or Southern Rhodesia.

British ship[33] wherever the ship might be. The competent authority could use a requisitioned ship in such manner as it thought expedient "in the interests of public safety, the defence of the realm or the efficient prosecution of the war or for maintaining supplies or services essential to the life of the community". The authority also had power to hold, sell or otherwise dispose of the ship as if it were the owner and as if the ship were free from any mortgage and in addition the authority could acquire a requisitioned ship.[34] Under Regulation 54 (Special Powers as to Ships and Aircraft) the competent authority had power to require any space or accommodation in a British ship[33] to be placed at its disposal and, if a ship was under charter to a British subject or company, the authority could by notice assume the rights and liabilities of the charterers under such charter.

The experience of the Great War had clearly demonstrated the inadequacy of partial control but nevertheless in September 1939, influenced by the over optimistic Board of Trade prediction with regard to the importing capacity of British shipping under wartime conditions, the Government decided that no general requisitioning of ships was needed. It was considered that the country's military and civil shipping needs could be met by selective requisitioning on a relatively small scale to meet the requirements of the armed forces and by a partial control of shipping through a negative licensing system which it was believed could ensure that shipping was available for essential imports and that freights could be controlled to avoid any inequality of sacrifice.

The Ship Licensing System was established as from 9th September 1939 by the Control of Trade by Sea Order[35] made by the Board of Trade under Defence Regulation 46 but, following the establishment of the Ministry of Shipping in October 1939, the original Order was revoked and replaced on 23rd November 1939 by a Ministry of Shipping Control of Trade by Sea (No. 2) Order 1939.[36] The No. 2 Order (as amended) provided that no British ship[37] was to proceed on any overseas voyage or any short sea voyage or any coasting voyage[38] except under the authority of a licence granted by the Minister of Shipping (or any person authorised by him) and such licence could be made subject to any of the conditions or limitations referred to in Regulation 46.[39] The flaw in the Ship Licensing system was that it only gave the Government a negative power of

34. In the event it was only in comparatively few cases that the Government exercised this power of compulsory purchase of British ships.

35. S.R. & O. 1939 No. 1090.

36. S.R. & O. 1939 No. 1671.

37. "British ship" meant any British ship registered in the United Kingdom, Channel Islands or Isle of Man having a gross tonnage of 100 tons or more but not fishing boats or any Government ship.

38. A coasting voyage was a voyage made wholly between ports in the U.K., Channel Islands and Isle of Man. A short sea voyage was a voyage between U.K. ports and ports on the Continental coast between St. Jean de Luz and Norvik including the Baltic. An overseas voyage was any voyage not a short sea voyage or a coasting voyage.

39. See. p. 141 *supra*.

control; the Licensing Authority could refuse permission for any particular voyage but this power of veto, apart from keeping tramp owners in a continual state of uncertainty, failed to ensure that tonnage could be promptly directed into the dangerous and less financially attractive trades involving war priority cargoes such as wheat and ore.[40] Furthermore, although the negative control over freights prevented profiteering,[41] it did result in serious inequalities between different owners.[42]

The inadequacies of the licensing system and the need for a positive control of shipping were emphasised in an adjournment debate on the Ministry of Shipping on 14th November 1939[43]; there were strong criticisms of the low level of the controlled freights paid to British owners as compared with the high rates paid to neutral foreign competitors and it was argued that British owners must be allowed sufficient profit to enable them to build up reserves for replacement. Immediately after this debate the Ministry of Shipping completed a Report on the shipping situation in the light of the actual circumstances then prevailing[44]; this re-examination provided a salutary correction to the over-optimistic pre-war appreciation and formed a more realistic appraisal of the importing capacity of the British merchant fleet and the extent to which assistance from neutral tonnage was likely to be available. In addition the Ministry was moving towards the view that the licensing system, except in relation to the coastal and short sea trades, was failing to meet the wartime needs and that to enlist the full capacity of the merchant navy in the war effort demanded a positive control through general requisitioning of all deep-sea tonnage.

On 4th January 1940 the Ministry of Shipping announced that, as from 1st January 1940, the Government had decided to introduce a policy of general requisition of deep-sea liners and to extend and ultimately apply generally the policy of requisitioning deep-sea tramps. All deep-sea liners, upon completing their discharge in the United Kingdom after 31st January 1940, automatically came under the Liner Requisition Scheme which was substantially the same as the scheme introduced in the latter part of the Great War.[45] The requisitioning of tramps was a more gradual process but by 18th March 1940 the Minister was able to confirm that "before long substantially the whole of our tramp tonnage will be operating under requisition apart from tonnage in the coastal and short sea trades".[46] All coastal and short sea trade vessels continued, free

40. As a result the Government had to requisition ships to import ore and grain.

41. The original controlled rates were so low in relation to rapidly rising operating costs that in November 1939 they were increased by 30 per cent.

42. P. Debs. 5 Ser., Vol. 351, c.607.

43. *Ibid.*

44. Ministry of Shipping Memorandum of 15th November 1939—Public Record Office File WP(G)(39) 89–GAB 67.

45. See p. 97 and fn. 17 *supra.*

46. P. Debs. 5 Ser., Vol. 358, c.1685.

from requisition, to operate under the licensing system until October 1940 when the general requisitioning of all coastal and short sea liners was introduced. On the other hand coasting and short sea tramps remained generally free from requisition[47] throughout the whole period of the war but they were, of course, always subject to the licensing system and rigidly controlled freights. Throughout 1940 tanker operations continued to be controlled only by the voyage licensing system but at the end of that year the Ministry decided that it must have the same power of positive control over tankers as it had over dry cargo ships and accordingly, as from 1st January 1941, all British ocean-going tankers were brought under general requisition.

Although the War Cabinet had approved the general requisitioning policy, they remained reluctant to accept the Ministry of Shipping's view that the shortage of shipping called for drastic cuts in the import programme. Accordingly, in December 1939, the Lord Privy Seal was requested to make an independent assessment of the shipping situation and his Report of 23rd January 1940[48] expressed full agreement with the Ministry's judgement as to the importing capacity of the available British and neutral tonnage in the first year of war and emphasised that shipping difficulties in the second year of the war were likely to be greater than in the first. The War Cabinet then accepted the necessity for a reduction of imports below the level fixed by reference to the over optimistic Board of Trade pre-war forecast.

Although, since the beginning of the war, requisitioning of ships had been continuing on an ever increasing scale, some eight months were to elapse before the Minister of Shipping and the shipowners' representatives were at last able to reach agreement on the rates of hire which were to be paid for requisitioned vessels in accordance with the formula laid down in Section 4 of the Compensation (Defence) Act 1939. Even before the commencement of the war there had been discussions between the Board of Trade and shipowners' representatives and, after the outbreak of war, the shipowners appointed a Co-ordinating Committee which concluded that the requisition hire should cover operating costs plus a percentage based on the first cost of each vessel to cover normal depreciation, a moderate return on capital and some small margin as a reserve towards the increased cost of replacement. Negotiations between the shipowners and the Government reopened at the end of 1939 but it was not until 30th April 1940 that the Minister of Shipping was able to announce in the House that rates of hire for liners and tramps had been agreed and to give brief particulars.[49]

47. Except for a considerable number of vessels specifically requisitioned by the Services and a limited number requisitioned for delivery of coal to the South Coast.

48. "The extent to which shipping considerations call for a review of our import programme" Public Record Office WP(40) 64—in WP(40) 21–WP(40) 70, Vol. V, p. 231.

49. P. Debs. 5 Ser., Vol. 360, c.518.

In August 1940 the Ministry published a White Paper[50] which, after making some general comments on the course of the negotiations, set out in detail the agreed charterparty conditions and rates of hire for requisitioned vessels. Although the Government had devised a Tonnage Replacement Scheme[51] "designed to go some way towards enabling ships lost by war risks to be replaced", the shipowners had argued strongly that the requisition rates of hire should be fixed at a level which would enable adequate sums to be put to reserve for replacing ships lost by marine risks and for building new ships to replace those which during the war would become obsolete by reason of age and the additional "wear and tear" resulting from operations under wartime conditions. The Government, however, took the view that the rates of hire should be based only upon "a proper allowance for running expenses, a proper provision for current depreciation and a reasonable return upon capital" and could not agree that it would be proper to include any allowance towards building up provision for replacement in the future.[52] The White Paper did then go on to refer to the financial assistance to shipping which, but for the outbreak of war, it had been intended to give under the abortive British Shipping (Assistance) Bill 1939 and stated that "the necessity of maintaining the British Mercantile Marine in adequate strength and in a position of full competitive efficiency is recognised by His Majesty's Government to-day. They will therefore keep this question constantly in mind as one which it will be necessary to ask Parliament to deal with in due course."[53]

There were four standard forms of requisition charters; these comprised a general dry cargo charter for vessels carrying military stores and commercial cargoes for the Government, a general tanker charter governing the carriage of oil and petroleum on Government account, a passenger ship time charter for vessels employed as troop transports or hospital ships and a demise charter governing the requisition of vessels for service as armed merchant cruisers or for other naval commissioned service involving non-commercial use. Except for the demise charter,[54] the owners were responsible for finding, paying and victualling the crew, providing stores, maintaining the ship in an efficient state and insuring against marine risks whilst the requisitioning authority was required to pay for fuel, dues and war risks insurance and to redeliver the ship at the end of the charter period[55] in the same good order as when delivered, fair wear and tear and depreciation excepted.

50. "Memorandum on the War-Time Financial Arrangements between the Government and British Shipowners", Cmd. 6218, Parl. Papers 1939–40, Vol. 7.

51. Details were given in Cmd. 6218—see further p. 148 *infra*.

52. The Government's decision on this point was a continual source of grievance to British shipowners.

53. Throughout the war, and afterwards, the Government were to be constantly reminded of this declaration of future support for the British mercantile marine.

54. Under which the ship was wholly under the control of and operated by the requisitioning authority who was responsible for all operating costs and other outgoings.

55. Unless otherwise agreed, the charter period was not to extend beyond the expiration of six months from the cessation of hostilities.

The rates of time charter hire were founded on the principle of a "basic rate" covering average operating expenses with the addition of an allowance of five per cent for depreciation (six per cent for tankers) and five per cent for interest on capital, calculated in the case of liners on the actual first cost of the ship and in the case of tramps and tankers on an agreed average value for each class of tonnage. Increases in the basic rates were agreed from time to time during the war to cover increases in owners' operating expenses resulting from wartime conditions but the basic rate did not at any time do more than cover outgoings and contained no element of profit. The President of the Chamber of Shipping subsequently stated[56] that the acceptance of these rates "was in fact only finalised as a mark of patriotic action, shipowners agreeing to hand over their vessels for the benefit of their country without either securing the all-important principle of being adequately paid or receiving a satisfactory allowance for depreciation to enable them to renew their fleets after the war".

So much for British tonnage—but it was also necessary that the Government should "secure the control, by charter or otherwise, of all the free neutral shipping we can obtain".[57] However the Government's early efforts to time-charter neutral shipping were, in the early months of the war, highly unsuccessful; the freight market levels for free neutral ships had risen rapidly and the Government were unwilling to pay rates far in excess of those being paid to British owners. Eventually the Government was forced to accept that neutral tonnage would only be obtainable if the terms offered were sufficiently attractive but negotiations were inevitably protracted and by the end of March 1940 only about 400,000 tons of foreign tonnage had been brought under British control.[58] The German occupation of Denmark and Norway in April 1940, and the subsequent over-running of the Low Countries and France and the invasion of Greece transformed the neutral shipping situation. France and Denmark could be treated as technical enemies whilst the great shipowning countries of Norway, Holland, Belgium and, subsequently, Greece became allies.

On 20th August 1940 the Prime Minister was able to tell the Commons[59] that "the merchant tonnage under the British flag . . . is larger than when we began" and that "we have in addition under our control at least 4 million tons of shipping from the captive countries".[60] The extent to which the newly Allied merchant fleets, especially those of Norway and Holland, should come under British control was the subject of lengthy negotiations[61] but eventually agreement was reached whereby a proportion of the Norwegian and Dutch ships

56. Chamber of Shipping Annual Report 1940–41.

57. W. S. Churchill, *The Second World War* (London, 1948–52), Vol. I, p. 423.

58. *Merchant Shipping and the Demands of War*, *op. cit.*, Appendix VIII.

59. P. Debs. 5 Ser., Vol. 364, c.1164.

60. See *Merchant Shipping and the Demands of War*, Appendix VIII; *Statistical Digest of the War*, Table 115 and *Oil*, *op. cit.*, pp. 128–129.

61. See *Merchant Shipping and the Demands of War*, *op. cit.*, pp. 91–103.

were allowed to trade free (and earn very high freights) whilst the remainder, and greater part, were chartered to the British at rates substantially higher than those paid to British owners. On the other hand the French and Danish ships were transferred to British flag and treated the same as other British ships.

From the outset of war all shipbuilding and ship repairs were under complete Government control; the Restriction of the Repair of Ships Order 1939[62] provided that, except with the authority of a Board of Trade licence, no ships were to be repaired, altered or drydocked in the United Kingdom otherwise than to the order of any Government department and the Restriction of Construction of Ships Order 1939[63] provided that, except under the authority of a Board of Trade licence, no persons should construct or cause or permit to be constructed in the United Kingdom any ship otherwise than to the order of any Government department. On 19th October 1939 the new Ministry of Shipping took over responsibility for shipbuilding and ship repairs from the Board of Trade[64] but, since the Admiralty remained responsible for naval construction, it was shortly afterwards decided that the Admiralty should take charge of merchant shipbuilding and repairs so that one department only should decide on the allocations between naval and merchant shipbuilding and repairs. Accordingly, as from 1st February 1940, responsibility for merchant shipbuilding and repairs was transferred to the Admiralty[65] who continued to control the building and repair of all ships in the United Kingdom throughout the war.

At the outbreak of war the shipbuilding industry had substantial orders in hand for British owners[66] but, although the Government allowed most of these orders to be completed, thereafter private shipbuilding orders practically ceased. The Government itself placed orders for a large number of merchant ships and also increased the programme of naval construction[67] but the shipbuilding situation was severely criticised in Commons debates on 14th November 1939 and 18th March 1940[68]; doubts were raised as to the adequacy of shipyard capacity and the supply of skilled labour but the Government

62. S.R. & O. 1939 No. 1086 made on 4th September 1939 by the Board of Trade under Defence Regulation 55 which gave the Government wide powers of control over industry generally.

63. S.R. & O. 1939 No. 1087 made on 4th September 1939.

64. By virtue of the Ministry of Shipping (Transfer of Functions) Order 1939 (S.R. & O. 1939 No. 1480).

65. S.R. & O.'s 1939 Nos. 1086 and 1087 were revoked on 31st January 1940. On the same day the Admiralty made a new Restriction of Repairs of Ships Order 1940 (S.R. & O. 1940 No. 142) and a new Restriction of Construction of Ships Order 1940 (S.R. & O. 1940 No. 143).

66. About 150 tramps and 25 cargo liners were laid down in the first six months of 1939—largely as a result of the financial stimulus given by the Government in March 1939—see pp. 134 *et seq. supra*.

67. Provision had to be made for a far larger number of smaller naval vessels than had been envisaged in the pre-war planning. As a result there was a sacrifice of some merchant shipbuilding capacity and a slowing down of the programme for major naval ships.

68. P. Debs. 5 Ser., Vol. 353, c.607 and Vol. 358, c.1659.

spokesman, whilst conceding that there was a shortage of skilled labour, rightly contended that yard capacity was not a restrictive factor and went so far as to say that it was hoped to achieve a rate of production of merchant ships "far in advance of the rate of sinkings to be expected from the enemy".[69]

Although the Government still rejected the shipowners' argument that the rate of requisition hire should be increased to provide for the cost of post-war replacement, the Government, as a gesture towards the replacement of ships lost by war risks, evolved a Tonnage Replacement Scheme of which details were published in August 1940.[70] For war risks insurance purposes the value of a ship was divided into two parts—"a basic value" representing the ship's pre-war value less normal depreciation and an increased value "being the increase in insurance value since the outbreak of war[71]; in the event of a ship being lost by war risks[72] only the basic value would then be paid to the owner whilst the increased value would be retained by the Ministry of Shipping in an interest bearing account. The retained increased value money would then only be paid out as and when the owners were prepared to use such money, in conjunction with the corresponding basic value amount, for the purpose of replacement tonnage.[73] Shipowners regarded the scheme as wholly inadequate and continued to urge the Government "to find some means of setting aside during the war the money required for the rehabilitation of British shipping after the war".[74]

From 1941 until the ending of hostilities substantially the whole of the British mercantile marine,[75] both dry cargo and tankers, was under full requisition by the Government and, in addition, a significant amount of Allied tonnage was under British Government control.[76] However, although the Government had complete control over the movements of, and cargoes carried by, the British and Allied merchant fleet, for the most part the day-to-day operating and maintenance of the vessels remained the responsibility of a

69. A surprisingly optimistic statement made by the Parliamentary Secretary to the Admiralty on 18th March 1940—but at the time losses from enemy action were unexpectedly low.

70. Cmd. 6218. The Scheme was embodied in a Government Tonnage Replacement Account Agreement (Appendix 2 of Cmd. 6218) and in a series of Agreements between the Ministry of Shipping and the War Risks Associations (Parl. Papers 1939–40(148)—(173), Vol. 10 modifying the Agreements made in September 1939.

71. In the case of a vessel first acquired after September 1939, its basic value was its first cost and its increased value would be the increase in value since the date of acquisition.

72. Or by marine risks if the Government was responsible for any total loss as under the terms of a demise charter.

73. The owners lost their right to the increased value if the replacement tonnage was not ordered within seven years from the end of the war.

74. Chamber of Shipping Annual Report 1941–42, pp. 69–71.

75. Excepting coasting and short sea tramps.

76. In June 1944 tonnage belonging to U.K. and colonial owners and controlled by the Government amounted to 11,873,000 gross tons, foreign tonnage demise and time chartered to the Government amounted to 5.823 million gross tons and 608,000 gross tons of foreign tonnage was under requisition by the Government, ("Statistical Digest of the War", Table 152).

large number of shipowners whose activities in this connection were much circumscribed by the multifarious shipping controls and restrictions imposed by the original 1939 Defence Regulations and the numerous amendments and additions made to them throughout the war years. Apart from Regulation 19, which gave power to stop a ship leaving a U.K. port, and Regulations 53 and 54 containing the requisitioning powers, most of the provisions relating to shipping and seamen were eventually contained between Regulations 43 and 47D but in addition shipowners were subject to numerous statutory orders made under the authority of the Defence Regulations which covered a wide diversity of shipping matters and there were also some Orders in Council made under the Royal Prerogative for the purpose of enforcing the economic blockade of the enemy countries.

Apart from the difficulties of conforming to this formidable code of controls and restrictions and the strain of operating under wartime conditions, shipowners were continually worried about the problem of replacing the ever increasing numbers of their ships lost by enemy action. Since the outbreak of war nearly all the orders for the building of new merchant ships had been for Government account and owners viewed with some misgivings the growth of the Government owned merchant fleet and the decline of their own tonnage. So, following their less than enthusiastic acceptance of the Government's Tonnage Replacement Scheme, the shipowners contended that, since they were compelled to allow the Government to retain a significant part of the insurance monies resulting from their war risk losses, they should be allowed during the war to purchase the new ships which had been, and were still being, built for Government ownership instead of waiting until after the war, when prices would be far higher, to replace their lost tonnage.

For some time the Government rejected the shipowners' request but eventually, in March 1941, the Minister of Shipping stated that "the general question of the disposal of ships already built and building to the order of the Ministry is under urgent consideration"[77]; nevertheless more than a year elapsed before, in May 1942, the Ministry of War Transport[78] published a Memorandum[79] of the Scheme under which British shipowners who had lost tonnage since the outbreak of war through marine or war risks might enter into an agreement with the Ministry of War Transport to purchase new tonnage built or to be built during the war on Government account. The actual transfer of the vessels to private ownership was to be deferred until after the war[80] but each

77. P. Debs. 5 Ser., Vol. 370, c.447.

78. By an Order in Council made on 9th May 1941, The Ministers of the Crown (Minister of War Transport) Order 1941 (S.R. & O. 1941 No. 654), a Ministry of War Transport was established and all the functions of both the Ministry of Shipping and the Ministry of Transport were transferred to the new Ministry.

79. Cmd. 6357, Parl. Papers 1941–42, Vol. 5.

80. The vessel was to be delivered to the new owner after discharge of cargo on the voyage current at the date of cessation of hostilities.

eligible owner wishing to buy could enter into a contract of sale and purchase with the Government and the owner to whom a vessel was allotted would then be appointed manager of such vessel. The price of any vessel sold, in payment of which monies standing to the credit of the Government Tonnage Replacement Account might be used, was to be the cost of construction less normal depreciation from the date of delivery by the builder to the Government until the post-war date of delivery by the Government to the purchaser.

The scheme provided for vessels to be allocated to owners in chronological order of loss[81] but the amount of tonnage to be made available to British owners was dependent on the arrangements made with Allied governments for enabling them similarly to replace a proportion of the tonnage which they had lost in the war effort. In July 1942 the Government published a further Memorandum[82] giving details of the arrangements whereby Allied governments who had made vessels available to the Ministry of War Transport would be offered the opportunity of partially replacing lost tonnage by purchasing a proportion of the new vessels built for the Government and of the second-hand vessels purchased by the Government from foreign flags. The terms of the Allied government Scheme differed in certain respects from the parallel British Scheme[83] and in fixing the amount of tonnage for sale to Allied governments regard was to be had to the proportion which losses of Allied tonnage bore to losses of British tonnage. By the summer of 1942 the first allocation to British owners, covering ships delivered to the Government up to 30th September 1941, had been completed and deliveries for the remainder of 1941 were allocated to Allied governments; thereafter allocations were made to both British owners and Allied governments in respect of ships delivered to the British Government in 1942 and subsequently.[84]

Owing mainly to the shortage of shipbuilding labour and materials,[85] the 1940 output of merchant ships had been disappointing[86] but over the next three years a continuing improvement in the labour supply, the diversion of more materials to the shipyards and minor modifications in the naval building programme all combined to increase the output of merchant ships for 1941, 1942 and 1943 to a level approximating to that of the pre-war target figure of 1.2 million gross tons per annum.[87] However, in spite of this welcome

81. Further details governing the basis of allocation were set out in the Appendix to Cmd. 6357.

82. Cmd. 6373, Parl. Papers 1941–42, Vol. 5.

83. For example an Allied government could call for a vessel to be transferred to its own flag if a complete crew of its own nationality was available to man it.

84. By March 1943 61 Government ships had been allocated to British owners (P. Debs. 5 Ser., Vol. 387, c.676).

85. P. Debs. 5 Ser., Vol. 367, c.1054.

86. 810,000 gross tons as compared with just over 1 million gross tons in 1938 (*Statistical Digest of the War*, Table 113).

87. The output of merchant ships from U.K. yards was: 1941–1.156 million g.t.; 1942–1.301 million g.t. and 1943–1.204 million g.t. (*Statistical Digest of the War*, Table 113).

improvement in annual output, British merchant ship losses in 1940, 1941 and 1942 were, largely as a result of the U boat campaign, on such a vast and increasing scale[88] that the improved deliveries from the U.K. yards still fell far short of adequate replacement.

Although the Government were only too well aware that "shipping was at once the strong hold and sole foundation of our war strategy",[89] for a variety of reasons it did not prove possible to achieve any appreciable increase in the annual rate of output of merchant ships. A large amount of labour and materials had to be diverted from shipbuilding to the vital task of repairing damaged ships and converting existing ships for war service and conditions; as a result the numbers employed in the repair and conversion work were generally at least half as many again as those engaged in building new ships[90] and, since the facilities in the repair establishments proved inadequate, much repair work had to be carried out in shipbuilding yards which inevitably delayed both the naval and merchant new-building programme. In addition, at the outbreak of war, many shipbuilding yards and marine engineering works were old fashioned, ill equipped and generally suffering from inadequate capital expenditure; it was not until 1942 that some modernisation schemes were carried out and the benefits were not experienced until late in 1943.

Between 1939 and 1945 the merchant shipbuilding programme was never sacrificed, as it had been between 1914 and 1916, to the demands for more naval vessels but in 1942 the scale of losses from enemy action necessitated the building of more escort vessels and in the following year it was decided to reduce merchant shipbuilding in the U.K. and concentrate more on the building of the specialised naval and combat vessels needed for the invasion of Europe.[91] However, in spite of all the difficulties, the performance of British shipyards in the Second World War was better than it had been in the Great War; on 1st November 1944[92] the First Lord of the Admiralty stated that, although there had been fewer shipyards and fewer shipyard workers than in the Great War, the output of both naval vessels and merchant ships had been greater.[93]

88. The losses (from all causes but mainly war risks) were 1940–2.725 million g.t.; 1941–3,047 million g.t. and 1942–3,695 million g.t. (Cmd. 6564, Parl. Papers 1943–44, Vol. 8).

89. *Second World War*, *op. cit.*, Vol. IV, p. 176.

90. For the detailed figures see *Factories and Plant*, *op. cit.*, p. 44.

91. See letter from Roosevelt to Churchill of 7th June 1943 (P. Debs. 5 Ser., Vol.391, c.2088). As a result the U.K. output of new merchant ships fell to 1.014 million g.t. in 1944 and to only 894,000 g.t. in 1945.

92. P. Debs. 5 Ser., Vol.404, c.815.

93. For the first four years of the Second World War naval building had amounted to 1.685 million tons compared with 1.596 million tons in the first four years of the Great War and merchant shipbuilding for the period 1940–43 totalled 4,415,668 tons compared with 3.770 million tons for the period 1915–18.

The Allied shipping and shipbuilding situation was significantly changed for the better as a result of the United States entering the war following the Japanese attack on Pearl Harbour in December 1941. At a meeting in Washington the Prime Minister and the President agreed[94] that Combined Shipping Adjustment Boards should be established in Washington and London and that the United States should commence a vast expansion of its merchant shipbuilding programme with a view to meeting the merchant shipping needs of both countries.[95] The Combined Shipping Adjustment Boards inevitably suffered from initial teething problems and it was not until 1943 that the Anglo-American shipping collaboration really achieved success[96]; the turning point came in June 1943 when the President agreed that 15 to 20 new ships per month should, for the following 10 months, be transferred to the British flag for temporary wartime duty and from then onwards the increase in the supply of new ships and the diminution in the scale of losses from enemy action brought about a steady improvement in the Allied shipping position.

In August 1944, following the liberation of much of France and Belgium, the Government published the text of an International Agreement on the Principles having reference to the Continuance of Co-ordinated Control of Merchant Shipping.[97] The Contracting Parties accepted, as a common responsibility, the provision of shipping for all military and other tasks necessary for, and arising out of, the completion of the war in Europe and the Far East and for the supplying of all the liberated areas as well as the United Nations and territories under their authority. There was to be a central authority,[98] coming into operation upon the general suspension of hostilities with Germany, and the Agreement was to continue until six months after the general suspension of hostilities in Europe or the Far East, whichever was the later, unless unanimously determined earlier.

On 9th May 1945 the war in Europe came to an end and on 15th August 1945 hostilities ended in the Far East; an Admiralty statement, issued in 1947, showed that between 3rd September 1939 and 2nd September 1945 2539 British merchant ships[99] having an aggregate gross tonnage of 11,831,410 had

94. See Cmd. 6332, Parl. Papers 1941–42, Vol. 9.

95. In 1943 deliveries of new American built dry cargo ships amounted to 13.5 million deadweight tons.

96. For details of Anglo-American shipping co-operation see *British War Economy*, *op. cit.*, Chapter XIV, *Merchant Shipping and the Demands of War*, *op. cit.*, Chapters XII to XVII and *Oil*, *op. cit.*, Parts IV and V.

97. Cmd. 6556,, Parl. Papers 1943–44, Vol. 8. The original contracting parties were Belgium, Canada, Greece, Netherlands, Norway, Poland, United Kingdom, United States and the French Committee of National Liberation.

98. This was to comprise a United Maritime Council and a United Maritime Executive Board (U.K., U.S.A., Netherlands and Norway).

99. Vessels registered in the U.K. and the Commonwealth.

been lost through war causes[100]; and in addition 226 vessels totalling 633,000 gross tons had been lost from marine risks.[101] U.K. owners had lost nearly three quarters of the deep sea tramps and about half of the liners and tankers which they had owned at the beginning of the war and, although some of the wartime losses had been made good by replacements during the war, at June 1945 the vessels on the U.K. register (excluding returnable tonnage)[102] amounted to 12.659 million gross tons—more than 5 million gross tons below the June 1939 figure of 17,891,134 gross tons.

It was not only in quantity but, of no less importance, in quality as well that the British mercantile marine had been diminished by the war. Many of the pre-war ships that had survived had been seriously damaged and all were suffering from the strains of wartime operations. There was also the problem of obsolescence and the fact that the majority of the war-built ships were unsuited to peacetime trading in general and to the traditional British trades in particular. Moreover the merchant fleet, as it stood in 1945, was notably lacking in balance; there was a shortage of cargo liners and smaller tramps owing to the fact that very few of these types of vessels had been built during the war.

British tonnage lost in the Second World War was substantially more than it had been in the Great War and, as had been the case between 1914 and 1918, British merchant shipping losses were considerably in excess of the Allied and Neutral losses from enemy action which amounted in total to 9,760,000 gross tons.[103] However, although the world war losses of merchant ships had been around 32 million tons,[104] in June 1946 world tonnage was estimated to be 72.9 million[105] which, largely owing to the huge wartime output of the American shipyards, was 11.5 million tons more than the estimated world tonnage of about 66.4 million tons in September 1939[106]; but the proportions of world tonnage owned by the major maritime powers in 1946 were very different from what they had been in 1939. Owing mainly to the comparatively modest scale of American war losses and the large wartime additions to the American merchant fleet, the American share of the world fleet had risen in 1946 to 56.1 per cent, compared with 14.2 per cent in 1939, whilst the United Kingdom's share had fallen from 27.5 per cent in 1939 to 18.3 per cent in

100. Of this total 245 vessels aggregating 760,000 g.t. were owned and registered in Commonwealth countries. The total also includes 399 war-built vessels of 2.180 million g.t. owned by the Ministry of War Transport.

101. See M. G. Kendall, "Losses of U.K. Merchant Ships in World War II", *Economica*, New Series, Vol. 15 (November 1948), p. 289. Kendall points out that probably half the vessels lost by marine risks would not have been so lost in peace time.

102. Returnable tonnage (mainly ships returnable to other flags or registers) amounted to 3.115 million tons.

103. Chamber of Shipping Annual Report 1945–46, p. 101.

104. The figure includes losses of enemy tonnage estimated at 10 million tons.

105. Chamber of Shipping Annual Report 1946–47, p. 111.

106. Chamber of Shipping Annual Report 1947–48, p. 128.

1946. The fleets of other major maritime countries all showed substantial declines but the United Kingdom's decline, owing to her wartime acquisitions of tonnage, was proportionately less than that of her principal maritime competitors.[107]

The financial experience of British shipowners in the Second World War was very different from what it had been in the Great War; this time, thanks to freights being controlled from the outset, there was no question of prodigious profits being made and, owing to the early introduction of the policy of general requisitioning, all owners received equality of treatment or, as they might have put it, suffered an equality of sacrifice. Although the basic rate was frequently adjusted upwards throughout the war period, the increases did no more than cover the continuing rises in operating costs; the only element of profit was the five per cent return on capital and the further five per cent for depreciation. In June 1945 the Commons Select Committee on National Expenditure reviewed the wartime financial arrangements with British shipowners as outlined in Cmd 6218 and in their Report[108] stated that in general these had proved fair and reasonable and that it did not appear that the earnings of shipping companies had been disproportionate to those of other enterprises engaged on war services.[109]

Shipping, like every other business, had to make its direct tax contribution towards the cost of war; by May 1940 Excess Profits Tax ("EPT") had risen to a rate of 100 per cent where it remained for the rest of the war and by April 1941 the standard rate of income tax reached 10 shillings in the pound where it also stayed for the remainder of the war. The 1939 EPT legislation had been so drafted that by mischance, owing to the depressed state of shipping in most of the relevant pre-war years, the profits standard for most shipping companies would have been unfairly low but this inequity was quickly appreciated and the shipowners' EPT position was alleviated in the Finance Act 1940.[110] Thus wartime shipping profits were taxed no more, and no less, than those of other sectors of industry but shipowners considered that, as the only major industry whose capital assets had sustained such crippling losses from enemy action, they were entitled to ask for special tax alleviation to assist their post-war replacement programme. The Government did not grant shipping any special tax relief but the Income Tax Act 1945[111] did give to shipping, along with other industries, a special initial allowance of 20 per cent of the cost of new

107. For details of the percentage declines see *British Shipping and World Competition*, *op. cit.*, p. 140.

108. Fifth Report from the Select Committee on National Expenditure, Parl. Papers 1944–45 (100), Vol. 3.

109. See also *British Shipping and World Competition*, *op. cit.*, p. 147.

110. 3 & 4 Geo. VI, c.29 (Section 27).

111. 8 & 9 Geo. VI, c.32 (Section 15).

plant and machinery[112] which was to be in addition to the ships' annual wear and tear allowance of six per cent.

During the war period the Government, Parliament and the leaders of the maritime industries naturally concentrated their attention on the vital war contribution of shipping and shipbuilding but it was not forgotten that when peace came it was no less important that there should be a merchant navy adequate in strength and fully efficient. It is noteworthy that, at the height of the war, both Houses of Parliament, on a number of occasions, temporarily turned aside from wartime problems and focused their attention on post-war policies for shipping and shipbuilding; on all sides there was anxiety that the mistakes in policy following the Great War and the neglect of the maritime industries in the inter-war period should not be repeated but the shipowners and the Government critics in Parliament wanted precise details of the Government's post-war reconstruction plans rather than just fair words and promises.

It was generally agreed that there must be vigorous action post-war to get our trade and industry going and that the prosperity of merchant shipping would depend on an expansion of international trade and the elimination of unfair and restrictive practices. The Government were repeatedly asked to state their intentions regarding the post-war size of the merchant navy. The reply, given in July 1943, was that the merchant navy must be at least as large as pre-war but that it was premature to formulate post-war policy in detail[113]; the size would ultimately depend on the volume of international trade and the ability of shipowners to use their initiative in recapturing their traditional trades, seeking out new trades and evolving new and efficient methods of construction and operation. Even in October 1944[114] Lord Leathers, Minister of War Transport, stated in the Lords that the Government thought it "too early to determine in detail what will be necessary to secure the welfare of the shipping industry or the shipbuilding industry which closely depends upon it".

Shipowners were continually reminding the Government of the pledge made in 1940 with regard to the post-war future of the British mercantile marine[115] and it was emphasised that, with shipbuilding costs at least double the pre-war level, it would be difficult, owing to the controlled level of insurance recoveries, the restricted wartime profits and the burden of taxation, to replace lost and obsolescent tonnage and restore the balance of the merchant fleet without Government assistance in some form. There was also concern regarding the future of the Government owned merchant fleet which, at 30th June 1945,

112. This expression included ships. Since the initial allowance was only to be given for new ships acquired on or after 6th April 1944, shipowners were anxious to know if the allowance would be given in respect of Government owned ships which owners had agreed to purchase with post-war delivery. On 26th September 1944 the Chancellor stated that the new allowance would apply to the purchase post-war of Government owned tonnage (P. Debs. 5 Ser., Vol.403, c.36).

113. P. Debs. 5 Ser., Vol. 391, c.305.

114. P. Debs. (HL) 5 Ser., Vol.133, c.358.

115. Cmd. 6218—see p. 145 *supra*.

was of formidable size[116]; there were fears of post-war nationalisation of the shipping industry or that the Government fleet would compete with private shipping and, although the Government had expressed no such intention, in shipping circles it was felt that a future Labour Government might have different ideas.

As regards foreign competition, British owners were primarily worried about American post-war shipping policy; by 1945 the United States was by far the largest shipowning nation but much of their surplus tonnage was regarded as unsuitable for British trades and the Chamber of Shipping urged that it should be scrapped or at least put to reserve.[117] In addition, in order to enable British shipping to re-establish its trading after the war, the Government were asked to ensure that British ships were released from requisition as soon as possible, and in any case no later than Allied shipping, and that Allied and Neutral ships should make a proper contribution to the task of post-war rehabilitation so that British shipping should suffer no disadvantage.

The immediate post-war future of the shipbuilding industry was viewed with less concern; it was thought probable that British yards would be kept fully occupied for some years in replacing lost tonnage, in building the specialised ships omitted from the war construction programme and in reconditioning the war-damaged ships. The Government made it clear that Admiralty control over shipbuilding would continue for some time after the war and it was hoped that a stable shipbuilding programme could be achieved through a new Shipbuilding Committee[118] which would advise the Government on all matters relating to priorities for building as between different types of merchant vessels and on the allocation of shipbuilding facilities between British, Allied and Neutral owners. [119] The Government accepted that a large and efficient industry was necessary both for reasons of national security and as a help for exports but, in order to maintain an industry large enough for defence needs, orders from British owners alone were not enough and the shipbuilders would have to go after foreign orders with competitive prices.[120]

In winding up a debate on shipping and shipbuilding in the Lords on 4th October 1944,[121] Lord Leathers emphasised that it was essential for Britain,

116. 601 vessels aggregating 3.402 million gross tons.

117. Lord Leathers thought it probable that the United States government would sell their specialised ships to U.S. nationals only and would offer their utility Liberty ships to British and other foreign owners.

118. Comprising representatives from the Admiralty, Ministry of War Transport, shipbuilders, shipowners and shipbuilding workers.

119. Statement by the First Lord of the Admiralty on 1st November 1944 (P. Debs. 5 Ser., Vol. 404, c.871).

120. On 24th October 1944 (P. Debs. 5 Ser., Vol. 404, c.30) the President of the Board of Trade stated that guarantees for export of ships were not excluded under the Export Guarantees Act 1939 but that "such guarantees must be given with great discretion at any rate until our own merchant fleet has been fully re-established after the war".

121. P. Debs. (HL) 5 Ser., Vol. 133, c.312.

both in war and peace, to have an efficient merchant navy which must be at least as large as before the war and so much larger as British enterprise could make it in a world from which it was hoped obstacles to freedom of trade would have been removed. The Government was ready to collaborate with other like-minded governments in establishing conditions under which the shipping of the world could be efficiently and economically carried on under conditions of fair competition and Lord Leathers concluded by giving an assurance that "the Government are determined that the British Merchant Navy, ships, officers and men, shall be reconstituted as a large and efficient fleet. We shall see that the industry and those who work in it shall have fair play." However, in spite of the promise given in 1940, the Government made no commitment of financial support to assist in the replacement of tonnage.

Britain's leading naval historian[122] had no doubt about one of the most important conclusions to be drawn from Britain's experience in the Second World War: "No other lesson is as clear as the importance to a maritime power of a large and modern Merchant Navy; and it must have behind it industrial capacity and skilled labour to build new ships and to repair those that have suffered damage. Nor is the existence of reserves of trained seamen to man the merchantmen any less important than the provision of the ships themselves; for in all maritime wars casualties amongst merchant seamen have been extremely heavy. In peace-time, when the economics of seaborne trade are the deciding influences on the design and production of merchant ships, this is too often forgotten but as soon as a war breaks out the old truth once again becomes forcibly clear."

122. Stephen Roskill, *The War at Sea*, Vol. III, Part II, p. 402.

CHAPTER 8

YEARS OF PLENTY—AND THEN THE LEAN YEARS

The beginning of the transition from war to peace was marked in July 1945 by the coming to power of a Labour Government supported by a large Parliamentary majority and it was not long before the new administration announced its post-war policies in relation to a number of matters which were of major concern to shipowners and shipbuilders.

A statement in the Commons by the Lord President of the Council on 19th November 1945[1] dispelled the fear that the new Government might intend to nationalise the shipping industry and on 18th December 1945[2] the First Lord of the Admiralty confirmed that shipbuilding would not be included in the Government's nationalisation proposals. The new Minister of War Transport, Alfred Barnes, announced in the Commons on 18th December 1945[3] that tankers would be released from requisition on completion of voyages after the end of 1945, that dry cargo ships[4] would likewise be released on termination of voyages after 2nd March 1946 but that for a transitional period the released ships would remain subject to licence control; he added that passenger and other ships employed in direct military or naval service would remain under requisition for as long as necessary. Mr Barnes also stated that he proposed to adjust the terms on which the remainder of the Government owned ships[5] would be offered to British owners and on 24th January 1946, in a written answer,[6] he outlined the new scheme under which owners would be invited to tender for the ships available for disposal. However the new Minister was just as reluctant as his predecessor to give any precise indication of what the Government considered the size of the post-war merchant navy should be[7]

1. P. Debs, 5 Ser., Vol. 416, c.35.
2. *Ibid.*, Vol. 416, c.2063.
3. *Ibid.*, Vol. 417, c.1124.
4. Other than those employed in trooping or other direct military or naval service.
5. A proportion of the Government fleet had already been sold, with deferred delivery, to British owners and Allied Governments in accordance with the Scheme set forth in Cmd. 6357 and Cmd. 6373—see pp. 149–150 *supra*.
6. P. Debs. 5 Ser., Vol. 418, c.(90).
7. See P. Debs. 5 Ser., Vol. 418, c.106.

and, again like his predecessor, was silent on the possibility of financial assistance for the replacement of lost tonnage.

The building and repair of ships in the United Kingdom continued to be subject to Admiralty licence control but the Government made clear its commitment to the future well-being of the shipbuilding industry[8] and set up a new Shipbuilding Advisory Committee to advise on all matters affecting the efficiency and stability of the industry. As a result of the restrictions imposed by the Exchange Control Act 1947[9] and the Control of Borrowing Order 1947,[10] for some years after the war it was not possible for British owners to build new ships abroad and likewise, except in an emergency, repairs in foreign yards were also prohibited; this meant that, owing to the surfeit of work in British yards, owners were handicapped by high costs and long delays. The Government also retained its power to restrict the sale of ships abroad[11] and the inability to raise funds by the sale of old ships to foreign buyers made it more difficult for British owners to finance their replacement tonnage.

In 1946, as in 1919, the main problem facing the British shipping industry was the replacement of its lost and obsolescent tonnage. It was clear, in spite of the pledge given in 1940, that no Government grants or loans would be forthcoming and, with the cost of new ships being well above twice their pre-war level, owners were faced with a serious financial burden in view of the fact that requisition hire had only allowed for normal depreciation based on historic cost and the Government Tonnage Replacement Scheme made no allowance for increases in the cost of replacement after the date on which a ship had been lost.[12] Nevertheless, in this transition period, the replacement of tonnage does not appear to have been inhibited by lack of funds; in the main the acquisition of new and second-hand ships were financed in the traditional British manner from the owners' total loss recoveries, depreciation and ploughed back profits without resort to the available outside borrowing.

Most of the orders for new ships were placed by the liner owners since they had only been able to buy second-hand a fraction of the specialised tonnage they needed; the tramp owners, mindful of the disastrous slump of 1920–21, were inclined to hold off in the belief that prices were bound to fall.[13] However British yards were far from lacking business; at the end of 1947 ships under

8. P. Debs. 5 Ser., Vol. 420, c.549.

9. 10 & 11 Geo. VI, c.14—which put on a permanent footing the exchange control system imposed by the Defence (Finance) Regulations 1939.

10. SI 1947 No. 945 made under Section 1 of the Borrowing (Control and Guarantees) Act 1946 (9 & 10 Geo. VI, c.58).

11. Under the Ships and Aircraft (Transfer Restrictions) Act 1939. It was not until 1958 that a general sanction was given for the sale abroad of most types of ships and the Act did not expire until the end of 1974.

12. See "Losses of Merchant Ships in World War II", *loc. cit.* and *British Shipping and World Competition*, *op. cit.*, pp. 148–151.

13. In the event this belief unfortunately proved to be ill-founded.

construction amounted to 2.137 million gross tons and in 1949, with employment in shipbuilding and marine engineering having recovered to near its pre-1914 level,[14] U.K. output rose to 1.354 million gross tons, more than 43 per cent of world output,[15] and for a brief period Britain had recovered her dominant shipbuilding position. Deliveries of new ships to British owners in 1948 and 1949 totalled nearly 1.7 million gross tons and, with the purchases of Government owned ships, some 200 American tramps and a number of ex-enemy ships, by June 1949 the tonnage on the U.K. register stood at 18.1 million gross tons compared with 17.9 million gross tons in 1939.[16]

Although, in terms of quantity, U.K. tonnage was back to its pre-war level, the same could not be said of its character and quality; out of more than 1,000 ships sold by the Government to British owners only very few were deep sea cargo liners and the war-built tramps bought from the Government and from the United States often proved uneconomic and ill-suited to the traditional British peacetime trades. There was also a lack of balance in the age distribution; whereas about one-quarter of liner tonnage and one-fifth of tanker tonnage had been built post-war, only six per cent of deep-sea tramp tonnage had been built between 1946 and 1949 and nearly half of this tramp tonnage was of wartime construction. Nevertheless the Rochdale Committee considered that in none of the major maritime countries, with the exception of the U.S.A., did shipowners appear to have come out of the war in a substantially more favourable position than those in the U.K.[17] and Sturmey asserted that by the end of 1948 the British fleet was relatively as strongly placed as in 1939 and that there was "no prima facie reason why British shipping should not have retained its relative position, at least at the 1939 level".[18] Sadly events were to prove otherwise.

During the course of 1946 nearly all British merchant tonnage, other than passenger ships,[19] was released from requisition but continued for some time to be subject to a system of freight control, licensing and direction. The control system was applied to the various types of ships in different ways[20] and was initially administered by the Ministry of Transport but as from 1st October 1947 responsibility for the allocation of tonnage to the various Government programmes was transferred to the industry itself although the Minister

14. *British Industries and their Organisation* , *op. cit.*, p. 133.
15. Chamber of Shipping Annual Report 1949–50.
16. General Council of British Shipping, *Survey of British Shipping 1960*, Appendix A. World tonnage in 1949 was about 82.6 million g.t. so the U.K. proportion was 21.9 per cent compared with 26.1 per cent in 1939; but excluding the American reserve fleet the U.K. proportion in 1949 was 26.4 per cent.
17. Cmd. 4337, para. 46.
18. *British Shipping and World Competition*, p. 159. D. H. Aldcroft took the same view—see his *British Transport since 1914*, (London, 1975), p. 236.
19. 93 passenger ships of over 2,000 tons were still under requisition in October 1946—P. Debs., Vol. 427, c.600.
20. For details see the Chamber of Shipping's Annual Report 1946–47.

retained his powers of licensing, direction and control of freights.[21] In this transitional control period shipowners had to contend with a number of operational problems. Although the Minister had stated[22] that shipping could return to normal commercial practices, including the arrangement of charters through brokers on the Baltic Exchange, so long as controlled freights and Government bulk buying and monopoly chartering continued there was limited scope for brokers to conduct chartering business in their customary manner and likewise there was no free market for the sale of second-hand tonnage abroad since it was not until the end of 1948 that permission was given for the sale of the oldest ships to foreign buyers. Another post-war problem was the coal shortage which at the beginning of 1947 was so severe that there was a complete ban on exports[23] and owners of coal burning ships had to revert to a policy of double bunkering abroad. There was also concern regarding the slow turnround of ships in U.K. ports and although, at the end of 1947, the Minister appointed a Working Party to examine the causes of delay, it was not until the spring of 1949 that the Chamber of Shipping was able to report some improvement.[24]

Before the end of 1948 the tonnage position had so improved that the Government agreed that, although the power of control would be retained,[25] all British owners would, as from 1st December 1948, be granted general trading licences under which they would be free to engage in any deep-sea or short sea trades at rates of freight depending solely on market conditions.[26] For some months after decontrol rates remained steady but in the latter part of 1949 there was a marked fall and many shipowners, mindful of their disastrous experience in the post-Great War period, feared that, once the strong post-Second World War demand for goods and services had been met, there would again be a serious trade recession and a depressed shipping market. In the event the trading pattern of the inter-war years was not repeated; by 1948 the volume by weight of world seaborne trade had already recovered to its 1938 level and thereafter the total volume (dry cargo and tanker cargo) continued to expand until 1957 without any serious hiatus.[27]

The growth of tanker cargo was both more consistent and greater than the growth of dry cargo. Between 1950 and 1957 total seaborne trade increased

21. Chamber of Shipping Annual Report 1947–48.

22. P. Debs. 5 Ser., Vol. 424. c.75.

23. For the whole of 1947 coal exports were only just over 1 million tons and although by 1949 coal exports had risen to nearly 14 million tons, thereafter they were never higher. This dramatic decline in coal exports was a serious blow to tramp shipping; between 1933 and 1938 the annual average export figure had been more than 40 million tons.

24. Chamber of Shipping Annual Report 1948–49.

25. Under the Control of Trade by Sea (No. 2) Order 1939.

26. In the coasting trade, tramp freight rates for Government cargoes continued to be controlled until June 1952.

27. For detailed figures of world seaborne trade over the years 1937, 1938 and from 1948 to 1958 see the GCBS 1960, Survey Appendix B.

by approximately 76 per cent but, whilst the aggregate growth of tanker cargo over this period was 86.6 per cent, the aggregate growth of dry cargo was only 63.3 per cent. This steady growth in world trade, especially the increasing demand for oil, combined with the artificial stimuli of the Korean War of 1950 and the first closure of the Suez Canal in 1956, all resulted in the years from 1950 and 1957 being generally the most prosperous period for British shipping within living memory although most of the profits came from the dry cargo trades since unfortunately British owners participated only to a very limited extent in the tanker boom and were even said to have "a distaste for tankers which they scarcely regarded as ships at all".[28] Nevertheless, in money terms and by comparison with the inter-war period, the decade following the de-requisition was one of plenty for British shipping but, in terms of the ever increasing cost of replacing tonnage and the continuing rise in operating costs, shipping profits and dividends were by no means excessive.[29] The post-war prosperity enjoyed by British shipowners was reflected only to a limited extent by the increase of tonnage on the U.K. register; by mid-1956 U.K. tonnage stood at 18.8 million g.r.t.[30] which represented a growth of less than seven per cent since mid-1949 but over the same period world tonnage had grown by over 28 per cent to 102.7 million g.r.t.[31] so that in seven years the United Kingdom's share of world tonnage had fallen from 21.9 per cent to 18.3 per cent. Moreover, if the small ships of under 500 g.r.t. are excluded, the modest growth in U.K. tonnage was represented entirely by tankers since dry cargo tonnage of over 500 g.r.t. was not only well below its pre-war level but was even slightly less than it had been at the end of 1949.[32] This insignificant post-war growth of the U.K. merchant fleet and the decline in its proportion of world tonnage were not the only causes for concern; in each of the three main sectors of the British deep-sea industry there were other factors which tended to blunt the competitive edge of U.K. shipping in the post-war world.

Although, between 1946 and 1956, more than 4 million tons of new liners had been built in British yards, the design and specifications of the new passenger ships did not make them suitable for the expanding cruise market and insufficient account had been taken of the ever increasing long term impact of air travel.[33] Most of the new cargo liners were of the traditional pre-war type and were ill-suited to the post-war pattern of world trade; in addition the liner

28. Political & Economic Planning (P.E.P.) "The British Shipping Industry", *Planning*, Vol. XXV, No. 437 (November 1959). See also Rochdale Report, para. 67.

29. See *British Shipping and World Competition* Tables 27 and 28 and Rochdale Report, Table 18.3 and para. 1255.

30. Vessels of 100 g.r.t. and over.

31. Vessels of 100 g.r.t. and over including the U.S. Reserve Fleet (estimated at about 14 million tons) but excluding U.S. tonnage on the Great Lakes.

32. For a comparison of the growth of the world's principal merchant fleets see the table in P.E.P.'s "The British Shipping Industry", *loc. cit.*

33. See Rochdale Report, para. 316.

owners tended to cling to their familiar pre-war trades and failed to look for new opportunities.[34]

In the post-war period tramp owners had not only made an incorrect assessment of the future pattern of the freight market but had also been wrong in their belief that the prices of new ships would fall; as a result only a little more than 900,000 g.r.t. of new tramp shipping was built between 1948 and 1956[35] and the new orders placed in the 1950s were at prices far in excess of those prevailing in the immediate post-war years. Moreover the new tonnage ordered comprised in most cases the same general-purpose vessels of around 8,000 to 10,000 deadweight tons which British tramp owners had traditionally used in the inter-war years but the changing pattern of post-war trade, particularly the virtual disappearance of U.K. coal exports and the growing demand for larger and faster ships to carry in quantity both dry and liquid bulk commodities, meant that there was less employment for the traditional tramp.

The one sector of British shipping in which there was substantial absolute growth was tankers; by the end of 1956 U.K. gross tanker tonnage stood at 5.33 million tons—a growth of about 76 per cent since 1939—but relatively the picture was very different since the rate of growth of foreign tanker tonnage was approximately double the British rate. In addition nearly three quarters of the U.K tanker fleet was owned by oil companies[36] and there is little doubt that the disinclination of British shipowners to enter the tanker field resulted in them missing valuable opportunities.[37] The growth of oil imports into the United Kingdom and the shortage of independently owned British tankers, particularly of the larger size, meant that the oil companies were forced to charter foreign tonnage for the carriage of oil to the United Kingdom although they had consistently wished to charter more ships from U.K. independent owners.[38]

The post-war years up to 1959 were also a period of exceptional prosperity for the British shipbuilding industry. By the end of 1949 the tonnage of the British mercantile marine was back to its pre-war level and, since there was also a decline in freight rates, it was feared that there would be a decline in orders for new ships. In the event the outbreak of the war in Korea in June 1950 and the steady increase in world oil consumption resulted in large orders, especially for tankers, being placed by both British and foreign owners; in 1951 new orders for merchant ships in U.K. yards reached the record figure of 4.152 million gross tons and between 1952 and 1958 the British order books for merchant ships[39] at 31st December in each year ranged between a

34. Rochdale Report, para. 64 and D. H. Aldcroft *British Transport since 1914* (London, 1975), p. 250.

35. Rochdale Report, para. 499.

36. *Ibid.*, paras. 556–559.

37. *Ibid.* para. 573.

38. *Ibid.* para. 571.

39. Vessels of 1,000 g.r.t. and over.

high of 6.181 million gross tons in 1952 and a low of 3.947 million tons in 1954.[40]

In spite of this abundance of orders, the output of ships from U.K. yards failed to exceed by very much the level attained in the late 1940s and never achieved the annual output of the five years prior to the Great War. In terms of annual tonnage completed, the output of British yards from 1950 to 1958 remained more or less static between a high of 1.496 million gross tons in 1954 and a low of 1.25 million in 1953; in contrast, world output showed a steady and substantial growth over the same period and as a result the United Kingdom's share of world tonnage output fell from 42.7 per cent in 1950 to 16.2 per cent in 1958 when world output was 9.059 million tons compared with a U.K. output of 1.464 million tons.[41] Far from being attributable to a lack of orders, this rapid decline in the relative importance of the U.K. industry was due to the inability of British yards to expand output[42] in spite of the fact that since the end of the war there had been substantial capital expenditure on improving plant and equipment.[43]

Quite apart from the short-term failure to increase production, the unprecedented size of the order book seems to have engendered an unwarranted degree of complacency on the part of both the shipbuilders and the Government and to have obscured the urgent need for action to ensure that British yards would be able to meet the increasing competitive threat from foreign builders. Following the exceptional volume of new orders placed in 1951, over the next few years there was a serious fall in new orders from foreign owners, many of them hitherto loyal British customers, who felt compelled by commercial considerations to place their orders in yards outside the United Kingdom.

There were several reasons why foreign owners regarded the British yards as having become uncompetitive. In the first place the unwillingness of British builders to offer fixed prices and to quote only on a "cost plus" basis meant that an owner had little idea how much his ship would eventually cost whereas foreign builders, with shorter delivery dates and fewer labour problems, would normally agree to a fixed price—sometimes even without escalation. Of at least equal importance was the lack of short delivery dates and the failure to deliver on time; the large order book combined with low output meant that delivery dates in British yards were far longer than those of their competitors and in addition British builders were beginning to get an unenviable reputation for failing, often by a wide margin, to meet even the far-off delivery dates. In the case of simple types of ships, such as tankers, British prices were higher than those quoted by European and Japanese builders and although, from

40. See Appendix 1 of the Report of the Shipbuilding Inquiry Committee 1965–66 (Geddes Committee), Cmnd 2937, Parl. Papers 1965–66, Vol. 7.
41. Geddes Report, Appendix K.
42. *British Industries and their Organisation*, *op. cit.*, p. 133.
43. See P. Debs. (H. L.) 5 Ser., Vol. 524, cc.2057–2058 and Geddes Report, para. 276.

1953 onwards, there was some improvement in the British credit facilities available to foreign owners, some years were to elapse before U.K. shipbuilding finance became as attractive as that available in Japan and the principal European shipbuilding countries.

During the early 1950s there were also indications that British builders might have difficulty in retaining the monopoly of the home market that they had enjoyed in the post-war period up to 1951.[44] Between 1951 and 1956, during which period British owners were allowed to build in Europe,[45] the bulk of new orders from British owners were still placed with U.K. yards but the need to remain competitive in an international market was beginning to overcome the long-established tradition of building at home.[46] So, for much the same reasons, both foreign and British customers of the U.K. yards began to look elsewhere; for the years 1950–58 the launchings per annum for export by the U.K. yards were on average 31.4 per cent of total launchings but over the next four years the average launchings for export had fallen drastically to only 14.6 per cent of total launchings.[47]

At the end of 1956 British yards still had an order book of around 5.2 million tons but in that year the tonnage launched from Japanese yards was greater than that launched from British yards.[48] It was the first occasion on which the annual U.K. shipbuilding output in peacetime had ever been exceeded by that of another country, and it was only nine years previously that a Government spokesman had proudly stated that the United Kingdom's shipbuilding industry was building more ships than all the rest of the world put together.[49]

During the post-war period up to 1957, whilst British shipping was enjoying generally prosperous trading conditions, both the Government and the shipowners were agreed that there was no need for the granting of any State subsidy to the industry along the lines of the abortive British Shipping (Assistance) Bill 1939 or otherwise. It was common knowledge that a number of Britain's foreign maritime competitors received direct monetary subsidies from their respective governments[50] but at this time British owners felt that foreign subsidies were not seriously affecting them and were far less damaging than other kinds of flag discrimination and the growing threat from the flags of convenience.

44. During this period British owners were not permitted to build abroad.

45. The import of ships from Japan was not permitted until late 1956.

46. In 1955 and again in 1956 British owners had placed orders for 500,000 tons of new ships in foreign yards (Chamber of Shipping Annual Reports 1955–56 and 1956–57). In 1955 the Government rejected opposition requests that the import of foreign ships should be prohibited (P. Debs. 5 Ser., Vol. 544, cc.563 and 1180).

47. Geddes Report, Appendix H.

48. *ibid.*

49. P. Debs. 5 Ser. Vol. 152, c. 360.

50. The United States were by far the worst offenders but financial help to shipping was also given by France, Italy, Spain and Japan—see Rochdale Report, paras. 170–182.

In the field of taxation, however, there was a fundamental divergence of views between the shipping industry and the Government. The shipowners argued that, owing to certain factors which affected shipping but not other industries, the impact of taxation was such that, in the absence of special alleviation, it was impossible to maintain, let alone expand, the British merchant fleet; the problem was the high rate of taxation of profits,[51] the calculation of depreciation by reference to the historic cost of a ship rather than its replacement value[52] and the unprecedented rise in the cost of new tonnage.[53] The industry continually pressed its case for special tax alleviation in direct talks with the Government, in its evidence to the Millard Tucker Committee on the Taxation of Trading Profits[54] and the Royal Commission on the Taxation of Profits and Income[55] and through those who pleaded its cause in Parliament.[56]

The shipowners' main arguments for justifying special treatment was that the losses suffered by the merchant marine in two World Wars were far in excess of those sustained by any other industry, that an adequate and efficient merchant navy was an essential part of our defence and that British shipping made a vital contribution to the balance of payments; it was also pointed out that the increase in the cost of new ships was greater than the increase in other types of capital equipment, that obsolete ships could not be replaced by degrees, that in shipping nearly all its capital was locked up in plant and machinery, that some other traditional maritime countries enjoyed more favourable tax treatment and that ships operating under flags of convenience paid no tax at all.

Eventually the persistent efforts of the shipowners bought a modest reward. By the Finance Act 1954[57] it was provided that for new machinery and plant[58] the initial allowance was to be replaced by an investment allowance at the rate of 20 per cent which would not, as the initial allowance had done, reduce the value on which annual allowances were granted.[59] In the spring of 1956 the

51. In 1949 profits (after depreciation) retained in a business were subject to income tax and profits tax amounting to 51.25 per cent.

52. As from 6th April 1949 depreciation allowances on ships were based on 100 per cent of the cost of the ship and the initial allowance was increased from 20 per cent to 40 per cent—but this did no more than accelerate the depreciation which could be charged.

53. In 1954 the shipbuilding price was more than four times its 1938 level.

54. The Millard Tucker Committee's Report (Cmd. 8189, Parl. Papers 1950–51, Vol. 20) rejected the shipowners' proposals.

55. The Commission did not accept the shipping industry's proposal that depreciation allowances should be based on current replacement values—see Final Report, Cmd. 9474, Parl. Papers 1955–56, Vol. 27.

56. Particularly P. Debs. 5 Ser., Vol. 508, c.2011 and Vol. 524, c.1999—Also P. Debs. (H. L.) 5 Ser., Vol. 169, c.731; Vol. 184, c.1119 and Vol. 194, c.19.

57. 2 & 3 Eliz. II, c.44 s.16 and Schedule 2.

58. This expression included new ships.

59. Thus as from 1954 the total investment and annual allowance amounted to 120 per cent of a new ship's cost.

Chancellor announced that, for industry generally, investment allowances were to be withdrawn but the Finance Act 1956[60] provided that in the case of ships alone they were to be retained. Later in 1956 the Chamber of Shipping pressed for further tax relief and by the Finance Act 1957[61] the investment allowance for new ships was increased to 40 per cent—in the words of the Chancellor "a unique step for a unique industry which is the lifeline of our country".[62]

Notwithstanding the taxation benefit from the granting of investment allowances, British owners felt that they were still far from being in a position of equality with the tax-free flags of convenience tonnage which, in the mid-1950s, was expanding at an alarming rate.[63] It was thus not surprising that some owners should consider the possibility of establishing subsidiary enterprises in British Colonies such as Bermuda or the Bahamas where there was virtually no taxation; moreover ships owned by Bermudan or Bahamian resident shipping subsidiaries of U.K. companies could still fly the British flag and be registered at a U.K. port in just the same way as ships owned by resident U.K. companies.

There was, however, a legal obstacle which deterred all but a handful from venturing on this escape route; Section 468 of the Income Tax Act 1952,[64] which made unlawful certain transactions which might result in the avoidance of liability to U.K. tax, prohibited, save with Treasury consent, the trade or business or any part of the trade or business of a body corporate resident in the United Kingdom being transferred to a person not so resident.[65] Although it was also provided[66] that a mere transfer of assets by a body corporate not resulting in a substantial change in the character or extent of the trade or business of that body corporate should not be treated as a transfer of the trade or business, the Treasury interpreted this proviso so widely that, if a resident shipping company merely transferred one out of several ships it owned to a Bermudan subsidiary, it was regarded as resulting in a substantial change in the character or extent of its trade or business.

A further impediment arose from the Treasury view that there could be a constructive transfer of a trade or business if no physical assets were transferred; thus even if a U.K. liner company set up an overseas subsidiary to operate with new ships on a line never operated by its parent, the Treasury would regard the transaction as involving a transfer of part of the trade or

60. 4 & 5 Eliz. II, c.54, s.15(2).

61. 5 & 6 Eliz. II, c.49, s.15.

62. See Budget speech 1957—P. Debs. 5 Ser., Vol. 568, c.995.

63. The tonnage registered under the flags of Liberia and Panama in December 1959 was almost five times greater than it had been in December 1949—see GCBS 1960 Survey, Appendix H.

64. Subsequently Section 482 of the Income and Corporation Taxes Act 1970 and later Section 765 of the Income and Corporation Taxes Act 1988.

65. Section 468(1)(b). A resident Colonial shipowning company would be a "person not so resident" in the United Kingdom.

66. Section 468(9).

business of the U.K. parent. So the Treasury interpretation of Section 468, and the fact that a breach of the section was a criminal offence carrying heavy penalties, proved a sufficient deterrent to all but the boldest of entrepreneurs; all representations to the Government for the removal of the restrictions went unheeded and even the Rochdale Committee saw "no merit, rather the reverse" in the establishment of overseas subsidiaries by U.K. shipping companies.[67]

By the mid-1950s some British owners, who had hitherto held back, decided that they had no alternative but to replace their obsolete dry cargo tonnage and/or to branch out into tanker operations but their internal resources were by this time quite inadequate to meet the ever increasing cost of new tonnage and, in order to fund the building of new ships in British yards, they had no alternative but to seek finance from some outside source.[68] There was however a difficulty in raising the medium-term loans needed for a shipbuilding contract since the British banks lent too short and the other financial institutions lent too long; foreign owners building in the United Kingdom were usually able to get medium-term finance from British banks largely because they could offer guarantees from the Government's Export Credit Guarantees Department ("ECGD")[69] but British owners were not so well placed.[70]

The Government was not at this time prepared to fill the gap by granting shipbuilding loans along the lines provided for in the British Shipping (Assistance) Bill 1939 but in an adjournment debate on the 22nd January 1957,[71] when concern was expressed as to whether adequate finance would be available over the following 10 years for British shipbuilding programmes, the Government spokesman pointed out that medium-term loans were available from Ship Mortgage Finance Company ("SMFC")[72] but he nevertheless agreed that a gap did exist and undertook that the Government would encourage the institutions to provide medium-term finance for the building of ships for British owners in U.K. yards.

In 1956 the events leading up to the Anglo-French military intervention in Egypt and the subsequent closure of the Suez Canal had a major impact on British shipping and shipbuilding. At the beginning of 1956 the Tramp Freight Guide (1952=100) was standing at 144.3 for voyage charters and 138.0 for time charters; by December 1956 the voyage charter index had reached 189.4 and in January 1957 the time charter index had risen to 216.3.[73] Nearly 80

67. Rochdale Report, para. 1394.

68. Not only independent owners but even the major oil companies were in need of finance to fund their shipbuilding programmes.

69. Although during the 1950s the terms of ECGD-backed loans were not as favourable as the loans available in Japan and some European countries to finance new ships.

70. On the other hand British owners had no difficulty in obtaining loans abroad for the building of ships in foreign countries.

71. P. Debs. 5 Ser., Vol. 563, c.153.

72. SMFC had been formed in 1951, with capital provided by U.K. banks and institutions, to provide loans for ships built in U.K. shipyards.

73. GCBS 1960 Survey, Appendix F.

British ships were requisitioned by the British Government for transport purposes in connection with the Suez military operations—the requisitioning being effected not by means of statutory powers, although these still existed under the Defence Regulations, but by the exercise of the Royal Prerogative.[74] The shortage of tonnage resulting from the Canal closure and the strength of the freight market combined to create a flood of new orders for British shipyards[75] and by the end of 1957 the order book had reached nearly 7.5 million g.r.t. of which considerably more than half was represented by tankers.[76]

The Suez freight boom proved relatively short lived; by April 1957, coinciding with the reopening of the Canal, the Tramp Freight Indices were beginning to slide rapidly and by December 1957 the voyage index was as low as 71.6 and the time charter index even lower at 63.0. During the early months of 1958 the depression in the freight market became even worse and there was a sharp rise in the amount of tonnage laid up for lack of employment; there seemed no hope of any quick return to the years of plenty which had been enjoyed for most of the post-war period and it was all too clear that the lean years had now come with a vengeance[77] and that shipping was confronted with a depression more severe and prolonged than anything experienced since the early 1930s.[78] Once again it was the old story of too many ships chasing too little cargo and with the same inevitable consequences but this depression, unlike that of the 1930s, was caused not so much by any slump in world trade but far more by a world over-ordering of new tonnage inspired by artificial aid, nationalism and mistaken opportunism.[79]

In 1958 the weight of tanker cargo carried in the world's seaborne trade continued its regular post-war expansion but the weight of dry cargo carried fell substantially from 510 million metric tons in 1957 to 480 million in 1958; there was a slight recovery in dry cargo tonnage in the following year but the 1959 figure at 490 million tons was still well below the 1957 level.[80] On the other hand in 1958 the world output of new ships reached a record figure of over 9 million g.r.t. and was only a little less in the following year[81]; thus, whilst world dry cargo tonnage was falling, world shipping tonnage continued

74. Requisition of Ships Order made on 3rd August 1956. See also *Port Line* v *Ben Line* [1958] 2 QB 146.

75. Mostly from British owners. Owing to the size of the British order book and the stagnation of British output, most new orders by foreign owners went to Japanese and West European yards.

76. Geddes Report, Appendix I.

77. See the speech of Lord Winter in a Lords debate on the merchant marine in March 1958 —P. Debs (H. L.) 5 Ser., Vol. 208, c.322.

78. In March 1958 100 members of the Commons supported a Motion stating that "in view of the unique position of British shipping as the lifeline of an island nation" there should be further Government measures to strengthen its competitive power (P. Debs. 5 Ser., Vol. 583, c.378).

79. See Sir Nicholas Cayzer, "The Challenge to British Shipping" in *Institute of Transport Journal* Vol. 30 (1963).

80. Chamber of Shipping Annual Report 1971, Statistical Table 33.

81. Geddes Report, Appendix K.

to grow apace. By the end of 1959 world tonnage amounted to 118.1 million g.r.t. compared with 106.7 million at the end of 1957 although in the same two-year period U.K. tonnage only increased from 18.3 million g.r.t. at the end of 1957 to 19.4 million g.r.t. at the end of 1959.[82] This world over-building resulted in the annual average of the tramp voyage freight index falling from a 1956 peak of 157.0 to 67.1 in 1958 and 71.9 in 1959.[83]

From 1960 onwards world seaborne trade resumed its growth; between 1960 and 1967 it rose steadily from 1,080 million tons per annum to 1870 million tons per annum but, whereas in 1960 tanker cargo and dry cargo each stood at 540 million tons, by 1967 tanker cargo had increased to 1,020 million tons whilst dry cargo had only increased to 850 million tons.[84] World shipping tonnage also rose substantially from 123.296 million g.r.t. in 1960 to 174.472 million in 1967 but total U.K. tonnage in 1967 was only slightly more than it had been in 1960 and even this small increase was solely attributable to tankers, since dry cargo tonnage fell by nearly 700,000 tons and the United Kingdom's share of world tonnage declined from 16.4 per cent in 1960 to 11.7 per cent in 1967.[85] Mainly on account of the continuing growth in world shipping tonnage and the delivery of increasing numbers of larger bulk carriers with lower operating costs,[86] the expansion of world trade had only a minimal effect on the freight market; rates during the early 1960s continued to be severely depressed and, although between 1963 and 1967 there was a modest improvement, for shipping in general, and for deep-sea tramps in particular, the decade from 1958 to 1967 afforded few opportunities for making profits of the order achieved between 1952 and 1957.

As the figures demonstrate, the contribution by British owners to the excess of world tonnage was negligible; between 1958 and 1968 the percentage increase in U.K. tonnage was only eight per cent whereas the fleets of West European countries (excluding France, Italy and Spain) increased by 79 per cent—the same rate of expansion as the world average.[87] In view of the very low level of profitability which British shipping achieved between 1958 and 1969,[88] it is hardly surprising that British owners were disinclined to increase their tonnage but since, as the Rochdale Report makes clear,[89] the profits from the operation of ore carriers and tankers were substantially higher than the profits made by cargo liners and general-purpose tramps, the profitability of British shipping would have been improved if more owners had invested in

82. Figures taken from Chamber of Shipping Annual Reports for ships of 500 g.t. and over excluding lake and river tonnage and miscellaneous craft.

83. GCBS 1960 Survey, Appendix F.

84. Chamber of Shipping Annual Report 1971, Statistical Table 33.

85. *Ibid.*, Statistical Tables 5(A), (B) and (C).

86. Rochdale Report, paras. 527–528.

87. *Ibid*, Table 4.3.

88. *Ibid.*, Chapter 18 and Appendix 13.

89. *Ibid.*, Table 18.4 and Chart 18.1.

bulk carriers instead of, as most did, continuing to order traditional ships for the dwindling traditional trades.

The effect of the shipping depression on the British shipbuilding industry soon became apparent; in 1958 the amount of new orders fell alarmingly to little more than 500,000 g.r.t., as compared with an average of over 2 million tons of new orders annually in the previous three years,[90] and new orders over the following four years averaged little more than 500,000 g.r.t. a year.[91] At the beginning of 1958 the British order book had stood at around 5.75 million g.r.t., representing 16.6 per cent of the world order book but although, over the next five years, there was a general decline in world orders for new ships, the British yards suffered disproportionately so that by the end of 1962 the British order book had fallen to some 2 million g.r.t. which represented about 11 per cent of the world order book.[92]

The drastic decline in new orders was by no means the only reason for concern. The output achievements of the industry remained as unimpressive, both in absolute and relative terms, as they had been since the end of the war; launchings between 1959 and 1966, at an annual average of only a little over 1.1 million g.r.t., were even lower than in the period 1950 to 1958 and, whilst U.K. output was declining, world output rose substantially from 8.697 million g.r.t. in 1959 to 14.105 million g.r.t. in 1966 with the result that the British share of world output fell from 15.9 per cent in 1959 to only 7.6 per cent in 1966. British yards were losing their foreign customers; in the period 1959 to 1966 the proportion of merchant ships completed in the United Kingdom for export was, on average, only around one-sixth of total output compared with a proportion of nearly one-third for export between 1950 and 1958. To make matters worse some U.K. owners, particularly those ordering bulk carriers and tankers, felt that they could no longer ignore the more favourable terms offered by foreign builders; from 1957 onwards a significant proportion of the new ships completed for U.K. owners came from foreign yards with the result that there were several years in which imports of foreign-built ships for U.K. owners exceeded exports of British built ships for foreign owners.

The continuing fall in the U.K. order book combined with the failure to step up output resulted in a steady decline in the numbers employed; excluding the Royal Dockyards, the number employed in shipbuilding and ship repairing fell from 197,000 in 1956 to 129,000 in 1963.[93] The financial position of the industry was also causing concern; although the captive market for Royal Navy orders remained an important and profitable source of business,[94] some

90. P. Debs. 5 Ser., Vol. 598, c.(123).
91. Chamber of Shipping Annual Reports.
92. Geddes Report, Appendix I.
93. Geddes Report, Appendix E—which also showed a serious decline in the number employed in marine engineering.
94. Geddes Report, para. 65.

British builders, in an endeavour to remain on competitive terms with foreign yards for merchant ship orders, quoted prices which allowed nothing for profit and in some cases did not even adequately cover overhead charges. This factor, combined with increasing costs and the poor returns from new capital expenditure,[95] resulted in a steady fall in the industry's profitability.[96] Thus at the end of the 1950s the fall in the order book and in shipyard employment together with the growing tendency for both British and foreign owners to favour foreign yards all combined to put increasing pressure on the Government to make a thorough investigation of the industry's problems and to take some positive remedial action.

The Government's first response was to decide that departmental responsibility for shipbuilding and ship repairing should be transferred from the Admiralty to the Ministry of Transport and thus be brought under the same management as shipping.[97] Then in May 1960 the Minister of Transport established a special Sub-Committee of the Shipbuilding Advisory Committee "to review the prospects of and the problems facing the shipbuilding and ship repairing industry and to make recommendations".[98] The Sub-Committee's Report ("the SAC Report") was published in March 1961[99] and some four months later the Minister announced[100] that the Government had appointed a leading firm of chartered accountants, Peat Marwick Mitchell & Co. ("Peats") to analyse the reasons why British owners were placing more orders abroad; Peats' Report was published in October 1961.[101] The SAC and Peats' Reports, the contemporaneous debates in the Commons[102] and ministerial statements were generally in agreement that there were four vital areas in which British builders were not competitive with their foreign rivals. British prices, especially for the less sophisticated ships, were often higher[103] and there was a reluctance to quote fixed prices; British delivery dates were longer and, owing to industrial disputes, were unreliable and seldom guaranteed; credit facilities were much more favourable in most foreign shipbuilding countries; and the poor state of labour relations had damaged the industry's reputation, increased building costs and caused delays in production.

95. *Ibid.*, paras. 35, 276 and 280.

96. See J. R. Parkinson, "Financial Prospects of Shipbuilding after Geddes", *Journal of Industrial Economy*, Vol. 17 (1968).

97. P. Debs. 5 Ser., Vol. 614, c.463. Transfer of Functions (Construction of Ships) Order 1959 (S.I. 1959 No. 1829) dated 30th October 1959.

98. P. Debs. 5 Ser., Vol. 620, c.1315 and Vol. 624, c.41.

99. HMSO, 10th March 1961.

100. P. Debs. 5 Ser., Vol. 644, c.596.

101. HMSO, 10th October 1961.

102. P. Debs. 5 Ser., Vol. 632, c.169 and Vol. 644, c.596.

103. A Report by the Dept. of Scientific and Industrial Research on the Research and Development Requirements of the Shipbuilding and Marine Engineering Industries (HMSO 1960) estimated that 1958–59 British prices were 10 to 40 per cent higher that those quoted by foreign builders. As regards the vessels covered by Peats' Report, the best U.K. tender prices were between four and 30 per cent higher than the accepted foreign tender.

Apart from the question of credit facilities, the Government considered that it was for shipbuilding management and unions to put their own house in order. Although it was known that some foreign governments were subsidising their shipbuilding industries, at this time British Government policy was opposed to subsidies in general[104] and also to giving British owners financial incentives to induce them to place orders with British rather than foreign yards[105]; and without subsidies there was little the Government could do to make British prices more competitive. Even more so was the question of shorter and guaranteed delivery dates outside the Government's sphere of influence; it was felt that earlier and prompt deliveries could only be achieved by far better co-operation between management and unions and to this end the Minister of Labour set up a working party to consider practical measures for improving industrial relations.

From 1958 onwards the British shipping industry had been unsuccessfully campaigning for the provision of long term finance for the building of ships in U.K. yards[106] but it was not until almost a year after the publication of the SAC Report, with its emphasis on the urgent needs of both U.K. and foreign owners for competitive credit facilities, that the Government took some action and even then it was only to announce new improved arrangements for the finance of export shipbuilding contracts covered by direct ECGD bank guarantees.[107] Not surprisingly British owners regarded the improved ECGD facilities as only increasing the disparity between them and their foreign competitors but, although they continued to press for better credit facilities for home owners,[108] it was not until May 1963 that there was an announcement heralding the Government's change of heart.[109]

The Minister of Transport stated that, with the primary object of promoting employment in the shipyards, the Government was prepared, for a limited period of one year, to make loans to finance new orders by British owners in U.K. shipyards; initially £30 million would be made available but the Government would be prepared to consider increasing this amount. The new scheme—known as the Shipbuilding Credit Scheme—was to start at once[110] and under it British owners would have credit facilities at least as good as those given to foreigners ordering in British yards. The new scheme received a prompt and enthusiastic response; in July 1963 the amount of the credit was increased to £60 million,[111] in October 1963 it was increased further to £75

104. P. Debs. 5 Ser., Vol. 646, c.741.
105. *Ibid.*
106. See P. Debs. 5 Ser., Vol. 589, c.1321 and Vol. 596, c.697 and P. Debs. (H. L.), Vol. 220, c.872.
107. P. Debs. 5 Ser., Vol. 652, c.52.
108. P. Debs. 5 Ser., Vol. 653, c.1526; Vol. 668, c.393; Vol. 669, c.1225 and Vol. 677, c.422.
109. P. Debs. 5 Ser., Vol. 678, c.1326.
110. The Scheme was subsequently authorised by the Shipbuilding Credit Act 1964.
111. P. Debs 5 Ser., Vol. 681, c.1461.

million[112] and in December 1963 the Minister announced that the whole of the £75 million had been allotted and that approximately 800,000 g.r.t. of new ships would be built in U.K. yards under the Shipbuilding Credit Scheme.[113]

The main features of the scheme were given by the Minister on 15th January 1964 when the Shipbuilding Credit Bill received its Second Reading. [114] Loans were to be made only to U.K. shipowners to finance the building of ships in U.K. yards; advances would be up to a maximum of 80 per cent of the contract price, repayable over 10 years, secured by a first mortgage of the new ship and, if necessary, by mortgages of other ships and would carry interest at the prevailing Government rates; the amounts lent were not to exceed in the aggregate £75 million and no loan was to be made after 31st May 1964 unless application had been made before that date. The Minister pointed out that, although the main objective of the scheme was to tide the shipbuilding industry over a crisis by providing immediate additional work, it would also help British owners to modernise their fleet.

Within its limited objectives the scheme was undoubtedly a success. In the year ending 30th June 1964 orders placed by U.K. owners in U.K. yards totalled 1.67 million g.r.t. and, although not all this new tonnage was financed under the scheme, it cannot be doubted that many orders were stimulated by the availability of Government finance and that without the scheme "a substantial industry might scarcely have survived".[115] For the time being the situation in the shipyards, as regards levels of ships under construction and employment, was greatly improved but the Government were concerned that the prices quoted by the builders would not yield a margin of profit sufficient for the longer-term health of the industry. The ending of the scheme resulted in a sharp reduction in new orders placed by U.K. owners and, since orders from foreign owners also fell substantially, at the end of 1964 the U.K. order book was only marginally higher than it had been at the end of 1963.[116]

Meanwhile, in October 1964, a new Labour Government had taken office and had decided that ministerial responsibility for shipping and shipbuilding should be transferred to the Board of Trade.[117] The new Government also took immediate steps to encourage exports; the Finance (No. 2) Act 1964 provided for export rebates which, in the case of shipbuilding, meant that builders could claim a rebate of two per cent of the contract price on their sales to overseas customers.[118] During the first half of 1965 the Government

112. This increase was to accommodate the proposed loan of £17.6 million to Cunard to finance a replacement for the *Queen Mary*.

113. P. Debs. 5 Ser., Vol. 685, c.(187). The tonnage later increased to 900,000 g.r.t.

114. P. Debs. 5 Ser., Vol. 687, c.232.

115. Geddes Report, para. 37.

116. *Ibid.*, Appendix I.

117. Transfer of Functions (Shipping and Construction of Ships) Order 1965 (SI 1965 No. 145).

118. The Government rejected the suggestion that a similar rebate should be given in respect of ships built for U.K. owners. The anomaly was subsequently corrected by the Finance Act 1966.

also announced further improvements in the export credit facilities for ships built for overseas owners[119] but repeated requests for the granting of similar credit facilities for British owners were rejected and, in an adjournment debate on shipbuilding in May 1965,[120] the Government merely emphasised that, with the help of the improved ECGD facilities, there had been a great increase in export orders as a result of which the industry's order book had risen to 2.5 million g.r.t.—the highest level since 1961.

During 1965 the new orders from overseas owners reached the exceptionally high level of 1.1 million g.r.t.[121] and, whilst foreign owners were no doubt attracted by the improved credit facilities, another factor may well have been the willingness of British yards to cut prices; the Geddes Committee considered that many of the orders taken would not be remunerative enough to cover costs and described the year 1965 as one of "profitless prosperity".[122] On the other hand, throughout 1965 and into the early months of 1966, the Government remained adamant in their refusal to grant British owners credit facilities comparable to those enjoyed by their foreign competitors[123]; as a result orders in 1965 by U.K. owners in U.K. yards fell to only 678,000 g.r.t. whilst in the same year U.K. orders placed abroad rose to 920,000 g.r.t. and there can be little doubt that the availability of far more favourable credit facilities was an important factor in influencing some British owners to build new ships abroad.[124]

Although, from 1958 onwards, there was continuing concern, both within Parliament and outside, at the absolute and relative decline of both the shipping and shipbuilding industries, up to 1965 the political emphasis in the domestic field was centred on shipbuilding. The main reason for this special Government concern for the prosperity of the shipbuilding industry was the fear of increased unemployment, since nearly all the principal shipyards were located in areas where unemployment tended to be well above the national average. The problems of the shipping industry were not neglected, but the Government considered that shipping had received substantial financial help from the introduction and subsequent doubling of the investment allowance, that the shipowners' continual pleas for improved credit facilities for the building of ships at home had been met, albeit for a short period only, by the loans made available under the Shipbuilding Credit Act 1964 and that the emphasis needed to be placed more on attempts to solve British shipping's difficulties in the

119. See P. Debs. 5 Ser., Vol. 705, c.(242) and Vol. 710, c.687.
120. P. Debs. 5 Ser., Vol. 713, c.801.
121. Compared with only 120,000 g.r.t. in 1964—see Chamber of Shipping Annual Report 1971, Statistical Table 19.
122. Geddes Report, paras. 39–41.
123. See P. Debs. 5 Ser, Vol. 717, c.(156) and Vol. 724, c.(121).
124. Price differential was another important factor—see, for example, P. Debs. 5 Ser., Vol. 710, c.(78).

international sphere—especially in regard to foreign discriminating practices.[125]

Whilst British shipowners welcomed the 1957 increase of the investment allowance, unfortunately it coincided with the beginning of period of severe depression and capital allowances were of little use if there were no profits against which they could be offset; in addition the investment allowance was of little help to the smaller tramp owners who, unlike the larger liner operators, did not have a more or less continuous building programme. Accordingly, in 1958, the shipowners put forward proposals for further tax relief[126] but, although the Chancellor assured the industry that the Government recognised "its paramount importance to this nation", in the event no further significant tax alleviation was forthcoming. In their 1960 Survey the General Council of British Shipping again asked the Government for additional tax relief but, apart from some small fiscal concessions in 1963 and 1964, there was no substantial change in shipping's tax position until the Finance Act 1965, and the new corporation tax then introduced for all U.K. companies in place of income tax and profits tax was by no means favourable to shipping companies.

The new tax system placed a heavier burden on companies that had a relatively low level of profits and distributed a comparatively high proportion of those profits by way of dividend. Before the 1965 Budget the shipowners recognised that most shipping companies would fall into this category but their representations to the Chancellor were all to no avail in spite of the Chancellor acknowledging that many shipping companies would be worse off under the new system, "some of them severely". However the Finance Act 1965 did provide that, in respect of future capital expenditure on new ships, the shipowner should be entitled to "free" depreciation—i.e. that he should be free to decide how much of the writing-down allowances[127] should be used in each year for the purpose of reducing or eliminating his corporation tax liability in respect of the profits for that year[128]—and for some years shipping was the only U.K. industry which qualified for free depreciation.

In the period up to 1965 the only financial assistance provided by the Government for shipowners in general was the credit facilities, up to the total limit of £75 million, made available under the Shipbuilding Credit Act 1964 and it is worthy of note that these Government loans, apart from the interest element,[129] involved neither subsidy nor, in the event, financial loss.[130] There

125. See further Chapter 9 *infra.*

126. These included the suggestion that shipowners should be allowed to set off unused capital allowances against the taxed profits of earlier years.

127. In 1965 these amounted to 140 per cent of the cost of the new ship.

128. See Rochdale Report, para. 1368.

129. The interest rate varied between 4½ and 5⅜ per cent. The commercial rate of interest was substantially higher.

130. By 31st March 1977 all the loans had been fully repaid—see the National Loan Funds Account 1976–77, Supplementary Statements, p. 37.

was, however, one British shipowning company to which, yet again, exceptional Government financial aid was accorded and which was still regarded as a very special case; as in 1902[131] and in the 1930s,[132] the favoured beneficiary was Cunard, whose Board at the end of the 1950s was planning to build a new passenger liner to replace the ageing *Queen Mary* and had submitted proposals to the Minister of Transport for Government assistance.

After taking advice from a Committee chaired by Lord Chandos,[133] in the autumn of 1960 the Minister announced that the cost of the new ship was estimated at a maximum of £30 million, that Cunard would contribute £12 million and that, subject to the necessary legislation, the balance would be financed by a Government loan of £18 million.[134] In March 1961 the Agreement between the Government and Cunard for the financing of the new liner was published[135] and on 1st May 1961 the North Atlantic Shipping Bill, authorising the loan to Cunard, had its Second Reading[136]; although there were some Conservative backbenchers, both in the Commons and the Lords, who felt that the loan was contrary to Britain's general shipping policy and that in any case it was wrong in principle to subsidise one shipowner only, the Bill passed rapidly through all its stages in both Houses and the Royal Assent to the North Atlantic Shipping Act 1961 was given on 27th July 1961.

Some three months later, in a surprising volte-face, the Cunard Board informed the Government that they had decided that they were not able at that time to place an order for the ship to replace the *Queen Mary*[137] and the Minister told the House that Cunard had asked the Government to hold open the question of financial assistance until the Board had completed its reappraisal. Nearly two years later, on 24th July 1963,[138] the Minister announced that Cunard were proposing to build a vessel of 58,500 g.r.t., known as Q.4, at a cost of £22 million and had asked the Government for a loan of £18 million repayable over 25 years with interest at 4 per cent per annum; the Minister stated that Cunard's new proposal was not acceptable to the Government but that Cunard was free to apply for a loan under the Shipbuilding Credit Scheme. In the event Cunard did apply for and was granted a loan of £17.6 million under the Shipbuilding Credit Scheme and, in order to accommodate Cunard, the lending limit in the Shipbuilding Credit Act 1964 was increased to £75 million.

131. Government assistance for *Mauretania* and *Lusitania*—see pp. 85 *et seq. supra*.
132. Government assistance for *Queen Mary* and *Queen Elizabeth*—see pp. 112 *et seq. supra*.
133. The Chandos Committee Report was never published but a summary of the Committee's main conclusions were given to the House—see P. Debs. 5 Ser, Vol. 623, c.1437.
134. P. Debs. 5 Ser., Vol. 627, c.2341 and Vol. 629, c.361.
135. Cmnd. 1319, Parl. Papers 1960–61, Vol. 17.
136. P. Debs. 5 Ser., Vol. 639, c.914.
137. The reasons given by the Cunard Board for this reversal of their previous decision was a slump in the passenger trade and an enormous rise in operating costs.
138. P. Debs. 5 Ser., Vol. 681, c.1461.

Progress in preparing the Q.4 specification was slow and it was not until 30th December 1964 that Cunard signed the Q.4 building contract with John Brown of Clydebank for a vessel increased in size to 65,000 g.r.t. and increased in price to £25.427 million subject to escalation. Predictably the ultimate purchase price for Q.4, now named *Queen Elizabeth* 2, proved to be greatly in excess of the contract price and in June 1967 Cunard approached the Government seeking further finance[139]; it was subsequently announced that the Government had agreed to lend Cunard up to £24 million and that, since such a loan could not be made under the Shipbuilding Credit Act 1964,[140] it was proposed that the necessary legislative authority should be obtained by the insertion of a special Clause in the Industrial Expansion Bill[141] which was due to be submitted to Parliament early in 1968.

The Industrial Expansion Act 1968 became law on 30th July 1968[142] and Section 9, headed "Finance for Queen Elizabeth 2", authorised the Board of Trade to lend up to £24 million to the Cunard Group at an interest rate of 4½ per cent per annum.[143] So, after more than eight years, and with the need for no less than three Acts of Parliament, the way was at last clear for the taxpayer to fund the building of the new Cunarder but, both in shipping circles and in Parliament, there were some who felt that, after more than a century of favoured treatment at the hands of the Government, it was time that Cunard should cease to be regarded as a sacred cow; as one member of the Commons remarked, a sacred cow is an object of great veneration but is generally of very little economic use.

139. P. Debs. 5 Ser., Vol. 748, c.551.

140. Because it would mean exceeding the limit of £75 million in the Act and because the terms of the loan were far more favourable to the borrower than would have been possible under the Act.

141. The main purpose of the Bill had nothing to do with the financing of Q.4. The special Clause inserted to authorise the loans to Cunard bore no relationship to the other provisions of the Bill.

142. None too soon—since *Queen Elizabeth 2* was completed and delivered in November 1968.

143. This lending rate was below that charged to most other shipowners under the Shipbuilding Credit Act 1964 and was at least 2 to 2½ per cent below the current market rate.

CHAPTER 9

BRITISH EXTERNAL SHIPPING POLICY AND FOREIGN COMPETITION

Although, during the depression of the 1930s, the Government had exceptionally granted temporary operating subsidies to British tramp shipping,[1] in general the inter-war period marked no change in the firm conviction of both the Government and British shipowners that Britain should adhere to her long established policy of freedom of the seas, which had been strongly endorsed in the 1918 Report of the Departmental Committee,[2] and that a reversion to any form of flag discrimination would be contrary to the best interests of British shipping. In the aftermath of the Second World War it was soon made clear that the Government, with the full support of the British shipping industry, intended to pursue the same external shipping policy.

In 1948, at a United Nations Maritime Conference, the United Kingdom had been active in promoting a Convention for the establishment of an Intergovernmental Maritime Consultative Organisation ("IMCO")[3] one of whose main objectives was "to encourage the removal of discriminatory action and unnecessary restriction by Governments affecting shipping engaged in international trade so as to promote the availability of shipping service to the commerce of the world without discrimination". In the same year the Organisation for European Economic Co-operation ("OEEC"), formed by the United Kingdom and 16 other European countries,[4] took a positive stand against flag discrimination by emphasising that it should always be the aim of member countries that "liberal and competitive commercial and shipping practices and procedures should be followed in international trade and that normal commercial considerations should alone determine the method and flag of shipment". The British Government responded in Memoranda submitted to the OEEC in December 1948[5] stating that the shipping policy of the United

1. See pp. 121 *et seq. supra.*
2. Cd. 9092, Final Report, para 397.
3. Cmd. 7412, Parl. Papers 1947–48, Vol. 28. IMCO was set up as a special agency of the United Nations which was to be concerned solely with shipping matters requiring international intervention by Governments.
4. See Cmd. 7388, Parl. Papers 1947–48, Vol. 27.
5. Cmd. 7572, Parl. Papers 1948–49, Vol. 34.

Kingdom was directed to the removal of all obstacles to the free international circulation of shipping.

The British Government's external shipping policy remained the same regardless of the political colour of the party for the time being in power. In 1950 a Labour Minister of Transport stated that the Government were opposed to discriminatory practices in the field of shipping and that it was their policy to maintain and promote, by international agreement and other means, the principles of free interchange of shipping services in world commerce without discrimination as to flag[6]; in 1953 a Conservative Minister of Transport stated that the Government were constantly endeavouring to promote the most favourable conditions for the prosperity of British shipping by pressing for the removal of discriminatory practices and by working for an expansion of world trade.[7]

These and other later ministerial statements of policy coincided closely with the views of both the Chamber of Shipping and the officials of the Ministry of Transport with whom, through the years, the Chamber had "built up a remarkably close and happy relationship".[8] The Departmental view, as summarised by Sir Gilmour Jenkins,[9] was that the Government's activities in support of British shipping should be "directed towards maintaining throughout the world the conditions in which our ships can compete fairly with ships of other flags without interference by other Governments"[10] and in 1960 the General Council of British Shipping declared that British shipowners shared with the Government the ideal that international trade should be conducted under a system of economic freedom and without discrimination.[11] Thus the shipping industry and the Government shared the same philosophy but shipowners felt that there was little that they alone could do to halt the growing trend towards protectionism and that the solution of the problem must lie ultimately in the hands of the British Government and the governments of the other traditional maritime countries.

It was generally agreed that the most serious danger to British shipping was the increasing tendency of some foreign governments to favour their national shipping by discriminatory preferential treatment of various kinds. Flag discrimination, though difficult to define comprehensively, was not difficult to recognise when encountered; the General Council of British Shipping[12] described it as comprising "a wide variety of acts and pressures exerted by

6. P. Debs. 5 Ser., Vol. 481, c.73.
7. *Ibid.*, Vol. 513, c.458.
8. Chamber of Shipping Annual Report 1956–57, p. 241.
9. Permanent Secretary, Ministry of Transport, 1947–57.
10. Sir Gilmour Jenkins, *The Ministry of Transport and Civil Aviation* (London, 1959), p. 44.
11. GCBS 1960 Survey, para. 60.
12. *Ibid.* para. 63.

Governments designed to direct cargoes to ships of the national flag regardless of commercial considerations which normally govern the routing of cargoes".[13] The measures taken by certain governments to protect their national shipping were many and varied[14] but the most objectionable, and most common, form of protection was that which excluded British ships from certain types of business by the reservation of cargoes to national ships either unilaterally[15] or through bilateral agreement.[16] Gilmour Jenkins described this practice as "the most objectionable and pernicious discriminating device" and there was constant pressure on the Government to solve "one of the most serious and intractable problems" facing the shipping industry.[17]

Throughout the 1950s there was no lack of Government will to secure the removal of all forms of flag discrimination[18] and in 1955 the Minister stated that representations had been made to 23 countries[19] but it seemed that little progress could be made by unilateral protest or persuasion and that the only real hope lay in trying to secure international agreement. The OEEC had taken a firm stand and its West European members were mostly strongly opposed to flag discrimination but the hope of achieving progress through IMCO came to nothing and indeed some of the IMCO members were among the worst offenders.[20] There remained the possibility of taking retaliatory measures but most British owners were reluctant to abandon their freedom of the seas philosophy; in a 1955 Lords debate on the shipping industry[21] Lord Runciman, a leading shipowner, pointed out that the adoption of any direct forms of protection might provoke harmful retaliation bearing in mind that two-fifths of the cargoes carried by British ships were in the cross trades and the Government reply made it clear that there was no question of giving preferential treatment to British shipping.

Flag discrimination continued to be a major problem throughout the 1960s; British shipowners regarded it as the most invidious and indeed the more insidious form of artificial government stimulus[22] and this was a view shared by successive Conservative and Labour administrations whose statements betray no lack of determination to safeguard the competitive freedom of British

13. The description given by the International Chamber of Shipping was "any action by governments which restricts the freedom of traders to choose the ships in which cargoes may be carried and thus places impediments in the path of the free flow of international trade".
14. For examples see GCBS 1960 Survey, Appendix O.
15. See, for example, the United States Cargo Preference Act 1954.
16. See GCBS 1960 Survey, p. 73.
17. *Ibid.*, para. 61 and Rochdale Report, para. 148.
18. P. Debs. 5 Ser., Vol. 489, c.1887 and Vol. 508, c.2018.
19. *Ibid.*, Vol. 538, c.2073.
20. See GCBS 1960 Survey, paras. 73 and 74 and Chamber of Shipping Annual Report 1956–57, p. 62.
21. P. Debs. (HL) 5 Ser., Vol. 194, c.19.
22. See speech of Lord Geddes in 1968 Lords debate on the shipping industry—P. Debs. (HL) 5 Ser., Vol. 220, c.872.

shipping.[23] The most harmful form of protection was still cargo reservation and the main proponent of this practice was the United States whose shipping policy, as declared in several Shipping Acts,[24] was to foster the development and encourage the maintenance of a national marine to carry the greater part of its commerce. The American Cargo Preference Act of 1954 (Public Law 664) required at least 50 per cent by weight of certain specified import and export cargoes to be carried in United States flag commercial vessels and, although there were many other countries who, either unilaterally by legislative controls or through the medium of bilateral trade treaties, discriminated by way of cargo preference in favour of their own national fleets, the Rochdale Committee estimated that the volume of cargo reserved to U.S. vessels by unilateral protectionist measures represented two-fifths of the cargoes subject to discriminatory measures by all governments, apart from those of Communist countries.[25]

The problem of how best to counter flag discrimination was one not capable of easy solution more particularly since it could not be alleged that either the bilateral trade agreements or the unilateral legislation constituted violations of international law.[26] The member countries of the Organisation for Economic Co-operation and Development[27] ("OECD"), with the significant exception of the United States, had agreed that their shipping policy should be based on "the principle of free circulation of shipping in international trade in free and fair competition" and in general OECD members, again excepting the United States, did not indulge in discriminatory practices. However, although one of the main purposes of IMCO was to discourage flag discrimination, so many of its member countries made reservations regarding this particular objective that in practice IMCO activities have been largely confined to technical matters and flag discrimination has been ignored.[28] So it seemed that the only course open was for the Government, by itself or through OECD, to endeavour by persuasion and protest to convince offenders that freedom rather than protectionism was in the best interests of all countries.

At the end of the 1950s the main diplomatic effort was directed against the United States and in June 1959 there were inter-governmental talks in Washington between the United Kingdom, the United States and some of the European maritime countries[29]; the Minister's report to the House on his

23. See, for example, P. Debs. 5 Ser., Vol. 619, c.1290; Vol. 627 c.(159) and Vol. 644, c.611. See also Cmnd. 2764, Parl. Papers 1964–65, Vol. 30 (Part I Ch. 12, para. 38) and P. Debs. (HL) 5 Ser., Vol. 290, c.1228.

24. U.S. Shipping Act 1916 and U.S. Merchant Marine Acts of 1920, 1928 and 1936.

25. Rochdale Report, para. 151 and on flag discrimination see paras. 147–163 and Appendix 4.

26. See E. Lauterpacht, "The Contemporary Practice of the United Kingdom in the field of International Law", *International and Comparative Law Quarterly*, Vol. 4 (1956).

27. OECD succeeded OEEC in December 1961.

28. See *British Shipping Laws* (London, 1967), Vol. 13, paras. 307–310 and 825–836.

29. Belgium, Denmark, France, West Germany, Italy, Netherlands, Norway and Sweden.

return from Washington[30] showed that little progress had been made and the Minister subsequently stated[31] that all the European countries were to make joint representations to the United States as a follow-up to the Washington talks. Government efforts were by no means confined to the United States; in May 1959 the Minister informed the House[32] that, since 1st June 1954, 47 formal protests regarding discrimination against British shipping had been made in 26 foreign countries and at the end of 1959 the Minister stated[33] that during the previous 10 years the Government had made 74 formal protests about flag discrimination to the governments of 31 foreign countries and added that all possible steps had been taken, often in co-operation with other European governments, to combat such discrimination.

The general feeling of disappointment at the unsatisfactory outcome of the Washington conference was reflected in a Lords debate on the shipping industry in February 1960[34] when it was suggested that a stronger shipping policy was needed. The Minister replying to the debate stated that the Government were considering the possibility of retaliation but emphasised that, before taking any measures of this kind, there was need to consider carefully, in conjunction with other like-minded governments, what the wider repercussions of such a change of policy might be. Later in 1960 there was further evidence of the ineffectiveness of the diplomatic campaign against flag discrimination. A grain agreement was concluded between the United States and India involving the shipment of 17 million tons of grain to India; under the U.S. Public Law 664 50 per cent of the grain had to be shipped in American ships and the Indian government insisted that the remaining 50 per cent had to be shipped in Indian ships.

Faced with this flagrant example of how British shipping was being excluded from even the possibility of participating in the carriage of this huge volume of cargo, the General Council of British Shipping recommended[35] that, in order to meet the steadily deteriorating flag discrimination position, the Government should equip itself with such general powers as it needed for the effective application of counter measures. Ministerial statements made during 1961 did not suggest that the Government was urgently considering the adoption of a more vigorous policy[36] and in a further Commons shipping debate in February 1962[37] the Government were again pressed to take some positive action; the Minister pointed out that retaliation might do the United Kingdom more harm than good but added that he was prepared to consider taking enabling powers

30. P. Debs. 5 Ser., Vol. 607, c.(45).
31. *Ibid.*, Vol. 609, c.407.
32. *Ibid.*, Vol. 605, c.(39).
33. *Ibid.*, Vol. 615, c.(159).
34. P. Debs. (HL) 5 Ser., Vol. 220, c.872.
35. GCBS 1960 Survey, para. 89(C).
36. See P. Debs 5 Ser., Vol. 634, c.(57) and, c.(148); Vol. 637, c.1332 and Vol. 644, c.596.
37. P. Debs 5 Ser., Vol. 653, c.1526.

if shipowners themselves knew in what way they wanted such powers to be exercised.[38]

In the same debate attention was also focused on the serious position in which British and European liner operators trading under conference arrangements to the United States had been placed as a result of the recent enactment of the U.S. Public Law 87–346 (the Bonner Act)[39] and the manner of its implementation by the American Federal Maritime Commission[40] ("FMC"). The trouble had its origin in a 1958 decision of the U.S. Supreme Court[41] which cast doubts on the legality, under the U.S. anti-trust laws, of the dual rate contracts between British and European conference lines and American shippers.[42] The Bonner Act legalised dual rate contracts, but only if their terms were approved by the FMC, and the Act also required tariff rates to be filed with the FMC, provided for the filing with the FMC of conference agreements and ordered the FMC to disapprove, correct or modify any agreements which it found to be "unjustly discriminatory or unfair as between carriers, shippers, exporters, importers or ports or between exporters from the United States or their foreign competitors or to operate to the detriment of the commerce of the United States or to be contrary to the Public Interest".[43]

It was hoped that the FMC would perform their functions in a liberal and practical manner but the draft regulations for putting into effect the FMC's powers under the Bonner Act showed that this hope was ill-founded.[44] In March 1962 a meeting of British and European shipping ministers strongly criticised the activities of the FMC[45] and British liner owners were instructed by the Ministry of Transport not to produce documents requested by the FMC on the grounds that the documents were not within the jurisdiction of the United States and that it would be contrary to the public interest of the United Kingdom to produce them. Subsequently, in a Commons debate on international shipping,[46] the Minister stated that the British Government could not accept unilateral regulation of international shipping by one country and that a collective European policy was the best way of opposing it; the Prime Minister also sent a Memorandum on the subject to the President.[47]

38. In fact the Government already had powers with which to retaliate under the Customs Consolidation Act 1853.

39. The Bonner Act amended the U.S. Shipping Act 1916.

40. A newly formed agency of the U.S. Congress which was constituted in August 1961 and charged with the task of administering the regulatory provisions of the U.S. Shipping Act 1916 as amended.

41. *Federal Maritime Board* v *Isbrandtsen*, 354 U.S. 481.

42. Dual rate contract was a type of "loyalty" arrangement under which shippers paid a reduced rate for a specific period during which they undertook to send all their shipments by conference lines.

43. I.e. contrary to the public interest of the United States.

44. See Chamber of Shipping Annual Report 1961–62, p. 66.

45. P. Debs 5 Ser., Vol. 655, c.1313.

46. *Ibid.*, Vol. 659, c.399.

47. *Ibid.*, Vol. 659, c.632.

In spite of the collective European diplomatic action, the situation regarding the activities of the FMC and flag discrimination in general showed no signs of improvement; a recent President of the Chamber of Shipping was even driven to say that "the day might well come when as a nation we shall have to consider some return to the Navigation Acts to protect our vital interests".[48] The Government were not prepared to support such a change in policy; early in 1963 they rejected Parliamentary requests that there should be provisions in trade treaties for a proportion of U.K. imports to be carried in British ships[49] or that increased duty should be charged on goods brought to the United Kingdom in ships registered in any country practising flag discrimination against British ships.[50] Nevertheless the FMC's continuing disregard of the interests of other maritime nations did result in increased unity of action on the part of the governments of the United Kingdom, nine European countries[51] and Japan; there was also close and more effective collaboration between the liner operators of the same countries through the Committee of European Shipowners ("CES") whose principal objective was to secure and maintain a fair and effective conference system in the United States trades.

During 1963 commercial relationships between the countries of the Consultative Shipping Group and the United States progressively worsened. There was another flagrant case of American cargo preference involving a shipment of 4 million tons of wheat to Russia subject to the condition that 50 per cent was to be carried in American flag ships. Later in the year the FMC served orders on the liner owners requiring them, under threat of penalties, to produce a wide range of documents and information which lay outside the jurisdiction of the United States' and in addition the FMC endeavoured unilaterally, in the interests of the United States commerce, to force changes in the conference freight rates. In December 1963, following a meeting of the CSG countries, Joint Notes were sent to the United States stating that the flag discrimination in the Russian wheat shipments represented a reversal of the declared policy of the United States to encourage freedom of opportunity for ships of all nations to compete in world trade[52] and that the signatories would restrain their nationals from complying with FMC requirements whenever such requirements constituted an infringement of sovereignty.

Matters were brought to a head when, in March 1964, the FMC announced that the only dual rate contract which could be used in trades to and from the

48. Sir Nicholas Cayzer, *loc. cit.*
49. P. Debs. 5 Ser., Vol. 672, c.224.
50. *Ibid.*, Vol. 675, c.4.
51. Belgium, Denmark, France, West Germany, Greece, Italy, Netherlands, Norway and Sweden. These countries together with the United Kingdom and Japan, subsequently became designated "the Consultative Shipping Group" (CSG).
52. P. Debs. 5 Ser., Vol. 685, c.(133).

United States had to be in a standard form prepared by the FMC[53]; the Minister of Transport told the Commons that there was complete solidarity between the European countries and Japan and that there should be no weakening of the principle that no one country could unilaterally impose its own laws on another[54] and, after a further meeting in Washington had brought no acceptable solution, in July 1964 the Minister announced the Government's intentions to bring in a Bill "to secure Her Majesty's jurisdiction against encroachment by certain foreign requirements in respect of the carriage of goods or passengers by sea and in respect of the production of documents and the furnishing of information".[55]

The Second Reading of the Shipping Contracts and Commercial Documents Bill took place on 15th July 1964[56]; the Bill rapidly passed through all its stages and received the Royal Assent on 31st July 1964.[57] The Act[58] provided firstly that if orders or directions were made by a foreign country for regulating the terms and conditions under which goods or passengers were carried by sea and, in the opinion of the Minister of Transport, these measures represented an infringement of United Kingdom sovereignty insofar as they applied to things to be done outside that foreign country, the Minister might make an order placing a duty on shipowners to report any such orders or directions made by a foreign country and the Minister could then prohibit compliance with such order or direction within the United Kingdom. It was further provided that certain Ministers of the Crown could prohibit the production to a foreign court, tribunal or authority of any commercial document not within the territorial jurisdiction of that foreign country or any commercial information to be obtained from documents not within that jurisdiction if, in the opinion of the Minister, the foreign requirement constituted an infringement of United Kingdom jurisdiction.[59]

The Act enabled British shipowners to negotiate, free from duress, an acceptable new form of contract which, although differing from the proposed FMC form, was eventually approved by the FMC.[60] Through the medium of OECD a compromise regarding the continued FMC demands for documents and information located outside the United States was reached whereby the FMC demands were considerably reduced and the countries of the Consultative Shipping Group agreed that they would endeavour to persuade their respective

53. In effect this meant that the FMC were even attempting to dictate the terms of commercial contracts entered into between British shipowners and shippers in the United Kingdom.
54. P. Debs. 5 Ser., Vol. 693, c.1303.
55. *Ibid.*, Vol. 698, c.411.
56. *Ibid.*, Vol. 698, c.1215.
57. Shipping Contracts and Commercial Documents Act 1964 (Ch. 87).
58. Which could be extended to dependencies outside the U.K.
59. The Government did forbid the production of documents and information within the U.K. which the FMC had demanded.
60. See Chamber of Shipping Annual Report 1964–65.

shipowners to submit information in aggregate form[61] for each conference to OECD who would then circulate it on a confidential basis to all OECD members—including the United States. In 1965, on the basis of the confidential information disclosed, the FMC alleged that the conference lines were guilty of freight discrimination against American exports to the United Kingdom. This allegation was strongly refuted by the British Government who, in conjunction with the other European governments concerned, also rejected a demand by the United States that the information circulated by OECD should be made public; nevertheless the U.S. government, in breach of the agreed confidentiality, released not only the consolidated figures but also individual figures relating to the carriage of 20 different commodities.[62]

In addition to the FMC imbroglio, 1964 marked other international developments in relation to both the conference liner system and flag discrimination. In the course of the first meeting of the United Nations Conference on Trade and Development ("UNCTAD"), a Shipping Working Party unanimously approved a Common Measure of Understanding on Shipping Questions[63] in which it was agreed that a liner conference system was necessary in order to secure stable rates and regular services but recommended closer co-operation between shippers and the conferences.[64] The Common Measure also welcomed the development of merchant marines in developing countries and their participation in liner conferences on equitable terms but added the caveat that such development should be "on the basis of sound economic criteria".

In spite of agreement on the Common Measure of Understanding, the UNCTAD meeting revealed a sharp difference of opinion between the developing countries and the traditional maritime powers with regard to flag discrimination in relation to the development of national fleets. The developing countries considered that Article 1(b) of the IMCO Convention[65] entitled them to give assistance and encouragement for the expansion and development of their national shipping and that preferential protective measures should be accepted as non-discriminatory in order that their merchant marines could play an increasing part in the transport of their cargoes. The traditional maritime

61. So as to avoid disclosure of individual details which, for competitive reasons, might be damaging.

62. See Chamber of Shipping Annual Report 1965–1966, p. 262.

63 Cmnd. 2417, Parl. Papers 1963–64, Vol. 32 (Annex AIV.22).

64. The European Conference Lines had already, in December 1963, agreed with European shippers a "Note of Understanding"—(see Chamber of Shipping Annual Report 1963–64) and this Note had been approved by the governments of the Consultative Shipping Group.

65. In this Article 1(b) it was stated that "assistance and encouragement given by a Government for the development of its national shipping and for purposes of security does not in itself constitute discrimination provided that such assistance and encouragement is not based on measures designed to restrict the freedom of shipping of all flags to take part in international trade". Some developing countries ignored the proviso and interpreted the Article as giving them liberty to indulge in cargo preference.

countries did not accept this view and instead made a recommendation, not supported by the developing countries, stating: "Shipping can best help the trade of developing countries by providing efficient transport at lowest possible cost. Free competition between shipowners is the way to ensure this. Interference with this freedom means higher costs or poorer service. No measure should therefore be taken to impede this freedom."

In April 1965 an UNCTAD Shipping Committee was established with representatives from both the principal shipping countries and the developing countries. At the first meeting of this Committee in November 1965 there was still a complete divergence of opinion as to what constituted "sound economic criteria" for the establishment of national fleets; the developing countries considered that economic criteria should not be related solely to profitability and continued to maintain that protection of national shipping should not be regarded as discriminatory. The developing countries also proposed that the Committee should investigate conference freight rates; this proposal was opposed by the maritime countries but, although it was then agreed that action should be postponed until the next meeting of the Committee in July 1966, at that meeting it was agreed by a large majority[66] that a study of conference freight rates should be carried out.[67]

During the second half of the 1960s the British Government, in co-operation with other CSG members and also through OECD, continued to pursue, by all diplomatic and other means short of outright retaliation, its traditional policy of freedom of the seas and equality of treatment for all flags. In June 1966 a meeting of the CSG Transport Ministers reaffirmed the necessity for intensified and co-ordinated efforts to combat the harmful effects of flag discrimination and in every OECD Annual Report during the 1960s there was mention of this increasing problem.[68] Shipowners of the CSG countries were also active in endeavouring to combat the activities of the FMC and the spread of flag discrimination; British shipowners in particular played a leading part in the work of the International Chamber of Shipping ("ICS"),[69] CES, the Committee of European National Shipowners Associations ("CENSA")[70] and the Committee of Liner Operations: South America ("COLOSA").[71]

The British Government also took individual action to resist further

66. Only the United Kingdom, Denmark, Netherlands, Norway and Sweden voted against.

67. However, it was accepted that the study should not oblige shipowners to reveal confidential information about their costs.

68. In 1969 OECD issued a special booklet on "Flag Discrimination".

69. For details of the work of the ICS see *British Shipping Laws*, *op. cit.*, Vol. 13, paras. 327 and 345–348 and Chamber of Shipping Annual Report 1965–66, p. 256.

70. CENSA was mainly concerned with the implementation of the shipowner/shipper Note of Understanding of 1963 (see fn. 64 *supra*) and the work of the UNCTAD shipping committee.

71. COLOSA co-ordinated the policies of the European lines trading to South America with a view to countering the growing flag discriminatory practices of the Latin American countries.

demands by the FMC[72] and, at the second full session of UNCTAD in February 1968, to secure the withdrawal of a resolution which would have condoned the use of discrimination by developing countries.[73] Nevertheless towards the end of the 1960s it was all too apparent that, in spite of all the individual and co- operative efforts, little progress had been made towards convincing the United States and the developing countries that fair and unrestricted competition in shipping was the best means of achieving a free flow and expansion of international trade. In 1970 some 30 non-Communist countries imposed flag discrimination in some form[74] and, short of taking retaliatory measures which the Government and most British shipowners were still reluctant to contemplate,[75] there was no way, other than by diplomatic means, in which the Government could prevent protectionist trade agreements between foreign countries or interfere with foreign discriminatory legislation unless it involved an attempt to invade British jurisdiction.

The effects of flag discrimination on the British shipping industry are not easy to quantify. Sturmey[76] and the Rochdale Committee[77] are not wholly *ad idem* in their calculations but there can be no doubt that British liners were deprived of business, that in some limited areas the effects on liner trades were serious and that British tramp ships extensively engaged in cross trading were also affected to some extent. However, when reporting in 1970, the Rochdale Committee concluded that up to that time the total impact of flag discrimination on U.K. shipping generally had not been particularly serious but added that it had had serious effects, particularly for cross traders, on individual routes subject to its full rigours and that it was important to view flag discrimination not simply in terms of then current conditions but rather as a practice which, if it proliferated, could damage the British shipping interest to a significant extent.[78]

Although cabotage—i.e. the reservation of a country's coastal trade to national flag ships—is really only another form of flag discrimination, it requires separate consideration since in most cases it does not involve restrictions on international trade and the right, under international law, for each country to decide whether or not foreigners should be allowed to trade in its territorial waters was clearly endorsed by the International Conventions of

72. See P. Debs. 5 Ser., Vol. 740, c.(93) and the Shipping Contracts (Foreign Measures) Order 1968 (S.I. 1968 No. 1382).

73. See P. Debs. (HL), Vol. 290, c.1228. However, at a meeting of the UNCTAD Shipping Committee in 1970 a resolution was passed stating that the developing countries had the right to "assist, promote and protect their mercantile marine".

74. Rochdale Report, para. 149 and Appendix 4. See also the OECD 1969 Report on Flag Discrimination.

75. See the speech of Lord Runciman—P. Debs (HL), Vol. 290, c.1264.

76. *British Shipping and World Competition*, *op. cit.*, pp. 201 *et seq.*

77. Rochdale Report, paras. 154 *et seq.*

78. *Ibid.*, paras. 161 and 162.

1921 and 1923.[79] In the 1960's cabotage was widely practised; a Board of Trade survey made in 1967[80] showed that 46 countries, out of the 76 covered, reserved their coastal trade to the national flag and those who adopted this kind of protectionism included a majority of the members of OECD,[81] Commonwealth countries such as India and Australia and a large number of developing countries.

In historical terms British shipowners were no strangers to cabotage: from 1562[82] and for some three centuries thereafter the English coasting trade had been restricted to English ships but in 1854 the monopoly was ended[83] and from then onwards foreign ships have been freely admitted to the United Kingdom's coasting trade. When, in 1854, the British coastal reservation was abolished, the Government had confidently expected that the United States and other foreign countries would reciprocate but in the event the United States not only maintained but later extended the reservation of its coastal trade[84]; France and Russia did likewise and, particularly after the Second World War, more and more countries adopted a cabotage policy.

If it would have served any useful purpose the United Kingdom could have retaliated by excluding from its domestic coasting trade all foreign ships or at least the ships of those countries which excluded British ships from their coasting trades. In 1902 a Commons Select Committee had advised the Government to consider such retaliatory measures[85] and in the 1930s depression there were repeated requests from British coasting owners for some measure of protection[86]; the Government did not respond and although, in 1962, the Minister of Transport did indicate his willingness to consider some degree of protection for the coasting trade if it would be of real benefit,[87] in the following year a Chamber of Shipping study of the incidence of foreign competition in the U.K. coasting trade concluded that, although the continued incursion of foreign ships sometimes caused concern, no change in existing policy on coastal reservation should be sought.[88] The matter was raised again in a 1968 Commons shipping debate but the Minister replying for the Government stated that in 1966 and 1967 the proportion of coastal dry cargo carried

79. See p. 115 *supra*.

80. Rochdale Report, para. 142.

81. In Western Europe only the United Kingdom, Belgium, Denmark, Netherlands and Norway did not reserve their coastal trades.

82. 5 Eliz. I, c.5—see p. 13 *supra*.

83. 17 & 18 Vict., c.5—see p. 49 *supra*.

84. By the 1960s the United States defined her reserved coastal trade as including not only that between the east and west coasts passing through the Panama Canal but also that to Alaska, Honolulu and the U.S. islands in the Caribbean (Rochdale Report, para. 141).

85. See p. 92 *supra*.

86. See the 1933 Report of the Tramp Shipping Committee—pp. 120 and 121 *supra*.

87. P. Debs. 5 Ser., Vol. 655, c.(73).

88. Chamber of Shipping Annual Report 1963–64, p. 76.

in foreign ships was only 3.3 per cent and that the proportion was still running at this low level.[89]

The Rochdale Committee considered the effects on British shipping of foreign reservation of coastal trades[90] and concluded that, except for a few coastal areas such as India and the United States "where goods are carried across thousands of miles of open water in deep sea vessels", the restrictions enforced by foreign governments did not have any significant effect on the prosperity of the U.K. shipping industry. The Committee accordingly saw no strong case for the reservation of the United Kingdom's coastal trade so, although a change of policy would involve neither a breach of international law nor flag discrimination in the customary sense of the term, the trade remained open to all; as the Committee observed, the Government's view was that to impose restrictions on foreign vessels operating round our own coasts would derogate, even if only slightly, from the Government's efforts to achieve the maximum of freedom of trade at sea.

Closely allied to the problems of flag discrimination and cabotage was the post-Second World War growth of the national fleets of the developing countries.[91] Between 1939 and 1968 the merchant fleets of developing countries increased from 1.7 million gross tons, representing three per cent of the world total, to 14.3 million gross tons, representing eight per cent of the world total,[92] whilst over the same period the U.K. fleet only increased from 16.9 million gross tons to 20.6 million gross tons and its share of the world total declined from 28.1 per cent to 11.5 per cent.[93] On the principle of equality of States, the developing countries, as sovereign powers, were as much entitled as the Western maritime powers to have their own national merchant marines[94] but to the CSG countries it seemed that in some instances the creation of these new fleets was merely an expression of national pride and had little economic justification when the developing countries were already well and efficiently supplied by long established shipping services.

The new, often State-owned, national shipping companies concentrated mainly on liner operations and the United Kingdom and other members of the conference lines found that, under threat of discrimination, they had no option but to admit the new national lines to a share of the available trade; the inevitable result was that the original members of the conference lost business

89. P. Debs. 5 Ser., Vol. 769, c.1194. See also Rochdale Report, para. 241.

90. Report, paras. 141–146.

91. The expression "developing countries" includes all countries except U.S.A., Canada, Western Europe (including the U.K., Irish Republic and Iceland), New Zealand, Australia, South Africa, Japan, Liberia, Panama, Lebanon, U.S.S.R. and other Eastern European countries, Republic of China, North Korea and North Vietnam (see Rochdale Report, para. 41, fn. 1).

92. Rochdale Report, Table 4.1.

93. *Ibid.*, Table 2.3.

94. Their right to have a national merchant fleet was recognised by Article 5 of the Geneva Convention on the High Seas of 1958 (Cmnd. 1929, Parl. Papers 1962–63, Vol. 37).

and in some cases the line ceased to be profitable. It was difficult for the West European liner operators to counter the belief that the creation of a national fleet was necessary for national prestige and prosperity but they did endeavour to demonstrate how adverse to world shipping and world trade was the pursuit of narrow nationalist and protectionist shipping policies and to emphasise that the supposed benefits to the balance of payments of the developing countries might well be illusory.[95]

Concerted action by the British and West European governments also achieved very little and, although the UNCTAD 1964 Measure of Understanding on Shipping Matters[96] had provided that new fleets should only be developed on the basis of sound economic criteria, in practice the growth of national fleets was all too often founded on subsidies and restrictions on the shippers' freedom of choice; moreover in 1970 a UNCTAD shipping resolution, which all members of the OECD unavailingly opposed, acknowledged the right of developing countries to assist, promote and protect their mercantile marines. So by 1970 no progress had been made towards convincing the developing countries that it was economically imprudent for them to create artificially supported fleets at a time when there was already a world tonnage surplus; the Rochdale Committee felt that they could not "properly question the general policy of a country deciding to foster a national fleet" but they doubted "whether economic arguments alone could have justified the establishment of some of the new fleets of recent years".[97]

Even more worrying to the shipowners of the traditional maritime powers than the growth of the new national fleets of the developing countries was the increasing competitive threat from the fleets of the U.S.S.R. and other countries in the Eastern Bloc. Even before the Second World War it had been the declared aim of the U.S.S.R. to build up its mercantile marine with the eventual objective of carrying the whole of its foreign trade—both imports and exports[98]—and in the period since 1945 the increase in the Russian merchant fleet had proceeded apace. In September 1939 it had totalled only 1.2 million gross tons (excluding ships of under 500 gross tons) but by December 1958 it had grown to 3.2 million gross tons and by December 1968 it had risen to 9.8 million gross tons and was still expanding at a rate of over 1 million tons a year.[99]

The Soviet Union's freighting organisation, Sovfrecht, ensured that, by insisting on f.o.b. purchases and c.i.f. sales, the growth of the State-owned

95. Because the developing countries had to buy their ships abroad and had to pay many of their operating costs in foreign currency.

96. See p. 189 *supra*.

97. Report, para. 168.

98. See the Chamber of Shipping's 1938 "Memorandum on British Shipping and Trade with Russia".

99. Rochdale Report, Table 2.3 and para. 74. Between 1938 and 1968 the rate of growth was 210 per cent compared with the world average growth of only 79 per cent (Rochdale Report, Table 4.3).

fleet was accompanied by a substantial increase in the volume of Soviet seaborne trade carried in national flag ships.[100] The Soviet authorities argued that their practice was not discriminatory and was merely exercising the "shippers' preference" but, since all Soviet cargoes were State owned, British shipowners considered that it was abundantly clear that considerations other than the official routing of cargo had prevailed.[101] In addition the U.S.S.R. entered into a number of bilateral trade treaties with countries outside the Eastern Bloc which were designed to ensure that goods moving between the two countries were carried only in Soviet ships or the ships of the other country in question.

Prior to the mid-1960s, the Eastern Bloc merchant fleets had concentrated their main effort on increasing their share of their own import and export trades but in 1968 the Chamber of Shipping reported that there was increasing intervention of Eastern Bloc tonnage in the cross-trades at uncompetitive freight rates[102] and in 1970 the Rochdale Committee pointed out that the Communist fleets were playing a minor, but growing, part in cross-trades and had sought to increase their participation in certain liner trades.[103] British owners felt that it was impossible for them alone to fight State owned shipping lines operating on a non-commercial basis[104] and that it must be for the Government to protect their legitimate trading interests; the trouble, as with other discriminatory practices, was that it was easier to state the problem than to find the means of resolving it.[105]

After flag discrimination, British owners regarded the next most serious threat to their competitive position as coming from the merchant fleets of the countries providing flags of convenience[106] which, in the period of 10 years from December 1958, increased at a greater rate than any of the traditional maritime countries with the exception of Japan. At December 1958 the tonnage registered under the flags of convenience totalled 15.6 million g.r.t. (15.6 per cent of world tonnage) but by December 1968 the flags of convenience tonnage

100. *Ibid.*, Table 4.2.
101. GCBS 1960 Survey, para. 66.
102. Chamber of Shipping Annual Report 1967–68, p. 115.
103. Rochdale Report, paras. 199 and 206.
104. The Rochdale Committee agreed the "no private company could withstand a determined effort by a government backed operator to take away his trade" (Report, para. 207).
105. A Treaty on Merchant Navigation between the United Kingdom and the U.S.S.R. came into force on 27th April 1972 (Cmnd. 5008, Parl. Papers 1971–72, Vol 38). Article 5 provided that the parties agreed to follow in international shipping the principles of free and fair competition and that each party would abstain from taking measures which would limit the opportunities for vessels of the other party to compete on equal terms for trade between each party's ports and between each party's ports and the ports of third countries. The Treaty appears to have made little difference to Soviet shipping policy.
106. In 1958 the OEEC identified Panama, Liberia, Costa Rica and Honduras as the flags of convenience countries (Rochdale Report, paras. 183–184). However, as from 31st December 1958 Costa Rica cancelled its registration facilities for foreign-owned tonnage and the Honduran foreign registered tonnage was relatively insignificant. Thus from 1959 onwards the expression "flags of convenience" is usually regarded as referring to ships registered under the flags of Liberia and Panama—sometimes called the Panlib ships.

had risen by over 110 per cent to a total of 32.9 million g.r.t. (18.3 per cent of world tonnage) whilst in the same period world tonnage increased by 79 per cent and U.K. tonnage by only eight per cent.[107]

This largely modern flags of convenience fleet, which had no natural connection with its nominal homes in Liberia and Panama, was in the main beneficially owned by nationals of the United States and Greece[108] and by 1958 it was causing such concern to British owners that the President of the Chamber of Shipping characterised it as "Public Enemy Number One".[109] It was considered that the tax immunity of the flags of convenience operators gave them an overwhelming advantage over their competitors in the maintaining and expansion of their fleets; in addition Panlib owners benefited from lower operating costs,[110] lack of any significant control by the Liberian and Panama authorities and the ability to poach the officers and crews that the maritime countries had recruited and trained at considerable expense.

In 1958 the British Government also regarded the competitive position of the British shipping industry as being menaced by the rapid growth of the tonnage operating tax free under the flags of convenience.[111] At international level the factor of most concern was that the Liberian and Panamanian governments did not have the power, the administrative machinery or indeed the desire to exercise effective control over their national flag ships particularly with regard to safety and crews' efficiency and conditions of service. The OEEC produced a study on flags of convenience,[112] recommendations were made at the 41st Maritime Session of the International Labour Conference[113] and the problem was discussed in detail at the 1958 Geneva Conference on the Law of the Sea arising from the proposal of the International Law Commission ("ILC")[114] that there should be acceptance in principle of the necessity of a "genuine link" between a State and any ship flying its flag.[115]

In its final draft of the Convention on the High Seas, the ILC, with the object of ensuring that each State had effective jurisdiction over the ships flying its flag, proposed that Article 5, dealing with the nationality of ships, should end

107. Rochdale Report, paras. 70 and 185 and Tables 2.3 and 4.3.

108. *British Shipping and World Competition*, *op. cit.*, Table 34 and Rochdale Report, para. 71.

109. See Chamber of Shipping Annual Reports 1957–58 and 1958–59.

110. Owing to lower manning scales, lower wages and no social security contributions.

111. See the 1958 shipping debates in the Commons (P. Debs. 5 Ser., Vol. 589, c.1321) and in the Lords (P. Debs. (HL) 5 Ser., Vol. 208, c.322).

112. "Study on the expansion of flags of convenience fleets and on various aspects thereof" (Paris, January 1958).

113. Seafarers' Engagement (Foreign Vessels) Recommendations (1958 No. 107) and Recommendations concerning Social Conditions and Safety of Seafarers in Relation to Registration of Ships (1958 No. 108).

114. An organ set up by the United Nations in 1947 to "promote the progressive development of international law and its codification".

115. For a detailed history of this proposal see H. Meyers, *The Nationality of Ships*, (The Hague, 1967), pp. 197 *et seq.*

with a sentence reading: "Nevertheless, for purposes of recognition of the national character of the ship by other States, there must exist a genuine link between the State and the Ship". This sentence provoked widely differing views when it was considered by a Conference Committee and eventually the Committee adopted an Italo-French proposal which was intended to make it clear that there could only be a "genuine link" if effective control over the ships was exercised by the flag state; it was accordingly proposed that the sentence should be supplemented by adding the phrase "in particular, the State must effectively exercise its jurisdiction and control over ships flying its flag in administrative, technical and social matters".

When the amended draft was considered at a plenary meeting of the Conference, certain delegates argued that the phrase "Nevertheless, for purposes of recognition of the national character of the ship by other States" offended against the principle of sovereignty; the phrase was rejected by a decisive majority and thereafter Article 5, with the offending phrase omitted, was adopted without any dissenting votes.[116] However in practice Article 5 came nowhere near to achieving the aspirations of those who had hoped it might signal the early demise of the flags of convenience; although the traditional maritime countries regarded Liberia and Panama as the most flagrant examples of the complete lack of any "genuine link", registration of ships under their flags continued and in 1960 their position was strengthened by a favourable decision of the International Court of Justice which held that both Liberia and Panama were among the eight largest shipowning nations and as such were entitled to a place on IMCO's Maritime Safety Committee.[117]

Flags of convenience were also discussed at the inter-governmental meeting on shipping policy in June 1959[118] but the talks produced no solution[119] and by the end of 1960 the General Council of British Shipping were confirmed in their view that, since no progress was being achieved by international action, British shipowners must look to the Government for action at national level to put the U.K. merchant fleet in a better position to meet the competition from the flags of convenience.[120] The GCBS accordingly asked the Government for additional tax relief for the shipping industry and freedom for U.K. shipowners to take full advantage of low taxation elsewhere in the Commonwealth.

The Government did not respond to the request for further tax relief; up to

116. In its final form (see Cmnd. 1929, Parl. Papers 1962–63, Vol. 37) the third sentence of Article 5 reads "There must exist a genuine link between the State and the ship; in particular the State must effectively exercise its jurisdiction and control in administrative, technical and social matters over ships flying its flag".

117. I.C.J. Reports 1960, p. 150.

118. See pp. 184–185 *supra*.

119. The official communiqué merely stated that "the complex problems arising from the rapid growth of tonnage registered under the so-called flags of convenience were considered and it was recognised that there was a need for further study and discussion".

120. GCBS 1960 Survey, para. 111.

1965, with the benefit of the existing 40 per cent investment allowance, shipping profits (if any) were so low that "little or no tax was paid"[121] and from 1966 to 1970, when shipowners were entitled to free depreciation and investment grant,[122] the Rochdale Committee concluded that the general tax position of the U.K. industry was at least as favourable as that of any of its major foreign competitors.[123] Neither did the Government repeal or relax the restrictions on transfers of business abroad imposed by Section 468 of the Income Tax Act 1952[124] and by the end of the 1960s the Rochdale Committee considered that it was "the view of the industry that a U.K. public company would probably prefer, in present circumstances, the combined worth of depreciation and investment grant to the possibility of operating under a flag of convenience"[125] and that the freedom from tax on profits which had previously given flags of convenience ships an advantage over their U.K. competitors had been countered by the tax arrangements made for U.K. shipping companies.[126]

By 1965 the Chamber of Shipping had reluctantly come to the conclusion that nothing could be done about the tax free fleets[127] and an OECD 1971 Report on Flags of Convenience confirmed that neither international measures nor national action by the traditional maritime countries had succeeded in countering the increasing growth of the flags of convenience fleets. This 1971 Report, and a further OECD Maritime Transport Committee Report in 1975, laid more emphasis on the threat from the avoidance of the more stringent manning and maintenance rules required and effectively enforced by the traditional maritime countries rather than on the unfair advantage of tax free operation; the 1975 Report particularly stressed the advantage to the flags of convenience fleets of economies in manning scales and personnel costs, from non-participation in officer and crew training and savings on social security.

In the late 1950s and early 1960s British owners also regarded excessive foreign government subsidies as yet another threat to the competitive position of British shipping and, as was the case with flag discrimination and flags of convenience, it was a problem not susceptible to easy solution since the main subsidiser was the United States and in addition some of the traditional maritime countries, members of the OECD such as France and Italy, had for long followed a policy of subsidising their national fleets. However, compared with flag discrimination, British owners considered subsidies to be the lesser of two evils; at least with subsidies the amount of government aid was usually quantifiable and, unlike cargo preference, subsidies did not eliminate the ability

121. Rochdale Report, para. 1362.
122. Investment grant was substituted for investment allowance in 1966—see further Chapter 10 *infra*.
123. Rochdale Report, paras. 1375 and 1393.
124. See page 168 *supra*.
125. Rochdale Report, para. 197.
126. *Ibid.*, para. 198.
127. Annual Report 1964–65, p. 289.

to compete although it might mean that competition was only possible on unequal terms.

In the United States subsidies had for long been a feature of the government's shipping policy; the Merchant Marine Act 1936 (Title VI), with the object of placing certain U.S. flag vessels on a parity with their foreign competitors, made provision for the granting of operating subsidies to cargo liners having scheduled sailings on established routes[128] and in 1968 these operating subsidies amounted to U.S. $200 million.[129] The same Act (Title V) provided for construction differential subsidies for the building in the United States of U.S. flag vessels to be used in U.S. foreign trades[130] and in addition a number of newly built U.S. merchant ships incorporated certain defence features, such as a capacity for higher speeds, and the entire cost of such features was borne by the U.S. Department of Defence.[131] During the 1960s both operating and construction subsidies were also paid by France, Italy, Japan, Spain, Canada and Australia although in some cases the amounts were modest compared with those paid by the United States.[132]

The problem of subsidies was dealt with in detail in the GCBS 1960 Survey[133] and the Government were urged to reach an understanding on shipping policy with the United States but in reality there was little hope of achieving much by international co-operation; even more than in the case of unilateral cargo preference measures, each country, as a sovereign power, could claim that aid to national maritime industries was a domestic matter which should not be subject to outside interference. There was thus left only one way in which foreign subsidies could be countered and that was by the British Government giving compensatory subsidies to British shipping but this was a form of aid to which British shipowners, except for a brief period during the depression of the 1930s, had for long been traditionally opposed; it was feared that, if the accepted British philosophy were to change, all the maritime countries could become involved in a subsidies race which would be to the detriment of all.[134]

However, although British owners were still averse to any form of general subsidisation, they did feel, having regard to the special support given to Cunard,[135] that financial aid could be justified in certain limited cases where a particular service or sector of the industry was under severe pressure from uncommercial foreign competition.[136] The Government did not respond

128. In 1970 the operating subsidy also became payable to bulk carriers.
129. Rochdale Report, para. 172. By 1971 the subsidies had risen to U.S. $268 million.
130. In 1967 the total was U.S. $80 million; by 1973 the total had risen to U.S. $186 million.
131. Rochdale Report, para. 174.
132. See Rochdale Report, paras. 175–178 and the 1969, 1971 and 1974 Reports on Maritime Subsidies by the U.S. Department of Commerce (Maritime Administration).
133. See paras. 90–107.
134. Chamber of Shipping Annual Report 1959–60, p. 241.
135. See pp. 178–179 *supra*.
136. See GCBS 1960 Survey, paras. 102 and 103.

favourably to this view[137] and during the second half of the 1960s complaints regarding foreign subsidies were noticeably muted; it seems probable that this was because the Government aid given to the British maritime industries from 1965 onwards by way of investment and other grants and through loans for shipbuilding had in total become so substantial that British owners no longer felt able to complain too loudly about the extent of foreign subsidies.

The investigations of the Rochdale Committee[138] revealed that over the 10 years from 1958 to 1968, a period in which the weight of cargo carried in the world's seaborne trade almost doubled,[139] the growth of U.K. registered tonnage was insignificant and compared very poorly with the increase in world tonnage. Excluding ships under 500 gross tons, the tonnage on the U.K. register increased by eight per cent from 19.2 million g.r.t. to 20.6 million g.r.t and the U.K. proportion of world tonnage fell from 19.2 per cent to 11.5 per cent; over the same period world tonnage increased by 79 per cent and all the fleets of Britain's major foreign competitors achieved increases which in relative terms were far in excess of the increase in the U.K. fleet.[140] It therefore remains to be considered as to what extent was the poor British performance attributable to unfair foreign competition resulting from such factors as flag discrimination, shipping subsidies and flags of convenience.

Certainly British shipowners regarded the relative decline of U.K. tonnage and its poor profitability as being in large measure due to foreign protectionist shipping policies and unfair competition. This was the underlying theme of the GCBS 1960 Survey[141] and the same complaint, together with protests at American interference with liner traffic, was constantly reiterated throughout the 1960s by the Chamber of Shipping and by spokesmen for the shipping interest in Parliament. Equally there can be no doubt that, during this period, the Government, whether Conservative or Labour and with full Parliamentary support, regarded foreign protectionism as damaging to the national shipping interest and although Government internal shipping policy which, apart from the Shipping Documents and Commercial Contracts Act 1964, stopped short of retaliatory measures, may not have been as forceful as some shipowners would have wished, it was clearly the will and purpose of the Government to support British shipping both at national level and through co-operation with the other traditional maritime countries.

On the other hand there were some political economists who felt that British

137. In 1961 the Prime Minister confirmed that Government policy was opposed to subsidies for shipping or shipbuilding (P Debs. 5 Ser., Vol. 646, c.741).

138. See Report, Tables 2.3 and 4.3.

139. See Tables 33 and 34 of the Statistical Tables in the Chamber of Shipping Annual Report 1971.

140. For example the percentage increase in the tonnage of Norway was 98 per cent, that of Liberia 144 per cent, that of Japan 245 per cent and that of Greece 326 per cent.

141. See p. 1, final paragraph.

owners were lacking in self criticism and were too much inclined to attribute their problems to unfair competition instead of recognising that the relative decline of U.K. shipping may also have been due to foreign enterprise and British conservatism.[142] Greek, Norwegian and German shipping, which was also unprotected and had to contend with the same unfair foreign competition, achieved far greater growth whereas the fleets of non-Communist countries indulging in subsidies and flag discrimination showed a poor rate of growth.[143] The general view of the critics of British shipping was that, whilst foreign discriminatory practices may have had some adverse effect on certain trades and routes, the overall effect on British shipping in general was not serious enough by itself to explain the stagnation in the growth of the U.K. fleet.

The Rochdale Committee accepted that the various forms of foreign protectionism had "in total reduced the opportunities for trading which would otherwise be available to our fleet and have increased the degree of competition prevailing" but they reached the general conclusion that these factors could not alone explain why the U.K. fleet grew but marginally when similarly placed Western European owners had "greatly increased their scale of operation during a period of expanding markets".[144] Like other critics the Committee felt that the U.K. industry's poor performance was partly due to internal constraints and the Report hints at management difficulties and errors of judgement: for example the failure to utilise the financial assistance available,[145] the tendency of liner owners to cling to their traditional dwindling trades instead of diversifying into new and expanding trades,[146] the lack of appreciation of air competition on the long distance passenger trade,[147] neglect of the enormously expanding trades for tankers and bulk carriers,[148] the ordering of ships of the wrong type at the wrong time[149] and the general lack of management expertise and enterprise.[150]

It is probably fair to say that it is generally accepted that in some measure foreign discriminatory practices did play a part in the relative decline of the U.K. merchant fleet in the period up to 1968. The area of disagreement centres on the extent to which these external constraints were necessarily responsible for the lack of growth; seeking to impress the Government, the owners did perhaps overstate their case whilst their critics may have treated the external problems too lightly. The *via media* of the Rochdale Committee may well

142. See *British Shipping and World Competition*, *op. cit.*, *British Transport since 1914*, *op. cit.* and the *British Shipping Industry*, *loc. cit.*
143. Rochdale Report, paras. 209, 210 and 214.
144. *Ibid.*, para. 218.
145. *Ibid.*, paras. 47, 1270 and 1280.
146. *Ibid.*, para. 64.
147. *Ibid.*, paras. 66 and 316.
148. *Ibid.*, para. 67.
149. *Ibid.*, para. 501.
150. *Ibid.*, paras. 219, 1172, 1208 and 1268.

represent the nearest approach to a correct assessment of both the situation up to 1968 and the possible increasing dangers thereafter.[151]

By the end of the 1960s it was apparent that the United Kingdom, the other Western European maritime powers and Japan had failed in their efforts to bring about even some moderation of national policies of flag discrimination and indeed there seemed to be a growing threat from the subsidised and protected fleets of the Eastern Bloc and the developing countries; as regards the latter, there were worrying signs that the UNCTAD Shipping Committee was supporting the view that the developing countries were entitled to encourage the growth of their infant fleets by protectionist measures.[152] The Rochdale Committee considered that there should be a multilateral inter-governmental agreement to establish "an agreed code of principles within which governments should develop their national shipping policies" and which would embody a general prohibition of flag discrimination in international trading and provisions to curtail operations under flags of convenience[153]; but at that time the likelihood of achieving an International Convention on these lines seemed remote and such indeed proved to be the case.

Another unresolved international shipping problem was in relation to the liner conference system. A Resolution on freight rates and conference practices had been passed at the Second Session of UNCTAD in 1968[154] and the Rochdale Committee, whilst approving the conference system in principle, did identify a number of defects and recommended that conference members covering trade to and from the U.K. should collectively accept a published code of conference practice covering admission of new members, publication of tariffs, provision of information about revenues and costs to representatives of the Government and shippers and consultation with the Government and shippers.[155] The Committee also suggested that it was desirable for there to be some international accord on a code of conduct for conferences generally[156] and in 1971 a meeting of the governments of the Consultative Shipping Group agreed that their shipowners should be requested to elaborate details of a code of conference practice in consultation with their shippers and present them to their governments for consideration before the end of 1971.[157]

151. *Ibid.*, paras. 1588–1592.
152. See p. 191 fn. 73 *supra*.
153. Rochdale Report, para. 1592.
154. Cmnd. 3649, p. 90, Parl. Papers 1967–68, Vol. 42.
155. Rochdale Report, paras. 481 and 485.
156. *Ibid.*, para. 484.
157. P Debs. 5 Ser., Vol 815. c.(23). See further p. 277 *infra*.

CHAPTER 10

RESURGENCE OF BRITISH SHIPPING AND REORGANISATION OF BRITISH SHIPBUILDING

On 22nd July 1967 a Committee, under the Chairmanship of Lord Rochdale, was officially appointed by the Labour Government to inquire into the organisation, structure, operation, efficiency and competitiveness of the United Kingdom shipping industry.[1] It was a momentous event in the history of British merchant shipping and was indeed the first comprehensive investigation of the shipping industry ever to be undertaken by an entirely independent body.[2] The origins of the decision to set up the inquiry are obscure; the industry thought it might be a by-product of the seamen's strike in 1966[3] which the President of the Board of Trade had described as proving the crucial importance of British shipping to the British economy[4] but a leading British owner[5] considered that public concern justified the inquiry because for the previous eight years profitability had been low, foreign fleets had been growing rapidly whilst the British fleet had stood still[6] and there was a suspicion that British shipping management was asleep.

When the Rochdale Committee commenced their inquiry they found that a wind of change was beginning to blow through the industry; at that time it seemed little more than a zephyr but three years later it had become a gale and "there was a new spirit of enterprise evident in the management of many

1. P. Debs. 5 Ser., Vol. 745, c.(98) and Vol. 748, c.(335). For the Committee's full terms of reference see Rochdale Report, p. xv.

2. None of the members of the Committee were connected with any British shipping or shipbuilding company.

3. See the First and Second Reports of the Court of Enquiry under Lord Pearson into the causes of the strike—Cmnd. 3025 and Cmnd. 3211, Parl. Papers 1966–67, Vol. 36. The strike inflicted severe damage to the national economy.

4. Chamber of Shipping Annual Report 1966–67, p. 159.

5. J. Lindsay Alexander of Ocean Steam Ship Company, "British Shipping in the Light of the Rochdale Report", *Institute of Transport Journal*, Vol. 33 (July 1970).

6. Between 1960 and 1967 world tonnage (merchant ships of 500 g.r.t. and over) had increased from 123.3 million tons to 174.5 million tons but over the same period U.K. tonnage had only grown marginally from 20.2 million tons to 20.375 million tons (Chamber of Shipping Annual Report 1971, Table 5(A) of the Statistical Tables).

shipping companies".[7] By early 1970, when the Committee made their Report, the manifestation of this new spirit had become apparent; in June 1970 U.K. registered tonnage[8] stood at 24.9 million g.r.t., an increase of 2.5 million g.r.t. since June 1968, and in September 1969 nearly 8 million g.r.t. of vessels were on order in home and overseas yards for U.K. registration.[9] The years of stagnation were at last over and during the next two years the growth continued; by June 1971 U.K. tonnage had increased to 26.4 million g.r.t. and in June 1972 it stood at 27.7 million g.r.t.[10] Moreover the growth was of the right kind, consisting mainly of container ships and larger tankers and bulk carriers, and in mid-1972 the average age of the U.K. owned and registered fleet had fallen to 6.9 years compared with 9.5 years in mid-1967.

Amongst the factors which brought about the remarkable increase in U.K. tonnage between 1968 and 1972 were the more rapid growth of world seaborne trade in the second half of the 1960s,[11] a rising trend in shipping profits[12] and the arrival in the higher levels of ship management of a generation unaffected by complacency, free from the memories of the inter-war years and eager to explore the possibilities of new trades with new ships financed from external sources. There can, however, be no doubt that two of the most important factors were the introduction in 1966 of cash investment grants in place of taxation investment allowances[13] and the ready availability of relatively inexpensive Government guaranteed home shipbuilding loans under the new 1967 Shipbuilding Credit Scheme.[14]

In a White Paper on Investment Incentives published on 17th January 1966[15] it was announced that investment allowances were to be withdrawn and were to be replaced for certain industries, including shipping, by a new system of investment grants.[16] The Finance Act 1966[17] abolished investment allowances in respect of expenditure incurred after 17th January 1966 save that a shipowner could still claim investment allowance under a contract entered into not later than 16th January 1966 provided the ship was brought into service

7. Rochdale Report, paras. 7 and 219.

8. Ships of 100 g.r.t. and over—Chamber of Shipping's *British Shipping Statistics 1973*, Table 1.5.

9. Rochdale Report, Table 3.3, which excludes ships of less than 500 g.r.t.

10. *British Shipping Statistics 1973*, Table 1.5. World tonnage also grew substantially—from 189.5 million g.r.t. in 1968 to 254 million g.r.t. in 1972.

11. The weight of cargo carried (excluding Great Lakes' trade) in million metric tons was 1,080 in 1960, 1,640 in 1965 and 2,560 in 1970—*British Shipping Statistics 1973*, Table 6.1.

12. See Rochdale Committee's "Financial Study", Report, Table 18.2.

13. See Rochdale Report, para. 1378.

14. See pp. 212 *et seq. infra*.

15. Cmnd. 2874, Parl. Papers 1965–66, Vol. 13.

16. Shipping was the only service industry within the new system because, as the Government spokesman in the Lords put it, "our maritime fleet plays a major part in balancing our payments by overseas earnings" (P. Debs. (HL), Vol. 276, c.1492).

17. 1966, c.18, s.35.

not later than 16th January 1968. Free depreciation for new ships[18] continued but writing-down allowances could only be claimed in respect of the cost of a new ship less the amount of any investment grant received for that ship.

The Industrial Development Bill giving effect to the new investment grants scheme, which was to be administered by the Board of Trade,[19] was the subject of lengthy debates in the Commons[20] but there was little criticism of the provisions dealing with shipping; thereafter the Bill passed rapidly through the Lords and received the Royal Assent on 12th August 1966.[21] Section 5 of the Act provided that the Board of Trade might make to any person[22] carrying on business in Great Britain a grant towards approved capital expenditure incurred in providing a new ship,[23] or converting an existing ship, for use for the purposes of that business.[24] The grant was to be at the rate of 20 per cent but by an Order coming into effect on 30th December 1966[25] the rate of grant was increased to 25 per cent in respect of expenditure incurred between 1st January 1967 and 31st December 1968. Section 8 of the Act gave a wide discretion to the Board of Trade with regard to the imposition of conditions on the recipients of grants and in the case of ships there were to be chartering restrictions.[26]

Doubts arose about the extent of the Board's discretion; "approved capital expenditure" was defined by Section 13 of the Act as "expenditure appearing to the Board to be of a capital nature and approved by them for the purposes of the grant" but did this mean that the Board had an absolute discretion in deciding whether or not any particular capital expenditure should be "approved" and, assuming capital expenditure was approved, did this mean that the Board was then bound to pay a grant since the Act provided that the Board "may" make a grant. Eventually these doubts were resolved by a decision of the House of Lords[27] who, in a unanimous opinion, held that "may" did not mean "shall", that no person had a right to receive grant and that Parliament had clearly given to the Board an unqualified discretion so that the Board was not bound to pay to every person who was eligible to receive a grant. Thus a clear distinction was drawn between the discretionary nature

18. See p. 177 *supra*.
19. The administration of investment grants was transferred to the Ministry of Technology in 1969 and then in 1970 to the Secretary of State for Trade and Industry.
20. P. Debs. 5 Ser., Vol. 728, c.941 and Vol. 732, c.380.
21. Industrial Development Act 1966, c.34.
22. In the case of a shipowning company it had to be incorporated and resident in Great Britain.
23. "New" meant "unused and not second-hand" and to be eligible for grant the ship had to be registered in the United Kingdom under Part I of the Merchant Shipping Act 1894.
24. A grant could also be made in respect of a new part for a ship but it had to be a significant addition of a capital nature.
25. The Industrial Development (Variation of Rate of Grant) Order 1966, SI 1569.
26. From the outset shipowners had misgivings about the manner in which the Board would exercise their discretion—see Chamber of Shipping Annual Report 1966–67, p. 60.
27. *British Oxygen Co. Ltd.* v. *Minister of Technology* ([1970] 3 All ER 165 HL).

of investment grants as compared with the former absolute entitlement to claim investment allowances.[28]

The purpose of the requirement that a company had to be "resident" in Great Britain was to ensure that only a shipowning company liable to U.K. taxation on its profits should be eligible for grant. For tax purposes a company is resident in the country where its central management and control actually abides, i.e. where its real business is carried on[29] and the great majority of U.K. shipowning companies were undoubtedly resident in Great Britain. However a number of enterprising foreign shipping entrepreneurs found the grant system so attractive[30] that they established new subsidiary companies in England[31] in order that these new companies, instead of their overseas parent, might order new ships, to be built in the United Kingdom or abroad,[32] and thus qualify for investment grants. Although these foreign-owned English subsidiaries usually had at least a majority of English resident directors and always held their board meetings in England, doubts might well have been raised as to whether in fact, whatever the Articles of Association might provide,[33] the important business decisions were taken by the directors in England or by the foreign shareholders abroad.[34] However it is believed that in no case did the Board challenge the investment grant claims of the new foreign owned "brass plate" subsidiaries on the grounds that they were not in law resident in Great Britain.

A similar doubt could well have arisen in relation to the requirement that, in order to be eligible for grant, the new ship had to be registered in England. Under the Merchant Shipping Act 1894 only a "British ship" is so capable of registration and Section 1 of the Act provides that a ship shall not be deemed a British ship unless the owning company is a body corporate established under and subject to the laws of some part of Her Majesty's Dominions and having its "principal place of business" in those Dominions. The test for ascertaining the location of a company's principal place of business is the same as that for establishing its residence, i.e. the country where the real business is carried on[35] but,

28. Section 16 of the Finance Act 1954 (as amended) provided that an investment allowance "*shall* be made".

29. See *De Beers Consolidated Mines Ltd.* v. *Howe* [1906] AC 455.

30. Not only the grant but also the ready availability of cheap finance.

31. The fact that all the shares in an English company were foreign owned did not, under the Act, disentitle the company from claiming grant.

32. A shipowning company was entitled to claim grant whether its new ships were built in the U.K. or elsewhere.

33. See for example Article 80 of Table A in the First Schedule to the Companies Act 1948.

34. If, on the facts, the central management and control of a company was exercised in a foreign country, that company would not be resident in Great Britain even if the acts of management were not irregular or unauthorised or unlawful—see *Unit Construction Co. Ltd.* v. *Bullock* [1960] AC 351.

35. In the Great War case of *The Polzeath* ([1916] P. 117 and 241) the court decided that in fact the English owning company was managed by the controlling shareholders in Germany, that the company's principal place of business was in Germany and that the ship was not therefore qualified to be a British ship.

in the case of some of the new foreign owned companies set up in the late 1960s to take advantage of the investment grant, it could well have been contended that on the facts the location of the effective management was in a foreign country.[36] In that case a ship owned by such a company would not be qualified to be registered as a British ship under the Merchant Shipping Act or to receive investment grant but, as far as is known, no challenge was made either by the Registrar of British Ships or by the Board of Trade.

In accordance with Section 8 of the Industrial Development Act, the Board imposed stringent, and in some cases impracticable, chartering conditions for the purpose of ensuring that the benefits from the operation of new ships did not flow abroad through, for example, the charter to a foreigner at below market rate. Within a five-year period from the date of a new vessel's delivery all charters, other than for a single voyage, had to be approved by the Board, demise charters to foreigners were prohibited, and the Board had also to approve any varying of the charters and the making of any sub-charters; any breach of the chartering conditions entitled the Board to require repayment of the whole of the grant but in most cases where a breach occurred the Board only demanded repayment of a proportionate part of the grant based on the relationship of the period of qualifying use to the five year period during which the chartering restrictions applied.[37]

The new system of grants had been introduced because the Government believed that cash grants would be an effective instrument for achieving the level of investment required in those sectors of industry, including shipping in particular, which could make the greatest contribution to strengthening the balance of payments.[38] However during the course of 1967 it was realised that new British ships, especially if built abroad, which were owned and operated by foreign controlled English companies might well contribute very little benefit to the balance of payments and might even result in a loss.[39] In January 1968 an attempt was made to rectify this situation by subjecting to a special Exchange Control scrutiny all applications for grant by foreign-controlled British companies which had commenced active business since the beginning of 1963 or which had since that date passed under foreign control; the purpose of this special scrutiny was to disallow payment of grant unless the applicant could demonstrate that the transaction, taken as a whole, was likely to be advantageous to the U.K. balance of payments in the short term.[40]

36. Some of these new companies were controlled by Norwegian or Greek shipowners and it hardly seems likely that they would have left the important management decisions to be taken by the English nominee directors on their own.

37. The Board also imposed other conditions, the breach of which involved the repayment of the whole or a proportionate part of the grant. For example repayment was required if, within five years of the delivery of the ship, it ceased to be used in the applicant's business.

38. Cmnd. 2874, para. 56.

39. Rochdale Report, para. 1380.

40. *Ibid.*, para. 1381.

The special scrutiny did have some modest deterrent effect but it did not really achieve its objective[41] and in November 1969 the Government felt compelled to take further action to ensure that investment grant was not given on ships where to do so would be detrimental to the balance of payments[42] and accordingly introduced the Industrial Development (Ships) Bill under which there was to be a new Treasury scrutiny applicable to all eligible ships, which would replace the limited Exchange Control scrutiny. Section 1 of the Industrial Development (Ships) Act 1970[43] provided that, if the Treasury were of the opinion that the granting of an application for investment grant under Section 5 of the 1966 Act would operate to the detriment of the United Kingdom in the matter of its balance of payments, they might direct the Minister of Technology[44] to refrain from granting it. The section was to apply to every shipping application received after 10th November 1969[45] other than, first, an application relating to a ship built or converted in the Convention area for the purposes of the European Free Trade Association Act 1960[46] or the Republic of Ireland or, secondly, where it was shown to the satisfaction of the Minister that the building or conversion of the ship was in fulfilment of a binding obligation incurred before 10th November 1969.

Apart from the United Kingdom itself, Denmark, Norway, Sweden and Finland were the only EFTA countries in which U.K. owners were likely to place shipbuilding orders so what the 1970 Act really amounted to was that, in respect of a ship built or converted outside the United Kingdom and these four Scandinavian countries, the payment of investment grant would depend upon the applicant passing the Treasury balance of payments test unless a contract for the building or conversion had been made before 10th November 1969. The 1970 Act was itself an enabling measure and the exact nature of the test was laid down in complex rules issued by the Treasury[47] which stated that the test was to consist of an evaluation of prospective balance of payments costs and benefits.[48]

It was difficult to be sure of the likely outcome of the test in any particular case but as a generalisation it could be said that a U.K. controlled company with the ship chartered on the open market would usually pass the test whereas a foreign controlled company might well fail if such factors as the source of

41. *Ibid.*, para. 1382.
42. P. Debs. 5 Ser., Vol. 792, c.117.
43. 1970, c.2.
44. By November 1969 the Minister of Technology had taken over the Board of Trade's functions under the 1966 Act.
45. The date of publication of the Bill.
46. Section 10 of the Act (8 & 9 Eliz. II, c.19) defined the Convention area as meaning Austria, Denmark, Great Britain, Northern Ireland, the Isle of Man, the Channel Islands, Liechtenstein, Norway with Spitzbergen, Portugal with the Azores and Madeira, Sweden and Switzerland. Subsequently Finland, Greenland and the Faroe Islands were included.
47. The Chamber of Shipping circular explaining the text ran to some 20 pages.
48. Rochdale Report, para. 1383 gives a brief description of the basis of the test.

finance, nationality of crews and location of management were adverse. Certainly the new Treasury test blocked some applications for grant that would otherwise have succeeded but on the other hand ships built in the U.K. or the EFTA countries were outside the ambit of the 1970 Act and in these cases there could still be a net loss to the balance of payments.[49]

Although the administration of the investment grant system did in some cases lead to abuse, it cannot be doubted that the new system "provided an enormous incentive for the expansion and re-equipment of the British mercantile marine".[50] The impact of investment grant on the placing of new orders by U.K. owners can best be shown by considering the figures for the period 1967 to 1970, since grants were first paid in April 1967 and, subject to minor exceptions, ceased to be payable in respect of expenditure under building contracts concluded on or after 27th October 1970,[51] and by comparing these figures with those for the two years immediately preceding the investment grant period. The following table shows the shipbuilding orders placed in U.K. and foreign yards by U.K. owners over the period 1965–70 and demonstrates the extent to which the availability of investment grant helped to produce a dramatic increase in orders:

Shipbuilding orders by U.K. owners in U.K. and foreign shipyards 1965–70 '000 g.r.t.[52]

Years	*Orders in U.K. yards*	*Orders in foreign yards*	*Total Orders*
1965	678	920	1,598
1966	314	870	1,184
1967	971	1,740	2,711
1968	1,452	1,010	2,462
1969	1,721	2,500	4,221
1970	1,449	4,870	6,319
1965–70	6,585	11,910	18,495

In respect of this unprecedented volume of new tonnage ordered by U.K. owners between 1966 and 1970, the total expenditure approved for grant purposes amounted to £870.9 million and grants paid up to 31st March 1971 totalled £196.8 million of which only £9.1 million was for conversions

49. *Ibid*., para. 1385.

50. From the speech of the President of the Chamber of Shipping on 25th February 1971. See also Rochdale Report, paras. 1378 and 1379, p. 315.

51. Investment and Building Grants Act 1971, Section 1—see further *infra*.

52. For orders in U.K. yards see *British Shipping Statistics 1973*, Table 3.4. For orders in foreign yards see Appendix C to the Report of the Shipbuilding Industry Board for the period 1st April to 31st December 1971 (Parl. Papers 1971–72 (316), Vol. 37).

and parts.[53] The annual investment grant reports did not disclose in what proportion the grants paid related to orders in the U.K. and foreign yards respectively but since, in terms of tonnage, nearly two thirds of the orders between 1967 and 1970 were placed in foreign yards, it seems probable that at least half of the grants paid were for ships built abroad. The fact that foreign shipbuilding contracts attracted grant at all gave rise to persistent criticism by the Conservative Opposition[54] who contended that the British shipbuilding industry would benefit greatly if investment grant was paid for home orders only; the reply of the Board of Trade Minister was that the purpose of the grant was not to assist British builders but to help British owners acquire first class modern ships and that owners must be free to get the best ship at the best price delivered on time with the right credit.

So investment grant continued to be paid in respect of foreign new buildings ordered by both British and non-resident controlled U.K. companies[55] and for the years 1969 and 1970 the total tonnage ordered for building abroad was more than double the tonnage ordered in British yards. It does not however follow that, if grant had been payable for British built ships only, the orders placed abroad would instead have been placed in British yards; in general the delivery dates quoted by foreign builders were much shorter than those offered by British builders,[56] many U.K. owners had more confidence in the ability of foreign yards to deliver on the contracted dates and there were substantial price differentials between the U.K. yards and their foreign competitors. It therefore seems unlikely that the restriction of grant to British built ships would have produced a significant increase in the orders placed with U.K. yards; more likely many of the ships ordered abroad would not have been built for U.K. registration at all.

The new Conservative Government, which came to power in June 1970, instituted a study of investment incentives for industry and in October published a White Paper on Investment Incentives[57] which stated that investment grant had not achieved its objectives since it benefited firms whether or not they were making profits and could result in uneconomic investment leading

53. For detailed figures over the period 17th January 1966 to 31st March 1971 see the Annual Reports required to be made under Section 12 of the 1966 Act—namely Report 1967–68 (Parl. Papers 1967–68 (420), Vol. 24), Report 1968–69 (Parl. Papers 1968–69 (329), Vol. 33), Reports 1969–70 and 1970–71 (Parl. Papers 1970–71 (124) and (580), Vol. 25).

54. See P. Debs. 5 Ser., Vol. 757, c.(120); Vol. 760, c.1368; Vol. 762, c.326 and c.377.

55. For details of the figures as at 30th September 1969 see P. Debs. 5 Ser., Vol. 781, c.(330).

56. Although, between 1967 and 1971 the U.K. order book rose dramatically, U.K. output in this period remained static at an annual average of 1.1 million g.r.t. (See *Booz-Allen and Hamilton Report on British Shipbuilding 1972* (HMSO), Exhibits 30 and 40). In contrast the output of Japan and some European builders rose substantially (*British Shipping Statistics* 1973 Table 3.3).

57. Cmnd. 4516, Parl. Papers 1970–71, Vol. 10.

to a waste of resources[58]; the Government had accordingly decided to replace investment grants with tax allowances and reductions. As regards shipping in particular, the White Paper referred to the general conclusions of the Rochdale Committee on investment grant[59] and especially to the Committee's opinion that in certain cases payment of grant could lead to a net loss to the balance of payments[60]; the Government considered that the Industrial Development (Ships) Act 1970 had reduced but not eliminated this problem and agreed with the Committee's view that it was still possible to circumvent the intention underlying the new test.

Although the Rochdale Committee had recommended that the level of special assistance for shipping should for the present be kept broadly unchanged and that as soon as practicable investment grants for ships should be withdrawn and replaced with investment allowances of the same nature as was applicable before 1966,[61] the Government did not agree with this view and had concluded that retention of free depreciation would present a reasonable degree of preferential treatment for ships in relation to the new arrangements for industry in general. This radical change of policy was a great disappointment to the shipping industry; the Chamber of Shipping emphasised that the surge of new orders between 1967 and 1970 had owed much to the stimulus provided by investment grants and that the proposed abolition of the grants system would bring about a serious decline in new orders. In addition shipowners felt aggrieved that the Government had rejected the Rochdale recommendation that the level of special assistance to the industry should be maintained.[62]

Unmoved by the shipowners' representations, the Government proceeded with the legislation required to implement its new policy. The Income and Corporation Tax (No. 2) Act 1970[63] reduced the charge of corporation tax from 45 per cent to 42½ per cent and also reduced the standard rate of income tax by five per cent. Then the Investment and Building Grants Act 1971[64] provided that, subject to certain exceptions, no grant was to be made under Part I of the Industrial Development Act 1966[65] in respect of expenditure on or after 27th October 1970 unless the Secretary of State was satisfied that such expenditure consisted of sums falling due under a contract made before 27th October 1970. The Act did however make three exceptions in relation to

58. The Government's reasons for abolishing investment grant were elaborated by the Chancellor of the Exchequer in a later debate—P. Debs. 5 Ser., Vol. 805, c.1097.
59. Rochdale Report, paras. 1378–1387 and 1393–1399.
60. *Ibid.*, para. 1385.
61. *Ibid.*, paras. 1356, 1359 and 1399.
62. Free depreciation on 100 per cent of a new ship's cost was far less beneficial than the investment and annual allowances totalling 140 per cent of cost available up to 1966.
63. 1970, c.54.
64. 1971, c.51.
65. Part I of the 1966 Act contained the provisions for grants in respect of new ships.

shipbuilding contracts; grant could be paid under a contract made after 27th October 1970 if such contract was in substitution for one made for a similar ship before that date,[66] an assignment of a contract after 27th October 1970 was permitted if the assignee was a company in the same group as the original contracting party and grant was payable in respect of extra items ordered after 27th October 1970 for a new ship which had been contracted before that date.

Thus in general no investment grant was claimable in respect of new building contracts made after 27th October 1970 and although, in the case of new ships, the Finance Act 1971[67] provided that there should be a first year allowance equal to the whole of the capital expenditure and that the allowance could be claimed on each instalment under a building contract as it fell due for payment[68] the withdrawal of the investment grant in October 1970 had the prejudicial effect on the British shipping and shipbuilding industries which many had predicted. A falling off in new orders by British shipowners was quickly manifest; the annual average of new tonnage ordered by U.K. companies from U.K. yards in 1971 and 1972 was only 716,000 g.r.t.,[69] compared with an annual average of 1.54 million g.r.t. for the three years 1968–70, and for the 12 months ending 31st January 1972 orders for U.K. flag in home and overseas yards totalled 2.34 million d.w.t. (3.1 per cent of world orders) whereas for the previous 12 months ending 31st January 1971 such orders totalled 8.66 million d.w.t. (10.7 per cent of world orders).[70]

The Chamber of Shipping regarded this drastic reduction in new orders as having serious implications for British maritime strength and at the end of 1971 they informed the Government of the need for some fresh incentive to stimulate renewed investment. The Government remained obdurate even when in 1972, at the invitation of the Government, shipowners and shipbuilders jointly submitted a new incentive scheme intended to benefit both industries; the Secretary of State said that he had concluded that the reintroduction of a general scheme of investment grant for shipping was not economically justifiable.[71] So with no further measures for the encouragement of new orders, U.K. orders for new tonnage continued to decline; in 1972 the orders placed by U.K. owners with U.K. builders totalled only 599,000 g.r.t.; except for 1966, this was the lowest yearly figure since 1963.[72]

Apart from investment grant, which was paid for ships built both at home

66. But only to the extent that the payments under the substituted contract did not exceed those payable under the original contract.

67. 1971, c.68.

68. Section 42(2). Under the special rules for new ships (para. 8 of Schedule 8) shipowners had the same degree of flexibility as they had had previously in relation to free depreciation.

69. Chamber of Shipping Annual Report 1972, Statistical Table 3.4.

70. *Ibid.*, Statistical Table 3.5 (ships of 1,000 g.r.t. and over).

71. P. Debs. 5 Ser., Vol. 842, c.(453).

72. Chamber of Shipping Annual Report 1972, Statistical Table 3.4.

and overseas, the other major factor which contributed to the surge of shipbuilding orders placed with U.K. yards by U.K. owners between 1967 and 1971 was the introduction in 1967 of new Government backed credit facilities for home owner building in home yards. The increase in orders which resulted from the 1964 Shipbuilding Credit Scheme[73] had proved no more than a temporary palliative; the ending of the scheme brought about a serious decline in orders from U.K. owners[74] and it became clear that British shipbuilders had failed to use the breathing space provided by the Scheme to improve their productivity and make themselves more competitive. Accordingly, early in 1965, the Labour Government announced[75] that Mr Reay Geddes had been appointed as Chairman of a Committee of Inquiry into the Shipbuilding Industry; the Committee's main task was "to establish what changes are necessary in organisation, in the methods of production, and any other factors affecting costs to make the shipbuilding industry competitive in world markets".

The Geddes Report was published in March 1966[76] and among the matters considered by the Committee was the question as to whether the Government should provide credit for home owners on the same terms as that available for overseas purchasers of British built ships.[77] Although the British shipping and shipbuilding industries strongly supported the extension of credit facilities to cover orders of ships in the United Kingdom by home owners,[78] the Geddes Committee did not favour the immediate introduction of a general scheme of credits for home owners[79] but instead, purely as a temporary measure, recommended that from mid-1967 to 1970 there should be provision of up to £30 million for financing home orders on a selective basis so as to assist the stability of the order books of shipbuilding firms undergoing rationalisation.[80] The Chamber of Shipping considered this recommendation to be inadequate in amount and too restrictive in character and strove to convince the Government that it was better for the balance of payments to operate more ships under the British flag than to build vessels on ECGD terms for foreign owners.

Early in 1967 there were signs that the Government might be relenting[81] and then on 15th February 1967 it was announced[82] that the Government had decided that there was a strong case for a credit scheme for British owners

73. See pp. 174 *et seq. supra.*
74. In the year ending 30th June 1964 orders totalled 1.6 million g.r.t.; in the next two years ending 30th June 1965 and 30th June 1966 the total of orders fell to 731,000 g.r.t. and 444,000 g.r.t. respectively (Chamber of Shipping Annual Report 1972, Statistical Table 3.4).
75. P. Debs. 5 Ser., Vol. 705, c.(272).
76. Cmnd. 2937, Parl. Papers 1965–66, Vol. 7.
77. The other matters covered by the Report are dealt with later—see pp. 217 *et seq. infra.*
78. Their reasons for doing so are given in para. 525 of the Report.
79. Report, para. 531.
80. *Ibid.*, para. 556.
81. P. Debs. 5 Ser., Vol. 739, c.21 and Vol. 740, c.1658.
82. *Ibid.*, Vol. 741, c.130.

going beyond that recommended by the Geddes Committee and that the Shipbuilding Industry Bill[83] would include a provision enabling the Minister of Technology[84] to guarantee loans to shipowners for the construction of ships in U.K. yards up to a total of £200 million at any one time.[85] Subsequently Section 7 of the Shipbuilding Industry Act 1967 provided that the Minister was empowered to guarantee the payment by any person resident or company incorporated in the United Kingdom of the principal or interest of a loan made for the purpose of financing the construction in a U.K. shipyard of a ship of not less than 100 g.r.t. and the equipment of that ship; the Section applied to any order placed after 15th February 1967, no guarantee was to be given except on the recommendation of the Shipbuilding Industry Board ("SIB"),[86] the terms and conditions of the guarantee were to be approved by the Treasury and the principal guaranteed was not to exceed £200 million.

The new facilities backed by the Section 7 guarantees clearly fulfilled British owners' long felt need for a competitive home credit scheme and proved to be an immediate and continuing success. The Act came into force on 28th June 1967 and in the second half of 1967 orders in U.K. yards from U.K. owners totalled 881,000 g.r.t compared with only 89,000 g.r.t. in the first half of that year.[87] The demand for Section 7 loans was so strong that by 31st March 1968 the SIB had already made recommendations to the Minister relating to 77 ships[88] and during the remainder of 1968 the demand for loans continued at such a high level that by the end of the year 52 guarantees amounting to £86 million had been given and 48 further guarantees bringing the total up to the maximum limit of £200 million were under negotiation or had been approved in principle.[89] In these circumstances the Government decided that the statutory limit would have to be raised to £400 million and in January 1969 a short Shipbuilding Industry Bill was introduced for this purpose.

The Bill, which was generally welcomed,[90] quickly passed through all its stages in both Houses without any divisions and received the Royal Assent on 6th March 1969.[91] The authorised increase in the guarantee limit to £400

83. This was the Bill to implement the recommendation of the Geddes Committee—see further pp. 218 *et seq. infra*.

84. Responsibility for the shipbuilding industry had been transferred from the Board of Trade to the Ministry of Technology on 21st November 1966.

85. The English and Scottish clearing banks were being asked to make their loans on the same terms as those applying to export credits backed by ECGD.

86. The SIB was established by Section 1 of the Shipbuilding Industry Act 1967—see further p. 219 *infra*.

87. *British Shipping Statistics 1973*, Table 3.4.

88. See First Report and Accounts of the SIB for the period ended 31st March 1968 (Parl. Papers 1967–68 (361), Vol. 31).

89. P. Debs. 5 Ser., Vol. 776, c.(109).

90. P. Debs. 5 Ser., Vol. 776, c.675.

91. Shipbuilding Industry Act 1969, Chapter 6.

million came none too soon; the SIB Report for the year ended 31st March 1969[92] disclosed that the Board had made recommendations for 188 ships having an estimated contract value of £363 million and considered that, if orders continued at the same rate, the new limit of £400 million would be rapidly reached. During the remainder of 1969 the spate of new orders did continue[93] and in January 1970 the Government stated that legislation would be introduced to increase the guarantee limit to £600 million.[94] In order to authorise such increase a further short Shipbuilding Industry Bill was introduced and passed its Second Reading on 30th April 1970[95] but a general election then ensued and the Bill was lost on the dissolution of Parliament.

Shortly after the Election the new Conservative Government confirmed that the Bill to raise the limit of guarantees would be reintroduced and in November 1970 the Secretary of State for Trade and Industry[96] announced that he was making an Order to extend the life of the SIB up to the end of 1971.[97] In February 1971 the Secretary of State announced that the guarantee limit was to be raised to £700 million, instead of £600 million as proposed by the previous administration, and for this sole purpose a further Shipbuilding Industry Bill received its Second Reading in April[98]; like its 1969 predecessor, the 1971 Bill passed quickly through all its stages and received the Royal Assent on 1st July 1971.[99] As in 1969, the new Act came none too soon; by 31st March 1971 the SIB had made recommendations for a total of 463 ships having a contract value of £981 million but the Board pointed out that the total amount guaranteed would be less because some orders might not be proceeded with and because guaranteed loans did not exceed 80 per cent of the contract value.[100]

Even before the passing of the 1971 Act the SIB considered that a limit of £700 million would prove insufficient and in August 1971 the Government announced[101] that it was intended to raise the limit for guaranteed loans to £1,000 million which it was thought should prove sufficient to provide finance

92. Parl. Papers 1968–69 (326), Vol. 45.
93. P. Debs. 5 Ser., Vol. 791, c.34.
94. P. Debs. 5 Ser., Vol. 794, c.511. The need for this further increase was emphasised by the SIB Report for the year ended 31st March 1970 (Parl. Papers 1970–71 (84), Vol. 49), which stated that the total of recommended guarantees up to that date was for 349 ships of an estimated contract value of £687 million.
95. P. Debs. 5 Ser., Vol. 800, c.1470.
96. John Davies, who had become the Minister responsible for shipbuilding on 20th October 1970—Secretary of State for Trade and Industry Order 1970 (SI 1970 No. 1537).
97. P. Debs. 5 Ser., Vol. 806, c.(1). Under Section 9 of the 1967 Act the SIB would otherwise have been dissolved on 31st December 1970. Had the extension not been made no further guarantees could have been given after 31st December 1970.
98. P. Debs. 5 Ser., Vol. 815, c.1381.
99. Shipbuilding Industry Act 1971, c.46.
100. SIB Report for the year ended 31st March 1971 (Parl. Papers 1970–71 (554), Vol. 49).
101. P. Debs. 5 Ser., Vol. 822, c.(315).

for all orders placed by U.K. owners in U.K. yards within the next five years.[102] The need for this further increase was made evident when the SIB, following its dissolution on 31st December 1971, published its Final Report[103]; this showed that during its lifetime—a period of four and a half years—the Board had recommended Government guarantees for bank loans in respect of 488 ships having an estimated total contract value of £1,095 million.[104] The Second Reading of the Industry Bill 1972 took place on 22nd May 1972[105]; the Bill was a far-reaching measure since, in addition to making provision for credits and grants for the construction of ships and mobile offshore installations in the United Kingdom,[106] provision was also made for the giving of selective financial assistance to industries in assisted areas and generally.[107]

Under Section 10 of the Industry Act 1972 (which replaced with modifications Section 7 of the Shipbuilding Industry Act 1967), the guarantee scheme was continued in much the same form[108] but with a substantially greater maximum financial limit; the aggregate of the liability at any time under guarantees given under Section 10 of the 1972 Act and Section 7 of the 1967 Act was not to exceed £1,000 million but there was power by Order to raise that limit to £1,400 million.[109] Section 10 of the 1972 Act also empowered the Secretary of State to make loans, within limits, to persons who were creditors in respect of any finance guaranteed by the Government under Section 10 of the 1972 Act or Section 7 of the 1967 Act.[110]

At its inception the 1967 Shipbuilding Credit Scheme did give rise to some administrative and legal problems; this was hardly surprising for such a novel major financing operation involving several Government departments, the SIB, the principal English and Scottish banks and the majority of British shipowners

102. Since the SIB was to be dissolved on 31st December 1971 it was apparent that the new legislation to increase the guarantee limit would also have to dispense with the requirement in Section 7 of the 1967 Act that there had to be a recommendation by the SIB before any guarantee could be given.

103. Parl. Papers 1971–72 (316), Vol. 37. Report for the nine months ended 31st December 1971.

104. As at 31st March 1972 the principal guaranteed amounted to just over £465 million (Parl. Papers 1972–73 (155), Vol. 16. Accounts re. Issues from National Loan Funds 1971–72, p. 101).

105. P. Debs. 5 Ser., Vol. 837, c.1008. Royal Assent to the Industry Act 1972 (c.63) was given on 9th August 1972.

106. Sections 10, 11 and 12 in Part III of the Bill. As to grants to shipbuilding under Section 11 see p. 231 *infra.*

107. Sections 7, 8 & 9 in Part II of the Bill. As to financial assistance for shipbuilders under Part II see pp. 232 *et seq. infra.*

108. There was no longer any time limit nor need for any SIB recommendation but the Secretary of State had to obtain the consent of the Treasury to the giving of any guarantee.

109. Such Order required the consent of the Treasury and the approval of the House of Commons. By the Ships and Mobile Offshore Installation Construction Credits (Increase of Limit) Order 1975 (SI 1975 No. 138) the limit was increased to £1,400 million.

110. This was to enable the Government to fund the lending banks if the total of the guaranteed loans exceeded the amount which the banks had from time to time agreed that they would provide from their own resources. By 31st March 1973 the Government had refinanced the banks to the extent of £50 million.

and shipbuilders. However the initial difficulties were soon overcome and, since the Treasury and the banks had agreed that the loans should be repayable over eight years from the delivery of the ship with interest at only 5½ per cent per annum, the scheme undoubtedly achieved one of its main objectives—to prevent British owners being forced to place their orders abroad in order to take advantage of better credit facilities. During the period of four and a half years from July 1967 to December 1971, when guaranteed loans were only given on the recommendation of the SIB, orders placed in U.K. yards by U.K. owners totalled 6.336 million g.r.t. compared with a total of 3.193 million g.r.t. during the four and a half years prior to July 1967[111]; since investment grant was equally available for ships built at home and abroad, it can hardly be doubted that if British credit facilities from mid-1967 onwards had not been comparable to those obtainable abroad, much of the tonnage ordered in U.K. yards would have been built overseas.

The SIB emphasised that the financial assistance provided under the 1967 scheme had been "a powerful stimulus to the placing of orders by British shipowners in British shipyards"[112] and the extent to which British builders were dependent on home orders between mid-1967 and the end of 1971 is amply borne out by the fact that, in terms of tonnage, more than 75 per cent of all the orders received in this period came from British owners[113]; if, through lack of adequate credit facilities, many of the orders had been diverted abroad, some British yards might well have not survived. So the 1967 scheme played a substantial part in keeping the British shipbuilding industry afloat but it is doubtful whether it achieved its other main objective which was to reinforce the reorganisation of the industry along the lines recommended in the Geddes Report and provided for in the Shipbuilding Industry Act 1967.

The Geddes Committee had proceeded upon the assumption that the world market for ships was likely to continue to grow, that a large part of the world market was open to a competitive British shipbuilding industry and that there was no natural or geographical obstacle to the British industry becoming fully competitive in world shipbuilding provided that those concerned were determined to make it so.[114] The Committee identified the major shortcomings in the industry and recommended the action required to make it efficient and competitive; the main recommendation for management was to carry out a fundamental structural reorganisation of the industry by concentrating its main strengths into four big and compact groups[115] and the unions, jointly with management, were recommended to establish new standards of general efficiency and performance,[116] to develop industrial and human

111. *British Shipping Statistics 1973*, Table 3.4.
112. SIB Report for year ended 31st March 1969. Parl. Papers 1968–69 (326), Vol. 45.
113. *British Shipping Statistics 1973*, Table 3.4.
114. Geddes Report, (Cmnd. 2937), paras. 78–94, 123 and 127.
115. Report, Chapters 17 and 18.
116. Along the lines of Chapters 8 to 17 of the Report.

relations[117] and to observe bargains in the spirit and the letter. In addition the unions were urged to review their structure with a view to achieving a situation in which all shipbuilding workers would be members of only five unions.[118]

As the industry's biggest customer the Government were recommended to segregate the orders for all naval ships of considerable size and complexity in three specialist yards only, instead of following the then existing practice whereby nine or 10 yards of the so-called warship group competed for naval orders to mix in with their merchant work.[119] The Committee also recommended the Government to adopt the practice followed in other countries by giving shipbuilders relief from indirect taxation, similar to export rebate, in respect of the sales of ships to home owners.[120] Lastly the Government were recommended to give substantial assistance, by way of grants and loans, to enable the reorganisation of the industry to be carried through quickly and efficiently but the Committee considered that financial assistance should be conditional upon the efforts made by both sides of the industry to make it internationally competitive and to this end the Committee advised the setting up of a Shipbuilding Industry Board to administer and control the Government assistance.[121]

As a first step towards implementing the recommendations made in the Geddes Report, the Finance Act 1966[122] provided for the granting of shipbuilders' relief at a rate to be prescribed[123] in respect of all ships of 80 g.r.t. and over delivered by U.K. builders on or after 12th September 1966.[124] Then on 9th August 1966,[125] just before the summer recess, the President of the Board of Trade announced that the Government had accepted the Geddes Report, that they were satisfied that both sides of the shipbuilding industry had accepted the Geddes recommendations and that legislation to establish a Shipbuilding Industry Board would be initiated. During the latter months of 1966 the Government was under pressure to introduce the necessary legislation and certainly the industry was in urgent need of aid with orders in the second half of the year falling to the exceptionally low figure of 131,000 g.r.t.[126] and output for 1966 only just over 1 million g.r.t.[127] However it was not until 9th

117. Along the lines of Chapter 21 of the Report.

118. Report, paras. 441–448.

119. *Ibid.*, Chapter 24.

120. *Ibid.*, paras. 533–536.

121. *Ibid.*, Chapter 26.

122. 1966, c.18 (Section 2).

123. By the Shipbuilders Relief (Prescribed Percentage) Order 1966 (SI 1966 No. 1026) the rate prescribed was two per cent of the ship's value.

124. If the ships were delivered to foreign purchasers the shipbuilders had the option of either claiming the shipbuilders' relief under the 1966 Act or the export rebate under the Finance (No. 2) Act 1964.

125. P. Debs. 5 Ser., Vol. 733, c.1400.

126. *British Shipping Statistics 1973*, Table 3.4.

127. *Ibid.*, Table 3.3. Japanese output for 1966 was 6.5 million g.r.t. and the output of both West Germany and Sweden exceeded that of the U.K.

March 1967 that the Shipbuilding Industry Bill had its Second Reading[128] but then the Bill passed rapidly through all its stages in both Houses and the Shipbuilding Industry Act 1967 received the Royal Assent on 28th June 1967.[129]

By Section 1 of the Act a Shipbuilding Industry Board was established "for the purpose of promoting the ability of the shipbuilding industry in the United Kingdom to compete in world markets". This was indeed the philosophy underlying the whole Act and in their First Report[130] the SIB stated that they regarded their main role as being "to initiate and stimulate action toward the Geddes objective of a reorganised competitive industry". Apart from their duties under Section 7 of the Act in connection with the administration of the Shipbuilding Credit Scheme,[131] the SIB was empowered under the Act to make grants up to a total of £20 million to shipbuilders or engine builders who were reorganising their resources with a view to increased efficiency[132] and to make loans of up to a total of £32.5 million to facilitate grouping schemes or for providing buildings and plant.[133] The SIB was also required by the Act to make regular Reports to Parliament covering (*inter alia*) the grants and loans which had been made and the recommendations made to the Minister in respect of Section 7 guarantees.[134]

The SIB decided that one of its main tasks was to encourage and financially assist the speedy rationalisation of the industry along the lines recommended in the Geddes Report[135] and by 31st March 1968[136] five yards on the Upper Clyde had merged to form Upper Clyde Shipbuilders, five companies on the Tyne and Tees had merged to form Swan Hunter Shipbuilders and two yards in Southampton had agreed to merge under the name of Vosper Thorneycroft. Progress towards further grouping continued over the next two years and by 31st March 1970 nearly all the structural reorganisation envisaged by the Geddes Committee had been completed[137]; the three yards on the Lower Clyde had merged to form Scott Lithgow, the yards on the Scottish east coast were grouped under Robb Caledon Shipbuilders, Swan Hunter had acquired Furness Shipbuilding, and, on the Wear, Austin & Pickersgill had acquired

128. P. Debs. 5 Ser., Vol. 742, c.1773.
129. 1967, c.40.
130. Parl. Papers 1967–68 (361), Vol. 31.
131. See pp. 214 *et seq. supra*.
132. Section 3. By Section 10 of the Industrial Expansion Act 1968 the financial limit was quadrupled and the scope of Section 3 was considerably extended.
133. Section 4. For any loans made under this Section the SIB could grant relief from interest up to the end of 1970.
134. Section 8. Under Section 10 the Minister was required to present Accounts to Parliament in respect of the financial transactions of the SIB.
135. Paras. 307 to 320 and Appendix P.
136. See SIB's First Report, Parl. Papers 1967–68 (361), Vol. 31.
137. See SIB's Second Report, Parl. Papers 1968–69 (326), Vol. 45 and Third Report, Parl. Papers 1970–71 (84), Vol. 49.

Bartrams and the other three Wearside yards had merged to form Doxford & Sunderland.

For the reorganised shipbuilding industry shortage of orders was not a problem. Influenced by such factors as investment grant, readily available cheap credit facilities for home and overseas buyers, the second closure of Suez, the devaluation of the pound and a general increase in world demand, the volume of new orders in 1968 amounted to 2.565 million g.r.t., the highest for a decade, and the orders for 1968 to 1970, totalling nearly 6.5 million g.r.t., was unprecedented in the industry's post-Second World War experience.[138] Unfortunately output did not rise to meet the demand with the result that the merchant order book rose from just over 2 million g.r.t. at the beginning of 1968 to nearly 5 million g.r.t. at the beginning of 1971.[139]

The Geddes Committee had hoped that, in two or three years after the major reorganisations, the output of the U.K. industry would have risen to 2.25 million g.r.t. per annum[140] but in the event U.K. output between 1967 and 1971 remained static at around an annual average of 1.1 million g.r.t.; indeed the average annual U.K. output had remained static at around 1.2 million g.r.t. since 1955 whilst in the period 1955 to 1971 world output had risen by over 10 per cent a year and the U.K. market share had declined from 27 per cent to five per cent.[141] In 1971 the SIB stated that it was much concerned at the low level of productivity and emphasised that there would have to be a continuing improvement in productivity as well as an increase in the volume of production if the U.K. industry was to enlarge its share of the world market.[142] However in 1972 U.K. output, at under 1.2 million g.r.t., was lower than in 1971 and the situation was made worse by the fact that orders in 1971 were only just over 1 million g.r.t. and in 1972 they fell to 839,000 g.r.t.[143]

The reorganised industry's failure to increase output was certainly not due to any lack of Government support. During its lifetime of four and a half years from mid-1967 to the end of 1971 the SIB, in addition to recommending Government guarantees in respect of 488 ships of an estimated total contract value of £1,095 million, had paid out to U.K. shipbuilders by way of grants and loans a total of nearly £43 million[144] but even finance on this scale proved to be insufficient to ensure the continuance of shipbuilding on the Upper Clyde, the Mersey and in Belfast. The operating losses sustained by Upper Clyde Shipbuilders, Cammell Laird and Harland & Wolff were so severe that,

138. *British Shipping Statistics 1973*, Table 3.4.
139. Booz-Allen Report, Exhibit 40.
140. Report, paras. 568–570.
141. Booz-Allen Report, p. 90 and Exhibit 30. Between 1955 and 1971 the U.K. was the only leading shipbuilding country which achieved no growth in output.
142. Report for year ended 31st March 1971, Parl. Papers 1970–71 (554), Vol. 49.
143. *British Shipping Statistics 1973*, Tables 3.3 and 3.4.
144. Out of this total nearly £28 million went to the yards on the Upper Clyde and in Belfast.

in order to prevent closure of these yards and to furnish further funds for necessary capital expenditure, the Government[145] felt compelled to provide additional financial support by way of grants, loans and equity capital which, for the period 1967 to mid-1972, amounted in all to nearly £117 million.[146]

Notwithstanding this massive financial support and the exceptionally full order book, in the period 1967 to 1971 many shipbuilding companies incurred substantial losses.[147] It had been hoped that the reorganisation of the industry would bring about a significant reduction in the cost of output but in the event operating costs escalated rapidly and major losses were incurred on fixed price contracts in which the allowances for increased costs over the building period often proved hopelessly inadequate.[148] Matters were made worse by late deliveries, which were the norm rather than the exception, and the increasing prevalence of labour disputes was, to no small extent, responsible for the industry's poor delivery record.[149] The Geddes Committee, in their review of industrial and human relations,[150] had emphasised that improvement in this field was "one of the prime conditions of the survival of shipbuilding as a live industry" but between 1967 and 1972 stoppages in the shipbuilding and marine engineering industries continued to compare badly with the national average.[151]

From the outset it had been anticipated that the integration and commercial development of the five yards on the Upper Clyde[152] would prove a formidable problem. Even before the completion of the Geddes Report there had been an ominous forewarning; at the end of 1965 a Treasury Guarantee for £1 million had been given to prevent the closure of Fairfields' Govan yard[153] and in the following year the Government had subscribed more than half the equity capital of, and made a loan of £940,000 to, a newly formed company called Fairfield (Glasgow) Limited to enable that company to acquire the assets and undertaking of the old Fairfields company and to continue shipbuilding in the Govan yard.[154]

Following its formation in September 1967 Upper Clyde Shipbuilders ("UCS") acquired the whole of the share capital of John Brown (Clydebank), Fairfield (Glasgow), Alex Stephens and Chas. Connell and 51 per cent of the

145. Labour up to June 1970; Conservative thereafter.

146. Booz-Allen Report, Exhibit 29. Out of this sum all but £6.4 million went to the Upper Clyde, Cammell Laird and Harland & Wolff. Only about one-third of the total of £160 million provided for the industry was used for capital investment.

147. Booz-Allen Report, Exhibit 71.

148. *Ibid.*, Chapter 17 *passim.*

149. *Ibid.*, p. 102 and Exhibit 39.

150. Report, Chapters 20 & 21.

151. Booz-Allen Report, p. 169 and Exhibit 68.

152. John Brown & Co. (Clydebank) Ltd., Yarrow (Shipbuilders) Ltd., Chas. Connell & Co. (Shipbuilders) Ltd. (Scotstoun yard), Alex Stephens & Sons (Linthouse yard) and Fairfield (Glasgow) Ltd. (Govan yard).

153. See P. Debs. 5 Ser., Vol. 718, c.1234 and Parl. Papers 1965–66 (2), Vol. 8.

154. See P. Debs. 5 Ser., Vol. 732, c.(294) and Vol. 737, c.(68).

share capital of Yarrow (Shipbuilders); on completion of the merger the share capital of UCS was owned 33 per cent by John Brown, 20 per cent by Yarrow, 10 per cent by Stephens, five per cent by Connells, 17 per cent by the Government[155] and the remainder by 10 private persons or trade unions. In the SIB's First Report for the period ended 31st March 1968 signs of unease regarding the future of UCS were already apparent[156] and by the time the Board made their Second Report for the year ended 31st March 1969[157] the alarm bells were ringing louder; losses which UCS were sustaining on both old and new contracts were far heavier than anticipated[158] and the severe strain on UCS's financial resources had only been temporarily alleviated by the Board making substantial grants and loans.

Throughout 1969 a large part of the SIB's time was taken up in wrestling with the problems of UCS; in June the Board accepted a revised UCS plan aimed at viability and made further grants and loans and subscribed £3 million for new shares but when, in the autumn, in spite of having by then received a total of some £13.8 million by way of grants, loans and share subscriptions, UCS sought further financial assistance from the SIB, on this occasion the Board decided that there were no commercial grounds to justify the Board's continued support. UCS thereupon applied for direct help from the Government and in December the Minister of Technology stated that the Government would provide loans not exceeding £7 million and would, if necessary, guarantee completion of new orders.[159] A loan of £7 million was advanced to UCS in February 1970[160] but it was wholly utilised in preventing the immediate insolvency of UCS and, although the labour force was reduced by 3,500, losses still continued and the financial position remained critical.

In June 1970 a new Conservative Government came to power and quickly made it clear that they intended to take a harder policy line in relation to "lame duck" companies but the newly created Department of Trade and Industry were soon embroiled in an Upper Clyde problem which put this philosophy under severe strain. A Government nominee on the Board of UCS reported that it was doubtful whether UCS could be profitable in the long term and questioned whether it was right that UCS should continue trading; in these circumstances the Government decided that for the time being they could not continue to issue guarantees in respect of orders placed with UCS and at the

155. The Government's shareholding in UCS resulted from the Government's holding in Fairfield.

156. See the Report of the Comptroller and Auditor General (paras. 8, 9, 11 and 12) appended to the SIB Report, (Parl. Papers 1967–68 (361), Vol. 31).

157. Parl. Papers 1968–69 (326), Vol. 45.

158. The underestimate was nearly £13.5 million.

159. P. Debs. 5 Ser., Vol. 793, c.662.

160. The terms of the loan were not revealed until one year later—see P. Debs. 5 Ser., Vol. 811, c.(185).

end of October 1970 the Chairman of UCS was so informed.[161] Over the next few months there were lengthy negotiations which culminated in February 1971 with the Secretary of State announcing[162] that the UCS cash flow position had been eased by shipowner customers of UCS making voluntary payments in excess of contract prices; in these circumstances the granting of guarantees was resumed but, with the Government refusing to provide any new public money, the future of UCS still remained doubtful.[163]

The crisis finally came to a head in June 1971 when the Chairman of UCS informed the Secretary of State that the company was insolvent and could no longer continue to trade; the Government thereupon decided that no purpose would be served by a further injection of funds into UCS and on 14th June 1971 UCS petitioned the Scottish court for the appointment of a provisional liquidator. This disastrous situation was reported to the Commons on 14th June[164] and on the following day there was a full debate[165] which was marked by bitter charges and counter-charges as to whether responsibility for the collapse lay with the Conservative Government or the previous Labour administration. However the Secretary of State made it clear that, with the co-operation of the provisional liquidator, the Government intended to bring about a reconstruction with a view to ensuring a viable and prosperous future for shipbuilding on the Upper Clyde; to this end he had appointed a group of experts[166] to advise what action could best be taken and, as an interim measure to enable work on some ships to continue, had agreed to advance £3 million to enable the provisional liquidator to keep all employees on the payroll.[167]

At the end of July 1971 the Government received and published the Advisory Group's Report[168] which was succinct and outspoken. The conclusion of the "four wise men" was that any continuation of UCS in its present form was wholly unjustified and they accordingly recommended that an end be made to UCS, that a successor company should be based on the Govan and Linthouse yards only and that the present UCS programme should be concentrated on Govan where they believed shipbuilding could be undertaken with good prospects of viability if there was full co-operation from the unions, adequate

161. P. Debs. 5 Ser., Vol. 819, c.35; Vol. 820, c.913 and Vol. 821, c.(157). The withholding of guarantees was a serious blow to UCS; for the reactions of the UCS Board see Jack McGill, *Crisis on the Clyde* (London, 1973), Chapter 8.

162. P. Debs. 5 Ser., Vol. 811, c.808.

163. *Ibid.*, Vol. 814, c.1054. See also *Crisis on the Clyde*, *op. cit.*, Chapter 9.

164. P. Debs. 5 Ser., Vol. 819, c.31.

165. *Ibid.*, Vol. 819, c.233.

166. They were Lord Robens (a former Labour minister), Sir Alexander Glen (a leading shipowner), Alexander McDonald (Chairman of Distillers) and David Macdonald (a director of Hill Samuel). They came to be known as "the four wise men".

167. P. Debs. 5 Ser., Vol. 820, c.(7)-(16).

168. Report of the Advisory Group on "Shipbuilding on the Upper Clyde", Parl. Papers 1970–71 (544), Vol. 49.

capital and satisfactory management. The Government accepted these conclusions[169] and at the end of September the Secretary of State announced the formation of a new company called Govan Shipbuilders which would be the vehicle for the Govan/Linthouse scheme[170]; a month later he reported to the House[171] that further advances were being made to the provisional liquidator, that the Government would give guarantees to shipowners to enable work at the yards to be maintained, that considerable public funds would be made available for investment in Govan Shipbuilders and that his Department had commissioned the merchant bankers Hill Samuel to undertake a feasibility study of the Govan/Linthouse scheme and to examine the possibility of the scheme being widened so as to include the Scotstoun yard.

At the end of February 1972 the Government received Hill Samuel's Report together with a covering letter from Lord Strathalmond, the Chairman of Govan Shipbuilders.[172] The consultants considered that the Govan, Scotstoun and Linthouse yards were capable, with considerable investment, of being transformed into a complex up to comparable European standards and the Secretary of State announced[173] that, subject to confirmation that Govan management had reached satisfactory agreement with the unions, the Government were prepared to propose legislation for carrying through the project which would involve £17 million to meet losses on orders and a further £18 million for investment in the yards and working capital. However the consultants considered that the maintenance of Clydebank as a competitive merchant yard was unrealistic but that there was American interest in acquiring this yard for the construction of oil drilling rigs.[174]

At last on 30th June 1972 it was announced[175] that the Govan management and the unions had concluded an agreement on working practices acceptable to the Government, that other conditions of Government support had been met and that the Government would provide Govan with adequate financial support[176] for five years or until Govan attained commercial viability—whichever period was the less; in addition a further loan would be made to the provisional liquidator to cover the interim period until the yards could be

169. P. Debs. 5 Ser., Vol. 822, c.791.

170. *Ibid.*, Vol. 823, c.176.

171. *Ibid.*, Vol. 823, c.724.

172. The Report and Lord Strathalmond's letter were published together—"Shipbuilding on the Upper Clyde" Cmnd. 4918, Parl. Papers 1971–72, Vol. 37.

173. P. Debs. 5 Ser., Vol. 832, cc.49–55.

174. The Clydebank yard was eventually sold to the Marathon Company of Houston but only as a result of the Government undertaking to provide substantial financial assistance—see P. Debs. 5 Ser., Vol. 836, c.(17) and *Crisis on the Clyde*, *op. cit.* Chapters 13 and 14.

175. P. Debs. 5 Ser., Vol. 839, c.(445).

176. The necessary finance was to be provided under the Industry Bill (then going through Parliament) when enacted.

transferred to Govan.[177] Thus the continuation, in a nationalised form, of shipbuilding on the Upper Clyde was for the time being assured but it can hardly be doubted that the Government's decision was largely based on political and social considerations and whether it could be justified on economic grounds or in the national interest was, to say the least, questionable.[178]

At the beginning of 1970 the Labour Government were also faced with a financial crisis in the yard operated by Cammell Laird Shipbuilders[179] on the Mersey which, mainly because of its geographical isolation from the three main shipbuilding areas, had been excluded from the positive recommendations in the Geddes Report for the creation of larger shipbuilding groups.[180] As a result of heavy losses on fixed price contracts in which wholly inadequate allowances had been made for rising costs over building periods greatly extended by late deliveries,[181] Cammell Laird was faced with a serious liquidity problem and appealed to the SIB for help. However the Board considered that its powers under the Shipbuilding Industry Act 1967 were not appropriate for a case such as Cammell Laird[182] and in these circumstances, the shipbuilders applied for direct Government assistance to prevent the closure of the yard.

In May 1970 the Government stated[183] that, to ensure the viability of the Cammell Laird yard, the Industrial Reorganisation Corporation ("IRC")[184] had agreed to make secured loans of up to £6 million to Laird Group provided that Cammell Laird ceased to be a subsidiary of the Laird Group.[185] The Government had accordingly agreed to purchase, at a cost of £1.5 million, 50 per cent of the share capital of Cammell Laird, leading shipowner customers had agreed to lend £765,000 to the Laird Group and the funds so received by the Laird Group were to be applied in relieving Cammell Laird of its existing and anticipated losses. A year later the IRC stated in its Final Report[186] that the Laird Group had agreed to make good actual losses on the current Cammell Laird order book up to a maximum of £7.2 million and that, in order to help the Laird Group meet these obligations, the IRC, at a cost of about £1.225 million, would subscribe for shares in the Laird Group and would also make a loan of up to £4.825 million.

177. Otherwise the liquidator was left to wrestle with the enormous UCS liabilities and the disgruntled UCS creditors who felt, with some justification, that the support which they had given to UCS up to the moment of its collapse merited something better than the Government's apparent disregard of their interests.

178. See Frank Broadway, *Upper Clyde Shipbuilders* (London, 1976).

179. A wholly owned subsidiary of Cammell Laird & Co. Ltd.

180. Geddes Report, paras. 319 and 320.

181. See Booz-Allen Report, pp. 102–3 and 177.

182. See SIB's Third Report, p. 7—Parl. Papers 1970–71 (84), Vol. 49.

183. P. Debs. 5 Ser., Vol. 801, c.590.

184. Established by the Industrial Reorganisation Corporation Act 1966.

185. See p. 12 of the IRC Report for the year ended 31st March 1970 (Parl. Papers 1969- 70 (310), Vol. 16) and Appendix I of the IRC's Final Report for the period 1st April 1970 to 30th April 1971 (Parl. Papers 1970–71 (443), Vol. 25).

186. *Loc. cit*,, p. 205.

In June 1970 a Conservative Government came to power and in July, in response to questions, it was confirmed[187] that the arrangements made regarding Cammell Laird would be honoured and that the 50 per cent holding in the equity of Cammell Laird would continue to be held by the Public Trustee on behalf of the Minister of Technology. A year later there was again a cash shortage[188] and following discussions between the Government and the Laird Group, the Secretary of State announced[189] that changes were being made in the top management of Cammell Laird and that, to enable the new management to retain the workforce and to carry out existing orders, the Government would provide a stand-by financial facility of £3 million over the course of the following year.

In April 1972 the new Minister for Industrial Development informed that House[190] that, after considering the new management's review of future prospects, the Government and the Laird Group had concluded that there were reasonable hopes for a viable future for Cammell Laird as a merchant shipbuilder and that it should be enabled to undertake a substantial programme of modernisation. The Government, provided it was satisfied that the management and unions were vigorously tackling the outstanding problems in the field of labour relations, was prepared in principle to finance the programme and, to enable initial steps towards modernisation to be taken without delay, would provide a further loan of £3 million. By the following September Booz-Allen & Hamilton, the consultants carrying out a general review of the shipbuilding industry on behalf of the Government, had reported favourably on Cammell Laird's modernisation plans and the Government agreed to provide Cammell Laird with up to £14 million under Section 7 of the Industry Act 1972[191]; thus by large-scale public expenditure and with half the equity passing into public ownership, the collapse of Cammell Laird was, for the time being, averted.

In the period up to 1972 the Belfast yard of Harland & Wolff, which had not been included in any of the other new shipbuilding groups,[192] was perhaps the most special case of all. The unhappy political and social state of Northern Ireland, and the extent to which Belfast was economically dependent on these famous shipbuilders as the largest employer of labour in the Province, made it a matter of critical importance to the U.K. and Northern Ireland Governments that shipbuilding in Belfast should continue to flourish. Even before the SIB had been constituted, Harland & Wolff's financial position was so

187. P. Debs. 5 Ser., Vol. 803, cc.1131 and 1145.

188. Losses on 12 merchant vessels and two LPG carriers in the period between 1969 and 1971 amounted to over £12 million (Booz-Allen Report, p. 87).

189. P. Debs. 5 Ser., Vol. 825, c.187.

190. P. Debs. 5 Ser., Vol. 835, c.1282.

191. The Act had received the Royal Assent on 9th August 1972—see further *infra* and Chapter 11.

192. See Geddes Report, para. 319 (C).

precarious that in 1966 the Northern Ireland Government was forced to advance a loan of £2 million and although, over the following three years, Harlands received more SIB assistance than any other shipbuilder, during that period insolvency was only averted by a further loan of £1.5 million from the Northern Ireland Government.

In its First Report[193] the SIB announced that it would support the construction in Belfast of a new building dock which would enable Harlands to compete for orders for large tankers and bulk carriers and by 31st March 1970[194] Harlands had received from the Board £8 million in loans and over £1 million in grants. During 1970, partly due to continuing losses on contracts, Harlands again ran into financial difficulties and, in spite of further SIB grants in excess of £5 million,[195] there were fears of collapse and rumours of takeover bids.[196] In March 1971 it was stated[197] that the Northern Ireland Government were intending to provide financial support for Harlands under its existing ownership[198] but with strengthened management and then in July it was announced[199] that, in order to enable the company to become fully viable, the Northern Ireland Ministry of Commerce were subscribing a par for £4 million shares of £1 each, which would give the Ministry 47.6 per cent of the equity, and would also be making a grant of an amount to be professionally assessed so as to ensure that the actual and prospective losses on the order book had been fully provided for.[200]

The U.K. and Northern Ireland Governments made it clear to Harlands that, once this financial support had been given, there would be no question of either Government accepting any responsibility for making good any deficiency in the company's resources should it get into any financial difficulties in the future. However nearly a year later, in May 1972, the Secretary of State for Northern Ireland announced[201] that Harlands new management[202] had put forward a plan for reorganisation and expansion at an estimated capital cost of £35 million of which a substantial proportion would be provided by the company from its own resources; the Government had agreed that the scheme should go ahead and were discussing with the company the terms and conditions on which the Government would provide financial assistance. Thus in

193. Parl. Papers 1967–68 (361), Vol. 31.
194. See SIB Report, for the year ended 31st March 1970—Parl. Papers 1970–71 (84), Vol. 49.
195. P. Debs. 5 Ser., Vol. 812, c.(308).
196. *Ibid.*, Vol. 808, c.(130).
197. *Ibid.*, Vol. 812, c.(459).
198. Harlands was a public quoted company with a large number of shareholders.
199. P. Debs. 5 Ser., Vol. 820, c.(340).
200. The grant eventually paid was £14.15 million which the assessors calculated would clear existing and anticipated losses on the fixed price contracts. Unfortunately the losses eventually proved to be much greater—see Chapter 11 *infra*.
201. P. Debs. 5 Ser., Vol. 836, c.579.
202. Lord Rochdale was part-time Chairman and Mr Iver Hoppe, a leading Danish shipbuilder, had been appointed Managing Director.

the period between 1967 and mid-1972 the Government assistance to Harlands, in one form or another, amounted to over £51 million[203] but, taking into account the exceptional conditions in the Province, the Government could hardly have refused this support and at least it could be said that more than 40 per cent was devoted to capital expenditure[204] which it was hoped would contribute to a more profitable future and increased employment.

The seriousness of the shipbuilding problems on the Upper Clyde, the Mersey and in Belfast gradually forced a change in the Conservative Government's initial firm commitment to a policy of non-intervention in commerce and industry. In March 1971, only nine months after coming to office, the Government were supporting the rescue operation for Harland & Wolff but this could perhaps be regarded as an exceptional case justified by the political condition of Northern Ireland and in the following month, in the debate on the Second Reading of the Shipbuilding Industry Bill,[205] the Minister was still declaring that, although the shipbuilders' relief would continue[206] and builders would continue to benefit from the extended home credit scheme, the Government did not consider that there was any justification for special assistance to the shipbuilding industry.

Within the following six months the interim financial support given to the UCS liquidator and to Cammell Laird suggested that cracks were appearing in the Government's facade and at the end of February 1972, in the course of a debate on employment,[207] the Government not only committed itself to an Upper Clyde financing of £35 million but also hinted at a softening of the hardline policy towards shipbuilding in general. Then in March 1972 came the publication of a White Paper on Industrial and Regional Development[208] which announced a radical change in Government policy not only towards shipbuilding but also to industry in general; there were to be improved tax allowances on capital expenditure, special regional development grants, selective financial assistance and, in order to relieve the shipbuilding industry's urgent difficulties and safeguard employment, U.K. shipbuilders were to be given tapering grants towards the construction of ships or mobile off-shore installations.[209]

In a debate immediately following the publication of the White Paper[210] the Secretary of State outlined the shipbuilding industry's financial problems,

203. Booz-Allen Report, Exhibit 29. This figure includes an estimate of the amount which the Government were expecting to contribute to Harland's expansion programme.

204. *Ibid.*

205. P. Debs. 5 Ser., Vol. 815, c.1381.

206. Shipbuilders' relief had been granted by the Finance Act 1966—see p. 218 *supra*. By April 1971 the relief given amounted to £17.7 million.

207. P. Debs. 5 Ser., Vol. 832, c.49.

208. Cmnd. 4942, Parl. Papers 1971–72, Vol. 18.

209. Provision for these construction grants was made in Section 11 of the Industry Act 1972—see Chapter 11 *infra*.

210. P. Debs. 5 Ser., Vol. 833, c.1551.

stressed the need for a major increase in productivity, better management and improvement in industrial relations, and gave a firm assurance that the Government were determined to see a continuing role for shipbuilding in the U.K. Proof of the sincerity of the Government's commitment to the industry was soon evidenced by the massive financial support given in 1972 to Govan, Cammell Laird and Harland & Wolff—and that was only a beginning. So, in a little more than two years after coming into office with a determination not to stage rescue operations or subsidise inefficient industries, the Conservative Government found itself in the position of having become not only a major shareholder in the shipbuilding industry[211] but also of having made provision for construction grants estimated at £50 million for the industry as a whole[212] and for loans and grants totalling over £100 million for the three lame ducks.[213]

211. The Government owned half the equity of Cammell Laird, 47.6 per cent of the equity of Harland & Wolff and the whole of the equity of Govan.

212. Apart from the old shipbuilding bounties given up to the end of the eighteenth century, this was the first time that a British Government had ever given direct construction grants to the industry in general.

213. Booz-Allen Report, pp. 87–88 and Exhibit 29. There were also contingent liabilities under the various guarantees given in support of the rescue operations.

CHAPTER 11

BRITISH SHIPBUILDING—THE FINAL SOLUTION?

The provisions of the Industry Act 1972[1] made it clear that, in a period of little more than two years, the philosophy underlying the Conservative Government's industrial policy, both in general and towards shipbuilding in particular, had fundamentally changed; the powers in Part II of the Act enabling the Government to give selective financial assistance for industry both in the assisted areas[2] and generally[3] were more far reaching than any measures of a similar character enacted since the end of the Second World War and in Part III of the Act, which related solely to the shipbuilding industry, Section 10 extended both the scope and monetary limit for the Government guarantees of shipbuilding credits for U.K. owners[4] hitherto given under the Shipbuilding Industry Acts 1967 and 1971[5] and Section 11 introduced a short term temporary scheme of tapering construction grants to alleviate the shipbuilders' more immediate financial problems and to provide a period of stability during which longer term policies to ensure the continuance of the industry could be developed.

The new grants were payable to builders in respect of the construction in the U.K. of a ship or mobile off-shore installation of the qualifying size[6] but only if construction on the berth had commenced before 1st January 1975 and the ship or installation had been delivered on or after 1st January 1972. Grant was to be paid where any part of the contract price fell to be treated as payable in 1972, 1973 or 1974[7] and the rate of grant was a percentage of the sum so treated as payable namely 10 per cent for 1972, four per cent for 1973 and three per cent for 1974; by 31st March 1976 a total of £46.2 million had been paid in construction grants since their inception.[8] The scheme was never

1. 1972, c.63. Royal Assent on 9th August 1972.
2. Section 7. Nearly all major British shipyards were located in the assisted areas.
3. Section 8.
4. See p. 216 *supra*.
5. These statutes were repealed.
6. As defined in Section 12 of the Act.
7. In accordance with a formula laid down in Section 11(2) of the Act.
8. See Industry Act Report for the year ended 31st March 1976—Parl. Papers 1975–76 (619), Vol. 17.

intended to be more than a short term measure of relief and although, during the latter part of 1972 and the early months of 1973, the Government were pressed to state their long term strategy for the industry, the Government were determined to await completion of the Booz-Allen Report and pressure was somewhat eased by an unexpected surge of new orders in the last quarter of 1972 and the first half of 1973.[9]

The Government received the Booz-Allen Report in February 1972[10] and in May it was announced[11] that an edited version of the Report would be published.[12] The consultants considered that the performance of the British shipbuilding industry in recent years had not been impressive and that it was in danger of falling behind its international competitors in terms of price, delivery, labour relations, technological development and capital investment; the Report was particularly critical as regards management, productivity and delivery performance and the consultants' general conclusion was that long-term development of the industry could only be achieved if Government support was combined with lasting improvements in management performance and capability.

After consultations on the Report had taken place with all interested parties, at the end of July[13] the Minister for Industrial Development made a definitive statement on the Government's longer term policy for shipbuilding. Both unions and employers had accepted that the major firms would only survive increasing competition if their weaknesses were remedied and the Government had concluded that the next step was for them to consider, under Section 7 of the Industry Act, proposals for individual projects in the assisted areas on the same basis, with one exception,[14] as for other industries. With the recent upturn of orders the industry should be better placed than the Report had envisaged to finance modernisation schemes but, although the industry was optimistic regarding the profitability of orders won over the previous six months, long order books did not mean that there were any grounds for complacency.

The Conservative Government shrugged off the arguments of the Labour Party and the TUC in favour of public ownership and for the last two years of their period in office used their powers under Section 7 of the Industry Act to give selective financial support to the three yards in which the Government

9. The total orders for the first nine months of 1972 were only 291,000 g.r.t.; in the last quarter of 1972 orders rose to 548,000 and for the first half of 1973 they soared to a total of 3.286 million g.r.t. (*British Shipping Statistics 1975*, Table 3.1). The surge reflected the rise in the freight market during the period—see *British Shipping Statistics 1975*, Table 5.5.

10. P. Debs. 5 Ser., Vol. 850, c.(979).

11. *Ibid.*, Vol 856, c.(347).

12. HMSO, 1973.

13. P. Debs. 5 Ser., Vol. 860, c.1157.

14. In the case of shipbuilding alone, loans at concessionary rates would be given for modernisation schemes which did not increase employment whereas for other industries concessionary loan rates were only granted for schemes which provided more jobs.

already had an equity interest.[15] For Govan the Government subscribed £5 million in equity capital, guaranteed a bank overdraft of £2 million and by 31st March 1974 had made advances totalling £8.5 million for working capital and a grant of £1.1 million to meet 1972 losses.[16] Cammell Laird, in accordance with the arrangements made in September 1972, was granted up to 31st March 1974 further interest-free loans totalling £6.3 million to finance its modernisation programme.[17] In the case of Harland & Wolff, it was announced in February and November 1973[18] that the Northern Ireland Government had made grants totalling £14.154 million to write off existing and anticipated contract losses and had provided finance for the modernisation scheme comprising grants of nearly £10.5 million, a long term loan of £5 million and a medium term loan facility of up to £8 million[19]; in addition the U.K. Government, at the end of 1973, provided guarantee facilities for a further £10 million and agreed to £10 million of Harland's existing debt being replaced by an issue of £8 million convertible preference stock.[20]

During the Conservative Government's term of office, a period roughly coinciding with the financial years 1970–71 to 1973–74, the financial aid made available to the shipbuilding industry by way of grants, loans and equity capital came to a total of nearly £110 million of which almost two-thirds went to the yards in which the State had an interest.[21] Unfortunately all too little of this assistance, or that previously provided by the SIB, was spent on modernisation or the provision of new facilities; in July 1972 the Committee of Public Accounts[22] concluded that much of the SIB assistance had been used "simply to meet company losses in order to avoid insolvency" and they expressed the hope that future assistance would be used more effectively towards establishing a viable shipbuilding industry but, in the period 1970–74, the Government, when faced with a situation in which yards would go under if cash was not supplied to meet past losses,[23] decided that, for the sake of employment, support would have to be given even though such support made no contribution

15. Govan, Cammell Laird and Harland & Wolff. Most of the assistance to Harlands was provided under Northern Ireland legislation.

16. See Industry Act Reports for the year ended 31st March 1973 (Parl. Papers 1972–73 (429), Vol. 12) and for the year ended 31st March 1974 (Parl. Papers 1974 (339), Vol. 7).

17. P. Debs. 5 Ser., Vol. 850, c.627 and Vol. 865, c.(239).

18. *Ibid.*

19. The grants were made under the Northern Ireland Industries Development Acts 1966 and 1971.

20. P. Debs. 5 Ser., Vol. 866, c.(467).

21. For details of the distribution of this aid see P. Debs. 5 Ser., Vol. 873, c.(248) and Vol 878, c.(17)–(24). The total of £110 million did not include shipbuilders' relief and aid available through schemes for industry in general such as investment grants and expenditure under the Local Employment Acts.

22. Third Report, Session 1971–72, Parl. Papers 1971–72 (447), Vol. 24.

23. Govan losses on fixed price contracts up to the end of 1973 were expected to be £22 million—see Third Report of the Committee of Public Accounts, Session 1974–75 (Parl. Papers 1974–75 (374), Vol. 2). Harlands 1973 Accounts showed a provision of £38 million for prospective losses on contracts entered into prior to 31st December 1973.

towards improving the industry's ability to compete in world markets.

Although the shipbuilding industry had accepted that the remedying of many of the major internal shortcomings identified by the Geddes Committee was a matter for action by management and workforce, many British shipbuilders believed that their ability to increase their penetration of overseas markets was severely handicapped by unfair foreign competition.[24] The Geddes Committee had pointed out that the shipbuilding industries in certain foreign countries enjoyed disproportionate advantages which distorted international trade in ships[25]; the Committee had accordingly recommended that every effort should be made to ensure that the British industry was not placed at a disadvantage by foreign government intervention and that, through OECD and otherwise, the British Government should endeavour "to reduce and eliminate assistance which withdraws sectors of the world market from international competition or gives a particular shipbuilding industry a dominating position in the world market".[26]

By mid-1969 some international progress had been made in the rationalisation of shipbuilding credits. An Understanding on Export Credits for Ships approved by the Council of OECD of 30th May 1969[27] provided that officially supported credits for ships should be limited to 80 per cent of contract value with repayments over a maximum of eight years from delivery and bearing interest at a minimum rate of 6 per cent per annum net of charges.[28] Although this OECD Understanding applied only to export credits, the terms of the 1967 U.K. Home Credit Scheme at all times conformed with the credit terms available through ECGD for foreign owners building in the U.K. and some, though not all,[29] of the OECD countries likewise brought their home credit terms into line with the OECD Understanding.

Thus by the beginning of the 1970s in OECD member countries export credits and, to some extent, home credits had mainly ceased to be within the area of unfair competition but direct construction subsidies continued to be paid by certain shipbuilding countries[30] and the licensing regulations and flag discriminatory practices of some foreign powers[31] continued to have an

24. See the Sixth Report (6th July 1972) of the Expenditure Committee on "Public Money in the Private Sector" (Parl. Papers 1971–72 (347), Vol. 27) and the Minutes of Evidence given to the Committee by several shipbuilders.

25. Report, Cmnd 2937 paras. 46, 49, 93, 94 and 522.

26. *Ibid.*, paras. 523 and 524.

27. The Understanding was accepted by the U.K., the major West European shipbuilding countries, Japan and Canada—but not the United States.

28. By a further OECD Understanding of 16th December 1970 the minimum rate of interest was increased to 7½ per cent net of charges.

29. Japan, France and Spain continued to charge lower rates of interest under their home credit schemes.

30. At that time principally by the United States, France, Italy, Spain and Canada.

31. For example France, Italy and Spain (licensing) and the United States, France and Japan (flag discrimination).

inhibiting effect on the ability of British shipbuilders to win export orders.[32] In a debate on 22nd April 1971,[33] in reply to Opposition criticism that nothing had been done to reduce unfair foreign competition, the Government suggested that the importance of foreign subsidies might be exaggerated but at the end of 1971 the Secretary of State affirmed[34] that Government policy was to support efforts within OECD to reach international agreement on the progressive reduction of all forms of government assistance which distorted competition.

It was however apparent that discussions within OECD were making little progress[35] and in March 1972 even the United Kingdom took the unprecedented and, in the view of some OECD members, retrograde step of announcing its intention to pay construction grants.[36] On the other hand in the summer of 1972 there was a modest move towards some limited international control in relation to the shipbuilding countries who were then members of the European Economic Community[37] or who were shortly to become so.[38] A Directive of the EEC Council made on 20th July 1972[39] declared that aid and intervention to assist shipbuilding were only to be considered as compatible with the common market if they consisted of credit facilities which satisfied the OECD Understanding or of any other form of aid or intervention which did not exceed five per cent of the contract price in 1972[40] or four per cent in 1973.[41]

At the end of 1972 the Government confirmed that Booz-Allen had been specifically briefed to consider the effects of worldwide government support for shipbuilding and Chapter 5 of the Booz-Allen Report was devoted to this topic. The consultants considered and analysed the government policies and practices for support of shipbuilding in 11 major shipbuilding countries[42] and reported (*inter alia*) that direct subsidies on the price of new ships were paid by the United Kingdom, the United States, France and Italy, that almost all shipbuilding nations offered credit terms which were more favourable than those available commercially and that the U.K., Italy, Japan and Sweden had given significant direct financial support for re-equipping shipyards and reorganising production.[43] The consultants concluded that U.K. subsidy and

32. For the general position in 1970 see the 1971 Review of Maritime Subsidies by the U.S. Department of Commerce—Maritime Administration.

33. P. Debs. 5 Ser., Vol. 815, c.1381.

34. *Ibid.*, Vol. 828, c.(232).

35. See P. Debs. 5 Ser., Vol. 826, c.11 and Vol. 831, c.(13).

36. P. Debs. 5 Ser., Vol. 833, c.1552 and Section 11, Industry Act 1972.

37. Belgium, France, Germany, Italy and the Netherlands.

38. The U.K., Denmark and Ireland became members on 1st January 1973.

39. No. 72/273/EEC published in the Official Journal No. L169/28 on 27th July 1972.

40. The Directive did not apply to the U.K. until 1973 and thus the U.K. was able to pay construction grants of 10 per cent in 1972.

41. There were some exemptions—e.g. certain grants by Italy and Ireland and grants when the excess was due to the operation of inflation insurance schemes.

42. Denmark, France, Germany, Italy, Japan, Netherlands, Norway, Spain, Sweden, U.K. and U.S.A.

43. See Report, Exhibits 20 and 29 (HMSO 1973).

credit arrangements compared favourably with those of other shipbuilding countries except the United States[44] but they pointed out that legislation, administrative practice or economic strength ensured that some countries i.e. Italy, Japan, Spain, United States and, to a lesser extent, France, bought ships only from their national builders; this meant that nearly one-third of the free world's demand for ships was not open to international competition and this substantially reduced the market available to U.K. shipbuilders.

So it seemed that the failure of British yards to attract a greater proportion of world orders was not due to lack of adequate Government financial support or credit facilities and although, as the Report pointed out, U.K. builders were excluded from certain markets, even in 1973, a world boom year for new orders, Britain made little significant penetration into the substantial foreign market which remained open[45] and over the four years 1970–73, as hitherto, orders from British owners remained a high proportion of the new merchant business secured by British yards—the figures (in thousands g.r.t.) being:[46]

Year	*Orders by U.K. owners*		*Orders by overseas owners*		*Total Orders*
	g.r.t.	*% of total*	*g.r.t.*	*% of total*	*g.r.t.*
1970	1,449	81.9	320	18.1	1,769
1971	833	81.1	194	18.9	1,027
1972	599	71.5	239	28.5	839
1973	3,721	85.4	637	14.6	4,358

However, although British orders continued to be the mainstay of U.K. shipbuilding, British owners also continued to place far more orders abroad than they did at home. The orders for merchant ships of 100 g.r.t. or more for U.K. registry on the books of U.K. and overseas shipbuilders at the end of March in each of the years 1968–72 (in thousands g.r.t.) was as follows[47]:

Country of build	*1968*	*1969*	*1970*	*1971*	*1972*
U.K.	1,470	2,948	3,454	3,522	2,602
Japan	1,944	2,005	2,395	3,222	2,964
Other overseas countries	1,686	2,715	3,454	6,317	5,980
Total for U.K. Registry	5,100	7,668	9,303	13,061	11,546

44. See Report, Exhibit 19.
45. All the flags of convenience and, in Western Europe, Norway, Germany, Sweden, Denmark and the Netherlands. World new orders in 1973 totalled 72.809 million g.r.t. of which under six per cent (4.358 million g.r.t.) were secured by U.K. builders and only 14.6 per cent of orders placed with U.K. builders were from overseas customers.
46. *British Shipping Statistics 1975*, Table 3.1.
47. P. Debs. 5 Ser., Vol. 838, c.(406). The Table on p. 67 of the Booz-Allen Report showed that among countries which both built and imported ships, only Norway, in the period 1966–71, imported a higher proportion of its requirements than did the U.K.

Provided that all major factors were roughly equal, there was a natural tendency on the part of most British owners to build at home rather than abroad.[48] In terms of technical competence and quality British yards, for most types of ships, were generally considered to be at least the equal of foreign yards but there were two factors, berth availability and delivery reliability, which played an important part in influencing the decisions of shipowners, both British and foreign,[49] and in this area British builders compared unfavourably with their foreign competitors. U.K. yards were handicapped by their long order books and their apparent inability to increase output and improve productivity whereas foreign builders, who also had long order books, were able to raise their output and could thus gain a significant advantage by quoting much earlier delivery dates.[50] Of at least equal importance to the time between an order and a delivery date was the owner's confidence in the builder meeting his commitment and a shipbuilder's demonstrated ability to deliver on time was often a decisive factor[51]; Japanese and some other foreign yards had an enviable reputation for prompt deliveries whereas many owners, British and foreign, had little confidence that U.K. builders would meet their contractual delivery dates.[52]

Price was another significant factor but British owners were generally not deterred from placing orders in the U.K. by a modest price differential; there were, however, substantial price differences between the U.K. and Japan in the case of the larger tankers and bulk carriers which often meant that the U.K. yards lost orders. Moreover, even if the difference in quoted prices was small, owners feared that the eventual U.K. price would turn out to be very much higher than the corresponding foreign price by reason of escalation during the longer U.K. delivery period and the likelihood of the ship not being delivered on time. Thus it seems that the decline of the U.K. industry in the early 1970s cannot be mainly attributed to lack of support by the British Government or, with certain exceptions, excessive support or unfair preference by foreign governments. The principal reasons for the failure of U.K. builders to win more orders were to be found in factors largely outside the Government's sphere of influence—namely static output,[53] poor labour

48. It was more convenient to supervise building in home yards, it avoided currency risks and many U.K. owners had long traditional links with certain U.K. builders.

49. See Booz-Allen Report, Chapters 6 and 7.

50. Since 1955 U.K. output had remained, at best, static whilst world output had grown at an average of 10 per cent per annum—see *British Shipping Statistics 1975*, Table 3.5.

51. See Booz-Allen Report, pp. 72–73.

52. *Ibid.*, pp. 74–75. The U.K. industry's poor delivery record over the period 1967–71 is shown on pp. 102–103 of the Report.

53. The Geddes Committee had hoped (see Report, paras. 567–568) that by 1972–75 British output would have been raised to 2.25 million gross tons per annum representing an estimated market share of 12.5 per cent. In the event annual output 1972–75 did not even reach 1.2 million gross tons and the U.K. market share was only 4.5 per cent or less.

relations,[54] low productivity,[55] later deliveries and inadequate financial control.

In the early 1970s there was also some concern regarding the state of the British ship repairing industry which had not benefited from the special direct financing aid bestowed upon shipbuilding. The number employed in ship repairing had fallen from 50,000 in 1961 to 20,000 in 1971 and this recession was attributed to the trend to larger vessels for which U.K. facilities were not always adequate, the decrease in age of British ships with consequent reduced need for repairs and the industry's reputation for failing to meet completion dates. Early in 1972 the Government rejected a request for special financial help for ship repairing[56] but at the end of the year the Minister for Industrial Development announced[57] that the Government was commissioning a study by independent consultants, P A Management Consultants, who would examine the current state and future prospects of the repairing industry in the light of world markets and competition. During 1973 there were warnings of a severe crisis with loss of orders and widespread unemployment[58] but the Government were awaiting the consultants' Report and when, in December 1973, this was received, the Minister announced that he would not make a statement until the Report had been discussed with all interested parties.[59] The matter was then overtaken by the February 1974 general election and action on the Report became a problem for the new Labour Government.

The Labour Party's manifesto for the general election of February 1974 made clear the Party's intention of taking the shipbuilding, ship repairing and marine engineering industries into public ownership and, when the Labour Government entered office in March 1974, the task of implementing this policy fell to the new Secretary of State for Industry,[60] Anthony Wedgwood Benn.[61] At the beginning of 1974 the merchant order book of the British shipbuilding industry was at an unprecedentedly high level; U.K. yards had on order 365 ships of an aggregate gross tonnage of just over 7.5 million[62] and, although new orders declined sharply during 1974, with output likely to remain at

54. The industry's strike record compared badly with the national average—see Booz-Allen Report, p. 169.

55. In 1975 it was stated (P. Debs. 5 Ser., Vol. 901, c.1454) that output per employee had been static since 1968 whereas with all our major foreign competitors output per employee had increased between 20 per cent and 90 per cent.

56. P. Debs. 5 Ser., Vol. 829, c.12.

57. *Ibid.*, Vol. 848, c.(447).

58. *Ibid.*, Vol. 854, c.10 and Vol. 856, c.33.

59. *Ibid.*, Vol. 866, c.(327) and Vol. 867, c.(36).

60. In place of the Department of Trade & Industry, the Labour Government created the new Departments for Industry, Trade and Prices & Consumer Protection—see Secretary of State (New Departments) Order 1974 (SI 1974 No. 692) and P. Debs. 5 Ser., Vol. 871, c.(178).

61. He had been previously responsible for shipbuilding as Minister of Technology in the 1966–70 Labour administration.

62. *British Shipping Statistics 1976–77*, Table 3.7.

around 1.16 million per annum[63] it seemed that for most yards there was work for years ahead. Unfortunately, as recent experience had shown, orders could be one thing and profits quite something else; moreover the accelerating fall in world and U.K. new orders[64] resulting from the Arab oil crisis raised fears that a serious over-capacity of world shipbuilding would manifest itself sooner than anticipated.[65]

Like their Conservative predecessors in 1970, the new Labour Government soon found themselves faced with crisis situations in particular shipbuilding areas and in addition action was needed on the consultants' Report on the Ship Repairing Industries. These problems, and the fact that the Government were in a minority in the Commons, delayed a statement of the Government's proposals for public ownership until 31st July 1974 when Mr Benn announced[66] that the Government believed that nationalisation of the major companies, including the specialist engine builders, offered the only effective prospect of enabling British shipbuilding and ship repairing not only to survive but to prosper in the highly competitive world markets; he added that fair compensation would be paid and that a discussion paper[67] was being circulated to all interested parties.

In October, at the second general election of 1974, the Labour Government was returned with an increased majority and on 30th April 1975 the Aircraft and Shipbuilding Industries Bill[68] was published and had its formal First Reading. Although the Government had hoped that the Bill would pass in the current session, on which basis the vesting date for public ownership would be early in 1976, in July 1975 Mr Eric Varley, who had succeeded Mr Benn at the Department of Industry, stated[69] that, owing to pressure of other legislation, it was not possible for the Bill to complete its passage in the current session and thus it was not until 2nd December 1975 that the Second Reading debate took place.[70] Thereafter the Bill's progress through Parliament[71] was so protracted and beset by so many unforeseen problems that it was not until 17th March 1977 that the Bill in an emasculated form reached the statute book[72] and the shipbuilding industry vesting date did not arrive until 1st July

63. The average annual output for the period 1971 to 1973.

64. *British Shipping Statistics 1975*, Tables 3.1 and 3.2.

65. World production in 1974 was 33.541 million g.r.t.—more than four times the level in 1960 (see *British Shipping Statistics 1975*, Table 3.5). Even before the oil crisis Booz-Allen (Report, Chapter 3) had forecast the probability of world capacity becoming vastly in excess of demand by 1980.

66. P. Debs. 5 Ser., Vol. 878, c.808.

67. The paper, which was not generally published, listed the companies which the Government intended should be taken into public ownership.

68. Parl. Papers 1974–75, Vol. 1 (Bill 151).

69. P. Debs. 5 Ser., Vol. 894, c.(355).

70. P. Debs. 5 Ser., Vol. 901, c.1446.

71. As to which see pp. 250 *et seq. infra*.

72. 1977, Chapter 3.

1977[73]—roughly three years after the first announcement of the Government's nationalisation proposals.

In this seemingly almost endless twilight period prior to full nationalisation, the Government were forced to deal *ad hoc* with several emergency situations and the first of these concerned the shipbuilding, ship repairing and marine engineering businesses on the River Wear of Sunderland Shipbuilders Limited[74] which had by then become a subsidiary of Court Line Limited, an old established shipowning company which, in the early 1970s, had diversified into the aircraft and holiday travel business and had also acquired the shipbuilding business of Appledore Shipbuilders in Devon. Although Sunderland Shipbuilders was one of the more successful businesses in the U.K. industry, early in 1974 the other interests, particularly holiday travel, of its parent Court Line ran into serious trouble and in June the directors of Court Line approached the Government for assistance to deal with the Group's financial difficulties which were threatening employment in the shipyards, the order book for ships and holidays for hundreds of thousands of people.

At the end of June and early in July[75] the Secretary of State informed the House that, under its powers in Section 7 of the Industry Act 1972, the Government was acquiring, for a sum of £16 million, the whole of the shipbuilding, ship repairing and marine engineering businesses of Sunderland and Appledore[76] and that the taking of these companies into public ownership would save over 9,000 jobs, £133 million of shipbuilding orders and make possible the completion of £48 million expected further orders. The Court Line Board had expressed confidence that these arrangements would safeguard the holiday operations but it subsequently transpired that the financial position of the remaining companies in the Court Line Group had already deteriorated to such an extent that, after the severance of the shipbuilding and other interests acquired by the Government, nothing would save the Group from collapse which, when it occurred, brought in its wake loss and chaos to thousands of intending holidaymakers. Eventually the matter was referred to the Parliamentary Commissioner for Administration[77] and in addition the affairs of Court Line were referred to the Board of Trade for investigation by inspectors appointed under Section 165 of the Companies Act 1948.[78]

73. This date was fixed by the Aircraft and Shipbuilding Industries (Shipbuilding Vesting Date) Order 1977 (SI 1977 No. 540).

74. Previously named Doxford & Sunderland Ltd.—see p. 220 *supra*.

75. P. Debs. 5 Ser., Vol. 875, c.1356 and Vol. 876, cc.(7) and (304).

76. The main operations taken into public ownership were Sunderland Shipbuilding, Appledore Shipbuilding, N. E. Coast Ship Repairers, Doxford Engines, Wolsington Steel, KL Marine Equipment and Sunderland Forge.

77. See his Fifth Report, Session 1974–75 (Parl. Papers 1974–75 (498), Vol. 29 and P. Debs. 5 Ser., Vol. 896, c.1812 and Vol. 897, c.532.

78. The Inspectors made an Interim Report in July 1975 and a Final Report early in 1978 (HMSO, 1978).

The next crisis facing the Labour Government was Harland & Wolff whose affairs were found to have deteriorated disastrously. Following the collapse of the Northern Ireland Executive in mid-July 1974, the United Kingdom Government assumed responsibility for direct rule of the Province[79] and on 22nd July[80] the Secretary of State for Northern Ireland informed the House that the previous proposals for providing assistance had proved to be inadequate and that the Belfast yard would have to close unless further Government financial support was given. Eight months later, on 26th March 1975, the Minister made a further statement[81] in which he disclosed that the Government intended to nationalise Harlands by acquiring all its remaining share capital and that there was need for an interim Order[82] to enable urgent payments to be made to the yard to cover further losses on contracts[83] and to provide finance for the completion of the modernisation programme.

A draft of the Shipbuilding Industry (Northern Ireland) Order 1975 was approved by the Commons on 8th May 1975[84] and the Order came into force on 27th May 1975.[85] The Order authorised the provision of financial assistance to Harland & Wolff, up to a maximum of £40 million, for the purpose of assisting or promoting the carrying on of its business if, in the opinion of the Department of Commerce, such provision was "likely to provide, maintain or safeguard employment in Northern Ireland". During the next two months financial assistance totalling £5.7 million was made to Harlands and then on 1st August 1975 a draft of the Shipbuilding Industry (No. 2) (Northern Ireland) Order 1975 was submitted to the Commons for approval. The Order provided (*inter alia*) that on 13th August 1975 all the company's securities, other than those already Government owned, were to vest in the Department of Commerce[86] and that, up to 31st March 1979, the Department was authorised to give financial assistance, up to a maximum of £60 million, in any of the various forms specified in the Order.

In recommending to the Commons that the No. 2 Order should be approved[87] the Minister pointed out that Harlands had failed to make a profit over the previous 10 years and that total Government assistance between 1966 and March 1975 was just over £81 million of which £22 million was of the

79. By the Northern Ireland Act 1974 under which the Queen was empowered, by Order in Council, to make laws for Northern Ireland during a specified period.
80. P. Debs. 5 Ser., Vol. 877, c.1060.
81. P. Debs. 5 Ser., Vol. 889, c.496.
82. Made under para. 1 of Schedule I to the 1974 Act.
83. It was estimated that a provision of £60 million would be needed to cover prospective losses on contracts entered into before 31st December 1973.
84. P. Debs. 5 Ser., Vol. 891, c.1759. It had previously been approved by the Lords.
85. 1975 SI 814 (N.I. 5).
86. The compensation to be paid to those owning the securities was 8p for each £1 of preference stock and 9p for each £1 of ordinary stock.
87. P. Debs. 5 Ser., Vol. 896, c.2474.

standard type[88]; of the balance £33 million had been provided to develop the new facilities at the yard and £26 million had been used to save the yard from closure. He added that a further £8 million had been provided since March 1975 and that, if all the further £60 million made available under the Order was taken up, Harlands would then have received between January 1966 and March 1979 a total of £119 million in special assistance plus £23 million of standard assistance to date. The Minister emphasised that, apart from the £60 million new money under the Order, there would be no more special aid; Government guarantees would be withdrawn and thereafter the company must operate within the principles of limited liability under the Northern Ireland Companies Act.[89]

There was considerable debate about the reasons for the financial disaster and where responsibility lay but in the end the draft Order was approved without a division and the Order was made and came into operation on 13th August 1975.[90] Just over a year later it was reported to the House[91] that, out of the £60 million authorised, £37 million had so far been advanced but that it was impossible to say how long the balance would last since much depended on the extent of the losses on existing contracts. Between August 1975 and March 1977 Harlands had not made any new contracts[92] but in April 1977 it was announced[93] that the builders had secured an order from Shell for two LPG carriers together worth between £60 and £70 million. Subsequently the Government were questioned regarding the profitability of the Shell contracts[94] and in reply the Minister stated that the latest forecast indicated that the price paid should cover the construction cost; he added, with regard to the Government's financial assistance to the yard, that although it was originally expected that the £60 million would only last until the end of 1978, it seemed possible that it would last beyond that date.

The Labour Government also soon found that the financial provision that their predecessors had made for Govan Shipbuilders would be wholly inadequate. In June 1972 the Conservative Government had estimated £35 million for Government support over five years and, although this sum represented £42.2 million at 1975 survey prices, by the end of June 1975 £37.5 million had been expended; Govan were forecasting no profits until 1978 and in

88. I.e. grants available generally to all industries in Northern Ireland and grants made to U.K. shipbuilders generally, e.g. construction grants.

89. The Minister clearly wished to make it plain that Harlands would not be a nationalised corporation and that the Government would accept no liability to creditors beyond the £60 million authorised by the Order.

90. 1975 SI No. 1309 (N.I. No. 14).

91. P. Debs. 5 Ser., Vol. 917, c.63–64.

92. It had been a condition of the No. 2 Order that no new contracts were to be made without Government approval and that such approval would not be given for loss-making contracts.

93. P. Debs. 5 Ser., Vol. 930, c.(322–323).

94. P. Debs. 5 Ser., Vol. 935 (2), c.1836–1837.

August 1975 the Secretary of State informed the Commons[95] that, in addition to the £4.7 million remaining from the original provision, the Government would lend a further £6.9 million for completing the capital development and would also provide £10.3 million to cover losses on existing contracts in 1975, 1976 and 1977. Govan was named in Schedule 2 of the Aircraft and Shipbuilding Industries Act 1977 as one of the companies whose securities were to vest in the State-owned British Shipbuilders on 1st July 1977[96] and on 29th June 1977 it was announced[97] that before the vesting date £14 million of Govan's outstanding loans would be converted into shares, the remainder of Govan's loans amounting to £9.25 million would be converted into grants to meet past losses and a further grant of £6.6 million would be paid in respect of losses outstanding at 30th June 1977.[98]

The provision of £14 million made in 1972 to enable Cammell Laird to carry out its modernisation programme also proved inadequate. In May 1975 the Committee of Public Accounts pointed out[99] that, owing to contractual and industrial relations disputes, the capital cost of the modernisation was likely to be far in excess of the original estimate and during the year ended 31st March 1976 further advances were made which brought the total Section 7 loan for the modernisation programme up to £13.43 million.[100] Although the company had traded profitably for four years since 1972, it could not itself finance the increased cost of the modernisation scheme and in August 1976 the Industry Minister stated[101] that, as from the nationalisation vesting date, British Shipbuilders would complete the modernisation and accept responsibility for expenditure on it but to cover the interim period Cammell Laird would be given up to a maximum of £6 million in direct assistance under Section 7 if this should be needed to meet the cost of the programme up to vesting day and that in addition a Section 7 guarantee would be given in respect of a bank overdraft facility of £3 million.

The change of Government in 1974 did not result in any slackening of the efforts by the UCS liquidator to persuade the Government to accept responsibility for the debts of some £7 million owing to those who had supplied UCS with goods and services. Although the liquidator's initial attempt in 1972 had met with no success,[102] the liquidator commissioned an investigation into the

95. P. Debs. 5 Ser., Vol. 897, c.(506).

96. Although Govan had from its inception always been wholly Government owned.

97. P. Debs. 5 Ser., Vol.934, c.(217–218).

98. Thus Govan was released from liability in respect of its Section 7 loans and all its losses, totalling £28.47 million, incurred up to the vesting date were covered by Section 7 grants—see Industry Act Report for the year ended 31st March 1978, Parl. Papers 1977–78 HC, 653.

99. See paras. 66–68 of the Committee's Third Report, Session 1974–75. Parl. Papers 1974–75 (374), Vol. 22 and Treasury Minute thereon—Cmnd. 6298, Parl. Papers 1974–75, Vol. 22.

100. See Industry Act Report for the year ended 31st March 1976—Parl. Papers 1975–76, (619) Vol. 17.

101. P. Debs. 5 Ser., Vol. 916 (2), c.(795).

102. See P. Debs. 5 Ser., Vol. 832, c.(282–283).

UCS situation by Professor David Flint[103] whose Report was submitted to the Secretary of State in 1975.[104] Professor Flint reached the conclusion that there was no contravention, by the UCS Board or the Government, of Section 332 of the Companies Act 1948 but he was extremely critical of the role played by the SIB and successive Governments whom he considered could not "escape sharing in the responsibility for the company continuing to trade as it faced successive crises with imminent prospects of collapse and liquidation". Mr Benn was unimpressed and in a Parliamentary reply[105] stated that there was no legal case against the Government and that he did not accept that the UCS creditors had any moral claim. Undaunted the liquidator then asked the Parliamentary Commissioner for Administration to investigate the matter but the Ombudsman was advised that such an investigation fell outside his jurisdiction and so, in spite of what seemed to many to be at least a strong moral case, the UCS creditors and their liquidator failed to persuade the Government to accept responsibility.

In March 1974 the new Labour Industry Secretary also found awaiting him the Report by P A Management Consultants on the Ship Repairing Industry[106] and in June Mr Benn stated[107] that an edited version of the Report was being published[108] and that the Government would have early consultations with all interested parties. The Report was a depressing one: outdated facilities, poor labour relations, weak marketing, low profitability and failures to meet completion dates all meant that the British industry was continually losing ground to its Continental competitors. However the consultants felt there was scope for improvement but only with substantially higher investment in modern facilities which the industry would be unable itself to fund. Progress accordingly depended upon Government support but of this there was little sign; the successive Industry Ministers referred to the Report as justifying the nationalisation of the major ship repairers[109] but otherwise, over the period of three years following publication of the Report, nothing was done by way of financial support or otherwise to encourage the much needed modernisation of the industry.

Outside Parliament British shipowners made clear their opposition to the nationalisation of the ship repairing industry.[110] As, by far, the industry's main customers,[111] they felt that they were entitled to tell the Government that, in

103. Professor of Accountancy at Glasgow University.

104. Professor Flint's Report was never officially published but it appeared in the newspapers —see *The Sunday Times*, 16th March 1975, p. 53.

105. P. Debs. 5 Ser., Vol. 888, c.(478).

106. See p. 238 *supra*.

107. P. Debs. 5 Ser., Vol. 875, c.(9).

108. HMSO, 1974.

109. See P. Debs. 5 Ser., Vol. 878, c.808–809, Vol. 886, c.34 and Vol. 901, c.1457–1458.

110. See General Council of British Shipping Annual Report 1975–76, p. 81.

111. In 1975 the total value of U.K. repair work was £150 million of which only £30 million was for foreign ships (P. Debs. 5 Ser., Vol. 915, c.(640)).

their view, the problems of ship repairing were quite distinct from those of shipbuilding and that to take the principal ship repairers into public ownership was against the interests of the industry, its customers and its employees. Opposition to the nationalisation of ship repairing was led, on behalf of the industry itself, by the Ship Repairers National Association and by some of the 12 companies on the nationalisation list[112]—notably Bristol Channel Ship Repairers whose campaign, led by its Chairman, Christopher Bailey, and supported by his workforce, was on an unprecedented scale and was at least partly responsible for the length of the Parliamentary struggle to get the Nationalisation Bill on the statute book and for the Government's reluctant acquiescence in the deletion of ship repairing from the Bill before it at last received the Royal Assent.[113]

It was, to say the least, unfortunate that the unexpected lacuna of some three years between Labour's advent to power in February 1974 and the eventual arrival of the Nationalisation Bill on the statute book in March 1977 should have coincided with a period of exceptional and increasing difficulty for both British and world shipbuilding. In these uncertain years U.K. shipbuilders were ill fitted to contend with the serious decline in new orders; in 1975 they had dwindled to only 67,000 g.r.t. compared with 4.358 million g.r.t. in 1973[114] and, in spite of output still remaining static,[115] the U.K. order book had fallen from 7.519 million g.r.t. at the end of 1973 to 2.946 million g.r.t. at the end of 1976.[116] In addition heavy losses were still being incurred on unprofitable fixed-price contracts and it was felt that, prior to nationalisation, there was an urgent need to evolve a strategy for a co-ordinated national shipbuilding policy.

In the first two years of the Labour Government's term of office no new measures for assisting shipbuilding were introduced but, in addition to funding the rescue operations for Sunderland Shipbuilders, Harlands, Govan and Cammell Laird, selective assistance under Section 7 of the Industry Act 1972 was given to a number of other yards.[117] Construction grants continued to be paid under Section 11 of the Industry Act[118] and, to meet the continuing strong demand for shipbuilding guarantees under Section 10 of the Act, the limit of £1,000 million was raised in February 1975 to £1,400 million[119] and, in order

112. Named in Part I of Schedule 2 to the Aircraft and Shipbuilding Industries Bill published on 30th April 1975.

113. See further *infra*.

114. *British Shipping Statistics 1975*, Table 3.1.

115. The average annual output for the period 1973–76 was 1.234 million g.r.t. (*British Shipping Statistics 1976–77*, Table 3.10).

116. *British Shipping Statistics 1976–77*, Table 3.7.

117. A loan of £9 million was made to Austin & Pickersgill to assist the modernisation of their yard and a loan of £6 million was made to Marathon U.K. to assist its acquisition and modernisation of John Brown's Clydebank yard. Financial help was also given to some smaller yards.

118. See pp. 231–232 *supra*.

119. See p. 216 fn. 109 *supra*.

to provide for further increase if needed, Section 23 of the Industry Act 1975 empowered the Secretary of State to make orders increasing the limit up to a maximum of £1,800 million.

As from 1st July 1974 the terms on which ECGD finance was available for foreign owners building in the U.K. was modified in accordance with a new OECD Understanding on Export Credits for Ships which provided that the credit was not to exceed 70 per cent of the ship's cost and was to be repayable over seven years with a minimum interest rate of 8 per cent net of all charges.[120] This less favourable finance hardly assisted the gaining of export orders, more particularly since British builders were convinced that in some foreign member countries the OECD Understanding was honoured more in the breach than in the observance, but in the spring of 1975 there was some small encouragement for exports by the introduction of a Government-backed insurance scheme which provided some measure of protection to a foreign buyer against a higher than expected rate of inflation.[121] However with new orders for U.K. yards dwindling to almost nothing[122] the scheme was of no immediate benefit and by the end of 1975 there were still no new Government proposals for aiding the hard-pressed industry.[123]

In April 1976 the Secretary of State announced[124] that the Government had been examining ways of utilising Section 7 of the Industry Act 1972 to help the U.K. shipbuilding industry and that he was introducing a scheme under which the Government would guarantee the refunding to shipowners of payments made during a vessel's construction if the yard should fail prior to nationalisation[125]; in addition the Cost Escalation Insurance Scheme, hitherto available only for ships built for export, was to be extended to ships built for British owners. By 31st March 1977[126] cost escalation guarantees had been given for the building of 14 ships having an aggregate value of £76.6 million and refund guarantees covering 14 ships of a total value of £80.8 million had also been given but, although these schemes were helpful, it was felt that they were unlikely to stimulate the much needed surge of new orders; the real problem lay in the inability of U.K. yards to match the low prices being quoted by Japanese and South Korean builders and it was in this area that there was

120. The terms on which finance was provided for U.K. owners under the Home Credit Scheme were also modified to accord with the July 1974 OECD Understanding.

121. See Section 3 of the Export Guarantees Amendment Act 1975.

122. Orders placed in U.K. yards during the second and third quarters of 1975 totalled only 12,000 g.r.t. (*British Shipping Statistics 1975*, Table 3.1).

123. See P. Debs. 5 Ser., Vol. 895, c.(6), Vol. 899, c.(237–238), Vol. 901, c.(48) and Vol. 901, c.1237.

124. P. Debs. 5 Ser., Vol. 909, c.647.

125. Some owners were being deterred from placing orders by the fear that a yard might fail before it was nationalised.

126. See Industry Act Report for the year ended 31st March 1977—Parl. Papers 1977–78, HC 545.

the urgent need for Government aid to close the gap which could not be bridged by commercial means alone.

During the mid-1970s the three specialist warship builders also had their problems although these were far less serious than those of the merchant shipbuilders. Following the recommendations made in both the 1966 Geddes Report[127] and the 1972 Booz-Allen Report,[128] the Conservative Government had accepted that, apart from Royal Fleet Auxiliaries and vessels smaller than frigates and destroyers, warship orders for the Royal Navy should be concentrated on Vickers, Yarrow and Vosper Thorneycroft and that there should be a phasing out of the warship building which, in 1973, was still being carried out by Cammell Laird, Swan Hunter and Scott Lithgow.[129] The three remaining warship builders had received very little Government financial aid in the decade 1967–1976 either from the SIB or under Section 7 of the Industry Act and ships for the Royal Navy were excluded from the Construction Grants Scheme; the warship builders were thus largely dependent on orders for the Royal Navy or on securing export naval orders.

The Labour Government initially continued the policy of concentrating Ministry of Defence orders for the larger ships on the three specialist yards[130] but the warship builders' prospects received a severe blow as a result of the cuts announced in the Government's 1974 Defence Review[131] which, it was later disclosed, would involve the deletion from the defence programme, as it had been in February 1974 when Labour came to power, of nine destroyers/frigates, two amphibious ships, three large fleet tankers and one support ship and the deferring of other contracts.[132] In the light of these defence cuts it was all the more important for the warship yards, all of whom were on the nationalisation list, to secure foreign naval orders and at the end of 1975 fears were expressed that public ownership could lose the warship builders some of the naval export business, valued at between £1,200 and £1,400 million, which was then under negotiation.[133]

During 1975 and 1976 the United Kingdom fully participated in the efforts which were being made in the EEC and the OECD to evolve some internationally acceptable policy for solving the massive over-capacity which had led to the worldwide shipbuilding crisis. In July 1975 there was a new EEC

127. Chapters 4 and 24.
128. Pp. 12–14.
129. See Lord Carrington's statement on warships ordering policy in the Lords on 23rd July 1973—P. Debs. 5 Ser., Vol. 344, c.1646.
130. But in 1977 there was a departure from the policy when the Ministry of Defence gave orders to Swan Hunter for three destroyers and a cruiser.
131. P. Debs. 5 Ser., Vol. 882, c.1355.
132. See 1975 Defence White Paper (Cmnd 5976, Parl. Papers 1974–75, Vol. 20) and P. Debs. 5 Ser., Vol. 919, c.(363–364).
133. See Report on p. 22 of *The Times*, 12th December 1975.

Directive on Aids to Shipbuilding[134] which approved home and export credit facilities conforming to the OECD Understanding of July 1974 and expressly prohibited "intervention measures to promote shipbuilding" other than conservatory and, approved by the Commission, "as a temporary solution for the rescue of shipbuilding and ship repairing undertakings". At an OECD shipbuilding working party meeting in April 1976 it was agreed that major shipbuilding countries should consider as a priority target a suitable reduction in their shipbuilding capacities and should not "take measures or grant aid likely to disturb the process of adapting the industry".

At the end of May 1976 a European Commission policy document stated that the EEC's first course should be to seek an international agreement for an orderly contraction of the world shipbuilding industry based on the OECD guidelines and Japan, whose 1975 output had been 50 per cent of world output and whose prices were alleged to be 30 or 40 per cent below European levels, was warned that, unless it was prepared to negotiate a contraction of its industry and a more equitable sharing of orders, the EEC might have to take unilateral action to protect the economic future of the Community's shipyards. After protracted discussions with the Japanese had taken place, the West European countries, at an OECD meeting in February 1977, accepted the limited concessions offered by the Japanese which involved an increase in the price of Japanese ships built for export, restrictions on exports to certain European countries whose shipbuilding industries were in severe difficulties and an undertaking to consider further curtailment of activity if these measures failed to achieve the desired result.[135]

Early in 1977, whilst the principal shipbuilding countries on the Continent were planning for long-term reductions in capacity[136] and short-term financial rescue operations, the British Government still remained entangled and preoccupied in the seemingly interminable Parliamentary struggle over the nationalisation of the industry. The shipbuilders and the unions were united in emphasising the urgent need for the Government to produce a survival policy in order to avert yard closures and eventually, after the Prime Minister had intervened in the crisis, the Minister for Industry, Mr Kaufman, announced on 24th February 1977[137] that, in order to bridge the price gap with competitors (other than in the EEC) who were undercutting U.K. builders, the Government would assist British yards to obtain orders by establishing, under the

134. No. 75/432/EEC published in the Official Journal of the European Communities, Vol. 18 L.192 on 24th July 1975. This Directive, which replaced the 1972 Directive (see p. 235 *supra*), was to apply until 31st December 1977.

135. See *The Times*, 9th February 1977.

136. Sweden and the Netherlands had already embarked on schemes to reduce output by 30 per cent.

137. P. Debs. 5 Ser., Vol. 926, c.1652.

powers in Part II of the Industry Act, an intervention fund of £65 million in grants.[138]

In his statement Mr Kaufman emphasised that, without this Government support, much of the U.K. merchant shipbuilding industry would close within two years and there would be heavy unemployment. The immediate concern was to secure orders and the new measure would alleviate the industrial and social effects of the world crisis but there would have to be a longer term strategy of modernisation and rationalisation following upon public ownership and the massive investment required could only be achieved under public ownership. The Government accepted that there would have to be some contraction, which would be alleviated by a redundancy scheme, but the Government had made it clear to the EEC and the OECD that the proposed across the board reductions for the British shipbuilding industry were unacceptable.[139]

Although there was a feeling that the new £65 million fund might be too little and too late, it was naturally welcomed by the shipbuilders[140] and the unions; by 31st March 1978 £55.8 million had been committed in grants under Section 7 to assist the securing of orders for 56 ships totalling 528,000 g.r.t.[141] and it seems likely that, without the help of the fund, new orders would have been substantially lower. Even so new orders for 1977 totalled only 429,000 g.r.t.—well less than half the 1977 output and not greatly in excess of the 1976 orders[142]—and the total of ships on order in U.K. yards at the end of 1977 was only 2.199 million g.r.t. which was by far the lowest end of year figure during the previous decade.[143] Not a happy augury for the nationalised British Shipbuilders which had the misfortune to enter into their inheritance at a time when both the U.K. and world shipbuilding industries were facing a crisis more severe than at any time since the depression of the 1930s.

Meanwhile, during the whole of 1976 and the early months of 1977 when the British shipbuilding and ship repairing industries were struggling to survive, the Labour Government, with their wafer thin majority, were much involved in a no less difficult struggle—to get through Parliament, against every delaying tactic that the Opposition could devise, the Aircraft and Shipbuilding Industries Bill. The Bill provided (*inter alia*) for the vesting in a new public corporation named "British Shipbuilders" of all the securities of the shipbuilding,

138. The European Commission had been informed of the intention to introduce this fund which the Government considered conformed with the U.K.'s obligations under the Treaty of Rome.

139. In EEC and OECD circles it was being suggested that all shipbuilding member countries should cut their output by the same fixed percentage.

140. British shipowners feared that the fund might encourage the building of further surplus tonnage and that foreign owners might use the fund to acquire relatively cheap ships which would be a competitive threat to British ships.

141. See Industry Act Report for the year ended 31st March 1978—Parl. Papers 1977–78, HC 653. A substantial part of this commitment was in respect of the controversial Polish contract for 24 ships—see P. Debs. 5 Ser., Vol. 941, c.53.

142. *British Shipping Statistics 1976–77*, Tables 3.1 and 3.10.

143. *Ibid.*, Table 3.7.

ship repairing and marine engineering companies named in Part I of Schedule 2 of the Bill, being companies which on 31st July 1974 fulfilled the conditions in Part II of that Schedule. In relation to shipbuilding this meant that all the major shipbuilding companies in Great Britain, including those already wholly or partly Government owned, would, on the shipbuilding industry vesting date, become wholly owned subsidiaries of British Shipbuilders.[144]

The debate on the Second Reading of the Bill took place on 2nd December 1975.[145] In moving the Second Reading, the Secretary of State for Industry, Mr Varley, recounted the unhappy history of the U.K. shipbuilding industry over the previous 20 years,[146] outlined the bleak prospects for world shipbuilding and argued that, without public ownership, the U.K. industry could not survive; since 1966 a total of £299 million[147] had been given or committed to U.K. shipbuilders but the industry was still suffering from outdated facilities, bad labour relations, weak financial control, low productivity[148] and late deliveries. The Conservative Opposition speakers, led by Mr Michael Heseltine, strongly opposed the nationalisation proposals and contended that the world shipbuilding problems were caused by over-capacity which public ownership would not help the U.K. industry to overcome; they also argued that the problems of the ship repairing industry differed from those of shipbuilding and that it was best left alone and there was criticism of the compensation provisions[149] as being inadequate and inequitable.

The Bill passed its Second Reading by 280 votes to 275 and was sent to Standing Committee D whose consideration of the Bill was of unprecedented duration. The Committee commenced its deliberations on 11th December 1975 and did not end them until 13th May 1976 by which time there had been 58 sittings.[150] During this marathon numerous amendments were moved by the Conservatives[151] but, in 105 divisions, not one amendment was carried against the Government. Whilst the Committee were still engaged on its scrutiny, the Secretary of State proceeded with the setting up of an Organising Committee whose primary task was to work in close consultation with the Government, the managements and the trade unions in preparing detailed

144. Northern Ireland was excluded from the Bill. Harland & Wolff, which had become wholly Government owned in August 1975, thus remained independent of British Shipbuilders.

145. P. Debs. 5 Ser., Vol. 901, c.1446.

146. In 1955 U.K. output was 26 per cent of world output; in 1975 it was less than four per cent. Britain was the only major shipbuilding country which had not achieved any growth in output in the past 20 years. (*British Shipping Statistics 1976–77*, Table 3.10).

147. This did not include £30 million provided for UCS but did include £47 million of construction grants. Of the balance of £252 million some £220 million (87 per cent) had been allocated to companies wholly or partly in public ownership (P. Debs. 5 Ser., Vol. 902, cc.(63) and (318)).

148. Since 1968 U.K. output per employee had been static.

149. See Clauses 35–41 and Schedule 5 of the Bill.

150. Involving 140 sitting hours.

151. These included attempts to exclude the warship builders and ship repairers from the scope of the Bill and, conversely, to include Harland & Wolff.

plans for vesting and for the initial organisation of British Shipbuilders. Admiral Sir Anthony Griffin, Chairman designate of British Shipbuilders, was appointed Chairman of the Organising Committee, Mr Graham Day, Managing Director of Cammell Laird and Chief Executive designate of British Shipbuilders, was appointed a Deputy Chairman of the Organising Committee and Mr Ken Griffin, a leading trade unionist, was also appointed a Deputy Chairman.[152]

Following the completion of the Committee stage, the Bill was due to come up for Report in the Commons on 26th May 1976 but on the previous day a Conservative member, Mr Maxwell Hyslop, presented a petition by a member of Yarrow (Shipbuilders) Ltd.[153] claiming that the Bill was a hybrid[154] and that, in accordance with Commons Standing Orders, it should be referred to a Select Committee or a Joint Committee as the House might order.[155] The basis of the hybridity claim was that Marathon Shipbuilding (U.K.) Ltd.[156] was not named in the Bill as one of the companies to be nationalised and should have been because it fulfilled the qualifying condition for a shipbuilding company in paragraph 2(1) of Part II of Schedule 2 to the Bill. The Speaker first ruled that the submission did not support a case for hybridity but on the following day, having been given further information, he reversed his previous ruling and declared that the Bill was *prima facie* hybrid.[157]

On the basis of the Speaker's new ruling the Opposition maintained that the Bill should be sent to the Examiners to receive petitions from interested parties and that it should be referred to a Select Committee. The Government response was to propose a motion[158] that any Standing Orders relating to private business should be dispensed with whereupon the Opposition moved an amendment endorsing the Speaker's ruling that the rights of private citizens might be affected by the Bill and that the normal procedure as laid down in Standing Orders should be followed. In the debate the Government argued that it was only a "hairline hybridity" which could be rectified by an amendment at the Report stage whilst the Opposition arguments centred on the constitutional importance of safeguarding the rights of the subject. The voting on the Opposition amendment was a tie—303 votes to 303—whereupon, in accordance with precedent, the Speaker give his casting vote against the amendment; the

152. P. Debs. 5 Ser., Vol. 907, c.(625). Subsequently two full-time and three part-time members were appointed to the Organising Committee—see P. Debs. 5 Ser., Vol. 910, c.(465).

153. A shipbuilding company named in Part I of Schedule 2 of the Bill.

154. I.e. that it was a Public Bill which affected a particular private interest in a manner different from the private interests of other persons or bodies of the same category or class.

155. P. Debs. 5 Ser., Vol. 912, c.299.

156. Which had acquired the Clydebank shipyard from the UCS liquidator on 8th August 1972 and was using the yard for the construction of off-shore drilling rigs.

157. P. Debs. 5 Ser., Vol. 912, c.445.

158. *Ibid.*, Vol. 912, c.632.

House then voted on the Government motion which, to the surprise of the Opposition, was carried by 304 votes to 303.[159]

The Conservative Opposition considered that the vote had been lost as a result of a breach in the pairing arrangements and on 23rd June the Prime Minister, Mr James Callaghan, stated[160] that, owing to a misunderstanding on the pairing arrangements, the Opposition had a well-founded sense of grievance and that the Government would provide an opportunity for the issue to be considered and put to the vote again. On 29th June there was a lengthy debate on an Opposition motion to refer the Bill to a Select Committee[161]; the arguments were much concerned with hybridity and procedural questions and on this occasion the Opposition motion was decisively defeated by 311 votes to 297.[162] The way was thus left clear for the Government to proceed with the Report stage and Third Reading and, after another long and acrimonious debate,[163] the House approved by 311 votes to 294 a Government guillotine motion allowing only three days discussion for the Report and Third Reading.

The Report stage of the Bill, as amended in Standing Committee, began on 27th July 1976 and continued on the following two days.[164] Government amendments to overcome the hybridity problem[165] were carried by 300 votes to 287 but a Plaid Cymru amendment, supported by the Conservatives, to cut out the nationalisation of the ship repairing companies was defeated by 302 to 296 and the Report stage was concluded with the defeat, by 313 votes to 303, of a Conservative amendment for excluding the warship builders from the scope of the Bill. The House then passed to a debate on the Third Reading[166] when much the same arguments for and against the Bill were again recited by the same protagonists and eventually the Bill passed its Third Reading but only by the narrow margin of three votes.

In the Lords the Minister moving the Second Reading of the Bill on 28th September 1976[167] rehearsed the now familiar Government arguments in favour of the Bill and emphasised that, as a major merchant shipping country with a large volume of seaborne trade and also as a naval power, it was essential for the United Kingdom to maintain a home base for shipbuilding and that the Government were determined to ensure a viable and competitive industry. The principal spokesman for the Conservative Opposition, Lord Carr, stated that the Conservatives were strongly opposed to the Bill which they would

159. Whereupon, as Hansard put it, "Grave disorder having arisen in the House, the Speaker suspended the sitting for 20 minutes".

160. P. Debs. 5 Ser., Vol. 913, c.1361.

161. *Ibid.*, Vol. 914, c.218.

162. Largely owing to abstentions by Scottish Nationalists and Plaid Cymru both of whom had previously voted against the Government.

163. P. Debs. 5 Ser., Vol. 915, c.1527.

164. *Ibid.*, Vol. 916, cc.265, 661 and 892.

165. By excluding a mobile off-shore installation from the definition of "ship" in Schedule 2.

166. P. Debs. 5 Ser., Vol. 916, c.981.

167. P. Debs. 5 Ser. (HL), Vol. 373, c.1634.

examine thoroughly and propose a large number of amendments; he also warned that there was a possible hybridity in relation to the list of ship repairing companies in Schedule 2 of the Bill.[168] Cross-bench speeches from two leading shipowners[169] made clear the shipping industry's opposition to the nationalisation of the ship repairers and Lord Shinwell, the nonagenarian Labour peer with expert knowledge of the industry, took the view that neither the ship repairers nor the warship builders should be nationalised.

The Bill passed its Second Reading without a division and was committed to a Committee of the whole House but, before the Committee stage began, the Leader of the House, Lord Peart, gave detailed answers[170] to the hybridity questions that had been raised and stated that the Government were satisfied that no amendments to Schedule 2 were necessary. The Committee stage commenced on 11th October[171] and at an early stage the Conservatives criticised the Government's answers to the hybridity allegations and argued that, in view of the doubts, the Bill should go to the Examiners. The Lords then considered Opposition amendments for the removal from the Bill of the ship repairers but Lord Melchett, the Minister in charge of the Bill, strongly resisted this change and the amendments were withdrawn.[172] The Committee stage was resumed on 14th October[173] when the Liberals, supported by the Conservatives, moved an amendment for excluding the warship builders and the marine engine builders but the Government front bench argued that the naval builders, as the most profitable sector, had to be included and that the engine builders could not be divorced from the shipbuilders on whom they were almost entirely dependent.[174] At the conclusion of the second day of the Committee Stage[175] the Government gave written answers to the hybridity arguments in relation to the ship repairers and Lord Peart said that the Government remained entirely satisfied that Schedule 2 was correctly drafted and did not involve any element of hybridity. The Committee stage continued for a further three days[176] and, after a number of amendments had been carried against the Government, the Committee proceedings concluded with the contentious Schedule 2 being left unamended.

168. The particular hybridity argument had not been raised in the Commons. In the Lords the Conservatives maintained that three ship repairing companies named in Part I of Schedule 2 did not fall within the qualifying conditions and that, conversely, there were two companies, not named in the Bill, which did comply with the qualifying conditions.

169. Lord Inverforth, Chairman of Andrew Weir, and the Earl of Inchcape, Chairman of P & O and President of the General Council of British Shipping.

170. P. Debs. 5 Ser. (HL), Vol. 374, c.1481.

171. *Ibid.*, Vol. 375, cc.11–95 and 118–193.

172. They were reintroduced at the Report stage—see *infra.*

173. P. Debs. 5 Ser. (HL), Vol. 375, cc.461–536 and 561–633.

174. This amendment was also withdrawn but a new amendment for the exclusion of the warship builders was moved on Report.

175. P. Debs. 5 Ser. (HL), Vol. 375, cc.633–639.

176. *Ibid.*, Vol. 375, cc.763–851, 869–1117, 1343–1463 and Vol. 376, cc.81–259.

The Lords commenced the Report stage of the Bill on 1st November[177] and considered a number of Conservative amendments designed to cut out ship repairing; these were again strongly opposed by Lord Melchett but were carried against the Government by 73 votes to 34. Before the House rose the Government answered in detail[178] further written questions on hybridity which had been raised by Lord Colville, a member of the Bar, and once again Lord Peart reiterated the Government's confidence that Schedule 2 did not involve any element of hybridity. The consideration of the Bill on Report continued on 3rd November[179] and again on 5th November[180] when the Report stage was concluded; on both days there were a substantial number of Government and Opposition amendments of which the most significant were the carrying against the Government, by 74 votes to 45, of an amendment for leaving out the specialist warship builders and the agreement, without a division, of the amendment for leaving out the ship repairing companies.[181]

The Lords' debate on the Third Reading of the Bill took place on 9th November.[182] Lord Melchett accused the Opposition of delaying tactics which made it more difficult to draw up a strategy that would ensure that the industry was able to compete in world markets but Lord Carr denied that there had been any undue delay since the Bill had passed through all its stages in six weeks and one third of the 90 amendments had been either amendments proposed by the Government or Opposition amendments accepted by the Government without a division. Winding up for the Government, Lord Melchett maintained that the Lords had wrecked the Bill and warned that when the Bill returned to the Commons the Government would repair the damage that had been done. The Bill was then passed and returned to the Commons.

The Bill's sojourn in the Commons was brief. On 11th November the Commons considered the Lords' amendments[183] and, although on some of the divisions the Government majority was slender,[184] at the end of the six hours allotted for the debate[185] the Commons had disagreed all the Lords' amendments on matters of major principle[186] and in substance the Bill had been restored to the original form in which it had left the Commons in July. The Bill then started on the first of the five journeys that it was destined to make

177. *Ibid.*, Vol. 376, cc.879–1065.
178. *Ibid.*, Vol. 376, c.1066.
179. *Ibid.*, Vol. 376, c.1262.
180. *Ibid.*, Vol. 376, c.1628.
181. Lord Colville observed that, since ship repairing had been omitted from the Bill, there was no longer any need for him to deal with the problem of hybridity.
182. P. Debs. 5 Ser. (HL), Vol. 377, c.187.
183. P. Debs. 5 Ser., Vol. 919, c.670.
184. On the division regarding the amendment for leaving out ship repairing the Government had a majority of one.
185. See P. Debs. 5 Ser., Vol. 919, c.94.
186. Including those removing the warship builders and ship repairers and changing the compensation formula.

along the corridors of Westminster during the ensuing 10 days. On 12th November the Lords received the Bill back from the Commons and considered it on 16th November.[187] The debate was lengthy but in the end the Lords only insisted on their amendments relative to the exclusion of the 12 named ship repairers[188] and the ship repairing business of Vosper Thorneycroft[189]; both on industrial grounds and because of the hybridity problem the Government were pressed to agree that nationalisation of the ship repairers should be abandoned but Lord Melchett refused to give way and asserted that the Government was perfectly clear that the Bill was not a hybrid.

The Bill then went back to the Commons where, on 18th November,[190] the Lords' amendments were rejected by a margin of two votes. On the morning of 22nd November, the last day of the session, the Bill was once more before the Lords[191] for consideration of the Commons' reasons for disagreeing with the amendment on which the Lords had insisted. In support of a Government motion that the Lords should no longer insist on their amendments Lord Melchett said that the Government would make no concessions and that, if the Lords persisted in their resolve to delete ship repairing, the Bill would fall in the current session but would be reintroduced at the beginning of the next Session.[192] In reply Lord Campbell said that the House was now only insisting on the removal of the ship repairing industry but the Government had decided it must be all or nothing and it was no use blaming the Lords for delay. The House then divided and the Government motion was disagreed by 197 votes to 90; the Bill was then returned to the Commons and on the afternoon of the same day[193] the Commons approved, by 276 votes to 268, a Government motion that the House insisted on its disagreement with the Lords' amendments. Later in the afternoon the Bill once more arrived back in the Lords[194] and thereupon Parliament was prorogued to 24th November and the session ended.

On 26th November, two days after the opening of the new Session, the Bill was re-introduced[195] and on 1st December there was a Government Procedure Motion[196] designed to ensure the rapid passage of the Bill through the Commons. In opposing the motion the Conservatives concentrated on the hybridity issue and pointed out that the Bill had been declared *prima facie* hybrid by

187. P. Debs. 5 Ser. (HL), Vol. 377, c.1119.
188. The Lords agreed not to insist on the exclusion of the warship builders.
189. Vospers had a warship building and ship repairing business. The Lords felt it wrong for the ship repairing side to be nationalised.
190. P. Debs. 5 Ser., Vol. 919, c.1608.
191. P. Debs. 5 Ser. (HL), Vol. 377, c.1656.
192. Under the Parliament Acts 1911 and 1949 the Lords could then delay the Bill until the end of the next Session.
193. P. Debs. 5 Ser., Vol. 919, c.1890.
194. P. Debs. 5 Ser. (HL), Vol. 377, c.1743.
195. P. Debs. 5 Ser., Vol. 921, c.346.
196. *Ibid.*, Vol. 921, c.934.

the Public Bill Office.[197] The Leader of the House, Mr Michael Foot, said that the case for hybridity was not proved and in the Government's view there were not such doubts as would justify a reference to the Examiners; the Government motion was then carried by 286 votes to 268 and the House proceeded immediately to the Second Reading[198] at which, after a brief debate, the Bill was passed by 285 votes to 279.

On 7th December, after approval of a Business motion[199] and the formal passing of the Committee Stage,[200] the Conservatives moved amendments for leaving out the ship repairing companies and the Vosper repair business[201] but both amendments were defeated by 281 votes to 279. Mr Kaufman then moved the Third Reading[202] and the Government were warned by the Opposition that, in view of the judgement of the Public Bills Office about the *prima facie* hybridity, the Bill, when it reached the Lords, would automatically be referred to the Examiners; the warning was disregarded and the Bill then passed its Third Reading by a margin of three votes. The Bill was brought to the Lords on 8th December, formally read a first time, ordered to be printed and referred to the Examiners[203]; the Bill then disappeared from sight for a period of over two months during which time the Examiners[204] were engaged on deciding whether or not the Bill was hybrid.

On 17th February 1977[205] the Lords ordered that the Examiners' Certificate that certain Standing Orders should apply to the Bill and had not been complied with should be referred to the Standing Order Committee and that the Examiners' Statement of their reasons should be printed.[206] The main finding of the Examiners was that the Bill was hybrid in respect of the omission of Westminster Dredging Company[207] and because the condition of turnover[208] was not germane to the subject matter of the Bill so far as it related to the ship repairing companies. On 23rd February the Standing Order Committee published their Report[209] stating that the Standing Orders not complied with be dispensed with and that the Bill be allowed to proceed on condition that a notice was published in national newspapers giving details of the procedure

197. The Order Paper contained the words "Second Reading (to be reported upon by the Examiners").

198. P. Debs. 5 Ser., Vol. 921, c.1013.

199. *Ibid.*, Vol. 922, c.236.

200. *Ibid.*, c.258.

201. These amendments were exactly the same as the Lords' amendments which the Commons had rejected on 18th November.

202. P. Debs. 5 Ser., Vol. 922, c.375.

203. P. Debs. 5 Ser. (HL), Vol. 378, c.671.

204. Two officers of the Lords and two officers of the Commons.

205. P. Debs. 5 Ser. (HL), Vol. 379, c.1844.

206. HL 71.

207. Because Westminster fulfilled the criteria in para. 3 of Part II of Schedule 2.

208. As set out in para. 3(1)(C) of Part II of Schedule 2.

209. HL 79.

for objecting to the Bill in accordance with the usual practice relating to Private Bills.[210]

The characterisation of the Bill as a hybrid soon induced the Cabinet to climb down on ship repairing. On 2nd March Lord Peart stated[211] that, in view of the hybridity findings and the damaging delay that would ensue, the Government had reluctantly decided that the ship repairing companies should be dropped from the Bill. Events in the Lords then moved with remarkable rapidity. The Second Reading took place on 8th March[212] and at the Committee stage on 10th March[213] the amendments to Schedule 2 for omitting all references to the ship repairing companies were agreed without a division; the debate on the Third Reading then took place[214] and the Bill was passed and returned to the Commons. Matters moved no less swiftly in the Commons. On 15th March[215] the Lords' amendments to Schedule 2 were quickly agreed[216] and on 17th March 1977 the Bill received the Royal Assent; at long last "a body corporate to be called British Shipbuilders" was legally constituted.

It was not until more than three months later that, on 1st July 1977,[217] British Shipbuilders entered into its inheritance and during this hiatus the Secretary of State had to make two policy decisions of importance to the future of the new corporation. The first of these related to the location of British Shipbuilders' headquarters which, two years previously, it had been said would be "in an assisted area with a tradition of shipbuilding"[218]; since then there seemed to have grown up a general impression that the headquarters would be on Merseyside but in April 1977 the Secretary of State announced[219] that the headquarters would be in the North East at a location to be decided by British Shipbuilders.[220] The other problem was to find someone with the necessary expertise who would be willing to accept the appointment of Chief Executive in place of Graham Day who had resigned in December 1976.[221] In the end, Mr Michael Casey, an Under Secretary at the Industry Department, was

210. On the same day the House ordered that any Petition should be deposited by 18th March 1977 (P. Debs. 5 Ser. (HL), Vol. 380, c.355).

211. P. Debs. 5 Ser. (HL), Vol. 380, c.641.

212. *Ibid.*, c.915. The House had previously agreed that no petitions against the Bill should be heard and that there should be no publication.

213. *Ibid.*, c.1165.

214. *Ibid.*, c.2276.

215. P. Debs. 5 Ser., Vol. 927, c.365.

216. The Government had previously rejected Conservative requests that Vospers should be permitted to extract their ship repair business.

217. The designated vesting date by virtue of the Aircraft and Shipbuilding Industry (Shipbuilding Vesting Date) Order 1977 (SI 1977 No. 540).

218. P. Debs. 5 Ser., Vol. 888, c.1156.

219. *Ibid.*, Vol. 930, c.(96).

220. They were eventually located in Newcastle but the corporation also had an office in London.

221. P. Debs. 5 Ser., Vol. 922, c.626. Mr Day's decision was largely as a result of the delay in the Bill becoming law.

chosen and the formal announcement of his appointment in June 1977 also gave the full composition of the Board as then constituted.[222]

Prior to the vesting date it was announced that, as a result of the negotiations with the respective owners, British Shipbuilders were acquiring four ship repairing companies[223]—namely R. H. Green and Silley Wear, London Graving Dock,[224] Scott Lithgow Drydocks[225] and Wallsend Slipway and Engineering[226]; since the shares of the ship repairing companies which had become publicly owned in 1974 and 1975[227] were also being transferred to British Shipbuilders, it could be said that by the Vesting Date, in spite of the omission of the ship repairing companies from the Act, a substantial part of the ship repairing industry had been nationalised. Another development before vesting date related to the arrangements for payment of compensation to the shareholders of the nationalised shipbuilding and engineering companies[228]; it was announced[229] that the accountants appointed by the Government, Whinney, Murray & Co., were collecting the information needed for their valuation and that the timing of the compensation payments would depend on the progress of the negotiations.

At last came the shipbuilding industry vesting date—a momentous day for those fiercely independent shipbuilders and engine builders, many of them household names throughout the maritime world for a century or more, who then began, as a unified industry under the aegis of British Shipbuilders, a new era in which it was hoped that U.K. shipbuilders could re-establish themselves as a competitive and profitable world force. In mid-1977 however the prospects were bleak; for the 12 months ending June 1977 new orders for U.K. yards amounted to only 345,000 g.r.t.[230] and the order book was dwindling rapidly.[231] For the time being longer term strategic plans for modernisation and rationalisation had to take second place; the pressing need was to obtain new and profitable orders and British Shipbuilders made it clear that vigorous marketing was to be accorded top priority.

Unfortunately, the world order book, like that of the U.K., was also falling fast[232] and it was in the context of the world over-capacity and dearth of

222. *Ibid.*, Vol. 933, c.(148). There were still vacancies as a result of the three full-time members having resigned in January 1977.

223. All of whom had originally been listed for nationalisation.

224. P. Debs. 5 Ser., Vol. 928, c.(627).

225. *Ibid.*, Vol. 929, c.(221).

226. *Ibid.*, Vol. 936, c.1477.

227. Both Sunderland Shipbuilding and Harland & Wolff had ship repairing businesses.

228. See Sections 35–41 and Schedule 5 of the Act.

229. P. Debs. 5 Ser., Vol. 932, c.(267).

230. *British Shipping Statistics 1976–77*, Table 3.1. 79 per cent of these new orders were for U.K. owners.

231. *British Shipping Statistics 1976–77*, Table 3.7. At the end of 1976 the U.K. order book stood at 2.946 million g.r.t.; by the end of 1977 it had fallen to 2.199 million g.r.t.

232. At the end of 1977 the world order book was reduced to 36.7 million g.r.t compared with 82.3 million g.r.t. at the end of 1975 and 55.4 million g.r.t. at the end of 1976 (*British Shipping Statistics 1976–77*, Table 3.7).

orders that the Government hoped that, with support from the new intervention fund,[233] British yards would be able to quote prices more in line with their competitors outside Europe. There was, however, some apprehension as to the likely extent of the demands which British Shipbuilders would make on the public purse[234]; there was already a provision of £65 million to subsidise the winning of orders and it was probable that further provisions for the same purpose would be required. In addition it was clear that some yards would soon need additional working capital, heavy losses expected to be incurred on pre-nationalisation contracts would have to be funded and, in the longer term, further capital would be needed for modernisation and to bring about the orderly contraction of the industry to which the Government were committed.

It was soon apparent that nationalisation was no easy panacea for the ailing shipbuilding industry. The first accounts of British Shipbuilders, for the period from 1st July 1977 to 31st March 1978, showed a loss, before interest and tax, of £104 million after crediting intervention fund assistance of £46.6 million[235] but the loss, which in reality amounted to some £150 million, was accentuated by a provision of £47 million for losses on contracts made before nationalisation. On the other hand, although British Shipbuilders had assured the Department of Industry that post-nationalisation orders secured with assistance from the fund would not be taken at below break-even prices, in the event a further provision of another £47 million had to be made for losses on orders accepted with support from the fund.[236]

Throughout 1978 demand for new ships continued to decline and by the end of the year the world order book had fallen to 25.8 million g.r.t.—its lowest level since 1965; new orders in U.K. yards totalled only 246,000 g.r.t. and at December 1978 the U.K. order book had declined to 1.2 million g.r.t.[237] The failure of British yards to win more orders was mainly due to the fact that U.K. construction costs were far higher than those of many of their foreign competitors so that although, with EEC approval, the intervention fund had been renewed for 1978 at an annual rate of £85 million,[238] during the year ended 31st March 1979[239] only £15 million had been committed in grants to

233. See pp. 248–249 *supra.*

234. Not only British Shipbuilders but also the publicly owned Harland & Wolff for whom the Northern Ireland Office remained responsible.

235. This assistance, which often amounted to 30 per cent of a quoted price, had been expressly approved by the European Commission—see Article 6 of the European Council's Fourth Directive on Aid to Shipbuilding, 78/338/EEC published in OJ 1978 L.98. The manner in which the Fund was administered was severely criticised by the Auditor General (Parl. Papers 1978–79, HC 138) and by the Committee of Public Accounts (Parl. Papers 1979–80, HC 173 and Cmnd. 7788).

236. A substantial part of these losses related to the order for the 28 Polish ships which was criticised by the Public Accounts Committee.

237. *British Shipping Statistics 1979–80*, Table 3.7.

238. However the EEC did stipulate that the permitted rate of subsidy on individual orders should be reduced from 30 per cent to 25 per cent of the tendered price.

239. See Industry Act Report for the year ended 31st March 1979, Parl. Papers 1979–80, HC 206.

secure orders for eight ships totalling 49,000 g.r.t. because, even with help from the fund, British builders were still unable to match the prices quoted by their competitors.

On 30th June 1978 the Secretary of State had determined[240] that for the year ended 31st March 1979 British Shipbuilders should seek to limit its losses to £45 million and the Accounts for 1978–79 showed a trading loss, before interest and tax, of £49.5 million and revealed outstanding losses of £101.14 million as compared with the statutory borrowing limit of £200 million.[241] The Accounts emphasised the importance of the contribution made by the warship group; Vickers, Vosper Thorneycroft and Yarrow showed profits aggregating more than £22 million whereas the merchant shipbuilding companies nearly all showed poor results and three of the largest—Scott Lithgow, Govan and Swan Hunter—made losses ranging between £11.7 million and £15.7 million. The 1978–79 Report also stated that, since vesting day, the number employed in merchant shipbuilding had fallen from 38,000 to under 28,000[242] and, following the making, in August 1978, of Orders implementing the Shipbuilding (Redundancy Payments) Act 1978,[243] both British Shipbuilders and Harland & Wolff were empowered to make special redundancy payments to those leaving the industry as a result of closures or rundowns.

At the end of 1978 British Shipbuilders submitted to the Government their corporate plan for the future of the industry but, prior to the dissolution of Parliament on 5th April 1979, the Labour Government had not announced their conclusions on a long term strategy for the industry. However on 4th April 1979[244] the Secretary of State did give details of various short term measures of support; these comprised the extension of the intervention fund at the annual rate of £85 million but subject to the requirement that British Shipbuilders should operate for 1979–80 within a total loss limit of £100 million after crediting fund assistance, the bringing forward of public sector orders, support within OECD for improved credit terms, aid for ship repairing by extending the home credit scheme to include conversions by U.K. owners[245] and the extension of the redundancy payments scheme to July 1981.

240. In accordance with his powers under Section 10 of the Aircraft and Shipbuilding Industries Act 1977.

241. See Section 11(7) of the 1977 Act.

242. Employment at Harland & Wolff had fallen from 10,000 in 1974 to 7,700 in March 1979.

243. Shipbuilding Redundancy Payment Orders 1978 (SI 1978 No. 1191 for Great Britain and SI 1978 No. 1127 for Northern Ireland). These 1978 Orders authorised the payment of special redundancy for a period of two years (July 1977 to July 1979). Further Orders made in 1979 extended the period to July 1981 and Section 5 of the Industry Act 1980 enabled the period to be extended to July 1983. The period was further extended by the Shipbuilding Act 1982.

244. P. Debs. 5 Ser., Vol. 965, c.(829).

245. Effect was given to the extension of the Home Credit Scheme by Section 2 of the Shipbuilding Act 1979—see pp. 262–263 *infra*.

Meanwhile since August 1975 the Northern Ireland Department of Commerce had continued to provide Harland & Wolff with the financial assistance, limited to £60 million in the period up to 31st March 1979, which had been authorised by the Shipbuilding Industry (No. 2) (Northern Ireland) Order 1975.[246] By 31st March 1977 drawings against the £60 million limit amounted to £32.7 million and total issues to Harlands from public funds from 1st January 1966 to 31st March 1977 totalled £125.6 million.[247] Over the following two financial years around £13.7 million was provided by way of further assistance to Harlands[248] and then on 7th March 1979, shortly before the expiry of the 1975 Order, the Northern Ireland Minister of State informed the Commons[249] that the continuing worldwide shipbuilding crisis meant that Harlands would for some time need Government financial assistance in order to survive. Parliament thereupon approved the Aircraft and Shipbuilding Industries (Northern Ireland) Order 1979[250] which empowered the Department of Commerce to give financial aid for an unlimited period and without specifying any amount.[251]

On taking office at the beginning of May 1979 the new Conservative Administration required time to consider British Shipbuilders' corporate plan and it was not until 23rd July 1979[252] that Adam Butler, the Minister of State at the Department of Industry, was able to make a detailed policy statement. With substantial over-capacity in the shipbuilding industry worldwide, further contraction of domestic merchant shipbuilding was inevitable and British Shipbuilders advised reduction of capacity to an annual rate of 430,000 g.r.t.[253] with manpower falling to 20,000. The Government were prepared to put public funds for a two year period behind the industry's own effort to achieve viability and were proposing an intervention fund of £120 million to cover the next two years[254]; the Government would also use the same additional measures of support as had been announced by their predecessors just prior to the dissolution of Parliament.[255]

As regards British Shipbuilders' financial position, the Government decided

246. See pp. 241–242 *supra*.

247. See Northern Ireland Appropriation Accounts 1976–77 (Parl. Papers 1977–78, HC 89).

248. See Northern Ireland Appropriation Accounts 1977–78 (Parl. Papers 1978–79, HC 79) and 1978–79 (Parl. Papers 1979–80, HC 314).

249. P. Debs. 5 Ser., Vol. 963, c.1415.

250. SI 1979 No. 294.

251. The lack of a precise financial limit was because the Government was still negotiating with the European Commission as to the extent of the support which could be given.

252. P. Debs. 5 Ser., Vol. 971, c.41.

253. U.K. output in 1978 had been 1.133 million g.r.t. (*British Shipping Statistics 1979–80*, Table 3.12).

254. On 23rd October 1979 (P. Debs. 5 Ser., Vol. 972, c.(135)) it was announced that the European Commission had approved the fund on the basis that £65 million could be made available for a period of 12 months from 16th July 1979 and that from 16th July 1980 to 31st December 1980 the fund could run at an annual rate of £55 million.

255. See p. 260 *supra*.

that, for the purpose of Section 15 of the 1977 Act, the corporation should have a nil commencing capital debt and that, in accordance with Section 16 of the Act, it should be financed by public dividend capital.[256] For the financial year 1979–80 there was no change in the trading loss limit of £100 million (after intervention fund assistance) proposed by the previous Administration but for the financial year 1980–81 the Secretary of State determined that British Shipbuilders should seek to limit its trading loss to £90 million before crediting intervention fund assistance. By mid-July 1979 the corporation's borrowing had risen to £160 million and it was clear that the existing limit on borrowing and public dividend capital of £200 million specified in Section 11(2) of the Act would soon be exceeded; accordingly on 25th July 1979 the Commons approved an Order[257] increasing the limit to the maximum of £300 million permitted by the 1977 Act.

On 23rd July 1979 there was also a statement by the Northern Ireland Under Secretary on the future of Harland & Wolff.[258] He emphasised that the much needed new orders would not be obtained, even at subsidised prices, unless delivery dates were met and that poor productivity had resulted in heavy trading losses which the Government could not continue to cover indefinitely. However the Government had decided to propose to the EEC Commission that there should be an intervention fund for subsidies on new orders won by the Belfast yard over the next two years[259] and that for the current year, up to an overall limit of £22 million, the Government would continue to fund losses and other expenditure. In the event Harland's trading loss for 1978 turned out to be £21.4 million and, with the trading loss for 1979 expected to be in excess of £24 million, the aid of £22 million was rapidly used up.

In November 1979 the Commons debated the Second Reading of another Shipbuilding Bill.[260] It was explained that by January 1980 British Shipbuilders' borrowing and public dividend capital were expected to exceed the existing statutory limit of £300 million and the Bill accordingly amended Section 11(2) of the 1977 Act so as to increase the limit to £500 million with power for a further increase by Order to £600 million. The Bill also amended Section 10 of the Industry Act 1972 so as to extend the Home Credit Scheme to conversions of U.K. ships in U.K. yards and thus give some help to the ship repairers; loans of up to 80 per cent of the contract price repayable over five years[261] with interest at 7½ per cent per annum would be made available for

256. See P. Debs., Vol. 972, c.(18). The corporation was not required to pay any dividends on its capital until it became profitable.

257. British Shipbuilders' Borrowing Powers (Increase of Limit) Order 1979, SI No. 961.

258. P. Debs. 5 Ser., Vol. 971, c.(31).

259. It was subsequently announced that the European Commission had approved a new intervention fund of £25 million for Harlands on the same terms as the fund already approved for British Shipbuilders.

260. P. Debs. 5 Ser., Vol. 972, c.1481.

261. For very large orders of special importance credit might be extended to eight and a half years.

conversions of ships over 5,000 g.r.t. and for mobile off-shore installations. The Bill passed quickly through all its stages in both Houses and received the Royal Assent on 20th December 1979.[262]

For shipbuilding worldwide the new orders placed in 1979 showed a marked improvement over those for 1978, an exceptionally poor year, and at the end of 1979 the world order book stood at 28.3 million g.r.t. as compared with 25.8 million g.r.t. at the end of 1978.[263] The figures for the U.K. industry were less encouraging: even with help from the intervention fund[264] new orders in 1979 totalled only 231,000 g.r.t. (all for U.K. registration)[265] and at the end of the year orders in hand were only 762,000 g.r.t. compared with 1.2 million g.r.t. at the end of 1978.[263] The 1979–80 results of British Shipbuilders were also disappointing; only the warship builders made profits[266] and, in spite of continuing reductions in manpower[267] and the closure of some yards, the trading loss (after crediting intervention fund receipts) was nearly £110 million and the loss for the year (after extraordinary items) was over £152 million.[268] It was certainly not an opportune moment for the Conservative Government to implement the statement in their election manifesto that the nationalised shipbuilding companies would be returned to private ownership; with the industry facing a period of continuing uncertainty about its future shape and viability, the Government decided in August 1980 that privatisation would have to be deferred.[269]

With the benefit of continuing support from the intervention fund,[270] in 1980 U.K. shipbuilders won orders totalling 503,000 g.r.t.[271]—a considerable improvement on the previous two years—and the order book at the end of 1980, 858,000 g.r.t.,[272] was slightly higher than at the end of 1979. The 1980–81 results of British Shipbuilders were likewise much better than those of the previous year; for 1980–81 the trading loss was £41 million (after crediting

262. Shipbuilding Act 1979 (Ch. 59). The financial limit in Section 11(7) of the 1977 Act was raised by Order to £600 million in 1981, was increased to £700 million by the Shipbuilding Act 1982 and was increased again to £1,000 million by the British Shipbuilding (Borrowing Powers) Act 1983.

263. *British Shipping Statistics 1979–80*, Table 3.7.

264. During the year ended 31st March 1980 grants of £35 million were offered—see Industry Act Report, for the year ending 31st March 1980, Parl. Papers 1979–80, HC 772.

265. *British Shipping Statistics 1979–80*, Table 3.1.

266. Vosper £22 million, Vickers £14.5 million and Yarrow £6.7 million.

267. The merchant shipbuilding workforce had been reduced from 39,000 in July 1977 to 20,500 in March 1980. The ship repairing workforce had also been nearly halved over the same period.

268. There was a provision of £69 million in respect of losses incurred to 31st March 1980 and a further provision of £52 million in respect of future losses on contracts in hand at 31st March 1980.

269. See P. Debs. 5 Ser., Vol. 990, c.(289).

270. Grants of £44 million were offered in the year ending 31/3/81—see Industry Act Report for that year, Parl. Papers 1980–81, HC 460.

271. *British Shipping Statistics 1981*, Table 3.1.

272. *Ibid*., Table 3.7.

intervention fund receipts of £44 million) and, with the Chairman expecting an improvement in 1981–82,[273] the Secretary of State determined that in the year ending 31st March 1982 British Shipbuilders should seek to limit any trading loss (before interest, tax and extraordinary items) to £25 million after crediting intervention fund assistance.[274] However in Belfast Harlands continued to make heavy losses as a result of falls in productivity and serious slippage in delivery dates; in July 1980 the Commons were told[275] that in order to keep the yard going Government finance of £42.5 million would have to be made available in 1980/81.

In the early 1980s the most fundamental problem facing the U.K. shipbuilding industry was still largely outside its control. Worldwide there was a substantial over-capacity of shipping due to the over-ordering of new tonnage in the early 1970s and the relative stagnation of world trade since 1973; as a result in the world shipbuilding market there remained a serious imbalance between supply and demand. The key to survival was the winning of profitable orders in the face of fierce foreign competition. With help from the intervention fund and the recently improved OECD credit terms,[276] British yards could offer a financial package which was often competitive at world level but to shipowners price and credit were by no means the only consideration; of no less importance was the question of delivery date and it was in this area that most British shipbuilders compared unfavourably with their overseas rivals.

The value of Government financial assistance was wholly dependent on the winning of new orders and no amount of Government funding would help the industry unless British shipbuilders could satisfy their potential customers, both British and foreign, that they could deliver ships when the customers wanted them. Many British yards took far longer to build a standard type ship than their foreign competitors and for many years British yards had failed, sometimes by a margin of a year or more, even to meet the often far-off contracted delivery dates. In his evidence given to the Public Accounts Committee in March 1980[277] the Permanent Secretary of the Industry Department agreed that "one of the tragedies of recent years had been poor delivery dates" and stated that, although Britain had a number of yards which were well equipped with modern buildings and machinery, the industry would not become profitable until those yards achieved a productivity approaching that of their competitors.

Certainly the continuing failure of the State owned yards to win a fair share

273. See P. Debs. 5 Ser., Vol. 992, cc.622–640.

274. P. Debs. 5 Ser., Vol. 994, c.(75).

275. *Ibid.*, Vol. 987, c.(534).

276. As from 1st December 1979 the members of the OECD had agreed that the 1974 Understanding on shipbuilding credits should be revised so as to permit loans of 80 per cent of contract price repayable over eight and a half years with interest at 8 per cent.

277. Parl. Papers 1979–80, HC 186, xxi.

of world orders[278] could not be attributed to any lack of Government financial support; by November 1980 the public dividend capital provided for British Shipbuilders since vesting day (a period of less than three and a half years) amounted to £316 million,[279] in July 1981 it was announced[280] that since March 1975 (when Harland & Wolff became publicly owned) the payments made to and commitments given to the Belfast yard amounted to £206 million and between February 1977 and March 1981 the payments from the intervention fund to the U.K. shipbuilding industry totalled £105.5 million.[281] However the question remained as to whether the Government would be prepared to continue indefinitely the provision of financial support at this level; it was generally accepted that it would be some years before there was a real equilibrium between capacity and demand in world shipbuilding and meanwhile, in spite of constant ministerial exhortation,[282] the merchant yards showed little sign of achieving the substantial improvements in production and efficiency which were needed to give them the prospect of a viable future.

So what may be the long-term future of the British shipbuilding industry? The case for the retention of the naval yards seems unanswerable; they are an essential strategic resource, they have an export potential and they are profitable. If the merchant yards can achieve their declared objective—a thriving, profitable and competitive industry fully capable of trading successfully in the world market—*cadit quaestio*; but in 1981 the hope of achieving such an objective in the foreseeable future seemed remote indeed and it was clear that for some years merchant shipbuilding would only be able to survive with substantial Government aid. After coming to power in 1979 the Conservative Government had undertaken that for two years it would put public funds behind the industry's own efforts to achieve viability but when, in 1981, this period expired there was no hint of any cessation, or even reduction, of Government financial support and it remained difficult to believe that any British Government could seriously contemplate the possibility of pursuing a policy which might lead to the cessation of all merchant shipbuilding in the United Kingdom.

278. In 1981 new orders for U.K. yards totalled only 479,000 g.r.t. and the U.K. order book at the end of 1981 (1.140 million g.r.t.) amounted to only 3.23 per cent of the world order book.

279. P. Debs. 5 Ser., Vol. 996, c.(271). By March 1982 the public dividend capital had risen to £453 million (see, Parl. Papers 1981–82, HC 146, Accounts relating to Issues from the National Loan Fund).

280. P. Debs. 6 Ser., Vol. 7, c.(477).

281. See Industry Act Report for year ended 31st March 1981—Parl. Papers 1980–81, HC 460.

282. See, for example, P. Debs. 5 Ser., Vol. 992, c.622 and P. Debs. 6 Ser., Vol. 8, c.1590.

CHAPTER 12

THE RISE AND DECLINE OF BRITISH SHIPPING

Between 1958 and 1968 the weight of cargo carried in the world's seaborne trade had more than doubled[1] and between 1968 and 1973 there was a similar rate of expansion—from 2,071 million tonnes in 1968 to 3,233 million tonnes in 1973.[2] During the period from 1968 to 1973 there was also a substantial increase in the tonnage of the world merchant fleet—from 189.534 million g.r.t. in 1968 to 274.835 million g.r.t. in 1973.[3] From 1974 onwards the situation changed radically for the worse; on the one hand the 1973 oil crisis provoked a drastic fall in oil consumption and a general trade recession whilst on the other hand, due to over-ordering, of tankers in particular, and the unjustified expansion of world shipbuilding capacity, world merchant tonnage in general, but especially tanker tonnage, had continued to grow apace.

Thus by 1976, whilst the weight of world seaborne cargo, 3,312 million tonnes, was little more than it had been in 1973,[4] the world merchant fleet as at 1st July 1976 had increased in three years by some 28.76 per cent to 353.895 million g.r.t.[5] with the inevitable result that there was a serious tanker surplus and to a lesser extent, some surplus dry cargo tonnage.[6] To make matters worse, new vessels delivered from world yards in 1976

1. See Chamber of Shipping Annual Report 1971, Statistical Table 33.
2. *British Shipping Statistics 1976–77*, Table 6.1.
3. *British Shipping Statistics 1975*, Table 1.4. The breakdown as between dry cargo and tanker tonnage was:

Year	*1968*	*1973*	*(000 g.r.t.)*
Dry Cargo	116,301	156,283	
Tanker	73,233	118,552	
All Ships	189,534	274,835	

4. *British Shipping Statistics 1976–77*, Table 6.1. The weight of tanker cargo in 1976 was 76 million tonnes less than in 1973.
5. *Ibid.*, Table 1.4. The breakdown as between dry cargo and tanker tonnage (in millions g.r.t.). was: Dry Cargo 180.968; Tanker 172.927. All Ships 353.895. Thus between 1973 and 1976 tanker tonnage had increased by some 46 per cent.
6. Shipping laid up at 31st December 1976 totalled 19.355 million g.r.t. of which 3.539 million g.r.t. was dry cargo tonnage and 15.816 million g.r.t. was tanker tonnage (*British Shipping Statistics 1976–77*, Table 4.1).

totalled 34 million g.r.t., of which 20 million g.r.t. was represented by tankers,[7] and, at the end of 1976, ships on order throughout the world totalled 90 million deadweight tons of which 39 million d.w.t. was represented by tankers.[8] So, although in 1976 world new orders had fallen drastically to around 13–14 million g.r.t., it looked as if it was going to be many years before the serious imbalance between tonnage and cargo would be corrected.

After 20 years of stagnation following the ending of the Second World War, tonnage on the U.K. register at last showed rapid growth corresponding to that of world tonnage; between July 1968 and July 1972 the increase was from 21.402 million g.r.t. to 27.693 million g.r.t.[9] Partly owing to the withdrawal of investment grant,[10] in 1971, and even more so in 1972, new orders for U.K. registration were at a level well below that of 1970[11] but nevertheless at the end of 1972 there were still 269 ships aggregating over 20 million deadweight tons on order in U.K. and foreign yards for registration under the U.K. flag.[12] During the first nine months of 1973 both the dry cargo and tanker freight markets were exceptionally strong[13] and this produced a flood of new orders; in the 12 months ending 31st October 1973 new tonnage ordered for U.K. registration totalled 10.513 million d.w.t.[14] Then came the oil crisis and, during the ensuing depression, new orders for U.K. flag dwindled away; in 1974 they fell to 3.175 million d.w.t. and in 1975 they were only 803,000 d.w.t.[15]

Largely as a result of the orders placed in 1973 and earlier, U.K. registered tonnage continued its growth between 1972 and 1976 and in July 1976 reached a peak of 53.047 million d.w.t. and although in July 1977 there was a significant fall to 50.662 d.w.t.[16] this decline was attributable not so much to reductions in deliveries of new tonnage as to increased sales of old ships for breaking up and to foreign buyers[17] which were to some extent prompted by owners coming under financial pressure as a result of the prolonged

7. *British Shipping Statistics 1976–77*, Table 3.12.

8. *Ibid.*, Table 3.5.

9. *British Shipping Statistics 1975*, Table 1.4. However only 1 million tons of this increase was dry cargo.

10. See pp. 210–211 *supra*.

11. For the 12-monthly period ending 31st October in each year the new order figures (in deadweight tons) were 1970: 8.25 million; 1971: 4.34 million; 1972: 1.49 million—see Chamber of Shipping Annual Report 1972, Statistical Table 3.5.

12. *British Shipping Statistics 1976–77*, Table 3.6.

13. In the last quarter of 1973 the Tramp Time Charter Index (1968=100) rose to a peak of 358. (*British Shipping Statistics 1975*, Table 5.5.) By the end of 1974 the Tanker World Scale index had fallen from 400 to 25.

14. *British Shipping Statistics 1975*, Table 3.2.

15. *Ibid.*, 12 months ending 31st October for each year.

16. For the figures (in d.w.t. and g.r.t.) between 1972 and 1977 see *British Shipping Statistics 1976–77*, Table 1.4.

17. For details of the additions to and removals from the U.K. owned and registered fleet for the year ending 30 June in 1976 and 1977 see *British Shipping Statistics 1976–77*, Table 2.3.

depression.[18] Nevertheless in the period from 1965 to 1976 the U.K. registered fleet had grown from 29.223 million d.w.t. to 53.047 million d.w.t.[19] an increase of about 81.5 per cent; by any reckoning this was a vast improvement over the performance of the previous 20 years and in 1976 the fleet was not only larger but also better balanced and more modern.[20]

At the end of 1972, a year in which orders for new tonnage by British owners had fallen to an exceptionally low level,[21] the Chamber of Shipping continued to emphasise the need for the restoration of investment allowances[22] or some other form of investment stimulus but the Conservative Government seemed only interested in schemes which might be of joint benefit to British shipowners and shipbuilders—more especially the latter—and the Secretary of State emphasised that the Government would give no aid to shipowners that might result in increased orders for foreign yards.[23] However, notwithstanding the misgivings voiced by the Chamber of Shipping, the improvement in market conditions in 1973 resulted in a spate of new orders[24] and in such circumstances it was not surprising that the Government made it clear that there was no possibility of reintroducing an investment grant scheme for shipping.[25] No change in this aspect of domestic shipping policy resulted from the coming to power of a Labour Government in 1974; the Shipping Minister stated in May that there was no intention of introducing any new measures to encourage British shipping.[26]

Nevertheless although, subject to minor exceptions, no investment grant could be made in respect of expenditure on a new ship on or after 27th October 1970 unless such expenditure fell due under a building contract made before 27th October 1970,[27] payments of investment grants were still being made more than 10 years later. This long running-down period was due to the fact that at 31st March 1971 approximately 13 million g.r.t. of new ships were on order for U.K. registry in British and foreign yards[28] and by far the greater part of this tonnage had been contracted for prior to 27th October 1970 and was thus eligible for grant. As a result investment grants paid in respect of shipping for the years after 31st March 1971 were in total more than double the grants paid before that date; between 17th January 1966 and 31st March 1971 grants paid for new ships amounted to £196.832 million whereas from

18. The figures for the Tramp Time Charter Index (1968=100) were 1973: 253; 1974: 284; 1975: 122 and 1976: 129 (see *British Shipping Statistics 1976–77*, Table 5.7).
19. *British Shipping Statistics 1976–77*, Table 1.4.
20. *Ibid.*, Table 2.3.
21. See fn. 11 *supra.*
22. As recommended by the Rochdale Committee—see Report, para. 1395.
23. P. Debs. 5 Ser., Vol. 847, c.893.
24. See *British Shipping Statistics 1975*, Table 3.2
25. P. Debs. 5 Ser., Vol. 857, c.13.
26. *Ibid.*, Vol.874, c.(341)
27. Investment Building Grants Act 1971—see pp. 211–212 *supra.*
28. See P. Debs. 5 Ser., Vol. 838, c.(406)

1st April 1971 to 31st March 1982 shipping grants came to a total of £432.788 million.[29]

Between 1975 and 1977, with freight markets still depressed and substantial tonnage laid up, there was a severe decline in the level of new ship orders for U.K. registration. Total orders (home and abroad) in 1975 were only some 800,000 deadweight tons[30] and 1975 orders by U.K. owners in U.K. yards amounted to a negligible 43,000 g.r.t.[31]; in 1977 total orders (home and abroad) were even less at 590,000 tons deadweight and, although in that year the home proportion was appreciably higher, orders for U.K. flag in U.K. yards still only amounted to 452,00 d.w.t.[32] This drop in new orders, particularly for those placed in U.K. yards, did not result in the introduction of any new investment incentives for U.K. owners. The Government's mind was concentrated on the problem of the shipbuilding industry and the introduction in 1976 of the Government schemes of refund guarantees and cost escalation insurances[33] together with the setting up in February 1977 of the intervention fund[34] were all designed to assist U.K. shipbuilders in securing orders that would otherwise have been placed abroad; as the GCBS pointed out, the intervention fund did not benefit owners—it only enabled U.K. yards to narrow the gap between their break-even prices and the prices quoted by foreign countries outside the EEC.

However, from 1972 onwards into the 1980s, Government guaranteed loans for the building of new ships in U.K. yards to the order of U.K. owners continued to be available under Section 10 of the Industry Act 1972.[35] In order to meet the growing demand, the limit of £1,000 million (exclusive of interest) on the aggregate of the liability of the Secretary of State under the guarantees as specified in the 1972 Act was increased in 1975 to £1,400 million[36] and by Section 23 of the Industry Act 1975 the Secretary of State was empowered by order to increase this limit to £1,800 million. Up to 1974, in accordance with the terms of the OECD Understanding of December 1970, loans under the Home Credit Scheme were given for up to 80 per cent of the contract price repayable over eight years with interest at 7 per cent per annum but as from 1st July 1974, as a result of a new OECD Understanding, the maximum amount of a loan was reduced to 70 per cent of the price and the loan was to

29. See Industry Act Report for the year ended 31st March 1982—Parl Papers 1981–82, Vol. 46, HCP 503. The Annual Reports do not disclose what proportion of these total shipping grants of nearly £630 million were paid in respect of new ships built in foreign yards but probably around half of the total grant related to new ships built abroad.

30. *British Shipping Statistics 1975*, 12 months ending 31st October 1975, Table 3.2.

31. *Ibid*., Table 3.1.

32. *British Shipping Statistics 1976–77*, Table 3.2.

33. See p. 246 *supra*.

34. See pp. 248–249 *supra*.

35. See p. 216 *supra*.

36. Ships and Mobile Offshore Installations Constructions Credit (Increase of Limit) Order 1975 (SI 1975 No. 138).

be repayable over seven years with interest at 8 per cent. Subsequently, as from 1st December 1979 when there was a revised OECD Understanding, credit terms were improved so as to again permit loans up to 80 per cent of the price repayable over eight and a half years.

Under Section 16 of the 1972 Act the Secretary of State was required to make an annual report to Parliament showing the total amount of the liabilities under guarantees given pursuant to Section 7 of the Shipbuilding Act 1967 and Section 10 of the 1972 Act. The first two Reports[37] showed that in the financial years 1972–74 guarantees totalling some £268 million had been given and that, after allowing for repayments, the guarantees current at 31st March 1974 amounted to over £642 million. During the year ended 31st March 1975[38] an exceptionally large amount, over £226 million, was newly guaranteed, in the following financial year new guarantees totalled some £182 million and by 31st March 1976 the outstanding liability in respect of current guarantees amounted to some £895.5 million.[39]

Prior to 1976 there had been no default under the Shipbuilding Credit Scheme but in July 1976 concern arose as a result of a serious deterioration in the financial position of Maritime Fruit Carriers ("MFC"), an Israeli-American entrepreneurial Group which, through the medium of U.K. subsidiaries, had placed a large number of orders with U.K. yards in the early 1970s,[40] and it was reported that the Secretary of State had authorised two mortgagee banks to take possession of six MFC ships.[41] During the following six months there were intense negotiations with a view to disposing of the MFC operating ships and also to find buyers for two large tankers on order for MFC with Scott Lithgow and eventually, in July 1977, the Department of Industry reported[42] that, although MFC had defaulted on repayment of loans on eight completed ships, these ships had all been sold and that no losses or calls on Government guarantees had resulted. However the Department of Industry incurred both losses and further heavy liabilities in connection with the arrangements for the taking over of the two MFC/Scott Lithgow contracts.[43]

In the latter part of 1977, with the shipping recession showing no signs of nearing its end, there were indications that even some of the smaller and old established tramp shipping companies were having difficulty in servicing their Section 10 loans out of earnings so severely reduced that in some cases they

37. Parl Papers 1972–73 (429), Vol. 12 and Parl. Papers 1974 (339), Vol. 7.
38. See Industry Act Report—Parl. Papers 1974–75 (620), Vol. 14.
39. See Industry Act Report—Parl. Paper 1975–76 (619), Vol. 17.
40. At 31st December 1975 no less than 35 per cent of the new tonnage on order in U.K. yards was for account of MFC—see P. Debs. 5 Ser., Vol. 905, c.(385).
41. P. Debs. 5 Ser., Vol. 916 (2), c.(86).
42. Industry Act Report for the year ended 31st March 1977, Parl. Papers 1976–77, HCP 545.
43. *Ibid.*, The sale of the first tanker involved a loss of £3–4 million and the giving of a Government guarantee amounting to £4.5 million. The sale of the second ship involved a grant of £5 million from the intervention fund and the giving of a Government performance guarantee under which the contingent liability amounted to £17 million.

were barely covering operating costs let alone providing for depreciation. Eventually, on 8th May 1978, the Trade Secretary announced[44] that he was prepared, on a selective basis, to consider a limited extension of Government guarantees for loans to shipping companies which had short-term problems but which were expected, with the aid of such moratoria, to come through the recession as viable entities.[45] The Government's decision to give this modest help was prompted by concern regarding forced sales abroad of modern ships merely to raise money to service loans and the resulting redundancies among seamen.

The Industry Act Report for the year ended 31st March 1978[46] revealed no further defaults but, for the first time, a fall in new orders and an increase in loan repayments resulted in the amount of guarantees outstanding at the end of the year, around £888 million, being less than it had been 12 months previously.[47] However by 31st March 1979 the outstanding liability under guarantees had risen again to around £944 million[48] and the Report for the following year[49] showed a figure slightly higher at around £945 million; this 1979–80 Report also stated that temporary help by deferring capital repayments had been given to four companies which had outstanding loans totalling £34.5 million. In October 1980 arrangements were introduced to encourage early repayment of guaranteed loans by allowing a discount on the outstanding capital and up to 31st March 1982 the annual Reports[50] showed that guaranteed loans of some £112 million had been repaid earlier and that the discounts had amounted to £18.7 million; the Report for the year ended 31st March 1982 also showed that during the year new guarantees totalling £298 million had been given and that the outstanding liability at the end of the year has risen to £1,003 million.

Thus in 1982 the demand for guaranteed loans by U.K. owners placing orders in U.K. yards was as strong as ever and since, in the period from the end of the Second World War, orders from U.K. owners had consistently been the mainstay of the U.K. shipbuilding industry,[51] there seemed every probability that, with no end in sight for the dearth of orders and the intense overseas competition, the Home Shipbuilding Credit Scheme would continue

44. P. Debs. 5 Ser., Vol. 949, c.(328)—See also Industry Act Report for the year ended 31st March 1979, Parl. Papers 1978–79, HCP 206.

45. Under the scheme capital repayments were deferred for up to three years but interest was still payable during the moratorium.

46. Parl. Papers 1977–78, HCP 653.

47. At 31st March 1977 the amount outstanding had been £932 million.

48. Industry Act Report for the year ended 31st March 1979, Parl. Papers 1978–79, HCP 206.

49. Industry Act Report for the year ended 31st March 1980, Parl. Papers 1979–80, HCP 772.

50. Industry Act Reports for the years ended 31st March 1981 and 31st March 1982, Parl. Papers 1981–82, HCP 460 and Parl. Papers 1982–83, HCP 503.

51. For example in the years 1960 to 1981 U.K. yards completed new ships aggregating 23.179 million g.r.t. of which 16.415 million g.r.t. (about 71 per cent) were for U.K. registry (*British Shipping Statistics 1981*, Table 3.11).

more or less indefinitely. There can be little doubt that the scheme, instituted in 1967, had achieved its main objective—namely to assist the British shipbuilding industry in obtaining orders from British owners by providing adequate finance on competitive terms. Between June 1967 and December 1971 the Shipbuilding Industry Board had recommended the giving of Government guarantees in respect of 488 new ships of an estimated total contract value of £1,095 million[52] and in the period 1st April 1972 to 31st March 1982 441 Government guarantees were given to support loans to U.K. owners aggregating approximately £1,761 million[53]; if British owners had not been able to obtain home credit terms comparable to those available overseas it can hardly be doubted that much of the considerable volume of tonnage financed under the Home Credit Schemes would not have been built in British yards.

Apart from the finance made available under the Home Credit Schemes, during the 1970s, after the ending of investment grants the only modest encouragement given to shipowners for the building of new tonnage was the first-year capital allowance which was equal to the whole of the expenditure incurred on or after 27th October 1970 on the provision of a new ship[54] and which, under the special rules applicable to new ships,[55] could be used as and when the shipowners wished. In the early 1970s the traditional pattern for the use of this free depreciation was for the shipping company to set off the first year allowance against its own trading profits and other taxable income so that for some years after the delivery of a new ship—the period depending on the state of the freight market, the level of operating costs and interest charges—the owner's profits, otherwise subject to corporation tax, would be absorbed and the owner would thus enjoy a "tax holiday" in the early years of the ship's operational life.

However from 1975 onwards this traditional pattern became financially less beneficial as a result of various events which seriously reduced the level of shipping profits; the cost of new ships, and the consequent interest charges on borrowing, increased substantially, from 1973 the oil crisis and other factors caused an alarming escalation in operating costs and the freight market, due to over-tonnaging and the general trade recession, was depressed. For many shipowners this all meant a low level of profit, or even no profit at all, with the result that little benefit accrued from the first-year allowance because there were little or no taxable profits against which it could be off-set. In these circumstances some owners sought other means whereby they could finance a higher proportion of a new ship's cost over a longer period and accelerate the tax advantages accruing from the first-year allowance.

52. See Report of the SIB for the nine months ended 31st December 1971, Parl. Papers 1971–72 (316), Vol. 37.

53. See the Industry Act Reports covering this period.

54. Finance Act 1971, Section 44.

55. *Ibid.*, Section 49 and Schedule 8, para. 8.

One favoured solution was ship leasing which enabled a shipping company wishing to have the use of a new ship over the whole of its economic life to obtain what was in effect long term finance for a period far in excess of that available for a normal ship mortgage loan. The lessor, normally a bank or other financial institution, would contract for a new ship and on delivery would become the owners and as such able to claim the 100 per cent first year capital allowance. The ship would then be let on demise charter to the ship operator for 15 or even 20 years and the lessor, having substantial profits against which it could immediately utilise the whole of the capital allowance, would be able to quote a rate of charter hire which reflected, at least in part, the tax saving benefit which the lessor had obtained. Under such an arrangement the ship operator did not have to provide any capital, the cost of the ship was spread over a long period and the charter hire was reduced by the immediate utilisation of the whole of the capital allowance.

An alternative method of ensuring the prompt and effective use of the first year allowance in cases where the shipowner's profit level was inadequate was by means of the utilisation of the group relief provisions in Sections 258 to 264 of the Taxes Act 1970. This shipping group relief scheme involved five or fewer U.K. resident companies, having substantial taxable profits, forming a consortium company which would then enter into a contract for the building of a new ship. On delivery the new ship would be let on demise charter to the shipping operator and, through a Group Relief Agreement, the consortium company would surrender to its members the tax losses resulting from the claiming of the first-year allowance. The consortium members would then achieve a tax saving and, after retaining a discount, would make a group relief payment to the consortium company of a sum equal to the tax saved; this payment would then be utilised in partially financing the cost of the new ship and would make possible a reduction in charter hire. Although a number of these schemes were carried through, their scope was eventually restricted by anti-tax avoidance legislation which affected both group relief and leasing transactions.[56]

Although, during the 1970s, there was little evidence of any positive Government encouragement for the British shipping industry in the domestic field, there were soon signs that the Government was prepared to take a firmer line in its external shipping policy. At the Ministerial Meeting of the Consultative Shipping Group ("CSG")[57] in Japan in February 1971[58] the member governments were united in their adherence to a liberal international shipping policy

56. See Finance Act 1973 (Sections 28 to 31 and Schedule 12) and Finance Act 1975 (Section 41).

57. Comprising the governments of Belgium, Denmark, Finland, West Germany, Greece, Italy, Japan, the Netherlands, Norway, Sweden and the United Kingdom.

58. For a full record of the Ministerial Decisions see Chamber of Shipping Annual Report 1971, Appendix 1.

based on the principle of free circulation of shipping in international trade in free and fair competition[59] and reaffirmed their belief in the principles of freedom of choice of flag by shippers and freedom of shipowners to compete for all cargoes. The Ministers noted with concern that flag preference and cargo reservation had become more widespread and agreed that, in case an equitable solution could not be reached with a government practising flag preference, the 12 CSG governments should remain free to take in any trade, either individually or preferably on a co-ordinated basis, such counter measures as they considered necessary to preserve the freedom of trade and shipping as well as to protect the interests of their shippers and shipowners.[60]

In spite of the harder line taken by the CSG in Tokyo, it became even more evident that the diplomatic efforts of the United Kingdom and other CSG countries to halt the growth of flag discriminatory practices were achieving very little and by the end of 1972 British shipowners and other members of CENSA[61] felt that the time had arrived for the traditional maritime powers to act more positively against the protectionist policies of other countries by arming themselves with countervailing legislation and making it clear that, if it proved necessary, they were prepared to take retaliatory action. It was also hoped that with the accession, on 1st January 1973, of the United Kingdom, Denmark and Ireland to the European Economic Community, the greatly increased shipping strength of the EEC would encourage a first attempt at developing a common shipping policy which (*inter alia*) would be directed against flag discrimination.

Although at a meeting of CSG Ministers in London in September 1973 it was agreed that officials should prepare recommendations on the counter-measures necessary to protect the CSG countries against flag discrimination resulting from unilateral government action, the British Government decided to wait no longer; on 1st November 1973 the Conservative administration presented to the Commons a Merchant Shipping Bill which clearly showed that there was to be a radical change in British foreign shipping policy. Part III of the Bill gave the Secretary of State far-reaching powers to take counter-measures against flag discrimination or other action by foreign governments[62] where U.K. shipping or trade interests were affected or where required to meet the U.K.'s international obligations. The Secretary of State was authorised to make orders under which he could be empowered to obtain information,[63] to regulate the

59. This principle was the basis of the OECD Code of Liberalisation adopted by the Council of the OECD in December 1961.

60. The Committee of European National Shipowners' Association (CENSA) endorsed the conclusions of the CSG Ministers—see Chamber of Shipping Annual Report 1971, Appendix II.

61. At the end of 1972 the membership of CENSA comprised the National Shipowners' Association of the 12 CSG countries and also the Spanish Shipowners' Association.

62. I.e. "the government of any country outside the U.K.".

63. Orders for obtaining information were subject to a negative resolution of the Commons whereas all other Orders had to be approved by an affirmative resolution.

carriage of goods,[64] to levy charges on ships,[65] to refuse admittance of ships to U.K. ports and to approve or disapprove agreements.[66] Customs and Excise officers were authorised to enforce any orders made under Part III[67] and the Bill also provided for the repeal of Sections 324 to 326, 330 and 331 of the Customs Consolidation Act 1853.[68]

The Second Reading of the Bill[69] was moved by Michael Heseltine, the Minister of State responsible for shipping, who stated that, although the U.K. continued to believe that the common interest of all countries in the efficient carriage of world seaborne trade was best served where exporters were not compelled by law to support a particular flag, this view was not generally accepted, unilateral intervention by foreign governments was increasing and British shipping was suffering as a result of flag discrimination. The time had come to provide for protection; the Government expected and hoped that the powers would be rarely used but they would not hesitate to use them if necessary in the last resort.[70] The Labour Opposition did not vote against Part III of the Bill, although their spokesman observed that the Bill showed that the United Kingdom was shifting from its long-held belief in trade liberalisation and the maximum freedom for shipping, but, before the Committee stage had been completed, Parliament was dissolved and at the ensuing February 1974 general election the Labour Party was returned to power.

In May 1974 the Labour Government reintroduced the Bill in the Lords where, on the Second Reading,[71] the Government spokesman stated that Part III of the Bill was unchanged. The Bill passed quickly through all its stages in the Lords and when the Bill had its unopposed Second Reading in the Commons[72] the speaker on the Government side showed that there was no real divergence of view between left and right in regard to Britain's foreign shipping policy. The Bill received the Royal Assent on 31st July 1974[73] but it was not until well into 1979 that a Commencement Order was made[74] bringing into operation Part III of the Act with effect from 1st August 1979. In the meantime

64. For example by directing that certain goods could only be carried in British ships as had been the case under the old Navigation Laws.

65. So as to render more costly the import of goods on foreign ships.

66. Including charterparties and conference agreements.

67. Schedule 4 of the Bill.

68. The retaliatory powers in the new Bill were very much wider than those contained in the Customs Consolidation Act 1853 (pp. 50–51 *supra*) which it is believed have never been invoked. The whole of the 1853 Act was eventually repealed in 1986 (see p. 51, fn. 156 *supra*)

69. P. Debs. 5 Ser., Vol. 865, c.610.

70. Other maritime countries already had contingency powers of this kind and the powers in Part III of the Bill had been approved by all the other CSG countries and by the Chamber of Shipping and the British Shippers' Council.

71. P. Debs. (HL) 5 Ser., Vol. 351, c.1250.

72. P. Debs. 5 Ser., Vol. 876, c.1091.

73. Merchant Shipping Act 1974, c.43.

74. Merchant Shipping Act 1974 (Commencement No. 4) Order 1979 (SI 1979 No. 808).

the Secretary of State's powers under Part III had been strengthened and clarified by Section 40 of the Merchant Shipping Act 1979 which was also brought into operation on 1st August 1979.[75]

The far-reaching countervailing powers conferred on the Secretary of State by the 1974 Act which, if invoked to their fullest extent, would involve measures for the protection of the merchant navy going beyond even the monopolistic provisions of the Navigation Acts, clearly indicated that by the mid-1970s flag discrimination, often backed by non-commercial subsidies, was the most serious cause for concern to both British shipowners and the British Government. Flags of convenience were no longer regarded as "Public Enemy No. 1"; in the depressed trading conditions tax free operations did not give any great advantage and, although the flags of convenience tonnage had continued to grow, this had not inhibited the growth of the U.K. merchant fleet. The lack of control exercised by Liberia and Panama in relation to such matters as safety, pollution, crew conditions and manning levels did create problems[76] but flag discrimination had come to be regarded as by far the most serious of the evils facing the traditional maritime powers and increasingly through the 1970s the three main areas of greatest concern were the Code of Conduct for Liner Conferences and other activities of UNCTAD, the threat from the Eastern Bloc and the regulatory practices and protectionist policies of the United States.

Following the request made by the CSG Ministers at their Tokyo meeting in February 1971,[77] a draft Code of Liner Conference Practice was prepared by the Joint Standing Committee of CENSA and the European Shippers' Councils and submitted to the CSG governments. The Code was based on the principle of self-regulation in the belief that the public interest would best be served if the shipping industries, in consultation with their customers, were left free to conduct their own affairs within the framework of the Code.[78] The draft was approved by the CSG governments in November 1971 and by the end of the following year the CSG Code had been adopted by over 40 liner conferences serving the CSG countries. A copy of the CSG Code was sent to UNCTAD for consideration in advance of its third quadrennial session, due to take place in Santiago in August 1972, at which the main shipping matter was the formation and the adoption of a United Nations Code of Conduct for Liner Conferences based on proposals submitted by the UNCTAD Secretariat

75. Merchant Shipping Act 1979 (Commencement No. 1) Order 1979 (SI 1979 No.807).

76. See (i) 1975 Report on Flags of Convenience by the OECD Maritime Transport Committee; (ii) ILO 1976 Convention on safety standards, social security measures and shipboard employment and living conditions and (iii) Resolution of the European Parliament on 10th February 1977 (OJ 1977, c.57) re. Flags of Convenience.

77. See p. 202 *supra*.

78. The main features of the CSG Code are summarised on pp. 28–30 of the Chamber of Shipping Annual Report 1971.

which included arbitrary cargo-sharing rules and increased governmental control of international shipping.[79]

At the UNCTAD Santiago Conference the British representatives urged that the CSG Code should form the basis for an effective world code based on the principles of free enterprise and self-regulation but, after lengthy and controversial discussion, the developing countries (the so called Group of 77) rejected the CSG Code and the Conference thereupon passed, by a majority of 77 to 19,[80] a resolution[81] requesting the U.N. General Assembly to convene a Conference of Plenipotentiaries to adopt a Liner Conference Code which fully took into account the needs and problems of the developing countries. At a meeting of the U.N. General Assembly in December 1972 a resolution similar to that carried at Santiago was duly passed[82] and in November and December 1973 the Conference of Plenipotentiaries took place in Geneva and considered a Code previously drafted by a preparatory committee.[83]

Although the Conference lasted for five weeks, it was unable to complete its task and reconvened in March 1974. Eventually on 6th April 1974 a Convention on a Code of Conduct for Liner Conferences was adopted by 72 votes to seven[84]; the United Kingdom voted against adoption[85] and in a concluding statement the U.K. representative severely criticised the cargo sharing proposals in Article 2 (4).[86] Article 48 of the Convention provided that it was to remain open for signature from 1st July 1974 to 30th June 1975 and should thereafter remain open for accession. By Article 49 the Convention was to enter into force six months after the date on which not less than 24 states, the combined tonnage of which amounted to at least 25 per cent of world liner tonnage,[87] had become contracting parties.[88] The British Government, with the full support of British liner owners, made it clear that they had no intention of ratifying the Convention[89] and although, by early 1979, 34 States had ratified

79. The CSG countries were highly critical of many features of these proposals.

80. The United Kingdom, the United States and all the other OECD countries voted against the Resolution.

81. The full text of the resolution and the draft Code annexed is set out in Cmnd. 5134, Parl. Papers 1972–73, Vol. 35.

82. See Cmnd. 5236, Parl. Papers 1972–73, Vol. 35.

83. This draft was based on that previously prepared by the UNCTAD Secretariat.

84. The full text of the Convention is set out in U.N. Document TD/Code/10.

85. As did Denmark, Finland, Norway, Sweden, Switzerland and the United States. Canada, Greece, Italy, the Netherlands and New Zealand abstained but France, Belgium and West Germany voted in favour.

86. This established the so-called 40:40:20 Rule whereby, in a conference trade between two countries, 40 per cent of the trade would be allocated to the national lines of each country leaving only 20 per cent available to third flag lines.

87. As set out in Table 2 of *Lloyds Register Statistical Tables 1973*. The world liner tonnage total was 72,694,191 g.r.t. of which the U.K. total was 6,576,469 g.r.t.

88. By either (*a*) signature without reservation or (*b*) signature subject to and followed by ratification or (*c*) accession.

89. P. Debs. 5 Ser., Vol. 893, c.(296)

or acceded to the Convention, they represented only 6.35 per cent of world liner tonnage.[90]

The adoption of the Code, with France, West Germany and Belgium voting in favour, prompted the European Commission to consider whether the Code's cargo-sharing provisions were compatible with the Treaty of Rome and, although some Community members considered that the Treaty had no application to shipping unless and until the Council established a common sea transport policy,[91] the Commission took the view that the general rules of the Treaty, where relevant, did apply to shipping and in April 1974 this view was upheld by a decision of the European Court of Justice.[92] The Commission thereupon contended that certain aspects of the Code were incompatible with the obligations of EEC members under the Treaty and requested that members should refrain from signing or ratifying the Convention pending a decision by the Council of Ministers on the joint action to be taken by all members. No Council decision was forthcoming by the signature deadline of 30th June 1975 and, in view of this, the French, Belgian and West German governments signed the Convention but only subject to ratification; subsequently in 1976 the three countries undertook with the Commission that they would not unilaterally ratify the Convention before 1979.

Meanwhile British liner owners, whilst remaining firm in their opposition to the Convention, were trying to work out some compromise solution which might prove acceptable to both developed and developing countries and early in 1977 the British Government and the GCBS put forward a proposal, for consideration by EEC governments and their shipowners, that trades between developed countries—mainly but not exclusively OECD members—should continue to be based on the liberal principles in the CSG Code but that, as an exception to this general rule, the developed countries should offer to the developing countries an agreed share in their own cargoes. However it soon became clear that the British proposal, which became known as the "alternative approach", was attracting insufficient support and although, in September 1977, a European Council Decision[93] set up a consultation procedure on relations between members and third countries in shipping matters and on action relating to such matters in international organisations, some time was to elapse before the British Government and British shipowners were prepared to moderate their opposition both to the U.N. Code and to the draft of an accession Regulation submitted by the European Commission to the Council in December 1977.[94]

Nevertheless, whilst still favouring their "alternative approach", the GCBS

90. General Council of British Shipping Annual Report 1978–79, p. 34.
91. Which it was empowered to do under Article 84(2) of the Treaty.
92. Case 167/73, *European Commission* v *France*. OJ 1974 No. C.70.
93. Council Decision 77/587/EEC published in OJ 1977 L.239.
94. See OJ 1978, C.35, p. 3.

expressed willingness to undertake a constructive study of the Commission's proposed Regulation[95] and eventually, after much discussion between EEC members at government and shipowner level, a compromise, generally known as the Brussels Package, was agreed and on 15th May 1979 the European Council promulgated a Regulation[96] detailing the terms upon which Member States should ratify, or accede to, the U.N. Convention. The Community position in relation to the Code which was finally adopted included the provisions to which British shipowners attached the most importance; the Regulation stated first that the ratification of the Convention by Member States should be subject to the reservation that the 40:40:20 cargo-sharing provisions, and certain other rigid features of the Code, should not apply to conference trades between Member States or between Member States and other non-EEC OECD countries which were parties to the Code and were prepared to offer reciprocity and secondly that the trades between Member States and developing countries should be governed by the cargo-sharing system but that the share of such trade falling to Community lines should be redistributed on a commercial basis and that the lines of other OECD countries should, subject to reciprocity, be allowed to participate in the redistribution process.

However it was not until October 1983 that the U.N. Liner Code Convention entered into force following ratification by West Germany and the Netherlands in the previous April. Meanwhile the Merchant Shipping (Liner Conference) Act 1982, which enabled the United Kingdom to accede to the Convention subject to the Brussels Package reservation, had received the Royal Assent in July 1982 but, owing to technical problems, the Regulations needed to implement the Code were not approved by Parliament until January 1985 and it was not until December 1985 that the Convention came into force for the United Kingdom. Although the acquiescence of British liner owners had been noticeably reluctant, they had finally come round to the view that the cargo sharing provisions, rather than unilateral cargo reservations, might prove to be a better way of satisfying the aspirations of the developing countries.

By the end of the 1970s other activities of UNCTAD were also proving a source of concern to West European shipowners and their governments. At the fifth UNCTAD Conference in Manila in May 1979[97] the developing countries, building upon their cargo sharing achievements in the Liner Code, proposed a resolution which was intended to ensure that the carriage of bulk cargoes in the regular import and export trades of two countries should be reserved and to be shared equally between the trading countries in question. All the EEC and OECD countries voted against the resolution on the grounds that the proposed compulsory sharing of bulk cargoes was directly opposed to the freely competitive environment which was an essential feature of the bulk

95. See GCBS Annual Report 1977–78.
96. Regulation (EEC) No.954/79 published in OJ 1979 L.121.
97. Cmnd. 7675, Parl. Papers 1979–80.

market and would substantially increase the costs of transportation. The UNCTAD Secretariat and the Third World countries did not allow the matter to rest; they continued to argue that there were barriers preventing them from carrying a reasonable proportion of their primary products whereas the Western maritime powers maintained there were no obstacles and strongly opposed the introduction of cargo reservation measures in the bulk trades.[98]

Another Third World proposal, linked with the reservation of bulk trades, was for the phasing out of flags of convenience—or open registries as they had come to be called. A large proportion of the world's wet and dry bulk carriers were registered under flags of convenience and, at the UNCTAD Manila Conference in 1979 and subsequently, the developing countries contended that the open registry vessels were an impediment to the Third World obtaining a fair share of their own bulk trades. In 1980, at a special session of the UNCTAD Shipping Committee, the developing countries, supported by the Communist Bloc, proposed the setting of conditions for the registration of ships which, if adopted, would lead to the eventual elimination of open registries and in June of the following year the Shipping Committee, against the opposition of all the OECD countries, passed a resolution calling for an international convention which would impose economic requirements for shipping registration on all states and would provide for the closure of ports to ships of non-complying countries.

All the OECD governments and their shipowners opposed any requirements for an economic link between a ship and her flag State which they considered to be a matter of national sovereignty; as the GCBS pointed out,[99] these requirements would not only eliminate open registries but also the one-third of the British fleet represented by foreign-owned tonnage. Between October 1980 and July 1981 the question of the phasing out of flags of convenience and the effect of the proposed convention on British shipping was raised in Parliament on several occasions[100]; the Government emphasised that their policy was based on the need to preserve the British shipping industry and the jobs that depended on it, that this object would not be served by attacking the countries operating open shipping registries and that the Government wished to see the preservation of competitive international conditions for shipping in which each nation was free to set its own conditions for admission to its register subject to the full observance of internationally agreed safety standards.

Throughout the 1970s British liner operators were feeling a growing concern at the increasing threat from the merchant shipping of the Eastern Bloc; in

98. See GCBS Annual Reports 1979–80 to 1981–82.

99. See Annual Report 1982–83, p. 27.

100. Commons P. Debs. 5 Ser., Vol. 991, c.(378) and c.(961), Vol. 992, c.(315), Vol. 999, c.(309) and P. Debs. 6 Ser., Vol. 5, c.628, Vol. 7, c.559 and Vol 8, c.32. Lords P. Debs. 5 Ser., Vol. 421, c.1065.

1968 the Soviet merchant fleet had stood at 9.8 million g.r t.[101] but by July 1981 Soviet merchant tonnage had increased to 15.7 million g.r t. of which nearly half was represented by cargo liner-type tonnage.[102] Following the ratification in 1972 of the Anglo-Soviet Treaty on Merchant Navigation,[103] the problems of cargo sharing and the level of freights in the direct trade between the U.K. and the U.S.S.R. were discussed at every meeting of the Joint U.K.–Soviet Maritime Commission but there was little progress towards correcting the gross imbalance in the Soviet Union's favour. In 1977 the Soviet Shipping Minister did go so far as to agree that there should be a move towards "parity of carrying as between U.K. and Soviet vessels in bilateral trades between the U.K. and U.S.S.R."[104] but subsequent negotiations proved unproductive and five years later no less than 90 per cent of the bilateral trades was still being carried in Soviet ships.[105]

By the mid 1970s the non-commercial activities of Eastern Bloc shipping competing on most of the major world liner–cargo conference routes were causing increasing anxiety to British and other Western European shipowners who felt that concerted action by their governments was essential to counter the economic and strategic threat resulting from the price cutting and other non-commercial shipping policies being pursued by the U.S.S.R. and their Comecon partners and by the increasing amount of container traffic from Europe to the Far East which was being carried at subsidised rates on the trans-siberian railway. Early in 1977 there were the first overt signs that the European Community was becoming aware of the problem; resolutions passed by the European Parliament[106] called upon the Commission to assess the threat posed to Community shipowners by the practices of Comecon and other State trading companies and to submit proposals for the establishment of a common programme of action against flag discrimination.

It was not, however, until April 1978 that the Commission submitted to the European Council its proposal for a Decision concerning the activities of certain State trading countries in cargo liner shipping[107] which provided (*inter alia*) for the establishment of a monitoring system to collect data and for the possibility of the Council taking appropriate countervailing measures. Although the draft Decision was welcomed in the Commons as a modest first step,[108] strong opposition from France resulted in the Decision concerning the activities of certain third countries in the field of cargo shipping finally adopted

101. Rochdale Report, Table 4.2.
102. *British Shipping Statistics 1981*, Tables 1.1 and 1.4.
103. See p. 195, fn. 105 *supra.*
104. P. Debs. 5 Ser., Vol. 938, c.(26).
105. See the speech of the Shipping Minister in an adjournment debate on the merchant fleet in November 1982—P. Debs. 6 Ser., Vol. 32, c.1103
106. OJ 1977, C.57, p. 57 and C.118, p. 41.
107. OJ 1978, C.198, p. 3—see also a report in *The Times*, 7th April 1978.
108. P. Debs. 5 Ser., Vol. 951, c.591.

by the Council in September 1978[109] being a much weakened version of the Commission's original proposal.[110] Moreover this Decision was executory only and no monitoring action was taken until a further Council Decision made in December 1978[111] specified the information which Member States were to collect over the two year period 1979 and 1980 and the areas to be monitored which were limited to the Europe-East Africa and Europe-Central America trades only.

The Council's Decision contained no mention of the Commission's recommendation that there should be a study of possible counter-measures against unfair Comecon competition although a Resolution of the European Parliament[112] emphasised that the setting up of the two year monitoring system should not be used as a pretext for not taking counter-measures in the meantime should the practices of certain countries prove to be jeopardising the Community's maritime interests. In a House of Lords debate in June 1979,[113] it was also stressed that the Community should have countervailing measures ready to put into effect without delay in case of need and the British Government agreed that there was need for more concerted and effective action by the EEC; unfortunately there was disunity, if not disarray, among the Member States in spite of the fact that the growth of the Soviet merchant fleet, its distortion of the shipping market and the increase in capacity of the trans-siberian railway were not only a commercial threat to Community shipping but also a potential military threat to the NATO powers.

At the beginning of the 1970s the regulatory activities of the United States Federal Maritime Commission ("FMC"), which had given rise to many problems for the British and West European liner operators during the previous decade,[114] showed no signs of diminishing.[115] At the CSG meeting in Tokyo in February 1971[116] the Ministers of the 12 CSG countries agreed that there should be consultation with the United States with a view to settling the many difficulties arising from what their communiqué termed "the relationship between the U.S. regulatory policy and other aspects of U.S. shipping policy". There was a belief that the regulatory measures inspired by the U.S. anti-trust laws were not only intended to prevent unfair foreign discrimination against U.S. commerce but also to sustain the U.S. merchant marine. Certainly, in the early 1970s, there was a flood of protectionist shipping legislation before

109. Decision 78/774/EEC, OJ 1978 L.258, p. 35.
110. See P. Debs. 5 Ser., Vol. 958, c.(731–733).
111. Decision 79/4/EEC, OJ 1979 L.5, p. 31.
112. OJ 1978, C.259.
113. P. Debs. (HL) 5 Ser., Vol. 400, c.1114.
114. See Chapter 9 *passim*.
115. See Chamber of Shipping's Annual Report 1971, p. 66.
116. See pp. 274–275 *supra*.

Congress which was designed to increase U.S. shipping's participation in the carriage of its foreign trade.[117]

During 1973 the United States conducted a "Ship American" cargo promotion campaign and the FMC promoted a Bill aimed at regulating freight rates of foreign carriers and empowering the FMC to reject a rate filed by a foreign flag operator if it was lower than that of any national flag operator in the same trade. CSG representations had little effect and matters really came to a head in 1976 when, in addition to the FMC instituting a new investigation into alleged conference malpractices, the U.S. Department of Justice initiated a Grand Jury investigation into ocean transport in the North Atlantic trade between the U.S. and Europe. In addition there was renewed pressure for reserving a proportion of U.S. oil imports for U.S. built national flag tankers and a move to extend the U.S. cabotage restrictions which were already creating a number of difficulties for CSG shipowners.

Vigorous opposition to the investigation of the North Atlantic shipping conferences was initiated by the CSG. Following the issuing by the U.S. Department of Justice of subpoenas for documents from most of the British and European shipping companies involved in the North Atlantic trade, protests were made by the British and other West European governments who maintained that the United States had no right to attempt unilaterally to regulate international shipping. The British note of protest also drew attention to the Government's powers under the Shipping Contracts and Commercial Documents Act 1964[118] and subsequently it was stated in the Commons[119] that the Secretary of State had given directions under Section 2 of the Act to those in the U.K. who had received subpoenas prohibiting disclosure of documents located in the U.K. or any information compiled from such documents.

The increasing concern of the CSG governments and their shipowners at the escalating scale of the U.S. government's attacks on the conference system and the increasing protectionist tendency of other U.S. shipping policies eventually resulted in the U.S. administration agreeing that there should be a meeting in Washington with CSG representatives in May 1978. The CSG countries hoped to establish a long-term *modus vivendi* with the U.S. but, although the Americans did agree to the setting up of a working party to examine liner shipping problems, they refused to give any assurance that current anti-conference activities would be suspended[120] and in the following year there was a sharp deterioration in commercial shipping relations between the United States and

117. The measures included Cargo Preference Bills aimed at reserving all U.S. government-generated cargo and a proportion of U.S. oil imports to American flag ships, a further Bill making shipping rate disparities illegal and a new system of tax "deferral" which gave a freight advantage to U.S. lines in the American trade—see P. Debs. 5 Ser., Vol. 857, c.17.

118. See p. 188 *supra*.

119. P. Debs. 5 Ser., Vol. 919, c.(195).

120. See GCBS Annual Report 1978–79, p. 36.

Europe[121] as a result of heavy fines totalling over £1 million being imposed on British nationals and British shipping companies who were alleged to be in breach of the Sherman Anti-Trust Act of 1890 by having conspired to fix freight rates on goods shipped between Europe and America without the rates having been first approved by the FMC.[122]

The British Government considered that no offence had been committed under international law and the Trade Secretary made a strong protest to the U.S. government in which it was stated that the British Government considered it to be wrong in principle for the U.S. to seek to exercise unilateral control over shipping between the U.K. and the U.S. in disregard of British economic interests and shipping policies and that the U.K. was reviewing its attitudes towards the U.S. on anti-trust questions and the enforcement in the U.K. of U.S. anti-trust judgments. No progress was made when, in November 1979, there were further talks between the CSG governments and the U.S. administration and, whilst these discussions were taking place, the Commons gave a Second Reading to the Protection of Trading Interests Bill.[123] The Bill, which repealed the Shipping Contracts and Commercial Documents Act 1964, built on the powers in the 1964 Act and extended them to other areas of trade; it had as its main objective the improvement of the defence of the U.K. against attempts by other countries to enforce their economic and commercial policies outside their own territories and imposed restrictions on the enforcement in the U.K. of certain overseas judgments.[124]

In the early 1980s British shipping, with tonnage on the U.K. register having already fallen far below its 1976 peak, faced a difficult and uncertain future. Although from 1974 to 1978 there was a continuing and substantial decline in the world shipbuilding order books,[125] the backlog resulting from the large volume of world orders placed in the euphoria of the early 1970s resulted in a continuing flow of new vessels from the world's shipyards and in consequence, at July 1981, world tonnage had risen to 683.5 million d.w.t. as compared with around 598.5 million d.w.t. in July 1976.[126] Unfortunately in the period 1976 to 1979 there was only a modest growth in world seaborne trade and this was followed by a fall in 1980 and again in 1981 back to the 1978 level;[127] there was thus no alleviation of the severe world shipping depression—the worst since the 1930s—and at the end of 1981 the total of

121. See the speech of Lord Rochdale in the Lords debate on 21st June 1979, P. Debs. (HL) 5 Ser., Vol. 400, c.1114.

122. See GCBS Annual Report 1979–80, p. 14 and P. Debs. 6 Ser., Vol. 12, c.(2).

123. P. Debs. 5 Ser., Vol. 973, c.1533.

124. The Protection of Trading Interests Act 1980 received the Royal Assent on 20th March 1980.

125. From 120.7 million g.r.t. at the end of December 1974 to 25.9 million g.r.t. at the end of December 1978—*British Shipping Statistics 1981*, Table 3.7.

126. *British Shipping Statistics 1981*, Table 1.4.

127. *Ibid.*, Table 6.1 and *British Shipping Facts and Figures 1984*.

world tonnage laid up amounted 27.4 million d.w.t. of which 24.6 million d.w.t. was represented by tankers.[128]

There was no possibility of the British shipping industry being insulated from the world wide depression. From 1977 onwards new shipbuilding orders for U.K. registration continued at low levels[129] and, with operating costs continually rising, the trading results of even the financially strongest of British shipowners were so poor that, in order to meet their commitments and remain viable, a substantial number of ships, some comparatively modern, had to be sold to foreign buyers. So, from 1978 onwards, the comparatively small amount of new tonnage coming on to the U.K. register[130] was far outweighed by the existing tonnage being sold abroad[131] and in consequence the U.K. registered merchant fleet, which at mid-1976 had totalled 53.047 million d.w.t., had by mid-1981 fallen to 40.473 million d.w.t.—a decline of nearly 24 per cent—and its position amongst the major world merchant fleets had fallen to fifth place after Liberia, Greece, Japan and Panama.[132]

In the spring of 1982 the GCBS reported[133] that more tonnage had been lost to the U.K. owned and registered merchant fleet in 1981 than in any other year previously and that this fleet now represented a mere 4.3 per cent of the world fleet as compared with 40 per cent in 1913, 26 per cent in 1939, 18 per cent in 1945 and nine per cent in 1975. With few exceptions British shipowners were not ordering any new ships[134] and there were clear indications that sales of U.K. registered ships to foreign countries or British dependencies were likely to continue on a substantial scale. In these circumstances there seemed every likelihood that for the foreseeable future there would be a continuation of the decline that had commenced in 1977. One of the main reasons for this decline was the world trade depression on the one hand and the still growing world surplus of tonnage on the other. This had inevitably led to a dramatic fall in tanker and dry cargo rates and British owners were not prepared to keep ships—still less order new ships—unless they could be profitably employed. Another factor particularly relevant to the decline of the U.K. fleet was the fall in commercial competitiveness; over 1980 and 1981 the earnings of British

128. *British Shipping Statistics 1981*, Table 4.1.

129. 1977: 590,000 d.w.t.; 1979: 1.223 million d.w.t.; 1980: 1.949 million d.w.t.; 1981: 982,000 d.w.t. See *British Shipping Statistics 1976–77, 1979–80* and *1981*, Table 3.2.

130. The new tonnage delivered to the U.K. owned and registered fleet between January 1978 and July 1981 totalled only 2.1 million g.r.t. (*British Shipping Statistics 1981*, Table 3.13).

131. Between January 1978 and December 1981 transfers of U.K. registered ships to foreign flags totalled 12 million g.r.t. (P. Debs. 6 Ser., Vol. 12, c.(140) and Vol 31, c.(24). Most of these transfers were believed to be outright sales but the statistics did not distinguish outright sales from those cases in which a British owner retained beneficial ownership.

132. *British Shipping Statistics 1981*, Table 1.4.

133. See Annual Report 1981–82.

134. Orders placed for the U.K. owned and registered fleet amounted to only 21 ships totalling 318,000 d.w.t. in 1982 and 18 ships totalling 363,000 d.w.t. in 1983 (*British Shipping Facts and Figures 1984*).

seamen had increased by some 30 per cent and it was a formidable task for British owners to compete against foreign ships on which the crew costs were in some cases only half those of the British.[135] There were also the continuing problems of flag discrimination and other forms of protectionism by a number of foreign countries and the non-commercial shipping activities of the Eastern Bloc.

On the domestic front the Government took no action to stem, still less reverse, the persistent decline in U.K. tonnage; in both the 1981 and 1982 Budgets the Government failed to respond to the shipowners' request that, in order to encourage the acquisition of new or second-hand tonnage, the investment allowance for new ships should be restored and free depreciation for second-hand ships introduced. The GCBS also continued to feel misgivings regarding the impact on shipping of the Government's shipbuilding policy; whilst accepting that the ailing nationalised merchant yards could not survive without Government aid, it was felt that the shipping recession would only be prolonged if the continuing output of subsidised new tonnage was not accompanied by more positive and urgent action on the part of the British and foreign governments to reduce subsidies and the worldwide surplus shipbuilding capacity. In addition there were certain cases in which British owners believed that Government funds were being used to put them at a disadvantage with foreign competitors[136] and there was criticism on the use of overseas aid funds to secure orders for U.K. yards.

Notwithstanding the economic importance of shipping's net contribution to the balance of payments,[137] the Government, whilst expressing concern at the continuing decline of U.K shipping, felt that the size of the merchant fleet must be determined by market forces and that it should be mainly for the industry itself to ensure that it was commercially competitive. Both at the time of the 1981 seamen's strike and subsequently Ministers continually emphasised the necessity for a reduction in operating costs generally, and labour costs in particular, so as to enable British shipping to compete on equal terms with its foreign competitors but shipowners, whilst accepting that such action was urgently needed to enable profitable operation under the U.K. flag to continue, found it no easy task to persuade the officers' and seamen's unions that future security of employment depended upon a moderation of wage demands.

135. At the time of the seamen's strike early in 1981 the Government emphasised that the U.K. shipping industry had to operate in a strongly competitive worldwide market and that the future size of the U.K. fleet depended primarily on its operating costs being internationally competitive (P. Debs. 5 Ser., Vol. 996, c.1136).

136. The most notorious case was the Polish shipbuilding contract which cost the taxpayer £72 million for subsidising the building of 24 ships for Poland in U.K. yards. The contract was severely criticised by the Committee of Public Accounts in its 19th Report for 1979–80, HC 737.

137. In 1981 the net direct contribution was £1,123 million and in addition U.K. owned ships carried imports of £450 million which were gross savings.

In the international field the Government fully accepted that British shipowners could not on their own contend with the non-commercial and protectionist practices of foreign governments. In co-operation with the CSG countries the Government continued to resist foreign protectionism and cargo reservation in all their manifest forms but it maintained its belief that the continuation and enlargement of the open trading system throughout the world must be achieved without resort to subsidies—to which British shipowners were in any case traditionally opposed—or any reversion to protectionism. Under the Merchant Shipping Act 1974 (as amended) the Government possessed wide countervailing powers which, if fully invoked, could lead to measures for the protection of British shipping going well beyond even those contained in the Navigation Acts but both the Government and most shipowners believed that the exercise of such powers would inevitably lead to foreign retaliation and would thus be likely to restrict the cross-trading opportunities from which came more than two thirds of the U.K. fleets gross overseas earnings.

So much for the peacetime problems of the merchant navy but what of the role of the Fourth Service in time of war or other emergency? In 1980 the U.K. relied on foreign shipping for nearly 70 per cent (by weight) of its imports and over 60 per cent (by weight) of its exports[138]; in shipping and political circles there was concern as to whether the reduced and still declining U.K. merchant fleet would be of sufficient size and consist of the right types to supply the country's wartime needs at home as well as to play its essential part as the fourth arm of defence in support of the fighting services; there were also fears of a shortage of trained seamen since the fall in tonnage had inevitably resulted in a drastic reduction in the numbers of officers and ratings.[139] However Government spokesmen gave repeated assurances that the adequacy, in size and shape, of the merchant fleet for defence purposes was constantly kept under review and that the Government remained confident that, in spite of its decline, the merchant navy remained capable of fulfilling the duties that it would be called upon to perform in an emergency. British shipowners still had some misgivings and in their Review of British Shipping at the end of 1981 the GCBS felt it opportune to give a reminder that "in normal times the country tends to forget how important the Merchant Navy is in times of crisis" and, with what turned out to be remarkable prescience, raised the question of whether the merchant navy would again be called upon to form its vital task as the fourth arm of defence; it was a question to which a positive answer was to be given sooner than almost anyone could have expected.

138. See *British Shipping Statistics 1981*, Table 7.5.

139. Between 31st December 1977 and 31st December 1981 the number of officers had fallen from 37,740 to 29,232, the number of cadets from 6,887 to 4,663 and the number of ratings from 32,593 to 28,862 (*British Shipping Statistics 1981*, Table 8.1).

EPILOGUE

THE FALKLANDS—AND AFTER

Far-call'd our navies melt away–
On dune and headland sinks the fire–
Lo, all our pomp of yesterday
Is one with Nineveh and Tyre

On Saturday 3rd April 1982 both Houses of Parliament were recalled for an emergency session[1] because, in the words of the Prime Minister, "For the first time for many years, British sovereign territory has been invaded by a foreign power"; she reported that, after several days of rising tension, the armed forces of Argentina had attacked the Falkland Islands and established military control of the Islands. The Prime Minister went on to emphasise that it was the Government's objective to see that the Islands were freed from occupation and returned to British administration as soon as possible; to this end the Government had decided that a large task force would sail as soon as all preparations had been completed.

It was immediately apparent that the naval task force would have to include a substantial number of merchant ships to act as troop carriers and to provide the necessary logistical support for the armed forces. To this end, at a Privy Council meeting at Windsor Castle on Sunday 4th April 1982, the Queen, in exercise of her prerogative powers for the defence of the realm, signed the Requisitioning of Ships Order 1982 which enabled the Government to "requisition for Her Majesty's service any British ship and anything on board such ship wherever the ship may be".[2] On the following day the Commons were told that the P & O liner *Canberra* was being transferred to naval control that afternoon and that other merchant ships would be requisitioned and chartered as necessary.[3]

The taking up of ships from trade proceeded rapidly and efficiently in accordance with long-standing contingency plans made to meet national emergencies. As the General Council of British Shipping subsequently reported: [4] "The Merchant Navy went to war in 48 hours. That first weekend in April

1. Commons P. Debs. 6 Ser., Vol. 21, c.633 and Lords P. Debs. 5 Ser., Vol. 428, c.1577.
2. The Order stated that "British ship" meant a ship registered in the United Kingdom, the Isle of Man, the Channel Islands, any Colony and any country outside Her Majesty's Dominions in which Her Majesty has jurisdiction in right of the Government of the United Kingdom.
3. P. Debs. 5 Ser., Vol. 21, c.688.
4. GCBS Annual Report 1982–83, p. 60.

the industry swung into its traditional role as the fourth arm of defence. No questions were asked, ships were made available and the crews volunteered. Decisions were taken that weekend to requisition or charter 15 ships." On 7th April the Defence Secretary thanked the shipping industry for its co-operation and support[5] and on 14th April the Prime Minister stated in the Commons that "Recourse to the merchant marine is traditional in time of naval emergency and its response has been whole hearted on this occasion as in the past".[6]

As time passed there was inevitably the need for more ships to sustain a task force 8,000 miles from the United Kingdom and at the height of the Falklands campaign there were 54 British-owned and British-crewed ships supporting the Task Force in a wide variety of roles. This is not the place for a detailed account of the exemplary manner in which the merchant navy played its vital part in the Falklands task force; suffice it to say that, when announcing in the Commons on 15th June 1982 the surrender of the Argentinean forces, the Prime Minister was the first to acknowledge the enormous debt owed to the merchant marine[7] and subsequently the importance of the merchant navy as the fourth arm of defence was emphasised by Sir John Fieldhouse, Commander-in-Chief, Fleet, and Commander, Falkland Islands Task Force, who stated "I cannot say too often or too clearly how important has been the merchant navy's contribution to our efforts. Without the ships taken up from trade, the operation could not have been undertaken and I hope this message is clearly understood by the British nation."[8]

The Falklands campaign revived memories of the merchant navy's indispensable contribution to ultimate success in the two World Wars and resulted in further action, both within and outside Parliament, to alert the Government to the urgent need for measures first to halt and then to reverse the continuing decline in the United Kingdom's merchant fleet.

Within a week from the Argentinean capitulation the Government were asked to "initiate a review of the adequacy of the size and capability of the merchant shipping fleet following the events in the Falkland Islands" and in his reply Iain Sproat, the Trade Minister responsible for shipping, stated that he was keen that the relevant experience gained from the fleet's role in support of the Falkland Islands' operation should be thoroughly studied and that he was writing to the GCBS and the maritime unions inviting them to give their views on the lessons to be learnt.[9] At the end of July there was a short adjournment debate on the merchant navy[10] in which concern was expressed at both

5. P. Debs. 5 Ser., Vol. 21, c.1046.
6. *Ibid.*, c.1147
7. P. Debs. 5 Ser., Vol. 25, c.731.
8. There were other tributes by Ministers—see P. Debs. 5 Ser., Vol. 28, cc.49 and 1520.
9. P. Debs., Vol 26, cc.(4) and (107).
10. P. Debs., Vol 28, c.1513.

the decline of the U.K. merchant fleet[11] and also in the numbers of British seamen[12]; it was put to the Government that the Falklands conflict had shown once again that the merchant navy was an essential part of Britain's defence strategy and that steps should be taken to ensure there was no further decline. In his reply the Armed Forces Minister, whilst fully acknowledging the magnificent achievement of the merchant fleet, pointed out that the size of the merchant navy was a matter for the Department of Transport and considered that any action required should await the publication of the White Paper on the lessons to be learned from the Falklands operation.

Outside Parliament a significant event was the formation of a new association, having no party political affiliation, named the British Maritime League. The creation of this new maritime action group had resulted from a meeting of maritime experts convened by Admiral of the Fleet Lord Hill-Norton, a former Chief of the Defence Staff,[13] and the Council of the League comprised a wide cross-section of expertise in all aspects of British maritime affairs. Echoing the philosophy underlying the old Navigation Laws, one of the main purposes of the League was to make clear that adequate maritime forces were not only essential to the security and peace of the nation but also to its wealth and prosperity and its initial primary objective was to reverse the rapid decline in all Britain's maritime capabilities. In February 1983 the League published its First Report, entitled "British Maritime Policy", in which the Council attempted to analyse the causes of the decline and the Report's main recommendations were that positive and coherent national maritime policies should be agreed on an all-party political basis and that a Maritime Affairs Committee of the Cabinet should be established under the Prime Minister to initiate co-ordinate and direct these policies and their implementation.[14]

Meanwhile, during the latter part of 1982 and the early months of 1983, concern over the decline of the U.K. registered merchant fleet was kept well to the forefront in Parliament. On 25th November 1982 there was another adjournment debate,[15] initiated by Edward Du Cann, who emphasised Britain's total dependence on the "safe and timely arrival of our ships" and called upon the Government, in the national interest, to take action to restore British maritime pre-eminence. In his reply the Shipping Minister, Iain Sproat, acknowledged that the continuing decline was a matter for great concern but

11. Between 1975 and March 1982 the U.K. owned and registered fleet (500 g.r.t. and over) had fallen from 50 million d.w.t. to 29.6 million d.w.t. (*British Shipping Review 1982*).

12. For the figures see p. 288 fn. 139 *supra*.

13. By coincidence this first meeting took place on 30th March 1982 just prior to the Argentinean invasion of the Falklands.

14. In evidence to the Commons Industry and Trade Committee, British Shipbuilders also suggested that there should be a total maritime policy embracing shipping and shipbuilding (see para. 37 of the Committee's First Report—Parl. Papers 1981–82, HCP 192); the Government Reply (Parl. Papers 1981–82, HCP 381) showed little enthusiasm for this suggestion.

15. P. Debs. 6 Ser., Vol. 32, c.1103.

pointed out that, with too many ships chasing too few cargoes, there were no easy solutions; the Government were not going to abandon free trade principles—protectionism and shipping subsidies were no answer—but the Government were strongly opposing the UNCTAD proposals against flags of convenience which, if adopted, would severely damage the U.K. registered fleet of which 45 per cent was beneficially owned abroad.[16]

On 14th December 1982 the Government published a White Paper entitled "The Falklands Campaign: The Lessons"[17] which acknowledged the crucial role played by the merchant navy and stated that a working party of the Shipping Defence Advisory Committee was examining ways in which merchant ships likely to be required in any future emergency might be designed, modified or equipped for possible use in support of the armed forces or for self-defence. The White Paper was debated in both the Commons[18] and the Lords[19] and, in the Upper House particularly, several peers emphasised the need for positive Government action in support of both the shipping and shipbuilding industries; Lord Hill-Norton (President of the British Maritime League) complained that the White Paper had given quite inadequate attention to the over-riding importance of ensuring that the vital support of merchant ships would be available in the future and from the Opposition benches he was strongly supported by Lord Shinwell. The reply from Lord Belstead, the Government spokesman, was disappointing; the Government appreciated the importance of merchant vessels and the question of their future availability was under active consideration.

In January and February 1983 the Shipping Minister was subjected to further questions regarding the decline of the U.K. fleet[20] and these culminated on 14th February in a request that he should list the action he had implemented or initiated during the previous 12 months to assist the British merchant navy. In a lengthy written reply[21] Mr Sproat first emphasised his concern at the decline of the merchant navy which he attributed to the worldwide shipping recession, growing protectionism of certain foreign governments and loss of commercial competitiveness by the British fleet. The Minister then listed the steps taken in the international field including continued opposition to the UNCTAD proposals directed against the open registries, negotiations with the major maritime countries to resist pressure on the open trading system and progress towards the U.K.'s accession to the U.N. Liner Code on the terms of the Brussels Package which would mean that over 75 per cent of the world's liner shipping would remain free of the Code's cargo sharing provisions. On the domestic front the Minister outlined the measures he was taking to help

16. For an analysis of the ownership of the U.K. registered fleet at 30th September 1982 see P. Debs. 6 Ser., Vol. 35 cc.(253–4).
17. Cmnd. 8758, Parl. Papers 1982–83.
18. On 21st December 1982—P. Debs. 6 Ser., Vol. 34, c.845.
19. On 17th January 1983 P. Debs. (HL) 5 Ser., Vol. 437, c.1186.
20. P. Debs. 6 Ser., Vol. 35, c.657, Vol 36, c.389 and Vol 36, c.(51).
21. *Ibid.*, Vol. 37, c.(57).

the U.K. fleet to become more competitive but he concluded by making it clear that the Government would not resort to protectionism and subsidy which, "however beguiling in the short term, would be disastrous to the long term prospects of our merchant navy".

In the meantime the GCBS and the seafaring unions had responded to the Governments request for their views regarding the future of the merchant fleet; the shipowners had reiterated their request for an investment allowance for new ships, improved capital allowances for second-hand ships and help related to the employment of U.K. seafarers[22] whilst the unions had proposed State ownership, protectionism and State subsidy. On 18th March 1983 the Minister was asked what view he had reached on these representations and in another lengthy written reply[23] Mr Sproat rejected in forthright terms any form of nationalised shipping line, operating subsidies, controls to require shippers to use British ships, a cabotage regime for U.K. ports, any other form of protectionism or cargo reservation or any improvement in what he described the "U.K.'s very favourable tax regime for shipping". The Government believed that British shipping must become competitive on a true commercial basis and that this could only be achieved if management analysed and selected the areas of world shipping in which a competitive U.K. merchant fleet could still have an important role.

A few days later, in yet another adjournment debate on merchant shipping,[24] John Prescott, the Labour spokesman, rejected the suggestion that the decline of the U.K. fleet was due to high crew costs and manning levels and criticised those British owners who were transferring ships to open registrations to obtain the advantage of lower manning levels and safety standards. In his reply Iain Sproat maintained his view that British manning costs were uncompetitively high,[25] and again pointed out that, if open registrations were to be banned, the U.K. flag would suffer since 45 per cent of the British merchant fleet was beneficially owned abroad. Further questioning of the Minister in April and early May elicited written statements that light dues were to be cut by 10 per cent for 1983–84 so as to reduce the cost burden on British ships,[26] that the Government were not prepared to see British cruise operators damaged by uncommercial Soviet competition out of U.K. ports[27] and that cabotage by certain EEC countries was contrary to the non-discrimination spirit of the Treaty of Rome.[28]

22. For further details of the GCBS proposals see their Annual Report 1982–83, p. 16.
23. P. Debs. 6 Ser., Vol. 39, c.(290).
24. P. Debs. 6 Ser., Vol. 40, c.417.
25. In a later reply (P. Debs. 6 Ser., Vol. 41, c.589) he added that 25 per cent of British ships were overmanned in comparison with our best European competitors.
26. P. Debs. 6 Ser., Vol. 40, c.(135).
27. P. Debs. 6 Ser., Vol. 42, c.(106).
28. *Ibid.*, c.(192). U.K. ships were free to compete in the coastal trades of the Netherlands, Belgium and Ireland but were still excluded from the coastal trades of France, West Germany, Greece, Italy and (except for limited cases) Denmark.

On 13th May 1983 Parliament was dissolved for the June 1983 general election but, just prior to the dissolution, Iain Sproat gave what turned out to be his last ministerial answer.[29] In reply to yet another question on the decline of the merchant navy,[30] the Minister reiterated that the decline would not be reversed by subsidies or protectionism,[31] and added that, whilst the aggregate of foreign subsidies and the policies of certain foreign governments did affect our competitive position, it was not a major reason, nor even hardly a minor reason, for the superiority of other merchant navies at present larger than ours; the main reason our fleet was declining was that it was uncompetitive *vis-à-vis* the best European fleets and the main constituent part of that uncompetitiveness was high crew costs.

The Falklands campaign also emphasised the strategic importance of the British shipbuilding industry; the ships taken up from trade had to be fitted out to refuel at sea, 19 of them had helicopter platforms fitted, several were fitted with Harrier decks and other adaptations were needed for their service with the Royal Navy. All this work was carried out by the shipyard workers with remarkable efficiency and dispatch and their efforts made an important contribution to the rapid mobilisation and departure of the Task Force.[32] However, the Falklands apart, the two years leading up to the general election of June 1983 unfortunately showed little, if any, prospect of significant long-term improvement in the fortunes of British shipbuilders; there was still a world trade recession, still the same gross imbalance in world shipbuilding between capacity and demand and, for the British merchant yards, still the same problem of winning orders against Far East competition.

Nevertheless the Report and Accounts of British Shipbuilders for the years ended 31st March 1982 did show an improvement over the preceding year; the trading loss (after crediting Intervention Fund assistance of £46.9 million) was reduced to £19.79 million[33] and new orders for merchant ships, totalling 373,000 c.g.r.t., were greater than in any other year since nationalisation. However in February 1982 the Report from the Trade and Industry Committee[34] showed the extent to which the business of British Shipbuilders had been reduced; since 1977 nine shipyards, 38 building berths, three engine building facilities and three ship repairing companies had been closed with a loss of 20,700 jobs. Even so the continued existence of British Shipbuilders remained totally dependent on Government financial support; in November 1981, on the Second Reading of the Shipbuilding Bill, the Shipbuilding Minister, Norman

29. He was narrowly defeated at the general election.

30. P. Debs. 6 Ser., Vol. 42, c.(405).

31. Particularly since 60 per cent of the earnings of U.K. ships came from cross-trading and much of this would be lost if foreign governments took counter-protectionist action.

32. Due acknowledgment of the shipbuilding industry's efforts were made by several speakers in the Lords debate—see P. Debs. (HL) 5 Ser., Vol. 437 cc.1210 and 1233.

33. The warship yards had made a profit of £38.5 million.

34. Parl. Papers 1981–82, HCP 192.

Lamont, stated that British Shipbuilders' total losses since vesting amounted to £341 million, that by March 1981 Government support by way of public dividend capital, intervention fund and redundancy payments had reached £500 million and that the Bill was needed so as to raise British Shipbuilders's borrowing limit to £700 million with provisions for a further increase to £800 million by Order.[35]

The closure of the Belfast shipyard of Harland & Wolff was likewise only prevented by substantial Government financial support; in a debate on 1st December 1981[36] the Northern Ireland Minister gave an assurance that such support would continue but emphasised the urgent need to obtain new orders so as to avoid a hiatus in production.[37] Some months later, in a debate on 26th July 1982,[38] the Minister stated that more than £47 million would be provided from public funds for Harland & Wolff in 1982–83 and that this was on top of about £270 million of assistance which had been provided since 1966; in view of the particular problems of Harland & Wolff in Northern Ireland the Government were providing a higher level of aid than was available for other U.K. shipyards and in the event Government assistance for Harlands in 1982–83 was in excess of £57 million.[39]

Although, in August 1980, the Government had decided that the return of shipbuilding to private ownership would have to be deferred, Ministers subsequently made it clear that it was still the Government's firm intention to proceed with the privatisation of the industry when the time was opportune.[40] Eventually, in November 1982, the Government moved the Second Reading of the British Shipbuilders Bill[41] which firstly removed the constraints imposed in the 1977 Act by replacing the corporation's statutory duties to engage in shipbuilding and related activities by powers to do so and secondly made privatisation possible by empowering the Secretary of State, subject to a negative resolution in either House, to direct the corporation to dispose of assets and parts of it undertaking and to limit or cease activities. However, although the Bill enabled any part of the undertaking of British Shipbuilders to be returned to the private sector, the Government's immediate intentions were limited to the privatisation of the profitable warship building yards since the unprofitable merchant shipbuilding yards would not be attractive to the private

35. P. Debs 6 Ser., Vol. 13, c.166. The Shipbuilding Act 1982 received the Royal Assent on 25th February 1982. On 18th July 1983 the borrowing limit was increased to £800,000 by the British Shipbuilding Borrowing Powers (Increase of Limit) Order 1983. The 1982 Act also extended the period for the operation of the redundancy schemes for Great Britain and Northern Ireland under the Shipbuilding (Redundancy Payments) Act 1978.

36. P. Debs. 6 Ser., Vol. 14, c.156.

37. The urgent need for new orders was raised again in February 1982—see P. Debs. 6 Ser., Vol. 18, c.970.

38. P. Debs. 6 Ser., Vol. 28, c.862.

39. P. Debs. 6 Ser., Vol. 42, c.(276).

40. See for example P. Debs. 6 Ser., Vol. 13, c.166 and Vol 22, c.726.

41. P. Debs. 6 Ser., Vol. 32, c.282.

investor and the Government accepted that, for the time being, merchant shipbuilding would have to remain in the public sector and that support would have to continue for the foreseeable future.

The Bill was vigorously opposed and it was not until 9th May 1983, shortly before the dissolution of Parliament, that the British Shipbuilders Act 1983 received the Royal Assent. In the meantime, whilst the Bill was going through its various stages in both Houses, the severity of the problems oppressing the British shipbuilding industry resulted in four separate debates in the Commons.[42] There was no dissension regarding the seriousness of the situation since, in spite of the support from the intervention fund which made it possible for British yards to quote below cost, the world over-capacity in shipbuilding, the depression in trade and shipping, the superior Far East productivity[43] and unfair Far East competition all militated against British merchant yards obtaining sufficient orders to achieve profitability. One measure constantly advocated by the Labour Opposition was that British shipowners should be compelled to place their new ship orders with U.K. yards but the Government consistently took the view that, whilst they would try to persuade British owners to buy British, it would not be in the interests of the British shipping industry to compel them to do so; as the Minister pointed out, most British owners would prefer to buy British if the U.K. yards could offer commercially advantageous terms but if this was not the case they must be free to place orders elsewhere since otherwise they could not be competitive.

The deterioration in the fortunes of British Shipbuilders was also shown in the Report and Accounts for the year ended 31st March 1983. The loss, after crediting intervention fund assistance of £20.4 million but before interest and tax, was £117 million in spite of the fact that the warship yards had made a profit of £31.7 million. One difficulty was that full use could not be made of the intervention fund assistance that was available since, under the terms of the current EEC Directive,[44] aid was limited to 15 per cent of the cost price of the new ship and thus was insufficient to bridge the gap when there was a difference of 35 per cent between the building cost of a ship built in European yards and the selling price of a ship built in Far Eastern yards. Nevertheless it could not be said that British Shipbuilders lacked financial support; for the period 1977–78 to 1982–83 public dividend capital[45] amounted to £474 million, grants under Sections 7 and 8 of the Industry Act 1972 (as amended) to £160.8 million and

42. On 7th February 1983 (P. Debs. 6 Ser., Vol. 36, c.773), on 31st March 1983 (P. Debs. 6 Ser., Vol. 40, c.475), on 19th April 1983 (P. Debs. 6 Ser., Vol. 41, c.215) and on 29th April 1983 (P. Debs. 6 Ser., Vol. 41, c.1171).

43. Japanese labour productivity was between two and two and a half times greater than in U.K. yards (P. Debs. 6 Ser., Vol. 42, c.(312)).

44. EC Council Directive of 28th April 1981 on aid to shipbuilding (81/363/EEC) the operation of which, by Council Directive of 21st December 1982 (82/880/EEC), had been extended to 31st December 1984.

45. Including payments from the National Loans Fund and other loans.

payments under the redundancy scheme to £66 million.[46] In addition finance on competitive terms continued to be made available under the Home Credit Scheme[47] but loans were of little help if the orders could not be obtained.

The formation of the new Conservative Government in June 1983, following the general election, did not result in any significant shift in shipping policy. The Queen's Speech contained no reference to shipping and in July 1983,[48] when the Government were asked to take further steps to halt this decline of the British merchant navy, David Mitchell, the new junior Minister at the Transport Department with responsibility for shipping,[49] stated that, whilst concerned at the decline in the merchant fleet, the Government did not propose to protect or subsidise it[50] and that both sides of the industry must work together to improve its competitiveness. He added that in international negotiations the Government would continue to work for the widest possible access for British shipping to world trades and that it would continue to minimise the burden of regulation, consistent with safety, and to take action against unsafe foreign shipping in British ports.

The decline in the tonnage[51] owned and registered in the U.K. continued; in mid-1981 it had been 33.2 million d.w.t., in March 1982 29.6 million dwt and at the beginning of 1983 it amounted to 24.7 million tonnes deadweight but by the end of 1983 it had fallen further to 20.7 million deadweight which represented a reduction of 29.3 million deadweight (59 per cent) since the end of 1975.[52] However, although the greater part of the tonnage lost to the U.K. flag since 1975 was represented by ships sold to foreign buyers or for scrapping, increasingly during the 1980's there were a number of U.K. owners who, finding themselves unable to operate at even a modest profit under the U.K. flag with market conditions continuing to be severely depressed, decided that, if they were not the cease operations entirely, the only course open was to "flag out", i.e. to transfer their ships to an overseas port of registry, Commonwealth or foreign, so as to affect a substantial reduction in operating costs through being able to employ competitive labour.[53]

During the latter part of 1983 and continuing into 1984 the state of the

46. P. Debs. 6 Ser., Vol. 42, c.(389).

47. See Industry Act Reports for the years ended 31st March 1982 (Parl. Papers 1981–82, HCP 503) and 31st March 1983 (Parl. Papers 1982–83, HCP 72). The loan guarantees given for these two years amounted to £480 million and at 31st March 1983 the guarantees current totalled £1,032 million.

48. P. Debs. 6 Ser., Vol. 45, c.(246).

49. Following the general election responsibility for shipping had been transferred from the Department of Trade to the Department of Transport.

50. Apart from the subsidies which had for many years been given to the Scottish Highlands and Islands shipping services—see P. Debs. 6 Ser., Vol. 54 c.697 and Vol 61, c.(286).

51. Ships of 500 g.r.t. and over.

52. *British Shipping Review 1982* and *British Shipping Facts and Figures 1984* (GCBS).

53. In its *British Shipping Review 1982* the GCBS stated that a shipping company, to stay in business, "must be free to put its ships under the flag most likely to serve the success of the enterprise".

merchant navy remained a matter for much concern. The GCBS continued to campaign, without success, for a 40 per cent investment allowance for new ships[54] and free depreciation for second-hand ships and pressed for more vigorous Government action in opposing unfair subsidised competition and foreign protectionist measures.[55] In November 1983 the Lords debated[56] the Report of its European Communities Committee on EEC Competition Policy: Shipping[57]; Lord Rochdale, the Chairman of the Sub-Committee which prepared the Report, emphasised the importance, in both peace and war, of a substantial and competitive British merchant fleet and Lord Hill-Norton urged the need for a co-ordinated national maritime policy. Shipping also figured largely in a Commons transport debate in April 1984[58] when, in answering Opposition charges of Government responsibility for the shipping decline, the Transport Minister, Nicholas Ridley, attributed the decline since 1975 to substantially higher investment in preceding years, the world recession, the over-supply of new ships resulting from massive world shipbuilding subsidies and the protectionist policies of emergent nations.

To the dismay of the U.K. shipping industry, the 1984 Budget proposals contained disincentives to the ordering of new tonnage for the U.K. flag; the 100 per cent first-year allowance and free depreciation for new ships were to be phased out and in addition the Government intended to withdraw the 25 per cent foreign earnings tax relief from which the majority of British sea-farers had benefited since 1977. In spite of strong representations the Government initially refused to give way, although admitting that shipping companies could be disadvantaged by the capital allowance reductions,[59] but eventually the Government agreed that there were strategic reasons for treating shipping as a special case[60] and undertook that in the 1985 Finance Bill provision would be made for continuing the system of free depreciation for new ships which had been in existence since 1965.[61] However the free depreciation was only to relate to the new 25 per cent writing down allowance and the U.K. industry felt that the loss of the 100 per cent first-year allowance put them at a disadvantage compared with their foreign competitors.[62]

54. At the end of 1983 the order book for new ships to be U.K. owned and registered had fallen to 1 million d.w.t. (two per cent of the world order book)—the lowest level for many years (*British Shipping Facts and Figures 1984*).

55. The Government were reluctant to use their powers under Section 14 of the Merchant Shipping Act 1974 (as amended).

56. P. Debs. (HL) 5 Ser., Vol. 445, c.369.

57. Third Report 1983–84, HL 23.

58. P. Debs. 6 Ser., Vol. 58, c.757.

59. P. Debs. 6 Ser., Vol. 59 cc.308 and 314.

60. I.e. the requirement of merchant ships for military reinforcement and naval support; also to import the goods and services required if foreign shipping was not available.

61. P. Debs. 6 Ser., Vol. 63, cc.1084–1085.

62. *Ibid.*, cc.1117–1118. However the 1985 Finance Act did also provide that second-hand ships, as well as new ships, would qualify for free depreciation on a 25 per cent writing-down allowance basis.

Following the publication of the 1984 Defence Estimates,[63] which surprisingly contained no reference to merchant shipping, a Report of the Commons Defence Committee[64] raised doubts as to whether, with the decline in the numbers of ships and corresponding loss of personnel, defence needs could be met and requested that future Defence White Papers should contain details of the merchant fleet available for requisition in an emergency.[65] In the subsequent defence debate[66] Humphrey Atkins, the Chairman of the Defence Committee, enquired whether in an emergency the Government could be able to lay their hands on those ships which were beneficially owned in the U.K. but registered under foreign flags; the Government failed to give an adequate answer to this question and also refused to give any assurance that the next White Paper would give details of the merchant ships available in an emergency.

Fears about whether the declining merchant fleet would still be able to fulfil its traditional role as the fourth arm of defence were not allayed by the Prime Minister's statement[67] that she readily accepted that the merchant navy was very important for our defence and that the Government kept under continuous and detailed review the requirements of HM Forces for support by merchant ships and the availability of ships with the specifications capable of meeting those requirements. In November 1984, in the course of a debate on the Royal Navy,[68] Du Cann announced the formation of an all-party Maritime Affairs Group whose purpose was to draw the attention of Government and Parliament to matters of significant and national importance in maritime affairs. The Defence Minister agreed that the merchant navy was critical to the operational effectiveness of the Royal Navy and gave an assurance that, except for mine-sweepers, the size of the merchant navy was at present adequate for defence needs though this might not be the case if the decline continued for several more years; he added that the Department of Transport, in conjunction with the Ministry of Defence, was launching an in-depth study into the likely future trends in the size of the British mercantile marine.[69]

Less than three weeks later there was a Commons debate on the British shipping industry[70] in which Du Cann and other members of the all-party Maritime Group spoke in support of a motion which asked the House to

63. Cmnd. 9227, Parl. Papers 1983–84.
64. First Report 1983–84, HCP 436 (paras. 49–53).
65. The Report pointed out that certain ships needed in an emergency might be out of reach when required.
66. P. Debs. 6 Ser., Vol. 62, c.36.
67. P. Debs. 6 Ser., Vol. 64, c.818 (24th July 1984).
68. *Ibid.*, Vol. 68, c.1119.
69. It was later explained (see P. Debs. 6 Ser., Vol. 69, c.(339)) that the object of the survey was first to review the number of ships in particular categories required for defence purposes and secondly to seek to establish how many ships of the appropriate types were likely to be available in the short and medium term. See also P. Debs. (HL) 5 Ser., Vol. 460, c.569.
70. P. Debs. 6 Ser., Vol. 70, c.30.

recognise the importance of the shipping industry to the U.K.'s trade, commerce and defence needs and, in view of the decline of the merchant fleet, asked the Government to state its policies for helping the industry to improve its international competitive position. In replying to the debate the Shipping Minister stated that the Government shared the concern at the decline of the merchant fleet[71] and was intending to minimise the burdens imposed on U.K. operators by some fairer method of sharing the costs of lights and buoys, by reform of pilotage and by reducing the costs of moving ships into the U.K. flag. Since 58 per cent of the U.K. fleet's earning came from cross-trades, the Government was trying to ensure that U.K. owners had fair and open markets[72]; in this connection the Government was supporting the EEC efforts to provide fairer trading and competition within Europe[73] and hoped that the United States and OECD would shortly agree to act together against new protectionist devices. As regards defence, the Minister contended that, in addition to the U.K. fleet, the Government had requisitioning powers over 400 vessels registered in overseas dependencies and 250 further vessels which were flagged out to foreign registries but beneficially owned by U.K. interests; however doubts were expressed as to whether these flagged out ships could in practice be requisitioned or whether, even if they could, there would be the crews to man them.[74]

The 1985 Defence Estimates[75] confidently asserted that there were still sufficient ships in each category (except deep sea trawlers) to meet defence needs but, with the U.K. owned and registered fleet (500 g.r.t. and over) having declined still further to 647 ships having a deadweight tonnage of 16.6 million,[76] the Commons Defence Committee produced a special Report on the Use of Merchant Shipping for Defence Purposes.[77] The Report pointed out that the defence purposes for which merchant shipping was needed included the trans-Atlantic re-inforcement of Europe, the re-inforcement of Europe from the U.K. and direct support of the Royal Navy but there was also a need for economic shipping to service the civil supply of the U.K. and Europe in

71. By December 1984 the U.K. owned and registered fleet (ships over 500 g.r.t.) had fallen to 689 ships having a deadweight tonnage of 18.38 million and in 1984 orders for new ships amounted to only 258,000 d.w.t. (*British Shipping Facts and Figures 1985* (GCBS)).

72. Immediately following this shipping debate there was a further debate (P. Debs. 6 Ser., Vol. 70, c.72) in which the House approved the Merchant Shipping (Liner Conference) Regulations which enabled the U.K. to accede to the U.N. Liner Conference Convention as modified by the Brussels package (EC Reg. No. 954/79).

73. In recent Parliamentary answers (see P. Debs. 6 Ser., Vol. 62, c.(364) and Vol 68, c.(358)) it had been stated that Denmark, France, West Germany, Greece and Italy still reserved their coastal trades for their own ships. The Government regarded cabotage as contrary to the spirit of the Treaty of Rome.

74. It was thought probable that the foreign crews on the flagged out ships would refuse to serve on them in wartime.

75. Cmnd. 9430, Parl. Papers 1984–85.

76. Figures for June 1985—see *British Shipping Review 1985*, p. 3.

77. First Report of Defence Committee 1984–85, HCP 114.

time of war. The Committee accepted that there would be no real problems in requisitioning by Royal Prerogative the vessels registered in the U.K. and Dependent Territories but considered that the Government view that ships flagged out to foreign registries but still U.K. beneficially owned were also available for requisition was at best arguable and that it was unsafe to place reliance on the availability of this category for requisition. The Report concluded that, when the consultants' study had been completed,[78] there should be a formal statement of Government policy covering (*inter alia*) the future number of vessels in the categories required for defence purposes, the extent of the requirement for economic shipping, the categories of shipping available for requisition and the legal powers proposed to be used and the likely future availability of trained officers and seamen.

The Defence Committee's Report was strongly endorsed by British shipowners[79] and was warmly welcomed by the all-party Maritime Group when the Defence White Paper was debated in June 1985.[80] From both sides of the House doubts were cast on the assertions in the Defence White Paper; John Silkin from the Labour front bench questioned whether the merchant navy could meet either defence needs or feed and supply the U.K. in a prolonged war and Du Cann agreed that in wartime Britain would have too few ships to support a war economy and supply and reinforce our forces. Misgivings were also expressed regarding the shortage of seafarers[81] and a leading shipowner referred to a recent statement by the President of the GCBS that a quarter of British-owned shipping was registered outside the U.K. and that the proportion was still rising. In reply the Defence Minister admitted that the decline in the merchant fleet was causing the Government concern but he reiterated that the fleet was still adequate to meet foreseeable defence needs; he added that the SEA Group study on the availability of merchant shipping for defence would shortly be completed and in the event an edited version of the study was placed in the Commons library shortly before the 1985 summer recess.[82] In reply to a question from Du Cann the Prime Minister stated that she was very much aware of the importance of the merchant fleet to the defence of the country and that she was taking a close interest in the SEA Group Report.[83]

78. The Government had arranged for the study to be made by the Shipping Economics Advisory ("SEA") Group—a division of Lloyd's of London Press. For the SEA Groups terms of reference see fn. 69 *supra*.

79. See *British Shipping Review 1985*, pp. 14–15.

80. P. Debs. 6 Ser., Vol. 80, c.896.

81. In March 1985 the number of merchant seamen was 37,000 compared with 71,000 in March 1980 (P. Debs. (HL) 5 Ser., Vol. 464, c.945). In 1939 the number was 159,000.

82. P. Debs. 6 Ser., Vol. 83, c.(447). See also 1986 Defence Estimates, p. 303 *infra*.

83. P. Debs. 6 Ser., Vol. 83, c.859. In July 1984 the Prime Minister, after meeting a number of leading British shipowners, wrote to the President of the GCBS saying "I hope that I left you in no doubt about the importance which I attach to the role of British shipping in peace as in war".

In the international shipping field 1985 witnessed the taking by the EEC of a first step towards a common shipping policy. In March the European Commission published their proposals for a Community Maritime Policy[84] comprising six legal instruments to liberalise the Community's internal shipping market and to permit Member States to act in concert in countering protectionism and unfair competition from outside the Community.[85] The proposals included a regulation for liberalising cabotage in all Community States; with the U.K. coastal trade having been open to all countries since 1850, British shipowners particularly welcomed the proposed removal of their exclusion from the coastal trades of those Community States which still reserved this trade to their national flag but it was anticipated that there would be strong opposition to this particular proposal and such indeed proved to be the case. The EC proposals were debated and approved in the Commons in March 1986[86] and, after being subjected to detailed scrutiny by the Lords European Communities Committee,[87] were likewise debated and approved in principle by the Lords in May 1986.[88] It was not, however, until December 1986 that the Transport Secretary was able to announce that the EC Transport Council had agreed a package of four measures as the first stages in the development of a common shipping policy.[89]

Two of the new regulations, which eventually came into force from July 1987, dealt with external shipping policy. The first (EC Regulation 4058/86) provided for the Community taking concerted action to combat protectionism by other countries and the second (EC Regulation 4057/86) enabled the Community to protect its liner shipping from unfair pricing practices by State-owned or supported shipping companies. The other two regulations concerned internal Community shipping relations. The third (EC Regulation 4056/86) applied the Treaty's competition rules to Community shipping but tramp shipping was specifically excluded and, subject to conditions, liner conferences were also exempted from the operation of these rules. The fourth (EC Regulation 4055/86), perhaps the most significant and which proved the most contentious, declared the freedom to provide shipping services in international trades to, from and between Member States and provided for the progressive phasing out, over a period up to the end of 1992, of unilateral cargo reservation[90] and discriminatory cargo-sharing arrangements in agreements

84. EC Document No. 5635/85.
85. P. Debs. 6 Ser., Vol. 79, c.(60).
86. P. Debs. 6 Ser., Vol. 93, c.815.
87. "Report on European Maritime Transport Policy", ninth Report 1985–86, (HL) 106.
88. P. Debs. (HL) 5 Ser., Vol. 474, c.514.
89. P. Debs. 6 Ser., Vol. 107, c.(531).
90. France, Spain and Portugal reserved "government" cargoes to national flag ships, France reserved 66 per cent of her crude oil imports and 40 per cent of her coal imports to French flag ships and Spain reserved various cargoes (oil, cereals and tobacco) to Spanish ships (see P. Debs. 6 Ser., Vol. 100, c.(550)).

between Member States and third countries[91]; but the Council failed to reach agreement on the elimination of restrictions in the national coastal trades of certain Member States and this omission of the Commission's original proposal for the liberation of all Community cabotage trades naturally left British owners with a strong sense of injustice.[92]

During the Parliamentary session 1985–86 there was no slackening of the pressure on the Government to take more positive action to halt the continuing decline of the U.K. merchant fleet; the GCBS reported that at the end of 1985 the U.K. owned and registered fleet (500 g.r.t. and over) had decreased to 627 ships of 15.9 million deadweight tonnes and that during the whole of 1985 the only new orders for U.K. registration were for six ferries of varying sizes and six general cargo ships totalling 15,000 dwt. In January 1986 there was an adjournment debate on the merchant service[93] prompted by the announcement by British Petroleum that its bulk fleet of 30 vessels was to be transferred to Bermudan registry and would be manned by three international agencies; concern was expressed about the defence implications and about the effect of the closure of BP Shipping's training facilities. In replying to the debate the Shipping Minister agreed that in the long term this was an issue of significance for defence and pointed out that the Government and GCBS had begun to look into the availability and training of seafarers.

In February 1986 the annual debate on the Royal Navy[94] provided a further opportunity for the Parliamentary Maritime Group to press the Government for constructive action. The Minister for the Armed Forces continued to maintain that the size of the British flagged merchant marine was sufficient to enable the U.K. to discharge her NATO obligations but, when challenged, he conceded that NATO requirements were quite separate from the wider requirements to maintain the economy in time of war and speakers on both sides of the House remained more convinced than ever of the need to reverse the decline. The 1986 Defence Estimates[95] stated that the SEA Group study of future trends into those parts of the merchant fleet for which there was a defence requirement indicated that for the foreseeable future such requirement was likely to be met but the subsequent Report of the Defence Committee[96] pointed out that the White Paper took no account of the requirement for economic shipping carrying essential civil supplies in time of war and added

91. Belgium, France, West Germany, Italy, Portugal and Spain had bi-lateral cargo-sharing agreements of various kinds with certain developing countries (P. Debs. 6 Ser., Vol. 100, c.(550)).

92. France, Greece, Italy, Portugal and Spain all reserved their cabotage trades to national flag ships. Denmark and West Germany had similar restrictions but in practice waived them for U.K. flag vessels. The British Government had warned that it might take unilateral action and GCBS felt that either there should be a case taken to the European Court or a closure of the U.K. coast.

93. P. Debs. 6 Ser., Vol. 90, c.423.

94. P. Debs. 6 Ser., Vol. 91, c.470.

95. Cmnd. 9763, Parl. Papers 1985–86.

96. Second Report of Defence Committee 1985–86, HCP 399 (paras. 100–105).

that Government policy as a whole appeared to pay little regard to the implication, in terms of national freedom of action, of dependence on other nations for merchant shipping.[97]

In March 1986 the Prime Minister was faced with questions on the implications of the decline, with regard to both defence and economics, and requests for corrective action; in her replies[98] she reiterated that the merchant fleet remained capable of meeting all the needs of the armed forces, pointed out that many of the factors leading to the fleets reduction were outside the control of either the industry or the Government and asserted that the Government were working to reduce the burden of costs and marine regulations and in international negotiations was endeavouring to create conditions that would give opportunities to British ships. In the summer and early autumn the Prime Minister gave like replies to similar questions[99] but in June 1986, in the course of a debate on the Defence Estimates,[100] the Government failed to respond to a request by Humphrey Atkins, Chairman of the Defence Committee, for a formal statement of Government policy covering such matters as numbers of ships, the availability of ships, the legal powers over ships and other matters referred to in his Committee's 1985 Report on Merchant Shipping (HCP 114). In his 1986 Budget the Chancellor likewise failed to give any encouragement for the acquisition of tonnage to be registered in the U.K. by refusing the shipowners' proposal that there should be a special extra 50 per cent allowance for new and second-hand ships and a roll-over relief for balancing charges to enable funds to be retained within a business for further investment.

As had been the case with shipping, the general election of June 1983 did not result in any change in the Conservative Government's policy for the British shipbuilding industry; in a July debate[101] to approve an Order increasing the borrowing limit of British Shipbuilders from £700 million to £800 million, Norman Lamont, who continued as Shipbuilding Minister, made it clear that the Government still intended to privatise the warship yards, that the merchant yards must improve their competitiveness but that in the meantime the Government would have to continue its financial support in order to enable the industry to survive.[102] In answering earlier questions[103] the Minister had stated that the Government was considering a request by British Shipbuilders for special emergency help to enable new orders to be obtained during the

97. In relation to the U.K.'s seaborne trade, by 1985 only 25 per cent of U.K. imports and 17 per cent of U.K. exports by tonne miles were carried in U.K. ships (*British Shipping Review 1985*).

98. P. Debs. 6 Ser., Vol. 93, c.148 and c.(213).

99. P. Debs. 6 Ser., Vol. 99, c.(288); Vol 100, c.(591) and Vol. 102, cc.1289–1292. She also stated that the National Union of Seamen had demanded salaries and restrictive practices that had priced its members out of British shipping.

100. P. Debs. 6 Ser., Vol. 100, c.712.

101. P. Debs. 6 Ser., Vol. 46, c.130.

102. Since 1979 BS had received nearly £750 million in Government support.

103. P. Debs. 6 Ser., Vol. 44, c.561.

recession and, in a statement made just before the 1983 summer recess,[104] the Minister said that, in view of the depressed state of the market,[105] the Government was asking the European Commission to approve, for a temporary period, the increase in the rate of intervention fund support above the existing level of 17 per cent in order to bridge the gap between U.K. building costs and Far Eastern selling prices.

The first privatisation of a major British Shipbuilders yard came much sooner than expected and, far from being the deliberate outcome of Government policy, was forced upon the BS management by the severity of the financial losses sustained and anticipated at Scott Lithgows arising out of the building of a semi-submersible drilling rig for Britoil. The first formal announcement of the impending disaster came just before Christmas 1983[106] and a month after, as the situation rapidly deteriorated, there was a full debate, initiated by the Opposition,[107] in which the Government spokesman made it clear that there would be no intervention in the dispute that had arisen between Britoil and Scott Lithgow but that the Government would encourage a private sector takeover of the yard. A few days later, in yet another shipbuilding debate,[108] there was mention of a proposed takeover by Trafalgar House, the parent company of Cunard, and on 9th February 1984 it was announced[109] that BS and Trafalgar House had reached a conditional agreement on the acquisition of Scott Lithgow. Finally, at the end of March 1984,[110] Norman Lamont announced that the Government had consented to the sale of Scott Lithgow to Trafalgar House; the purchase price for the virtually bankrupt yard was to be £12 million but the net cost to the Government of the deal was estimated to be £71 million[111] which was broadly the same as the cost of closing down the yard.

Meanwhile, towards the end of 1983, the continuing losses of BS had necessitated the passing of the British Shipbuilders (Borrowing Powers) Act 1983[112] which increased the limit on external finance (i.e. Government grants) from £800 million to £1 billion with provision for the limit to be further raised to £1.2 billion by successive steps of up to £100 million. It was not long before the new limit of £1 billion proved insufficient; on 27th June 1984[113] the Commons approved an Order increasing the limit to £1,100 million and in

104. *Ibid.*, Vol. 46, c.1355.
105. In 1982 world new orders had fallen by 20 per cent and BS new orders were their lowest ever.
106. P. Debs. 6 Ser., Vol. 51, c.281 and c.591.
107. *Ibid.*, Vol. 52, c.781.
108. *Ibid.*, Vol. 53, c.287.
109. *Ibid.*, Vol. 53, c.1021.
110. *Ibid.*, Vol. 57, c.289.
111. This was in addition to the sum of around £165 million already provided by taxpayers for Scott Lithgow since nationalisation (P. Debs. 6 Ser., Vol. 53, c.400)
112. Royal Assent, 21st December 1983. For Commons Second Reading debate see P. Debs. 6 Ser., Vol. 47, c.750.
113. P. Debs. 6 Ser., Vol. 62, c.1093.

the course of the debate the Minister stated that BS was getting out of ship repairing, which had been a heavy lossmaker, had closed three small loss-making yards and would be concentrating resources on its mainstream business of merchant ships and engines. A month later the Secretary of State announced[114] that for 1983–84, after crediting £11.3 million from the intervention fund, BS had made a trading loss, the worst since nationalisation, of £161 million, of which £75 million had been contributed by Scott Lithgow, that only 117,000 c.g.r.t. of new orders, the lowest ever, had been won in that year and that it had been decided that BS should sell its warship building interests,[115] making substantial progress towards privatisation by 31st March 1985 and completing it by 31st March 1986. At the same time, in reply to a question, the Prime Minister stated that it was important to keep a merchant shipbuilding capacity in the U.K. for strategic reasons.[116]

In November 1984 there was a further debate on an Opposition motion deploring the deepening crisis in the shipbuilding industry and demanding urgent Government action.[117] The Government spokesman pointed out that £1,170 million had been provided for BS since 1979, that the EEC had agreed an extension until the end of 1986 of the fifth Directive on Shipbuilding Aids but that regretfully the Commission had not yet agreed an improved rate of support from the intervention fund; the Minister also reiterated that the Government was committed to maintaining the maximum competitive and efficient shipbuilding industry but that much needed orders would only be placed if customers were confident about performance, delivery and price.

In January 1985 there was the Second Reading of a short Shipbuilding Bill[118] which was a technical measure to extend by 18 months the life of the shipbuilding redundancy payment schemes[119] and to write off certain irrecoverable outstanding loans made by the Shipbuilding Industry Board to Upper Clyde Shipbuilders in the period 1968–72.[120] In the following month the Commons approved yet another Order[121] increasing from £1,100 million to £1,200 million, the maximum permitted under the 1983 Act, the borrowing limit of BS; in introducing the Order[122] the Under Secretary warned that, if BS continued to be unprofitable, there would be a need for legislation to extend the borrowing limit still further but that, on a more hopeful note, the disposal of the loss-making ship repairing companies was nearing completion and the

114. P. Debs. 6 Ser., Vol. 64, c.998—see also BS Report and Accounts 1983–84.

115. The yards to be sold were the warship yards of Vickers, Yarrow, Vosper Thorneycroft, Hall Russell and Brooke Marine plus the mixed yards of Cammell Laird and Swan Hunter. The warship building profits for 1983–84 were £44 million.

116. P. Debs. 6 Ser., Vol. 64, c.819.

117. *Ibid.*, Vol. 68, c.832.

118. P. Debs. 6 Ser., Vol. 70, c.790.

119. Introduced by the Shipbuilding (Redundancy Payments) Act 1978.

120. The Shipbuilding Act 1985 received the Royal Assent on 27th March 1985.

121. British Shipbuilders Borrowing Powers (Increase of Limit) Order 1985.

122. P. Debs. 6 Ser., Vol. 74, c.294.

new orders recently obtained by BS made it likely that the stated order target of 200,000 c.g.r.t. for 1984–85 would be attained.

The Government's plan for the future of the shipbuilding industry was stated succinctly by the Prime Minister to be "first to concentrate available resources on the most successful yards in order to create a cost-effective and efficient merchant shipbuilding industry and secondly to privatise the warship building yards by 31st March 1986"[123]; but, as one of the Departmental Ministers subsequently emphasised,[124] the future of the merchant yards depended primarily on the state of the international market and the degree to which U.K. shipbuilders were competitive within that market. However the prospects for meeting Far East competition were enhanced by the announcement, in July 1985,[125] that for orders taken between July 1984 and December 1986 the European Commission had approved an increased rate of up to 20.5 per cent assistance from the intervention fund[126] plus two per cent shipbuilders' relief and had indicated that it would be prepared to consider higher payments on a case by case basis particularly for orders where there was no EC competition.

Shortly before the end of the 1984–85 session the Government stated[127] that it accepted British Shipbuilders' plan to continue to concentrate resources on a stable cost-effective mainstream merchant shipbuilding business particularly since this strategy had enabled BS to reduce its trading loss for 1984–85 (after crediting £22 million from the intervention fund) to £25 million and to secure new orders for merchant ships of around 233,000 c.g.r.t.[128] The Opposition was however much disquieted by the Cunard announcement that the re-engining and renovation of the QE2 was to be carried out in a West German shipyard at a cost of some £80 million but the Speaker rejected a request for an emergency debate[129] and a Minister subsequently stated[130] that, as no U.K. yard had been able to offer to carry out the work,[131] the contract had had to be placed abroad but that some 30 per cent of the total cost would be spent in the U.K.

As had been the case for many years, the survival of shipbuilding in Northern Ireland was only made possible by the continuation of substantial subsidies to

123. P. Debs. 6 Ser., Vol. 77, c.(504). By October 1985 (see P. Debs. 6 Ser., Vol. 84, c.(157)) there had been good progress in the disposal of the warship yards. Yarrow and Brooke Marine had been sold and negotiations were taking place for the sale of Hall Russell, Swan Hunter and Vosper Thorneycroft.

124. P. Debs. 6 Ser., Vol. 80, c.453.

125. *Ibid.*, Vol. 82, c.(275).

126. For vessels over 70,000 d.w.t. to be built by Harland & Wolff the payment from the intervention fund could be increased to 25.5 per cent.

127. P. Debs. 6 Ser., Vol. 84, c.(309).

128. See BS Report and Accounts for 1984–85. The Government subsidy to BS for 1984–85 was £154 million excluding the cost of the sale of Scott Lithgow to Trafalgar House.

129. P. Debs. 6 Ser., Vol. 84, c.671.

130. *Ibid.*, Vol. 84, c.(476).

131. The timescale fixed by Cunard was so short that no British yard even considered tendering for the work.

the State-owned Harland & Wolff. Payments made under the Aircraft and Shipbuilding Industries (Northern Ireland) Order 1979 were £40 million in 1983–84 and £37.5 million in 1984–85[132]; for 1985–86 the Government were proposing to make £36.5 million, inclusive of intervention fund payments, available for the Belfast yard[133] and at the end of 1985 a Northern Ireland Minister stated that the order book was very creditable and that the Government would give Harland & Wolff all possible encouragement and support in their search for orders.[134] In the spring of 1986 the extent and implications of Government support were called into question in connection with the competition between the Belfast yard and the recently privatised Swan Hunters for a valuable Royal Navy order for an AOR (auxiliary oil replenishment) vessel. In spite of a Government assurance that competition for the order would be fair,[135] an unsuccessful attempt was made to have the matter debated as an emergency[136] and in an adjournment debate on the following day[137] it was alleged that Harland & Wolff were only able to quote a lower price because of cross-subsidy. In the event the order went to Belfast and the Minister stated that Harland's bid had been reviewed by an independent firm who had concluded that the tender was comprehensively costed, contained a profit margin and did not benefit in any way from cross-subsidy.[138]

In April 1986 the Government were able to announce[139] that all the warship yards had been returned to the private sector by the 31st March 1986 target date[140] but at the end of April the continuing deterioration in the finances of the merchant yards necessitated the introduction of yet another Borrowing Powers Bill[141] increasing the borrowing limit of British Shipbuilders to £1,300 million with powers to raise it to £1,400 million.[142] In May it was announced[143] that, in the absence of new orders, BS could not maintain its current capacity and that by the end of 1986 a number of small yards would have to be closed with resulting 3,500 redundancies by March 1987.[144] Later

132. P. Debs. 6 Ser., Vol. 84, c.(280) and c.(490).

133. *Ibid.*, Vol. 86, c.(10).

134. *Ibid.*, Vol. 88, c.1055.

135. P. Debs. 6 Ser., Vol. 93, c.881.

136. *Ibid.*, Vol. 94, c.621.

137. *Ibid.*, c.851.

138. *Ibid.*, c.1063. It was later announced (P. Debs. 6 Ser., Vol. 96, c.434) that Swan Hunter would be given a preferential opportunity to bid for a second AOR ship and in the latter part of 1987 a contract for such ship was awarded to Swan Hunter—notwithstanding protests from Northern Ireland.

139. P. Debs. 6 Ser., Vol. 95, c.871.

140. Gross sale proceeds exceeded £120 million but the sales resulted in a book loss to BS of £248 million.

141. P. Debs. 6 Ser., Vol. 96, c.681.

142. British Shipbuilders (Borrowing Powers) Act 1986 (Royal Assent, 26th June 1986).

143. P. Debs. 6 Ser., Vol. 97, c.705.

144. This meant that in March 1987 BS would have 6,500 employees, H & W 4,000, warship yards 27,000 and private sector (small ships) 2,000. At the time of nationalisation there were 44,800 employed in merchant ship and engine building and 87,500 in the whole of BS.

in May there was a full-scale debate on the shipbuilding industry[145] in the course of which Government spokesmen emphasised the worldwide cutbacks in shipyards, reaffirmed continuing financial support for the U.K. merchant yards, promised improved credit arrangements in the hope of obtaining more foreign orders and undertook to see what help could be given to British owners in order to encourage them to place more orders with U.K. yards.[146] The Opposition, on the other hand, with some support from Conservative backbenchers, stressed that the U.K. required a strong shipbuilding industry for trade and defence and called upon the Government to bring forward public sector orders and adopt measures to secure sufficient orders from home and abroad so as to maintain the industry's existing capacity and workforce.

In July 1986 British Shipbuilders reported a trading loss for 1985–86 of £125 million after crediting intervention fund support of only £5.8 million[147] and its corporate plan covering the years 1986–87 to 1989–90 was intended to allow British Shipbuilders to maintain its business at the size it would reach after the restructuring then taking place; the Government accepted the plan but emphasised that its success would depend on sufficient orders being won.[148] By December 1986 the continuing rapid deterioration in BS's finances[149] necessitated the raising yet again of the corporation's borrowing limit from £1,300 million to £1,400 million;[150] the Minister stated[151] that for 1986–87 a limit of £155 million had been placed on the financing needs of BS's continuing business but only two months later the figure had been increased to £244 million.[152] Early in December the Commons also considered[153] a draft of the EEC Sixth Directive on Aid to Shipbuilding[154] which the Government considered an improvement on the Fifth Directive in that it controlled all subventions (not only direct production aid as in the Fifth Directive) so as to ensure fair competition between EC yards. However the increased aid ceiling of 26 per cent cost was considered too low to enable EC yards to compete with Far East prices and when, later in the month, the Council of Industry Ministers approved the Sixth Directive,[155] it sanctioned, for the first 12 months, direct

145. P. Debs. 6 Ser., Vol. 98, c.412.

146. See also the replies given by the Prime Minister to questions on 15th and 20th May (P. Debs. 6 Ser., Vol. 97, c.848 and Vol 98, c.(178).

147. See BS Annual Report 1985–86.

148. P. Debs. 6 Ser., Vol. 102, c.(351). Orders secured during 1985–86 were only 23,000 c.g.t.

149. Largely due to one customer going into receivership and delays in securing new orders; in 1986 BS had won around 90,000 c.g.t. of orders.

150. British Shipbuilders' Borrowing Powers (Increase of Limit) Order 1986.

151. P. Debs. 6 Ser., Vol. 107, c.145.

152. *Ibid.*, Vol. 110, c.(524).

153. *Ibid.*, Vol. 107, c.123.

154. EC Docs 9470/86 and 9470/1/86.

155. 87/167/EC, which was to last for four years from 1st January 1987. At the end of 1990 a further Council Directive (90/684/EC) was made to regulate state aid to shipbuilding for the years 1991 to 1993 (inclusive) – see OJ L374, 31st December 1990, pp. 13–33 and a helpful summary on p. 39 of the *Law Society Gazette* of 1st May 1991.

support of up to 28 per cent of the value of the contract before aid which represented 39 per cent of the resulting contract price.[156]

During the year ended 31st March 1987 British Shipbuilders had disposed of the South Bank yard at Middlesbrough of Smith's Dock, the Troon yard of Appledore Ferguson Shipbuilders and the Wallsend works of Clark Kincaid; these disposals left British Shipbuilders with only four merchant ship and engine building subsidiaries—Govan Shipbuilders in Glasgow, North East Shipbuilders ("NESL") with four yards in Sunderland, Appledore Ferguson Shipbuilders with yards in Appledore and Port Glasgow and Clark Kincaid's engine building works in Greenock. For 1986–87 the BS trading loss, after intervention fund assistance of £20.8 million, amounted to £148 million[157] and, following the June 1987 general election, it was not long before the newly elected Commons were told that there was urgent need for another British Shipbuilders (Borrowing Powers) Bill which would raise the existing borrowing limit of £1,400 million to £1,550 million with provision for further increases up to £1,800 million.[158] In moving the Second Reading of the Bill[159] the new Minister with responsibility for shipbuilding, Kenneth Clarke, stated that, although since 1979 British Shipbuilders had received Government support of more than £1.75 billion, the root cause of the problem was a world market dominated by massive excess capacity in both shipping and shipbuilding; in the case of shipping there were great tonnages laid up, rates depressed and returns on capital low whilst for world shipbuilding, with a merchant capacity of 18 million tonnes a year, in 1986 new orders totalled only 9 million tonnes, of which the U.K. share was two per cent,[160] and there was no prospect of an upturn in demand until 1990 at the earliest. Thus the problem was not one facing the U.K. alone; France was reduced to one yard, Sweden had abandoned shipbuilding, several West German yards had gone into liquidation and the Japanese were cutting capacity by at least 20 per cent. The Government had decided that for 1987–88 British Shipbuilders must try to operate within an external finance limit of £118 million and its survival depended on its ability to win orders, to improve its performance and to reduce costs.

156. P. Debs. 6 Ser., Vol. 108, c.(198). The U.K. scheme for shipbuilding assistance, as approved by the EEC (see P. Debs. 6 Ser., Vol. 131, c.(18)) provided for direct aid of up to 28 per cent of cost (including two per cent shipbuilders' relief) for vessels costing more than £10 million but only up to 20 per cent of cost for ships costing less than £10 million. The agreed credit terms for home and export orders, based on an OECD Understanding, were for loans up to 80 per cent of contract price repayable over eight and half years with interest at 7.5 per cent per annum.

157. See BS Annual Report 1986–87. For the period April to September 1987 the loss was £23 million.

158. The additional £200 million borrowing authorised by the 1986 Act had been wholly utilised in 12 months; the largest elements were £50 million lost on contracts in progress and £40 million as a result of a shipowner customer going into receivership.

159. P. Debs 6 Ser., Vol. 119, c.545. The British Shipbuilders (Borrowing Powers) Act 1987 eventually received the Royal Assent on 23rd July 1987.

160. The Japanese share was 41 per cent, Korea 14 per cent and the EEC 15 per cent.

In the ensuing debate it was generally agreed that British Shipbuilders should pursue its new strategy of concentrating on more specialised and sophisticated ships and the Opposition emphasised that, with the merchant yards reduced to only seven employing fewer than 6,000 men, there should be no question of any further reduction in capacity.[161] The Government were urged to take the lead in tackling the problem of world over-capacity[162] but at the same time there were requests for incentives, credits and a favourable tax regime to persuade British owners to place orders with U.K. yards and to keep their ships under the U.K. flag. There was also the usual Opposition demand that British owners should be compelled to buy British and the usual Government response that, if U.K. owners were compelled to build at home, what would happen if other countries did likewise; in any case 70 per cent of the tonnage ordered for U.K. registration in 1986 was placed in U.K. yards but, in view of the depressed shipping market resulting from the over-supply of ships, there was little incentive for U.K. owners to order any new tonnage.[163]

In April 1988 a statement by the Chancellor of the Duchy of Lancaster[164] revealed more detail of the Government's policy with regard to the future of BS' few remaining merchant yards. Mr Clarke informed the House that Kvaerner Industries, a Norwegian company at the forefront of gas ship technology, was in negotiation with British Shipbuilders for the purchase of the Govan yard, that another party had expressed interest in the Appledore yard and that the Government would welcome any serious approach for the purchase of NESL which was experiencing serious contractual difficulties with its programme for the building of a series of Danish ferries. The following month there was a shipbuilding debate[165] on a Labour Opposition motion calling upon the Government to affirm its commitment to British merchant shipbuilding and a Government amendment welcoming the prospect of returning the British Shipbuilders merchant yards to the private sector; in the course of the debate the Government Spokesman reported that there was purchasing interest in the Ferguson yard at Port Glasgow and the Clark Kincaid engine works, confirmed that funding for British Shipbuilders would continue, pointed out that there was a substantial shipbuilding capacity outside the British Shipbuilders yards[166] and expressed the view that a return of the remaining British Shipbuilders yards to the private sector was the realistic way to secure their long term future.

161. In 1986 deliveries of new ships from UK merchant yards amounted to only 99,000 g.r.t. —0.6 per cent of world output. (British Maritime League, 1987 Annual Report)

162. In a short policy statement issued in September 1987, the British Maritime League likewise urged the Government to mount an immediate international initiative to reduce the world over-supply of ships.

163. In 1986 orders of new tonnage for UK registration amounted to only 4,000 d.w.t.(GCBS Annual Report 1986–87).

164. P. Debs. 6 Ser., Vol. 131, c.554.

165. *Ibid.*, Vol. 133, c.1106.

166. Mr Clarke maintained that the U.K. still had a substantial shipbuilding capacity for war or peace and that the thriving privatised warship yards were all capable of building merchant ships.

Later in May there was yet another debate on shipbuilding on the Lower Clyde[167] and then, at the end of June, Kenneth Clarke, in a written answer,[168] stated that the Government had approved the sale of the Govan yard to a Kvaerner subsidiary upon the basis that, with intervention fund support, Kvaerner would order two gas ships (with option for two more) and would develop Govan as its centre for gas ship technology.[169] The closure of the Govan yard was thus averted but there was still serious doubts regarding the future of the Sunderland yards of NESL where lay-offs had already begun; the dispute with the Danish ferry owners was still dragging on and, in reply to an Opposition request that intervention fund support should be given to an order for new ships which Cuban owners were considering placing with NESL, Mr Clarke pointed out that no price had yet been negotiated with the Cubans and emphasised that it would be reckless for Government financial support to be given to British Shipbuilders if the contracts were concluded on terms unacceptable to the taxpayers and with the likelihood that the taxpayer would pay more for the ships than the Cubans.[170]

Towards the end of July 1988, shortly before the summer recess, there was a debate on the draft of an Order, proposed to be made under the British Shipbuilders (Borrowing Powers) Act 1987, to increase the BS borrowing limit from £1,550 million to £1,700 million.[171] In seeking approval of the Order, the Chancellor of the Duchy of Lancaster told the House that British Shipbuilders continued to consume alarming sums[172] and that this history of continuing losses provided the background for the Government's belief that the remaining British Shipbuilders businesses capable of survival would be managed more efficiently in the private sector. The Government was looking for serious purchasers with sensible business plans and substantial financial backing—the aim being to return every part of the business to the private sector on a basis that was fair to the purchaser, the taxpayer and the workforce. British Shipbuilders expected bids for Appledore from at least two groups interested in continuing merchant shipbuilding at the yard, interest had also been expressed in the Ferguson yard at Port Glasgow and the Clark Kincaid engine works and a number of parties had shown interest in acquiring all or part of NESL facilities

167. P. Debs. 6 Ser., Vol. 134, c.623.

168. *Ibid.*, Vol. 136, c.(25).

169. The sale was due to be completed in August. Kvaerner would pay £6 million but the cost of disposal for BS would be up to £25 million and the liabilities of Govan would remain with BS. The unions had agreed to a reduction of up to 500 in the Govan workforce.

170. P. Debs. 6 Ser., Vol. 137, c.337. Previous Cuban orders had cost the taxpayer around 16–17 per cent of the contract price in addition to intervention fund support.

171. P. Debs. 6 Ser., Vol. 137, c.1377.

172. Almost £1.8 billion since 1979. Of the £150 million provided by the 1987 Act, around £100 million had already been spent—largely in meeting contract losses on every order and under-recovered overheads due to shortage of orders and work.

at Sunderland. As regards the possible Cuban orders, the Government had refused BS's application for intervention fund support because it was not satisfied that NESL could build to cost but such support for a purchaser of the Sunderland yards would be considered because then it would be such purchaser, rather than the taxpayer, who would have to bear any contract losses.

The Government decided that bids for NESL would have to be submitted by 30th September 1988 and on that date it was reported[173] that bids from four interested parties were being submitted but that hopes of saving the Sunderland yards were not high. Towards the end of October, the new Minister with responsibility for shipbuilding[174] stated that a number of bids had been received for NESL and that these were still being evaluated.[175] Two weeks later, in a Commons statement,[176] Mr Newton announced that none of the original four bids for NESL had been found acceptable but that in the past few days three new expressions of interest in a possible purchase had been made and, in a last effort to find a viable way forward for the Sunderland yards, the Government had agreed with the British Shipbuilders Chairman that an opportunity should be given to establish, by the end of November, whether any of these new proposals could be developed into a firm basis for negotiation. The Minister also mentioned that good progress had been made in the negotiations for the sale of Clark Kincaid, the Appledore yard and the Ferguson yard at Port Glasgow.

In a further statement early in December[177] the Chancellor of the Duchy of Lancaster informed the Commons that British Shipbuilders and its independent financial advisers had concluded that none of the three new proposals for NESL could form the basis for a viable future for merchant shipbuilding in Sunderland; the Government accordingly saw no further prospect of maintaining NESL in its present form and had decided that the yards would progressively close as work ran out and that a new enterprise zone for Sunderland would be established. The following week there was a shipbuilding debate[178] on a Government motion approving the progress made towards returning to the private sector the shipbuilding yards and other facilities owned by British Shipbuilders and an Opposition amendment condemning the decision to close NESL and regretting the "unnecessary and untimely demise of British merchant shipbuilding". In the course of the debate the Minister re-emphasised that none of the proposals for NESL showed sufficient

173. In *The Times*.

174. Mr Tony Newton had been appointed Chancellor of the Duchy of Lancaster in place of Mr Kenneth Clarke.

175. P. Debs. 6 Ser., Vol. 139, c.286 and c.(300).

176. *Ibid.*, Vol. 140, c.745.

177. *Ibid.*, Vol. 143, c.315. See also P. Debs. (HL) 5 Ser., Vol. 502 c.612.

178. P. Debs. 6 Ser., Vol. 143, c.924.

financial resources or sufficient work for the future and that the best course lay in the measures being taken to encourage new enterprises on Wearside; Mr Newton also ridiculed the Opposition's suggestion that the country would no longer be able to build for its own merchant fleet and pointed out that there would still remain not only important civil yards such as Govan and Harland & Wolff but also military yards such as Swan Hunter with substantial merchant shipbuilding capacity which could be utilised if a demand arose for merchant ships which could be sold at satisfactory prices.

During the first half of 1989 further progress was made in the disposal of BS's remaining subsidiaries; by February the Government reported that BS had sold Clark Kincaid and the Appledore yard[179] and by April British Shipbuilders had also disposed of Sunderland Forge and British Shipbuilders Training and were considering bids for Ferguson Shipbuilders and Marine Design Consultants.[180] Then in June Mr Newton stated in a written answer[181] that there had been expressions of interest in some or all of the NESL yards for shipbuilding, ship repairing and general engineering and that British Shipbuilders had been asked to evaluate these new proposals; subsequently, in mid-July,[182] Mr Newton informed the House that British Shipbuilders considered that one of the four bids for NESL could represent a basis for new and substantial shipbuilding activity but that elucidation was needed before clear advice could be given on the prospects of secure employment and that, taking into account the approval already given by the European Commission in relation to the proposed closure of NESL and the creation of an enterprise zone in Sunderland, the Government had concluded that an enterprise zone was in the best long-term interests of Sunderland. The Opposition continued to pursue the matter; during the latter part of July further written questions were raised[183] and, just before the summer recess, there was a debate[184] in which the Opposition attempted to reverse the Government's decision not to accept the latest bids for NESL; however the response of Douglas Hogg, the new Minister of State at the Department of Trade and Industry, was that he agreed with Mr Newton's decision to close NESL and to go ahead with the creation of the enterprise zone in Sunderland.

Meanwhile, over the previous two years, the politically sensitive State-owned yard in Belfast was still only able to survive with continuing Government

179. *Ibid.*, Vol. 147, c.(820).

180. P. Debs. 6 Ser., Vol. 151, c.(188). Subsequently, in June, it was reported that the HLD Group were entering into negotiations for the purchase of the Ferguson yard (see P. Debs. 6 Ser., Vol. 155, c.(17)).

181. P. Debs. 6 Ser., Vol. 154, c.(146).

182. P. Debs. 6 Ser., Vol. 156, c.1148.

183. See P. Debs. 6 Ser., Vol. 156, c.(574) and Vol.157, cc.(126), (271), (273), (582), (824) and (1083).

184. P. Debs. 6 Ser., Vol. 157, c.1269

financial support. For 1986–87 £68 million was provided to cover Harland & Wolff's trading losses and redundancy costs[185] and the original provision of £40.5 million for 1987–88[186] was subsequently increased by a further £18.1 million to cover delays in the building programme and losses on contracts.[187] Nevertheless the yard's loss for the year to the end of March 1988 was only £25 million, as compared with £75.6 million in the previous year, and in the spring of 1988 Ulster hopes for a more secure future for the yard were raised by an announcement by the Indian shipowner Mr Ravi Tikkoo of a plan for Harlands to build the world's largest cruise ship (to be named *Ultimate Dream*) with an estimated contract value of about £295 million. However this grandiose *Ultimate Dream* project was dependent on a Government subsidy of 28 per cent[188] plus ECGD backed finance being forthcoming and the initial response from the Northern Ireland Office, which perhaps feared a repetition of the De Lorean financial fiasco, was not too encouraging.

At the end of May 1988,[189] in replying to requests from Northern Ireland members that the Government should support the *Ultimate Dream* project, the Northern Ireland Industry Minister stated that the costing was not yet completed and that Harlands had made no formal approach to the Northern Ireland office for contract support nor to ECGD for credit facilities; the Government would review thoroughly and carefully any eventual application and, because of the continuing high level of support needed to keep the yard in business, would also seriously consider any proposals for privatisation. A month later, in a written answer,[190] the Government stated that the future of Harlands was heavily dependent on whether the builders, the Government and Tikkoo Cruise Line could come to mutual agreement as to whether the *Ultimate Dream* could be economically built in Belfast; the Government has received preliminary costings and were making their own assessment to consider whether and to what extent they might provide contract support; Mr Tikkoo had also expressed interest in taking over Harlands and this privatisation proposal would be considered in the context of the Government's assessment of the *Ultimate Dream* project.

Shortly before Parliament adjourned for the 1988 summer recess, in the course of a debate on the Northern Ireland economy,[191] there was a plea for

185. P. Debs. 6 Ser., Vol. 106, c.(161). 4460 employees were made redundant between 1st January 1979 and 31st December 1986.

186. P. Debs. 6 Ser., Vol. 120, c.469.

187. P. Debs. 6 Ser., Vol. 123, c.885–886. This additional support was said to be necessary because the yard's facilities were best suited to larger ships but that, owing to Far East competition, H & W had had to turn to smaller and more sophisticated ships.

188. The maximum allowed under the EEC Sixth Directive—see fns 155 and 156 *supra*.

189. See P. Debs. 6 Ser., Vol. 134, c.633.

190. P. Debs. 6 Ser., Vol. 136, c.(339).

191. *Ibid.*, Vol. 138, c.605.

Harlands to remain in the public sector but in reply the Secretary of State said that the yard's future depended on getting orders and that privatisation was the right way to proceed; in a written answer[192] Mr King added that the Government had appointed merchant bankers to advise on possible privatisation, that discussion had taken place with Tikkoo Cruise Line and that a number of other parties had also expressed initial interest. However, when the Commons reassembled on 19th October, Mr King announced that the privatisation talks with Mr Tikkoo had collapsed, that his plans to build the cruise liner had likewise been abandoned but that active privatisation negotiations with other parties were still taking place.[193] It was also mentioned that Mr John Parker, the Chairman of Harlands, had put forward a management/employee buy-out proposal and in mid-November it was reported[194] that the Sealink shipping group had invited Harlands to tender for the building of five ferries but that any order for these ships was subject to clarification of the Government's position on the ownership of the yard and to the provision of the standard level of subsidy from the intervention fund.

At the end of 1988 and during the early months of 1989 there were indications of positive progress in the negotiations for the privatisation of Harlands[195] and eventually, at the end of March, the Secretary of State informed the House[196] that the Government had approved the sale of Harland & Wolff to Mr Parker's management/employee buy-out (MEBO) team supported by Mr Fred Olsen, the prominent Norwegian shipowner. Mr King explained that the MEBO team and Mr Olsen would subscribe for the £15 million share capital of a new company which would acquire the assets and undertaking of Harland & Wolff for £6 million net book value and that the Government would advance to the new company £60 million of loan stock and provide grant assistance of £38.75 million towards the cost of rationalising the activities of the yard; the new company would complete the vessel ordered by BP and the AOR vessel for the Ministry of Defence and Mr Olsen had agreed to order three tankers of about 150,000 d.w.t. each which would provide work for the yard up to the end of 1992.[197]

The sale was (*inter alia*) subject to the approval of the EEC and the Norwegian government and was also dependent on the support of Harland's employees but shortly before the 1989 summer recess the Northern Ireland

192. *Ibid.*, Vol. 138, c.(561).

193. See *The Times*, 20th October and 8th November 1988.

194. See *The Sunday Times*, 13th November 1988.

195. P. Debs. 6 Ser., Vol. 144 c.(450) and c.(752), Vol.146, c.1124 and Vol.148, c.981.

196. P. Debs. 6 Ser., Vol. 149, c.1089. See also Third Report of the Trade & Industry Committee (1988–89, HCP 131) and Government Response (HCP 353).

197. The Government had agreed to give intervention aid, within EEC permitted limits, towards the cost of these tankers and Mr Olsen and the Government were equally to support the pre-delivery financing—see P. Debs. 6 Ser., Vol. 152, c.(509) and Vol.153, c.(141). Existing liabilities of Harland & Wolff were to remain with the old company.

Industry Minister stated in a written answer[198] that EEC approval was expected at the beginning of August and that, subject to the satisfactory conclusion of other pre-contract conditions, it was hoped to complete the sale in September. It therefore seems probable that, after some 14 years under State ownership involving considerable cost to public funds,[199] the future of merchant shipbuilding in Belfast will once again rest with the newly privatised Harland & Wolff.

The Accounts of British Shipbuilders for 1987–88[200] showed a trading loss, after crediting £32 million from the intervention fund, of £110 million,[201] a total loss for the year of £259 million[202] and an accumulated loss at 31st March 1988 of £1,604 million. The Chairman (*inter alia*) reported the return to the private sector of the Govan and Appledore shipyards and the marine engineering works at Greenock, the impending closure of the NESL yards at Sunderland and the negotiations for the sale of the Ferguson yard at Port Glasgow. As regards employment, he also reported that during the year ended 31st March 1989 the numbers employed had fallen from 6,290 to 993 but added that 2,390 jobs had been saved in the disposal of subsidiaries and that at the end of April 1989 895 jobs had been found for employees made redundant at NESL.

So, as 1989 drew towards its close, substantially all the remaining merchant yards in the United Kingdom were back in private hands and British Shipbuilders was nearing the end of its short and unprofitable life.[203] In July 1988 the Government had expressed the hope that, as a result of the British Shipbuilders disposals, Britain would have a merchant shipbuilding industry with a promising future into the 1990s and beyond.[204] The Falklands campaign had been a salutary reminder that, from a strategic viewpoint, there could be no denying the necessity for a technologically advanced home naval and merchant shipbuilding industry able to supply replacements and effect repairs but, on commercial grounds as well, the continuation of merchant shipbuilding in the U.K. is surely needed to ensure that British shipowners do not become entirely dependent on foreign shipbuilders for their new tonnage. Having spent so

198. P. Debs. 6 Ser., Vol. 157, c.(357).

199. Between 1975 and 1989 Harlands received around £450 million from public funds. There will be further substantial Government expenditure in connection with the yard's return to the private sector.

200. Published in May 1989 because it was decided that the Accounts should be prepared on a closure basis and that the completion of the Accounts should be delayed so that the effect of closure could be assessed.

201. There was a loss of £42 million arising from the cancellation of the Danish Ferries contract and a loss of £38 million from under utilised labour and under-recovered overhead costs.

202. Including an extra-ordinary item of £136 million reflecting the estimated costs of disposal and closure of subsidiaries and closure of Head Office.

203. Since 1979 BS had cost the taxpayer some £2 billion.

204. See Kenneth Clarke's speech on 21st July 1988—P. Debs. 6 Ser., Vol. 137, c.1377.

much to maintain a nationalised industry, it is difficult to conceive that in the future the Government will deny to the privatised industry such support as may be needed to ensure that the U.K. maintains an adequate capability for the building of both naval and merchant ships.

Although the uncertainty about the future of merchant shipbuilding in the U.K. was worry enough, at the beginning of the 1986–87 Parliamentary session there was even more concern at the Government's apparent failure to recognise the seriousness of the continuing decline in the U.K. merchant fleet; at 30th November 1986 the deadweight tonnage of the U.K. owned and registered fleet (500 g.r.t. and over) had fallen to 10.1 million,[205] a decline of 6.5 million d.w.t. since June 1985, but the GCBS estimated that 4.1 million d.w.t. of shipping controlled by U.K. companies was registered in British overseas territories and that 2.5 million d.w.t. of shipping similarly controlled was registered in foreign countries.[206] In a written reply to questions from Du Cann[207] the Prime Minister again affirmed that there were sufficient vessels to meet MoD requirements but that requirements for civil supply had to be viewed in NATO terms and had to take into account the overall NATO demand and supply including overseas registered shipping beneficially owned in NATO countries. However the Prime Minister added that in 1985 the total tonnage of the merchant fleets of NATO members had fallen by 30.7 million d.w.t. and that the NATO Planning Board for Ocean Shipping had drawn the attention of the North Atlantic Council to the implications for the Alliance of this trend.

There was no less concern at the serious decline in the numbers of British seafarers; in 1985 the total for officers, ratings and cadets had been around 34,600[208] but by November 1986 the total had fallen substantially to around 27,500.[209] In December 1986 the Government were asked what steps were being taken to ensure the availability of adequate manpower on British merchant vessels in time of war or emergency and in a written reply[210] the Secretary of State for Transport, John Moore, stated that he was consulting shipowners' and seafarers' representatives about ways in which the Government might help with training and with the costs of transporting crews to and from vessels

205. Including 3 million d.w.t. registered in the Isle of Man and Channel Islands.

206. See *British Shipping Review 1987* Figure A which also shows the decline of the fleet since 1975.

207. P. Debs. 6 Ser., Vol. 106, c.(158).

208. Cmnd. 9763, Vol. 2, Table 1.4.

209. P. Debs. 6 Ser., Vol. 106, c.(589). The breakdown of the figures was as follows:

	November 1986	*1985 (Cmnd 9763)*
Officers	11,637	15,023
Ratings	15,225	18,595
Cadets	668	1,016
	27,530	34,634

210. P. Debs. 6 Ser., Vol. 107, c.(156).

operating away from the U.K. and that these measures should contribute to the retention of British nationals on board British vessels. The Minister added that in an emergency it might be necessary to replace foreign seafarers on some ships with U.K. nationals and that to facilitate this the Government proposed to create a Merchant Navy Reserve of trained personnel willing to return to sea if needed.[211]

Another significant event in the autumn of 1986 was the decision of the Commons Transport Committee to make a detailed Inquiry into the Decline in the U.K. Registered Merchant Fleet. The Committee's terms of reference included the increase of "flagging out", protectionism and fiscal incentives offered to shipowners, the international competitiveness of the U.K. fleet and ports and cabotage but, although the Committee took a substantial amount of oral and written evidence,[212] it was prevented from taking further evidence by the dissolution of Parliament in May 1987 and was unable to make a full report. However in its Interim Report[213] the Committee gave statistics for the U.K. and world merchant fleets over the period 1960–86[214] and stated that the decline of the U.K. fleet had reached a point where there was deep concern over the prospects for the fleet's continued existence as a major international trading fleet; the Committee stressed the question of decline was of great importance and recommended their successor Committee to take up the inquiry and pursue it as a matter of urgency.

In February 1987 much of the annual debate on the Royal Navy[215] was devoted to the problems of the merchant navy and from both sides of the House the view was expressed that the Government's proposals for assisting with training and repatriation costs, although welcome, would not be enough to halt, still less reverse, the decline in the U.K. registered tonnage. As in previous debates Government spokesmen concentrated on the defence aspects and paid little regard to the economic argument, the undesirability of a trading nation being largely dependent on foreign shipping,[216] and the need for a more favourable fiscal regime, such as that enjoyed before 1984, to encourage British owners to invest in new or second-hand tonnage. Doubts were also expressed as to whether ships registered under foreign flags but indirectly beneficially owned by U.K. interests could legally be requisitioned in an emergency and in reply it was stated that the Government were having discussions on this subject with three major open registry states.

211. Further details of these proposals were given in a speech by the Minister to the GCBS on 10th December 1986—see Cm. 239 (Annex A), Parl. Papers 1987–88.

212. Including detailed Memoranda and oral evidence from GCBS, the British Maritime League and the Department of Transport.

213. Parl. Papers 1986–87, HC 94, i-xii.

214. Interim Report, Table 1.

215. P. Debs. 6 Ser., Vol. 109, c.701.

216. It was pointed out that the volume of UK seaborne trade had grown by 20 per cent in the past decade but that the UK flag share had fallen from more than 33 per cent to less than 25 per cent.

Another matter which came to the fore in the early months of 1987 was the light dues imposed on merchant shipping entering U.K. ports to fund the cost of lighthouses, navigational markers and buoys. For well over a hundred years shipowners had been contending that this was a burden which should be borne by the Exchequer but successive Governments had remained unmoved in spite of the fact that Select Committees in 1860 and 1902 and the Committee on Shipping and Shipbuilding in 1918 had all recommended that light dues should be abolished. Since the Prime Minister had indicated that the Government were working to reduce the burden of costs borne by U.K. owners,[217] the GCBS hoped that light dues were one expense which could at last be removed but instead it was announced in a written answer[218] that in 1987–88 light dues were to be increased by just under 14 per cent in order to bring revenue into line with current operating costs. In April 1987, when the Lords debated[219] the Regulations giving effect to the increase[220] it was pointed out that no other North European countries except Sweden and Ireland imposed this burden on shipping and that light dues deterred shipowners from using British ports[221]; in reply the Shipping Minister stated that there was no prospect of transferring the cost to the Exchequer, that the Government thought it right that the cost should be borne by the user but that the Government hoped to achieve a major cost reduction in lighthouse services. Subsequently, in November 1988,[222] the Minister of Transport stated that in April 1989 he hoped to implement the changes in the Light Dues Regulations recommended by a working party and would at the same time introduce a general reduction in light dues—but that the costs would still have to be borne by the users. Then in February 1989 the Minister announced[223] that the reduction in costs achieved by the lighthouse authorities would permit an overall reduction of just over 10 per cent in the light dues to be collected in 1989–90 and that in real terms light dues would then be 40 per cent lower than eight years previously.

In April 1987, shortly prior to the dissolution of Parliament, there was further questioning in the Commons regarding the Governments shipping policy[224]; reference was made to the GCBS forecast that by 1995 the U.K. fleet might be reduced to only 100 ships[225] but the Government made it clear that

217. P. Debs. 6 Ser., Vol. 99, c.(286).
218. *Ibid.*, Vol. 109, c.(663).
219. P. Debs. (HL) 5 Ser., Vol. 486, c.1205.
220. Merchant Shipping (Light Dues) (Amendment) Regulations 1987 (SI 1987 No 244) which as from 1st April 1987 increased the amount of dues payable under the Merchant Shipping (Light Dues) Regulations 1981 (SI 1981 No. 354). Later in 1987 the 1981 Regulations were as from 1st June 1987 further amended by the Merchant Shipping (Light Dues) (Amendment No 2) Regulations 1987 (SI 1987 No. 746).
221. The cost of providing the lighthouse services in 1987–88 was expected to be £60 million.
222. P. Debs. 6 Ser., Vol. 140, c.671.
223. *Ibid.*, Vol. 147, c.(557).
224. P. Debs. 6 Ser., Vol. 114, c.2.
225. *British Shipping Review 1987*.

the measures announced in December 1986 were considered adequate and that there was little hope of an improved tax regime. In the Lords the Government were also questioned as to what action was being taken on the NATO Report of the decline in the Western merchant fleet[226] and in reply the Government stated that it was hoped that the creation of a Merchant Navy Reserve and assistance with training and repatriation costs would encourage owners to keep their ships on the U.K. register. The Government added that the NATO suggestion for creating a strategic merchant navy reserve of ships was under consideration but would be costly and, when asked if there should not be concern on economic as well as national grounds about the collapse of the merchant navy, the reply given was that flagging out was mainly to obtain cheaper crew costs and that it would be expensive to subsidise these costs in order to keep ships on the U.K. register.

Before the dissolution of Parliament there was also a further reminder of the strategic importance of the merchant navy in a Defence Committee Report on Implementing the Lessons of the Falkland Campaign.[227] The Report stressed the need for more peacetime liaison between the Merchant and Royal Navies, reiterated that the merchant navy represented an essential element of the U.K.'s defence capability and stated that in a war within the NATO area its role would be even more significant than in the Falklands campaign. In its Response to the Report[228] the Government acknowledged the vital role played by the merchant navy in the Falklands, recognised the need for good liaison between the Merchant and Royal Navies and reaffirmed that the use of merchant shipping for military purposes in an emergency had long been an essential part of defence planning.

Following the general election of June 1987, a notable event at the opening of the new Parliament was the statement in the Queen's Speech[229] that measures would be introduced to assist the merchant shipping industry. It was not until the autumn that the long-awaited Merchant Shipping Bill was published and introduced into the Lords but in the meantime, prior to the summer recess, the continuing decline in the U.K. registered fleet gave rise to further questions in the Commons and a full scale debate in the Lords.

When questioned in the Commons as to the adequacy of merchant ships to fulfil their defence role[230] the Shipping Minister, in a written reply, gave figures for the ships on the U.K. register (including Isle of Man and Channel Islands) which, together with the unspecified number of ships registered in the Dependent Territories, would be available for use in war and added that the availability of shipping for defence purposes was closely monitored and (rather

226. P. Debs. (HL) 5 Ser., Vol. 486, c.689.
227. Fourth Report of the Defence Committee 1986–87, HCP 345-I.
228. Cm. 228 (published in October 1987).
229. P. Debs. 6 Ser., Vol. 118, c.38.
230. P. Debs. 6 Ser., Vol. 118, c.(123).

cryptically) that a number of initiatives were being taken to help to ensure the future adequacy of these resources.[231] The Government were also asked what plans they had to arrest the annual decline of the merchant fleet[232] and in another written reply the Minister said that the Government's interest was twofold: first to ensure adequate merchant shipping resources to meet the country's needs in emergency or war to which end the new measures were aimed at encouraging the retention of British seafarers on British owned vessels: secondly to help the competitive position of the U.K. fleet for which purpose initiatives had been taken at EEC and wider international levels to provide an improved access to trading opportunities. As regards the EEC failure to agree on the liberalisation of its cabotage trade, the Prime Minister, in a written answer,[233] stated that the Secretary of State was considering options for redressing the present imbalance of access to cabotage markets including mounting a case in the European Court of Justice; she added that it was patently unfair that some European governments should be able to reserve their cabotage trade to domestic operators[234] when other governments like the U.K. operated an open cabotage market.

In July, at the opening of a Lords debate on the state of the mercantile marine,[235] it was stated by an Opposition peer that trading tonnage (ships in excess of 500 g.r.t.) beneficially owned by British interests amounted to some 18 million d.w.t. of which only 6 million d.w.t. was registered in mainland Britain whilst the remainder was registered in the Isle of Man, the Channel Islands, British Dependent Territories and foreign countries.[236] Lord Geddes, a leading shipowner, welcomed the proposals in the new Merchant Shipping Bill but added that they did not really start to address the problem; what was needed to halt the decline were two tax changes—sale proceeds to be tax free if reinvested in shipping and a 50 per cent first-year ship allowance for investment in new or second-hand tonnage. Other speakers sought a restoration of the pre-1984 tax concession for seamen and cast doubts on the practical validity of the statement in the 1987 Defence Estimates[237] that it would be possible by legislation to extend the power of requisitioning to ships on foreign

231. This may have been a reference to the negotiations with open registry states with regard to requisitioning.

232. P. Debs. 6 Ser., Vol. 119, c.(181).

233. *Ibid.*, Vol. 120, c.(355).

234. As Britain had done for some 300 years up to 1854!

235. P. Debs. (HL) 5 Ser., Vol. 488, c.1072.

236. These were not official figures and some doubted their accuracy.

237. Parl. Papers 1986–87, Cm. 101 published on 6th May 1987 just before the dissolution of Parliament. The figures in Table 1.3 of Volume 2 of the 1987 Defence Estimates for ships on the U.K. and Dependent Territories registers were severely criticised by the British Maritime League in its 1987 Annual Report as being misleading, out of date and giving a false sense of security.

registers which were beneficially owned by British operators.[238] In replying to the debate Lord Brabazon, the Shipping Minister, said that the Government had no control over the principal causes of decline—massive imbalance between supply and demand resulting in severely depressed charter rates, increased competition from Third World countries with lower crew costs and changes in trading patterns[239]—and that, whilst the Government did not encourage flagging out, the alternative of getting out of tanker and bulk carrier trades was even less attractive. It was Government policy to break down trade barriers and promote fair competition, to accelerate the second stage of the EEC Common Shipping Policy which was to harmonise Community aids and strengthen the position of the Community shipping industry and to work to open European closed cabotage trades.

The Merchant Shipping Bill[240] was published in late October 1987 and was accompanied by a White Paper[241] describing the legislative proposals in the Bill. In order to ensure that strategic requirements for shipping and for trained seafarers could be met, the Bill provided for financial assistance (of an unspecified amount) for the training of cadets and the cost of flying out crews to ships operating in distant waters[242] and also for the establishment of a Merchant Navy Reserve (MNR)[243]; it was hoped that these measures would help to reverse the decline in the number of officer cadets undergoing training, make it more attractive for shipowners to employ British officers and ratings and help to ensure adequate future availability of merchant seamen to meet the U.K.'s commercial and defence needs in time of emergency. To enable the Government[244] to take more effective action again unfair competition in international shipping services from other countries, the Bill strengthened the powers already available for this purpose under Part III and Schedule 4 of the Merchant Shipping Act 1974 as amended by the Merchant Shipping Act

238. Owing to the dissolution of Parliament there was no Report by the Commons Select Committee on Defence on the 1987 Defence Estimates. However in a defence debate on 27 October 1987 (P. Debs. 6 Ser., Vol. 121, c.205) the Minister winding up the debate reiterated (c.271) that under prerogative powers the Government could requisition ships on the Dependent Territories registers as well as the on U.K. register and that emergency legislation would enable the Government to requisition ships on foreign registers if such ships were beneficially owned by British operators. He added that, in spite of the decline in the British merchant fleet, the Government were confident that defence needs could still be met.

239. Such as the switch to the European Community as our major trading area and the reduction in long-haul oil cargoes.

240. HL Bill 22.

241. Cm. 239, Parl. Papers 1987–88.

242. I.e. outside the Limited European Trading Area (roughly from Bergen to Cadiz).

243. The intention was that the MNR should be a body of qualified and experienced seafarers who could be called upon to crew merchant vessels in time of tension or war.

244. Together with other Member States of the European Community if co-ordinated action was required under the EC Regulations agreed in December 1986—see p. 302 *supra*.

1979[245] and, with a view to reducing the costs burden of light dues, the Bill made a number of changes in the legislation dealing with the administration of lighthouses. The Bill also made radical changes in the law relating to ship registration in the U.K.,[246] introduced new arrangements for ship registration in the Dependent Territories[247] and reformed the law on the registration of fishing vessels.[248] Lastly the Bill introduced a number of new provisions relating to safety of navigation,[249] pollution of the sea, investigation of marine accidents and inquiries into the fitness or conduct of officers.

The Bill had its Second Reading in the Lords on 10th November 1987[250] and in opening the debate the Shipping Minister stated that he hoped that the schemes for training and crew relief costs would commence as early as possible in the financial year 1988–89 and gave details of the financial provisions that had been made[251]; he also explained that the new Merchant Navy Reserve would plan to recruit former seafarers who had taken up shore-based jobs. The provisions in the Bill for training, crew relief costs and the establishment of a Merchant Navy Reserve were generally welcomed from both sides of the House but it was likewise the general view that these measures would not amount to very much in alleviating the problems of the British shipping industry. For the Opposition Lord Underhill said that the officers' union felt there was nothing in the Bill that would reverse or even arrest the disastrous decline in the British merchant fleet and, whilst approving the extension of the Government retaliatory powers, he wished to know what action was being taken on the cabotage problems in a number of Community countries. Lord Simon, a leading shipowner, referred to the new Merchant Navy Reserve and suggested it was perhaps even more necessary to ensure that, in an emergency, we had sufficient merchant vessels for these reservists to man; it was far more important to increase the size of the fleet than to provide a reserve of crews for ships that did not exist.

Other speakers, from both Government and Opposition benches, gave thanks

245. See pp. 275–277 *supra*. Amongst other things Clause 36 of the Bill extended the retaliatory powers to the carriage of passengers. During the Lords' Report stage the scope of the Clause was further enlarged so as to enable retaliatory action to be taken in relation to any services provided by means of ships—i.e. not only, as the 1974 Act and the Bill had provided, to services related to the carriage of cargo and passengers.

246. Substantial amendments were to be made to Part I of the Merchant Shipping Act 1894. Registration under the British flag of a ship owned by qualified individuals or companies would no longer be mandatory.

247. Designed to improve the safety standards of ships registered in the Dependent Territories.

248. Particularly to prevent foreign owned (mainly Spanish) fishing vessels being registered in the U.K. and fishing against U.K. quotas. See further pp. 340 *et seq. infra*.

249. Some of these were recommendations made in the Report of the Investigation into the loss of the *Herald of Free Enterprise*.

250. P. Debs. (HL) 5 Ser., Vol. 489, c.1292.

251. £2.5 million for training and £3.5 million crew relief costs in 1988–89 rising to £3.5 million and £5 million respectively in 1989–90.

for the small mercies in the Bill but were strongly of the view that further Government action was necessary to tackle the problem of world over-tonnaging, possibly by giving financial incentives to encourage scrapping, and to persuade British owners to refrain from further flagging out by removing the existing fiscal and other disincentives to registration under the U.K. flag. Lord Strathcona, a member of the Council of the British Maritime League, put to the Minister the straight question—"how dedicated are the Government to maintaining a viable merchant shipping industry?"—but in replying to the debate Lord Brabazon added little to what he had said in the July debate on the state of the mercantile marine.[252] Whilst reaffirming the Government's whole-hearted commitment to the promotion of free trade, the Minister firmly rejected any kind of subsidy but said that the Government would continue to reduce the burden of unnecessary maritime regulation of the industry. He added that he was not convinced by the argument that there was no incentive to build for operation under the British flag; he believed that the reducing burden of taxation and the greater willingness of the seafaring unions to negotiate realistically meant that British owners would be able to compete in many trades with British registered ships. The Minister also mentioned the possibility of going to the European Court of Justice to challenge the closed cabotage regimes of a number of Community States and felt that this course was preferable to the alternative of closing U.K. coasts to those whose coasts were closed against British ships.

The Bill was considered by the Lords in Committee on 24th and 26th November and on Report on 14th December 1987[253]; a large number of amendments were made but these were mostly of a technical or drafting nature and were in many cases proposed by the Government. However substantial and noteworthy amendments, proposed by the Government, were made to Clauses 3 and 4 of the Bill[254] which defined the persons qualified to be owners of British ships and set out the conditions to be fulfilled for the purpose of determining whether a ship was entitled to be registered under Part I of the 1894 Act in the United Kingdom. Under the Bill as originally drafted, Commonwealth companies and citizens were no longer qualified, as they had been under the 1894 Act, to place a ship directly on the U.K. register[255] since the Bill limited "qualified persons" to U.K. and Dependent Territory companies and citizens; in order to temper this restriction the Government amendments[256] removed the requirement for a ship to be wholly owned by qualified persons and instead provided for non-qualified persons (Commonwealth or foreign companies or citizens) to own a minority of shares in a U.K. registered ship but only if a majority of shares in the ship (i.e. at

252. P. Debs. (HL) 5 Ser., Vol. 488, cc.1098–1105—see pp. 322–323 *supra*.
253. P. Debs. (HL) 5 Ser., Vol. 490 cc.540 and 744 and Vol. 491, c.437.
254. With consequential amendments in other parts of the Bill.
255. Although they could still do so indirectly by forming a U.K. subsidiary which could then be registered as the owner.
256. Which the Minister stated satisfied the wishes of the GCBS.

least 33 shares out of 64) were owned by qualified persons. The House agreed the amendments without demur and there was no mention by the Minister or anyone else that to allow a foreigner to have a direct share in a British ship was making a radical change in a principle of English law which had for centuries been regarded as sacrosanct.

The Navigation Act 1660 had defined English ships as such ships "as do truly and without fraud belong only to the People of England or Ireland, Dominion of Wales or Town of Berwick on Tweed" and the Registration Acts 1786 to 1845 had all provided that a British ship had to be wholly owned by a British subject and that the owner had to swear not only that he was "truly and bona fide a subject of Great Britain" but also that no foreigner had any interest in the ship. Following the repeal of the Navigation Laws, the Merchant Shipping Acts 1854 and 1894 retained this principle of exclusivity and provided that a ship only qualified as a British ship if she was owned wholly by British subjects or bodies corporate established under and subject to the laws of some part of Her Majesty's Dominions and having their principal place of business in those Dominions; the 1854 and 1894 Acts also provided that the owner must declare that no unqualified person or body of persons was entitled as owner to any legal or beneficial interest in the ship or any share therein.[257]

It remains to be seen whether this right for a foreigner to own directly a minority of the shares in a U.K. registered ship may in the future create difficulty in relation to the requisitioning of ships under the Royal Prerogative since this power is founded upon a British subject's duty of allegiance to the Crown and hitherto it has been the governing principle in all the legislation that it is not consistent with public policy to allow persons who owe no allegiance to the Crown to directly own any share in a British ship.[258] During the Bill's Third Reading in the Lords,[259] Lord Brabazon, in his winding-up speech shortly before the Bill was passed, made a brief reference to the useful flexibility which would be provided by the amendments allowing foreign interests to hold minority shares in British ships[260] but when, on 28th January 1988,

257. Section 17 of the Status of Aliens Act 1914 also provides that an alien (i.e. anyone who is not a British subject) is not qualified to be the owner of a British ship. Perhaps surprisingly, this provision was not repealed by the Merchant Shipping Act 1988 because the Department of Transport took the view that Section 17 of the Aliens Act only prohibits an alien from being the sole owner of a British ship and does not disqualify an alien from owning a minority interest in a British ship.

258. The Minister did not explain in detail the need for these far-reaching amendments to the Bill. It is clear that under the 1894 Act and the Bill as originally drafted a foreign company could establish a subsidiary in the U.K. and that ships owned by that subsidiary could be entered on the U.K. register provided the subsidiary had its principal place of business in the U.K..

259. On 11th January 1988—P. Debs. (HL) 5 Ser., Vol. 491, c.925.

260. It is understood that these amendments were made at the request of the GCBS to make possible a particular joint venture project which, partly for tax reasons, necessitated the joint owners of a ship (British, Australian and foreign) being directly registered in the U.K. However the Department of Transport believes that this new right for a foreigner to have a direct minority interest in a British ship will also facilitate other EEC and Commonwealth joint ventures.

the Bill had its Second Reading in the Commons,[261] there was no reference by Ministers or any other speaker to the radical change which these Government amendments would make to Britain's long-established defence policy designed to ensure that British ships, being wholly owned by British subjects, would, in an emergency, be immediately available for service under the Crown.[262]

In other respects the non-ministerial speeches from both sides of the House during the Commons debate on the Bill's Second Reading were notable for the unanimity of the view that, apart from the modest measures to assist in the training of officer cadets and the repatriation of crews and to set up a Merchant Navy Reserve of seamen, the Bill failed to tackle the real problem of the decline in the British merchant fleet. Figures were quoted, and not challenged, to show that the U.K. registered fleet had, by the end of 1987, fallen to around 6 million tonnes deadweight and that, even taking into account the ships on the registers of the Isle of Man, Channel Islands and the British Dependent Territories together with the ships, beneficially British-owned, flagged out to foreign registries, the total was still only about 17 million tonnes deadweight.[263] Requests were made for fiscal measures to encourage the ordering of new ships by British owners, incentives for the scrapping of old tonnage, action to assist British coastal shipping having regard to the cabotage policies of some Community countries, assistance on running costs particularly in relation to British crews, the creation of a strategic reserve of merchant ships[264] and assurances that the merchant fleet was still adequate for all the needs of an emergency[265] and that in a crisis it would be practically possible to obtain the use of U.K. owned ships registered under foreign flags.[266] In

261. P. Debs. 6 Ser., Vol. 126, c.504.

262. As indeed happened as recently as 1982 when the Falklands Task Force was assembled. It is understood that the Department of Transport do not foresee any difficulty in requisitioning ships in which foreigners are part owners since the controlling interest would have to be owned by British subjects and there would also be a British master, chief officer and first engineer.

263. The figures given by GCBS in their *Shipping Facts 1988* for the U.K. owned trading fleet (500 g.r.t. and above) at the end of 1987 were slightly different—namely:

Register	*No.*	*m. d.w.t.*
Mainland U.K.	386	6.0
Crown Dependencies*	77	3.5
Dependent Territories**	99	6.3
Foreign	93	1.8
Total	655	17.6

* Isle of Man and Channel Islands

** Mainly Bermuda, Cayman Islands, Gibraltar and Hong Kong.

264. This had been proposed by the Government just prior to the Second World War in Clause 6 of the British Shipping (Assistance) Bill 1939—see p. 135 *supra*.

265. In his winding up speech the Minister indicated that a question to the Ministry of Defence would receive a satisfactory answer.

266. In the course of a defence debate on 27th October 1987 (P. Debs. 6 Ser., Vol. 121, c.271) a Junior Defence Minister had stated that emergency legislation would enable the Government to requisition ships on foreign registers if they were beneficially owned by British operators. He added that, despite the decline in the British merchant fleet, the Government were confident that defence needs could still be met.

replying to the debate the Minister for Public Transport, David Mitchell, gave an assurance that the points made in the debate would be drawn to the attention of the Chancellor of the Exchequer and said that there were now grounds for hoping that the cabotage problem could be solved; otherwise the Minister gave no indication that the Government were intending to take any further action to stem the continuing decline in the British merchant fleet.

During the Commons Committee and Report stages of the Bill some progress was made towards dealing with the cabotage problem. At the Seventh Sitting of the Standing Committee on 3rd March 1988 Sir David Price, a former Minister having considerable shipping expertise, proposed a new Clause under which restrictions would be placed on access to the U.K. coasting trade for ships registered under the flags of those members of the European Community who excluded British ships from their coasting trades. The Minister for Public Transport agreed that the time had come for legislative action to correct the imbalance and undertook to bring forward on Report a new Clause giving the Secretary of State power to introduce a test of establishment for shipping companies wishing to engage in the U.K. cabotage trade. On Report[267] the Secretary of State proposed a new Clause giving him an enabling power to prohibit the provision of coastal shipping services unless such services were to be provided from a permanent place of business in the British Isles but at the same time he emphasised that the Government's primary objective on cabotage remained liberalisation throughout the European Community.[268]

The Merchant Shipping Act 1988 received the Royal Assent on 3rd May 1988[269] and on the same day there was published a Scheme for Department of Transport Assistance for Merchant Navy Officer Training.[270] The objectives of the scheme, which was to give effect to Section 26 of the Act, were first to increase the number of officers being trained and secondly to build on and develop existing training arrangements and the use already being made by the industry of Government assistance under the Youth Training Scheme; the new scheme was to be managed by the GCBS and the budget was to be £2.5 million

267. P. Debs. 6 Ser., Vol. 130, c.1164.

268. The new Clause, together with another new Clause providing for enforcement, were approved by the Commons and the Lords without a division and became Sections 39 and 40 of the Act. In 1986 the value of the U.K. cabotage market was estimated to be £440 million (of which U.K. shipping had some 72 per cent) whilst the total cabotage market of the European Community was estimated at £1,450 million.

269. The Act was not to come into force until a Commencement Order was made under Section 58(2) or, in the case of Part II of the Act (dealing with the registration of fishing vessels), on the coming into force of the first regulations under Section 13 making provision for the new system of registration. By 1st April 1989 almost the whole Act had been brought into force as a result of three Commencement Orders (SIs 88/1010, 88/1907 and 89/353) and the coming into force of the Merchant Shipping (Registration of Fishing Vessels) Regulations 1988 (SI 88/1926).

270. See P. Debs. 6 Ser., Vol. 132, c.(410).

for 1988–89 and £3.5 million for 1989–90. Then, shortly before the summer recess, the Secretary of State announced[271] details of the scheme, under Section 27 of the Act, for Department of Transport assistance with crew relief costs; with the object of making it more attractive to employ British crews, as from 1st September 1988 ship operators would be reimbursed half the cost of flying out and repatriating crews of U.K., Isle of Man and Channel Islands ships operating outside the European trading area provided such crews were ordinarily resident in the U.K., Isle of Man, Channel Islands or Irish Republic. However, the Government has not yet exercised the power in Section 39 to prohibit the provision of coastal shipping services which are not British based and is instead continuing with its diplomatic effort for the full liberalisation of cabotage in all European Community countries.[272]

Although the provisions in the 1988 Act for assistance with training and crew relief costs and for the establishment of a Merchant Navy Reserve were a welcome indication that the Government accepted the need for some action towards stemming the decline in ships and men, considerable doubt was felt, both within and outside Parliament, as to whether these relatively modest measures would be sufficient. There was concern that the Government's mind was too much concentrated only on the strategic need for merchant shipping in war or an emergency; in a Memorandum submitted to the Transport Committee in February 1987[273] the Department of Transport had expressed the view that any case for assistance to the shipping industry must be strategic since it had no compelling economic basis but in their evidence to the same Committee both the GCBS and the British Maritime League were strongly of the opinion that on economic grounds alone an island trading nation such as Britain needed a strong and profitable merchant shipping industry.[274] In the event 1988 proved to be a year in which exceptional pressure from many different sources continued to be put on the Government to take further positive steps to reverse the decline of the U.K. merchant marine.

At the beginning of December 1987, whilst the Lords were considering the Merchant Shipping Bill in Committee, the composition of the new Commons Select Committee on Transport was at last approved.[275] In accordance with

271. P. Debs. 6 Ser., Vol. 138, c.(251).

272. In reply to a question on 13th March 1989 (P. Debs 6 Ser., Vol. 149, c.6) the Minister of Transport said that the primary objective remained liberalisation through a binding Community Regulation but that he would certainly use his powers under Section 39 in the last resort. The cabotage problem was due to be discussed at the EEC Transport Council in June 1989.

273. Parl. Papers 1986–87, HC 94, i-xii.

274. See also the British Maritime Charitable Foundation's publication *The Merchant Fleet and Britain's Economy* (1988) in which the conclusion is reached that the continuing decline of the U.K. shipping industry is a matter of real concern to the U.K. economy.

275. P. Debs. 6 Ser., Vol. 123, c.1039. There had been considerable delay in reconstituting all the Commons' Select Committees.

the recommendation made by their predecessors, the new Committee decided to continue the Inquiry into the Decline of the U.K. merchant fleet and in this connection to have particular regard to the view of the 1986–87 Committee[276] that central to such inquiry "must be the question whether the U.K. needs a merchant fleet and, if so, whether the U.K. Government should provide support for the shipping industry beyond that which it provides for other industries". The new Committee took a considerable amount of further evidence, both oral and written, and published their Report on 21st June 1988.[277]

The Report (Section II) first dealt with the statistics of the decline in the U.K. registered merchant fleet (ships of 500 g.r.t. and over) which showed (*inter alia*) a fall in deadweight tonnage from 51.9 million at the end of 1975 to 11.2 million at the end of 1986, a reduction in the U.K. proportion of world tonnage from 9.7 per cent at mid-1975 to 1.8 per cent at mid-1987,[278] the increasing age of the U.K. fleet and a fall in the number of seafarers (officers and ratings) employed in U.K. registered ships from 73,400 in 1975 to 23,800 in March 1988. In Section III of their Report the Committee examined the reasons for the decline which they attributed partly to international influences, such as changes in world demand for shipping,[279] changes in trade patterns, technological advances and world over-capacity.[280] After dealing with certain safety matters,[281], Section V of the Report posed the question "Does the Decline Matter?"; after noting, and agreeing with, the Department of Transport's view that, for strategic reasons,[282] there was a continuing need for a substantial British merchant marine to meet defence and civil resupply purposes, the Committee went on to state that, unlike the Department of Transport, they believed that there were economic arguments for maintaining a U.K. registered fleet—for example the impact on trade, the danger of being largely dependent on others to move U.K. imports and exports, shipping's contribution to the U.K. balance of payments, employment in shipping and ancillary industries and loss of international influence. The Committee also gave figures of the "flagging out" of the U.K. owned trading fleet (ships of 500 g.r.t.

276. See their Interim Report, Parl. Papers 1986–87, HC 94.

277. Parl. Papers 1987–88, HCP 303.

278. In relation to other large fleets the U.K. fleet had fallen from first place (21.3 per cent) in 1950 to eleventh place (two per cent) in January 1987.

279. See the figures in Table 10 ("International Seaborne Trade"), Table 11 ("International Seaborne Trade of the U.K.") and Table 12 ("Percentage of U.K. imports and exports carried by U.K. vessels".).

280. Due mainly to governmental subsidising of world shipyards without commercial justification.

281. See Section IV of the Report.

282. The trans-Atlantic reinforcement of Europe, the reinforcement of Europe from the U.K., direct support of the Royal Navy and the civil supply of the U.K. and Europe in time of tension and war.

and over)[283] and expressed concern as to whether, for defence purposes, the Government could rely on requisitioned U.K. owned vessels registered in the Dependent Territories and foreign countries returning expeditiously and whether there would be sufficient U.K. seafarers available to man them.[284]

Section VII of the Report set out the Committee's Conclusions and Recommendations. The Committee believed that the case for a merchant fleet on both strategic and economic grounds was unarguable, that the time for action had arrived, that the Government must take steps to ensure that a core fleet, of a size sufficient to fulfil its strategic and economic roles, was maintained and that there was a case for the Government to provide assistance to enable the U.K. shipping industry to compete more fairly with that of the rest of the world. The Committee's recommendations, which they hoped would help to ensure the continued existence of the merchant fleet, included roll-over relief for balancing charges,[285] a substantial raising of the Business Expansion Scheme limit of £5 million,[286] a reduction in employers' National Insurance contributions for foreign-going seafarers,[287] amendment of the Regulations

283. See Table 24 of the Report, of which the following is an extract:

U.K. Owned Trading Fleet (500 g.r.t. and over)

	31.12.75			*31.8.87*		
	m. d.w.t.	*%*	*No.*	*m. d.w.t.*	*%*	*No.*
U.K. Owned and U.K. mainland registered	50	100	1614	5.9	35	400
U.K. Owned and registered in Crown Dependencies	Included in above but negligible			3.2	19	75
U.K. Owned and registered in Dependent Territories	N/A			6.2	37	85
U.K. Owned and foreign registered	N/A			1.6	9	75
Total	50.0	100	1614	16.9	100	635

284. The Committee were particularly concerned at the figures for officer recruitment (Table 26) of which the following is an extract

Year	*Deck Cadets*		*Engineer Cadets*	
	New Entry	*Under Training*	*New Entry*	*Under Training*
1970	1220	4384	846	3064
1987	43	243	50	257

By December 1988 the critical shortage of junior officers was becoming apparent and it was announced (see P. Debs. 6 Ser., Vol. 142, c.(357)) that the Department of Transport was proposing to change the certification requirements so as to allow holders of EEC certificates of competency to serve as junior officers on U.K. ships.

285. Report, para. 121.

286. *Ibid.*, para. 122.

287. *Ibid.*, para. 136.

relating to seafarers' personal taxation[288] and a doubling of the sum made available by the Government for training.[289]

In their observations on the Report, published on 26th October 1988,[290] the Government did not accept any of these particular recommendations but on the other hand the Government did not dissent from the Committee's view that, if necessary, the powers in the recent Merchant Shipping Act with regard to U.K. cabotage should be used,[291] agreed with the suggestion for a campaign to reverse the decline in numbers entering the shipping industry[292] and undertook to consider the possibility of periodic training for the new Merchant Navy Reserve.[293] In reply to the Committee's misgivings regarding the repatriation of U.K. owned vessels registered in foreign countries in the event of crisis or war,[294] the Government referred to the Understanding already reached with the Bahamas and expressed the hope that similar agreements would be concluded with Liberia, Panama and Vanuatu later in the year.[295] With regard to the seafarers' taxation, the Government pointed to the changes made in the 1988 Finance Bill which would enable many more seafarers to qualify for tax relief and should make it more attractive to employ U.K. seafarers in deep-sea trades. Perhaps more significant than anything else, the Government did fully accept that it had a responsibility for ensuring that the merchant fleet should continue to be able to meet the nation's defence requirements[296] and expressed the belief that the steps already taken[297] constituted a clear commitment to ensure that the shipping industry continued to be in a position to provide sufficient seafarers and ships to meet the country's needs in time of emergency.

Earlier in June 1988 the Select Committee on Defence published a further Report on the "Defence Requirements for Merchant Shipping".[298] Although in the 1988 Statement on the Defence Estimates[299] the Ministry of Defence had yet again declared that, despite the decline in the numbers of ships on the

288. *Ibid.*, para. 143.
289. *Ibid.*, para. 148.
290. Parl. Papers 1987–88, HCP 681.
291. Report, para. 124.
292. *Ibid.*, para. 149.
293. *Ibid.*, para. 159.
294. *Ibid.*, para. 153.
295. In the course of a defence debate on merchant shipping on 7th July 1988 (P. Debs 6 Ser., Vol. 136, c.1261) the Minister for the Armed Forces said that the Bahamas had agreed that they would waive their sovereign authority over U.K. owned ships. Subsequently, in a written reply on 2nd March 1989 (P. Debs 6 Ser., Vol. 148, c.(295)), it was stated that the Liberian and Vanuatuan governments had agreed to allow British-owned ships to be made available to the British Government in the event of hostilities provided the owners had agreed to make named ships available in return for Government reinsurance against war risks.
296. The Government made no reference to the economic arguments for maintaining an adequate U.K. registered fleet.
297. In the Merchant Shipping Act 1988 and the Finance Act 1988 and in the negotiations with the open registry states.
298. Fourth Report of the Defence Committee 1987–88, HCP 476.
299. Parl. Papers 1987–88, Cm. 344 (Part I, para. 319).

U.K. and Dependent Territories registers, there were still sufficient ships to meet the needs of the armed forces in wartime,[300] the Defence Committee, in the introduction to their Fourth Report, expressed the belief that the implications for our national and collective security of the continuing decline in the British merchant navy and in the merchant fleets of our NATO allies were alarming. The Committee felt there might be a conflict between the requirements of economic shipping and of trans-Atlantic reinforcement[301] and considered that, even if the Dependent Territories shipping were fully available, there would be difficulty in meeting the economic shipping requirement[302]; the Committee also expressed doubts as to whether foreign-registered ships beneficially British-owned could be requisitioned under the Royal Prerogative[303] and queried whether, even if the Government had made agreements with the foreign countries in question, those countries would have the necessary capability if the owners and/or crews were unco-operative. In their conclusion[304] the Committee stated that they had looked in vain for evidence of clear direction in the Government's policy with regard to the merchant fleet and its "availability for all purposes in wartime" and expressed the view that it was essential that "policy on this subject should be directed by the Prime Minister as the only Minister in a position to take a broad overview and, where necessary, to cut across departmental boundaries".[305]

Shortly after the publication of the Defence Committee's Report Sir David Price asked the Prime Minister for her response to the Committee's view that the decline in the merchant fleet had alarming implications for the U.K.'s national and collective security and that only she was in a position to take a broad overview of a national maritime policy; in her written reply[306] the Prime Minister stated that she and her colleagues had regularly examined the implications of the decline in recent years and had already introduced a number of measures to safeguard the national interest. A week later, in a debate on the defence needs for merchant shipping,[307] the Chairman of the Defence Committee, Mr Michael Mates, re-emphasised the salient points in his Committee's Fourth Report but in his reply to the debate the Minister for the Armed Forces contended that at no time had the supply of ships available from

300. In their 1988 Annual Report the British Maritime League disputed this statement as "misleading and complacent"—particularly since it gave no indication that the requirements of economic shipping had been taken into account and made no reference to the acute shortage of trained U.K. seafarers.

301. Fourth Report, Part II, para. 36.

302. *Ibid.*, Part III, paras. 35 and 36.

303. *Ibid.*, para. 49. In evidence the Department of Transport had admitted that "it was very concerned about the use of the prerogative in a number of cases" and whether it could be made to stick.

304. Report, Part III, paras. 72 and 73.

305. This was also a view which the BML had been expressing for several years.

306. P. Debs 6 Ser., Vol. 136, c.(315)—on 30th June 1988.

307. *Ibid.*, c.1261.

the U.K. and Dependent Territories fallen below the level needed to meet British national defence needs[308] and that NATO was studying the shipping capability of the allies with regard to reinforcement of Europe from the United States and the resupply of the civil economies of the NATO countries. Subsequently, in October 1988, the Government published their detailed Reply to the Defence Committee's Report[309] in which it was pointed out that the size of the U.K. owned fleet had remained stable for more than a year,[310] that the industry had returned to profitability,[311] that the tonnage of new orders had risen[312] and that, whilst there was some concern regarding the availability of British crews for defence tasks, for some non-sensitive economic resupply cargoes friendly neutral crews would be acceptable. The Government concluded its Reply by stating that national and NATO requirements in an emergency were being carefully considered in the light of current and possible future trends in the size of the U.K. owned merchant fleet and the Government believed that the measures introduced[313] were a cumulative and adequate response to the situation as it had developed.

Apart from the Merchant Shipping and Finance Acts, the Reports of the Transport and Defence Committees and the Government Replies to such Reports, the year 1988 was notable for the pressure that was continuously applied on the Government from outside Parliament. In addition to the oral and written evidence submitted to the Transport and Defence Committees, and also to the Foreign Affairs Committee in connection with British shipping in the Gulf War, GCBS published a major policy paper on *The Future of the British Merchant Fleet*[314] which sought "to analyze the options open to Government to influence the size, composition and commercial viability of that fleet in the future"[315] and continued its "vigorous advocacy of the defence and economic case for action to stimulate future investment in British-owned

308. I.e. support of the Royal Navy and reinforcement of Europe from the U.K.

309. Parl. Papers 1987–88, HCP 674.

310. The GCBS end year figures for the U.K. owned trading fleet (500 g.r.t. and above) were: 1986–17.8 million d.w.t.; 1987–17.6 million d.w.t.; 1988–16.5 million d.w.t. (Shipping Facts 1989).

311. In mid 1986 the combined Index of Cargo Rates (1976=100) was 85 but by the end of 1987 the index had risen to 176 and at the end of the first quarter of 1988 it stood at 234.

312. GCBS figures for new orders were: 1986–4,000 d.w.t.; 1987–10,000 d.w.t. and 1988–136,000 d.w.t. (shipping facts 1989). The GCBS Annual Report 1988–89 emphasised that new orders were far below the level needed to replace the ageing fleet over any reasonable timespan.

313. Particularly those in the Merchant Shipping Act 1988 and in the Finance Act 1988 which the Government expected would encourage the employment of British seafarers in deep-sea trades. In the Finance Act there had also been an extension to the Business Expansion Scheme whereby the £5 million higher limit was made available to companies operating their own ships as well as to those letting ships on charter.

314. GCBS (December 1987).

315. The options suggested were aids for reinvestment (particularly roll-over relief for balancing charges on new and second-hand ships), aids for running costs over and above those proposed in the Merchant Shipping Bill and other measures, such as the opening of the European cabotage trades to British ships, which would improve the competitive environment for British shipping.

ships".[316] The British Maritime League also submitted oral and written evidence to the Transport and Defence Committees and in February 1988 wrote to the Prime Minister enclosing a policy paper on "The National Importance of Restoring Britain's Maritime Capabilities" which (*inter alia*) recommended that the Government should formulate a national policy aimed at restoring profitability to shipping, should act with other maritime nations to reduce the over-supply of ships throughout the world and should establish equality of opportunity for British shipowners.[317]

In March 1988 the British Maritime Charitable Foundation ("BMCF"), a charitable body associated with the BML, whose role is to research, inform and educate on all matters concerning the U.K.'s maritime activities and problems, published three major research reports respectively entitled *Why the Ships Went—Supplement 1983–1987*,[318] *The Merchant Fleet and Britain's Economy* and *The Merchant Fleet and Deterrence*.[319] These Reports provided the basis for a BML Conference on "A Future for Merchant Shipping" held in London on 20th April 1988 which was attended by representatives of every sector of U.K. maritime interests[320] and, following the Conference, the BML President wrote again to the Prime Minister reporting on the major points discussed[321] and emphasising that there was a unanimous call for the Government to declare publicly that a properly balanced maritime capability was vital to the nation, that there was a consequential necessity to develop a realistic national maritime policy and that the Government should take the lead in every appropriate regional and international body seeking to implement that policy.

Following this further approach to the Prime Minister, a meeting took place on 13th July 1988 between the Secretary of State for Transport, Mr Paul Channon, and BML representatives. Mr Channon made it clear that, in the view of the Government, the only justification for a merchant fleet was on defence grounds and that the Government did not accept the economic case for a merchant shipping industry. However, as a result of this meeting, the BML was asked to prepare for Mr Channon an agreed list of the actions

316. See GCBS Annual Report 1987–88 and the Presidential Address of Mr (now Sir) Ian Denholm on 26th May 1988.

317. A summary of this BML paper is set out in the *BML Newsletter*, 1/88. The Prime Minister responded to the BML letter on 4th March 1988 but further correspondence was then postponed until after a BML Conference on "A Future for Merchant Shipping" due to be held on 20th April 1988—see further *infra*.

318. This Report, commissioned by the Department of Transport, is an update of the *Why the Ships Went* study published by BMCF and Lloyds of London Press in 1986. The two Reports analyse the reasons for the decline of the U.K. registered merchant fleet over the period 1978 to 1987.

319. A resumé of these three Reports is set out in *BML Newsletter*, 2/88, p. 4.

320. At the Conference the BML presented its responses and recommendations arising out of the BMCF Reports and papers were also presented by GCBS, the Nautical Institute and Professor R. Goss of the Department of Maritime Studies, University of Wales.

321. A summary of these points is set out in *BML Newsletter*, 3/88, p. 4.

believed to be required by as many as possible of the different interests involved in merchant shipping in order to arrest the decline and restore conditions in which the U.K. fleet could compete on equal terms with all-comers. In addition, it was agreed that BMCF should undertake a follow-on research project to establish the extent of the manpower problem and a further related study to try to establish the smallest size of merchant fleet that would be capable of sustaining adequate infrastructure, facilities for education and training, research and development and administration as well as providing the trained seafarers needed in many key occupations beyond shipping itself.[322]

In October 1988 the BML sent to the Secretary of State their paper setting out "Proposals for Action to Maintain a Strategic Merchant Marine and to Preserve the United Kingdom's Maritime Infrastructure".[323] The paper stated that the objective of the actions proposed was "to arrest the continuing decline and to restore commercial health to the industry" and expressed the view that "the best way to meet the defence requirements in times of tension and war is to have a profitable Industry and Fleet in peacetime serving economic needs, both national and international". It was also emphasised that the detailed proposals,[324] most of which required Government action, were the minimum required to provide a climate in which the Industry could be profitable, could flourish and be successful and in which recruitment was encouraged and seafarers were trained, thereby maintaining a strategic fleet of ships and a pool of manpower to man them.

So far the BML paper has unfortunately not evoked any positive Government response. In the Annual Report of the BML Council for 1989 it was stated that, since the submission of the paper, there had been correspondence and meetings with officials out of which it became clear that the Department of Transport did not agree with the League's view that there were already far too few vessels available to meet the demands of national defence, NATO reinforcement and supply and economic shipping. The BML Report added that, until the Government accepted the need to arrest the decline of the U.K. fleet, there could be little hope of persuading Ministers to adopt some of the measures needed to enable the fleet to compete on level terms with its international competitors; the Department had done all in its power to avoid taking any action and its present position was to await the results of the NATO Study

322. See Annual Report of BML Council (1988).

323. The paper embodied the consensus views of the GCBS, the Marine Society, the Nautical Institute, the National Union of Marine Aviation and Sea Transport Officers (NUMAST) and the National Union of Seamen (NUS), the Institute of Marine Engineers and the Royal Institution of Naval Architects as well as those of the League.

324. These were set out under the following headings:
I Promotion of the Industry; II Competing on Equal Terms; III EEC Shipping Policy; IV Training and Manpower; V International Measures; VI Direct Subsidies in order to maintain particular ship types and seafarers for strategic reasons (particularly advocated by the GCBS); VII Defence Measures; VIII Flag Control, Coastal Cabotage and Ferries; IX Research and Development.

on Supply and Demand for Merchant Shipping due no earlier than mid-1990.

During the Parliamentary session 1988–89 concern continued to be expressed in the Lords and Commons regarding the state of the British mercantile marine—both ships and men. In November 1988 the Minister for the Armed Forces accepted that there was concern regarding the NATO contribution to the merchant shipping section of the Alliance[325] but when replying to a debate on the Royal Navy in February 1989[326] the same Minister, whilst admitting the continuing decline in the merchant fleet, continued to maintain that national defence requirements could still be met and argued that the full effect of the measures taken by the Government[327] had yet to be seen. Shortly afterwards a Transport Minister stated[328] that the scheme for financial assistance towards the cost of training future merchant navy officers had begun to show encouraging results[329] but the current shortage of junior officers was revealed by his further statement[330] that officers holding certificates of competence issued by any of the EEC States or Norway would be allowed to serve in junior officers' posts in U.K. vessels.

The feeling in the Commons in mid-1989 was reflected in an early day motion, signed by well over 200 members, which in July 1989 was quoted by Mr Peter Shore, the Chairman of the Parliamentary Maritime Group, during the debate on the 1989 Finance Bill[331]; the motion (*inter alia*) urged "the primary importance, with an ageing fleet, of the early provision of fiscal and other measures to encourage British shipping companies to undertake the substantial re-investment in ships which will be needed if the decline of the British-owned and controlled merchant fleet is not to accelerate again over the years immediately ahead". Mr Shore was moving a new Clause providing for the reintroduction of a 50 per cent first-year allowance for capital expenditure on new ships[332]; he argued that the maintenance of a large, modern and efficient merchant navy was essential to the well being and security of an island nation, that it was a paradox that the U.K., a nation more dependent on shipping than any other European country, should alone among West European nations offer no protection or assistance to its merchant fleet and that, since a large part of the existing world fleet would have to be replaced over the next decade, there was a major opportunity to revive our fleet and incentives to invest must be strengthened to enable the U.K. to gain a substantial share of

325. P. Debs. 6 Ser., Vol. 142, c.562.

326. *Ibid.*, Vol. 148, c.163.

327. In the Merchant Shipping Act 1988 and the Finance Act 1988.

328. P. Debs. 6 Ser., Vol. 148, c.(497)

329. The cadet entry to colleges had almost doubled to 279 in the current academic year; but the BML calculated that, to maintain the number of officers required by the greatly reduced fleet, the entry rate needed to rise to at least 1,000 a year.

330. P. Debs. 6 Ser., Vol. 149, c.(119).

331. *Ibid.*, Vol. 156, c.909.

332. This was an incentive for which the GCBS had been pressing the Government for some years—see GCBS Annual Report 1988–89.

new shipping. Mr Shore's new Clause was supported by Conservative and Labour backbenchers who referred to the Reports of the Transport and Defence Select Committees but the Government remained unimpressed; a Treasury Minister argued that the decline in the fleet was due to excess capacity and over investment rather than fiscal reasons and rejected the new Clause on the ground that it would go against the whole thrust of the Government's business tax reforms.

Meanwhile, in the 1989 Statement of the Defence Estimates[333] published in May, the Ministry of Defence reported[334] that in the past year the fall in the number of merchant ships on the U.K. and Dependent Territories registers suitable for defence purposes had slowed but that it remained to be seen if the present return to relative stability, at a level still generally above that needed to meet the wartime needs of the British armed forces, would last.[335] The Statement[336] also gave the figures for merchant vessels available for defence purposes (vessels in the categories required for defence purposes, available within the required timescales and capable of being requisitioned under the Royal Prerogative) and the yearly average of the manpower figures for 1988 which showed a fall of some 3,700 from the 1987 figures.[337] The Defence Estimates were debated in the Lords in July[338] and a number of peers expressed concern at the decline in ships and men of the British and NATO merchant navies; Admiral Lord Hill-Norton, a Past President of the BML, characterised the paragraphs dealing with the merchant fleet as "actively misleading and foolishly optimistic" and said that the figures were both serious for defence and the effect on our formerly worldwide maritime commercial presence; Lord Colnbrook (formerly Humphrey Atkins) and other speakers contended that, even if enough ships and men could be scraped together for military operations, there would be nothing left for civilian supply and to keep essential industries going. In his reply to the debate the Minister, Lord Trefgarne, agreed that NATO was concerned at the shortage of vessels for trans-Atlantic reinforcement and civil resupply but gave no indication of any positive measures being taken to solve the problem.

Simultaneously with this Lords' debate, the Commons Defence Committee

333. Parl. Papers 1988–89, Cm. 675, Parts I and II.

334. Part I, para. 332.

335. The Ministry felt that the signs were encouraging but in para. 334 it was admitted that there was still a NATO shortage of vessels for all purposes including trans-Atlantic reinforcement.

336. Part II, Table 3.1.

337. The figures for the two years were as follows:

	1987 (Cm. 344)	*1988 (Cm. 675)*
Officers	10,978	9,568
Ratings	15,835	13,638
Cadets	554	428
Total	27,367	23,634

338. P. Debs. (HL) 5. Ser., Vol. 510, c.432.

published their 1989 Report on the "Availability of Merchant Shipping for Defence Purposes".[339] The Report showed that between May 1988 and 31st March 1989 the numbers of ships (over 500 g.r.t.) registered in the U.K., the Crown Dependencies and the Dependent Territories had declined by 7.2 per cent[340] and referred to the GCBS forecast of a further fall in the size of the British controlled merchant fleet of some 25 per cent by 1992.[341] The numbers of British seafarers also continued to decline[342]; at 30th June 1989 the total was estimated to be 22,000 and, although the level of cadet recruitment in 1988–89 showed some improvement on 1987, it was clearly too small to sustain even the present reduced number of officers. The Committee remained concerned that the Government's confidence[343] was not fully justified by the evidence and concluded their Report by stating that the decline in the British merchant fleet continued at a worrying pace, not only from a defence point of view but also from the wider economic and employment perspective; the Committee regretted that, for the sixth year in succession, they had had to report a worsening situation and they urged the Government to take effective steps to reverse the decline.[344]

In addition to the concern regarding defence, the Government was pressed to take action for the purpose of ensuring that, in relation to foreign competition, the British shipping industry should enjoy what was often termed a level playing field. At the end of November 1988 in reply to a question from Sir David Price,[345] the Minister for Public Transport (Mr Michael Portillo) stated that the Government were pressing for the liberalisation of the cabotage trades of six EEC countries and were awaiting details of the Commission's proposals

339. Ninth Report (Session 1988–89), HCP 495.
340. The detailed figures were as follows:

	May 1988	*31st March 1989*
U.K. Trading	402	374
U.K. Non-Trading	504	482
Channel Islands & Isle of Man	113	117
Dependent Territories	585	515
	1604	1488

341. See GCBS Annual Report 1988–89, p. 16.
342. See figures in fn. 337 *supra*.
343. As expressed in the Government's Reply (Parl. Papers 1987–88, HCP 674) to the Committee's previous Report (Parl. Papers 1987–88, HCP 476)—see pp. 332 *et seq. supra*.
344. There was a Commons debate on the 1989 Defence Estimates on 18–19th October 1989 (P. Debs. 6 Ser., Vol. 158, cc.143–233 and 287–362) but no Minister made any reference to this July 1989 Report of the Defence Committee or indeed any mention of merchant shipping at all. However, on 19th October 1989 Sir David Price put a written question to the Prime Minister (P. Debs. 6 Ser., Vol. 158, c.(227)) in which he referred to the Defence Committee's Report and asked what steps she intended to take to reverse the decline. Sir Geoffrey Howe (replying for the Prime Minister) said that the Government had already introduced a number of measures to help the industry and that the effect of such measures depended to a large extent on the practical response of the industry, which the Government awaited with interest.
345. P. Debs. 6 Ser., Vol. 142, c.(165).

for measures to tackle the decline of European fleets and to improve their competitiveness. Then, early in March 1989,[346] Mr Portillo gave details of seafarers' tax concessions which benefited the operations of Danish and Swedish fleets[347] and said that the EEC Commission had been asked to consider the compatibility of the Danish arrangements with EEC competition rules. A week later, in reply to a further question from Sir David Price,[348] Mr Portillo said that his Department had registered with the Commission their strong opposition to any preferential treatment for intra-Community shipping and were waiting for the Commission to produce proposals on the harmonisation of State aids.

In May 1989 the GCBS published a paper entitled *A Level Playing Field for Merchant Shipping?* which set out in detail the various forms of aid given by nearly 70 foreign countries to the ships flying their flags.[349] The paper showed that at least two thirds of world shipping operated under national shipping policies which discriminated in their favour and accordingly for British shipowners the competition was not fair and neither was the playing field level. What the industry needed from the Government was a package of measures of broadly equivalent overall effect to those available to the main foreign competitors and only the Government was in a position either to persuade other governments to remove the advantages they gave to their own fleets or to broadly off-set these advantages. In the same month the GCBS published a further paper entitled *British Shipping and the Balance of Payments* in which details were given of the industry's contribution to the balance of payments[350] and it was argued that, with the U.K. facing the largest balance of payments deficit for many years, the Government should encourage the growth of the U.K. owned merchant fleet by creating conditions in which British owners could compete fairly; if this were done the GCBS believed that the industry was fully capable of making a substantial contribution to the U.K.'s economic success, not least in the realm of the balance of payments.

During 1989 there was another important international shipping matter, with significant constitutional implications, resulting from proceedings for judicial review brought against the Secretary of State for Transport by a

346. *Ibid.*, Vol. 148, c.(409).

347. Subsequently (see P. Debs. 6 Ser., Vol. 149, c.(450) a Treasury Minister stated that the earnings of Greek ratings were exempt from tax, that there was a special low rate for Greek officers and that in some other EEC countries (Belgium, Denmark, Germany and the Netherlands) the tax liability of seafarers formed the basis for calculating a subsidy in favour of the employing shipowner.

348. P. Debs. 6 Ser., Vol. 149, c.(112).

349. The areas in which unfair preference and protection were given to foreign shipping were grouped under the following headings:
(*a*) Shipbuilding Credit Schemes; (*b*) Taxes on Business; (*c*) Taxes on People; (*d*) Subsidies and (*e*) Cargo Reservations.

350. Even with the decline in the size of the U.K. fleet, in 1987 a total positive contribution of over £1.3 billion was still made to the balance of payments.

number of Spanish controlled U.K. fishing companies who challenged the legality of the new statutory regime for the registration of British fishing vessels[351] on the ground that it contravened the provisions of the Treaty of Rome and the European Communities Act 1972. The 95 deep sea fishing vessels owned by the Spanish controlled companies had been registered as British under the Merchant Shipping Act 1894[352] but they did not satisfy one or more of the conditions under Section 14 of 1988 Act[353] and thus failed to qualify for re-registration under that Act. The matter came before a Divisional Court which on 10th March 1989 decided that a preliminary ruling as regards the compatibility of the British nationality requirements in Section 14 of the 1988 Act with Community law should be obtained from the European Court of Justice and ordered that, pending final judgment, the operation of Part II of the 1988 Act and the 1988 Regulations be disapplied and that the Secretary of State be restrained from enforcing them against the shipowners.[354] The Secretary of State appealed to the Court of Appeal who allowed his appeal[355] and the shipowners thereupon appealed to the House of Lords who, whilst agreeing that a preliminary ruling should be sought from the European Court, held unanimously that the Divisional Court had no power to make an order declaring an Act of Parliament not to be the law until some uncertain future date.[356]

The Spanish fishermen (through the Commission) then commenced an action in the European Court[357] for a declaration that, by imposing the British nationality requirements in Section 14 of the 1988 Act, the U.K. had failed to fulfil its obligations under Articles 52 and 221 of the EEC Treaty which prohibited discrimination on the ground of nationality. By a separate application (Case C-221/89) they also sought an Order requiring the U.K. to suspend the application of these British nationality requirements and on 10th October 1989[358] the President of the European Court made an Interim Order requiring the U.K. to suspend, until judgment in the main proceedings, the application of the British

351. Part II of the Merchant Shipping Act 1988 and the Merchant Shipping (Registration of Fishing Vessels) Regulations 1988 (SI 1988 No. 1926) both of which came into force on 1st December 1988.

352. Fishing vessels registered as British under the Merchant Shipping Act 1894 were required to be re-registered under the 1988 Act by 31st March 1989.

353. Because the vessels were managed and controlled from Spain and most of the shareholders and directors of the owning companies were by Spanish nationals.

354. *R.* v *Secretary of State for Transport, ex parte Factortame* [1989] 2 CMLR 353. This meant, in effect, that the 95 vessels were to be treated as still registered as British fishing vessels (under the 1894 Act) and as such could continue to fish against the British quota of fish protected under the Common Fisheries Policy.

355. See *The Times*, 24th March 1989.

356. See *The Times*, 19th May 1989 and [1990] 2 AC 85. The Lords also decided that the Divisional Court did not have jurisdiction to grant an interim injunction against the Crown in proceedings for judicial review.

357. Case 246/89.

358. See *The Times*, 28th October 1989.

nationality requirements in Section 14(1), (2) and (7) of the Merchant Shipping Act 1988 as regards the nationals of other Member States and in respect of fishing vessels which, until 31st March 1988, were pursuing a fishing activity under the British flag and with a British fishing licence.

In order to give effect to the President's Interim Order, the Shipping Minister, on 25th October 1989[359] put to the Commons a motion for approving the draft of the Merchant Shipping Act 1988 (Amendment) Order 1989[360] which, pending delivery of the judgment of the European Court in the main proceedings, suspended the requirement in the 1988 Act that the owners, charterers, managers and operators of British fishing vessels must either be British nationals or, in the case of a company, have at least 75 per cent of its shares legally and beneficially owned by British nationals and at least 75 per cent of its directors as British nationals.[361] Mr McLoughlin emphasised that the Order did not affect the requirements in Section 14 that such persons must be resident and domiciled in the U.K. and that vessels must be managed and their operations directed and controlled from within the U.K.; it was not possible to say what number of vessels would become eligible but it seemed likely that many vessels would not be able to meet the requirements that remained in force. From both sides of the House there was concern at the constitutional implications for Parliament of what was described as a humiliating defeat[362] and at the prospect of the Spanish being once again able to catch fish against the British quota but in the end the Order was approved by a small majority and came into force on 2nd November 1989.[363]

For the British a more acceptable manifestation of the activities of the European Commission was the publication in August 1989 of the Commis-

359. P. Debs. 6 Ser., Vol. 158, c.993.

360. The Order was in exercise of the powers of the Crown under Section 2(2) of the European Communities Act 1972 which empowered Her Majesty by Order in Council to make provision for the purpose of implementing any Community obligation of the U.K.

361. The Order only applied to vessels fishing under the British flag up to 31st March 1989 and owned by nationals of EC Member States.

362. The House was far from reassured by the Solicitor-General's undertaking that the Government would try to overturn the President's Interim Order in the main proceedings in the European Court.

363. SI 89/2006. The Interim Order of the President of the European Court was affirmed by the full Court (Case C-213/89) on 19th June 1990 (see European Law Report on p. 31 of *The Times* of 20th June 1990 and [1991] 1 AC 603). The case then went back to the House of Lords who on 9th July 1990 made an order granting the Spanish applicants interim relief pending final determination of the issues raised (see p. 31 of *The Times* of 12th October 1990 and [1991] 1 All ER 70). Subsequently on 24th July 1991 ([1991] 3 All ER 769—Case C-213/89) the European Court held, first, that the statutory system governing the registration of British fishing vessels set out in Part II of the 1988 Act and the 1988 Regulations was contrary to Community law, in particular Article 52 of the Treaty of Rome because there was discrimination on the grounds of nationality, and was therefore ineffective in relation to nationals of other member states and, secondly, that it was not contrary to Community law for a member state to stipulate, as a condition for registration of a fishing vessel, that the vessel must be managed and its operations directed and controlled from within that member state.

sion's long-awaited proposals for the second stage of the Common Maritime Transport Policy.[364] These proposals[365] were set out in a document entitled "A Future for the Community Shipping Industry; Measures to improve the Operating Conditions of Community Shipping" and a second document entitled "Financial and Fiscal Measures Covering Shipping Operations with Ships Registered in the Community". The first document comprised three draft Regulations which respectively provided for the establishment of a Community ship register to be named Euros, the definition of a Community shipowner and the liberalisation of cabotage throughout the Community; there was also a Recommendation for improving Port State Control in order to discourage sub-standard ships.[366] The second document described the Commission's approach to State aids and explained the manner in which the Commission proposed to police State aid for shipping in order to ensure that such aid was compatible with the Common Market.[367]

These Community documents were debated in the Commons at the end of November 1989[368] on a Government motion which also sought endorsement of the Government's commitment to liberal shipping policies and to the opening of the coastal and offshore markets (cabotage) of France, Greece, Italy, Spain and Portugal and its opposition to subsidies for shipping and its support for policies which would promote vigorous competitive United Kingdom and Community shipping fleets. In opening the debate the Shipping Minister stated that the Government did not consider that the proposals would improve the competitiveness of the European shipping industry and in particular did not favour the Euros ship register idea which, having been criticised by a majority of the Ministers at a meeting of the Transport Council, was expected to wither away. On the other hand the Government strongly supported the liberalisation of cabotage but considered that the draft Regulation contained totally unacceptable conditions introduced to protect inefficient operations in some

364. The four Regulations comprising the first stage of the CMTP had come into force in 1987 —see pp. 302–303 *supra*. At the beginning of 1989, as a result of an investigation by the Commission under Article 7 of Regulation 4057/86, Council Regulation 15/89 of 4th January 1989 imposed a redressive duty on containerised cargo transported in the liner service between the Community and Australia by Hyundai Merchant Marine Company of South Korea. The investigation by the Commission was prompted by complaints by EC liner companies that Hyundai was able to charge low freight rates because of subsidies paid by the South Korean government and other non-commercial advantages.

365. EC Docs 8367/89 and 8368/89.

366. A Memorandum of Understanding on Port State Control, which had been signed by all littoral EC countries, provided that each country should achieve an annual total of inspections corresponding to 25 per cent of the estimated number of individual foreign merchant ships entering its ports in a 12 months period. The U.K. has always exceeded the 25 per cent figure—see P. Debs. 6 Ser., Vol. 159, c.(94).

367. See Article 92 of the Treaty of Rome.

368. P. Debs. 6 Ser., Vol. 162, c.790. For the GCBS reaction to the Commission's proposals see their "Shipping Factsheet No. 9" (1989) and for the views of the BML see their 1989 Annual Report, p. 4.

Member States; coastal trades along mainland coasts in Europe must be unconditionally opened up to all Community vessels and, if such a move continued to be blocked by some Member States, the U.K. might be forced to take retaliatory action by invoking the powers available in Section 39 of the Merchant Shipping Act 1988.[369] Mr McLoughlin added that the Government would continue to oppose the provision of subsidies, particularly to intra-EC shipping, and expected the Commission to take a rigorous view of State aids in the shipping sector; existing State aids should be challenged and no new ones permitted.

Although the Opposition speakers did not disagree with the Government views on the cabotage question, the Shadow Transport Minister, Mr Prescott, charged the Government with major responsibility for the decline in U.K. owned tonnage and the numbers of British seamen since 1979, for failing to heed the warnings given by the Defence Committee in its 1988 and 1989 Reports and for ignoring the opinion of the Community's Economic and Social Committee that the objective of the Community's shipping policy should be to "produce a sufficient incentive for Community shipowners to register their ships within the Community and to man those ships, to the highest possible proportion, with Community seafarers". Mr Prescott pointed out that the merchant fleets of some other EC members had declined far less as a result of the provision of financial incentives and the Labour Party was in favour of the U.K. giving subsidies so as to increase the merchant marine to a level sufficient to meet the country's economic and strategic requirements.[370] Another Labour speaker asked the Minister whether, in view of the objection taken to the British nationality requirements for fishing vessels in Section 14 of the Merchant Shipping Act 1988, he anticipated problems from the European Commission in relation to the British nationality requirements relating to the merchant ships in Section 3 of the Act; perhaps wisely, the Minister did not reply and at the conclusion of the debate the Government's motion was carried by 128 votes to 79.

So, as the British merchant marine enters the 1990s, what are the prospects for its revival. At March 1990 the U.K. owned trading fleet (500 g.r.t. and above) comprised 583 trading ships of 15.4 million d.w.t.[371] and at September

369. See p. 328 *supra*.

370. In the Labour Party's policy document entitled "Moving into the Nineties" it was stated that a Labour Government would probably set up a State-owned merchant shipping company as part of a programme to reverse the decline of the U.K. fleet.

371. See GCBS Annual Report 1989/90. Thus there has been a further fall since mid-1989 when the figures were as follows:

Register	*No.*	*m. d.w.t.*
Mainland U.K.	339	5.0
Crown Dependencies	77	3.0
Dependent Territories	86	5.6
Foreign	99	2.1
Total	601	15.7

1989 the number of seafarers had fallen again to 9,300 officers and 12,850 ratings;[372] moreover the British fleet was an ageing one[373] and orders for new ships remained far below the rate required for renewal.[374] Nevertheless, in a GCBS Memorandum of December 1989 entitled "British Shipping—The Way Ahead",[375] British owners expressed the view that, with the recent significant improvements in shipping markets in most sectors of the industry and the growth in world trade, there was now a "small window of opportunity" for British owners to modernise the fleet by placing orders at today's relatively favourable prices,[376] but that, to encourage investment in new building and the employment of more British seafarers, the Government must play its part in helping to create a more level playing field on which the industry could flourish. British owners did not seek long-term subsidies but, in order to match the assistance which many foreign governments gave to their shipping industries,[377] changes in Government policy were essential in order to enable owners to reinvest in new ships and in trained British seafarers; specifically the industry asked first for aids to investment by means of accelerated depreciation (100 per cent ship allowance as a first-year allowance), improved terms for roll-over relief for corporation tax and improvements in the Business Expansion Scheme and secondly for a reduction in manning costs by eliminating National Insurance and income tax liabilities in regard to sea-going employment which would enable owners to employ more British seafarers.

The early 1990s proved to be of special significance as regards the relationship between the Government and the British shipping industry. The most important event of 1990 was the setting up in May, by the Secretary of State for Transport,[378] of a Joint Working Party bringing together, in addition the industry itself, no less than five Ministries[379] and co-chaired by Cecil Parkinson and Lord Sterling, the then GCBS President and also Chairman of P & O. The Working Party's Report, entitled "Challenges and Opportunites", was

372. For the figures in 1987 and 1988 see fn. 337 *supra*.

373. At the beginning of 1990 the U.K. registered fleet had an overall age of over 13 years (GCBS Annual Report 1989/90).

374. In 1988 orders placed by U.K. owners for U.K. registration amounted to only 14 ships totalling 136,000 d.w.t.

375. Presented by the GCBS President on 7th February 1990 and supported by 10 shipping factsheets respectively entitled:- No. 1 Shipping and the Balance of Payments, No. 2 Shipping and the Free Market, No. 3 Merchant Shipping and Defence, No. 4 British Shipping and the Channel Tunnel, No. 5. Light Dues: A Heavy Burden, No. 6 Cabotage, No. 7 VAT and Duty-Free in Shipping, No. 8 Ferry Safety, No. 9 European Community Shipping Policy, No. 10 Shipping Facts – 1989 Update.

376. The GCBS expect ship prices to increase dramatically in the next five years as old ships have to be replaced.

377. The fleets of Norway, Denmark and West Germany have grown significantly as a result of government support.

378. At that time Cecil Parkinson.

379. Transport, Defence, Trade and Industry, Foreign and Commonwealth and (as an observer) the Treasury.

published in September 1990 (HMSO) and concluded with the important statement that "British shipping is a vital national asset"; the Report also stated: "It is in our national interest that British shipping should win profitable business. The Gulf Crisis has brought back into sharp focus our strategic defence needs for British ships and British seafarers. A strong competitive British shipping industry is also good for the economy. Profitable investment in the up-turn of world trade will benefit the Balance of Payments.[380] It will create new jobs in seafaring and in land-side investment. It will strengthen the country's position as a leading seafaring nation."

Following the publication of this Report the Chamber of Shipping[381] made its annual fiscal submission for the 1991 Budget which proposed measures designed to encourage the rebuilding of the fleet and the recruitment and training of more high-quality British seafarers.[382] The measures attracted wide cross-party support[383] and in the debates on the Finance Bill two amendments were proposed for the purpose of giving statutory effect to the measures; unfortunately, to the disappointment of the industry and the many MPs supporting them, neither amendment was called by the Speaker at the Report stage of the Bill. However, the industry took some comfort from the assurances given by two Treasury Ministers during the latter stages of the debates on the Bill that: "an important defence issue is being addressed by Ministers"; "a statement will be made when a proper conclusion is reached"; and "we shall not hesitate to act and, if necessary, to spend if we consider that such action is justified by our defence requirements".[384]

Another important non-political event in 1991 was the Chamber of Shipping's major campaign to raise the profile of British Shipping and to increase public awareness of its importance to the nation. The campaign was supported by a widely circulated video – "The Seaway to Success" – and an accompanying brochure[385] and culminated in British Shipping Month when there were 16 events at ports evenly spread around the country at which school children and local people were invited to visit a wide range of ships.[386] In addition there were discussions and events on board the Royal Yacht *Britannia*

380. In 1990 British shipping made a direct gross contribution of almost £4 billion to the balance of payments and related activities in the City of London contributed a further £1.2 billion.

381. In the latter part of 1990 the GCBS decided that it would henceforth operate under the historic name of "The Chamber of Shipping" which had applied from 1873 to 1975.

382. Specifically temporary 100 per cent first year capital allowances for investment in ships for re-structuring purposes and for assistance with the employment costs of British seafarers through Income Tax relief.

383. An Early Day Motion was signed by 354 MPs.

384. No Government statement has yet been made, but there is speculation that the Government may be contemplating some form of "retainer payment" to British shipping companies designed to keep selected ships crewed by British seafarers on the UK Register.

385. Both video and brochure had an introduction by the Prince of Wales.

386. A comprehensive education pack for use in Primary Schools was also produced by the Chamber of Shipping in conjunction with the National Maritime Museum.

in the Pool of London at which both the Duke of Edinburgh and the Duke of York participated.

The Chamber of Shipping's Annual Report 1991, published in October 1991 and covering a 16 month period (May 1990 to September 1991), noted that, despite the absence of the favourable fiscal regimes enjoyed by many of its competitors in recent years, the rate of decline of the British fleet had slowed considerably.[387] The Report went on to point out that, in the year to June 1991, following several years of contraction, there was a net addition to the trading fleet of seven ships which, although only a small increase, nevertheless did represent a reversal of a seemingly inexorable downward trend; but the Report then added the caveat that the fleet was ageing and significant replacement tonnage was required if the good work of recent years was not to be wasted.[388]

Although still apparently reluctant to accept the economic case or even the argument, repeatedly advanced, that unless a sufficiently strong U.K. manned British merchant fleet is maintained in peacetime it will certainly not be available in an emergency, the Government did at least declare unequivocally in July 1988 that "it has a responsibility for ensuring that the Merchant Fleet should continue to be able to meet the nation's defence requirements".[389] This begs the question as to whether the present strength of the U.K. controlled fleet and the available numbers of trained British seafarers are sufficient to meet the country's strategic and economic needs in an emergency and it is perhaps salutary to recall the extent to which, in 1938–39, the Government seriously underestimated the demands for shipping in the Second World War. In Parliament there is a clear difference of opinion regarding the shipping defence capability between the Government on the one hand and backbenchers, from both the left and the right, in the Lords and Commons on the

387. The figures at June 1989, 1990 and 1991 (ships over 100 grt) were:

Register	*June 1989*		*June 1990*		*June 1991*	
	No.	*mdwt*	No.	*mdwt*	No.	*mdwt*
Mainland UK	532	5.1	491	4.2	478	3.7
Crown Dependencies	81	3.0	74	2.7	63	2.7
Dependent Territories	95	5.6	90	5.5	83	4.6
Foreign	118	2.1	128	3.4	166	4.3
TOTAL	826	15.8	783	15.7	790	15.3

388. The recent shipbuilding figures for UK owned trading fleet (all registers-ships over 100grt) were:

	June 1990		*Dec. 1990*		*June 1991*	
	No.	*dwt ('000)*	No.	*dwt ('000)*	No.	*dwt ('000)*
On order	37	2206	21	657	19	702
Under construction	13	164	22	238	12	38
Fitting out	7	51	7	146	8	57

389. See introduction to HCP 681 (Parl. Papers 1987–88).

other hand. Throughout the Parliamentary session 1988–1989 the Government consistently maintained,[390] as it had done in earlier years, that, notwithstanding the continuing decline in U.K. controlled shipping, national defence requirements could still be met[391] and that, although there was some shortage in officers and seamen, the full effect of the measures recently taken[392] had yet to be seen. However the Defence Committee,[393] the Transport Committee[394] and others who contributed to the debates in the Lords and Commons took an entirely contrary view; they believed that the fall in the numbers of ships and men meant that, in an emergency, defence and economic needs could not be met and urged the Government to take further action to reverse the decline.

Outside Parliament there was little, or no, difference of opinion. In September 1989 the GCBS published a paper entitled *British Shipping and Defence* in which grave doubts were expressed as to whether the U.K. controlled merchant fleet could supply the required numbers of ships and of trained British officers and seamen for both direct support to the armed forces and NATO trans-Atlantic reinforcement[395]—let alone economic resupply, i.e. supporting the requirements of the U.K.'s wartime industry and civil population.[396] Earlier, in April 1989, the BML circulated a short paper criticising the paragraphs on merchant shipping in the 1989 Defence Estimates as being "misleading, over-optimistic and complacent"[397] and in June 1989 both GCBS and BML representatives attended NATO's triennial conference Sea Link 89 at which there was circulated a BML paper entitled *World Trade, Military Logistics and Merchant Shipping: Demand and Supply* which spelt out the decline in NATO Member States' beneficially owned or controlled tonnage and the shortfall across the whole Alliance of a sufficient tonnage to fulfil wartime requirements.[398] Subsequent to Sea Link 89 the NATO Secretary General informed the BML that NATO was not waiting for the completion of the

390. See 1989 Defence Estimates (Parl. Papers 1988–89, Cm. 675); P. Debs. 6 Ser., Vol. 148, c.(497); Vol. 156, c.909 and Vol.158, c.(227) and P. Debs. (HL) 5 Ser., Vol. 510, c.432.

391. It was however admitted that NATO was concerned at the shortage of vessels for trans-Atlantic reinforcement and civil resupply.

392. In the Merchant Shipping Act 1988 and the Finance Act 1988.

393. See their 1989 Report on the "Availability of Merchant Shipping for Defence Purposes" (Parl. Papers 1988–89, HCP 495).

394. See their Report on the "Decline in the U.K. Registered Fleet" (Parl. Papers 1987–88, HCP 303).

395. Subsequently, in December 1989 (see paras. 71–74 of "British Shipping—The Way Ahead"), GCBS pointed out that paradoxically the new mood in Eastern Europe, forces reductions and American cut backs in Europe have shifted the emphasis more than ever to trans-Atlantic reinforcement and resupply—and so to merchant shipping.

396. The estimate made by GCBS was that in an emergency the U.K. was likely to be short of at least 300 to 400 ocean-going ships and this deficit would increase.

397. This paper is reproduced in the printed evidence for the Defence Committee's 1989 Report on merchant shipping (HCP 495).

398. This BML paper, like that of the GCBS, also concluded that there would be a large shortfall in U.K. shipping capacity to meet the likely wartime demands of U.K. civil resupply.

NATO Study on Supply and Demand for Shipping before attempting to deal with shipping problems within the Alliance.

Thus, outside Government circles, there remains a near unanimous view, in Parliament and elsewhere, that Britain needs a strong merchant fleet—both ships and men—in peace as much as in war. As the GCBS has pointed out,[399] a greatly reduced fleet must have a major adverse effect on our defence capability, balance of payments, employment, trade[400] and on shipbuilding and other maritime industries. The shipping industry cannot by itself reverse or even stem the decline; and although, in the Merchant Shipping and Finance Acts 1988, the Government has at least shown some small recognition of the industry's problems, far more Government action is required now at national and international level if Britain's maritime industries are to be revived before it is too late to do so. There have been no lack of suggestions as to what needs to be done in order to make it possible for the U.K. owned fleet to be increased and modernised and for U.K. registered ships to operate profitably with British crews[401] but at present it seems to British shipowners that, although the Government must be well aware that if they do not give support comparable to that given by foreign governments to their merchant marines, the U.K. owned fleet will continue to decline, the Government may still not be prepared to go much beyond the modest measures already taken which they appear to believe will suffice to ensure that the industry will still be able to provide sufficient ships and seafarers to meet the country's needs in an emergency.[402]

In its 1989 Report[403] the Defence Committee stated: "The availability of merchant shipping for defence purposes is governed by three key factors—the number of U.K. flag ships, their accessibility when they are needed and the availability of a pool of British seafarers to man them. There are grounds for concern on all three counts." The Shipping Minister has recently declared[404] that the Government does not agree with the Defence Committee's views but, since the defence of the realm is the primary duty of any British Government, surely the present Government, even if it should remain unwilling to recognise the strength of the economic case, must now pay due regard to the fact that it is not only the Defence Committee but also the Transport Committee and many others concerned from a national point of view with the future of the merchant navy who doubt whether present policies can ensure that in an emergency there will be sufficient vessels of the categories required and the

399. In its evidence to the Transport Committee.
400. In 1986 U.K. ships carried only 23 per cent by weight of U.K. imports and exports.
401. See in particular the evidence submitted to the Transport Committee (HCP 303) and the numerous GCBS and BML papers referred to above.
402. See the introduction to HCP 681 (Parl. Papers 1987–88).
403. Parl. Papers 1988–89, HCP 495.
404. On 29th November 1989—see P. Debs. 6 Ser., Vol. 162, c.808.

necessary trained U.K. seafarers available to man them.[405] Now is the time for the Government to demonstrate by action its belief in the sea and, under the direction of the Prime Minister, adopt a vigorous maritime policy which will recognise that, as in centuries past, profit and power must be jointly considered and that, as the old Navigation Laws repeatedly declared, the wealth, safety and strength of this kingdom still much depends upon a "multitude of ships" and a "large, constant and ready supply of seamen".[406]

In 1708, at a time when British merchant ships were sustaining heavy losses as a result of attacks by foreign powers, the House of Lords made the following address to Queen Anne: "May it please your Majesty: It is a most undoubted maxim that the honour, security and wealth of this kingdom does depend upon the protection and encouragement of trade and the improving and right managing of our naval strength. Other nations, who were formerly great and powerful at sea, have by negligence and misconduct lost their trade and seen their maritime strength entirely ruined. Therefore we do in the most earnest manner beseech your Majesty that the sea affair may always be your first and most peculiar care."[407] For those, mindful of the historical lessons of past centuries and the more recent experience of two World Wars, Suez and the Falklands, whose firm belief is that Britain still needs a strong merchant marine, it must remain their earnest request that, as in times past, Government will always regard the "sea affair" as their "first and most peculiar care" and that Parliament will give all necessary encouragement and support to "those that go down to the sea in ships and occupy their business in great waters".[408]

405. In view of the statements made by Treasury Ministers at the end of the 1991 Budget Debate, there is perhaps now a glimmer of hope – see fn 384 *supra*.

406. At least our future King needs no convincing! Apart from his Introduction to the Seaway to Success, in a speech on 29th November 1988 to the Honourable Company of Master Mariners, the Prince of Wales, as Master of the Company, dealt in some detail with the economic and strategic grounds "for supporting a significant British presence in seaborne trade" and emphasised the need for a healthy fleet to provide a core of trained committed mariners. In addition, in July 1989, the Duke of Edinburgh gave a dinner at Buckingham Palace to discuss "The State of the Merchant Navy".

407. House of Lords Debates, Vol. II, 1697–1714, p. 239.

408. Psalm 107.

BIBLIOGRAPHY

I. Books and Articles

II. Parliamentary Papers

III. Parliamentary Debates

IV. Government (Non-Parliamentary) and other Official Publications

I. BOOKS AND ARTICLES

Aldcroft, D. H., *Studies in British Transport History 1870–1970*, London, 1974.

——, *British Transport since 1914*, London, 1975.

Alexander, Sir J. L., "British Shipping in the Light of the Rochdale Report", *Institute of Transport Journal*, vol.33, 1970.

Allen, G. C., *British Industries and their Organisation*, 5th edn., London, 1970.

Anderson, Adam, *The Origins of Commerce*, London, 1764.

Anderson, Sir Donald, "British Shipping in 1964", *National Provincial Bank Review*, No. 65, 1964.

Behrens, C. B. A., *Merchant Shipping and the Demands of War*, (History of the Second World War, U.K. Civil Series, (ed. Sir Keith Hancock), London, 1955.

Brady, Alexander, *William Huskisson and Liberal Reform*, Oxford, 1928.

Brewster, Francis, *Essays on Trade and Navigation*, London, 1695.

Broadway, Frank, *Upper Clyde Shipbuilders*, London, 1976.

Brown, Lucy, *The Board of Trade and the Free Trade Movement*, 1830–1842, Oxford, 1958.

Cairncross, A. K. and Parkinson, J. R., "The Shipbuilding Industry" in Duncan Burn (ed.) *Structure of British Industry*, Cambridge, 1958.

Cayzer, Sir Nicholas, "The Challenge to British Shipping", *Institute of Transport Journal*, Vol. 30, 1963.

Child, Josiah, *A New Discourse of Trade*, 4th edn., London, 1740.

Churchill, E. F., "Dispensing Powers and Defence of the Realm", *Law Quarterly Review*, vol. 148.

Churchill, Sir W. S., *The Second World War*, 6 vols. London, 1948–52.

Clapham, Sir J. H., "The Last Years of the Navigation Acts", *English Historical Review*, vol. 25, 1910.

——, *Economic History of Modern Britain*, Cambridge, 1967.

Coke, Roger, *A Discourse of Trade*, London, 1670.

Cunningham, William, *The Growth of English Industry and Commerce in Modern Times*, 5th edn. Cambridge. 1910.

D'Avenant, Charles, *Political and Commercial Works*, London, 1695.

Davis, Ralph, *The Rise of the English Shipping Industry in the 17th and 18th Centuries*, Newton Abbot, 1972.

Decker, Mathew, *Causes of the Decline of Foreign Trade*, London, 1750.

Dickerson, O. M., *The Navigation Acts and the American Revolution*, Philadelphia, 1951.

Dyos, H. J. and Aldcroft, D. H., *British Transport*, Leicester, 1969.

Fayle, C. E., "The Proposed Revival of the Navigation Acts", *Edinburgh Review*, vol. 2, 1918.
——, *Seaborne Trade*, 3 vols. History of the Great War, London and New York, 1920–24.
——, *The War and the Shipping Industry*, London, 1927.
——, *Short History of the World's Shipping Industry*, London, 1934.
Firth, C. H. and Rait, R. S., (eds.) *Acts and Ordinances of the Interregnum 1642–1660*, 3 vols. London, 1911.
Fortrey, Samuel, *England's Interest and Improvement*, Cambridge, 1663.
Glover, J., "State of Tonnage during the First Decade under the Navigation Law of 1849", *Journal of the Statistical Society*, Vol. 26, March 1863.
——, "Tonnage Statistics of the Decade 1860–70", *Journal of the Royal Statistical Society*, vol. 35, June 1872.
——, "Tonnage Statistics of the Decade 1880–90", *Journal of the Royal Statistical Society*, vol. 55, June 1892.
Gordon, Barry, *Economic Doctrine and Tory Liberalism 1824–1839*, London, 1979.
Guisberg, B. W., "Shipping Subsidies", *Journal of the Royal Statistical Society*, vol. 64, 1901.
Hancock, W. K. and Gowing, M. M., *British War Economy* (History of the Second World War — U.K. Civil Series, ed. Sir Keith Hancock), London, 1949.
Harper, L. A., *The English Navigation Laws*, Columbia University Press, 1939.
Hertslet, L., *A Collection of Treaties and Conventions relating to Commerce and Navigation*, London, 1840.
Hilton, John, "Merchant Shipping and State Control", *Edinburgh Review*, vol. 1, 1918.
Hodson, J. L., *British Merchantmen at War*, London, 1949.
Holdsworth, Sir W. S., *The Relation between Commercial Legislation and National Defence Historically Considered*, Rhodes Lecture, University College, London, 25th February 1918.
——, "The Power of the Crown to Requisition British Ships in a National Emergency", *Law Quarterly Review*, vol. 25, 1919.
——, *A History of English Law*, London, 1938.
Hopkins, G. P., *National Service of British Seamen 1914–1919*, London, 1920.
Hornby, W., *Factories and Plant*, (History of the Second World War — U.K. Civil Series (ed. Sir Keith Hancock), London, 1958.
Hughes, P. L. and Larkin, J. F. (ed.), *Tudor Royal Proclamations*, Yale University Press, 1964.
Hunter, H. G., *How England got its Merchant Marine 1066–1776*, New York, 1935.
Hurd, Archibald, *The Merchant Navy*, History of the Great War, London, 1921.
Hyde, F. E., *Cunard and the North Atlantic 1840–1973*, London, 1975.
Jaffe, P., "World Trade and British Shipping" in M. Abrams (ed.), *Britain and her Export Trade*, London, 1946.
Jenkins, Sir Gilmour, *The Ministry of Transport and Civil Aviation*, London, 1959.
Jones, G. M., *Government Aid to Merchant Shipping*, U.S. Department of Commerce, 1925.
Jones, L., *Shipbuilding in Britain*, Cardiff, 1957.
Kendall, M. G., "Losses of U.K. Merchant Ships in World War II", *Economics* (New Series), vol. 15, November 1948.
Kirkaldy, Adam W., *British Shipping — its History, Organisation and Importance*, London, 1914.
Larkin, J. F. and Hughes, P. L. (ed.), *Stuart Royal Proclamations*, vol. 1, Oxford, 1973.
Larkin, J. F. (ed.), *Stuart Royal Proclamations*, vol. 2, Oxford, 1983.
Lauterpacht, E., "The Contemporary Practice of the United Kingdom in the Field of International Law", *International and Comparative Law Quarterly*, vol. 4, 1956.
Lindsay, W. S., *History of Merchant Shipping and Ancient Commerce*, 4 vols. London, 1874–76.
Lipson, E., *Economic History of England*, 12th edn. London, 1959.
Macdonagh, Oliver, *A Pattern of Government Growth 1800–1860*, London, 1961.
Mance, Sir H. O., *International Sea Transport*, London, 1945.
McGill, Jack, *Crisis on the Clyde*, London, 1973.
Mathias, Peter, *The First Industrial Nation*, London, 1969.
Meyers, H., *The Nationality of Ships*, The Hague, 1967.
Mitchell, B. R. and Deane, Phyllis, *Abstract of British Historical Statistics*, Cambridge, 1962.
Money, Sir Leo, "The Nationalisation of Shipping", *English Review*, vol. 28, 1919.
Murray, Evelyn, *The Post Office*, London, 1927.

Parkinson, J. R., "Financial Prospects of Shipbuilding after Geddes", *Journal of Industrial Economy*, vol. 17, 1968.
Payton-Smith, D. J., *Oil* (History of the Second World War — U.K. Civil Series (ed. Sir Keith Hancock), London, 1971.
Petty, Sir William, *Essays in Political Arithmetic*, London, 1699.
Philanglus (anon), *Brittannia Languens*, London, 1680.
Political & Economic Planning (PEP), "The British Shipping Industry", *Planning*, vol. 25, 1959.
Pollard, S., *The Economic History of British Shipbuilding 1870–1914*, unpublished Ph.D. thesis, University of London, 1951.
——, "Laissez-faire and Shipbuilding", *Economic History Review* (2nd Series) vol. 5, 1952–53.
Postan, M. M., *British War Production* (History of the Second World War — U.K. Civil Series (ed. Sir Keith Hancock), London, 1952.
Ricardo, J. L., *The Anatomy of the Navigation Laws*, London, 1847.
Robinson, Howard, *Carrying British Mail Overseas*, London, 1964.
Roskill, Capt. Stephen, *The War at Sea*, (U.K. Military Series of the Second World War), London, 1954.
Salter, Sir Arthur, *Allied Shipping Control*, Oxford, 1921.
Saugstad, J. E., *Shipping and Shipbuilding Subsidies*, U.S. Department of Commerce, 1932.
Savage, C. I., *Inland Transport* (History of the Second World War — U.K. Civil Series (ed. Sir Keith Hancock), London, 1957.
Savile, George (Marquess of Halifax), *A Rough Draft of a New Model at Sea*, 1694.
Singh, N. and Colinvaux, R., *Shipowners* (vol. 13 British Shipping Laws), London, 1967.
Smart, W., *Economic Annals of the Nineteenth Century*, 2 vols, London, 1917.
Smith, Adam, *An Inquiry into the Nature and Causes of the Wealth of Nations*, 1776 (ed. J. S. Nicholson), London, 1884.
Smith, Sir H. L., *The Board of Trade*, London, 1928.
Smith, Russel, *Influence of the Great War upon Shipping*, New York, 1919.
Stamp, Sir Josiah, *Taxation during the War*, London, 1932.
Sturmey, S. G., *British Shipping and World Competition*, London, 1962.
Thornton, R. H., *British Shipping*, 1st edn., Cambridge 1939 and 2nd edn., Cambridge, 1959.
Trevelyan, Sir G. M., *History of England*, 3rd edn., London, 1945.
Usher, A. P., "The Growth of English Shipping 1572–1922", *Quarterly Journal of Economics*, vol. 42, 1929.
Vale, V., "The Government and the Cunard Contract of 1903", *Journal of Transport History*, (New Series), vol. 5, February 1979.

II PARLIAMENTARY PAPERS (CHRONOLOGICALLY ARRANGED)

1820
Report of the 1820 Select Committee on Foreign Trade; (300), vol. 2.

1821
Report of the 1821 Select Committee on Foreign Trade; (186), vol. 6.

1833
Report of the Select Committee on Manufactures, Commerce and Shipping; (690), vol. 6.

1835
Report of the Select Committee on Timber Duties; (519), vol. 19.

1836
Report of the Select Committee on Shipwrecks; (567), vol. 17.

1840
Report of the Select Committee on Import Duties; (601), vol. 5.

1843

Report of the Select Committee on Shipwrecks; (549), vol. 9.

1844

Report of the Select Committee on the State of the Commercial Marine; (545), vol. 8.

1846

Report of the Select Committee on the Halifax and Boston Mails; (563), vol. 15.

1847

Reports of the Commons' Select Committee on the Navigation Laws; (232), (246), (329), (556) and (678), vol. 10.

1847/48

Reports of the Lords' Select Committee on the Navigation Laws; HL(340), (431), and (754), vol. 20, Part II.

Exchange of Correspondence; Lord Palmerston and the American Ambassador; (901), vol. 59.

Papers relating to the Commercial Marine of Great Britain; (913), vol. 59.

1849

Lord Palmerston's Note to Foreign Governments and their Replies re: proposed Repeal of the Navigation Laws; Command 1029, 1030, 1036, 1038, 1041 & 1048, vol. 51.

Report of the Select Committee on the Contract Packet Service; (571), vol. 12.

1851

Reports of the Select Committee on Steam Communication with India, China, Australia and New Zealand; (372) and (605), vol. 21.

Report of the Select Committee on the Passenger Acts; (632), vol. 19.

Report of Admiralty Commission on Irish Packet Station; Command 1391, vol. 25.

1853

Report of Treasury Committee of Enquiry on Contract Packets; (195), vol. 95.

1859

Report of Royal Commission on Manning the Navy; Command 2469, vol. 6 (1st Session).

Address to the Queen by British Shipowners and subsequent Correspondence in reference thereto; Command 2494, vol. 25.

1860

Report of the Select Committee on Government Mail Contracts with Steam Packet Companies; (328), vol. 14.

Report of the Select Committee on the State of Merchant Shipping; (530), vol. 13.

1867

Correspondence respecting the Operations of the French Navigation Laws on Merchant Shipping; (3773), vol. 74.

1868/69

Report of the Select Committee on the Cunard and Inman Contracts; (106), vol. 6.

1870

Statistical Abstracts for the United Kingdom 1840–1854 and 1855–1869; C.144 and C.145, vol. 68.

1872

Correspondence between the Board of Trade and British Consulates Abroad; C.630, vol. 53.

1874
Final Report of the Royal Commission on Unseaworthy Ships; C.1027, vol. 34.

1876
Report on Legislation Concerning Merchant Ships and Seamen; C.1398, vol. 66.

1881
Tables of the Progress of British Merchant Shipping 1820–1880; (125), vol. 82.

1884/85
Report of the Committee on the Building and Repair of Ships for the Navy; C.4219, vol. 14.

1885
Report of the Board of Trade Load Line Committee; C.4566, vol. 69.

1887
Report of the Admiralty Committee on Naval Contracts; C.4987, vol. 16.
Subventions of Merchant Steamers for State Purposes; C.5006, vol. 52.
Report of Royal Commission on Losses of Ships and Lives at Sea; C.5227, vol. 43.

1889
Report respecting Bounties or Subsidies in European Countries in aid of the construction or running of ships; C.5667, vol. 76.

1890/91
Mail Packet Service Expenditure; (33), vol. 48.

1895
Admiralty Returns on Royal Naval Building Programme; (260) and (460), Sess. 2, vol. 65.
Report of Postmaster General on (*inter alia*) Payments for Foreign and Colonial Packet Services; C.7852 (Appendix G), vol. 26.
Report on Foreign State Bounties on the construction and running of ships; C.7898, vol. 13.

1898
Report on Foreign State Bounties on the construction and running of ships and on foreign preferential railway rates; C.8720, vol. 92.

1900
Contract between the Crown Agents for the Colonies and Elder Dempster & Co.; Cd. 175, vol. 55.

1901
First Report of the Select Committee on Foreign Subsidies to Steamship Companies and Sailing Vessels; (300), vol. 8.
Reports on Foreign State Bounties for Shipbuilding; Cd. 596, vol. 80.

1902
Report on Merchant Ships as Armed Cruisers; (218), vol. 92.
Second Report of the Select Committee on Foreign Subsidies to Steamship Companies and Sailing Vessels; (385), vol. 9.
Report of Committee on Arrears of Naval Shipbuilding; Cd. 1055, vol. 61.
Report of Admiralty Committee on Mercantile Cruisers; Cd. 1379, vol. 92.

1903
Report of Naval Reserves Committee; Cd. 1491, vol. 40.

Report of Board of Trade Committee on the Employment of Lascars and Foreigners in the British Merchant Service; Cd. 1607, vol. 62.

Agreement between the Government and Cunard re *Mauretania* and *Lusitania*; Cd. 1703, vol. 36.

Agreement between the Government, International Mercantile Marine, Ocean Steam Navigation and others; Cd. 1704, vol. 63.

1905

Report of the Select Committee on the extent to which British Statutory Regulations should be made applicable to Foreign Vessels; (269), vol. 7.

1907

Return of Exchequer Payments re Steamship Subsidies for Foreign and Colonial Services; (359), vol. 47.

1908

Report of a Treasury Committee on a National Guarantee for the War Risks of Shipping; Cd. 4161, vol. 58.

1909

Report of Royal Commission on Shipping Rings; Cd. 4668, vol. 47.

1912/13

Admiralty Return re Naval Building; (300), vol. 53.

1913

Report on Foreign Bounties and Subsidies in respect of Shipbuilding, Shipping and Navigation; Cd. 6899, vol. 40.

Progress of Merchant Shipping in the United Kingdom and Principal Maritime Countries; Cd. 7033, vol. 60.

1914

Return of Exchequer Payments re Steamship Subsidies for Foreign and Colonial Services; (156), vol. 70.

Admiralty Return re Naval Building; (410), vol. 54.

Report of a Sub-Committee of the Committee of Imperial Defence on the Insurance of British Shipping in Time of War; Cd. 7560, vol. 70.

Annual Statement of the Navigation and Shipping of the United Kingdom; Cd. 7616, vol. 82.

1914/16

Agreements made under Government War Risks Insurance Scheme for Shipping; Cd. 7838, vol. 55.

1917/18

Final Report of the Dominions Royal Commission; Cd. 8462, vol. 10.

1918

Reports of the Board of Trade Departmental Committee on the Shipping and Shipbuilding Industries; Cd. 9092, vol. 13.

Merchant Tonnage and the Submarine; Cd. 9009 and Cd. 9221, vol. 22.

1919

Government War Risks Insurance Scheme for Shipping. Preliminary Statement of Results; Cmd. 98, vol. 32.

Treaty of Versailles; Cmd. 153, vol. 53.

1922

International Convention Concerning Freedom of Transit; Cmd. 1992, vol. 24.

International Convention Concerning Rights of Navigable Waterways; Cmd. 1993, vol. 24.

1923

Report of the Imperial Economic Conference 1923; Cmd. 2009, vol. 10.

International Convention Concerning Regime of Maritime Ports; Cmd. 2141, vol. 27.

1924

Return of Sums payable out of the Exchequer in the year ending 5th April 1924 re Steamship Subsidies for Foreign and Colonial Services; (147), vol. 13.

1927

Report of Treasury Guarantees given under the Trade Facilities Acts 1921–26; (61), vol. 13.

1928

Contract between Postmaster General and Cunard re sea mails to the United States; (95), vol. 13.

Contract between Postmaster General and Oceanic Steam Navigation re sea mails to the United States; (96), vol. 13.

1928/29

Contract between the Postmaster General and D. Macbrayne re passenger, cargo and mail service in the Western Islands and Highlands of Scotland; (4), vol. 16.

Statistical Abstract for the United Kingdom 1929; Cmd. 3253, vol. 21.

Final Report of the Balfour Committee on Industry and Trade; Cmd. 3282, vol. 7.

1930/31

Memorandum explaining Financial Resolution re Cunard Insurance Agreement; Cmd. 3706, vol. 25.

Final Report of the Royal Commission on Transport; Cmd. 3751, vol. 17.

1931/32

Revenue Departments Appropriation Accounts; (7), vol. 18.

Imperial Economic Conference (Ottawa 1932). Proceedings and Agreements between the United Kingdom and the Dominions; Cmd. 4174, vol. 10.

1933/34

Agreement (30 Dec. 1933) between Cunard, Oceanic and the Treasury; Cmd. 4502, vol. 16.

North Atlantic Shipping, Memorandum on proposed Financial Resolution; Cmd. 4516, vol. 18.

Outline of Scrapping and Rebuilding Scheme for British Cargo Vessels; Cmd. 4647, vol. 18.

1934/35

Memorandum on Financial Resolutions re Assistance to British Shipping; Cmd. 4754, vol. 14.

First Report of the Tramp Shipping Advisory Committee; Cmd. 5004, vol. 11.

1935/36

Mail Contract (1 April 1936) between the Postmaster General and Cunard White Star; (92), vol. 15.

Memorandum on Financial Resolution re Continuance of Tramp Shipping Subsidy (1936); Cmd. 5082, vol. 13.

Second Report of the Tramp Shipping Advisory Committee; Cmd. 5084, vol. 13.

Statement of Distribution of Tramp Shipping Subsidy (1935); Cmd. 5129, vol. 13.

Third Report of the Tramp Shipping Advisory Committee; Cmd. 5291, vol. 13.

1936/37

Account of Advance under Part II of the British Shipping (Assistance) Act 1935 for period ended 31 March 1936; (8), vol. 16.

Memorandum on Financial Resolutions re Continuance of Tramp Shipping Subsidy (1937); Cmd. 5357, vol. 21.
Fourth Report of the Tramp Shipping Advisory Committee; Cmd. 5363, vol. 13.
Agreement (15 Feb 1937) between Cunard White Star and the Treasury; Cmd. 5397, vol. 21.
Statement of Distribution of Tramp Shipping Subsidy (1936); Cmd. 5420, vol. 16.
Report of the Ships' Replacement Committee; Cmd. 5459, vol. 13.
Fifth Report of the Tramp Shipping Advisory Committee; Cmd. 5555, vol. 13.

1937/38

Accounts of Advances under Part II of the British Shipping (Assistance) Act 1935 for the periods ended 31 March 1937 and 31 March 1938; (1) and (145), vol. 16.
Defence White Paper (1938); Cmd. 5682, vol. 17.
Agreement (16 Feb 1938) between Cunard White Star and the Treasury; Cmd. 5725, vol. 21.
Sixth Report of the Tramp Shipping Advisory Committee; Cmd. 5750, vol. 13.

1938/39

Postal Subventions for Overseas Mails in 1937. Revenue Department's Appropriation Accounts; (19), vol. 20.
Provisional Scheme for the Re-Insurance of the Marine Insurance Market by the Board of Trade in respect of King's Enemy Risks on Cargoes; Cmd. 6002, vol. 21.
Bilateral Trade Agreement between the U.K. and the U.S.A.; Cmd. 6048, vol. 28.
Draft Agreement between the Board of Trade and War Risks Associations for the Re-Insurance of King's Enemy Risks; Cmd. 6058, vol. 21.
Agreements between the Board of Trade and British War Risks Associations; (182) to (194), vol. 21.
Proposals for the Assistance of British Shipping (1939); Cmd. 6060, vol. 18.
British Shipping Assistance Bill 1939; (Bill 198), vol. 1.

1939/40

Memorandum on the War-Time Financial Arrangements between the Government and British Shipowners; Cmd. 6218, vol. 7.
Supplemental Agreements between the Ministry of Shipping and the British War Risks Associations; (148) to (173), vol. 10.

1941/42

Agreements between the Prime Minister and the President of the United States (Jan 1942); Cmd. 6332, vol. 9.
Memorandum on Scheme for purchase by British Shipowners of new vessels built on Government Account; Cmd. 6357, vol. 5.
Memorandum on Scheme for purchase of merchant vessels by Allied Governments from His Majesty's Government; Cmd. 6373, vol. 5.

1943/44

International Agreement on Principles re Continuance of Co-ordinated Control of Merchant Shipping; Cmd. 6556, vol. 8.
Statistics of the War Effort of the United Kingdom; Cmd. 6564, vol. 8.

1944/45

Fifth Report of the Select Committee on National Expenditure; (100), vol. 3.

1947/48

Convention for the Formation of the Organisation for European Economic Co-operation ("OEEC"); Cmd. 7388, vol. 27.
Convention for the Formation of the Intergovernmental Maritime Consultative Organisation ("IMCO"), Cmd. 7412, vol. 28.

1948/49

British Government Memorandum to OEEC re British Shipping Policy; Cmd. 7572, vol. 34.

1950/51

Report of Committee on the Taxation of Trading Profits (Millard Tucker Committee); Cmd. 8189, vol. 20.

1953/54

Cunard Insurance Fund Closure; (220), vol. 20.

1955/56

Final Report of the Royal Commission on the Taxation of Profits and Income; Cmd. 9474, vol. 27.

1960/61

Agreement between the Government and Cunard re Finance for replacement of *Queen Mary*; Cmnd. 1319, vol. 17.

1961/62

Final Report of Treasury Guarantees given under the Trade Facilities Acts 1921 to 1926; (183), vol. 25.

1962/63

Geneva Convention on the High Seas (1958); Cmnd. 1929, vol. 37.

1963/64

Report on First Meeting of the United Nations Conference on Trade and Development (UNCTAD); Cmnd. 2417, vol. 32.

1964/65

National Plan; Cmnd. 2764, vol. 30.

1965/66

White Paper on Investment Incentives; Cmnd. 2874, vol. 13.

Report of Shipbuilding Inquiry Committee (Geddes Committee); Cmnd. 2937, vol. 7.

1966/67

First and Second Reports of the Court of Enquiry under Lord Pearson into the causes of the seamen's strike; Cmnd. 3025 and Cmnd. 3211, vol. 36.

1967/68

Report on Second Meeting of UNCTAD; Cmnd. 3649, vol. 42.

Industrial Development Act 1966, Annual Report 1967/68; (420), vol. 24.

Shipbuilding Industry Board. First Report and Accounts for the period ended 31 March 1968; (361), vol. 31.

1968/69

Industrial Development Act 1966, Annual Report 1968/69; (329), vol. 33.

Shipbuilding Industry Board, Report and Accounts for the year ended 31 March 1969; (326), vol. 45.

1969/70

Report of the Committee of Inquiry into Shipping (Rochdale Committee); Cmnd. 4337, vol. 27.

Industrial Reorganisation Corporation, Report for the year ended 31 March 1970; (310), vol. 16.

1970/71

Industrial Development Act 1966, Annual Reports 1969/70 and 1970/71; (124) and (580), vol. 25.

White Paper on Investment Incentives; Cmnd. 4516, vol. 10.
Shipbuilding Industry Board, Report and Accounts for the year ended 31 March 1970; (84), vol. 49.
Shipbuilding Industry Board, Report and Accounts for the year ended 31 March 1971; (554), vol. 49.
Report of Advisory Group on Shipbuilding on the Upper Clyde; (544), vol. 49.
Industrial Reorganisation Corporation; Final Report for the period 1 April 1970 to 30 April 1971; (443), vol. 25.

1971/72
Shipbuilding Industry Board, Report and Accounts for the period 1 April to 31 December 1971; (316), vol. 37.
Committee of Public Accounts, Third Report Session 1971/72; (447), vol. 24.
Expenditure Committee on Public Money in the Private Sector; (347), vol. 27.
Shipbuilding on the Upper Clyde, Report by Hill Samuel & Co. Ltd.; Cmnd. 4918, vol. 37.
White Paper on Industrial and Regional Development; Cmnd. 4942, vol. 18.
Treaty on Merchant Navigation, U.K. and U.S.S.R.; Cmnd. 5008, vol. 38.

1972/73
Accounts re Issues from the National Loans Fund 1971/72, Statement of Guarantees under the Shipbuilding Industry Acts 1967 and 1971 for the year ended 31 March 1972; (155), vol. 16.
Industry Act 1972, Report for the year ended 31 March 1973; (429), vol. 12.
Report of Proceedings at UNCTAD 1972 Santiago Conference; Cmnd. 5134, vol. 35.
Report of Proceedings at the 27th Session of the United Nations General Assembly — Sept. to Dec. 1972; Cmnd. 5236, vol. 35.

1974
Industry Act 1972. Report for the year ended 31 March 1974; (339), vol. 7.

1974/75
Committee of Public Accounts. Third Report Session 1974/75; (374), vol. 22.
Parliamentary Commissioner for Administration. Fifth Report Session 1974/75. (498), vol. 29.
Defence White Paper; Cmnd. 5976, vol. 20.
Treasury Minute on Third Report of Committee of Public Accounts; Cmnd. 6298, vol. 22.
Industry Act 1972, Report for the year ended 31 March 1975; (620), vol. 14.

1975/76
Industry Act 1972, Report for the year ended 31 March 1976; (619), vol. 17.

1976/77
Industry Act 1972, Report for the year ended 31 March 1977; (545), vol. 16.

1977/78
Industry Act 1972, Report for the year ended 31 March 1978; (653), vol. 18.
Northern Ireland Appropriation Accounts 1976/77; (89), vol. 26.

1978/79
Report by the Auditor General on the Administration of the Intervention Fund, Appropriation Accounts (vol. 2.) 1977/78; (138), vol. 11.
Northern Ireland Appropriation Accounts 1977/78; (79), vol. 11.

1979/80
Committee of Public Accounts, First Report Session 1979/80; (173), vol. 15.
Treasury Minute on First Report of the Committee of Public Accounts; Cmnd. 7788, vol. 16.
Industry Act 1972, Report for the year ended 31 March 1979; (206), vol. 16.
Industry Act 1972, Report for the year ended 31 March 1980; (772), vol. 49.
Northern Ireland Appropriation Accounts 1978/79; (314), vol. 20.

Committee of Public Accounts, Twenty fourth Report Session 1979/80; (763), vol. 48.
Committee of Public Accounts. Nineteenth Report Session 1979/80; (737), vol. 47.
Report of Proceedings at UNCTAD 1979 Manila Conference; Cmnd. 7675, vol. 62.

1980/81
Industry Act 1972, Report for the year ended 31 March 1981; (460), vol. 39.

1981/82
Accounts relating to Issues from the National Loans Fund; HC 200.
Industry Act 1972, Report for the year ended 31 March 1982; HC 503.
Industry and Trade Committee, First Report on British Shipbuilders; HC 192.
Government Reply to the First Report of the Industry and Trade Committee; HC 381.

1982/83
Defence White Paper — "The Falklands Campaign: The Lessons"; Cmnd. 8758.
Industry Act 1972, Report for the year ended 31 March 1983; HC 72.

1983/84
Defence Estimates 1984; Cmnd. 9227.
Defence Committee First Report 1983/84; HC 436.
House of Lords European Communities Committee, Third Report on EEC Competition Policy: Shipping; HL 23.

1984/85
Defence Estimates 1985; Cmnd. 9430.
Defence Committee First Report on the Use of Merchant Shipping for Defence Purposes; HC 114.

1985/86
House of Lords European Communities Committee, Ninth Report on European Maritime Transport Policy; HL 106.
Defence Estimates 1986; Cmnd. 9763.
Defence Committee Second Report 1985/86; HC 399.

1986/87
Transport Committee, Interim Report on the Decline in the U.K. Registered Fleet; HC 94 i–xii.
Defence Committee. Fourth Report on Implementing the Lessons of the Falklands Campaign; HC 345—I.
Government Response to the Fourth Report of the Defence Committee; Cm. 228.
Defence Estimates 1987; Cm. 101.

1987/88
Trade & Industry Committee, Evidence re British Shipbuilders; HC 519.
White Paper, Merchant Shipping Bill; Cm. 239.
Transport Committee, Report on the Decline in the U.K. Registered Fleet; HC 303 (3 vols).
Government Observations on the Transport Committee's Report on the Decline of the U.K. Registered Fleet; HC 681.
Defence Committee, Fourth Report on the Defence Requirements for Merchant Shipping; HC 476.
Government Reply to the Fourth Report of the Defence Committee; HC 674.
Defence Estimates 1988; Cm. 344.

1988/89
Trade and Industry Committee, Report on Privatisation of Harland & Wolff; HC 131.
Government Response to the Report of the Trade & Industry Committee on the Privatisation of Harland & Wolff; HC 353.
Defence Estimates 1989; Cm. 675.
Defence Committee, Fourth Report 1988/89 (on the 1989 Defence Estimates); HC 383.

Defence Committee, Ninth Report 1988/89 (on the Availability of Merchant Shipping for Defence Purposes); HC 495.

III PARLIAMENTARY DEBATES (HANSARD)

1. New Series (NS), vols. 1 to 25. 21 April 1820 to 23 July 1830.
2. Third Series (3 Ser), vols. 1 to 356. 26 October 1830 to 5 August 1891.
3. Fourth Series (4 Ser), vols. 1 to 199. 9 February 1892 to 21 December 1908.
4. Fifth Series (5 Ser), House of Lords from 16 February 1909 (and continuing).
5. Fifth Series (5 Ser), House of Commons vols. 1 to 1000. 16 February 1909 to 13 March 1981.
6. Sixth Series (6 Ser), House of Commons from 16 March 1981 (and continuing).

IV GOVERNMENT (NON-PARLIAMENTARY) AND OTHER OFFICIAL PUBLICATIONS

HMSO Publications

Balfour Committee on Industry and Trade, Survey of Metal Industries; 1927.
Balfour Committee on Industry and Trade, Survey of Factors on Industrial and Commercial Efficiency; 1927.
Report of Imperial Shipping Committee on British Shipping in the Orient; 1939.
Statistical Digest of the War; 1951.
Report of the Department of Scientific and Industrial Research on the Research and Development Requirements of the Shipbuilding Industry; 1960.
Report of the Sub-Committee of the Shipbuilding Advisory Committee on Prospects of the Shipbuilding and Ship Repairing Industry; 1961.
Report of Peat, Marwick, Mitchell & Co. on Shipbuilding Orders placed abroad by British Owners; 1961.
British Shipbuilding 1972, Report to the Department of Trade & Industry by Booz-Allen & Hamilton; 1973.
U.K. Ship Repairing Industry, Report to the Department of Trade by P.A. Management Consultants Ltd; 1974.
Interim and Final Reports of Board of Trade Inspectors into the affairs of Court Line Ltd.; 1978.
British Shipbuilders, Annual Reports and Accounts 1977 to 1988.
British Shipping: Challenges and Opportunities; 1990.

Chamber of Shipping of the United Kingdom

Annual Reports for various years up to 1974 and then 1991.

Chamber of Shipping of the United Kingdom and the Liverpool Steam Ship Owners Association

Joint Committee's Report on the measures requisite for the maintenance of the British Merchant Marine; July 1917.
Joint Shipping Policy Committee's Report on proposals for the support of British Shipping (January 1939) accompanied by the following Reports of Fact Finding Committees:
Report of the Deep Sea Tramp Committee
Summary of Replies to Deep Sea Liner Questionnaire
Report of the Near Continental Trades and Russia Committee
Report of the Coasting Committee
Report of the Tanker Committee
Report on Shipping and Shipbuilding
Memorandum on Shipping and Shipbuilding Subsidies

General Council of British Shipping ("GCBS")

Survey of British Shipping with Recommendations as to Policy; December 1960.
Annual Reports 1971 to 1990.

British Shipping Statistics 1975, 1976/77, 1979/80 and 1981.
British Shipping Facts and Figures 1984 and 1985.
Shipping Facts 1988 and 1989.
British Shipping Review 1978 to 1987.
The Future of the British Merchant Fleet; December 1987.
British Shipping and the Balance of Payments; May 1989.
A Level Playing Field for British Shipping?; May 1989.
Merchant Shipping and Defence; September 1989.
British Shipping—The Way Ahead; December 1989.
British Shipping Factsheets; December 1989 (Comprising: No. 1 Shipping and the Balance of Payments, No. 2 Shipping and the Free Market, No. 3 Merchant Shipping and Defence, No. 4 British Shipping and the Channel Tunnel, No. 5 Light Dues: A Heavy Burden, No. 6 Cabotage, No. 7 VAT and Duty – Free in Shipping, No. 8 Ferry Safety, No. 9 European Community Shipping Policy and No. 10 Shipping Facts—1989 (Update).
The Seaway to Success; September 1990.

U.S. Department of Commerce—Maritime Administration
Review of Maritime Subsidies 1971.

European Economic Community
Council Aid to Shipbuilding Directive No. 72/273/EEC; OJ No. L169/28 (27 July 1972).
Council Aid to Shipbuilding Directive No. 75/432/EEC; OJ No. L192 (24 July 1975).
Council Aid to Shipbuilding Directive No. 78/338/EEC; OJ 1978 No. L98.
Council Decision No. 78/774/EEC (OJ 1978 No. L258) and Council Decision No. 79/4/EEC (OJ 1979 No. L5) both concerning the activities of certain third countries in the field of cargo shipping.
Council Regulation No. 954/79 ("the Brussels package") concerning ratification of UN Convention on a Code of Conduct for Liner Conferences; OJ No. L121 (17 May 1979).
Council Aid to Shipbuilding Directive No. 81/363/EEC (28 April 1981) OJ No. L137 as extended by Council Directive No. 82/880/EEC (21 December 1982) OJ No. L371.
Council Aid to Shipbuilding Directive No. 87/167/EC (January 1987).
Proposals for a Community Maritime Policy (EC Doc. No. 5635/85—March 1985).
First phase of EEC Common Shipping Policy comprising Regulations 4055/86, 4056/86, 4057/86 and 4058/86 (July 1986).
Proposals for the second stage of the Common Maritime Transport Policy (EC Docs 8367/89 and 8368/89—August 1989).
Council Aid to Shipbuilding Directive No. 90/684/EC (December 1990) OJ L374.

United Nations
Convention on a Code of Conduct for Liner Conferences; UN Doc. TD/Code/10 (April 1974).
Convention on Conditions for Registration of Ships; UN Doc. TD/RS/CONF.23 (February 1986).

British Maritime League ("BML") (Since February 1991 the name has been changed to *British Maritime Foundation ("BMF").)*
Annual Reports 1982 to 1990.
Newsletters 1982 to 1991.
British Maritime Policy; February 1983.
British Owned Merchant Shipping; November 1983.
An Examination of the Causes of Decline of the British Merchant Fleet since 1975; September 1984.
Britain does Need a Merchant Shipping Industry; June 1984.
British Shipbuilding Policy; July 1985.
The Merchant Shipping Industry—Recommendations for Actions to Restore Profitability; April 1986.
The National Importance of Restoring Britain's Maritime Capabilities; January 1988.
The United Kingdom Merchant Shipping Industry—Proposals for Action; October 1988.
World Trade, Military Logistics and Merchant Shipping—Demand and Supply; June 1989.

Increasing British Shippings' Contribution to the Economy; January 1990.
The Adverse Effects of the Taxation and Social Security Systems on the Recruitment and Retention of British Foreign-Going Seafarers; June 1990.
The Merchant Navy Reserve; June 1991.

British Maritime Charitable Foundation ('BMCF")
Why the Ships Went (covering the years 1978/83); March 1986.
Why the Ships Went—Supplement 1983/87; March 1988.
The Merchant Fleet and Britain's Economy; March 1988.
The Merchant Fleet and Deterrence; March 1988.
The U.K. Shipping Industry—Critical Levels Study; 1990.

Lloyd's Register of Shipping
The Fleet Controlled by the European Community; 1990.

INDEX